The Sovereignty of the Sea

The "British Seas," according to Selden.

The Sovereignty of the Sea

An Historical Account of the Claims of England to the Dominion of the British Seas, and of the Evolution of the Territorial Waters: with special reference to the Rights of Fishing and the Naval Salute

BY

THOMAS WEMYSS FULTON

LECTURER ON THE
SCIENTIFIC STUDY OF FISHERY PROBLEMS, THE UNIVERSITY OF ABERDEEN

WITH ILLUSTRATIONS

THE LAWBOOK EXCHANGE, LTD.
Clark, New Jersey

ISBN 9781584772323 (hardcover)
ISBN 9781616190842 (paperback)

Lawbook Exchange edition 2010

The quality of this reprint is equivalent to the quality of the original work.

THE LAWBOOK EXCHANGE, LTD.
33 Terminal Avenue
Clark, New Jersey 07066-1321

Please see our website for a selection of our other publications and fine facsimile reprints of classic works of legal history:
www.lawbookexchange.com

Library of Congress Cataloging-in-Publication Data

Fulton, Thomas Wemyss.
The sovereignty of the sea: an historical account of the claims of England to the dominion of the British seas, and of the evolution of the territorial waters, with special reference to the rights of fishing and the naval salute / by Thomas Wemyss Fulton.
p. cm.
Originally published: Edinburgh: W. Blackwood and Sons, 1911.
Includes index.
ISBN 1-58477-232-8 (cloth: alk. paper)
1. Territorial waters—Great Britain—History. I. Title.

KZA154O .F85 2002
341 .4'48'0941—dc2l 2002024324

Printed in the United States of America on acid-free paper

The Sovereignty of the Sea

An Historical Account of the Claims of England to the Dominion of the British Seas, and of the Evolution of the Territorial Waters: with special reference to the Rights of Fishing and the Naval Salute

BY

THOMAS WEMYSS FULTON

LECTURER ON THE
SCIENTIFIC STUDY OF FISHERY PROBLEMS, THE UNIVERSITY OF ABERDEEN

WITH ILLUSTRATIONS

William Blackwood and Sons
Edinburgh and London
1911

I DEDICATE THIS BOOK TO

MY WIFE

PREFACE.

In this book I have endeavoured to bring together from all available sources such information as exists as to the claims formerly made to the sovereignty of the British Seas, and to trace the evolution of the territorial waters in recent times. The work was originally undertaken with the intention of dealing only with these subjects so far as they related to the sea fisheries, but it soon became apparent that to restrict the scope in this way would involve considerable disadvantages, and would enable only a partial picture to be presented. For though during a large part of the period with which the book is concerned, the question of the fishery was the main question in determining the claim to sea sovereignty, and is the one of the greatest frequency at the present day with respect to the territorial waters, it was by no means the only one. The freedom of commerce to regions more or less remote; the jurisdiction of a State in the sea which washed its shores or which it claimed as belonging to it; the naval salute or homage to the flag, and various other matters, were commonly bound up with the question of the fisheries. It was therefore deemed more satisfactory to treat the subject as a whole, even though this necessarily involved much additional labour.

The book is divided into two sections, the first comprising an historical account of the pretensions to the dominion of the sea; the second dealing with the relic of such pretensions, the territorial waters, more particularly in the aspect which they present under the Law of Nations and in relation to the rights of fishing. With some doubtful exceptions, the claim to a special sovereignty or dominion over the so-called British Seas was a doctrine of the Stuarts, introduced from Scotland to England with that dynasty, and terminating with it. It was aimed in particular against the Dutch, whose commerce, shipping, wealth, and power were believed to be derived from the fisheries which they carried on along the coasts of this country. Hence a very considerable part of the work refers to the dealings and negotiations with that people as to the liberty of fishing and the homage to the flag. Such pretensions to extensive maritime sovereignty gradually decayed and disappeared, but the troubles and disputes as to the rightful jurisdiction of a State in the waters adjacent to its coasts have continued to the present day, and are dealt with in the second section of the book. Scarcely a year passes that does not witness one or more international differences of this kind, notably with respect to fisheries, and in various quarters of the globe—it may be now on the coasts of Portugal and Spain, or in the Pacific and South America, or again at the White Sea, each case giving rise to international negotiations and discussions as to the common usage and the Law of Nations.

One great group of such questions, which for long formed a troublesome heritage of the British Foreign Office, concerns the fisheries on the coasts of British North America. Under various treaties, some of them old, France and the United States possess special rights in these fisheries, the true nature of which has occasioned numerous disputes. It is a happy circumstance of recent years that those differences have now been composed. The agreement with France in 1905 settled the question of the fishery rights of that Power at Newfoundland, and the Award of the Permanent Court of International Arbitration at The Hague in the North Atlantic Coast Fisheries Arbitration, which was made last autumn while this work was passing through the press, has in a manner equally satisfactory settled the difficulties with the United States,—a fortunate result due in great part to the exceedingly able, lucid, and temperate presentation of the British case by Sir Robert Finlay, but chiefly, it cannot be doubted, to the growing feeling of goodwill between the two great branches of the Anglo-Saxon race. It is to be hoped that similar differences now pending and to come, as to the fisheries on other coasts, may be adjusted in a corresponding spirit of amity and compromise. The fish in the sea, as Dr Nansen has said, are not the property of any particular nation. They are, if the word may be used, international, and it would therefore be as just as it would be auspicious if all such questions were dealt with in a spirit of international brotherhood, with due regard to the interests of the coast population on the one hand, and the legitimate rights of the enterprising fishermen from other nations on the other. To this end the joint fishery investigations at present being conducted under the guidance of a Council of representatives of the western and northern Powers of Europe may be expected to contribute, if only by providing that full and precise information, without which an effective and equitable arrangement is difficult.

As far as possible, I have gone to original sources for my information; the State Papers in the Record Office, the MSS. in the British Museum, and those preserved at Hatfield—access to which was courteously granted by the late Marquess of Salisbury—have been laid under contribution. References to the various authorities are given for practically all the statements in the book; and in the Appendix are printed, either entire or in part, some of the more important documents which are cited.

Among foreign friends and colleagues to whom my thanks are due for information kindly given during the progress of the work, I must mention four, who, alas! are no longer with us: Professor A. F. Marion, Marseilles; Professor Enrico H. Giglioli, of Florence, for long the esteemed President of the Commissione consultiva per la pesca, Rome; Secretary of State M. Vladimir I. Weschniakow, President of the Société Impériale Russe de pisciculture et de pêche, St Petersburg; and Dr

Rudolf Lundberg, Stockholm, all very willingly complied with my requests for information. Among others who have aided me from time to time are Dr Georges Roché, Paris; Dr Eugène Canu, Boulogne-sur-mer; Señor Rafael Gutierrez Vela, Madrid; Dr Cav. Enrico Giacobini, of the Ministry of Agriculture, Rome; Dr F. Heincke, Heligoland; Dr Johan Hjort, Bergen; and Captain C. F. Drechsel, Copenhagen. My thanks are also due to Dr Fridtjof Nansen, formerly the Norwegian Minister in London; to M. J. Irgens, his successor; and to Dr T. Baty, Honorary Secretary to the International Law Association, London, for copies of documents and laws relative to the Scandinavian limits of the territorial sea; and likewise to Mr R. M. Bartleman, the American Consul-General at Buenos Aires, for papers referring to the extensive claims recently advanced by the Argentine Republic for the regulation of the fisheries in the adjacent seas.

Very specially have I to thank my friend, Dr P. P. C. Hoek, the Scientific Adviser for the Fisheries of the Netherlands, and the Commissioner appointed by The Hague Tribunal in the North Atlantic Fisheries Arbitration, for his valued assistance and advice. Dr Hoek was good enough to read over the proofs of the book, and I am indebted to him for a number of emendations and improvements which his knowledge of Dutch fisheries and history enabled him to suggest.

In transcribing records and preparing the index, and in some other ways, I have been assisted by my wife.

I feel that an acknowledgment is due to my publishers for the patience and consideration they have shown in the delay which, for several reasons, has occurred in the completion of the book.

It is right to add that I alone am responsible for all the opinions expressed, unless when otherwise stated.

T. WEMYSS FULTON.

41 Queen's Road, Aberdeen,
January 1911.

CONTENTS.

INTRODUCTION.

SECTION I.—THE HISTORY OF THE CLAIMS TO THE SOVEREIGNTY OF THE SEA.

CHAPTER I.

EARLY HISTORY.

CHAPTER II.

THE FISHERIES.

CHAPTER III.

UNDER THE TUDORS.

CHAPTER IV.

UNDER THE STUARTS. JAMES I. A NEW POLICY.

CHAPTER V.

JAMES I.—*continued.* DISPUTES WITH THE DUTCH.

CHAPTER VI.

CHARLES I. FISHERIES AND RESERVED WATERS.

CHAPTER VII.

CHARLES I.—*continued.* THE NAVY.

CHAPTER VIII.

CHARLES I.—*continued.* THE NAVY.

CHAPTER IX.

CHARLES I.—*continued.* THE JURIDICAL CONTROVERSIES.

CHAPTER X.

THE PARLIAMENT, THE COMMONWEALTH, AND THE PROTECTORATE.

THE FIRST DUTCH WAR.

CHAPTER XI.

THE PARLIAMENT, THE COMMONWEALTH, AND THE PROTECTORATE —*continued*.

THE PEACE NEGOTIATIONS.

CHAPTER XII.

CHARLES II.

THE SECOND DUTCH WAR.

CHAPTER XIII.

CHARLES II.—*continued.*

THE THIRD DUTCH WAR.

CHAPTER XIV.

JAMES II. AND AFTER.

SECTION II.—THE TERRITORIAL WATERS.

CHAPTER I.

THE HISTORICAL EVOLUTION OF THE TERRITORIAL SEA.

CHAPTER II.

GENERAL ADOPTION OF THE THREE-MILE LIMIT.

CHAPTER III.

THE FISHERY CONVENTIONS.

CHAPTER IV.

THE MODERN PRACTICE OF STATES AND THE OPINIONS OF RECENT PUBLICISTS.

CHAPTER V.

THE INADEQUACY OF THE THREE-MILE LIMIT FOR FISHERY REGULATIONS.

APPENDIX.

LIST OF ILLUSTRATIONS.

THE SOVEREIGNTY OF THE SEA.

INTRODUCTION.

ONE of the most prominent and characteristic features in English history relates to the sea and maritime affairs, and the reason is not far to seek. The geographical situation of the country—everywhere surrounded by the waves, separated on the one side from the Continent by a narrow strait and open on the other to the great ocean—made it almost inevitable. And to the advantage of insularity was added the potent influence of race. A great part, if not the larger part, of our blood has come from the old Scandinavian peoples,—the sea-wolves, as the Roman poet said, whose school was the sea and who lived on the pillage of the world; and it is to this circumstance even more perhaps than to the accident of position that we owe our maritime and naval supremacy and the vast empire scattered around the globe. Running through the web of English history one perceives the connecting thread of maritime interest and occupation interwoven with the national life, and at all times affecting the national policy. First and foremost was the necessity of securing the land from invasion; then came the duty of safeguarding shipping and commerce; and with regard to those fundamental interests, the language used by our rulers centuries ago was the same as that which is used by our statesmen to-day. The sea must be "kept." That has been the maxim and watchword of national policy throughout the ages, and the recognition of its truth was by no means confined to rulers and statesmen. The people at large have always been as convinced and as resolved that the supremacy or dominion on the sea should be maintained as were those in whose hands was placed the guidance of the affairs of the state. Again and again, when owing to mismanagement of the national resources, the poverty of the exchequer, or from some other cause, the supremacy at sea was endangered or temporarily lost, one will find the people clamouring for steps to be taken to maintain it. On the other hand, such was the deep and abiding sentiment with respect to the sovereignty of the sea, when this king or that wished to embark upon a policy or engage in a war for an object that was secret or unpopular, there was no better method of deceiving the people than by declaring that the dominion of the sea was in danger. Thrice in the compass of a single generation the nation was plunged into war with the object of maintaining it.

One thus finds in English history a great deal which refers to the sovereignty of the sea, although the words were not always used to signify the same thing. Most commonly perhaps they meant a mastery or supremacy by force of arms, —what is now so much spoken of as sea-power. In times of peace, the strength of the navy should be such as to safeguard the commerce that came to the realm and went from it, thus enabling merchants and traders to carry on their traffic in security. In time of war, the fleets should be strong enough to sweep the seas, so that, as it has been described, the bounds of the empire should then be the coasts of the enemy. But, more strictly, the sovereignty of the sea was a political sovereignty that existed as a matter of right, and was duly recognised as such, apart from an actual predominance of naval power at the time, just as the sovereignty of a state exists on land, though in both cases its maintenance may depend upon the sword. In this sense, the sovereignty of the sea signified the same sole power of jurisdiction and rule as obtained on land, and also, in its extreme form, an exclusive property in the sea as part of the territory of the realm,—very much indeed like the rights that are now admitted by the law of nations to appertain to the so-called territorial waters of a state. Many things and many interests were thus embraced in the term besides the question of naval ascendency. There were jurisdictions of various kinds and for various purposes. There was the important subject of the fisheries in the waters adjacent to the coasts, or, it might be, in distant regions. There was the still more important question of the freedom or restriction of commerce and navigation from one European country to another, or to the remote countries in the east or west which had been opened up to commercial enterprise by the discoveries of the early navigators. There was, moreover, another subject which was specially characteristic of the English pretensions to the dominion of the seas, and which gave rise to more trouble than all the others combined, and that was the demand that foreign vessels on meeting with a ship of the king's should lower their top-sails and strike their flag as a token and acknowledgment of that dominion.

Although according to the Roman law the sea was common and free to all, in the middle ages many seas had become more or less effectively appropriated, and Civilian writers began to assign to maritime states, as a principle of law, a certain jurisdiction in the waters adjacent to their coasts. The distance to which such jurisdiction was allowed by those writers was variously stated. Very commonly it extended to sixty or one hundred miles from the land, and thus included all the bordering sea within which navigation was practically confined. Sometimes the principle governing the ownership of rivers was transferred in theory to the sea, the possession of the opposite shores by the same state being held to entitle that state to the sovereignty over the intervening water; or, if it possessed only one shore, to the same right as far as the mid-line. In most cases, however, the appropriation of the sea was effected by force and legalised afterwards, if legalised at all, and the disputes on the subject between different nations not infrequently led to sanguinary wars.

The most notable instances are to be found among the early Italian Republics. Long before the end of the thirteenth century Venice, eminent for her commerce, wealth, and maritime power, assumed the sovereignty over the whole of the Adriatic, though she was not in possession of both the shores, and after repeated appeals to the sword she was able to enforce the right to levy tribute on the ships of other peoples which navigated the Gulf, or to prohibit their passage altogether. The neighbouring cities and commonwealths were soon compelled to agree to her claim, which was eventually recognised by the other Powers of Europe and by the Pope. The right of Venice to the dominion of the Adriatic, arising in this way by force, became firmly established by custom and treaty; and even after she had fallen from her greatness and was hardly able to sustain her claim by the sword, it was still for a time admitted by other nations, who looked upon the Republic as forming a useful barrier to the farther extension of the Turk in Europe and as a scourge to the Saracen pirates.[1] On the other side of the Italian peninsula, the Republic of Genoa advanced a similar claim to the dominion of the Ligurian Sea, and some of the other Mediterranean states followed the example in the waters with which they were most immediately concerned.

Then in the north of Europe, Denmark and Sweden, and later Poland, contended for or shared in the dominion of the Baltic. The Sound and the Belts fell into the possession of Denmark, the Bothnian Gulf passed under the rule of Sweden; and all the northern seas between Norway on the one hand, and the Shetland Isles, Iceland, Greenland, and Spitzbergen on the other, were claimed by Norway and later by Denmark, on the principle referred to above, that possession was held of the opposite shores. The Scandinavian claims to maritime dominion are probably indeed the most important in history. They led to several wars; they were the cause of many international treaties and of innumerable disputes about fishery, trading, and navigation; they were the last to be abandoned. Until about half a century ago Denmark still exacted a toll from ships passing through the Sound,—a tribute which at one time was a heavy burden on the trade to and from the Baltic.

Still more extensive were the claims put forward by Spain and Portugal. In the sixteenth century these Powers, in virtue

[1] The possession by Venice of this maritime sovereignty was symbolised each year for many centuries by the picturesque ceremony of "espousing" the Adriatic. On Ascension Day the Doge was rowed to the strains of music in a magnificent gilded state barge, the *Bucentaur*, to the channel of Lido, where he cast a ring into the water, exclaiming as he did so, "We espouse thee, O Sea, in sign of a real and perpetual dominion" ("Desponsamus te mare in signum veri perpetuique dominii"). The Papal nuncio and representatives of other states assisted at the ceremony.

of Bulls of the Pope and the Treaty of Tordesillas, divided the great oceans between them. Spain claimed the exclusive right of navigation in the western portion of the Atlantic, in the Gulf of Mexico, and in the Pacific. Portugal assumed a similar right in the Atlantic south of Morocco and in the Indian Ocean. It was those preposterous pretensions to the dominion of the immense waters of the globe that caused the great juridical controversies regarding *mare clausum* and *mare liberum*, from which modern international law took its rise. The task of Grotius in demolishing them by argument was, however, materially facilitated by the exploits of Drake, Hawkins, and Cavendish on the part of the English, and of Jakob van Heemskerk on the part of the Dutch; and, as we shall show, the credit of having first asserted the freedom of the seas in the sense now universally recognised, belongs rather to our own Queen Elizabeth than to the Dutch publicist.

In thus appropriating the seas adjacent to their territories, or which formed the means of communication with them, the various nations were doubtless impelled by consideration of their own immediate interests. Sometimes it helped to secure the safety of their coasts or commerce; in other cases it enabled them to levy tribute on foreign shipping traversing the appropriated waters, and thus to increase their revenues; or it allowed them to preserve the fisheries for the exclusive use of their own subjects. In most instances, however, the principal object appears to have been to maintain a monopoly of trade and commerce as far as possible in their own hands, in accordance with the commercial spirit of the times.

But when the matter is more carefully examined in its historical aspects, a less selfish explanation may be found of the tendency to appropriate seas in the middle ages. In the state of wild anarchy which prevailed after the break-up of the Roman empire, pirates swarmed along every coast where booty might be had. Scandinavian rovers infested the Baltic, the North Sea, and the Channel; Saracens and Greeks preyed upon the commerce of the Mediterranean; everywhere the navigation of trading vessels was exposed to constant peril from the attacks of freebooters. The sea was then common only in the sense of being universally open to depredation.[1] The lawless-

[1] Twiss, *The Law of Nations in Time of War*, 142. Maine, *International Law*, 76.

ness and insecurity that reigned on the sea led merchants, in the absence of effective sovereign authority, to form associations among themselves for mutual protection, and to maintain by force the security of navigation in the common interest. Independent princes at first made use of the armed fleets of those voluntary associations, and later, as their power grew stronger and better organised, they took over the duty of policing the neighbouring seas under an admiralty jurisdiction of their own, which enforced the maritime laws and customs, such as the Laws of Oleron, that had been gradually developed among the merchant associations. In the thirteenth century this duty of exercising supreme admiralty jurisdiction on the neighbouring sea came to be regarded as a prerogative of sovereign power,[1] and it was only a short step further to the assertion of an exclusive dominion. It was natural that this assumption of sovereignty on the sea should first be made by the great trading cities of Italy, who then controlled the important traffic between the east and the west, and whose shipping was to be found in all the ports of Christendom. It was also natural that the Italian jurists should be the first to attempt to give it a legal sanction, by assigning a large part of the bordering sea for the exercise of those sovereign functions which were originally confined to the maintenance of order and the punishment of delinquents. There is little doubt that the assumption of sovereign jurisdiction in this way was advantageous to navigation and commerce in those times, though later, with the extension of commercial intercourse and the increased security of the sea, it became burdensome and unnecessary.

There are good reasons for the belief that the English claims to the sovereignty of the sea originated in this humble way—by the exercise of jurisdiction in the interests of peaceful commerce—some time after the Norman Conquest, and in all probability first of all in the Channel or the Straits of Dover. The earliest indication of it is to be found in the much-discussed ordinance which King John issued in 1201. By that ordinance any ships or vessels, "laden or empty," which refused "at sea" to lower their sails when ordered to do so by the king's lieutenant or admiral in any voyage appointed by the Council, and resisted the demand, were to be reputed

[1] Twiss, *op. cit.*, 143, 144. Reddie, *Maritime International Law*, i. 41.

as enemies, and the ships, vessels, and goods were to be seized and forfeited and the crews punished. This is the first evidence of the custom of lowering the top-sails and striking the flag which afterwards became so notorious as a supposed acknowledgment of the English sovereignty of the sea; and it is to be noted that, in later times at least, the vessel had not only to strike, but had also to "lie by the lee." Considering the prevalence of piracy and the jurisdiction exercised by the state for its suppression, as above described, and in view likewise of the special measures taken by John to encourage and safeguard foreign commerce, the most reasonable explanation of the origin of the custom is that the demand for the sail to be lowered—and the largest vessels then had but one mast and a single sail—was to enable the king's officers, who were there to maintain the security of navigation, to ascertain the true nature of the vessel which they challenged, whether it was a peaceful trader or a pirate. In all ages piratical vessels have been generally swift, and, if we judge from later times, the ships used in the navy were generally slow: the command to a vessel to lower its sails was thus made in order to deprive it of the power of escaping until the king's officers had satisfied themselves as to its *bona fides*, and was equivalent to the gun that was fired in later times in connection with "visit and search." Shortly before the ordinance was issued, John sent writs to the Mayor and Commonalty of London and to all the Sheriffs of England instructing that all merchants, of what nation soever, should have safe conduct to pass into and repass from England, and to enjoy peace and security.[1] It is noteworthy that in the first record relating to the seizure of a vessel for not lowering its sail (a Flemish herring smack, in 1402) it was pled on its behalf that it was not armed, and that the sail had been dropped at the first command. It is also noteworthy that the ordinance of John was placed in the *Black Book of the Admiralty* immediately after the mercantile marine laws.

Further evidence as to this sort of jurisdiction in the so-called "Sea of England" is to be found in the reign of Edward I., at the end of the thirteenth century and the beginning of the next, in the reign of Edward III., and later,

[1] Nicolas, *Hist. Navy*, i. 157.

more particularly in the famous rolls, "On the Supremacy of the Sea of England and the Right of the Office of Admiralty in the same," as well as in the *Black Book*. The rolls referred to show that England had the sovereign jurisdiction in regard to the maintenance of peace and security in the Sea of England, but there is no evidence to indicate that that Sea extended far from the coast, or that the rights exercised differed from those put in force by other maritime states in the waters adjoining their territory. A great deal was made later of these rolls and of the ordinance of John, as proving that the Angevin or Plantagenet kings possessed the sovereignty of the sea; but beyond the jurisdiction in question, which doubtless was exercised in the Straits of Dover and perhaps in the Channel when the coasts on each side were in the possession of the crown, there is a lack of evidence to prove that any claim of the kind was made. In those times the kings of England were not infrequently styled Lords of the Sea, but this appears to have been either because of the existence of this "sovereign lordship" in the neighbouring waters, or, more usually, because they held at the time the actual command and mastery of the seas in a military sense. There were long periods when nothing was heard of any pretension by England to a special sovereignty of the sea, and, in point of fact, the characteristic features of appropriation were always absent. No tribute was levied on foreign shipping passing through the Channel or the narrow seas, even when both coasts were held by the king, as was done by Denmark at the Sound and by Venice in the Adriatic. After the battle of Agincourt, when Henry V. had been recognised by the Treaty of Troyes as the future king of France and the power of England was predominant, the proposal of Parliament that such tribute should be levied was set aside. Foreign ships of war freely navigated the adjacent seas without asking or receiving permission to do so. The sea fisheries, moreover, were not appropriated. All people were at liberty to come and share in them, and this freedom to fish on the English coast was expressly provided for in a long series of treaties with foreign Powers. The so-called sovereignty of the seas exercised by England thus differed from the actual sovereignty enjoyed by Venice and the northern states of Europe, whose rights were, moreover, recognised in numerous treaties with other nations.

Until the accession of the Stuarts indeed, any pretension of England to a sovereignty in the sea had but little international importance. The custom of lowering the sail by vessels encountering a king's ship, which probably, as above described, originated in a practical way, had grown into a ceremony in which the top-sails were dropped and the flag hauled down; but it is evident that this was done, even in Tudor times, rather as a matter of "honour" and respect than as an acknowledgment of maritime sovereignty. But after the Stuarts came to the throne the claim of England to the sovereignty of the sea became prominent in international affairs. The doctrine may be said to have been introduced by this dynasty and to have expired with it. One of the first acts of James I. was to cause to be laid down on charts the precise limits of the bays or "chambers" along the English coast, within which all hostile actions of belligerents were prohibited. This sensible proceeding, which had reference to the continuance of the war between the United Provinces and Spain (from which James had himself withdrawn), is not to be regarded as in any sense an assertion of maritime sovereignty or jurisdiction beyond what was customary; and it does not appear that any other prince or state contested the right of the king to treat these bays and arms of the sea as territorial in respect of neutrality. The limits of the "King's Chambers" were fixed by a jury of thirteen skilled men, appointed by the Trinity House, according to their knowledge of what had been the custom in the past; and there is little doubt that the limits they adopted merely defined in an exact way what was previously held to be the waters under the special jurisdiction of the crown, or, in other words, the "Sea of England," though the latter doubtless included, at times at least, the Straits of Dover and perhaps the Channel as well.

But James went further than this. In 1609 he issued a proclamation in which he laid claim to the fisheries along the British and Irish coasts, and prohibited all foreigners from fishing on those coasts until they had demanded and obtained licenses from him or his commissioners. This policy of exclusive fishing, though in complete agreement with the views held in Scotland as to the waters "reserved" for the sole use of the inhabitants, was a reversal of the long-settled practice in England, where fishing in the sea was free. It is from this time that one may date the beginning of the English pretension to the sovereignty of the sea. The proclamation and the policy were aimed against the Dutch, the great commercial people of those times. Their ever-increasing herring fishery along the British coast was one of the principal sources of their wealth and power; by means of it indeed, according to their own accounts, they were able to maintain their vast commerce and shipping. The action of James may be looked upon as the first blow in the great contest between the English and the Dutch for maritime and commercial supremacy, which was prolonged throughout the seventeenth century; and the ready acceptance of the new policy by the English people was owing to the fact that the conditions had been gradually preparing for it in the preceding reign, while the two nations were still bound together in alliance against Catholic Spain. With the new development of commercial enterprise the English found the Dutch their competitors in trade in all parts of the globe to which they ventured. The feeling of jealousy that was thus engendered was embittered by the belief that they were often circumvented by the Dutch by unfair means, and this feeling deepened with every year as the century advanced. It was thus against the Dutch that the English pretension to the sovereignty of the sea was specially directed, and it eventually culminated in war. From various circumstances, and not least perhaps from the timid character of James when force was necessary, the policy of preventing the Dutch from fishing on the British coasts was not carried into effect in his lifetime. But with the tenacity that was a curious feature in his nature, his claim to the fisheries was kept alive and formed the subject of mutually irritating negotiations throughout the whole of his reign.

Under Charles I. the English pretension rapidly developed and reached its greatest height, in connection more particularly with the ship-money fleets. The need of an efficient navy for the most elementary duty of safeguarding the sea had been made fully manifest by the frequent and flagrant violations of the king's sovereignty in his "chambers," and even in the ports and harbours, both by the Dutch and Dunkirkers. And some of the reasons which were used to justify the formation of a powerful fleet, far beyond the requirements necessary to enforce the ordinary jurisdiction, were sound enough. Without it, it was said, the kingdom could not be made safe, whereas if the king had the command of the seas he would be able to cause his neighbours "to stand upon their guard" whenever he thought fit; and it could not be doubted that those who would encroach upon him by sea would do it by land also when they saw their time. But the pretensions of Charles went far beyond this. He had caused the records in the Tower to be searched for evidence of the ancient supremacy exercised by the crown in the Sea of England, and when they were found they were interpreted in the widest possible sense. Charles assumed the *rôle* of the Plantagenets with a good deal added. The bounds of the Sea of England were extended to the coasts of the Continent, and over all the intervening water the king was to enforce an absolute sovereignty. No foreign fleets or men-of-war were to be allowed to "keep any guard" in them, to offer any violence, or to take prize or booty. All passing through them were to be "in pace Domini Regis," in the peace and under the protection of the King of England, who was Lord of the Seas, ruling over them as part of his territory, and he would take care that there was no interruption of lawful intercourse. And as an acknowledgment of this sovereignty, all foreign ships or vessels meeting with a king's ship in "those his seas" were to lower their top-sails and strike their flag as they passed by. Charles even proposed to levy tribute on the foreign ships that passed through "his seas," but by the advice of the Admiralty this was to be only voluntary, in payment for waftage or convoy.

These extraordinary pretensions Selden attempted to justify in his book, *Mare Clausum*, but Charles was unable to carry them into effect. It is pitiful to read of the proceedings of the great ship-money fleets, created under circumstances so memorable in English history, roaming about the Channel in their vain attempts to compel the French men-of-war to strike their flags, and in the North Sea forcing the king's licenses on the poor Dutch herring fishermen. The Earl of Northumberland succeeded in the latter mission, against which the Dutch Government strongly protested, and there is no doubt that if the policy had been persisted in, the first Dutch war would have been antedated by some fifteen years.

At this period and during nearly all the remainder of the century the greatest prominence was given to the striking of the flag, which had continued to be a matter of small importance in the reign of James. It was now claimed as a token and acknowledgment of England's sovereignty of the sea, and it was insisted on with the utmost arrogance. The "honour of the flag" burned like a fever in the veins of the English naval commanders, who vied with one another in enforcing the ceremony, not merely in the Channel or near the English coast, but in the roads and off the ports on the Continent; and the records relating to their achievements in this respect were treasured up in the archives of the Admiralty, to be used again and again in later diplomatic negotiations as to the rights of England to the sovereignty of the sea. Dutch ships, and in particular the men-of-war, made little scruple about performing the "homage." The Government of the United Provinces were keenly concerned about their commerce and fisheries, and so long as the English pretension did not menace these substantial interests they were willing to show "respect" to the English flag—never, however, as an acknowledgment of any supposed sovereignty of the sea.

While Charles was on the throne no serious international consequences resulted from the enforcement of the salute. The Dutch, as has been said, readily rendered it, and by the prudent policy of Richelieu the French ships were kept out of the way; and not very long thereafter Charles was stripped of his sovereignty on land as well as on the sea. But a little later it had noteworthy results. It was the reluctance of Lieutenant-Admiral Tromp to lower his flag to Blake in their historic meeting in the Straits of Dover in 1652 that precipitated the first Dutch war. By this time the States-General of the United Provinces, and the State of Holland in particular, had considerably abated their readiness to render the "homage of the flag," even as a mark of respect, thinking that it might be construed as an acknowledgment on their part that the Republic of the Netherlands was inferior to the Republic of England. They had dallied with the subject when it was brought before them in connection with the instructions to their fleets, and had refrained deliberately from giving precise orders about it. The Commonwealth, on the other hand, assigned as much importance to the striking of the flag as Charles had ever done, considering that it touched their dignity as well as their sovereignty in the seas, and the instructions they issued to the naval commanders were practically the same as those that had been given to the ship-money fleets. Even the godly Barebones' Parliament of 1653, which looked upon the Dutch as a carnal and worldly people, held it necessary that the seas should be secured and preserved as peaceable as the land, as a preparation for the coming of Christ and the personal reign. The traditional sentiment of the English nation respecting supremacy at sea had never been stronger; their jealousy of the commercial pre-eminence of the Dutch was never keener. In the prolonged negotiations that preceded the conclusion of peace, Cromwell, who, until he became Lord Protector, acted as spokesman for the Council, put the questions relating to the dominion of the sea in the foreground. The draft articles which he submitted to the Dutch for their acceptance, while permitting their merchant vessels to navigate the British seas (a provision offensive in itself), proposed to limit the number of their men-of-war that might be allowed to pass through those seas, and if occasion arose for a larger number, the Dutch Government were to give three months' notice to the Commonwealth and obtain consent before they put them forth. Their men-of-war, as well as their merchant vessels, were to submit to be visited and searched. The Dutch were to have liberty to fish upon the British coasts on payment of an annual sum for the privilege. They were to render the honour of the flag to any ship of the Parliament. Of all these demands the only one that was conceded was the last, and it was a small triumph for Cromwell that he was able, for the first time, to bind another nation to this ceremony by the formal stipulation of a treaty. The Dutch, however, were able to eliminate from the article the words representing that the striking of the flag was an acknowledgment of England's sovereignty of the sea; and it was pointed out in Holland that they had undertaken to do nothing more than they had previously done.

After the Restoration the pretension to the sovereignty of the sea was continued with almost as much zeal as before. Charles II. did not indeed lay claim to an absolute dominion over the British seas, such as his father had done in the earlier part of his reign. But on all occasions when the opportunity offered, he held to his alleged right to levy tribute for the liberty of fishing on the British coasts, but without the least success. And as for the right to the "honour of the flag," if it was not exacted with the same arrogance as it had been earlier in the century, it came now to be more than ever before a subject of importance in international relations, especially with the United Provinces. De Witt, the able Minister who directed Dutch affairs, was very desirous to arrive at a definite understanding about it, for he saw that to leave in ambiguity a matter which England regarded as touching her national honour would be to imperil the peaceful relations between the two countries. His object was to have a well-considered regulation prepared and agreed to, so that the points in ambiguity might be made clear, and also to provide that if the Dutch saluted first the English should then return the salute; and he stipulated that the striking of the flag or any agreement about it must not be looked upon as an acknowledgment of England's so-called sovereignty of the sea; the Dutch, he said, "would rather die" than admit it. One of the points which was in obscurity was whether a whole fleet or squadron of the States was to strike to any single ship of the king's, even if it was a frigate or a ketch, which did not customarily carry the royal flag in the main-top, or only to an admiral's ship or one carrying the royal flag. De Witt let it be known in the clearest manner that in his opinion it was intolerable that an English frigate or ketch could claim to force a whole Dutch fleet to strike to it. A few years later, when Charles wished to give effect to his secret compact with Louis XIV. by waging war against the United Provinces, it was necessary to hoodwink the English people as to this flagrant breach of treaty obligations. He therefore contrived, as the means of picking a quarrel with the Dutch, a dispute about the honour of the flag, and he sent, not a frigate, but his yacht, the *Merlin*, to force the whole Dutch fleet to strike to it, and thus to raise a clamour in England, as he hoped, about the sovereignty of the sea being flouted and endangered. In the third Dutch war which followed, the United Provinces maintained the contest at sea with credit and success against both the English and the French. For domestic reasons Charles was forced to make a separate peace, and in the long negotiations with that object the question of the sovereignty of the sea was brought prominently forward. An attempt was made again to induce the Dutch to agree to pay an annual sum of £12,000 for the privilege of fishing on the British coasts, but the only concession obtained from them related to the striking of the flag. The article in the treaty of peace which dealt with this differed from the corresponding article in previous treaties. The term "the British Seas" was omitted, and it was agreed that even squadrons of the Dutch should strike to any single ship of the king's in "any of the seas" from Cape Finisterre to Van Staten in Norway; but it was to be done as an "honour" to the king's flag, and not as an acknowledgment of his alleged sovereignty of the sea. The Dutch, indeed, offered to strike in the same way all the world over.

After this time the English claim to the sovereignty of the sea began to lose its importance. In subsequent treaties with the Dutch Republic, even as late as 1784, a clause was inserted providing for the salute, but it had become merely a matter of form and precedent. The ceremony, in truth, had grown to be a political encumbrance, and after the battle of Trafalgar, when British supremacy at sea was unquestioned, the clause relating to the enforcement of the salute was quietly dropped out of the Admiralty instructions.

It is remarkable that throughout the whole of the long period in which England claimed sovereignty in some form or other over the so-called "Sea of England," or the "British Seas," no authoritative definition was ever given of the extent of sea included in the term. In the case of the Adriatic there was no difficulty in understanding the limits within which

Venice assumed maritime dominion, for the Adriatic is a narrow landlocked gulf whose boundaries were obvious. It was much the same with the claims put forward by Denmark. Both shores of the Sound were in her possession, and both coasts of the northern or Norwegian Sea. But with our island, washed everywhere by the waves, no such natural boundaries existed. Except when the crown possessed the opposite coast of France, England was isolated; and the Sea of England, so frequently referred to from the thirteenth to the seventeenth century, like the British Seas later, remained only a political expression, not officially described or represented on charts. Reasons have been given above for supposing that the Sea of England prior to the accession of the Stuarts included the waters of the King's Chambers as defined by James, and perhaps also at times the Straits of Dover and it may be the Channel, though precise evidence is lacking. In the seventeenth century, when the term the British Seas was commonly used, it is clear that the boundaries assigned to them were as vague and fluctuating as the sovereignty exercised over them. They expanded and contracted according to the naval power at the time and the condition of international affairs. Sometimes the whole sea up to the continental coasts was claimed as British; at other times the claim was restricted to the Channel or the Straits of Dover, and to a more or less narrow but undefined belt along the coast; not unfrequently it seemed to vanish altogether, at least as a thing to be regarded in international affairs. In the earlier records in which the sea is referred to in connection with English law or jurisdiction, it is evident that a certain part was held to appertain to the crown. In an article in the *Black Book of the Admiralty* which is ascribed to the reign of Henry I. (A.D. 1100-1135), reference is made to "the sea belonging to the king of England"; in John's ordinance of 1201 the term was simply "the sea" (*la mer*), but very commonly it was "our sea," or the "sea of England," or "the sea under the dominion or jurisdiction of the king"; while the declaration is often made that the kings of England are lords of the sea or of the English sea.[1] Similar phrases

[1] "Il sera banny hors dAngleterre et de mer appartenant au roi dAngleterre," Article in *Black Book*, i. 58, ascribed to the reign of Henry I. (A.D. 1100-1135);

were used in later times. Thus Queen Elizabeth spoke of "our seas of England and Ireland," and James of "his seas" and "streams," as did also Charles I.; and such terms as "the adjacent sea," the "environing seas," the "ambient seas," and "the seas flowing about the isle," were not uncommonly used.[1] Still more common and scarcely more definite was the term the "Four Seas of England," or simply the "Four Seas," which was employed as early as the thirteenth century in law books, statutes, and official documents, as indicating the boundaries of the realm in connection with legal proceedings. Within the four seas (*infra* or *intra quatuor maria;* dedeinz les quaters meers) was to be within the realm; and without the four seas (*extra quatuor maria,* oultre les quaters meers) was to be without the realm.[2]

In the seventeenth century, when the English pretension to the sovereignty of the sea was at its height, Coke, Selden, Prynne, and others maintained that to be on the four seas, as well as within them, was to be within the realm, under the jurisdiction of the Admiralty, and this doctrine was held, at least formally, as late as 1830.[3] Rarely the "Three Seas" are mentioned,[4] and less rarely the "Two Seas," by which was

"Ad piscandum in mari nostro, prope Jernemuth," Edward I., A.D. 1295, *Fœdera,* ii. 688; "la meer Dengleterre," A.D. 1306, *Chanc. Rolls, Misc. Treaties,* &c., Bd. 14, No. 15; "super mare Anglicanum" (*Rot. Pat.,* 14 Edw. II., pt. ii. m. 26, d.), A.D. 1320, &c., &c.; "partibus maris infra regnum nostrum Angliæ," A.D. 1317, Edw. II., *Fœdera,* iii. 469; A.D. 1406, Hen. IV., giving freedom of fishing, "ubicumque supra mare, per et infra dominia, jurisdictiones, et districtus nostra"; "Seigneur de la mer," A.D. 1320, *Fœdera,* iii. 852; "reges Angliæ domini maris Anglicani circumquaque," A.D. 1336, *Rot. Scot.,* i. 442; "domini maris et transmarini passagii," A.D. 1336, *Fœdera,* iv. 721; "le roi de la mier," A.D. 1372, *Rot. Parl.,* ii. 311; "seigneurs del meer," A.D. 1420, *ibid.,* iv. 126, &c., &c.

[1] *Fœdera,* xvi. 395; *State Papers, Dom.* 1604, 11, 40; *Fœdera,* xix. 211; *Libelle of Englyshe Polycye;* Dee, *General and Rare Memorials,* 6; *State Papers, Dom.* 1662, 66, 50, "It is a fundamental Maxime of England, that the sea flowing about the Isle of Great Britaine is of the same dominion with the isle"; "the dominion of the ambient seas."

[2] *Rot. Escheat.,* 41 Hen. III., A.D. 1259, referred to by Coke, 1. 107*a*; Bracton, *Legibus et Consuetudinibus Angliæ,* lib. v. c. xxx. fol. 437 (A.D. *circa* 1259); *Statutes of the Realm,* 18 Edw. I. Stat. 4 (A.D. 1290); *Rot. Parl.,* 13 Ric. II., "deinz les quatre miers Dengleterre," &c.

[3] Hall, *On the Rights of the Crown in the Sea Shores of the Realm,* p. 1.

[4] "The guardian of his Majesty's three seas" (A.D. 1607). *Cæsar Papers, MS. Brit. Mus. Lansd.,* 142, fol. 373.

meant the two arms of the sea passing respectively between England and France, and England and Flanders, and corresponding to one of the meanings of the Narrow Sea.

The term, the Narrow Sea or the Narrow Seas, was applied at different times or by different writers to very various areas. In its original and more restricted sense it denoted the Straits of Dover; sometimes it signified only the southern sea or the Channel proper; at other times it included also the sea south of the Wash and the Texel; and yet again it was synonymous with the whole of the British seas in which dominion was claimed. In the political poem, *The Libelle of Englyshe Polycye,* which was written about 1436 with the object of rousing the nation to the paramount duty of "keeping the sea," the narrow sea is spoken of as lying between Dover and Calais,[1] as it is also in the records of the Privy Council for 1545, which mention the appointment of ships to "kepe the passage of the Narrow Seas."[2] Later in the same century, and very generally in the seventeenth century, it was used to include the Channel, as when the Earl of Salisbury in 1609 referred to "his Majesties narrow seas between England and France,"[3] and likewise the sea off the Dutch coast; and at this period the Admiralty usually distinguished between the guard of the Narrow Seas and that of the North Sea.

But in other cases, and very commonly in the seventeenth century, the Narrow Sea was equivalent to the marginal sea along the whole coast or to the "British Seas." Thus in one of James's proclamations in 1604 for preventing abuses in and about "the narrow seas," they are referred to as being commonly called the four English Seas, and this was repeated in a proclamation of Charles I. in 1633. So also Lord Chief Justice Hale in his treatise, *De Jure Maris,* describes the narrow sea, adjoining to the coast of England, as part of the waste and demesnes and dominions of the King of

[1] "Thene here I ende of the comoditees
Ffor whiche nede is well to kepe the sees;
Este and weste, sowthe and northe they be;
And chefely kepe the sharpe narowe see,
Betwene Dover and Caleise."

[2] *Acts of the Privy Council of England,* N.S., i. 232, 242.

[3] Winwood's *Memorials,* iii. 50.

England; and in another work he speaks of the narrow sea lying between us and France and the Netherlands.

After the union of the Crowns the "British Seas" were very often referred to, and there was equal want of definition of their limits as in the case of the Sea of England. The advocates of the English claims to the sovereignty of the sea assigned them a wide but vague extent, while the Dutch argued that the British Sea was the Channel, the Mare Britannicum of Ptolemy and others, the North Sea being distinct and known as Oceanus Germanicus. In many of the diplomatic negotiations that took place on the subject there were heated discussions as to the meaning of the term the "British Seas," and in point of fact the British representatives, like the Admiralty itself, were unable to define them. The only serious attempt which was made to define the Sea of England or the British Seas in relation to the claim to its sovereignty was made by Selden in 1635. It did not fail on the side of modesty, for according to him the Sea of England was "that which flows between England and the opposite shores and ports."[1] More particularly in the opening chapter of his second book he describes the British Sea (Oceanus Britannicus) as being divided into four parts according to the four quarters of the world. On the west lay the Vergivian Sea, also called the Deucaledonian Sea where it washes the coasts of Scotland, and in which Ireland is placed; on the east is the German Ocean, so called by Ptolemy because it lies opposite the German shore; on the south, between England and France, is the sea especially noted by Ptolemy as the British Sea, the Mare Britannicum; but in reality all the sea extending along the shores of France through the Bay of Aquitaine (Bay of Biscay) as far as the northern coast of Spain was British. Since the northern and western ocean stretches to a great distance, to America, Iceland, and Greenland, and to parts unknown, it could not "all be called British," but inasmuch as the King of Great Britain had very large rights in those seas, beyond the extent of the British name, it was not wholly to be left out of account. The indefiniteness of these boundaries to the north and west is obvious, but in a chart which he furnished,

[1] *Mare Clausum*, ii. c. xiii.

and which is reproduced in the frontispiece of this book, he presumably represented what he regarded as the British seas proper; and in several places in his work he expressly declared that the English sea and the English sovereignty of the sea extended to the opposite shores of the Continent.

Throughout almost the whole of the remainder of the century after the appearance of *Mare Clausum*, Selden's authority was paramount on all questions relating to the sovereignty of the sea, and his description of the extent of the British seas was very generally adopted, both by writers and by the Government, at least in theory. But it not infrequently happened on particular occasions when a precise definition of their extent was required, that only a vague declaration was forthcoming. Again and again one finds English admirals and naval commanders imploring the Admiralty to tell them the bounds of the British seas, so that needless broils about the salute might be avoided. As a rule, no reply was given to their inquiries; and when it was, it was usually so oracular as to be of little practical advantage. Thus the Earl of Lindsey, when placed in command of the first ship-money fleet, put the question to Secretary Coke, and was told that his Majesty's seas "are all about his dominions, and to the largest extent of those seas," and similar explanations were given on other occasions. There is evidence that neither the Admiralty nor the law officers of the crown were able to state what the boundaries of the British seas were, and sometimes the Trinity House was appealed to, with but little better result. In truth, it was part of the national policy to leave their boundaries undetermined. The free navigation of the North Sea and the Channel was of vital importance for many of the states of Europe, and three of them at least—the Netherlands, France, and Spain—had large interests in the fisheries on the British and Irish coasts. If this country had by a formal act of state assigned definite and wide boundaries to the British seas within which sovereignty was claimed, it would have led to frequent and hopeless wars or to constant humiliation. By leaving them vague and ambiguous the pretension to maritime sovereignty could be put forward and used as a political instrument when the navy was strong and occasion offered, and when the navy was weak the pretension might fall into the background without the national honour being unduly tarnished. But on the whole, the claim to the sovereignty of the so-called British seas became an anachronism and was allowed to die out from practical affairs, surviving only in the pages of historians, naval writers, and pamphleteers. During the almost constant naval wars in the eighteenth century a new principle came into being for the delimitation of the neutral waters of a state, the extent of the adjacent open sea that might be appropriated being determined by the range of guns from the shore. All the water within reach of cannon-shot could be protected and commanded by artillery on the land, and thus made susceptible of exclusive and permanent dominion. This principle was accepted very generally by the various maritime Powers as offering a just and equitable means of fixing the limits of their territorial waters, within which the bordering state had exclusive sovereign jurisdiction. It has also been accepted by the great majority of modern publicists, and the phrase of Bynkershoek, "terræ dominium finitur ubi finitur armorum vis," has become enshrined in the Law of Nations.

Later, and mainly through the action and practice of the United States of America and Great Britain since the end of the eighteenth century, the distance of three miles from shore was more or less formally adopted by most maritime states as equivalent to the range of guns, and as more definitely fixing the limits of their jurisdiction and rights for various purposes, and, in particular, for exclusive fishery. At the time the three-mile limit was introduced, that distance did indeed represent the farthest range of artillery, so that the boundary was the same in each case; and it was sufficient to secure to neutrals that their coasts should not be violated by the operations of belligerents carried on beyond three miles from the shore, while at the same time it furnished a practical measure of the extent of the protection that neutral Powers were bound to afford to the vessels of one belligerent from attacks by the other. But all this is changed. Guns are now able to throw shells to a distance of fifteen miles and more, and the three-mile limit has become quite inadequate to secure the coasts of a neutral from damage from the guns of belligerents engaged in hostilities in the waters near their shores. The argument is not uncommonly used that inasmuch as Great Britain is the predominant maritime Power, it is to her advantage that the territorial waters of all countries should be as narrow as possible. The wider the theatre the better chance for our navy, either in engaging the battle fleets of the enemy or in capturing his shipping. The importance of the change in the conditions referred to above is overlooked. There has been no great maritime war in Europe since the three-mile limit was adopted as the equivalent of the range of guns. If and when another maritime war unfortunately breaks out, it would be absurd to suppose that the neutral Powers within the sphere of possible operations would be content with a three-mile limit to safeguard the security of their coasts. As provided for in the rules drawn up by the Institute of International Law, their duty would be to prohibit all hostilities within such distance of their coasts as would render them secure, and this in turn would involve the immunity from capture within the same space of the merchant vessels of one of the belligerents by the vessels of the other. And thus if this country were engaged in a great maritime war, such as occurred a century or so ago, a very considerable belt of sea on neutral coasts would be closed to the operations of the fleet, and the conditions of naval warfare would be profoundly changed.

With regard to the other questions of sovereignty or exclusive rights in the seas washing the coasts of a country, it is becoming more and more recognised that there is no reason in nature why the boundary for one purpose should be the boundary for all purposes. Just as the three-mile limit is now obsolete in respect to belligerents and neutrals in time of war, so is it inadequate in all cases with regard to the protection and preservation of the sea fisheries. In the concluding chapters of this book it is shown that all recent inquiries by Parliament into the condition of the fisheries, especially of the North Sea, have resulted in proving the inadequacy of the present limit for fishery regulations, and in recommendations that the subject should be dealt with internationally by the various countries concerned.

SECTION I.

THE HISTORY OF THE CLAIMS TO THE SOVEREIGNTY OF THE SEA

CHAPTER I.

EARLY HISTORY.

When the claim of the English crown to the sovereignty of the British seas became a question of international importance in the early part of the seventeenth century, the records of history and the treasures of ancient learning were searched for evidence to establish its antiquity. Some of the greatest lawyers and scholars of the time took part in the task, and they were not always content with the endeavour to prove that the claim was in conformity with the laws of England as an old heritage of the crown, but they tried to trace it back to a remote past. Selden, who was incomparably the ablest and most illustrious champion of the English pretension, as well as Boroughs and Prynne and other writers of lesser note, laboured with more or less erudition and ingenuity to show that the British dominion in the adjoining seas was anterior to the Roman occupation. From the ancient Britons it was supposed to have passed to the Roman conquerors as part and parcel of the British empire, and to have been exercised by them during their possession of the island.[1] It is unnecessary to discuss the evidence and arguments for these contentions. They are for the most part drawn from scattered passages or even phrases in the writings of classical authors, to which a strained and improbable significance was assigned. An example may be given from Selden, who, in referring to the well-known passage in Solinus[2] in which Irish warriors are described as decking the hilts of their swords with the tusks

[1] Selden, *Mare Clausum*, lib. i. c. viii., lib. ii. cc. ii.-viii.

[2] *Polyhistor.*, c. xxiv.

of sea-beasts (walrus), first tries to show that the passage applied also to the Britons, and then argues that there must have been a great fishing and a large number of fishermen to provide sufficient material, the conclusion being that the British seas were "occupied" by navigation and fishing. In reality the walrus tusks came by barter from the north, and there is little or no evidence to show that the ancient Britons fished for anything except salmon. At the utmost it may be said that the Romans were masters of the British seas, or parts of them, in a military sense. During their occupation of Britain they were also in possession of Gaul, and thus held both coasts of the narrow sea, and no doubt exercised authority over it, as the Norman and Angevin kings under similar circumstances did later.

Throughout the Anglo-Saxon period of English history evidence of the existence of a sovereignty over the adjoining sea, or even of a pretension to it, is almost as unsatisfactory. Here again the authors who championed *mare clausum* professed to find in very ordinary events arguments in favour of their case. The seafaring habits of the Teutonic invaders and their daring and valour—they were described by the Roman poet as sea-wolves, fierce and cunning, with the sea as their school of war and the storm their friend—were regarded as proof that they possessed maritime sovereignty after their conquest of Britain. The Danegeld, a tax which was originally levied as a means of buying off the Danes, or of providing a fleet to resist their attacks, was thought by Selden to show the same thing.[1] So also with the fleets collected by Alfred, Edgar, Ethelred, and other English kings to oppose the invasions of the Northmen,—they were believed to have secured and maintained dominion over the sea. Even the beautiful lesson in humility which Cnut desired to convey to his courtiers when, seated in regal pomp on the seashore, he vainly commanded the inflowing tide to stay its course at his behest, was seized on for the same end. "Thou, O sea," said the great king, "art under my dominion, like the land on which I sit; nor is there any one who dares resist my commands. I therefore enjoin thee not to come up on my land, nor to presume to wet the feet or garments of thy lord." In these words Selden professed to find

[1] *Mare Clausum*, lib. ii. c. xi.

clear proof that Cnut claimed the British seas as part of his dominions.[1]

There appears to be only one instance before the Norman Conquest in regard to which *prima facie* evidence was produced that an English king expressly claimed the sovereignty of the sea, and as it is constantly quoted by later writers it may be worth while examining it. The chronicles agree that the naval power of England was specially manifested by King Edgar (A.D. 959-975), who is said to have possessed a fleet of several thousand vessels, with which he cruised every year along the English coasts. In the words of the Saxon Chronicle, "no fleet was so daring, nor army so strong, that mid the English nation took from him aught, the while that the noble king ruled on his throne."[2] According to William of Malmesbury, who wrote in the twelfth century, Edgar usually styled himself the sovereign lord of all Albion and of the maritime or insular kings dwelling round about,[3] the assumption being that he also exercised sovereignty over the intervening and surrounding seas. In a charter by which Edgar, in 964, granted large revenues to the Cathedral Church at Worcester, the claim to the ocean around Britain is more definite, and it is this version that is usually quoted by the writers maintaining the antiquity of the English rights.[4] The title thus said to have been used by Edgar is expressive enough, but an important difference in the wording of this part of the charter is to be found in the transcript printed by Coke in the Epistle to the Fourth Book of Reports, by Spelman,[5] Wilkins,[6] and by the more recent authorities on Anglo-Saxon charters, Kemble,[7] Thorpe,[8] and

[1] *Mare Clausum*, lib. ii. c. xii. "Canutus autem Rex suæ ditionis esse Oceanum Britannicum verbis expressissimis item est testatus." Prynne uses the same argument. *Animadversions on Coke's Fourth Institute*, 88.

[2] Ed. Petrie, 395.

[3] *Gesta Regum Anglorum*, i. 235; Eng. Hist. Soc. "Ego Edgarus totius Albionis Basileus nec non maritimorum seu insulanorum Regum circumhabitantium."

[4] "Ego Edgardus Anglorum Basileus omniumque Regum insularum, Oceanique Britanniam circumjacentis cunctarumque nationum quæ infra eam includuntur Imperator et Dominus," &c. Dee, *General and Rare Memorials*, 58, 60; Selden, *Mare Clausum*, ii. c. xii. (quoting from a charter of Inspeximus, *Rot. Pat.*, 1 Edw. IV., m. 23); Prynne, *op. cit.*, 87.

[5] *Concilia*, i. 432.

[6] *Ibid.*, i. 239.

[7] *Codex Diplomaticus*, ii. 404, vi. 237.

[8] *Diplomatarium Anglicum Ævi Saxonici*, 211.

Birch,[1] from which it appears that Edgar claimed to be, not lord of the sea, but of the islands in the sea.[2] This is the version given by Sir John Boroughs in his *Sovereignty of the British Seas,* and it is also mentioned by Selden. But, after all, the authenticity of the preamble of this charter is not well established. Kemble marks it as doubtful, a view supported by intrinsic evidence as to an imaginary conquest of Ireland. Thorpe is of opinion that the preamble was fabricated about 1155, when Henry II., in concert with Pope Adrian IV., was meditating the conquest of that island. It may therefore be concluded that King Edgar's assumption of maritime sovereignty had its source in a monkish fable, although he may have possessed the actual command of the sea in his time. Later on, the supposed *rôle* of Edgar among the Anglo-Saxon kings was a common argument for the English claims. He was looked upon as a sort of patron saint of the doctrine that the kings of England were lords of the sea. Charles I. put his effigy on the beak of his great ship, the *Sovereign of the Sea,* and inscribed his name in a motto on her guns. Oliver Cromwell, too, quoted his exploits to the Dutch ambassador in the course of the negotiations after the first war with Holland.

It is not to the Anglo-Saxon period of our history that we must look for the origin of the claims of England to the sovereignty of the sea, even in a purely military sense. At that time, for at least three centuries before the Norman Conquest, the Northmen and not the English were the real lords and masters of the sea. They offered an example of what is now so much spoken of as the influence of sea-power on history that is unsurpassed in later annals. Their leaders were styled sea-kings for the best of reasons. Their fleets darkened every coast from within the Arctic circle to the furthermost bounds of the Mediterranean. Through their command of the sea they took permanent possession of the larger part of England; they penetrated almost every great river in Europe—the Elbe, the Schelde, the Rhine, the Seine; they formed settlements from Friesland to Bordeaux; they discovered and planted colonies in Iceland (A.D. 861), Greenland

[1] *Cartularium Saxonicum,* iii. 377.

[2] "Insularum oceani quæ Brytanniam circumjacent."

(A.D. 985), and North America (A.D. 861); and they founded kingdoms or dynasties not only in England, but in France, Sicily, Ireland, and Russia.[1] In the presence of such irrepressible energy in maritime and warlike enterprises the English were not able to hold their own on the sea, far less to acquire dominion over it.

It is not until a considerable time after the Norman Conquest that valid evidence is to be found of the English claim to the sovereignty of the sea. Although obscurity surrounds the precise time and mode in which the pretension took its rise, there is little doubt that it originated in the period following the Conquest. The shores on both sides of the Channel were then brought under the same dominion. In the reign of Henry I. almost the whole of the Atlantic coast of France from Flanders to the Pyrenees was in the possession of the English crown, and for about four and a half centuries, until the loss of Calais in 1558, England held more or less territory in France. The Channel thus became in effect an English sea—the narrow sea—intervening between the continental and insular territories of the king, and it acquired high importance as the passage from one part of the realm to the other. It was in this connection and for the guarding of the coasts that the organisation of the Cinque Ports was developed by the Norman and Angevin kings.[2] Even after the loss of the French provinces, the continued possession of the Channel Islands and the usual possession of Calais kept alive the English claim to the narrow sea. The Conquest was, moreover, followed by a great increase in the stream of traffic between the two countries,[3] while fishermen from Normandy and Picardy, as well as from Flanders, came in large and increasing numbers to take part in the great herring fishery along the east coast of Scotland and England.

During the frequent wars with France from the commencement of the twelfth century onwards, the Channel acquired special significance from a military point of view, and it was

[1] Worsaae, *An Account of the Danes and Norwegians in England, Scotland, and Ireland;* Depping, *Histoire des Expéditions maritimes des Normands;* Beamish, *The Discovery of America.*

[2] Burrows, *Cinque Ports*, 62, 81.

[3] Cunningham, *The Growth of English Industry and Commerce during the Early and Middle Ages*, 173.

from this time that the importance of "keeping the narrow seas" began to be recognised in English policy. The command of the Channel was not only of value in safeguarding the coast. The Channel formed the great avenue of commerce between the north and south of Europe. The merchant vessels from Venice, Genoa, and the Mediterranean, from Spain and France, passed northwards through it on their way to Flanders and the Baltic, and those from the Hanseatic towns and northern parts had in like manner to traverse it in their southern voyages. The Channel was thus crowded with shipping in summer, and the nation which commanded it had the power of interrupting the commerce of other nations, and consequently retained a potent political weapon in its hands. It is this aspect of "keeping the narrow sea" which forms the burden of the remarkable old poem, *The Libelle of Englyshe Polycye.*

Moreover, in the period following the Norman Conquest another condition came into existence in connection with the security of the commerce passing through the Channel, which throws light on the origin of the English claim to sovereignty over it. As already mentioned, owing to the lawlessness that prevailed on the sea after the break-up of the Roman empire, when pirates and freebooters infested every coast, it became customary for merchants to associate themselves together for mutual protection. Their vessels sailed forth in fleets under the charge of an elected chief, called the "admiral," and armed vessels were frequently fitted out by them for the express purpose of purging the sea of pirates. In the course of time this duty of maintaining the police of the seas was taken over by sovereign princes, who exercised their jurisdiction through an admiralty, and put in force the old "laws of the sea" which had gradually grown up among the merchant associations.[1] In the thirteenth century this supreme admiralty jurisdiction came to be regarded among the principal states of Europe as a prerogative of sovereign power, and it is about this time and in this connection that we first find certain evidence of the claim of England to the sovereignty of the adjacent sea. The Plantagenet kings, or at all events some of them, asserted the right of "maintaining the ancient supremacy of the Crown over the Sea of England" by exercising jurisdiction

[1] Twiss, *The Law of Nations in Time of Peace*, 244; ibid., *In Time of War*, 142.

according to the old maritime laws, for the maintenance of "peace and justice amongst the people of every nation passing through the said sea." [1] It was the production of the old rolls concerning these claims by Sir John Boroughs, the Keeper of the Records in the reign of Charles I., which furnished that king with the material on which to base his pretension to the sovereignty of the sea.

The English writers of the seventeenth century who strove to prove that the kings of England anciently exercised an exclusive sovereign jurisdiction over the so-called Sea of England, as if it were a "territory or province of the realm," quoted largely from the old Admiralty records. Selden sought to show that they had perpetually enjoyed the dominion of the surrounding sea from the coming of the Normans from the fact that they had maintained a guard upon it.[2] The evidence adduced, however, merely proves that measures were taken for guarding the seas, defending the coasts, and suppressing piracy,—duties which were discharged, even in the same seas, by the Admiralty of other countries, as that of France. Such phrases as "to guard the seas," "to guard the sea and sea-coasts," are common enough in the early records of the Admiralty,[3] but they do not imply exclusive dominion. It was a duty common to neighbouring nations. In England, from the time of Henry I., at the beginning of the twelfth century, orders were given for the seas to be guarded as occasion required; and officers were appointed by Henry III. and other kings as Wardens, Keepers, and Guardians of the sea and sea-coasts, and also as Governors and Captains of the Navy, whose title was subsequently changed to Admiral in the latter part of the thirteenth century, following the practice of the merchant associations, as above mentioned. Much was made by the English writers of the appointment of admirals by the kings of England for safeguarding the sea. The first appears to have been appointed in 1297 with the title of Admiral of the Sea of the King of England,[4] but before this

[1] See p. 51.

[2] *Mare Clausum*, lib. ii. c. xiv.

[3] "Pour garder la mere," "la garde du meer," "la sauve garde du meer," "pro custodia maris," "de custodia maritimæ," &c. See *Proceedings and Ordinances of the Privy Council of England*; Nicolas, *History of the Royal Navy*; Prynne, *Animadversions*.

[4] *Fœdera*, i. 861; Nicolas, *op. cit.*, i. 279, 437.

time the King of Castile and Leon had appointed an admiral with similar duties, and an Admiral of all France was appointed about the year 1280.[1] So too with the equipment of fleets. Edward I. divided the ships charged with the guarding of the seas into three squadrons, each with an admiral,—a measure which, it was argued, showed his resolution to maintain his dominion of the sea. But the practice in France was similar. From an early period French fleets were equipped under "governors or custodians of the sea" (*præfectus maris*), "lieutenants-general of the sea and the shores thereof," and "admirals," and their maritime jurisdiction was regulated from at least the early part of the fourteenth century.[2] Selden laboured to show that the office of admiral and the admiralty jurisdiction had a different significance in France from what they had in England,[3] but on quite inadequate grounds.

Another class of evidence adduced by the English authors refers to the impressment of ships for the defence of the realm or the transport of troops on occasions of emergency. These duties were at first performed by the vessels of the Cinque Ports, in accordance with their charters; but as early at least as the reign of Richard I., ordinances were issued (at Grimsby) regulating the mode of arresting vessels and men for the service of the king,[4] and it became an established and common practice. Numerous instances occur which show that on such occasions foreign vessels were not exempt from arrest, though compensation was at least sometimes made to their owners.[5] The argument of the English writers that these arbitrary proceedings were evidence of the dominion exercised by the kings of England on their sea is rebutted by the practice in France. Froissart[6] tells us that the French adopted similar measures in 1386 when they were preparing for an invasion of England, and the practice was doubtless common enough, and justified by the emergency which occasioned it.

With regard to the most important attribute of maritime

1 Twiss, *The Law of Nations in Time of Peace*, 245.

2 *Vide* Twiss, *Black Book of the Admiralty*, i. 420.

3 *Op. cit.*, lib. ii. c. xviii.

4 Twiss, *ibid.*, i. 64.

5 Nicolas, *op. cit.*, i. 131, 231, ii. 45, 84, 130, 176; *Rot. Pat.*, 65 (1206); *Fœdera*, i. 96 (1208).

6 *Chronicles*, ii. 497.

sovereignty—the right to exclude others from an equal use of a particular sea by prohibiting navigation, at least of vessels of war, and from fishing in it, or by imposing dues and conditions for the liberty—there is scarcely a scrap of evidence to show that any authority of the kind was exercised by England in the adjacent seas. The circumstance is noteworthy, inasmuch as other countries which then enjoyed undoubted maritime sovereignty, did not permit unrestricted navigation or fishing in the seas specially under their control, as Venice in the Adriatic, and Denmark in the northern seas and in the Baltic. The evidence concerning the liberty of fishing in the sea along our coasts is dealt with in another chapter, but it may be said here that this liberty was provided for in a series of treaties with other Powers. As for liberty of navigation, it was asserted, or rather implied, by Selden, in guarded language, that the kings of England anciently possessed the power of refusing it;[1] but the evidence relates for the most part to passports and safe-conducts "by land and sea," and to the impressment of vessels, referred to above. There appears to be not a single fact to prove that the liberty of innocent navigation in the English seas was ever interfered with by the king. The Parliament of Ireland, it is true, passed an Act in 1465 prohibiting all foreign vessels "from going to fish at Ireland among the king's enemies" without first obtaining a license, on pain of forfeiture of the vessel. But it is clear from the preamble that the Act was passed because foreign vessels frequenting the Irish coast for fishing were supplying the king's enemies with money, arms, and provisions.

Nor is there any valid evidence that tribute was ever imposed on foreigners for liberty of navigation in the sea of England. A case frequently quoted to the contrary was the imposition of a duty by Richard II., in 1379, on merchant vessels and fishing smacks, to provide means for the defence of the eastern coast and the security of navigation and fishing. At that time the English navy had almost ceased to exist, through the mistaken policy of Edward III. in the latter part of his reign. In 1377 a French and Spanish fleet had not only scoured the seas, but plundered and burned Rye, Folkestone, Hastings, Plymouth, and other towns on the southern coast,

[1] *Op. cit.*, lib. ii. cc. xiii., xx.

which they ravaged. In the following year they continued their depredations on the English coast, and held such complete command of the sea that "no victualler, fishing boat, or any other, could pass or return without being taken."[1] In 1379, as the enemy still held the sea and the coast, Parliament, after consultation with the merchants, decreed that certain duties should be levied to provide means to secure the safeguarding of the sea, and among these was one on vessels laden with goods belonging to merchants of Prussia, Norway, or Scania. Selden says this ordinance applied to foreign as well as English vessels, which had therefore to pay for passage through the sea "just as one may exact payment for passage over one's field."[2] But there is no evidence that the tax was levied on other than English vessels; and in any case it is clear from the preamble that it was a voluntary arrangement, and probably made at the request of the merchants themselves, who had been petitioning the king and Parliament for protection.[3] It is noteworthy also that the keepers of the northern sea were not to convoy the vessels to or from Flanders and Calais unless they were paid for doing so.

An incident which occurred early in the next century shows the temper in which the Parliament regarded the sovereignty of the narrow sea, as well as the caution of the king. By that time the English navy had recovered its strength and France lay prostrate at the feet of Henry V., and the Parliament peti-

[1] *Rot. Parl.*, iii. 46*b*; Nicolas, *op. cit.*, ii. 260-280; Laughton, *Studies in Naval History*, 16-22. The Yarmouth herring fishing suffered severely in these years, and the fishermen equipped and armed vessels for their own defence,—*Chronicon Angliæ, ab* A.D. 1328 *usque ad annum* 1388, p. 170, Rolls Series.

[2] *Op. cit.*, lib. ii. c. xv.

[3] *Rot. Parl.*, iii. 63*b*, 391*a*; *Fœdera*, vii. 220. "C'este l'ordinance et grante par l'advis des Marchaundz de Londres, et des autres Marchaundz vers la North, par assent de touz Communes de Parlement par devant le Comte de Northumberland et le Meair de Londres, pur la garde et tuicion du Mier," &c. The specified dues throw some light on the commerce and fisheries of the period: (1) all vessels or crayers navigating the seas within the limits of the admiralty of the north were to pay a duty of sixpence a ton-tight, going and returning, with the exception of those bringing wines and goods from Flanders to London, or carrying wool and skins to Calais; (2) vessels laden with goods belonging to merchants of Prussia, Norway, or Scone (Scania) were to pay sixpence a last; (3) vessels carrying coals from Newcastle were to pay sixpence a ton every three months; (4) sixpence a-week per ton was to be paid by all vessels fishing for herrings within the said admiralty, and sixpence every three weeks per ton by boats fishing for other fish.

tioned the king to levy an impost on all foreign ships passing through the Channel, in emulation, no doubt, of the practice of the Danish kings at the Sound. It was a few years after the battle of Agincourt, and the Treaty of Troyes, by which Henry was recognised as the future king of France, had just been concluded. "The Commons pray," ran the petition, "that seeing our Sovereign Lord the King and his noble progenitors have ever been Lords of the Sea, and now by the grace of God it has come to pass that our said Lord the King is Lord of the shores on both sides of the sea, such tribute should be imposed on all strangers passing through the said sea, as may appear reasonable to the King for safeguarding the said sea."[1] The answer of the king was that he would consider it (*soit avise par le Roy*), the usual formula of refusal. In the following year Henry was again involved in war with France, and he died in 1422 and nothing more was heard of the proposal. But it is extremely doubtful if he or any other English king would have ventured to adopt the policy recommended by the Commons. The shipping that passed through the Channel was far more voluminous and important than that passing through the Sound, and the waterway could not be so easily commanded, as by guns from the shore. Any measure of the kind would doubtless have led to a combination of other maritime Powers against England, which would have been fatal to the attempt. It may be noted that the Parliament based their proposal on the king's possession of both shores; and this, in accordance with the opinions of the Italian lawyers of the preceding century, whose authority was great, carried with it the right of sovereignty over the intervening sea.

The statement in the petition that the kings of England had ever been lords of the sea is true at least to the extent that on several occasions previously the title was applied to them, and this was usually at times when they possessed actual supremacy and mastery over the seas in a special manner,

[1] A.D. 1420, *Rot. Parl.*, iv. 126. "Item, priount les ditz Communes, que par l'ou nostre très soverain seignour le Roy et ses nobles progenitours de tout temps ount esté seignours del meer, et ore par la grace de Dieu est venuz que nostre dit seignour le Roy est seignour des costes d'ambeparties del meer d'ordeigner que sur toutz estraungers passantz parmye le dit meer tiel imposition à l'oeps nostre dit seignour le Roy apprendre qui à luy semblera resonable, pur la salve garde del dit meer."

though it may also have implied the idea of sovereign jurisdiction. Nearly a century earlier than the above petition we find the same title used by Edward III., who is peculiarly identified with the naval glory of England, and he too refers to his progenitors as having been lords of the sea. In a mandate to his admirals in 1336, the king, after stating that twenty-six galleys of the enemy were reported to be on the coasts of Brittany and Normandy, said: "We, calling to mind that our progenitors, the Kings of England, were Lords of the English sea on every side, and also defenders against the invasions of enemies before these times; and it would greatly grieve us if our royal honour in such defence should be lost or in any way diminished in our time, which God forbid, and being desirous with the help of God to obviate such dangers and to provide for the safety and defence of our realm and people, and to restrain the malice of our enemies: We strictly require and charge you" to proceed against the galleys, &c.[1] Later in the same year, in a commission to certain nobles, prelates, and the Warden of the Cinque Ports respecting measures to be taken against the Scottish fleet, which was attacking merchant and other ships, and had ravaged Guernsey and Jersey, the king desired it to be remembered that his progenitors the kings of England, in similar disturbances between them and other lords of foreign lands, were in all bygone times "lords of the sea and of the passage across the sea," and he would be much afflicted if his royal honour should be in his time impaired.[2] These declarations, made in the first half of the fourteenth century, indicate clearly enough at least the pretension to special interest and jurisdiction in the narrow sea and the Straits of Dover on the part of the earlier kings. No English king deserved the title of Lord of the Sea better than Edward III. Only a few years after the above missives were written he gained the memorable victory over the French in the battle of Sluys, and in 1350 the

[1] *Rotuli Scotiæ*, i. 442, "Nos advertentes quod progenitores nostri reges Angliæ Domini Maris Anglicani circumquaque et etiam defensores contra hostium invasiones ante hæc tempora extiterint," &c. Part of the language of this mandate was copied by Charles I. in his ship-money writs. See p. 211.

[2] *Fœdera*, iv. 722. "Consideratio etiam quod progenitores nostri, Reges Angliæ, in hujusmodi turbationibus, inter ipsos et alios terrarum exterarum dominos motis, domini maris et transmarini passagii, totis præteritis temporibus, extiterunt," &c.

equally great victory over the Spaniards off Winchelsea ("Les Espagnols sur Mer"), commanding the fleet in person on each occasion.[1]

It appears to have been in connection with the former victory that Edward coined his famous gold noble, in which

Fig. 1.—*Edward's Noble.*

the obverse bears the effigy of the king, crowned, standing in a ship with a sword in one hand and a shield in the other, while the reverse bears the legend from St Luke, *Jesus autem transiens per medium eorum ibat*, "but Jesus, passing through the midst of them, went his way," which Nicolas thinks was meant to indicate the action of the king in passing through the French fleet at the battle of Sluys. The impress on the obverse has been usually regarded as symbolic of Edward's power and sovereignty on the sea. The unknown author of *The Libelle of Englyshe Polycye*, written some ninety years later, makes frequent reference to Edward's noble,—

> "Ffor iiii thynges our noble sheueth to me,
> Kyng, shype, and swerde, and pouer of the see,"[2]—

and it is always mentioned by the English writers on the sovereignty of the sea as evidence that Edward exercised

[1] Nicolas, *op. cit.*, ii. 49, 106.

[2] *Political Poems*, ii. 157. The author states that it was coined after Edward captured Calais, when

> "The see was kepte, and thereof he was lorde,
> Thus made he nobles coigned of recorde.'

But Edward did not take Calais till 1347, while the noble was issued in July 1344. Nicolas, *loc. cit.*

that sovereignty. A recent author[1] doubts whether there was any connection between Edward's noble and the battle of Sluys or the claim to the sovereignty of the sea; but at all events in the next century, in the reign of Henry VI., when the naval power of England had again sunk to a low point, the noble was made an object of jest and derision among foreigners, especially the Flemish and French. They told the English to take away the ship from their noble and put a sheep on it instead—an allusion, no doubt, to the growth of sheep-farming in England.[2]

If Edward intended to symbolise his naval power and sea sovereignty by the device on the gold noble in the early part of his reign, it was certainly inappropriate towards the end of it. The navy had been starved for the sake of the army, and when the Spaniards defeated the English fleet and were masters of the sea, complaints became rife as to the insecurity of the country. The king had then to listen to language from his Parliament to which he was unaccustomed, and which must have galled him. There are many instances in our history where the Commons have shown their spirit and temper when they thought the navy was inadequate for its duties, and on the occasion in question, in 1372, after granting a naval subsidy, they called the king's attention to the fact that while twenty years previously, and always before, the navy was so noble and so numerous in all the ports, coast towns, and rivers that the whole country deemed and called him King of the Sea,[3] and he and all his country were the more dreaded by sea and by land by reason of the said navy, it was then so decreased and weakened from various causes that there was scarcely sufficient to defend the country, if need were, against

[1] Oppenheim, *A History of the Administration of the Royal Navy*, i. 7.

[2] Cunningham, *op. cit.*, 361. In the *Libelle* it is asked—

> "Wher ben our shippes, wher ben our swerdes become?
> Our enmyes bid for the ship set a sheep";

and the rubric of an anonymous commentator states that the advice quoted was owing to the fact that while in the time of Edward III. the English were lords of the sea, they were now in these days mad (*vecordes*), vanquished, and for waging war and guarding the sea, like sheep. The jest is also alluded to by Capgrave, *Liber de Illustribus Henricis*, 135.

[3] "Tous les pays tenoient et appelloient nostre avandit seigneur, le Roi de la Mier."

royal power, by which there was great peril to all the realm.[1] From this complaint of the Parliament it would appear that the title of king or Lord of the Sea was applied in a popular sense, to signify the great sea-warrior who had overcome his enemies and made himself master of the sea.

There was another symbol or supposed symbol of the sovereignty of the sea, which later became exceedingly prominent — viz., the striking of the flag or the lowering of the top-sails to a king's ship, about which there is little to be found in the records of those times. It is nevertheless with this that the earliest of the records relating to the subject is concerned, and it is a very interesting one. The famous ordinance of King John which compelled the lowering of the sails has given rise to much controversy. It was first brought prominently to notice by Selden in 1635,[2] but it is also contained in the little work of Boroughs on the *Sovereignty of the British Seas,* which was written in 1633, although not published till 1651, and that author transcribed it from a manuscript in the possession of Sir Henry Marten, the Judge of the Court of Admiralty. Selden gave as his authority for it, "MS. Commentarius de Rebus Admiralitatis," without further specification, and its authenticity was questioned by contemporary critics. Prynne, who, like Boroughs, was Keeper of the Records, printed it in 1669 from the *Black Book of the Admiralty,*[3] and from the fact that the *Black Book* was lost until quite lately, and the existence of Selden's manuscript in the Bodleian Library was overlooked, and that used by Boroughs unknown, some recent authors have regarded the ordinance with suspicion.[4] The most elaborate account of the various manuscripts containing the ordinance of John is given by Sir Travers Twiss in the Introduction to the *Black Book of the Admiralty;* and through his efforts the original *Black Book,* lost for more than half a century, was found at the bottom of a chest in 1873.[5] Twiss gives the

[1] *Rot. Parl.*, ii. 311.

[2] *Mare Clausum*, lib. ii. c. xxvi.

[3] *Animadversions*, 108.

[4] Nicolas, *op. cit.*, i. 156, but cf. ii. 481; Hannay, *A Short History of the Royal Navy*, 15. Hannay, as well as the writer of the naval articles in *Social England* (i. 138), was not apparently aware of the labours of Sir Travers Twiss mentioned in the text.

[5] *The Black Book of the Admiralty*, i. Intro. xiii *et seq.*, 129; iii. Intro. i, x.

following free translation of the ordinance, made by the Registrar of the Admiralty Court in the reign of James II.:—

> ITEM, it was ordained at Hastynges for lawe and custome of the sea in the tyme of Kyng John, in the second yeare of his raigne, by the advice of his temporall lordes, that if the lieutenant of the king or the admirall of the king or his lieutenant in any voyage appointed by Common Counsell of the Kyngdom did at sea meet with any shyps or vessells laden or empty which would not stryke and lower their sailes at the command of the kyng's lieutenant, or the kyng's admirall, or his lieutenant, but makeing resistaunce against those of the ffleet, that if they can be taken that they be reputed as enemies, and their shyps, vessells, and goodes, taken and forfeited as goodes of enemies, albeit that the maysters or possessors thereof should afterwards come and alleadge the same ships, vessells, and goodes to be the goodes of friends of our lorde the kyng, and that the company therein be chastized by imprisonment of their bodies for their rebellion at discretion.[1]

This ordinance is the last of a series of articles in the third part of the *Black Book*, which contains Admiralty regulations, the Laws of Oleron, and other three ordinances of King John, as well as ordinances which purport to have been made in the reigns of Henry I., Richard I., and Edward I. The facts ascertained by Sir Travers Twiss show that of the six or seven extant manuscripts which contain the ordinance, the oldest was written before 1422 and probably about 1420,[2] and appears to have been drawn up for the use of Sir Thomas Beaufort, the Lord High Admiral. The manuscript used by

[1] "Item ordonne estoit a Hastynges pour loy et coustumes de mer ou temps du roy Johan lan de son regne second par advys de ses seigneurs temporelz que se le lieutenant en aucun voyage ordonne par commun conseil du royalme encontrent sur la mer aucunes nefz ou vesseaux chargees ou voide que ne veullent avaller et abbesser leurs trefs ou commandement du lieutenant du roy ou de ladmiral du roy, ou son lieutenant, mais combatant encontre iceulx de la flotte que silz puent estre pris quilz soient reputez comme ennemys et leurs nefs, vesseaulx, et bien pris et forfaitz comme biens des ennemys tout soit que les maistres ou possesseurs dicelles vouldroient venir apres et alleguer mesmes les nefs, vesseaulx, et biens estre biens des amys du roy nostre seigneur, et que le mayne estant en icelles soient chastiez par emprisonnement de leur corps pour leur rebellete par discrecion." The above is given by Twiss from the *Whitehall MS.* of the eighteenth century; it does not materially differ from the others. The *Cottonian MS.*, which is stated to be the earliest and purest, reads in both places "le lieutenant du roy ou ladmiralle du roy ou soun lieutenant."

[2] *The Black Book*, Intro. xix, lxxvii. It is *Vespasian MSS.*, B. xxii.

Selden was probably written between 1430 and 1440; that of the *Black Book* itself a little later, but still in the reign of Henry VI.[1] The others are not older than the seventeenth century. None of the manuscripts is therefore contemporaneous with the reign of John, but it is clear that the ordinance existed and was ascribed to John in the reign of Henry V., before 1422. Moreover, from intrinsic evidence it is proved that part of the *Black Book* originated in 1375, in the reign of Edward III., and that the compilation of other parts of it is still earlier. Pardessus,[2] the great authority on ancient marine laws, is of opinion that the part of the *Black Book* which includes the ordinance of John contains the results of the consultations with the judges in 1338 on the subject of the maritime laws, which were recorded in the roll, still preserved, of 12 Edward III., *De Superioritate Maris*—which also, as we shall see, claimed supremacy for the king in the sea of England. Twiss, however, thinks it was more probably compiled between 1360 and 1369. He is of opinion that the ordinance is authentic, and was in reality, as it purports, made by John at Hastings on 30th March 1201, and that it was transcribed into the compilation of the *Black Book* with the earlier ordinances of Henry I. and Richard I.

The arguments against the authenticity of the ordinance are mainly that it is written in the French language instead of in Latin, as was customary at the time; that there is no other evidence that John was ever at Hastings; and that the terms "king's admiral" or "king's lieutenant" are not to be found in contemporary documents. Twiss has shown that John and his Queen were at Canterbury on Easter Day 1201, and it is not an improbable conjecture that the king passed from Canterbury to Hastings, and thence to London—a supposition that Sir Thomas Duffus Hardy, the author of the *Itinerary of King John*, regards as quite possible. Twiss also explains in an elaborate argument that the circumstance of the ordinance being written in French offers no difficulty, if the compilation of the third part of the *Black Book* is assigned, as above stated, to the reign of Edward III.; but there might be some difficulty in deciding whether the ordinances attributed to Henry I., Richard I.,

[1] *The Black Book*, iii. Intro. viii, x. See p. 410.

[2] *Collection des Lois Maritimes*, iv. 199.

Edward I., and John were originally written in French as they now appear in the *Black Book,* or were at first drawn up in Latin and translated into French by the compilers.[1]

The best authority is therefore in favour of the authenticity of the ordinance; but whether it be held as genuine or apocryphal there is no doubt that in the reign of Henry V. it was incorporated among the official regulations of the Admiralty, and it is almost as certain, as Twiss and Pardessus believe, that it was contained in the Admiralty regulations in the reign of Edward III. The question whether it should be antedated one hundred and fifty years, or thereabout, and placed in the reign of John, or ascribed to the time of Edward III., when so much consideration was given to naval affairs, is perhaps of minor importance.

The language of the ordinance is worthy of close attention with regard to the claim to sovereignty in the narrow sea. Selden says that the ordinance shows it was held to be treason for any ship whatever not to acknowledge the dominion of the king of England in his own seas by lowering sails, and that the king prescribed penalties for infraction of the rule, just as if a crime were committed in some part of his territory on land.[2] In 1201 John still possessed both shores of the Channel, a circumstance which, according to the ideas of the time, conferred on him special rights in regard to it; and though the ordinance contains no qualification of the general term "at sea," it is probable that it applied in particular, and at first perhaps exclusively, to the waters between the two shores. There is nothing to show whether the ordinance applied to or was enforced against the war vessels of other princes navigating the narrow sea, which was the principal feature of the rule in later times. From the terms used it is probable that it applied only to merchant vessels,—a supposition that agrees with its place in the *Black Book* at the end of the articles entitled the Laws of Oleron, or the laws of the mercantile marine; and it was to be enforced only in voyages appointed by the Council. As already mentioned, it is reasonable to suppose that the lowering of the sail at the demand of a king's ship was to enable a suspected vessel to be overhauled, and the king's

[1] *Collection des Lois Maritimes*, i. Intro. pp. li, 129; iii. Intro. p. xi.

[2] *Mare Clausum*, lib. ii. c. xxvi.

officers to be satisfied whether it was engaged in piracy or in lawful trade.

Until the sixteenth century there is scarcely any evidence to show that the "right of the flag," as it came to be called, was enforced even in the Channel. The record of one such incident, however, exists, which occurred in 1402, in the reign of Henry IV.,—and thus, it is interesting to note, before the oldest extant manuscript containing John's ordinance was written,—and, curiously, the place where the lowering of the sails was demanded was not the Channel but the North Sea. In the year mentioned, the town of Bruges complained to the king and Council that a poor fisherman of Ostend, named John Willes, along with another from Briel, while fishing for herrings in the North Sea, had been captured by an English vessel and taken into Hull, notwithstanding that they were unarmed—a remark which is significant—and had lowered their sails at the moment the English had called to them.[1] It is singular that the earliest record of the "ceremony" refers to the humble herring-boats of Flanders. Later on we shall see that the lowering of top-sails and the striking of the flag became a burning question in international politics.

Of greater interest and importance than this question of the lowering of the sail or the ordinance of John is the claim put forward by the Plantagenet kings to sovereign lordship and jurisdiction in the "sea of England," for the maintenance of peaceful navigation and commerce,—a claim which may still be read in some of the rolls of Edward I. and Edward III. The great importance of these documents for the English pretension to dominion of the sea in the seventeenth century was shown by the fact that Boroughs, Selden, Coke, and Prynne all quote freely from them, Selden especially turning to them again and again for fresh quotation and argument. They are the more interesting since the claim to the sovereignty of the narrow sea in the reign of Edward I. could not, as Boroughs points out, be based on possession of both shores; the king was not then *Dominus utriusque ripæ,* as when Normandy belonged to the English crown. The rolls in question are still preserved in the

[1] "Quanquam tamen, ad primam vocem ipsorum Anglicorum, idem Johannes Willes velum suum declinavit," &c., *Fœdera*, viii. 273; "omnes tamen inermes, et velum suum, ad primum clamorem Anglicorum declinantes," *ibid.*, 277.

Record Office, and the earlier parchments appear to have been collected together in the reign of Edward III., in connection with the consultations that the judges held in 1338 on the subject of the maritime laws.[1]

The documents were first brought into prominence by Lord Coke[2] and Selden,[3] both of whom published parts of them. The handwriting belongs to the beginning of the fourteenth century, and its contents show that it must have been drawn up after 1304 and before 1307, in which year Edward I. died.

The events that preceded may be summarised as follows. During the war between Edward I. and Philip the Fair of France it was concluded between them in the year 1297 that notwithstanding the war there should be freedom of commerce on both sides, or a truce for merchants, known as sufferance of war, and in the following year certain persons were appointed by both kings to take cognisance of things done contrary to this truce, and to pass their judgments according to the law of merchants and the tenor of the sufferance referred to.[4] On 20th May 1303 a treaty of peace and alliance was signed at Paris,[5] the first article of which embodied a declaration of amity and mutual defence of all their respective rights, and the third that each would abstain from assisting or succouring the enemies of the other. A little later in the same year four agents or commissioners were appointed by Edward and four by Philip to hear complaints and decide upon them, and the English members were instructed to inquire into the "encroachments, injuries, and offences committed

[1] *Chancery Rolls, Misc. Treaties and Diplomatic*, Bdle. 14, No. 15. It is endorsed *De Superioritate Maris Angliæ et Jure Officii Admirallatus in eodem.* There are several copies on separate membranes in the bundle—viz., 1, 8, 12, 14, 15,—and they differ from one another, as indicated in the transcript in Appendix A. Prynne (*Animadversions*, 109) says that besides the roll in the Tower from which Lord Coke and Selden quoted, he discovered "an ancient copy of it in the White Tower Chapple," and among the Admiralty papers is a memorandum by Nicholas, undated, but before 1631, on the records in the Tower respecting the Laws of Oleron and the Sovereignty of the Seas, in which he says that "in ye little closset there" a record in French exists, dated in the time of Edw. I. or II., referring to the depredations of Grimbald. There is also a transcript in a collection of MSS. in the British Museum (*Harleian*, 4314) and a translation of the roll, in a hand of the seventeenth century, in *MS. Otho.* E. ix. fol. 14.

[2] *Fourth Institute*, cap. 22, p. 142.

[3] *Mare Clausum*, lib. ii. c. xxvii., xxviii., xx., xxiv.

[4] *Rot. Pat.*, 26 Edw. I., part 2, memb. 24, *in dorso.*

[5] *Fœdera*, i. 954.

on either side during the truce or sufferance between us and the said King of France, on the coasts of the sea of England and other neighbouring coasts, and also towards Normandy and other coasts of the sea more remote."[1] To these commissioners the following joint complaint or libel bears to have been submitted on behalf of England and certain mariners of other nations, charging one Reyner Grimbald or Grimaldi, a Genoese who is known to have been at the time in command of ships in the service of France operating against the Flemings, with seizing their merchants and merchandise contrary to the treaty at Paris:[2]—

Concerning the Supremacy of the Sea of England and the Right of the Office of Admiralty in the same.[3]

To you the Lords Auditors deputed by the Kings of England and of France to redress the wrongs done to the people of their kingdoms and of other lands subject to their dominions by sea and by land in time of peace and of truce The proctors of the prelates and nobles and of the admiral of the sea of England[4] and of the commonalties of cities and towns and of the merchants mariners messengers and pilgrims and of all others of the said realm of England and of other lands subject to the dominion of the said King of England and elsewhere, as of the coast of Genoa, Catalonia, Spain, Almaigne, Zeeland, Holland, Friesland, Denmark, and Norway, and of several other places of the Empire do declare, That whereas the Kings of England by right of the said kingdom, from a time whereof there is no memorial to the contrary, had been in peaceable possession of the

---

1 Selden, *op. cit.*, lib. ii. c. xxvii., quoting from *Rot. Pat.*, 31 Edw. I., m. 16, which reads as follows: "Des enterprises, mesprises, et forfaitz en Treue ou en Sufferance, entre nous et le dit Roi de Fraunce, dune part et dautre, es costeres de la mer Dengleterre et autres per decea et ausint per deuers Normandie et autres costeres de la mer per de la."

2 The King of France ordered John de Pedrogue, a celebrated seaman of Calais, to collect a fleet there and proceed with it to Holland against the Count of Flanders, who had invested Zierikzee. Included in the fleet were eleven Genoese galleys, under Reyner de Grimaldi, who was given the chief command by Philip, with the title of "Admiral," John de Pedrogue acting under him. Nicolas (*op. cit.*, i. 373) gives a description of the fight.

3 The translation, for which I am indebted to Miss E. Salisbury, is from membrane 12.

4 The expression is also used in a document of 1297, when Lord William de Leybourne is described as "Admiral of the sea of the said King of England." *Fœdera*, i. 861.

sovereign lordship of the sea of England and of the isles within the same, by ordinance and establishment of laws, statutes, and prohibitions of arms, and of ships otherwise furnished than merchant vessels, and to take surety and afford safeguard in all cases where need shall be, and by ordinance of all other actions necessary for the maintaining of peace, right, and equity among all manner of people as well of any other dominion as of their own passing thereby, and by sovereign guard and all manner of cognizance and justice high and low, concerning the said laws, statutes, ordinances, and prohibitions, and by all other actions that may appertain to the exercise of sovereign lordship in the places aforesaid. And A. de B.[1] deputed Admiral of the said sea by the King of England, and all other Admirals [appointed] by that same King of England and his ancestors heretofore Kings of England, had been in peaceable possession of the said sovereign guard with the cognizance and justice and all other the aforesaid appurtenances, except in case of appeal and complaint made of them to their sovereigns the Kings of England of default of right or of wrong judgment, and especially by putting hindrance (making prohibitions) and doing justice, taking surety of the peace of all manner of people using arms in the said sea, or carrying ships otherwise provided or furnished than appertained to a merchant ship, and in all other points wherein a man may have reasonable cause of suspicion towards them of robbery or other misdemeanours. And whereas the masters of the ships of the said kingdom of England in the absence of the said admirals had been in peaceable possession to take cognizance and to judge of all actions in the said sea between all manner of people according to the laws, statutes, and prohibitions, franchises and customs. And whereas in the first article of the alliance formerly made between the said Kings, in the treaties upon the last peace of Paris are comprised the words which follow in a schedule annexed to these presents.

> First, it is concluded and accorded between us and the messengers and proctors aforesaid in the name of the said Kings that the said Kings shall from this time forward be good, true, and loyal friends, and be aiding to one another against all men saving the Church of Rome in such manner that if any one or more, whosoever they be, will disturb, hinder, or molest the said Kings in the franchises, liberties, privileges, rights, dues, or customs of

[1] Coke (*op. cit.*, 143) states that this refers to "De Botertort," who, he says, was Admiral "of the sea coasting upon Yarmouth in Norfolk (right over against France) and of that station in *anno* 22 Edw. I." Nicolas (*op. cit.*, i. 270, 407) states that Sir John de Botetourt was made commander of the northern fleet in 1293, and in the following year, when Edward divided his fleet into three squadrons, the ships of Yarmouth and the adjacent ports were placed under his charge.

them and their kingdoms, they shall be good and loyal friends and allies against every man living, and ready to die to defend, keep, and maintain the franchises, liberties, privileges, rights, dues and customs aforesaid; Except (on the part of) the said King of England, Monsieur John, Duke of Brabant, in Brabant, and his heirs descended from him and the daughter of the King of England, and except (on behalf of) our said lord the King of France, the excellent Prince, Monsieur Albert, King of Almaigne [and] his heirs Kings of Almaigne, and Monsieur John, Count of Hainault in Hainault. And that the one shall not be of counsel nor aiding where the other may lose life, member, temporal estate, or honour.[1]

Monsieur Reymer Grymbaltz, Master of the navy of the said King of France, who calls himself admiral of the said sea, deputed by his lord aforesaid for his war against the Flemings did after the said alliance made and confirmed, and against the form and force of the same alliance and the intent of them that made it, by commission of the King of France wrongfully usurp the office of admiralty in the said sea of England and did exercise it for a year and more taking the people and merchants of the kingdom of England and elsewhere passing through the said sea with their goods, and committed the people so taken to the prison of his said lord the King of France, and by his judgment and award caused their goods and merchandises to be delivered to the receivers of the said King of France deputed for this purpose in the ports of his said kingdom, as to him forfeit and acquired. And the taking and detaining of the said people with their said goods and merchandises, and his said judgment and award concerning the forfeiture and acquest of them, he has justified before you, Lords Auditors, in writing, according to the authority of the said commission of the admiralty aforesaid by him thus usurped, and during a prohibition commonly made by the King of England by his power, according to the tenor of the third article (*sic*) of the alliance aforesaid, which contains the words below [above] written, requiring that he may thereupon be quit and absolved, to the great damage and prejudice of the said King of England and of the prelates and nobles and others above named, Wherefore the said proctors in the names of their said lords do pray [you Lords] Auditors aforesaid that you would cause due and speedy deliverance of the said people with their goods and merchandises thus taken and detained, to be made to the Admiral of the said King of England, to whom the cognizance thereof of right belongs, as above is said, so that, without disturbance from you or any

[1] The rest is on the back of the membrane.

other, he may take cognizance hereof and do that which belongs to his office aforesaid, and that the said Monsieur Reyner be condemned and constrained to make due satisfaction to all the persons wronged as aforesaid as, etc. [so far as he is able to do, and in his default his said lord the King of France, by whom he was deputed to the said office, and that after due satisfaction made for the said damages, the said Monsieur Reyner may be so duly punished for the violation of the said alliance that his punishment may be an example to others in times to come.[1]] Item, the said proctors require that whereas according to the ancient laws, franchises and customs of the realm of England, to the keeping whereof your said lord the King and his ancestors Kings of England were wont to be bound by their oaths. Their admirals of the sea of England with the masters and mariners of ships of ports of the coast of England, being in the armies of the said admirals, needed not to answer before any justices of the Kings aforesaid concerning actions in the sea abovesaid during their wars against their enemies. And the said admiral of your said lord the King and many of the masters and mariners of the ports aforesaid now being in his army against the [their] enemies of Scotland and their helpers and allies, by express commandment of your said lord the King, are accused before you by people of Normandy and Brittany and elsewhere concerning some actions in the said sea in time of truce and since the peace confirmed between the said Kings of England and France, and before the war begun between them as is said. It may please you to surcease the process already commenced against them and to forbear to commence a new one during the war abovesaid, that they may have no cause to complain to your said lord and to the prelates and nobles of his said realm, bound by their oath to keep and maintain the said laws, franchises, and customs.

Selden alludes to this document as proving that the right of dominion over the sea, and that ancient and confirmed by long prescription, was in express terms here acknowledged by almost all the neighbouring nations to belong to England.[2] This is, however, not quite justified, because there is no record at all to show any decision, or even whether the matter was

[1] The part within brackets is to be found on the membranes 1, 14*d*, and 15, but not on 12.

[2] *Mare Clausum*, lib. ii. c. xxvii. Hall, in his excellent *Treatise on International Law* (p. 141), and with reference apparently to this roll, says that exclusive dominion over the English seas by the English king was acknowledged as early as 1299 (*sic*), at a commission in Paris, by the representatives of the merchants and mariners of the countries mentioned in the above document.

ever brought to proof, and no mention is made of the proceedings by any English or French historian. There seems to be no doubt of the authenticity of the record. It is in the handwriting of the time, is preserved among the public records, and agrees with other circumstances elsewhere recorded. On the other hand, even the most complete copy[1] is only a draft, as Selden states, without date or seals; the admiral's initials only are given, and the citation of the first article of the treaty at Paris is not on a separate schedule as the text states, but is part of the text. Selden gives it as his opinion that it was a matter "of such moment" that it was thought better to make an end of it by agreement than to bring it to a trial.

Light is thrown on the above record by another of the proceedings before the Auditors deputed by the kings of England and France for the redress of the grievances between the subjects of the two countries, 27-33 Edward I.[2] It consists of a series of libels or complaints, which, as Mr Salisbury of the Record Office has been good enough to inform me, are in the handwriting of the time of Edward I., and are doubtless those, or part of those, on which the *De Superioritate* roll is based.[3] The complaints are sixteen in number, and they refer to the seizure of a number of ships and the removal of goods from them, between May 1298 and September 1303, at various places,—the foreland of Thanet, the mouth of the Thames, off Blakeney, off Kirkele, Scarborough, Dover, and Orfordness,—the goods, and sometimes the vessel, being taken to Calais. Most of the vessels were freighted from London to Brabant, or from the latter place to London, one from Winchelsea to Dieppe, another from Antwerp to London, a third from Berwick to London, a fourth from Scotland to Brabant, a fifth from Lynn to Scotland, a sixth from Antwerp to England, and another from Yarmouth to London; in two cases the crews were killed, and the ships as well as the goods disposed of. In most cases the complaints are laid against Johan Pederogh or John de Pederogue (see p. 45), Michel de Navare, and others, who appear to have been under Grimbald, but in some instances they are against the latter. The first is by

[1] See Appendix A.

[2] *Chancery Miscel. Rolls*, *France*, Bdl. 5, No. 6.

[3] See translation in Appendix B.

Richard Bush against "Reyner Grymaus," complaining of goods having been taken from a ship going from Winchelsea to Dieppe, in August 1301, by Michel de Navare and others of Calais, who took the goods thither and disposed of them. The "chevalier" denied this, and asserted he was "not in that country" at the time specified nor for nearly a year afterwards, and in the "rejoinder" note was taken of the answer "that he was not admiral till some time after the events specified." The eighth complaint refers to the seizure of goods from a ship going from Berwick to London in August 1303, off Blakeney, "by men from Calais." In reply John (Pederogh) says the demand concerns "mi sire Reniers de Grimaus" only, for he was then admiral, and said John was on shore at the date specified, and was only in the company of Reniers in Zealand and Holland. The twelfth complaint declares that the ship *Michele de Arwe,* from London to Brabant, with a cargo valued at £556, was seized "on the high seas" by Sire Reyner Grimbaud, admiral, in September 1303, taken to Normandy, and the crew sent to Calais and imprisoned. In reply the "chivaler" confesses he took such a ship, and seized it rightfully, as it was consorting with the enemies of France; and in response to the demand of one of the crew still in prison at Calais, he says he is there as a malefactor against the King of France, and that the commission of the deputies does not extend to such cases. The fourteenth complaint is by John de Chelchethe against Reyner de Grymaus, and John Pedrogh replies "as he did to William Servat," the latter name not occurring elsewhere in the record, a circumstance which points to these libels being only part of those brought before the commissioners.

It is to be noted that, with the exception of the *Michele de Arwe* above mentioned, which was taken "on the high seas,"—an elastic term,—all the ships were attacked near the English coast, and well within what may be called the sea of England, or the waters included in the King's Chambers in 1604, where the jurisdiction of the English Admiralty undoubtedly extended. In all cases, moreover, the goods seized belonged to Englishmen, though some of the ships were foreign.

Too much importance appears to have been attached to the roll *De Superioritate.* It furnishes no proof, or even reasonable probability, that any other Power acquiesced in an English claim to a specific sovereignty of the sea beyond what appears to have been customary among maritime states at the time. The point of the libel is that Grimbald seized shipping after the alliance was made and took people and goods to France, and was thus said to have usurped the sovereign lordship or jurisdiction of the English king or admiral in "the sea of England."

An important light is thrown on the nature of the jurisdiction exercised by the English admiral by the memorandum of 12 Edward III., in the same roll, the documents in which were collected together at the time it was written, in connection with the consultation of the judges to which it refers.[1] It recites that, among a number of other things, the King's Justiciaries were to be consulted as to the appropriate method of revising and continuing the form of proceedings instituted and ordained by Edward I. and his Council for maintaining and preserving the ancient supremacy of the crown in the sea of England and the right of the admiral's office over it, with the view of correcting, interpreting, declaring, and upholding the laws and statutes made formerly by his ancestors, the kings of England, for the maintenance of peace and justice among the people of all nations whatsoever passing through the sea of England, and to take cognisance of all attempts to the contrary in the same, and to punish delinquents and afford redress to the injured; which laws and statutes, the memorandum states, were by Richard I., on his return from the Holy Land, corrected, interpreted, and declared, and were published in the Island of Oleron and named in the French language *La Loy Oleroun.*[2]

[1] *Chancery Rolls, Misc.*, Bdle. 14, n. 15, memb. 4.

[2] "Infrascripti sunt articuli generales super quibus et fines ad quos Justiciarii domini nostri Regis sunt consulend', et dominus noster Rex de eorum consilio certificand' in Cancellar' sua in scriptis citra festum, &c.

"Item ad finem, quod resumatur et continuetur ad subditorum prosecucionem forma procedendi quondam ordinata et inchoata per avum Domini nostri Regis et ejus consilium ad retinendum et conservandum antiquam Superioritatem Maris Angliæ et jus officii Admirallatus in eodem, quoad corrigendum, interpretandum, declarandum, et conservandum leges et statuta per ejus antecessores Angliæ Reges dudum ordinata ad conservandum pacem et Justitiam inter omnes gentes nacionis cujuscunque per Mare Angliæ transeuntes, et ad cognoscendum super omnibus in contrarium attemptatis

This memorandum furnishes an important clue as to the nature of the jurisdiction exercised in the so-called sea of England. It is evident from the concluding part that the laws and statutes referred to are the mercantile marine laws, which were best known in this country as the Laws of Oleron, and are included in the *Black Book of the Admiralty* together with other articles peculiar to the English Admiralty.[1] They appear to have been published by Richard I. at the end of the twelfth century, at a time when the old customs of the sea began to be committed to writing, as rules proper to be observed by the admirals of his fleet for the punishment of delinquencies and the redress of wrongs committed on the sea. They were

in eodem, et ad puniendum delinquentes et dampna passis satisfaciendum; quæ quidem leges et statuta per Dominum Ricardum quondam Regem Angliæ in reditu suo a Terrâ Sancta correcta fuerunt, interpretata, declarata, et in Insula Oleron publicata, et nominata in Gallica lingua La loy Olyroun."

According to Godolphin (*A View of the Admiral Jurisdiction*, 1661), the "form of proceedings" refers to the statute of the Writ of Consultation, 24 Edw. I., with regard to the proceedings of the Courts. The following is on another membrane in the same roll (mem. 2*d*), which contains ordinances agreed upon between the masters and mariners of England, Bayonne, and Flanders, at Bruges, 8th March 1286. It is in the handwriting of the time of Edward III.

"Item a la fin qe veues et considerees les formes des proces et des lettres ordeinees per les consaillers le dit aiel nostres seigneur le Roi pur eux et la dite nacioun Dengleterre a recouerer et receuer les ditz subgitz aidaunz et alliez et a faire redresser a eux toux les damages a eux donez en Mier et en terre duraunz les dites trewes pees et confederaciouns et countre la forme dycelles par les ditz Fraunceys aidaunz et alliez et eschuire clamour de poeple sur la dite denatureste, &c., et les damages quiex de tiel clamour purroient auenir et especialment a retenir et meintener la souereignete qe ses ditz auncestres Rois Dengleterre soleyent auoir en la dite mier Dengleterre quant alamendement declaracioun et interpretacioun des lois per eux faites a gouerner toutes maneres des gentz passanz per la dite mier. Et primerement a son admirail et as meistres et mariners des nefs des Sync Portz Dengleterre et des autres terres annex a la Corone Dengleterre entendaunt a sa armee en la dite mier pur retenir et meyntenir la garde des lois auauntdites et la punisciou de toux faitz al encountre en la mier susdite Semblables formes des proces et lettres soient desors tenues od toux les amendementz quiex purrount estre ordeinez par le sage Counsail nostre Seignur le Roi a profist et honur de lui et des soens."

[1] Twiss (*Black Book of the Admiralty*, ii. xliii; ii. xi), who collected the old sea laws of Europe, states that the most ancient extant source of modern marine law are the Decisions of the Consuls of the Sea of the City of Trani, on the shores of the Adriatic, which purport to be of the date A.D. 1063; and that the next most ancient are the Judgments of Oleron, of which there are still copies, belonging to the reign of Edward II., in the archives of the Guildhall, for use no doubt in the City court, which administered the Law Merchant and the Law Maritime.

continued among the Admiralty regulations in subsequent reigns, and it was part of the duties of the admiral to see that they were duly observed in the seas within his jurisdiction. The powers of the admiral were extensive, as may be seen from the memorandum of the fourteenth century defining his office and duties, which has been published by Nicolas,[1] by those given by Twiss in the *Black Book*,[2] and later by Godolphin.[3]

At the time with which we are dealing the utmost lawlessness reigned on the sea, the depredations of undisguised freebooters being scarcely a greater evil than the constant acts of reprisal between the traders of different nations. It was a common practice for the seamen of different countries or cities to carry on hostilities with one another, and to enter into treaties of peace or truce without the sovereign on either side being concerned in their quarrels, except as mediators or umpires. In 1317, although there was peace between England and Flanders, the mutual reprisals of the seamen and merchants reached such a height that commercial intercourse was entirely suspended, and Edward II. and the Earl of Flanders had to actively interpose in order to bring about "peace" between their subjects.[4] A marked feature in the policy of Edward III. was the promotion and encouragement of foreign commerce, and quite a number of statutes were passed in his reign with that object, and to facilitate the entrance of foreign merchants into the realm. One of these, made six years after the consultation of the judges on the maritime laws, was specially passed to declare the sea open to all merchants.[5]

With these circumstances in view, it can be readily understood how desirable it was to have the maritime laws for the security of commerce and shipping carefully considered and

[1] *Op. cit.*, i. 484.

[2] *Op. cit.*

[3] *Op. cit.* The specification of the duties within the cognisance of the Admiralty occupies several pages; they included "all cases of seizures and captures made at sea, whether *jure belli publicis*, or *jure belli privati* by way of reprisals, or *jure nullo* by way of piracy . . . all causes of spoil and depredations at sea; robberies and pyracies," &c., &c.

[4] M'Pherson, *Annals of Commerce*, i. 475, 485, quoting from *Fœdera*.

[5] 18 Edw. III., st. 2, cap. 3. Several articles in the *Black Book* show the same desire to encourage foreign merchants, and severe penalties were prescribed for the robbing or wronging of foreign ships, or interference with their freedom to trade.

put in force; and a consideration of the whole case shows that the roll *De Superioritate Maris* deals with the maritime laws, the interpretation of the documents having been strained by the later advocates for the English claim to the sovereignty of the seas. It is interesting no doubt to learn that the King of England and his admiral exercised jurisdiction of the kind in the neighbouring sea at the early time referred to, but there is nothing in the case of Grimbald or in the other documents associated with it to indicate any claim to a sovereignty such as was enjoyed by Venice and Denmark. There was no attempt made to interfere with the innocent use of the so-called sea of England, or to exact dues for navigation or fishery. The jurisdiction extended only to the keeping of the peace and the security of the sea—duties exercised by other princes and states in like manner, and indeed now exercised by all countries within the waters under their control. This view is supported by the interpretation of Callis, who stated that the king ruled on the sea "by the laws imperial, as by the roll of Oleron and others," in all matters relating to shipping and merchants and mariners.[1] It would no doubt be of great interest if there were distinct evidence as to how far from the coast "the sea of England" extended. The records cited show that the vessels were seized close to the English coast, within the waters covered by the proclamations concerning the King's Chambers in the seventeenth century, and even within the narrow limits of the territorial waters as now usually defined. It is to be noted with reference to the vessel taken "on the high seas" that in the Court of Admiralty in the seventeenth century this phrase covered seizures made a few miles from the coast.

There is, however, one case which occurred in the fourteenth century which has been referred to as showing that the sea of England and the jurisdiction of the king extended far from the English coast, over indeed to the coast of Brittany. In the mutual aggressions of Flemish and English sailors, the robberies by the men of Rye of Flemish ships off "Craudon" and Orwell became so flagrant that commissioners on both sides were appointed in 1311, further proceedings were instituted in 1314,

[1] *The Reading of the Famous and Learned Robert Callis, Esqr., upon the Statute of Sewers*, 23 Hen. VIII., c. 5, &c., 1622; ed. 1824, p. 48.

and finally, in 1320, envoys from Flanders arrived in London during the sitting of Parliament, and a treaty was concluded. In this it is stated that divers merchants of Flanders, while "proceeding on the sea of England near Craudon,"[1] were robbed of their wines and merchandise by evil-doers of England, and that the goods had been brought to England. The Flemish envoys prayed the king, "of his lordship and royal power to cause right to be done and punishment awarded, since he is lord of the sea, and the said robbery was committed in the sea under his power."[2] The account goes on to state that the king and his council in Parliament, with the assent of the peers, agreed to appoint justices to inquire into the matter, and that those who were concerned in the robbery should be promptly punished.[3] Accordingly, in December 1320, the Keeper of the Cinque Ports and others were instructed to make inquiry regarding the pillaging of a Flemish ship, laden with wines and merchandise, said to have been committed by Englishmen on the sea of England, off Craudon, so that the malefactors might be brought to justice.[4] Selden, who gives the document in which the previous proceedings are also recited,[5] does not attempt to locate Craudon, which in other records in the rolls of Parliament in 1315 was also called "Carondon," "Crasdon," and "Grasdon"; but Nic-

1 "Sur la mere d'Engleterre, devers les parties de Craudon."

2 "Et prierent que le Roi, de sa seignurie et poer real, fait sente dreit et punissement del dit fait, de siccome il est seigneur de la mer, et la dite roberie fut fait sur la mer dans son poer, sicomme dessus est dit."

3 Nicolas, who gives the details referred to, says that there is no record of these proceedings in the rolls of Parliament. *Op. cit.*, i. 388.

4 "Et cum dicti nuncii ad tractandum de novo super hujusmodi dampnis per dictum dominum nostrum Regem admissi fuissent, ipsi nuncii, prout alii nuncii præfati Comitis, in tractatibus supradictis, inter cetera quæ requirebant, ante omnia supplicabant, ut dictus dominus Rex ad sectam suam de potestate sua Regia inquiri et justitiam faceret de quadam deprædatione quibusdam hominibus de Flandria nuper de vinis et aliis diversis mercimoniis suis super mare Anglicanum, versus partes de Crauden, infra potestatem dicti domini nostri Regis, per homines de regno Angliæ. Ut dicebant facta asserentes quod vina et mercimonia prædicta eisdem Flandrensibus deprædata adducta, fuerunt infra regnum et potestatem dicti domini Regis, et quod ipse est dominus dicti maris, et deprædatio prædicta facta fuit supra dictum mare infra potestatem suam." *Rot. Pat.*, 14 Edw. II., pt. ii. m. 26, *in dorso.* Selden quotes this document (lib. ii. c. xxix.), but his text varies from the above, thus: ". . . potestatem dicti domini Regis, et quod ad ipsum Regem pertinuit sic facere pro eo quod ipse est dominus dicti maris."

5 *Mare Clausum*, lib. ii. c. xxix. p. 282.

olas states that there was no place of that name on the sea coast of England, nor in any part of the territories of Edward II., and he identified it with a small seaport, since called "Crowdon," in Brittany, lying on the extreme part of the Point du Raz, about eight leagues west of Quimper, where he shows that the fleets returning to England with wines frequently took shelter.[1] If this explanation be correct, it would extend the "sea of England" more than 120 miles south of the Lizard, which, however, is still well within the limits which were claimed for it by Selden (see p. 19). Although, according to the English record, the Flemish envoys themselves described the sea off Craudon as part of the sea of England and under the jurisdiction of the king, it is evident that this admission would facilitate redress from England, and standing alone it is not of much weight. The whole value of the admission, moreover, depends on the position of the "Craudon" of the record; and it is remarkable, if it was really the Crowdon referred to by Nicolas, that that fact was unknown to Selden, to whom it would have furnished a very strong argument for his case.

[1] That "Crowdon" was in Brittany appears from a letter, dated from Plymouth, 9th December 1402, from Henry Beaufort, Bishop of Lincoln, the Earl of Somerset, and the Earl of Worcester, who were sent to escort Joan of Navarre, Duchess of Brittany, the second wife of Henry IV., to England. "Et par fin force pur un temps nous faut demurrer en Bretaigne car la ou nous avoioms envoie au dite nostre treshonuree et tresredoutee dame pur venir, noz niefs ne poiont ne osent aler en le temps dyver. Et faut qele eit un leisir pur venir pardevers nous, dont le havene que nous pensoms aler ove leide de Dieu est Crowdon."—*Proceedings and Ordinances of the Privy Council of England*, i. 190.

CHAPTER II.

THE FISHERIES.

It was with respect to the right of fishery on the British coasts that the claim to maritime sovereignty was revived in the seventeenth century, and with which it was chiefly concerned. The "honour of the flag," however gratifying to national pride or important in the international relations of England, was unprofitable, and served at best to stimulate and maintain the spirit of the nation for power and adventure on the sea. But the question of free or licensed fishing touched the profit as well as the "honour" of the king and the prosperity of the people, and hence the monarchs of the Stuart line, the Commonwealth, and the Protector strove to impose tribute on foreign fishermen for the liberty to fish in the British seas. This policy was in direct opposition to that which had long prevailed in England. It is shown below that the freedom of fishing on the English coast had been guaranteed to foreign fishermen by a series of treaties extending over some centuries, and that in point of fact the fishermen of various nations had immemorially frequented the British seas in large numbers, and there peacefully pursued their business of catching fish without molestation or interruption by the English Government. In some respects this liberty enjoyed was remarkable, when one considers the practice in many other countries and the value of the fisheries.

In the early and middle ages the sea fisheries were indeed much more important relatively than they are now. There was a greater demand for fish, and fishermen from various countries—from France, Flanders, Spain, and England—made long and distant voyages, extending to Iceland and even beyond the North Cape, in quest of fish. One reason for the great demand was the numerous fast-days enjoined by the Church; for although fish were eschewed by the ascetic monks of early times as dangerous to purity of soul, the fashion changed, and they were later consumed plentifully on the days of fast both by clergy and laity.[1] The fasts were strictly observed throughout Catholic Europe, and a large variety of sea and fresh-water fishes, as well as seals and cetaceans, were consumed on such occasions. Some of the large monastic establishments had their own staff of fishermen, and their fish-houses at seaports for the salting and curing of herring. Another reason for the extensive consumption of fish was the want of winter-roots and the scantiness of fodder in winter, so that it was impracticable to keep cattle and sheep for slaughtering throughout the winter. It was customary to kill them and salt the flesh in autumn; and thus fish, fresh, dried, smoked, or salted, formed a valued article of food in place of salted beef and mutton. Fish were also used to an extraordinary extent in victualling the army and navy, and in provisioning castles, the expense on this item of the commissariat generally equalling or exceeding that for beef, mutton, or pork.[2] The distribution even of fresh fish was also much better than might have been expected. Barges and boats carried them up the rivers, and pack-horses and waggons transported them throughout the country, so that even in inland counties the harvesters in the fields were supplied with herrings for their dinner.[3] In mediæval times, moreover, fishermen and fishing vessels constitued a considerable part of the naval force available for the defence of the kingdom, for offensive operations and the transport of soldiers. The fishermen of the Cinque Ports, who had the government of the great herring fair at Yarmouth, had also to provide vessels for the king's service under their charters. Later, when a permanent navy existed, the fisheries were looked upon as a very important "nursery" of seamen to man the fleets.

[1] Allard, *Du Poisson, considéré comme Aliment dans les Temps anciens et modernes.*

[2] Garrad, *The Arte of War.*

[3] In the itinerary of a journey from England made by a Scottish nobleman to join Edward I. in Scotland, it is recorded that herrings were purchased nearly every day—at Dunstable, Newport, Northampton, Leicester, Nottingham, Sherburn, &c. Sixty fresh herrings at York, nearly forty miles from the sea in a straight line, cost eightpence, and fresh haddocks and codlings were also bought.

The herring fishery was by far the most important of all the sea fisheries, and as this fish was found in greatest abundance on the British coasts, foreign fishermen were attracted hither in great numbers. It was with reference to the herring fishery that exclusive claims were raised by England in the seventeenth century, and it is desirable at the outset to understand the policy which was pursued previously in regard to it both in England and Scotland. At what period foreign fishermen first began to frequent the British coasts is uncertain; but we know that within fifty or sixty years of the Norman Conquest fishermen from Flanders and Normandy—and doubtless from other countries—visited our shores and carried on a fishery for herrings by means of drift-nets. An important fishery was established at the mouth of the Firth of Forth, on the east coast of Scotland, in the early part of the twelfth century, and it was shared by fishermen from England, Flanders, and France, who paid tithes to the monks of the priory on the Isle of May. This monastery was founded by King David I. before the middle of the twelfth century, and was endowed by him with the manor of Pittenweem in Fife, and by Cospatrick, the great Earl of Dunbar, with a house and "toft" at the village of Dunbar, both grants being of value in connection with the fishery. King William the Lion (A.D. 1165-1214) confirmed these grants, and addressed missives to "all his good subjects and the fishermen who fish round the Isle of May" commanding them to pay their tithes to the monks as they were paid in the time of his grandfather, King David (A.D. 1124-1153); and he prohibited them from fishing in their waters or using the island without license from the monks.[1] This very early claim to the right of exclusive fishing in the sea is characteristic of the policy of all the Scottish kings. It was repeated on several occasions, the royal mandate being sometimes addressed solely "to all fishermen who fish around the Isle of May"; and that some of them were foreigners appears to be shown not only by the statement above given, on the authority of contemporary monks, but by the size of the vessels, some of which had four hawsers, and paid much higher dues at the neighbouring

[1] "Prohibeo etiam firmiter ne quis decimas suas eis injuste detineat sicut habuerunt in tempore regis Davidis super meum forisfactum et ne quis in aquis eorum piscari presumat . . . nisi per eorum licentiam."

harbours than the local fishing-boats. We know also from contemporary Flemish records that as early as the first half of the twelfth century fishermen from Nieuport and other places in Flanders fished from large vessels for herrings with drift-nets in August and September in the northern parts of the North Sea.

The men from France and Flanders alluded to, no doubt continued to fish each season down the east coast of England to the mouth of the Thames, as they did later and do still. About the period mentioned, Yarmouth was a great fishing centre, and was frequented by foreign merchants—Flemings, French, Swedes, and Frieslanders—who purchased and cured herrings; but the earliest notice of foreign fishermen on the English coast is in the year 1274, shortly after Edward I. came to the throne. Complaint was then made that during a time of truce the English fishermen had been attacked by the Flemish disguised as fishermen and twelve hundred of them killed.[1] On the other hand, the Countess of Flanders complained that twenty-two of her subjects who had been fishing on the coast of England and Scotland, and had gone ashore at Berwick to rest themselves and get provisions, had been seized, with their nets, at Norham and thrown into the castle there.[2] About twenty years later, Edward I. issued a mandate to John de Botetourt, the Warden of the coast of Yarmouth, and to the bailiffs of that town, saying that he understood that many men from Holland, Zealand, and Friesland would shortly come "to fish in our sea off Yarmouth," and commanding them to make public proclamation once or twice a-week forbidding any molestation or injury to be done to them, but that they should rather be helped to pursue their fishing to advantage.[3] The number of English fishermen stated to have been killed by the Flemings in the encounter mentioned above, indicates how extensive the fishery then was. This also appears a few years later, when the Flemings resorted to a similar device; for in

[1] *Fœdera*, ii. 23. "Gent de Flaundres estre venuz sur mer, come Pescheurs," &c.

[2] *Ibid.*, ii. 37. The Flemish fishermen had probably gone up the Tweed after salmon.

[3] *Ibid.*, ii. 688, dated 28th September. "Quia intelleximus quod multi homines, de partibus Hollandiæ, Zelandiæ et etiam Frislandiæ, qui sunt de amicitia nostra, ad piscandum in mari nostro, prope Jernemuth," &c.

July 1296 above a thousand men of Flanders, and others of France, disguised as fishermen, were preparing to attack and burn Yarmouth and neighbouring places, and the bailiffs and men of the port were ordered to collect their ships to oppose them. These proceedings show the lawless state of the sea in those times. In the thirteenth century an extensive herring fishing was also carried on by the Scots on the east coast, especially in the Firth of Forth and the Moray Firth, and particularly by the men of Fife, and cargoes of herrings, cod, and haddocks, as well as salmon, were exported to England and chiefly to London, but also to Bordeaux, Rouen, Dieppe, and other ports in France.

From the foregoing it is clear that centuries before the question of *mare clausum* was raised, important fisheries were established along the east coast of England and Scotland, and that foreign fishermen took part in them. The number of French and Flemish fishermen attending the fishery must have been always great, because they had to furnish a large part of Catholic Europe with fish. But the number was increased after the fourteenth century, and especially in the fifteenth, from two causes. One was the decline of the great herring fishery at Scania, in the Baltic, upon which the Hanseatic League had risen to power and opulence, and which provided perhaps the greater part of continental Europe with salted and smoked herrings—Germany, Poland, Russia, part of France, and even to some extent Flanders and England. The Scanian herrings were esteemed the best, and the Hanse controlled the trade.[1] The other circumstance was the invention in the latter part of the fourteenth century by Beuckelsz, a native of Biervliet, in Zealand, of a greatly improved mode of curing herrings,—an invention which most materially aided the Dutch in taking the place of the Hansards in the herring industry, and in the commerce which it brought in its train. Some of the towns in the Low Countries early belonged to the Hanseatic League, and their fishermen were in the habit of going to the Scanian fishery;[2] but from the fifteenth century at least the herring fishery on the British coasts became by far the most import-

[1] Lundberg, *Det Stora sillfisket i Skåne under medeltiden och nyare tidens början.* Worms, *Hist. commerciale de la Ligue Hanséatique.*

[2] Fruin, *Tien Jaren uit den Tachtigjarigen Oorlog*, 181.

ant in Europe. It attracted foreign fishermen in increasing numbers, and gradually the Dutch came to take the leading part in it, displacing the Flemings and the men from Normandy and Picardy, and even to a large extent the English themselves. In 1512 we find Margaret of Savoy appealing to Henry VIII. to protect the fishermen of Holland, Zealand, and Friesland in their herring fishery, in which they were menaced by the Hanseatic towns, which were fitting out vessels to interrupt them; and in her letter she describes the herring fishery as the principal support of these states.[1] Towards the end of the century, when the Dutch had begun to call their herring fishery on the British coast their "great gold mine," another event occurred which tended still further to strengthen their hold on it by opening fresh markets on the Continent. This was the failure of the great Bohuslän fishery in Sweden, which continued barren for about seventy years.[2] They were also enabled to prosper in their fishery by the beneficent policy of the English sovereigns towards them up to the reign of James I., when the claim to the exclusive fishing in the British seas was put forward on behalf of the crown.

When this claim was advanced in the seventeenth century, it was argued that the sea fisheries had always belonged to the crown. Selden declared that "license had usually been granted to foreigners by the Kings of England to fish in the sea; and that the protection which the kings gave to fishermen, as in their own territory, was an ancient and manifest evidence of their maritime dominion."[3] The cases adduced in support of that contention are singularly few and unconvincing. One is the tax imposed by Richard II. in 1379 on fishing vessels, among others, in the admiralty of the north, but which, if it was imposed on foreign vessels at all, must have been done with their consent (see p. 33). Another relates to the arrangements which were occasionally made for "wafting" or guarding the fishermen at the Yarmouth fishing, and for which the fishermen thus protected had to pay,—an arrangement which

[1] *Brit. Mus. MSS. Galba*, B. iii. 16. Henry apparently acceded to the request; *vide* "John Heron's accompte for waftynge of the herring fleete in the parties of Norfolk and Suffolk, *anno quarto* R. Henrici VIII." *State Papers, Foreign and Domestic*, Hen. VIII., i. 1512.

[2] Ljungman, *Nägra ord om de stora Bohus-länska Sillfiskeri.*

[3] *Mare Clausum*, lib. ii. c. xxi.

was also adopted in the reign of Charles I. Thus, in 1482, Edward IV. invested certain persons, called Guardians, Conductors, and Wafters, with naval powers, to protect the fishermen "of whatever country they be, who shall desire to fish under the protection" of the said wardens on the coasts of Norfolk and Suffolk; and all those who took advantage of such protection had to pay an equal share of the cost of it; any other persons pretending to have power to protect the fishermen were to be apprehended. This arrangement was repeated in the reigns of Richard III. and Henry VII.[1] It is evident that the payment was only exigible from such foreign fishermen as took advantage of the protection offered to them; those who desired to fish without protection of the wardens were at liberty to do so. A more pertinent case is the Act of the Irish Parliament in 1465—also during the reign of Edward IV.—which has been previously alluded to.[2] It was passed to prevent aid being given to the king's enemies by foreign vessels that went to fish at Ireland. All foreign fishing vessels were prohibited from fishing on the Irish coast (except the north part of Wicklow) without first obtaining a license from the Lieutenant, his deputy, a "justice of the land," or other person authorised to grant it, upon pain of forfeiture of ship and goods. All foreign vessels allowed to fish, which were of twelve tons burthen "or less," and had a "drover" or boat, were to pay thirteen shillings and fourpence yearly for the maintenance of the king's wars in Ireland; smaller vessels, as "scarfes" or boats not having "drover nor lighter," and within the burthen of twelve tons, were to pay two shillings. This was obviously a temporary measure, designed for a special purpose, though clearly imposing a tax on foreign vessels; but there is not evidence to show whether it was enforced.

Other two instances referring to later times were adduced in support of the contention that the sea fisheries belonged to England, and they may be mentioned here. One was the state-

[1] *Rot. Pat.*, 22 Edw. IV., m. 2; *ibid.*, 2 Ric. III., i. m. 3; *ibid.*, 3 Hen. VII., part ii. *dorso; Mare Clausum*, lib. ii. xxi.

[2] *The Statutes at Large passed in the Parliaments held in Ireland*, i. 30. 5 Edw. IV., c. vi. "An Act that no Ship or other Vessel of any Foreign Country shall go to the Fishing in the Irish Countries, and for Custom to be paid of the Vessel that cometh from Foreign Lands to Fishing."

ment made by Camden about 1586,[1] and by Hitchcock some years earlier,[2] that the Hollanders and Zealanders before they began to fish for herrings off the east coast of England, first, "by ancient custom, asked leave of Scarborough Castle"; "for," adds Camden, "the English have always given them leave to fish, reserving the honour to themselves, and resigning, as if from slothfulness, the benefit to strangers." Neither Hitchcock nor Camden quotes any authority for the statement. Scarborough Castle was in early times an important stronghold on the north-east coast, and it is not unlikely that foreign fishermen, who were frequently at the port, found it to their interest to maintain friendly relations with the governor, and gave notice of their arrival, or perhaps asked leave to dry their nets and paid for the privilege. It was the practice for the governor to levy dues, in kind, on fish brought ashore, for Edward III., in 1347, ordered writs of attachment to lie against those who during the fishing season sold their fish at sea instead of bringing them to the town, thus defrauding the Castle of its dues. Another instance, which was frequently made use of in negotiations later with the Dutch on the question of the fishery, was an alleged lease for twenty-one years granted by Queen Mary to her husband Philip II. of Spain, by which his subjects received licenses to fish on the Irish coasts. The first trace of this story is found in a memorandum addressed to Lord Salisbury in 1609 by one Richard Rainsford, an agent for a fishery company,[3] in which it is said that £1000 per annum had been paid into the Irish Exchequer by Philip for the privilege, and that Sir Henry Fitton, the son of the treasurer at the time, could substantiate the statement "on oath if need is." No year is mentioned by any of those who put forward this story,[4] and no record of it is referred to. If not entirely apocryphal, and invented as an argument against the Dutch, who were subjects of Philip in the early part of his reign, it was probably constructed on a very slender basis.

There is, however, one interesting case, or series of cases, in

[1] *Britannia*, Gough's edition, ii. 248.

[2] *A Pollitique Platt*, &c.

[3] *State Papers, Dom.*, James I., xlviii. 94.

[4] Malines, *Lex Mercatoria*, 189, from whom Selden quotes it, with the remark, "There are some also who affirm that the King of Spain," &c. *Mare Clausum*, ii. c. xxx. It is also given by Boroughs and other writers.

which licenses to fish in the Channel were frequently granted by the Lord Warden of the Cinque Ports to a limited number of French fishermen, chiefly of Dieppe and Treport, for the ostensible purpose of supplying the king of France's table with fresh fish, and especially soles. It is stated that the French kings "time out of mind" had applied for such licenses,[1] and they were certainly granted under Elizabeth, the Stuart kings, and Oliver Cromwell. It is doubtful when the custom originated, but since the liberty of fishing was granted for a definite area or bank, called the Zowe or Sowe, off Rye and well out in the Channel, it was probably of considerable antiquity, and may have survived from the Norman or Angevin reigns. James also furnished similar licenses for the use of certain high personages, such as the Duchess of Guise and the French ex-ambassador; but the liberty was greatly abused, and was the cause of much friction and trouble with the English fishermen later.[2] The fact that such licenses were asked for by the French court on behalf of fishermen of Dieppe, Treport, Calais, and other ports on the coast of France, may indicate that the fisheries out in the Channel were at one time claimed by England. But it is possible it was only the survival of a custom adopted during the times when great lawlessness reigned on the seas, and when the men of the Cinque Ports were a terror to their neighbours. A license from the Lord Warden would be then a safeguard and protection.

Such are the cases which were adduced to prove the rights of the English crown to exclusive fishing in the British seas. On the other side there is an overwhelming body of testimony to show that the fishery was free. It may be noted in the

[1] *State Papers*, *Dom.*, Charles I., clxxx. 96.

[2] One of the licenses, which ran for a year, is printed in Appendix C. The Zowe was described in 1630 as "a bank which lies between Rye and Dieppe, and the outermost part is nearly one-third over the sea. This zowe which they call the small zowe is 3 leagues long and 3 broad, and 26 and 28 fathoms deep. The French make it 10 leagues, because they fish till they bring Beachy Head N., fayre Loo (? Fairlea, Fairlight) W.N.W., and fish in 30 fathoms." Sir H. Mainwaring to Coke, "A Short Discourse or Propositions concerning the French fishing uppon the Zowe, theyr abusing it, and the Remedy" (*ibid.*) It was described as the "chief nursery for turbetts, hollibatts, pearles (brill), soules, weavers and gurnetts." In Queen Elizabeth's time only four licenses were granted, but James increased the number to fourteen or fifteen. They were carefully entered in the records of Dover Castle and the Hundred Book of Rye.

first place that Bracton and the other early English lawyers, unlike those of the seventeenth century, made no claim for an exclusive fishery. They merely propounded the Roman law that the sea and the shores of the sea were common to all; that the right of fishing in rivers and ports was likewise free to all; and that animals, *feræ naturæ*, including fish, belonged to no person. The law laid down by Bracton and the others was not, of course, international; but if it had been in agreement with English jurisprudence in the twelfth and thirteenth centuries (as it was made to be in the seventeenth) to consider the sea fisheries as the property of the crown, that would have been declared, because Bracton was embodying the customary law of England, and adopted Roman law only when that failed him. He is careful to state that wreck of the sea and "great fish," such as sturgeons and whales, "belong to the lord the king himself by reason of his privilege" or prerogative, precisely on the ground that Callis, Coke, Selden, and Hale claimed the sea fisheries generally for the crown in the seventeenth century. Had any such right existed or been thought of in the reign of Henry III., Bracton could not have failed to incorporate it, since the king placed the archives and everything necessary at his disposal to enable him to embody the common law of England.[1] So also there is nothing in the rolls of Edward I. and Edward III., which deal with the sovereignty of the sea, to indicate any claim to the fisheries; nor is there in the Admiralty ordinances and regulations in the *Black Book*, although it was part of the duties of the admirals to supervise the sea fisheries and to enforce the laws relating to them.

But the assertion that the fisheries were free in those early times does not depend upon negative testimony. Liberty of fishing was guaranteed in various treaties concluded with foreign nations from the middle of the fourteenth century until the end of the sixteenth. The first of these was made in the reign of Edward III., and it was in keeping with the liberal policy of that monarch in regard to the promotion of foreign commerce. It was almost a necessity, for English fishermen were by themselves unable to meet the home demand for fish.

[1] Henrici de Bracton, *Legibus et Consuetudinibus Angliæ*, lib. i. c. 12; lib. iii. c. 3. *Rolls Series*, Introd., by Sir Travers Twiss, i. ii. Güterbock, *Henricus de Bracton und sein Verhältniss zum Römischen Rechte*, 14, 55.

Fish caught by foreigners were regularly imported into England, and such importation was encouraged by the crown and by Parliament until after the Reformation. Foreign fishermen were also encouraged, as is shown by the mandates of Edward I. and Edward II. above alluded to, and by many others.

The first of the formal treaties providing for liberty of fishing was concluded in 1351 between Edward III. and the king of Castile and towns on the coast of Castile and Biscay. Edward had signally defeated the Spanish fleet in the year before in the battle known as "L'Espagnols sur Mer," and in the truce for twenty years which followed, it was stipulated that there should be mutual freedom of commerce and navigation, and that the fishermen from Castile and Biscay should be at liberty to come freely and safely to fish in the ports of England and Brittany, and in all other places and ports, paying the dues and customs to the lords of the country.[1] Spanish fishermen do not appear to have taken part in the great herring fishing on the east coast,—Spaniards, indeed, have never cared for pickled or cured herrings, differing in this respect from the Teutonic races, but have preferred the mackerel, the pilchard, and the cod. The liberty of fishing conferred by the treaty was no doubt chiefly valuable to them with respect to their fishery off the Irish coast, the south-west coast of England, and along the coasts of Aquitaine and Brittany for sardines and mackerel. Two years later a similar treaty was concluded between Edward and the towns of Portugal and Algarve, in which liberty of fishing was stipulated in precisely the same terms,[2] and no doubt related to the same waters.

Early in the next century we find what seems to be the first of the numerous agreements as to the liberty of fishing for herrings in the narrow seas, quite a number of which were made in the comparatively short and troubled reign of Henry IV. In a truce concluded in 1403 between Henry and the King of France, it was provided that merchants, mariners, and fishermen should be free to pass to and through either kingdom

[1] *Fœdera*, v. 719. "Il est convenu, &c., &c. Item, que pessoners de la seignurie del roi de Castelle et del counte de Viscay peussent venir et pescher fraunchement et sauvement en les portz d'Engleterre et de Bretaigne, et en touz autres lieux et portz où ils vorrontz, paiantz les droits et les custumes à les seignurs du pais."

[2] *Ibid.*, v. 763.

without requiring letters of safe-conduct. Henry, therefore, issued a mandate to his admirals and other officers concerned, enjoining that during the current herring season the fishermen of both countries should freely fish for herrings and all other fish, from Gravelines and the Isle of Thanet down to the mouth of the Seine and Southampton, without hindrance or molestation, and that if they were chased by pirates or met with contrary winds they were to be allowed to take refuge in the ports within the area defined, and were to be well treated.[1] As the king's missive is dated 26th October, it appears that there was then, as there is now, a considerable winter herring fishing in the Channel. Three years later, on 5th October 1406, Henry took all the fishermen of France, Flanders, and Brittany, with their ships and boats, under his protection until 2nd February in the following year,—that is to say, during the winter herring fishery,—for which time they were to be allowed to fish freely and without molestation, and to carry away their fish, provided they did nothing to prejudice him or his kingdom.[2] Considering the weak condition of the English navy at the time—the security of the sea had been committed to the merchants on the east coast, a system which in this month of October was known to have failed—and the prevalence of pirates, it is unlikely that the protection of the king was of much avail.

In November of the same year, with reference to his treaty with France, Henry published another proclamation stating that, on the supplication of the burgesses and people of Flanders, it had been agreed that the fishermen of England and Flanders, and generally of all the realm of France, should, during the continuance of the treaty, go in safety to fish in the sea. To the end that the fishermen who travelled on the sea at great peril to gain their living might fish in greater security, and obtain sea fish for the sustenance of the people, it was ordained that for a year from the publication of the proclamation all the fishermen of England, of Calais, and of other towns and places belonging to the King of England, as well as the fisher-

[1] *Fœdera*, viii. 306, 336. "Q'en ceste presente harenguison les pescheurs de l'une part et d'autre puissent pescher plus seurement en la mer la harenk et toutz autres poissons, depuis hable de Grauelinguez et l'isle de Tanent, jusques a l'entree de la riviere de Saine, et au hable de Hautoune."

[2] *Ibid.*, viii. 451.

men of Flanders, Picardy, Normandy, and Brittany, and other parts of France, might go in peace over the whole sea to fish and gain their living, without any restraint or hindrance; provided no fraud was committed, and that English fishermen had the same privileges from Flanders, Picardy, Normandy, Brittany, and other parts of France. If the fishermen were driven into port by the violence of the wind, or other cause, they were to be received freely and treated reasonably, paying the dues and customs as of old, and be at liberty to return to their own ports. The king, therefore, commanded his admirals, captains, bailiffs, the commanders of castles and ports, and others concerned, to see that the provisions of the treaty were carried out.[1]

In the following year was concluded the first of the great series of Burgundy treaties, about which so much was to be heard in the diplomatic negotiations with the Dutch in the seventeenth century. Flanders was then part of the dominions of the Duke of Burgundy, who held it as a fief of France, and freedom of commerce and fishery was of the highest importance to his Flemish subjects. A treaty or convention was therefore drawn up between Henry's ambassadors and the Duke of Burgundy, dealing chiefly with commercial intercourse, in which the above-mentioned provisions for mutual liberty of fishing were embodied, in practically the same language, and comprising likewise the whole of France.[2] In 1408 the mutual freedom of fishing in the sea was twice confirmed,—in the prorogation of the truce with the Duke of Burgundy, and in the ratification by the King of France of the treaty between Henry and the Duke;[3] and it was again

[1] *Fœdera*, viii. 459. "Pro Piscatoribus, sub Dominio Ducis Burgundiæ: . . . toutz pescheurs, tant de nostre dit roiaume d'Engleterre et de Caleis, et dez autres noz villes et lieux, come dez ditz conte et paiis de Flandres, dez paiis de Picardie, de Normandie, et de Bretaigne, et generalment de tut le dit roiaume de Fraunce, puissent paisiblement aler par tout sur meer, pur peschier et gaigner lour vivre, saunz en estre reprins ne empeschiez en ascun manere . . . et par ainsi que semblablement soit fait et otroie, de lez dites parties de Flandres, Picardie, Normandie, Bretaigne, et autres del dit roiaume de Fraunce, a la seurte dez ditz pescheours de nostre dit roiaume d'Engleterre."

[2] *Ibid.*, viii. 469, 472. Dumont, *Corps Universel Diplomatique du Droit des Gens*, &c., II. i. 302. *Proc. and Ordinances of the Privy Council of England*, i. 282.

[3] *Ibid.*, viii. 530, 548, "Et les pescheurs generalment aler pescher sur mer pour gaignier leur vivre paisiblement."

confirmed at Amiens by John, Duke of Burgundy, in 1417, in the reign of Henry V.[1]

The various fishery truces and conventions of Henry IV., which were made at a time when great insecurity prevailed on the sea and depredations were committed on all hands, reflect credit on that able monarch, and notwithstanding the naval weakness in the early part of his reign, they must have had a favourable influence in fostering the sea fisheries. The sort of treatment that fishermen in those times had frequently to undergo is indicated in a complaint made to the king in 1410 that, notwithstanding the fishery truce with France, the men of Harfleur had seized an English fishing vessel of twenty-four tons, *Le Cogge Johan de Briggewauter*, and had thrown the master and fourteen of the crew into prison, without food and water, and held them to ransom for a hundred pounds.[2] Such occurrences were by no means uncommon, and it was customary for fishing vessels to go to sea armed,[3]—a provision which also enabled them on occasion to do a little piracy on their own account. It was sometimes difficult for the authorities to decide whether a vessel provided with fishing-lines and armed, as some were, with "minions, falcons, and falconettes," and having a good store of powder and bullets, had been equipped to catch fish or prey upon other vessels.

It does not appear that any treaty concerning liberty of fishing was made in the warlike reign of Henry V. (1413-1422); but, as stated above, this king confirmed the Burgundy treaty in 1417. In the succeeding reign of Henry VI., in 1439, a treaty was concluded for three years with Isabel of Portugal, as representing her husband, Philip, Duke of Burgundy, which provided for liberty in fishing in much the same language as in the treaty of Henry IV. It was stipulated that all the fishermen of England, Ireland, or Calais, as well as of Brabant and Flanders, should be free to go all over the sea for fishing, without any hindrance or molestation on either side, and that they should have free access to the ports of either, under the

[1] *Fœdera*, ix. 483.

[2] *Rot. Parl.*, iii. 643*b*.

[3] Pikes and bows and arrows were used. Later, in the early part of the seventeenth century, a regular part of the equipment of a herring-buss was half-pikes and muskets, an estimate for one being—ten half-pikes, £1; muskets with bandaleers, rests, and moulds, £6, with 6 lb. of gunpowder and 6 lb. of leaden bullets.

usual conditions. Although the Duke of Burgundy was also Count of Holland and Zealand, these states were not specifically included in this treaty, which was renewed in 1442 for other five years, and again, at Calais, in 1446, for a term of twelve years, in precisely the same terms, and the commonalties of Ghent, Bruges, Ypres, and of the French dominions promised to observe it.[1] In the renewal of the treaty of intercourse at Brussels, in 1468, by Edward IV. and the Duchess of Burgundy on behalf of her husband, Duke Charles, in addition to the mention of Brabant, Flanders, and Mechlin, words were added[2] which brought Holland and Zealand into the treaty, and thus formally gave them that liberty of fishing on the British, or at least the English, coast which they struggled so hard and so successfully to retain in the seventeenth century. The article on the fishery also declared that the fishermen should be at liberty to fish without being required to obtain any license, permission, or safe-conduct,[3] which appears to indicate that the practice of obtaining such letters for their security had been previously in vogue. In 1468, in the treaty of peace, at Péronne, between Louis XI. of France and Charles, Duke of Burgundy, a similar clause was inserted providing for the freedom of the herring fishery;[4] and in the ten years' truce

[1] *Fœdera*, x. 730, 736, 761, 791. The article on the fishery was as follows: "Que tous pescheurs, tant d'Engleterre, d'Irlande, et de Calais, comme des paiis de Brabant et de Flandres, pourront paisiblement aler par tout sur mer, pour peschier et gaignier leur vivre, sans empeschement ou destourber de l'une partie ne de l'autre. Et avec ce, se fortune ou autre aventure chassoit ou amenoit les diz pescheurs de la partie d'Engleterre, en aucun des ports, havres, destrois, et daugiers des dites paiis de Brabant ou de Flandres, ou les diz pescheurs des dites paiis de Brabant et de Flandres en aucuns des dites ports, havres, destrois, ou daugiers du royaume d'Engleterre, Yrland, et de Calais, que ilz y soient paisiblement et franchement receuz et traictiez raisonnablement d'une coste et d'autre, en paiant aux lieux, ou ils arriveront, les toulieux et devoirs accoustumez, et d'illec puissent liberalment retourner a tout leurs nefs, applois, et biens sans destourbier, arrest, ne empeschement; pourveu que, par les diz pescheurs, d'un coste et d'autre, ne soit commise aucune fraude, ou fait dommaige." Intercursus continuandus pro spatio duodecim annorum inter Anglos et Flandros, Gandanos, Iperos et civitatis de Brabant. *Ibid.*, xi. 143.

[2] "Et pur toutz sez autres paiis et seigneuries."

[3] "Et sans qu'il leur soit bosoigne sur ceo requirer ne opteiner ascune license, congie, ou saufconducte." 5 Jan. $\frac{1467}{1468}$. *Ibid.*, xi. 591, 592, 595, 609. Dumont, *op. cit.*, III. i. 592.

[4] Dumont, III. i. 400.

agreed upon in 1471 between Edward IV. and the King of France mutual liberty of commerce and fishing was stipulated during the continuance of the truce.[1] The treaty of 1467, above referred to, which included Holland and Zealand, was to last for thirty years, but by the death of Charles the Bold, and the marriage of Mary of Burgundy to Maximilian of Austria, it was deemed necessary to renew it with the new Duke; and this was done, and the compact declared to be perpetual, in 1478, the clause providing for the liberty of fishing remaining unaltered.[2]

It is thus clear from those numerous treaties that in the fifteenth century the liberty of fishing in the sea was so generally recognised by England that the principle might be regarded as having become a part of her international policy and custom. Towards the end of the century the Burgundy treaties were superseded by the great treaty of peace and commercial intercourse which was concluded in 1496 between Henry VII., the first of the Tudor sovereigns, and Philip, Archduke of Austria and Duke of Burgundy. This treaty, which became so well known later as the Great Intercourse (Intercursus Magnus, le Traité d'Entrecours, 't Groot Commercie-Tractaat), was the sheet-anchor of Dutch policy in relation to England in the seventeenth century, and was constantly appealed to by them in their diplomatic struggles with the Stuarts and with Cromwell. It was the price paid by Henry for the expulsion of Perkin Warbeck from Flanders, the provisions in regard to whom, when slightly modified by St John in 1651 to apply to the "rebels" of the Commonwealth, so startled the Dutch Government (see p. 387). The treaty was to be perpetual, and it actually endured for a century and a half. The article dealing with the liberty of fishing was couched in almost the same language as in the preceding treaties. The fishermen of both nations were to be at liberty to go in security to fish anywhere on the sea, without requiring any license or safe-conduct, and to have free use of one another's ports under stress of misfortune, weather or enemies,

[1] *Fœdera*, xi. 683.

[2] *Ibid.*, xii. 67. In 1484 Richard III. issued a commission to Thomas Lye, sergeant-at-arms, to make restitution for fishing-boats belonging to subjects of Maximilian, Duke of Austria, which had been taken, laden with fish, by English pirates. *Ibid.*, xii. 227.

on paying the ordinary dues.[1] As conservators for this treaty of peace and commerce, which was received with much rejoicing in the Low Countries, Henry appointed, among others, the mayors and aldermen of London and of a large number of towns, including Southampton, Sandwich, Dover, Winchelsea, Boston, Yarmouth, and Berwick; and the Archduke, on his side, appointed the burgomasters of Ghent, Bruges, Dunkirk, Antwerp, Dort, Delft, Leyden, Amsterdam, Briel, and others.

Several supplementary treaties dealing with commercial subjects were concluded between Henry VII. and Henry VIII. on the one side, and the Archduke of Burgundy on the other—viz., in 1499, 1506, 1515, and 1520.[2] While they confirmed in general terms the previous treaty, the clause referring to the freedom of fishery was not specifically mentioned, a circumstance which, considering the nature of the matters dealt with—the staple at Calais, the cloth trade, the Zealand tolls,—was not surprising. Nevertheless, the fact that treaties of commerce had been made with the Low Countries subsequent to the Intercursus Magnus, without containing a clause expressly renewing the liberty of fishing, was used later by English statesmen, as by Lord Bacon, as an argument that the provision of that treaty had thereby been rendered inoperative. But the policy of Henry VIII., and indeed of all the Tudor sovereigns, proved the contrary; liberty of fishing on the English coast was not called in question till James came to the throne.

We have already seen that Margaret of Savoy appealed to Henry VIII. in 1512 to protect the herring fishermen of the Low Countries from the attacks of the Hanseatic towns, and apparently with success. The same regard for the herring fishery

[1] "Item, conventum, concordatum et conclusum est quod piscatores utriusque partis partium prædictarum (cujuscunque conditionis existant) poterunt ubique ire, navigare per mare, secure piscari absque aliquo impedimento licentia seu salvo conductu: Et, si contingat aliquos ex piscatoribus unius partis per fortunam, tempestatem maris, vim hostium, aut alio modo compelli intrare aliquem portum vel districtum alterius partis, ibidem pacifice et amicabiliter recipientur et tractabuntur (solvendo in locis ubi applicabunt jura et theolonia prædicta) et ab illis portubus et locis poterunt libere recedere et redire, cum eorum navibus et bonis, sine impedimento vel contradictione quacunque; dummodo tamen per ipsos piscatores non committatur fraus neque dolus, seu per eos aliis dampnum minime fiat." 24 Feb. $\frac{1495}{1496}$. *Fœdera*, xii. 583. Dumont, III. ii. 338.

[2] *Fœdera*, xii. 714; xiii. 132, 539, 714.

was shown in a marked manner in 1521 in the negotiations between the Emperor Charles V. and King Francis I. of France. Cardinal Wolsey, who was the "mediator" between them, strongly urged the need of allowing the herring fishery to be free, safe, and unmolested. He made this stipulation one of the chief points of the proposed treaty. It is stated in a despatch which was sent to Charles V. by his ambassadors at Calais, where the negotiations were being conducted, that the Cardinal declared his intention to propose, among other things, security for the fishermen and cessation of hostility on the sea between England and Flanders, and that either party should be free from attack by the other in English ports. There was no difficulty about the fisheries, the ambassadors said, as they knew the Emperor wished it, and that his subjects would more willingly go to sea in that event than they then did under the protection of ships charged to defend them.[1] The French ambassadors also informed Francis that Wolsey pressed the point on them, and that they had ultimately agreed in order "to conciliate him, considering it can be revoked at pleasure, and will be profitable to those living on the coast of Normandy and Picardy, and without it they will not be able to pay their taxes."[2] It is clear from the political events that followed, that the great Cardinal, in stipulating for the security of the fishermen, had principally in view the interests of the Emperor, to whom the Netherlands belonged; but it was in perfect accord with established English policy. The agreement for the security of the herring fishery was embodied as a leading article in the formal treaty concluded between the two potentates in October of the same year, it being provided that until the end of the following January, even though the war should continue between the two countries, the fishermen of both parties should be allowed to fish unmolested and to go home in safety.[3] In the war which ensued, the French admirals did not push the advantage they had on the sea to extremes, but sold safe-conducts to the fishermen of the Netherlands, and allowed them to pursue their fishing. In several treaties and truces made in the

[1] Ships of war were used to convoy the herring-busses of Holland and Zealand at least as early as 1440.

[2] *Cal. State Papers, Foreign and Domestic*, iii. Nos. 1534, 1535.

[3] *Fœdera*, xiii. 752. Dumont, IV. i. 352.

next few years between the Powers named, it was provided that the herring fishery should be carried on freely and in security on both sides, even during the existence of hostilities. One of these, to last for eight months, was concluded in 1528 between Charles V., Francis I., Henry VIII., and Margaret of Austria, who represented Holland, Zealand, and Friesland, as well as Flanders.[1] It may perhaps be surmised that in the common concern about the winter herring fishery the influence of the Church was not without effect, so that the fish for Lent might not be wanting.

From the foregoing it is apparent that the kings of England, so far from claiming an exclusive right to the sea fisheries along the English coast, entered into a series of treaties with their neighbours, extending over a period of nearly two hundred years, by which freedom of fishing was mutually recognised and guaranteed. Throughout the reigns of the Plantagenet and Lancastrian kings, as well as under the Yorkists and Tudors, foreign fishermen were at liberty to fish freely in the English seas without requiring any license or paying any tribute. Not only so, but up to the middle of the sixteenth century, and especially in the time of the Plantagenet kings, they were encouraged to take part in the fisheries off our coasts, and to bring into the realm and freely trade in fish, both fresh and cured; and, in point of fact, a large proportion of the fish consumed in England was caught and sold by foreigners. It was not until after the Reformation, when the English fisheries began to decay, that protective measures were adopted in favour of the native fishermen; and it was not until the reign of James I. that any attempt was made to place restrictions on the liberty of fishing immemorially enjoyed by foreigners along the English coasts.

But when we turn to Scotland we find there was not only in that country an absence of the toleration which was extended in England to foreign fishermen, but that restrictive measures were in force from an early period. The claim made by the

[1] Dumont, IV. i. 515. "Pourront aussi les Sujets des Païs, Roiaumes, Terres et Seigneuries dessusdites, librement, et sans détourbier, ni empêchement, pêcher à harangs, et autres poissons en la mer, où ladite Treve aura lieu, et là où la pêche dudit harang s'adonera, comme ils faisoient avant la Guerre, et pourroient et sont accoûtumez de faire au tems de Paix."

Scottish kings in the twelfth century for the exclusive fishing in the sea around the Isle of May on behalf of the monks of the priory there, strikes the keynote of their policy in later times. This difference between the policy in England and Scotland might to some extent be due to the nature of the fishings. In the northern kingdom the herring fishery was confined almost entirely to the firths and lochs "within land": the native fishermen did not compete with the foreign vessels which carried on the fishery at a greater or lesser distance from the coast from the neighbourhood of the Shetlands to the Thames. The encroachments of the foreign fishermen, which sometimes occurred from the vagaries of the shoals, were thus resented. On the English coast the native fishery was carried on for the most part alongside the foreign fishermen, and the English fishermen were thus accustomed to the presence of the foreigners. In Scotland, moreover, the sea fisheries, and in particular the herring fishery, were of greater relative importance to the people than was the case in England, which possessed rich pastures and was essentially agricultural. Fishing was much more of a national pursuit, and besides supplying what was required for home consumption, Scotland was able to export large quantities of fish to other lands: in the fifteenth century the title "Piscinata Scotia" was referred to as an "old proverb." The fisheries, besides forming a not unimportant source of revenue to the crown, supplied a chief staple of the trade and commerce of the "royal burghs," which were always extremely jealous of their rights and privileges, and possessed great power. Hence the Acts of the Scottish Parliaments which dealt with sea fisheries—and they are numerous —breathe a much more exclusive spirit than those of England. Hence also the treaties and conventions between Scotland and the Netherlands did not extend to foreign fishermen the generous treatment which was so evident in the south. The earliest of those commercial agreements seems to have been made in 1291; others were concluded in 1321 and 1323, in the reign of Robert the Bruce, by which free ingress and egress were given to merchants to pass with their merchandise to any parts of the kingdom, "with their ships and goods"; and similar freedom of commercial intercourse was stipulated in 1371, 1401, 1407, 1412, 1416, and on numerous occasions subsequently.[1] These early agreements contain no provision about the fisheries, and nothing to indicate a desire on the part of the Scottish king or people to allow fishermen from the Low Countries to fish in the adjacent waters. The feeling of the coast population towards the foreigners was usually jealous and aggressive; attacks by the one and reprisal by the other were of frequent occurrence, especially in the fifteenth and sixteenth centuries. The Earl of Holland complained in 1410 that the Scots had attacked the fishermen of that province "when they went to sea to catch herrings in their fishing vessels and to gain their living like honest men"; and by way of reprisal he gave permission to the people of Brouershaven to attack and injure their "enemies," the Scots, wherever they could find them, on sea or land.[2] There is much testimony to show that in those times the Scottish fishermen were of a fierce and forceful disposition, and little inclined to tolerate the intrusion of foreign fishermen within what they claimed as their "reserved waters,"—that is, the firths and bays and a distance along the coast described as "a land kenning," which extended to fourteen miles or to twenty-eight miles from the shore. An indication of their treatment of those who intruded is afforded by a story told in one of the English State Papers on the authority "of the old Bishop of Ross, who came in with King James to England." He said that in the time of King James V. (A.D. 1513-1542) the Hollanders, who had only a verbal license to fish at twenty-eight miles off, came near the shore within the mouth of the Firth of Forth, "and there fished in despite of the king's command." James thereupon set out men-of-war and took so many of them that "he sent a baril ful of their heads into Holland, with their names fixed to their foreheads on cards," as a warning to their fellows.[3] This tale

[1] *Fœdera*, ii. 529, 545. Mieris, *Groot Charterboek der Graaven van Holland*, &c., ii. 268; iii. 257; iv. 223, 378, 692, 816. Kluit, *Historiæ Federum Belgii Federati*, 284. Yair, *An Account of the Scotch Trade in the Netherlands*, 6, 27, 36.

[2] Mieris, *op. cit.*, iv. 146. About this time the Scots also did their best to drive away English fishermen from their coasts. In 1400 they fitted out a small fleet under Sir Robert Logan for this purpose, but it was apparently insufficient, and Logan himself was captured by the men of Lynn. Walsingham, *Hist. Anglicana*, 364. In 1420 complaint was made to the English Parliament that the Scots had at divers times attacked and taken English fishing vessels. *Rot. Parl.*, iv. 127*a*.

[3] *State Papers, Dom.*, Charles I., clii. 63. See p. 218.

of savagery, probably apocryphal, no doubt originated in the conflicts and reprisals between the Dutch and the Scots which are known to have occurred in the reign of James V., and led to the treaty of 1541, in which, for the first time, there is a stipulation concerning the fisheries. For some years previously the relations of the Emperor Charles V. (in whose dominions the Low Countries were included) and the King of Scotland had been strained, owing to the renewal of the old alliance between Scotland and France. A number of armed vessels, under the command of Robert Foggo of Leith, cruised about and captured many Dutch herring-busses, especially those belonging to Schiedam and Briel. The States of Holland retaliated by seizing Scottish goods in Holland, and then James V. threatened that he would put an entire stop to their herring fishing on the coast of Scotland.[1] Owing to the war with France and the depredations of privateers, the Netherlands at that time had much difficulty in protecting their herring-busses, and the threat of the Scottish king speedily brought about negotiations. The States of Holland petitioned the Emperor to interfere,[2] alleging that the prohibition of their herring fishing by the King of Scotland was inconsistent with the freedom of navigation, and even with the treaties subsisting between them—which, however, as has been said, did not include the question of fishing. In the treaty which followed between James V. and the Emperor,[3] it was, amongst other things, agreed that means should be devised for reparation of the damages done on both sides "to merchants, fishers, and other traders or subjects," or to their ships and goods, in time of peace; and that mutual protection should be afforded to the fishermen against pirates. It contained no fishery clause like those in the English treaties, and not a word about the liberty of fishing. It can scarcely be doubted that the omission was deliberate, and that those conducting the negotiations on behalf of the Dutch wished to have a guarantee of the kind. We learn from the treaty that the last article in the instructions of the Scots ambassador con-

1 "Dat hy voorhadt, de haringvisscherij omtrent zyne kusten te beletten." Wagenaar, *Vaderlandsche Historie*, v. 209.

2 *Resol. Staten van Holl.*, $\frac{5}{15}$ September 1540. Bosgoed, *Bib. Pisc.*, 319.

3 Treaty of Binche, $\frac{9}{19}$ February $\frac{1540}{1541}$. Dumont, *op. cit.*, IV. ii. 208.

tained some proposal about the fishery. Its nature does not appear; but from the fact that it was not agreed to, and was reserved for further consideration on the part of the Emperor, it is not unlikely that it referred to the fixing of a limit within which the Dutch were not to fish.[1] The Scottish lawyer, Welwood, early in the next century referred to the "notorious covenant" which had been made with the Dutch, that they should not fish within eighty miles of the coast of Scotland, a statement that may have been a reminiscence of this proposal.

The peace was not of long duration. The Scots again attacked the Dutch fishermen on the coast of Scotland; the goods of Scotch merchants were in turn seized in the Netherlands, and their ships and seamen arrested, and arrangements were made by the Dutch to convoy their herring-busses with many ships of war.[2] On the representations of Rotterdam and Schiedam—towns which had a great stake in the herring fishery on the Scottish coast—a request was made to the Emperor, in the name of the States of Holland, asking him to arrange in his negotiations with the Scots for the restitution of the goods taken by them from the Hollander fishermen; and early in 1545 he was petitioned to conclude a truce with them on account of the herring and dogger (cod) fishing.[3] It was not until 1550 that another treaty was signed between the two countries,—also at Binche, on 15th December, on behalf of the Emperor Charles V. and Mary Stuart, Queen of Scotland. It confirmed all previous treaties, and contained provisions for mutual freedom of commerce and navigation without the need of any safe-conduct or license, general or special, and with liberty to make use of one another's ports, and also mutually to protect one another's subjects, including fishermen, from the attacks of pirates. The part referring to the fishery did not, however, differ from that in the previous

[1] "Et quant au dernier article de la commission du Sr. de Limdy [Lundy] ambassadeur, concernant le fait de la pescherie, ladite Dame Reine [the Queen Dowager of Hungary and Bohemia] veuille par bonne et meure deliberation proceder en telles et semblables affaires, se fera informer sur le contenu dudit article, pour aprés en ordonner comme il sera trouvé étre de raison, équité, et justice d'une part et d'autre pour la conservation de la paix et amitié mutuelle desdits Sieurs." *Op. cit.*, and see footnote next page.

[2] Wagenaar, *op. cit.*, 355.

[3] *Res. St. Holl.*, $\frac{\text{29 Nov.}}{\text{9 Dec.}}$ 1544; $\frac{\text{23 Feb.}}{\text{5 Mar.}}$ 1545, &c. Bosgoed, *op. cit.*, 320.

treaty, which it merely confirmed. "With regard to the fishery and the free use of the sea," it said, "that which was made, concluded, and agreed upon by the foresaid treaty made at Binche on the 19th February 1541, between the Most Serene Queen Mary (of Hungary and Bohemia) and the aforesaid ambassador of the King of Scotland, shall be truly and sincerely observed."[1] This treaty, which was called in the Netherlands "celebre fœdus," may be regarded as the Scottish counterpart of the Intercursus Magnus, concluded with England in 1496. The older Dutch writers, as Wagenaar and Plegher, professed to regard it as having guaranteed freedom of fishery on the coasts of Scotland in the same way; and it was cited by the Dutch ambassadors in the negotiations concerning the fishery in the seventeenth century in this sense. But in the English treaty freedom of fishing all over the sea was expressly covenanted in the most plain and explicit language, while the treaty with Scotland in 1550 merely confirmed a previous treaty which certainly did not confer liberty of fishing, though the phrase "the free use of the sea," now introduced in the preamble, might at first sight imply the contrary. Nothing more appears to have been heard of the proposal of the Scottish ambassador in 1541, which had been deferred for further deliberation.[2]

A treaty which took a still more important place in the subsequent disputes and negotiations respecting *mare clausum* and unlicensed fishing, and upon which the Dutch relied even more, at least in the reign of James, than they did on the Intercursus Magnus, was concluded with King James VI. in

[1] Dumont, IV. iii. 12. "Circa piscationem verò ac liberum usum maris, ea quæ per supradictum Tractatum anno 1541, 19 Februarii, Binchii inter Serenissimam Reginam Mariam et supra nominatum Oratorem Regis Scotiæ inita, conclusa ac conventa fuerint debite ac sincere observari debebunt."

[2] In 1618, when there was much searching of the records in Scotland (where they were kept in a most careless and slovenly manner) to establish the claim of James to the fishing in connection with the approaching visit of the Dutch ambassadors, the Earl of Dunfermline wrote to Lord Binning in London, forwarding a copy, in French, of the treaty of 1541, and said, "Albeit ye will perseive by the last article of the same annent the propositions of the fishings, the Queen of Hungarie and Bohemia, who was for the Emperour Governant of the Low Countries — we call her commonly Frow Mary — in that takes her to further advysement with her Councill, and no thing resolved if any further proceeding; *I pray God ye may find it otherwayes.*" *MSS. Advoc. Lib.*, 31. 2. 16.

1594, fifteen years before he issued, as king of England as well as of Scotland, his famous proclamation forbidding promiscuous and unlicensed fishing. On the occasion of the baptism of his son, Prince Henry, which took place at Stirling on 30th August 1594, the States-General despatched two ambassadors, Walraven van Brederode and Jacob Valck, laden with costly gifts, to take part in the ceremony, and also to do a little business with the king. The two previous treaties between Scotland and the Netherlands had been concluded at a time when the whole of that country had been under the rule of Charles V. In the interval it had passed into the possession of Philip of Spain, and then the northern provinces had revolted, thrown off the Spanish yoke, and formed the famous federal commonwealth of the seven United Provinces of Holland, Zealand, Utrecht, Gelderland, Over-Yssel, Friesland, and Groningen. It was thought to be desirable by the prudent Dutchmen to renew if possible on their own behalf the treaties with Scotland, especially as it was then recognised that James would succeed to the English throne. The ambassadors therefore brought with them a long draft treaty, in which the previous treaty of 1541 was recited and that of 1550 was given in full. James agreed to the confirmation of the previous treaties, and the ratification was signed at Edinburgh on 14th September 1594. In his declaration he stated that he had "seen, read, and examined" the treaty of peace and alliance made at Binche in 1550 between Charles V., Emperor of the Romans, in the capacity of sovereign of the Low Countries, and Queeen Mary, "his honoured dame and mother," and having found it very desirable, good, and beneficial for him and his country, it was to be observed inviolably for the good of the traffic and commerce of the subjects of the two nations; and he sincerely promised to observe the treaty and every clause and article in it. Then the easy-going monarch appears to have forgotten all about it. The document itself was lost, and when it was urgently wanted for the negotiations in the next century it could not be found, and nobody in this country seemed to know what it contained; it was even regarded by some—as the English ambassador at The Hague—as apocryphal. Although the Dutch relied much on this treaty, it contained no stipulation regarding liberty of fishing.

The treaty of 1550 was confirmed, by which it was provided that commerce and navigation were to be free; merchants were to be at liberty to pass safely and freely with their goods by land and sea, and to buy and sell; pirates were to be chased from the sea, and the subjects of either state, including fishermen, were to be mutually protected from their attacks; but the fishery clause was precisely the same as before.[1]

It is thus evident that there was a great difference between the English and the Scottish treaties with the Netherlands respecting the right of fishery. The former contained a separate clause, conceived in a broad and liberal spirit and again and again renewed, providing for mutual freedom of fishing everywhere on the seas, while no such agreement or anything like it was made on the part of Scotland. The Dutch fishing on the coast of Scotland was more important to them than their fishing on the English coast, and there is no doubt they strove to obtain the same privileges for it as they received in England. The omission of a corresponding clause in the Scottish treaties was in accordance with the long-settled policy of the Scottish kings and Parliaments, and it was that policy that James carried with him to England when he attempted to reverse the established practice with regard to the fisheries, and opened up the claims to *mare clausum*.

There is, unfortunately, little contemporary evidence as to the precise extent of the claim to the fisheries which was anciently put forward in Scotland. The Acts of the Scottish Parliaments do not help us very far, although they reveal the jealous and conservative spirit previously referred to. Many statutes were made prohibiting strangers from buying fish except such as were salted and barrelled, and then only at free burghs; concerning the "assize-herring," of which so much was to be heard; and the payment of customs by foreigners exporting fish. The language of some of the Acts implied a certain control over foreign fishermen on the sea,[2] and all that we know of

[1] The heads of the treaty and the ratifications are given by Dumont, *Corps Diplomatique*, V. i. 507. The treaty itself is published in full by Bor, *Vervolgh Vande Nederlantssche Oorlogen ende Geschiedenissen*, iv. fol. 48-52.

[2] *E.g.*, in 1573, that "all maner of fischeris that occupyis the sey and vtheris persounis quhatsumeuer" that catch herrings or white fish "vpon the coist or within the Ilis or outwith the samin within the Fyrthis" should bring them to free ports to be sold. *Acta Parl. Scot.*, iii. c. 7.

the practice and customs in Scotland makes it highly probable that these enactments were in point of fact enforced against foreign fishermen as far as they could be. The Scots were always particularly jealous about the fishings in the firths and lochs "within land." An important herring fishery of this kind was carried on in the lochs on the west coast, especially in Loch Broom and Loch Fyne, in autumn and winter, by fishermen from the Clyde, the Ayrshire coast, and Fifeshire, who built timber houses on shore where they cured the herrings; and this fishing was attended by Frenchmen, "Flemings," and English, who purchased the cured herrings or bought the fish and cured them themselves.[1] Wishing to catch the herrings for themselves, these "divers strangers" most earnestly petitioned Queen Mary in 1566 for "license to fish in the said lochs." But the Council, to whom the petition was referred, after consultation with the burghs, refused the request, and ordained that "no stranger of whatever nation they be come in the said lochs, nor use the commodity of the said fishing in any time to come, but the same to be reserved for the born subjects and natives of the realm," under pain of confiscation of ships and goods.[2] Some of the old Scots Acts, of the reign of James III. (1460-1488) and later, refer to previous statutes, which seem to be lost, respecting the herring fishery in the western seas; and they indicate that "letters" had sometimes been granted by the king favouring foreigners in some way, but whether by allowing them to fish there is unknown.

On the east coast, where the Dutch carried on their great herring-fishing from busses, there is evidence that a limit was early fixed within which they were not allowed to fish, but no contemporary records relating to it appear to have been preserved. It is probable that an arrangement was come to between them and the Scottish fishermen, possibly in the reign of James V. or even earlier, by which they were not to fish within sight of land. At the beginning of the seventeenth century, when the question of unrestricted fishing was raised in

[1] Leslie, *De Origine Moribus et Rebus Gestis Scotorum*, 24. A point of land near Inveraray in Loch Fyne was long known, and is still known, as Frenchman's Point or French Farl, the tradition being that it was to this place that herrings were brought to be sold and cured. *Old Statistical Account of Scotland*, v. 291.

[2] *Register Privy Council of Scotland*, i. 482.

an acute form, there was a remarkable unanimity of opinion in Scotland that the ancient and established custom was that foreigners were not allowed to carry on their operations within a "land-kenning" of the coast,—that is, not nearer than where they could discern the land from the top of their masts. This distance was usually placed at fourteen miles, but sometimes a double land-kenning, of twenty-eight miles, was claimed; and we shall see that the former distance was embodied in the Draft Treaty of Union with England in 1604, as well as proposed to the States-General as a provisional limit in 1619 (see p. 192), and declared by Parliament and the Privy Council of Scotland to be the bounds of the "reserved waters" belonging to Scotland. Welwood, a Scottish lawyer who wrote at the end of the sixteenth and the beginning of the seventeenth centuries, states that before his time, after "bloody quarrels" about sea affairs between the Scots and the Hollanders, the disputes were arranged on the understanding that in future the Hollanders were to keep at least eighty miles from the coast of Scotland, which, he says, they did for a long time. If they were driven nearer by stress of weather they paid a tax or tribute at the port of Aberdeen, where a castle was built for this and other reasons. This tax, he adds, was paid until by frequent dissensions at home and the audacity of the Hollanders the right was lost.[1] There is no very satisfactory evidence to show in how far the statements of Welwood were in accordance with the facts. In the records of the Privy Council a case is mentioned which might be interpreted in another way. In 1587 two English ships belonging to Shields, coming from the "easter seas" laden with fresh fish and bound for England, were seized and brought into port by one Thomas Davidson of Crail, apparently on the plea that they had been fishing too near the shore. The owners contended that the fish had been caught "upon the main sea, outwith his Majesty's dominions, where not only they but the subjects of all other princes had had a continual trade and fishing in all times bygone past the memory of man." But

[1] *De Dominio Maris*, 16. In another work Welwood says, "And for the eastern seas, direct from Scotland, what is more antiently notorious than that covenant twixt Scottish men and Hollanders, concerning the length of their approaching toward Scotland by way of fishing." *An Abridgement of All Sea Lawes*, c. 26.

even, it was argued on their behalf, if the fish had been caught within his Majesty's waters, still, in respect of the "continual trade" which strangers had had there in all time past, "there being no inhibition made or published to the contrary as yet," no such treatment should have been meted out to them.[1] This was in the reign of James VI.; and the most likely explanation, in the absence of information as to the decision taken by the Council, is that while no official proclamation forbidding fishing by foreigners had been promulgated, and no recent measures carried out to prevent them from doing so, it was believed that a certain part of the sea was reserved for the use of the Scottish fishermen, apart from the waters of firths and lochs.

The difference in the national policy of England and Scotland concerning foreigners fishing along our coasts prevailed until the Union of the crowns, when James introduced the Scottish ideas into England and soon endeavoured to transform them into practice. Meanwhile, under the Tudors, certain changes were slowly and silently taking place which paved the way for the new policy, and that too although, very shortly before, the freedom of the seas had been proclaimed and vindicated by Queen Elizabeth.

[1] *Register Privy Council of Scotland*, iv. 216.

CHAPTER III.

UNDER THE TUDORS.

THE policy of freedom of commercial intercourse, navigation, and fishery which was enunciated in the Intercursus Magnus and the treaties which preceded it, was faithfully observed throughout the sixteenth century. No attempt was made by any of the Tudor sovereigns to interfere with the liberty which foreigners enjoyed of fishing on the English coast; nor was any claim put forward by them to the dominion or lordship of the surrounding seas. On the contrary, throughout the greater part of the century, facilities were given for the peaceful exercise and encouragement of sea-fishing, even in time of war; while on several occasions the last and greatest of the monarchs of the Tudor line actively contested the old pretensions of Denmark to the sovereignty of the northern seas, and the more recent claims of Spain and Portugal to the exclusive right of navigating the great oceans. It was nevertheless during this century that changes occurred which made it easy for James early in the next to initiate a new policy of *mare clausum*, and to repudiate the provisions of the so-called Burgundy treaties. The most important of these changes was perhaps the decay which overtook the sea fisheries. Apart from their commercial and economic value, the fisheries were looked upon as indispensable for the maintenance of maritime power, and probably at no previous time had greater efforts been made to foster maritime power than under the Tudors. The hardy fishermen who navigated their barks to distant seas —to Iceland, to Wardhouse, round the North Cape, and now to Newfoundland—were trained in a school of seamanship which fitted them admirably to take their place for the naval defence of the country. Even the herring-smacks and the dogger-boats that fished in the North Sea and the Channel turned out mariners by no means to be despised,—men acquainted with the coasts and the tides, able to manage sails and educated to the sea. It was this aspect of the fisheries which was mostly regarded by the statesmen of those times, and for which the "political lent" and the protective legislation were designed.

The causes which led to the decay in the English fisheries were no doubt various, but perhaps the chief one, and the one on which most stress was laid in the latter part of the century, was the Reformation. The very large consumption of fish due to the observance of Lent and the numerous days of fasting, or fish-days, has been referred to (see p. 58). The suppression of the monasteries (1536-1539) and the dispersal of the inmates and dependants must alone have had considerable influence, but the relaxation of ecclesiastical rule among the laity which followed was much more detrimental to the fisheries. The decay of the sea-coast towns, so frequently spoken of in the reign of Elizabeth, was mainly attributed to this cause. Another influence which operated in the same direction, most markedly towards the end of the century, was the great growth of the fisheries and commerce of the Dutch. After the assertion of their independence of Spain (1581), commonly called the "abjuration of Philip," their fisheries developed with great rapidity. One of the first acts of the new Republic (1582) was the codification of the fishery statutes; and about this time they applied to the deep-sea herring fishery the name of Great or Grand Fishery (*Groote Visscherye*), as being "the chief industry of the country and principal gold-mine to its inhabitants," in contrast to the real gold-mines of Spain. They furnished the greater part of Europe with cured herrings and other fish, and the fish supply of England, and more particularly of London, fell to a large extent into their hands. Their herring fishery was carried on along our east coast, and the spectacle of great fleets of foreign fishing vessels frequenting our waters, while the native fisheries were falling to decay, roused envious and jealous feelings in the breasts of patriotic Englishmen.[1]

Under the Tudors the efforts made to foster the sea fisheries did not, as has been said, take the form of interfering with the

[1] Much information on the fisheries of the Netherlands will be found in Professor A. Beaujon's *History of Dutch Sea Fisheries*, 1884.

foreign fishermen. They were rather directed, on the one hand, to increase the consumption of fish by restoring the strict observance of Lent and fish-days, and, on the other hand, to check the importation of fish caught by foreigners. In this way it was hoped that the native fisheries would be stimulated to supply at least the home markets. As early as 1541—a year or two after the suppression of the monasteries—an Act was passed which apparently indicates that the decline in the fisheries had already set in, and that it was customary for the English people to purchase fish from foreigners rather than catch them for themselves. Heavy penalties were imposed on any person who should bring into the realm for sale fresh fish (except sturgeon, porpoise, and seal, which were then included in the term) which they had purchased from strangers in Flanders, Zealand, Picardy, France, or elsewhere beyond the sea, "or upon the sea between shore and shore"; but the buying of fish at Iceland, Scotland, Orkney, Shetland, Ireland, or Newfoundland—to all which places English vessels went—was not prohibited.[1] This statute was re-enacted four years later, and again by Edward VI. and Queen Mary.[2] In the reign of Elizabeth a number of similar statutes were made, with the object of favouring the native fishermen in their competition with foreigners.

About the same time as the first Act of Henry was passed we begin to get evidence of laxity in the observance of Lent and of measures taken to deal with it. Many persons, including noblemen, were brought before the Privy Council charged with having eaten flesh in Lent, and were committed to the Fleet. The mayor and aldermen of London were commanded to make inquisition throughout all the wards of the city as to the households in which flesh was used in Lent, and the butchers were required to furnish information as to the quantity of flesh sold by them, and to whom, in the same period.[3] This activity of the Privy Council foreshadowed the new policy of the "political lent" which was inaugurated a few years later in the reign of Edward VI., and with which the name of Cecil

[1] 33 Hen. VIII., c. 2.

[2] 37 Hen. VIII., c. 23; 5 & 6 Edw. VI., c. 17; 7 Edw. VI., c. 11; 1 Mary, st. 2, c. 13.

[3] *Acts of the Privy Council of England*, i. 103, 104, 106, 112, 114, *an.* 1543.

was associated. By this time it was clearly recognised that the religious changes that had taken place were prejudicial to the fisheries by lessening the consumption of fish, and in 1548 an "Act for Abstinence from Flesh" was passed, by which fines were imposed on those who did not observe the usual fast-days. The object of the measure was clearly explained. "One day or one kind of meat of itself," it said, "is not more holy, more pure, or more clean than another, for that all days and all meats be of their nature of one equal purity, cleanness, and holiness;" but "considering that due and godly abstinence is a mean to virtue, and to subdue men's bodies to their soul and spirit, and considering also especially that Fishers, and men using the trade of living by fishing in the sea, may thereby the rather be set on work," it was enacted that no person should eat flesh meat on Fridays, Saturdays, Ember-days, Lent, or on any other day which was accustomed a fish-day, under a penalty of ten shillings fine and ten days' imprisonment without flesh food.[1]

By this statute the political lent was established, and the policy of compelling the people to eat fish for the good of the fisheries and the navy was continued with more or less vigour for a century and a half. Sir William Cecil was especially active in its favour. He caused careful inquiries to be made into the condition of the decayed havens and sea-coast towns and the state of the fisheries. He was informed by the London fishmongers, to whom he had submitted a series of questions, that there was not so much fish then consumed "by a great quantity" as used to be the case, and that the number of vessels engaged in the fisheries had greatly decreased. On the latter point they referred to a return made about the twentieth year of the reign of Henry VIII., which showed that seven-score and odd ships then went to the Iceland fishery, about 80 crayers to Shetland, and about 220 crayers from Scarborough and other towns to the North Seas fishing, making a total of about 440 fishing vessels; while at the time they wrote—in the reign of Edward VI., and probably in 1552 or 1553—the number had fallen to about 133, of which 43 went to Iceland, 10 crayers to Shetland, and 80 to "the North Seas," showing a

[1] 2 & 3 Edw. VI., c. 19. Certain exceptions, of those licensed, ill, or very old, or in prison, were made.

decrease in the twenty-four or twenty-five years of about 307 "ships and crayers."[1] A similar story of the decay of the fisheries came from the east-coast towns. At Lynn, which was maintained chiefly by the Iceland and the herring fisheries, and which twenty or thirty years before sent out about thirty vessels to those fisheries, there were then only two Iceland barks, and no herring-smacks at all. It used to be able to furnish 300 mariners for the king's service, while now it could not supply more than twenty or thirty. And so at Burnham (where the fishing-boats had decreased from 26 to *nil*), Wells, Clee, Cromer, Yarmouth, and other Norfolk ports—all had greatly decayed. The fisheries and the shipping had fallen off, the "men of substance" had lost their money or left, the population had diminished, and even the houses were falling down. To a statesman like Cecil, who knew the value of the mariners bred at the fishing ports for manning the navy if need arose, and how a flourishing fishery multiplied shipping, such information must have been disquieting. He calculated that while within twenty years back there had been 150 ships for Iceland, 220 for the north seas, and 78 for "Shotland" (Shetland), the numbers had fallen when he wrote to 43 for Iceland, 75 for the north seas, and 9 for Shetland; and that the number of fishing vessels had decreased from 448 to 127.[2]

In replying to Cecil's second question as to the cause of the decay in the fisheries, the fishmongers said it was first of all due to the diminished consumption of fish, since the fish-days were not "duly observed as heretofore," which "took away such hope of gain as in time past they have had" in carry-

[1] *State Papers, Dom., Addenda*, Edw. VI., iv. 56. The paper, which is endorsed by Cecil, "The Answer of the Fishmongers," is undated, but that it belongs to the reign of Edward VI. (1547-1553) is proved by the words, "the reign of our late sovereign, Henry VIII." The return of 1528, referred to by the fishmongers, is among the State Papers (*Foreign and Domestic Letters and Papers*, Hen. VIII., iv. pt. 2, No. 5101). It states that 149 vessels went to the Iceland fishing, mostly from Yarmouth, Blakeney, Cromer, Dunwich, Walderswick, and Southwold; the herring-fishing in the North Sea employed 222, of which 110 belonged to the Cinque Ports, while 69 went to Shetland, the total being 440. Shetland lings were in those days greatly prized, and brought very high prices.

[2] *State Papers, Dom., Addenda*, Edw. VI., iv. 57. "The decaied Porte Townes wth nombers of good villages a longe by the sea cost of this realm, within these twentie or thirtie years;" undated, but belonging to the same period, with Cecil's calculations written on the back.

ing on the fisheries. A second reason they gave was the greater love "for ease and pleasure" than in former times, people now preferring to buy their fish from strangers rather than to "travail and venture for it themselves,"—a very common charge against Englishmen then and for a long time afterwards. As a third reason, they said the price of fish was regulated in various towns by the mayors and other officers in such a way that they were often forced to sell without sufficient profit, while Government purveyors made them part with their fish at nominal prices. It is to be noted that they made no complaint against foreign fishermen or the importation of foreign fish.

During the brief reign of Mary (1553-1558) Cecil was in the shade, but shortly after the accession of Elizabeth he again devoted attention to the decay of the fisheries and tried to apply fitting remedies. Among the State Papers of the year 1563 is a long and elaborate document, copiously revised by Cecil himself, which deals with the condition of shipping and fisheries, and obviously formed the basis and argument for the great Act made in the same year.[1] In this paper the decay of the navy both in ships and mariners was traced by Cecil to a variety of causes: the piracies of Turks and Moors on the Levant trade, the transference of the spice trade from the Venetians to the Portuguese and Spaniards, the Spanish law of bottomry, the augmentation by the King of Denmark of the tolls at the Sound and his recovery of Iceland, and the decay of the English fisheries. Herrings and other sea fish, he said, were now taken upon our coast by strangers, who brought them into the realm and sold them "to the very inhabitants of the parts that were used to be fishermen," while Englishmen had themselves been prohibited from exporting fish.[2] The remedies which Cecil proposed were that the importation of wines and woad should be allowed only in English ships; that English-

[1] *State Papers, Dom.*, Elizabeth, xxvii. 71, February 1563. Endorsed, "Arguments for Increase of the Navy," and "Arguments to prove that it is necessary for the restoring of the navy of England to have one Day more in ye weeke ordained to be a fish day, and that to be Wensday rather than any other."

[2] The exportation, without license, of herrings, among other things, had been forbidden by 1 & 2 Ph. and Mary, c. 5 (1554); but by 1 Eliz., c. 17, subjects were permitted to export sea fish taken by subjects in English ships free of customs for four years.

men should be prohibited from purchasing fresh herrings which had been caught by strangers; that they should be free to export and sell sea fish out of the realm; and, principally, that Wednesday should be made an additional fish-day. The decay of the fisheries, he said, was manifest on all the sea coast in the decay of the port towns, which soon would be "remedeless," and it was caused by diminished consumption of fish at home and the want of foreign markets.[1] On the other hand, Scotland, Norway, Denmark, Friesland, Zealand, Holland, and Flanders caught not only sufficient fish for themselves, but exported it to other countries, including England; while Spain provided herself by her fisheries on the south coast of Ireland, and France "aboundeth with fishermen" from her great fisheries at Newfoundland and Iceland.[2] Cecil's conclusion was that there was no likelihood for a long time of developing a flourishing export trade in fish, and that it would be necessary to institute another fish-day to increase the demand at home. On this part of his proposals he entered into a long argument, showing that in 1536 the 500 monasteries which paid tithes to the king, with a minimum number of 25,000 inmates, must have required a great supply of fish, as fish was then eaten on at least seventy-six days a year more than at the time when he wrote.[3]

By the great Act passed in 1563, "Touching certain Politic Constitutions made for the Maintenance of the Navy," Wednesday was added to the two fish-days previously enjoined by the statute of Edward VI., but only after long debate and opposition on the part of the "puritans."[4] The Act also contained

[1] "The causes of the decay of fishing must be the lack of the vse of fishing, which must be divided into ij partes, small eating of fisshe in ye Realme, and not selling of it abroad."

[2] The number of French vessels engaged in the Newfoundland fisheries is placed at 500, with 15,000 men; and over 100, with at least 1000 men, fished at Iceland for "herrings,"—but no doubt for cod and ling.

[3] There are many other memoranda amongst the State Papers, some in Cecil's handwriting, which deal with fish-days. One gives in detail a note of all the fish-days throughout the year, amounting to 186, and in addition "a number of sayntes evens were fastyng dayes that now be not observed." *Ibid.*, xxxi. 41, 42 (1563).

[4] 5 Eliz. c. 5. The debate on the Wednesday proposal lasted three days, the clause being ultimately carried by 179 to 97 (*Commons Journals*, i. 68). It was in view of the expected opposition that the long paper above referred to was prepared. The Wednesday was not put on quite the same footing as the Fridays and Saturdays, since "one only usual competent dish of flesh and no more" was allowed, provided that at the same table "three full competent usual dishes of sea fish

provisions to restrain foreign importation of fish, to encourage the export of English-caught fish by subjects, and to remove the complaints as to the action of purveyors and burdensome impositions—points on which the fishmongers had laid some stress. Herrings and other sea fish taken by Englishmen in English ships were to be freely exported without paying custom; no tax, toll, or restraint was to be imposed on fish taken and landed by subjects; it was made illegal to buy from strangers any herrings unless they were "sufficiently salted, packed, and casked"; only English vessels were to be allowed to carry coastwise any fish, victuals, or other goods; the cultivation of flax for fishing-nets was to be encouraged; and on the plea that there was "much deceitful packing" of cod and ling brought into the realm by aliens, the importation of these fish was forbidden, except only "loose, in bulk and by tale." Most of these provisions and prohibitions would operate against the Dutch, who had not only a large part of the trade in herrings with England, but practically the monopoly in supplying barrelled cod and ling.[1]

From this time forward the policy of protecting the native fisheries by checking the competition of foreigners went hand in hand with the encouragement of the consumption of fish by the compulsory observance of fish-days. Interfering as it did with established practice and conflicting trade interests, the Act aroused opposition in various quarters, especially on the part of those who were interested in the important commerce in cured cod-fish. In the year after it passed, the Queen's purveyors were unable to obtain in England sufficient supplies of fish for the navy and the royal service, and they were licensed to import cod-fish, lings, and green-cod, in barrels or casks, notwithstanding the prohibition in the Act,[2]—a privilege which had to be extended to all English subjects

of sundry kinds, either fresh or salt," were served and eaten "without fraud or covin." Another clause explained that the object was "meant politically for the increase of fishermen and mariners, and repairing of port towns and navigation, and not for any superstition "regarding choice of meats"; any one stating the contrary was to be punished.

[1] Among the imports of fish from the Low Countries at this time were "cods-heads, cod-fish, eels, 'gull-fish,' haddocks, herrings, ling, salmon, salt-fish, sturgeon, and 'staple-fish.'" Hall, *A History of the Customs Revenue in England*, ii. 237.

[2] *State Papers, Dom.*, Eliz., xxxv. 36.

a few years later with respect to fish caught in their own vessels "with cross-sails."[1] On the other hand, it was claimed that the Act had done good. The coast people of Norfolk and Suffolk informed the Council in 1568 that it had increased the trade in fish in these counties; and as the Act had been passed for four years only and continued at the Queen's pleasure, they petitioned that it should be renewed, and that provision should be made to put a stop to the importation by strangers of cod and ling in bulk, which were dried and sold under the name of Iceland fish, to the detriment of those engaged in the Iceland fishery, and also to ensure that fish-days should be better observed.[2] In the same year the Council instructed the magistrates of London, Hull, and Southampton, and the justices of various shires, to commit to jail any persons fraudulently dealing with foreign imported cod and ling as Iceland fish;[3] and three years later another Act was passed, giving effect to the wishes of the fishermen, and continuing the former Act for other six years.[4] It contained a new provision showing that complaints had been made about the vessels, some of them foreign, which came "pretending" to buy fresh herrings on the coast of Norfolk. To avoid "lewd outrages" by these "catches, mongers, and Picardes," in cutting and damaging the drift-nets of the fishermen, they were prohibited from anchoring between sunset and sunrise during the fishing season in the places where the boats were accustomed to fish.

Up to about this time no complaint seems to have been made against the foreign fishermen either by English fishermen or by statesmen or writers. The men from the Low Countries appear to have pursued their occupation in peace side by side with the Englishmen. But in 1570 the first note was heard of what became later almost a continuous lamentation. A petition was presented to the Privy Council asking that "letters" should be sent to Zealand and Holland, or ships of war despatched to protect the English fishermen from the evil doings of the Low Countrymen. "Otherwise," the petitioners said, "both wee and all others that entend fysshing in all partes of

[1] 13 Eliz., c. 11. [2] *State Papers, Dom.*, Eliz., xlviii. 83.

[3] *Hatfield MSS.*, i. 1177, 27th June 1568.

[4] 13 Eliz., c. 11. In the preamble it is said the former Act "is a very good Act, and greatly increased the navy and fishermen."

this realme shall be utterly undone, for that the fishermen Flemynges this yeire have so spoyled and mysused all the coaste men, that it hath so discomforted them" that they feared "the whole avoyadaunce of fysshing both for herring and other fysshing upon all the north coast of this realme."[1] Whether or not this complaint referred to the outrages described in the Act quoted above is uncertain, but probably it did not, as the Hollanders and Zealanders fished for themselves, and they were now becoming rather numerous. It does not appear that any special action was taken regarding the petition. It was Cecil's aim to increase the use of fish within the realm and to foster the native fisheries, but he had no desire to interfere with the liberty of fishing enjoyed by the Hollanders. Such action would have been contrary not only to the treaties but to the international policy of England at that time. On political and religious grounds the aid of the Dutch was needful in the struggle against the common enemy, Spain.

That the English people had become interested in the condition of the fisheries and somewhat jealous of the fleets of foreign vessels which fished along their coast may be inferred from the appearance at this time of two works—one by Captain Robert Hitchcock, and the other by the learned and unfortunate Dr John Dee. It is a curious circumstance that those authors, who wrote at the same period, should each have advocated one of the two lines of policy adopted in the next century. Hitchcock was all for freedom of fishing, for strangers and natives alike. His remedy was the creation of a great English fishery organisation to oust the Dutch from our seas. Dee, on the other hand, was emphatic in claiming *mare clausum* and an exclusive fishing for Englishmen, and in urging heavy taxation of foreigners who fished in the British seas.

Hitchcock was a gentleman and a soldier who, in 1553, as he himself tells us, while serving the Emperor Charles V. in his wars in the Low Countries, had observed with astonishment that the wealth and shipping of Zealand and Holland were due to their sea fisheries. Pondering on his discovery, he thought out a plan some years later by which a great national fishery might be established in England to supplant

[1] *State Papers, Dom.*, Eliz., lxxv. 16.

the Dutch, so that the wealth acquired by them in the British seas might go to profit his own countrymen. It was the first of the innumerable schemes of the kind which are to be found scattered over the economic literature of the next two centuries. Having reduced his plan to writing, he submitted it about the year 1573 to the Earl of Leicester, in 1575 to Queen Elizabeth, and in the following year he distributed copies to men of influence, in the hope "that God would stir up some good man to set out this work." It appears even to have been brought to the notice of Parliament by Sir Leonard Digges, but its consideration was deferred "for want of time."[1] The copy presented to the Queen is preserved among the Burghley Papers in the British Museum,[2] and the completed work, somewhat enlarged,—now very rare,—was published (in black-letter) on 1st January 1580 as "A New Year's Gift to England."[3]

The plan of Hitchcock was to borrow £80,000 for three years, when the whole amount would be repaid from the proceeds of the fish sold. The shires were to be arranged in eight groups, each group providing with its £10,000 fifty fishing vessels of not less than 70 tons burthen, or 400 altogether. These were to be built after the manner of "Flemysche Busses" and distributed at eighty ports around the coast; and at eight of the chief ports (London, Yarmouth, Hull, Newcastle, Chester, Bristol, Exeter, and Southampton) two "honest and substantial men of credit" were to be appointed chief officers, to act as treasurers, purveyors, and directors. Hitchcock estimated that each ship when ready for fishing would cost £200; the crews were to consist of a skilled master, twelve mariners or fisher-

[1] In the same year the author, at a dinner he gave at Westminster to the burgesses representing "all the stately port towns of England," explained the substance of his "plat"; several of them suggested that a subsidy should be raised on land and goods to set the scheme afloat; and the Speaker remarked that "a Parliament had been called for a less cause."

[2] *Burghley Papers*, A.D. 1572, *MSS. Lansd.* 14, No. 30. As the catalogue states, the signature is erased, and the paper is entered as anonymous; but careful scrutiny shows that it was signed "Robt. Hitchcock."

[3] *A Pollitique Platt for the honour of the Prince, the greate profite of the publique state, relief of the poore, preseruacion of the riche, reformation of Roges and Idle persones, and the wealthe of thousandes that knowes not howe to liue. Written for an* Newyeres gift *to Englande and the inhabitantes thereof,* by Robert Hitchcok, late of Cauersfeelde, in the Countie of Buckyngham, Gentleman. London, 1st Januarie 1580.

men, and twelve "strong lustie beggers or poore men taken upp through the land."[1] The scheme proposed that the busses should first fish for herrings on the coast of England and Ireland during the fourteen or fifteen weeks this fishing lasted, the herrings being cured and branded after the "Flemish" fashion. The busses were also to visit Newfoundland for cod and ling; or some were to go to Iceland, "Wardhouse,"[2] the north seas of England and Scotland, or to Ireland. It was intended to employ some of them in winter in exporting the surplus of cured fish to France, "or elsewhere." As for the all-important question of earnings, it was calculated that each buss would catch at least 50 lasts, or 600 barrels, of herrings, worth £10 a last; altogether £200,000 from this item,[3] and if two voyages were made, the amount would be doubled. It was supposed that each buss would bring back from Newfoundland 20,000 of the best "wet" fish and 10,000 dried—together worth £500; the same value was placed upon the 15,000 cod and 10,000 ling to be procured at Iceland, Wardhouse, or the north seas; and besides the fish, each ship was estimated to return with £50-£60 worth of cod-liver oil. Then with regard to the "vent" or sale of the fish, it was assumed that about half of the herrings, or 120,000 barrels, would be required for home consumption—not an exaggerated idea, for from other accounts it appears that London and the parts around it consumed about this time 60,000 barrels. Markets for the surplus herrings, it was believed, would be found at Normandy, Nantes, Bordeaux, and Rochelle. The profits were to be divided into shares, and besides paying off the borrowed capital and the interest (at 10 per cent), a stock of £8000 was to be formed at the eight chief ports,

[1] In the early MS. copy presented to the Queen the 400 vessels were to be from 100 to 200 tons, costing £400 each, and the crew was to consist of a master, nine mariners, and thirty "rogues and lustie vagabonds" obtained in the same forcible way.

[2] This place, frequently mentioned in old works and papers referring to the fisheries, was Vardö, or Vardöhuus, at the mouth of the Varangerfjord, Finmarken, on the north-east coast of Norway, or, as it was often described, Lapland. The king of Denmark had a castle on the island, and dues had to be paid for liberty to fish. A number of English vessels went there in spring, returning towards the end of summer.

[3] In France at this time, according to other records, Flemish herrings brought £25 per last; Yarmouth, £10; Irish, £18; "coast" herrings and Scotch, £11.

and £400 at the "225 decayed towns" in England and Wales for the philanthropic purpose of giving work to the poor. Nay, there was more. At the chief ports the surplus earnings were to provide a salary for "an honest, virtuous and learned man," who was to travel constantly about the coasts preaching to the people, "as the Apostles did." Among the indirect benefits to the nation Hitchcock included the transformation of idle vagabonds, of whom there were plenty, "daily increasing," into good subjects—some of the Members of Parliament thought this part of the scheme alone entitled it to national support,—the addition of 9000 mariners for manning the navy, the saving of coin spent on foreign fish, the increase of the Queen's customs, of commerce and navigation, and the repair of the decayed towns.

Such was the dream of this enthusiastic but thoroughly sincere old soldier: to expel the Hollanders from our seas by means of a national fishery organisation and to win back for England the wealth they gathered from her waters. At the time when he wrote, foreign fishermen were not nearly so numerous on our coasts as they became later. The herring-busses from the Low Countries which fished on the east coast numbered, he says, between 400 and 500, and the Englishmen "for feare of them," and of tempests, fished in small vessels near the shore, as he shows in a "similitude," here reproduced (fig. 2). Besides these, between 300 and 400 ships and barks from Biscay, Galicia, and Portugal fished off the south-west coast of Ireland from April to July, "near to Mackertymors country"; and also on the west and north-west coasts of Ireland for cod and ling from about Christmas to March. Hitchcock makes no complaint against the foreign fishermen for fishing in "her Majesty's seas." With a fine catholic generosity he indeed expressly says that all men of what country soever should be free to do so; that there was enough fish in the northern seas for all, even if there were 1000 sail more than there was. He believed that the English, by being so much nearer the fishing grounds, ought to be able to undersell the foreigner and get the markets and the trade.[1]

[1] The *Pollitique Platt* is earnest and even religious in tone, and it is obvious that the author spent much time in collecting the information and elaborating his scheme, which in all sincerity was meant for the good of his country. Even after

The scheme of Dr John Dee was very different from that of Hitchcock. A mathematician, an astrologer, a reputed magician, and, above all, an accomplished scholar, he looked at the subject from another point of view. Well acquainted with the writings of the Italian jurists and the practice of the Italian states, he expounded the view that the fisheries and the sovereignty in the British seas pertained to the crown of England, and that foreigners should be compelled to pay tribute for the liberty of

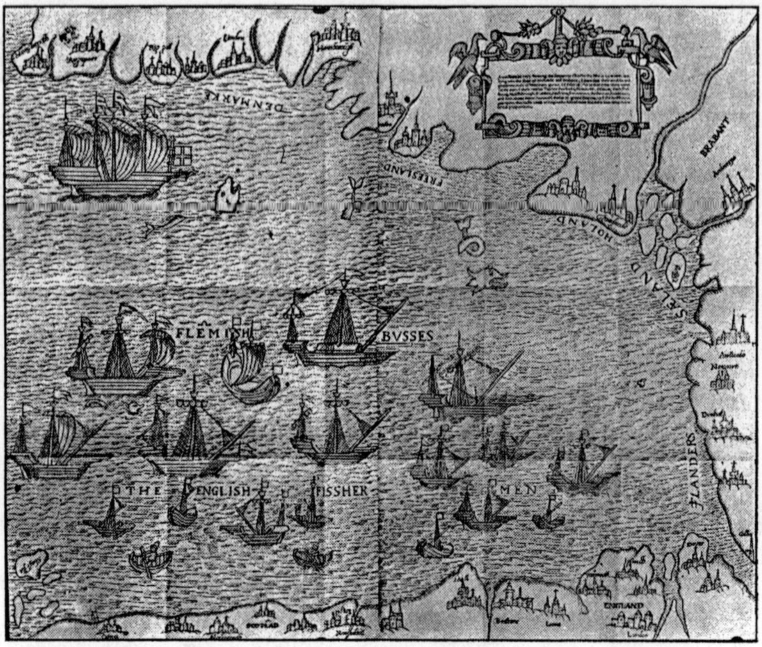

Fig. 2.—*Hitchcock's representation of the English and Flemish fisheries.*

fishing within them. It is the philosopher of Mortlake, indeed, who must be recognised as the literary pioneer of the claims to the sovereignty of the sea which were put forward by England in the seventeenth century. In 1577 he published a book

three centuries one learns with regret (from his letter preserved at Hatfield) that he had to petition the Privy Council, "for his relief and maintenance in these his now declining years" (1596), to cause every innkeeper, &c., to purchase from him, for sixpence, and put up publicly, a printed table, or "breviate," describing the "benefits that growe to this Realme by the Observance of Fish-Daies." . . .

entitled *General and Rare Memorials pertayning to the Perfect Arte of Navigation*,[1] in which he dealt with the fisheries and the boundaries of the British seas, and recommended that the tribute to be exacted from foreign fishermen should be expended in maintaining a navy to be called "The Petty Navy Royall," for keeping the seas and supervising the fisheries. "Should not forreyne fishermen," he asks, "(overboldly now and to to injuriously abusing oure riche fishings about England, Wales and Ireland), by the presence, oversight, power and industry of this Petty Navy Royal be made content; and judge themselves well apaid to enjoy, by our leave, some great portion of revenue to enrich themselves and their countries by, with fishing within the seas appertayning to oure ancient bounds and limits? Where now, to oure great shame and reproache, some of them do come in a manner home to our doors; and among them all, deprive us yearly of many hundred thousand pounds, whiche by our fishermen using the said fishings as chief, we might enjoy; and at length, by little and little, bring them (if we would deal so rigorously with them) to have as little portion of our peculiar commodity (to our Islandish Monarchy, by God and Nature assigned) as now they force our fishermen to be contented with; and yearly notwithstanding, doo at their fishing openly and ragingly use suche words of reproche toward our Prince and realm, as no true subject's hart can quietly digest; and besides that, offer such shamefull wrongs to the good laboursom people of this land, as is not (by any reason) to be born withall, or endured any longer: destroying their nets, cutting their cables to the los of their anchors; yea, and oftentymes of Barkes, men and all."[2] Here is the first note of a plaint which will become very common. He also accused the foreign fishermen, under colour of fishing, of making secret soundings of the channels and banks along our coast, to the great danger of the realm.

As for their fishing on the English coast, he says, erroneously, that the men from the Low Countries had frequented the herring fishing off Yarmouth for only thirty years (since 1540), since

[1] Better known by its running title, *The Brytish Monarchie.* It is a very rare work, only 100 copies having been printed. The author's own copy is in the British Museum.

[2] P. 7.

when their numbers had greatly increased. They had now become "very rich, strong, proud, and violent," so that the ships of Norfolk and Suffolk, next to the fishing places, were reduced in numbers by 140 sail, besides crayers and other craft. The number of Flemish herring-busses that came to our coast he placed at over 500, while there were about 100 French; and 300 or 400 "Flemings" fished for cod in the north seas, "within the English limits." Other foreigners, moreover, caught herrings on the Lancashire and Welsh coasts, and about 300 sail of Spaniards, besides Frenchmen, fished off Cape Clear and Blackrock in Ireland. All these fishings, said Dee, were "enjoyed as securely and freely from us by strangers, as if they were within their own King's peculiar sea limits; nay, rather as if those coasts, seas and bays were of their private and several purchases: to our unspeakable loss, discredit and discomfort, and to no small further danger in these peculiar times of most subtle treacheries and fickle fidelity." While admitting that the British seas were free for navigation, Dee held that the fisheries pertained to the crown of England, and that no foreigner had a right to cast a net in our sea without first obtaining leave from the Queen. To her belonged "the tenth" of all foreign fishings "within the royal limits and jurisdiction" in the British and Irish seas, and it was "a most reasonable and friendly request" that foreigners should pay that tenth in acknowledgment of the liberty to fish,—a tribute which he calculated would amount to £100,000 a-year, and which he urged should be devoted to the maintenance of the "Petty Navy Royal."

Dee was not only the first English writer who claimed the sovereignty of the sea and the fisheries for England; he was also the first who attempted to define their boundaries in detail. At the time when he wrote, it appears indeed to have been held in theory by some lawyers that the limit of the English seas extended to the mid-line between England and foreign coasts, except in the case of the Channel, where the water right up to the opposite shore was believed to be under the sovereignty of England. The doctrine, no doubt, was evolved from the opinions of the Italian jurists, whose authority was then very high (see p. 539), and from the political relations with France then and in former times. Two years before Dee published his book,

Plowden, an eminent lawyer, acting as counsel in a case concerning the rights on a manor to wreck of the sea, argued for the defendant that "the bounds of England" extended to the middle of the adjoining sea which surrounded the realm, but that the Queen had the exclusive jurisdiction on the sea between England and France by reason of her title to France, and so also with Ireland; whereas in other places, as towards Spain, she had only the moiety. It was the same, said Plowden, with the sea as with great rivers. But while Plowden allowed the "jurisdiction and governance of all things" to the Queen on the sea within the limits stated, he denied to her the right of property in it or in the land under it; it was common to all men, and she could not prohibit any one from fishing in it; the water and the land under it were things of no value, and "the fish are always removable from one place to another."[1]

Dee adopted the same opinion as to the limits, but held, as we have seen, that the fisheries were appropriated. The boundaries of the Queen's "peculiar seas," he said, were "in all places to be accounted directly to the myddle seas over betweene the sea-shores of her own kingdom (and of all petty Isles to the same kingdom appertayning) and the opposite sea-shores of all forrein princes: and in all seas lying immediately betweene any two of her own coasts or sea-shores, the whole breadth of the seas over (in such places) is, by all reason of justice, appropriate to her peculiar jurisdiction and sea royalty," even if the distance in such cases were 1000 miles or more.[2] On the other hand, according to Dee, neighbouring countries were to be allowed the same rights and interests in the moiety of the sea appropriate to their coasts.

[1] Sir John Constable's case. Moore, *Hist. Foreshore*, 225, from *Hargrave MSS.*, 15, fol. 95*d*. In the case for the crown the claim to the sea is very briefly put: "Car quant est floud est parcel del mere que est solement en le Roign et nemy en ascun subject; car est pur passage pur chescun, mes owner de ceo nul si non le Roign." Anderson, *Les Reports du Treserudite*, i. 86. (ed. 1664). In a MS. in the Cottonian collection (*Galba*, C. 11, "Acta inter Angliam et Belgium, 1564-1567") it is said the jurisdiction of the Prince in the adjoining sea extends for a distance of 100 miles unless (1) in seas lying between the territories of two princes which contain less than a hundred miles, in which case it extends to the mid-line —usq' ad mediũ eiusdem maris extenditur; (2) where another prince has a right to the whole sea. The authorities referred to are Bartolus, Angelus, Paulus de Castro, and Joan de Platea.

[2] *Op. cit.*, 21.

The limits of the British seas, and the sovereignty pertaining to them, were more fully described by Dr Dee some years later in a long unpublished letter or treatise addressed to Sir Edward Dyer,[1] who had apparently asked him for a fuller statement of his views on the subject. In his book Dee said little about the boundaries in the Channel, where the principle of the mid-line was complicated by two circumstances—the claim of Elizabeth to the French crown, and the possession by England of the Channel Islands. In his later treatise he says that presupposing "for doctrine's sake" that Calais was in the hands of Spain, and the northern coasts of Picardy and Normandy were appropriated by France (which was the case), then the boundary must be drawn in the very middle of the Channel between Dover and Calais, and then westwards in the middle line between the opposite coasts of England and of Picardy and Normandy, until it touched the middle of a straight line drawn between Portland and the island of Alderney. In this region, west of the line, inasmuch as the coasts of the Channel Islands and the opposite coast of England belonged to the Queen, her Majesty had "absolute, peculiar, and appropriate Sea Sovereignty and Jurisdiction Royall." The western boundary of this area of absolute sovereignty in the narrow seas coincided with a line drawn from Start Point to an "island" that Dee calls "Rocktow," which is unrepresented on charts, but which is probably a phonetic synonym for "Roches Douvres," a group of islets off the north coast of Brittany.[2] From the middle of this line the boundary passed westwards, again midway between the coasts of England and Brittany, until it touched the middle of a third straight line drawn from the north-west part of Ushant to about the Lizard. These were the limits on the supposition above referred to; but, "speaking more boldly in her Majesty's right," Dee declared that the whole sea between

[1] Two MS. copies exist, one bound up with Dee's copy of the *General and Rare Memorials* in the British Museum, which was sent to Dyer with the MS., the other in *Harleian MSS.* 249, fol. 95. The latter, which is a draft, is addressed "To my very honourable frende Syr Edward Dyer, Knight," and a note inscribed on it says, "Written by Dr John Dee, out of whose library I bought it after his death Aº Dº 1625, S.D." The title on both MSS. is ΘΑΛΑΤΤΟΚΑΡΤΙ'Α ΒΡΕΤΤΑΝΙΚΗ': *Miscelanea quædam extemporanea de Imperii Britannici Iurisdictione in Mari*; and both are dated 8th September 1597.

[2] Lat. 49° 6′ N., long. 2° 49′ W.

the south coast of England and the north coast of France—Picardy, Normandy, and Brittany—was under the Queen's "sea-jurisdiction and sovereignty absolute," inasmuch as she was a real monarch of France by direct inheritance and prior conquest, and therefore had right to the French coasts; and this "absolute sovereignty" served to "enlarge and warrant" the Queen's "Jurisdiction Respective" in the ocean to the west of France. So also the jurisdiction of the crown of England extended into the main ocean to the west of England and Ireland by reason of the possession of the shores; while the ocean around Scotland, inasmuch as that country was (he said) in olden times tributary to the English kings, yielded to her Majesty "a mightie portion of Sea Sovereignty," as it stretched away westwards to "that famous and very ancient Platonicall or Solonicall Atlantis." For the same reasons Dee claimed prerogative and jurisdiction for the Queen in the northern ocean, and between Scotland and the opposite coasts of Norway and Denmark, "at least to the mid-sea," and so to the southwards "half seas over" between the east coast of England and the coasts of Denmark, Friesland, and Holland, to the Straits of Dover.

Within the British seas as thus defined, Dee claimed that the crown of England had first of all sovereign jurisdiction, over foreigners as well as over subjects,[1] and part of the duty of the Petty Navy Royal—which, as stated, was to be maintained by taxing foreign fishermen—was to guard and protect foreign ships passing through our seas. This doctrine he based upon the law as laid down by the Italian jurists. Nor did he forget the purely naval side. Quoting the old proverb, "A sword keepeth peace," he argued that the presence of a fleet such as he suggested would cause other nations to respect us more than they did, and enable us to enjoy the royalty and sovereignty of the narrow seas and of our other seas better than the possession of Calais and Boulogne could do.

Dee's work was premature. His proposals that Elizabeth

[1] "All those that pass within our sea jurisdiction (either absolute or respective) and therein commit any notable offence against us may lawfully by our power be taken; and the same offenders may as lawfully and justly be punished, as if on our land territory an offence like, or of like degree of injury, were by them against us committed." "Absolute" jurisdiction applied to the sea where both coasts belonged to England; "respective" where it terminated half seas over.

should tax foreigners for fishing in the British seas and exercise jurisdiction over foreign vessels passing through them remained as much a dream as the scheme of Hitchcock.[1] It need not be supposed that such measures as Dee proposed were intrinsically distasteful either to the Queen or to Cecil. If a navy could have been acquired so easily, or a much less sum than £100,000 gathered from foreign fishermen in a "friendly" way, as Dee supposed, neither the sovereign nor the statesman was likely to let the chance go by. But they knew better than the philosopher, or than the Stuarts in the next century, that a policy of the kind would involve them in difficulties with other Powers,—with France and Spain as well as with the Protestant Netherlands.

So far from adopting any policy of this nature or making any claim to a special sovereignty in the surrounding seas, Elizabeth steadily opposed all claims which other nations put forward to *mare clausum*. Long before Grotius, she was the champion of the free sea, although it must be admitted that the action of the English Queen was no more based on considerations of the general good of mankind than were the efforts of the Dutch publicist: both had in view the interests of their native land. Elizabeth's motive was to secure liberty of trade and fishery for her subjects, which was threatened by the pretensions of Spain and Portugal on the one hand and by Denmark on the other. The Portuguese pretension was of long standing. When that nation in the latter half of the fifteenth century had pushed her way down the west coast of Africa and ultimately round the Cape of Good Hope to the East Indies, she obtained from the Pope various bulls securing her in her possessions, and granting sovereign authority to the crown of Portugal in all the lands it might discover in the Atlantic from Cape Bojador to the Indies. By an inhuman doctrine established during the Crusades, Christian princes were supposed to have the right to invade, ravage, and acquire the territories of infidel nations on the plea of extending the sway of the Christian Church; and the Pope, from his supreme authority over all temporal things, disposed of these heathen

[1] In 1597 Dee expressed his grief and surprise that so little had been done or attempted with regard to the sovereignty of the sea, "and so my labours (after a sort) vaynely employed." MS.

lands to such princes as might bring them under the dominion of the Church and propagate the true faith among the inhabitants. Immediately on the return of Columbus from his first voyage in 1493, the Spanish monarchs accordingly obtained a bull from Pope Alexander VI. confirming them in the newly-discovered regions; and in order to prevent disputes with Portugal as to the extent of their respective claims, another bull was issued, on 4th May 1493, containing the famous line of demarcation between their territories. This was an ideal straight line drawn from the North Pole to the South Pole, passing 100 leagues to the west of the Azores and Cape Verde Islands. All islands or lands discovered to the west of this line by the Spaniards, and which had not been in the possession of any Christian Power before the preceding Christmas, were to belong to the Spanish crown; and all territory discovered to the east of it was to belong to Portugal. The Pope, moreover, granted a monopoly of commerce within those immense regions to the respective crowns, so that other nations could not trade thither without license from the Spanish or Portuguese sovereigns.[1] Spaniards even were not allowed to go to the New World either to trade or form establishments without royal license and authority. Disputes arose between Spain and Portugal as to the equity of the Pope's line of demarcation, and by the Treaty of Tordesillas, 7th June 1494, they agreed that the inter-polar line should pass 370 leagues to the west of Cape Verde Islands.[2] The exclusive rights conferred by the Pope were rigorously enforced by Spain and Portugal. Navigation to their new possessions, or the carrying on of any trade or commerce with them, without royal license was made punishable by death and confiscation of goods.[3]

Early in her reign Elizabeth had occasion to protest against

[1] *Bullarium Romanum Novissimum*, i. 346. "Insulæ novi Orbis à Ferdinando Hispaniarum Rege, et Elisabeth Regina repertæ, et reperiendæ, conceduntur eisdem, propagandæ fidei Christianæ causa . . . omnes insulas et terras firmas inventas et inveniendas, detectas ad detegendas versus Occidentem et Meridiem fabricando, et construendo unam lineam à Polo Arctico scilicet Septentrione, ad Polum Antarcticum, scilicet Meridiem, sive terræ firmæ, et insulæ inventæ et inveniendæ sint versus Indiam aut versus aliam quamcumque partem, quæ linea distet à qualibet Insularum, quæ vulgariter nuncupantur de los Azores y cabo vierde, centum læucis versus Occidentem et Meridiem," &c. Art. 8, "prohibet aliis accessum ad illas insulas pro mercibus habendis absque Regis licentia."

[2] Harrisse, *The Diplomatic History of America*, 78.

[3] Selden, *Mare Clausum*, i. c. xvii.

the claims of Portugal, and had a heated dispute with King Sebastian about them.[1] Later, the daring exploits of Drake on the Spanish seas were more than a flagrant violation of Philip's pretension to *mare clausum* in the western Atlantic and the Pacific Oceans—a claim which Elizabeth refused to recognise. When Mendoza, the Spanish ambassador, complained to her in 1580 of Drake's depredations, and that English ships presumed to trade in the "Indian" seas, he was told in effect that the Spaniards, contrary to the Law of Nations, had prohibited the English from carrying on commerce in those regions, and had consequently drawn the mischief upon themselves. She was unable to understand, she said, why her subjects and those of other princes should be barred from the "Indies." She could not recognise the prerogative of the Bishop of Rome "that he should bind princes who owe him no obedience," and her subjects would continue to navigate "that vast ocean," since "the use of the sea and air is common to all; neither can any title to the ocean belong to any people or private man, forasmuch as neither nature nor regard of the public use permitteth any possession thereof."[2]

About the time when Drake left England, the question of the right of Spain to forbid the English to trade to the Indies had been considered. It was argued that the Pope's bull was void, for several reasons. The consent of the Pope had been conditional for the conversion of the natives, while the "usage of the Spaniards hath been otherwise." The bull could have no force in tending to the prejudice of a third party, because all princes by the Law of Nations had the right of navigation in the sea and the right of traffic, and the Pope could not deprive them of these rights. Besides, there had been agreements between Spain and England since the date of the bull that the subjects of each state might freely traffic in the dominions of the other; and the Spanish lawyers had come to the conclusion that the Venetians could not legally inhibit others from trading in the Adriatic, and therefore, by the same reasoning, neither could the Spaniards or Portuguese prohibit orderly and lawful traffic to their Indies.[3] Elizabeth has been charged with inconsistency on the ground that at the time

[1] Selden, *loc. cit.*

[2] Camden, *Annales*, 225 (ed. 1635).

[3] *Hatfield MSS.*, ii. 684. "Whether Your Majesty's Subjects may lawfully trade into the Indies." Undated, but calendered under the year 1578.

when she was asserting the freedom of the seas against the claims of Spain she was claiming for herself, "with very great energy," a similar dominion in the British seas.[1] The charge is quite unfounded. No claim was put forward by her to the sovereignty of the British seas. On the contrary, they were declared to be free for the navigation and fishery of all nations.

The policy of Elizabeth as to the freedom of the sea is revealed still more clearly in the negotiations with the King of Denmark as to the right of fishery at Iceland and in the northern seas. Denmark claimed not only the Sound and the Belts and the maritime dominion of the Baltic, with the right of controlling the navigation through them, but also the seas intervening between the coasts of Norway on the one hand and Iceland and Greenland on the other. A similar claim was made to the sea between Norway and the Orkney and Shetland Isles, at all events prior to 1468, when they were acquired by Scotland. Putting aside altogether the differences that arose with regard to the dues exacted at the Sound and in connection with the Baltic, a great many disputes had occurred between England and Norway and Denmark as to the right of Englishmen to trade and fish at Iceland and along the Norwegian coast, and many treaties were made between the two Powers regulating that right. From an early period numerous barks from Lynn, Yarmouth, Hull, Scarborough, and other east coast ports, and from Bristol, frequented the northern seas for fishing and buying fish, and for traffic, visiting not only Iceland, but Helgeland, Nordland, and Finmark, and going at least as far east as Wardhouse or Vardö. In 1415 Henry V., at the request of King Eric, and notwithstanding an earnest petition of the Commons to the contrary,[2] prohibited his subjects from going to Iceland or other islands belonging to Norway or Denmark;[3] in 1429 the King of Denmark prohibited English merchants from purchasing fish

[1] Hautefeuille, *Hist. des Origines, des Progrès, et des Variations du Droit maritime international*, 15. Hall, *A Treatise on International Law*, 142.

[2] *Rot. Parl.*, iv. 79*b*. The petition declared that owing to the fish having deserted the coasts where they used to be taken, the fishermen had been forced to go to Iceland and other places for six or seven years past in order to catch them. English fishermen, however, had frequented Iceland long before that time.

[3] *Fœdera*, ix. 322.

at Finmark, or elsewhere in his dominions than at Bergen, against which the English petitioned Henry VI.;[1] and in 1490 an important treaty was concluded between Henry VII. and King John II. of Denmark and Norway, by which English subjects were granted liberty to sail freely to Iceland for fishing or trading on paying the usual customs, provided that they obtained a renewal of their license to do so every seven years.[2] This treaty was renewed in 1523 between Henry VIII. and Christian II.,[3] but disputes frequently arose later, and several embassies were charged with composing the differences.

Apparently the English fishermen did not always conduct themselves with propriety. They were accused of committing various wrongs and injuries on the inhabitants, and in 1585, on the complaint of the King of Denmark, Queen Elizabeth issued an Order in Council reproving them for their excesses, and intimating that if they were continued the King of Denmark would interdict their fishing, and "punish such as shall without his license repair thither, and confiscate their ships and goods." The king, she said, had promised that if the English fishermen abstained from committing outrages and behaved themselves, and paid the customary duties, he would allow them to enjoy the liberties they had formerly possessed; and she commanded the principal officers at her ports to take bonds from all those going to Iceland or Wardhouse for their good behaviour.[4] But the disputes and difficulties continued. The English fishermen omitted to renew their licenses septenially,—in 1592 it was said they had not been obtained for twelve years, and the stipulation had been forgotten by those in authority,[5]—and the Danes began about 1593 to interrupt them in their fishing at Westmoney and in the sea off Iceland, and to seize their vessels. On complaint being made to the King of Denmark, he declared his willingness to allow the Englishmen to fish at Iceland under license, except at Westmoney (small islands on the south coast), where the fishing was reserved for his court.[6] At the close of the century

[1] *Rot. Parl.*, iv. 348, 378. 8 Hen. VI., c. 2.

[2] *Fœdera*, xii. 381.

[3] *Ibid.*, xiii. 798.

[4] *State Papers*, *Dom.*, Elizabeth, clxxx. 26, 15th July 1585.

[5] *Ibid.*, ccxlii. 92.

[6] *Fœdera*, xvi. 278. A license granted in 1570 to an Englishman, one Raymond Binge, for fishing at Iceland for seven years, gave permission for his boats to be

the Danes used stronger measures. In 1599 several English vessels were seized or molested. Five ships of Kingston-upon-Hull, while at Wardhouse for fish, as had been their custom for years, were met there by a small Danish fleet with the King of Denmark himself on board, who caused them to be seized as prize, took all the goods and effects of the Englishmen, beat some of the crew and put them in irons, and finally carried off four of the ships.[1] Other English vessels were driven away from their fishing on the high seas around Iceland, although far from the coast.

Elizabeth complained strongly of these acts of injustice as being contrary to the Law of Nations.[2] A Danish ambassador who came to England at this time tried to justify the prohibitions by reference to the treaty of 1583, by which permission had been given to English vessels to navigate the northern seas to Russia, but which did not grant any authority for fishing; and he requested the Queen to publish an edict inhibiting her subjects from fishing at Iceland or Wardhouse without the license of the King of Denmark, declaring that many English vessels persisted in carrying on the fishery without any license, contrary to the treaties. Reliance was also placed on an old treaty made in 1468 between Edward IV. and Christian I., in which it was stipulated that English vessels should not go farther north on the coast of Norway than Hagaland.[3] In the following year ambassadors were dispatched from England to negotiate an arrangement concerning the tolls levied at the Sound and the freedom of the northern seas for English fishermen,[4] and in a paper of 1602 conveying instructions to the ambassadors at Bremen we find an admirable exposition of the principles of the freedom of the seas.

After claiming that the treaties of 1490 and 1523 had given liberty of fishing to the English, the ambassadors were to

kept and wintered in the ports there, on payment of the customs and abstaining from trading, as well as freedom of fishing except where prohibited by royal edicts, reserved for the king's use, or granted to others. *Brit. Mus. Vespasian MSS.*, C. xiv. fol. 21.

[1] Complaint of the Mayor of Kingston-upon-Hull to Cecil, 2nd July 1599. *State Papers, Dom.*, cclxxi. 68.

[2] *Fœdera*, xvi. 395, 432.

[3] *Brit. Mus. Vespasian MSS.*, C. xiv. fol. 22. *Fœdera*, xvi. 431.

[4] *State Papers, Dom.*, cclxxiv.

declare that the Law of Nations allowed fishing in the sea everywhere, as well as the use of the ports and coasts of princes in amity for traffic and the avoiding of the dangers from tempests; so that if the English were debarred from the enjoyment of those common rights, it could only be in virtue of an agreement. But there was no such contract or agreement. On the contrary, by denying English subjects the right of fishing in the sea and despoiling them for so doing, the King of Denmark had injured them against the Law of Nations and the terms of the treaty. Moreover, with respect to the licenses the Queen declared that if her predecessors had "yielded" to take them, "it was more than by the Law of Nations was due"; they might have yielded for some special consideration; and in any case it could not be concluded that the right of fishing, "due by the Law of Nations," failed because licenses were omitted. As to the claim to the sea between Iceland and Norway on the ground that the King of Denmark possessed both coasts—the argument used by Dee and Plowden for the dominion of the English crown in the Channel—Elizabeth was emphatic. If it was supposed thereby "that for the property of a whole sea it is sufficient to have the banks on both sides, as in rivers," the ambassadors were to declare "that though property of sea, in some small distance from the coast, may yield some oversight and jurisdiction, yet use not princes to forbid passage or fishing, as is well seen in our Seas of England and Ireland, and in the Adriatic Sea of the Venetians, where we in ours and they in theirs, have property of command; and yet neither we in ours nor they in theirs, offer to forbid fishing, much less passage to ships of merchandise; the which by Law of Nations cannot be forbidden ordinarily; neither is it to be allowed that property of sea in whatsoever distance is consequent to the banks, as it happeneth in small rivers. For then, by like reason, the half of every sea should be appropriated to the next bank, as it happeneth in small rivers, where the banks are proper to divers men; whereby it would follow that no sea were common, the banks on every side being in the property of one or other; wherefore there remaineth no colour that Denmark may claim any property in those seas, to forbid passage or fishing therein."

The ambassadors were to declare that the Queen could not

agree that her subjects should be absolutely forbidden the seas, ports, or coasts in question for the use of fishing, "negotiation," and safety; she had never yielded any such right to Spain and Portugal for the Indian seas and havens. Nevertheless, if the King of Denmark for special reasons desired that she should "yield to some renewing of license," or that "some special place upon some special occasion" should be reserved for his own use, they were in their discretion and for the sake of amity to agree; but the manner of obtaining the license was to be defined in such a way that it would not be prejudicial to her subjects, nor "to the effect of some sufficient fishing," and the licenses were to be issued in the subject's name rather than in hers or the king's.[1] Denmark continued to insist upon her right to the trade with Iceland, and to the fisheries in the northern seas,[2] which became of greater importance early in the next century when the whale-fishing was established at Spitzbergen. The Danish claim to a very wide zone of territorial sea around Iceland was enforced until quite recent times.

The dispute between Elizabeth and the King of Denmark as to the rights of fishing in the North Atlantic bears a strong resemblance to that between James I. and the Dutch, which began a few years later, when the positions, however, were reversed, James insisting on his right to the fishery on the British coasts, while the Dutch used the arguments of Elizabeth in favour of the complete freedom of the seas. One difference in the two cases may be pointed out. England by agreeing to take licenses from the King of Denmark, in the treaties of 1490 and 1523, acknowledged the sovereignty of Denmark in northern waters, whereas the Netherlands never acknowledged the sovereignty of England in the British seas, within which the liberty of fishing had been expressly granted to them by the Burgundy treaties.

Meantime the condition of the English fisheries had not much improved, either under the restrictive legislation respecting imports and exports of fish or by the measures taken to enforce the political lent. The liberty given by the Act of 1571 for the importation of cod-fish was opposed to the interests of the Iceland trade, and gave rise to abuses. Great quantities

[1] *Fœdera*, xvi. 433.

[2] *Brit. Mus. Lansdowne MSS.*, 142, fol. 380.

of inferior fish were "engrossed" by English merchants abroad and brought into the realm, which was thus "furnished with foreign fish and herrings," while the Iceland fishery declined and the number of mariners available for the navy diminished. The importation of foreign salted fish or salted herrings by Englishmen or denizens was therefore prohibited; such fish were allowed to be brought by aliens alone, who were to pay additional customs, but fish from Iceland, Shetland, Newfoundland, and from the Scottish seas were still to be admitted.[1] But the attempt to keep out foreign fish failed in its object, the restrictions were found to be otherwise injurious, and they were repealed in 1597. "It had been hoped and expected," it was said in the preamble of the repealing Act,[2] "that the fishermen of this realm would in such sort have employed themselves to fishing, and to the building and preparing of such store of boats and shipping for that purpose, as that they should long ere this time have been able sufficiently to have victualled this realm with salted fish and herrings of their own taking, without any supply of aliens and strangers, to the great increase of mariners and maintenance of the navigation within this realm. Notwithstanding it is since found by experience that the navigation of this land is no whit bettered by means of that Act, nor any mariners increased, nor like to be increased by it; but contrary wise, the natural subjects of this realm being not able to furnish the tenth part of the same with salted fish of their own taking, the chief provision and victualling thereof with fish and herrings hath ever since the making of the same Statute been in the power and disposition of aliens and strangers, who thereby have much enriched themselves, greatly increased their navigation, and (taking advantage of the time) have extremely enhanced the prices of that victual[3] to the great hurt and impoverishing of the native subjects of this realm, and yet do serve the markets here in very evil sort," housing their fish till the price was raised to their liking. Thus the merchants in England were hindered in their trade, the navigation of the realm, "which was intended to be aug-

[1] 23 Eliz., c. 7, 1580-81. *Brit. Mus. Lansd. MSS.*, 14. [2] 39 Eliz., c. 10.

[3] The price of stock-fish had risen from £12 a last in 1584 to £18 and £20 in 1597, and the price of cured ling in the same time advanced from £3 to £5, 5s. per cwt. *State Papers, Dom.*, cclxv.

mented, hath been rather impaired than increased," and the price of fish had been greatly raised, to the general prejudice of the people. After this very thorough condemnation of its previous Act,[1] Parliament declared that as strangers and subjects were at liberty to export English-caught fish and herrings, it was only right to allow subjects as well as foreigners to bring in fish to provision their own country, and the previous Act was wholly repealed. Thus the condition reverted to what it had been before this course of legislation began.

It is equally doubtful whether the compulsory fish-days or political lent had much influence in fostering the fisheries. At first, if a return from the Trinity House can be trusted, the number of fishing-boats increased. They reported in January 1581 that since the previous Parliament there had been an increase along the coast from Newcastle to Portsmouth of 114 sail of fishing-boats, of between fifteen and forty tons, which was equal to the maintenance of a thousand additional seamen for the navy.[2] It is not improbable that an increase of the herring-boats occurred on the east coast at this time, but it was temporary, and more likely due to other provisions of the Act of 1563. Cecil's Wednesday, for which he had fought so hard, was abolished in 1584, while certain penalties for eating flesh in Lent, on Fridays, Saturdays, or other fish-days, were at the same time augmented;[3] but in 1593 all the penalties were greatly reduced.[4]

The policy of the political lent did not fail from want of efforts to enforce it. In London especially precautions were taken to have the law carried out, and the fishmongers were naturally active in their own interests. Taverns and inns were often raided; those who had flesh in their houses during Lent were often put in the pillory, and those who partook of it in the stocks; and butchers were frequently prosecuted for selling flesh on forbidden days. Those who were licensed to provide flesh in Lent for the sick were put under bond, and had to keep an account of every joint they sold; watchmen guarded the city gates lest any beef should be smuggled in.

[1] A commission of eleven peers, three bishops, and two law-officers had been appointed in 1593 for the repeal of the Act respecting the importation of salted fish and herrings. *Ibid.*, ccxliv. 84.

[2] *Ibid.*, cxlvii. 21, 22. [3] 27 Eliz., c. 11. [4] 35 Eliz., c. 7.

Similar measures were taken throughout the country. The sheriffs and justices of the peace were ordered by the Council to see that the Act was duly enforced, and innkeepers had to enter into recognisance to observe it.

But there is abundant testimony that the observance of the fish-days was evaded on all sides. The policy was against the temper of the people. So long as it had been a matter of religion and ecclesiastical rule they were faithfully observed. The motive was now too remote; and although the people were exhorted on grounds of "conscience" to eat fish on 153 days in the year in order to maintain the navy, and "great numbers" at first obeyed, the "universal multitude" always abstained, and their example was followed by the better classes. Many considered abstinence from flesh on fish-days to be "papistical"; others objected on economic grounds, saying they could maintain their families better and cheaper on flesh than on fish; and great numbers took advantage of the clauses in the Act granting license of exemption. The Lord Mayor was pestered by such applications, very commonly from noblemen and persons about the Court, even receiving them from the Queen herself, and in 1595 he begged that the Act might be repealed altogether.[1] Thus "Cecil's fasts," as the unpopular fish-days were vulgarly called, designed by the great statesman to increase the fisheries and strengthen the navy, became the butt of the popular dramatist, and served little purpose except, in the words of Ben Jonson, to "keep a man devoutly hungry all day, and at night to send him supperless to bed."[2] There is little doubt that the policy of the political lent, if it had been feasible, would have succeeded in its object. Edward Jennings at the end of the century calculated that shipping had diminished in the proportion of two to five since the time when fish-days were observed, and that the fisheries were reduced in the proportion of four-fifths in the same period; while the number of idle persons in England who had previously engaged in fishing in the sea was

[1] Jeninges, *A briefe discouery of the damages that happen to this Realme by disordered and vnlawfull diet*, 1593. Hitchcock, *A briefe note of the benefits that grow to this Realme by the observation of Fish-Daies*, *Hatfield MSS.*, 1595. *State Papers, Dom.*, cclxv. 25. *Remembrancia*, 391 *et seq.*

[2] *Every Man in His Humour*, Act 3, sc. 4.

estimated at 10,000. Even if those figures were exaggerated, they indicate, as Parliament admitted, that the measures hitherto taken to revive the fisheries had failed. It remained for King James to try another plan, that of exercising an effective sovereignty on the British seas by prohibiting foreign fishermen from fishing within them without taking license and paying tribute.

Before passing to the reign of James something must be said about one symbol of this sovereignty, as it was now regarded—the striking of the flag and top-sails. From the beginning of the fifteenth century, when the Flemish herring-boats, and no doubt others, lowered their sails to English ships (see p. 43), there appears to be no record of the ceremony until the middle of the next. In the reign of Henry VIII., although he was sometimes called "Lord of these seas,"[1] and ships were appointed to "keep the passage of the narrow sea," the honour of the flag was probably only occasionally enforced. But under Edward VI., during the Protectorate of Northumberland, we find it stated in the King's Journal that in April 1549 "the Flemings' men-of-war would have passed our ships without vailing bonnet, which they seeing shot at them, and drave them at length to vail bonnet and so depart"; and again in July of the following year, at Dieppe, the Flemish ships lowered their sails to an English man-of-war.[2] This appears to be the first recorded instance of foreign men-of-war saluting the ships of the King of England, and it is noteworthy that in the latter case it was performed in a French port by Flemish vessels.

That it was not always demanded in the absolute manner of later times is shown by orders issued by the Privy Council in 1552. The Baron de la Garde was in command of a French fleet of twelve men-of-war, and Sir Henry Dudley, whose force was weaker, asked how he should act "touching the preeminence of honnour to be gyven" when he met the Baron. The Council replied that "in respect of thamitie and that the sayd Baron is stronger then he uppon the sees sume tymes yelde and sume tymes receyve thonnour"; and he was told to use the

[1] Froude, *Hist. England*, iii. 69.

[2] King Edward's Journal, in Burnet, *Hist. Reformation*, ii. (v. of ed. 1865). Oppenheim, *Hist. Administration Roy. Navy*, 106.

Baron courteously, "and with such discression that the same yelding of the preeminence may be interpreted to be of curtesy rather then to the derogacion of the Kinges honnour."[1] It was the French who consistently and constantly opposed the English claim, and there is evidence that the salute was a point of rivalry between the two countries even at this time. An ordinance issued by Henry II. of France in 1555 (repeated by Henry III. in 1584) required all vessels to strike their sails to ships of the French navy whenever they met them at sea, and some Hamburgers were seized because they did not do so.[2] The honour appears to have been generally accorded by the Dutch in the reign of Elizabeth,[3] and compelled from the Spaniards. In 1554, in the reign of Mary, when the Spanish fleet was coming up Channel in all its bravery, with the royal flag flying on the Admiral's ship, and bringing Philip of Spain to marry the Queen of England, the English Admiral, Lord William Howard, fired a broadside into the Spaniard and forced him to lower his colours while in his presence.[4] And later, when Anne of Austria was on her way to Spain to marry Philip, the Spanish ships were fired on by Admiral Hawkins at Plymouth and forced to strike the flag and lower top-sails in like manner.[5] But it was not till the reign of Charles I. that this punctilio became of great international importance.

1 *Acts of the Privy Council of England*, iv. 37. 7th May 1552.

2 Selden, *Mare Clausum*, lib. ii. c. xxvi.

3 Raleigh, *A Discourse of the Invention of Ships*, Collected Works, viii. 326. Monson, *Naval Tracts*, in Churchill's *Collection of Voyages and Travels*, iii.

4 Monson, *op. cit.* Laughton, *Fortnightly Review*, Aug. 1866.

5 Froude, *op. cit.*, viii. 68. Laughton, *loc. cit.*

CHAPTER IV.

UNDER THE STUARTS. JAMES I. A NEW POLICY.

SHORTLY after the accession of James to the throne of England, the liberal policy of his predecessors as to the freedom of the sea suffered a marked change. In the previous century, under the Tudors, little was heard of the pretension to the sovereignty of the sea, with the exception of the striking of the flag to the royal ships in the narrow seas—a ceremony that was not peculiar to England. Foreigners then, as always before, enjoyed complete liberty of fishing on the coasts of England and Ireland, and no attempts had been made to exact tribute from them on the Scottish coasts. Queen Elizabeth, as has been shown, not only refrained from putting forward claims to the sovereignty of the sea, but on several occasions and in the most positive manner asserted the freedom of the seas for both navigation and fishing against the exclusive policy of Denmark and Spain. At the end of the Tudor period England was the great champion of *mare liberum*—long before the Dutch Republic had challenged the monopolies of the Portuguese either by the pen of Grotius or the guns of Jakob van Heemskerk.

But under James the old doctrine was revived, and something new was added in a claim to the fisheries along the British coasts. Before he had been a year in England he took measures, with the laudable object of defining the bays, or "King's Chambers," within which the hostile actions of belligerents were prohibited. In its essence this act was opposed to extensive claims to maritime sovereignty, because it restricted a most important attribute of such sovereignty to comparatively a narrow space in the adjacent sea, though a space much greater than that now comprised in the so-called territorial waters. In point of fact, throughout his reign no assertion was made to such a maritime sovereignty as was claimed by Charles I.[1] The measures referred to were in relation to neutrality in the war which continued between the United Provinces and Spain, James having promptly concluded peace with the latter Power. He issued a number of proclamations referring to privateering and depredations at sea, most of them being conceived in the interests of Spain; and in one of these, for the recall of British mariners in foreign service, dated 1st March 1604, the king forbad hostilities within his ports, havens, roads, creeks, or other places of his dominions, or so near to any of his ports or havens as might be reasonably construed to be within that title, limit, or precinct, as well as the hovering of men-of-war in the neighbourhood of such places; and he caused "plats" of the limits of his ports and jurisdiction to be prepared for the instruction of his officers concerned.[2]

Long before the time of James the harbours, roadsteads, and at all events some of the bays of a country were recognised as belonging to it, in the sense at least that hostilities of belligerent men-of-war or the capture of prizes were forbidden within them; they were "sanctuaries" under the jurisdiction and protection of the adjoining territory. With regard to the English Chambers, we find that in the treaty which Cardinal Wolsey drew up in 1521, when acting as mediator between the Emperor Charles V. and King Francis I. of France, it was stipulated that during the war between these two sovereigns, the ships, whether armed or unarmed, as well as the mariners, of either side should be secure from attack by the other Power in the harbours, bays, rivers, mouths of rivers, roads or stations for shipping, and especially in the Downs or other maritime place under the jurisdiction of the King of England.[3] There is

[1] An undated State Paper, calendared under the year 1604, entitled "Reglement for Preventing Abuses in and about the Narrow Seas," contains a claim by the king to a most absolute dominion over the Four Seas (*State Papers, Dom.*, James, xi. 40). It appears, however, to be merely a copy of the similar regulation prepared in 1633 by Sir Henry Martin (see p. 252). It is not contained in the volume of royal proclamations published in 1609, and is not referred to by Selden. It has no doubt been wrongly calendared.

[2] It is given in Appendix D, from *A Booke of Proclamations, published since the beginning of his Majesties most happy Reigne ouer England, &c., Vntill this present Moneth of Febr.* 3, *Anno. Dom.* 1609. *Cum Priuilegio*, p. 98.

[3] "Item, conventum et conclusum est, quod, dicto bello durante, nullus subditus principum prædictorum, intra portus et sinus maris quoscumque, flumina, ostia

little doubt that this article only embodied in a formal manner what had long been the practice of nations, the Downs being specially mentioned as the most important anchorage in the kingdom.

When James decided to mark out distinctly on a chart the boundaries of his neutral waters on the coast of England, the matter was submitted to the Trinity House, and a jury of thirteen men, specially skilled in maritime affairs, was appointed to prepare tables and charts showing the position and limits of the King's Chambers and ports and the sailing directions for the same, according to their knowledge of what had been the custom in the past. The charts and schedules were presented to Sir Julius Cæsar, the Judge of the High Court of Admiralty, on 4th March 1604, together with a sworn declaration that they represented the true boundaries.[1] The chambers formed were nominally twenty-six in number, the points or headlands selected by the surveyors being as follows, beginning at the northern extremity of the east coast and ending at the Isle of Man—Holy Island, Souter Point, Whitby, Flamborough Head, Spurn Point, Cromer, Winterton Ness, Caster Ness, Lowestoft, East Ness, Orfordness, the North Foreland, the South Foreland, Dungeness, Beachy Head, "Dunenoze" (Isle of Wight), Portland Bill, Start Point, Rame Head, Dodman Point, the Lizard, the Land's End, Milford, St David's Head, Bardsey Island, Holyhead, the Isle of Man. The extent of the "chambers" varies in different places; and while this is obviously due on

fluminum, gurgites, aquas dulces, stationes navium, et præsertim stationem vulgariter vocatam *les Dunes*, aut alia loca maritima quæcumque jurisdictioni dicti Regis Angliæ subjecta aliquam navem mercatoriam, onerariam, armatam vel non armatam, onustam seu vacuam, cujuscumque quantitatis aut oneris fuerit, de quacumque natione eadem navis extiterit, capere, spoliare, diripere, seu merces, victualia, aut armamenta quæcumque, ab eisdem navibus, aut earumdem nautis auferre, nec eisdem vim, violentiam, aut molestationem aliquam inferre possit, aut debeat," &c. Dumont, *Corps Diplomatique*, IV. i. 352.

[1] This interesting document is printed in Appendix E, from *State Papers, Dom.*, James I., vol. 13 (1605), No. 11; No. 12 is another of the same. It is not the original, but a copy, the names being all in the same hand as the body of the paper. Diligent search among the records has failed to furnish the "plott" referred to, but there is no reason to doubt that the reproduction of it by Selden (*Mare Clausum*, lib. ii. c. xxii.), and shown here on fig. 3, is an accurate representation. Selden states that the plott or chart was engraved, and copies sent to the officers concerned.

Fig. 3.—*Chart prepared by the Trinity House showing the bearings of the King's Chambers.* From Selden.

some parts of the coast to the contour, it is due on other parts to a selection of headlands, no doubt according to the custom which had grown up and was recognised among the officers and others concerned. Thus the great bay between Cornwall and Devon would have formed a natural "chamber" by a line, not so long as some of the others, between Start Point, or Prawl Point, and the Lizard, and which would have formed part of the girdle around the coast; whereas three chambers are formed along its shores. On the east coast the "chambers" are as a rule small,[1] the largest embracing the mouths of the Humber and the Thames; they are generally large on the south coast, and largest of all on the west coast, where the whole of the Bristol Channel was enclosed by the line from Land's End to Milford, a distance of nearly 100 nautical miles, the whole area containing about 3400 square nautical miles. This chamber, as well as those to the north of it, must have been of importance on account of the volume of shipping which passed through it.[2]

It is to be noted that the King's Chambers were confined to the coast of England, and, further, that they had no reference to the claim of James to property in his seas, so far at least as fisheries were concerned. They were strictly limited to questions of neutrality and jurisdiction, in view of the war then existing between Spain and the United Provinces and the frequent depredations of privateers. The chambers on the east coast, where the Dutch carried on their great herring fishery, were much too small to have any relation to the subject of unlicensed fishing; and at no time during the prolonged discussions on the fishery were the limits of the King's Chambers made use of in argument. Neutral protection, moreover, was strictly limited to the waters defined. It was in vain that Gentilis, the Spanish advocate in the Admiralty Prize Court, argued that the jurisdiction of England extended far beyond the limits of the "chambers," and ought therefore to be lawfully and justly applied in protecting Spanish vessels from

[1] It will be noticed from fig. 4, where the lines between the headlands are shown on a modern map, that some of the "chambers" on the east coast have entirely disappeared, no doubt owing to the erosion or silting up of the coast at those places during the last three hundred years.

[2] In stormy weather as many as 300 or 400 sail of Hollanders took refuge in St George's Channel at a time. *State Papers, Dom.*, xlv. 23 (1609).

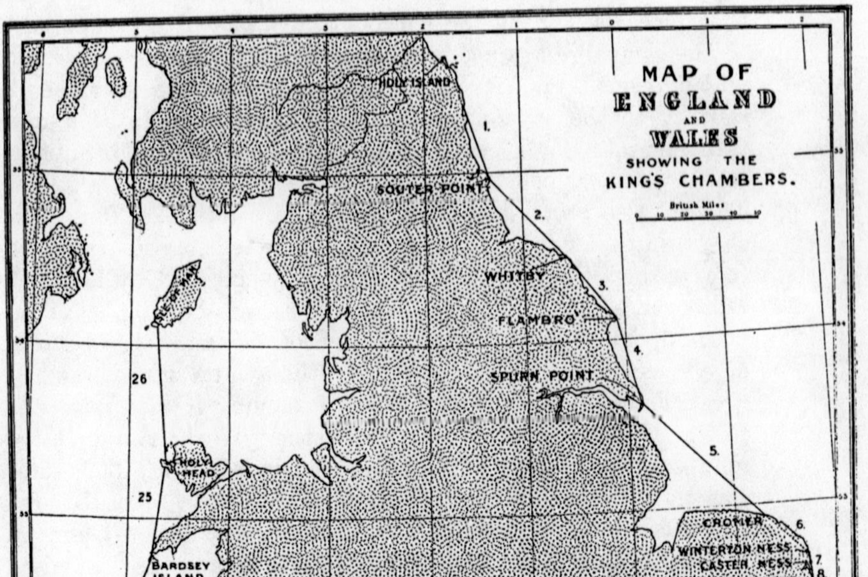

Fig. 4.—*Showing the King's Chambers on the Coast of England.*

the talons of the Dutch on the high seas. The judgment of the Court of Admiralty, so far as concerned the place of capture, was always based upon the consideration whether that place lay within or without the limits of a "chamber."

The campaign against foreigners fishing on the British coast, which opened up the claims of England in the seventeenth century to the sovereignty of the sea and introduced a new principle into English international policy, originated in another set of ideas, which James brought with him from Scotland. The Scottish people had been always very jealous of foreigners sharing in their fisheries, and, as we have seen, never consented to give them the liberty to fish, so freely accorded by England. Moreover, a tax or tribute, called the "assize-herring," was imposed upon the native fishermen in Scotland, and formed a part of the revenues of the crown. Although its value was not great, James conceived the idea of levying it also from the foreign fishermen, who frequented the British seas in large numbers, and before he formally demanded it in 1609, some curious negotiations took place with a syndicate of London merchants who proposed to form a fishery association based on the taxation of foreign fishermen, and in return they promised a handsome revenue to the king. The desire for an increased revenue may therefore have had something to do with the proposal to restrain unlicensed fishing on the British coasts. But neither this consideration, the practice in Scotland, nor the king's passion for his prerogative, fully accounts for the reversal of the long-settled policy of England, which was accomplished with the concurrence of the Privy Council, and, so far as may be judged, with the full approval of the people.

In truth, a great change had taken place in the national sentiment. England had now entered upon the long struggle for commercial and maritime supremacy, with the aim of increasing the power of the nation against all rivals.[1] It was obvious to every one that the great rival and competitor was the Dutch Republic, whose rapid rise to the first commercial state in Europe deeply impressed the minds of English statesmen and writers. In the reign of Elizabeth, the common interest of the two countries in opposing Spain prevented measures being taken to curb the growing power of the

[1] Cunningham, *The Growth of English Industry and Commerce*, i. 424.

Dutch. But early in the seventeenth century this motive had lost its force. James had promptly concluded peace with Spain, and even spoke of the Dutch as rebels.[1] Thus, during his reign arose that bitter rivalry and keen emulation of the Dutch which continued throughout nearly the whole century, and of which the English claim to the sovereignty of the sea may be looked upon as an important phase. It was against the United Provinces that the claim was directed, and as the Dutch themselves openly boasted that the sea fisheries were the foundation of their shipping, wealth, and power, it was to the sea fisheries that England first turned in her efforts to cripple them.

Those fisheries had greatly increased towards the end of the sixteenth and in the early part of the seventeenth century. An official account of the fisheries of Holland, Zealand, and Flanders in 1562 estimated the number of busses and fishing-boats at 700, of which Holland had 400, most of them being "great" busses of about 46 lasts burden.[2] Guicciardini, who visited the Low Countries about the same time, placed the fleet of busses at 700, each of which made three voyages, bringing back on an average 70 lasts of herrings, or a total of 588,000 barrels, valued at £441,000 sterling.[3] Another author of the period gave a list of towns whose prosperity and even existence depended upon the fishery;[4] and a little later Hitchcock, and, following him, Dee, stated that 400 or 500 busses came every year from the Low Countries to fish for herrings on the east coast of this country.[5] Those figures referred to the fisheries of the Netherlands as a whole, including Flanders, but during the war of independence, after the United Provinces threw off the yoke of Spain and secured command of the sea, the Flemish fisheries withered away. At Dunkirk, for example,

[1] Gardiner, *Hist. England*, i. 103.

[2] Declaratie van de visscherijen in Holland Zeeland en Vlaanderen. Fruin, *Tien Jaren uit den Tachtigjarigen Oorlog*, 1588-1598, p. 186.

[3] *Descrittione Di M. Lodovico Gvicciardini Patritio Florentino, Di Tvtti i Paesi Bassi, Altrimenti Detti Germania Inferiore*, Antwerp, 1567, p. 21. The value of the cod caught was placed at £150,000 sterling per annum.

[4] Hadrianus Junius, *Batavia*, p. 203. The work was written between 1565 and 1569, and published in 1588.

[5] Hitchcock, *A Pollitique Platt*. The author says that when he was at the wars in 1553, more than 400 busses were set forth from twelve towns in the Low Countries. Dee, *General and Rare Memorials*.

which sent 500 busses to the herring-fishing in 1532 and 400 in 1550, the fishermen at the beginning of the next century were scarcely able to supply the town with herrings.[1] The industry passed into the hands of the Dutch. At the end of Elizabeth's reign, so greatly had it prospered that 1500 busses went to the herring-fishing in 1601 from Holland and Zealand alone.[2]

From this time much attention was given by English writers to the Dutch fisheries, and on the whole they exaggerated their extent and the number of boats and vessels engaged in them. One of them, John Keymer, who was afterwards much quoted, professedly based his account upon his personal observations in the Netherlands about the year 1601. His statement appears to have been submitted to King James in 1605 or 1606, but it was not published until 1664. He said that the fishing fleet of the Hollanders numbered more than 4100 vessels, of which 100 were dogger-boats, 700 pinks and well-boats, 700 "strand-boats," 400 "euers," and 400 "galliotts, drivers, and tod-boats," and 1200 busses, afterwards increased to 2000. The pinks and well-boats, each from 60 to 100 tons burden, fished on the coasts of England and Scotland for cod and ling, while the busses, ranging from 60 to 200 tons burden, pursued the herring fishery along our east coast. There were also, according to this author, 400 Dutch vessels, called "Gaynes" and "Euers," which fished for herrings off Yarmouth; 1000 vessels, of from 50 to 100 tons, that caught cod and ling in his Majesty's seas; as well as 600 ships engaged in carrying cod and ling to London. Keymer also says that he had seen near 3000 sail of English, Scotch, French, Hollanders, Embdeners, Breemeners, and Hamburgers fishing *at one time* upon the coast of Scotland, Shetland, Orkney, Gattney (Caithness?), North Farrel, and Fowl (Fair) Isle, and divers other places.[3] In a later treatise which

[1] Faulconnier, *Description Historique de Dunkerque*, i. 47, 53, 121.

[2] Van Meteren, *Historie der Nederlandscher ende haerder Naburen Oorlogen* (1614), fol. 466. This author says the maritime power of the States was shown in the same year, when between 800 and 900 ships departed for the Baltic within the space of two or three days' tides.

[3] John Keymer's *Observation made upon the Dutch Fishing about the year* 1601. *Demonstrating that there is more Wealth raised out of Herrings and other Fish in his Majesties Seas, by the neighbouring Nations in one Year, then the King of Spain hath from the Indies in Four.* London, Printed from the original Manuscript,

Keymer wrote in 1620 and submitted to King James, it is also said that the Hollanders employed about 3000 ships and 50,000 people in fishing on the coasts of England, Scotland, and Ireland. This tract has usually been attributed to Sir Walter Raleigh and is published among his works, and it obtained celebrity in consequence, both in this country and on the Continent, but it was without doubt written by Keymer.[1] A more moderate

for Sir Edward Ford, in the year 1664. Keymer states that he found in Holland more than 20,000 sail of ships and "hoyes," more than was possessed by England, France, Spain, and other eight countries in Europe. The same figure is given by Sir Thomas Overbury, who visited the Netherlands in 1609 (*Observations in his Travels, upon the State of the Seventeen Provinces*, 1626).

[1] *Observations touching Trade and Commerce with the Hollander, and Other Nations; presented to King James, wherein is proved that our Sea and Land Commodities serve to enrich and strengthen other Countries against our own.* Raleigh's *Collected Works*, viii. 351. Oldys, in his Life of Raleigh, which was published in 1736, says there was some reason to doubt whether Sir Walter Raleigh was the author of this treatise: it was first printed in 1653, first associated with Raleigh's name by being bound up with his "Remains" in 1656, and first definitely said to be Raleigh's by Roger Coke in his *Detection of Court and State;* and he gives reasons

Fig. 5.—*Facsimile of Keymer's Signature to his 'Book of Observations.'*

for the opinion that it was written by John Keymer and not by Raleigh (*Collected Works*, i. 441). But, as Raleigh's latest biographer states, Raleigh still has the credit of it (Stebbing, *Sir Walter Raleigh*, 267). I have, however, found the original signed manuscript copy among the State Papers for 1620 (*State Papers, Dom.*, cxviii. 114, December 1620), and an unsigned and slightly altered copy among those for 1623 (*State Papers, Dom.*, clvii. 45). The original is endorsed, *Keymers booke of observacons for your moste excellent Matie touchinge trade and traffique beyond ye Seas and in England wherein he certaynly findeth y^{t} your sea and land Commodities doe scarve to inrich and strengthen other Cuntries agnst your Kingdome; wch were ye urgent causes why he endeavoured himselfe to take extraordynarie paynes for ye redresse: soe it maie stande wth your Maties good Likinge.* 1620. It is subscribed, "Your Maties most loyall and true harted Subject, John Keymer," and it is the same treatise as is published in Raleigh's *Works*, with a few trifling statement was made by another writer, Tobias Gentleman, who published the best work on the subject, in 1614, and was evidently well versed in the fisheries both of Holland and England. He states that 1000 sail of Hollanders came every

verbal differences, while the concluding sentence is omitted in the printed form —viz., "To conclude, England is a great and famous body and would be farr greater, richer and stronger, if the ten fingers were rightly imployed." Further proof exists that Keymer was the author of this much-discussed treatise. Its object was to show how the trade and revenue might be greatly increased, and the author begged the king to have a commission appointed to examine witnesses as to his proposals. This commission was appointed two years later, as appears from the following entry in the Grant Book in 1622: "20 Dec. Com̃ to Charles, pr. of Wales, John Bp. of Linc., Ld Keeper of ye g. seale, Lewis Duke of Lennox, Geo. Marquis Buck., &c. to hear the propositions which shall be made by John Keymer and to consider whether they will tend to the good of ye King, and commonwealth as is pretended" (*State Papers, Dom.*, Jas. I. (Grants), vol. 141, p. 352). There does not appear to be any further mention of the matter. This John Keymer is supposed to be the same as a person of that name who was licensed by Raleigh about 1584 to sell wines at Cambridge. Among the MSS. at Hatfield are letters from him, dated in 1598, to Cecil and the Earl of Essex, in which he speaks of his services, of "his travels and labours to find out the practises used beyond the seas to their advantage and our great danger and how to prevent the same," and of his works, one of which he said showed how to increase the Queen's treasure above £100,000 a year. He also corresponded with Carleton in 1619. In his address to the king, prefixed to the treatise of 1620, he mentions that "about fourteen or fifteen years past" he had presented him with "a book of such extraordinary importance for the honour and profit" of his Majesty and posterity, which was doubtless the earlier tract referred to above, and would fix its date about 1605 or 1606. He was also engaged on the fishery question about 1612 (doubtless in connection with the proposed society), because Tobias Gentleman, whose work was published in the spring of 1614, tells us that he was visited "some two yeares past" by "Maister John Keymar," who was collecting information about the fisheries, with the view of placing it before the Council (*Englands Way to Win Wealth*, 3).

The copy of Keymer's tract, which is among the State Papers of 1623, is unsigned, and is simply calendared as "Tract addressed to the King, consisting of observations made by the writer in his travels on the coasts," &c.; but the person who calendared the paper has written on it, in pencil, "q. By Sir Walter Cope (*ob.* 1614). See 1612, a letter or discourse to the King, to which this was attached," and has added the name "Walter Cope" at the end. The paper referred to (*State Papers, Dom.*, vol. 71, No. 89) has written on it in the old hand, "Sr Walter Cope to K.," and "Anno Domini 1612. A present for the Kinges most excellent Maiestie." It is only mentioned here because the draft of it, which is the next paper in the volume (No. 90) and has several corrections on the first page, bears the following note in one of the corners, "Nota Mr Chancellor and Malynes wife (?) the of Maye, Ralegh." The meaning is obscure, but perhaps it may be surmised from the contents that Malynes, who was at that time concerned with the fishery society proposals, had submitted it to Sir Walter Raleigh, and that ultimately it was presented to the king by Sir Walter Cope, who was on intimate terms with him.

year to fish for herrings in "his Majesty's streams"; that more than 600 of them were "great busses," some of 120 tons, most of about 100 tons; that the crews numbered from 16 to 24 men, so that there could not be less than 20,000 mariners altogether. In addition to the great fleet of busses, the Hollanders had "a huge number" of smaller vessels of from 20 to 50 tons burden, with crews of from 8 to 12 men, which were called "sword-pinks," "flat-bottoms," "Holland-toads," "Crabskuits," and "Yeuars," and fished for herrings along with the busses on the east coast from Shetland southwards, carrying home their catches or selling them at Yarmouth. Gentleman says there had been seen at one time, "and numbered," at Brassey Sound, in Shetland, where the busses rendezvoused, either going to sea or at sea within view, 2000 sail of busses and schuits, besides those that were out of sight. All these fished for herrings during the season "in his Majesty's seas." Then the pinks and well-boats, which caught cod and ling all the year round, numbered between 500 and 600; they were from 30 to 40 tons burden, and had crews of about 12 men each. There were also more than 200 "fly-boats" which fished with lines to the north-east of Shetland all the year round for ling, which were split and salted in bulk and were known as "Holland-lings," although, says Gentleman, they were really Shetland lings before they took them from his Majesty's seas. This author placed the total number of Dutch fishermen who fished off the British coasts at not less than 37,000, of whom 32,000 were engaged in the herring fishery, and 5000 in fishing for cod and ling.[1]

It would thus appear from the evidently honest account of Gentleman, that early in the reign of James fully 2000 Hollander busses and fishing vessels frequented the British seas. But the Dutch were not the only foreigners who reaped the harvest of fishes along our coasts. Fishermen likewise came from France, Spain, and Portugal, from Hamburg, Emden, and Bremen. The French herring-boats, from Normandy and Picardy, generally numbered about 100; sometimes there were

[1] *Englands Way to Win Wealth, and to employ Ships and Mariners; or, A plaine description what great profite it will bring vnto the Commonwealth of England, by the Erecting, Building, and aduenturing of Busses, to Sea, a Fishing: With a true Relation of the inestimable Wealth that is yearly taken out of his Majesty's Seas by the Hollanders, &c.*, by Tobias Gentleman, Fisherman and Mariner, London, 1614.

only 40, and they did not go so far north as the Hollanders.[1] Spanish, Portuguese, and French vessels fished for mackerel on the Irish coast and to the south-west of England, as well as for cod in the North Sea. Those from Hamburg, Bremen, and Emden took part in the herring fishery on the east coast, but they appear to have mostly confined their operations to the northern parts of Scotland. French and Flemish vessels also visited the western lochs of Scotland, both for fishing and for the purchase of fish.[2] The total number of foreign vessels thus fishing in the British seas at the time in question must have been large. In both of Keymer's treatises it is stated that there were 20,000, with 400,000 people. This estimate is obviously greatly exaggerated; but making all due allowances, it is certain that the fleets of foreign fishing vessels frequenting our coasts in the reign of James were of formidable extent. The great herring-busses, while fishing along the east coast of Scotland, were described in 1608 as occupying an area of the sea of at least 45 miles in length by 22 miles in breadth, within which space they allowed no others to shoot a net.[3]

[1] *State Papers, Dom.*, Jas. I., xlvii. 114.

[2] Keymer, *Observations on Dutch Fishing;* Gentleman, *op. cit.;* Buchanan, *Rerum Scot. Hist.*, lib. i. c. xlix.; Leslie, *De Origine Moribus et Rebus Gestis Scotorum*, 39; *Register Privy Council of Scotland*, ii. 656; *MSS. Advoc. Lib.*, 31. 2. 16.

[3] *State Papers, Dom.*, xxxii. 31. Other accounts are as follows. In 1609 the Earl of Salisbury wrote (erroneously) that while fifty or sixty years before only one or two hundred foreign vessels came to fish on the east coast, they then numbered two or three thousand sail (Winwood, *Memorials*, iii. 50). Sir William Monson in the same year placed the number of Hollander busses at 3000 and the number of men at over 30,000 (*State Papers, Dom.*, xlvii. 112, 114). Sir Nicholas Hales also estimated the number of men at 30,000 (*Ibid.*, xlv. 23; cclxxiv. 67). In the following year the Dutch ambassadors admitted that 20,000 men were employed in the great herring fishery, as well as other 40,000 in connection with it on shore (*Ibid.*, lxvii. 111). A little later, in 1616, the Secretary to the Duke of Lennox told the Dutch ambassador that in the previous June, 1500 or 1600 Hollander busses were at Shetland (*Add. MSS. Brit. Mus.*, 17,677, J, fol. 160). In 1618 the number fishing on the east coast of Scotland sometimes exceeded 2000 sail (*MSS. Advoc. Lib.*, 31. 2. 16). Malynes in 1622 placed the number of busses from Holland and Zealand at 2000 (*Consuetudo vel Lex Mercatoria*, 89). Two years later a Spanish agent described them as consisting of 2400 vessels, guarded by 40 men-of-war, and scattered over an area of 200 leagues (*State Papers, Dom.*, dxxi. 30). In 1629 Secretary Coke, who derived the information from a Scottish source, said the Hollander busses sometimes amounted to 3000 sail; three years later he put the number in connection with the fishery off Yarmouth at "above a thousand"; at this time the French vessels numbered 40 (*Ibid.*, Chas. I., clii. 63; ccxxix. 79). Beaujon (*op. cit.*, p. 64) expresses the opinion that 2000 busses were the maximum number.

The herring fishery of the Dutch along the British coast was known as the "great fishery" (*Groote Visscherye*), to distinguish it from the "small" or fresh-herring fishery which was pursued locally, and it was subjected to minute regulations. The busses collected at Bressay Sound in Shetland in the early part of June, but the fishing was not allowed to begin until St John's Day, on the 24th of the month, when the vessels departed in fleets for the fishing-grounds under the charge of "commodores" and guarded by men-of-war. As the season advanced the fishing was carried on farther and farther to the south. Until St James' Day (25th July) it was prosecuted in the neighbourhood of Shetland, Fair Isle, and as far south as Buchan Ness; from then until Elevation Day (14th September) it was from Buchan Ness to the coast of Northumberland; then southwards to the deep water off Yarmouth till St Catherine's Day (25th September); and so to the mouth of the Thames, the fishing usually coming to an end at the beginning of December. The "fleet" or train of nets was more than a mile in length, which necessitated the busses keeping some distance apart to prevent fouling; they were shot in the evening and hauled in the morning, when the crew began to salt and pack the herrings into barrels, which were then taken to Holland in "yagers," or carriers, repacked, branded, and exported to various countries. The smaller vessels which took part in the "fresh" herring fishery were employed especially off Yarmouth in the autumn, and they sold their herrings for ready money to the fish-curers with whom they were "hosted." On some occasions as many as 200 of those smaller Dutch vessels lay in Yarmouth harbour at a time. The boats that went for cod, ling, and haddock fished throughout the North Sea,—the smaller ones at the Dogger Bank as a rule, the larger on the Scottish coast and at Shetland. Hand-lines, baited with herring or lamprey, were used, the cod being either pickled, dried, or brought to land alive in wells, and these vessels furnished the larger part of the supply to London.

The quantity and value of the fish caught by the Dutch off the British coasts were variously stated. Keymer, in his first tract, estimated the quantity of herrings taken by the 2000 busses in the twenty-six weeks of their fishing at about 300,000 lasts (or 3,600,000 barrels) annually, and the value, at first hand, at

£3,600,000 sterling. But the merchants who exported the pickled herrings—and by far the greater quantity were exported [1]—are said to have charged from £16 to £36 a last, the eventual value as merchandise being estimated at not less than £5,000,000 sterling. In his later treatise the value of the herrings exported by the Dutch is placed lower, at about £1,768,000, the quantity being stated at from about 89,500 to 100,500 lasts, or from 1,074,000 to 1,206,000 barrels. Gentleman, whose work seems to have been the most trustworthy, estimated the quantity of herrings taken by the Dutch in the British seas at over 100,000 lasts or 1,200,000 barrels, the original value at £1,000,000 sterling and the gross value at twice that amount; "while we," he says, "take no more than to bait our hooks." Gentleman's estimate of the quantity may be taken as approximately correct, because in the present day the least effective of the vessels taking part in the Dutch herring fishery—namely, the old-fashioned flat-bottomed boats (*bommen*)—catch and cure on an average in a season about 660 barrels each, so that the quantity taken by a fleet of 2000 of such vessels would be about 1,320,000 barrels. But the old busses were of a superior type, keeled vessels (*hoekers, sloepen*), and the average catch of their modern representatives in a season is about 1060 barrels, which for a fleet of the same number would give a total yield of about 2,120,000 barrels, or over 176,000 lasts. Monson placed the value of the herrings exported from Holland to the Baltic at £800,000, and of those sent to other countries at £1,000,000,[2] while Sir Nicholas Hales in 1609 estimated the value of the exported herrings at £4,000,000, but raised it later, in 1634, to £6,000,000, owing to information received from Amsterdam.[3] Sir John Borough's estimate was still higher. He said that if account was taken of all the herrings, cod, ling, and other fish caught in the British seas by foreigners, the gross value would exceed £10,000,000 a year.

The larger figures above cited are unquestionably exagger-

[1] To Pomerania, Poland, "Spruceland," Denmark, Liefland, Russia, Sweden, Germany, Brabant, Flanders, France, "Lukeland," England, Greece, Egypt, Venice, Leghorn, and all over the Mediterranean, and even as far as Brazil.

[2] *State Papers, Dom.*, xlvii. 112.

[3] To the King's most excellent Majesty: A Declaration of the fishing of Herring, Cod, and Ling, and how much the favour or disfavour of Your Royal Majesty concerneth the Hollanders. *Ibid.*, xxxii. 30; cclxxix. 67.

ated, but even the lowest shows how very valuable the sea fisheries were to the Dutch at the beginning of the seventeenth century, for the total value of all the commodities exported from England in 1613 was placed at £2,487,435, and the value of the imports at £2,141,151.[1]

The English fisheries, which Cecil had laboured to revive, presented a striking contrast to the prosperous fishery of the foreigners. As in the days of Hitchcock, our fishermen shot their nets for herrings from small vessels near the shore, and on the east coast, at least, only in the period from September to November, with the exception of an occasional "summer" fishing.[2] They had very "sorry" nets and poor frail boats, and most of those going to the Yarmouth fishing from Yorkshire and Durham were only "five-men" cobles.[3] "The Hollander busses," it was said, "are greate and strong and able to brooke foul weather, whereas our cobles, crayers, and boats, being small and thin-sided, are easily swallowed by rough seas, not daringe to adventure far in fair weather by reason of their weaknesse for feare of stormes." The largest of the crayers were of 20 tons burden, their catch of herrings for a night being generally from one to three, and rarely as much as seven, lasts.[4] One can only guess at the number of fishing boats and vessels belonging to east coast ports at this time. Gentleman stated that the number of "North Sea boats" which fished for cod, and probably also for herrings, in autumn, was from 224 to 237 along the stretch of coast between the Thames and the Humber, the crews employed in them being between 1500 and 1600. The Iceland barks numbered about 125 in 1614; 20 of them, as well as 150 of the North Sea boats, belonged to Yarmouth. The town-clerk of that port, writing about the same time, said that they sent annually to Iceland and the north seas for cod and ling about 120 sail, while all the "ships, crayers, and fisher-boats" belonging to Yarmouth numbered 220; the able-bodied mariners and

[1] Misselden, *The Circle of Commerce, or the Balance of Trade*, 1623, p. 121. It may be said that the aggregate quantity of herrings now taken in the North Sea, and mostly by Scottish and English fishermen, equals about 3,500,000 barrels in a year.

[2] Manship, *History of Great Yarmouth*, 119, 121.

[3] Gentleman, *op. cit.*, 7, 32.

[4] Keymer, *Observations on Dutch Fishing*.

fishermen amounted to 1000.[1] The only other fisheries on the east coast were a small one for mackerel, which employed 40 boats at Yarmouth in the spring; a sprat fishery with bag-nets; while some small trawlers worked in the bays and estuaries. On the east coast of Scotland there was no native herring fishery except in the firths.

Compared with the great trade of the Dutch, the exports of fish from this country were insignificant and trifling in view of the quantity imported: in London alone no less than £12,000 was paid to the Hollanders for barrelled fish and Holland lings between the Christmas of 1613 and 18th February 1614. Scotland still sent tolerably large quantities of salmon, herrings, and salt fish to France, Spain, and elsewhere; but the exports from England were almost quite confined to red-herrings from Yarmouth and pilchards from Cornwall, —both sent to the Mediterranean, and very commonly in Dutch bottoms.[2] The English had no share whatever in the trade in pickled herrings or in pickled cod; they were indeed ignorant of the method of curing the latter.

From the foregoing it is not difficult to realise the feeling of irritation against the Dutch which began to gather in the breasts of the English people. They witnessed with envy the great fleets of alien fishing vessels which darkened their coasts every season and reaped a rich harvest in waters which they regarded as their own. "No king upon the earth," said Gentleman, "did yet ever see such a Fleet of his own subjects at any time, and yet this Fleet is there and then yearly to be seen. A most worthy sight it were, if they were my own countrymen!" Statesmen and economists saw in the extension of the Dutch fisheries a menace to the power and wealth of the nation. The fisheries formed a valuable nursery of seamen to man the mercantile marine and the royal navy; it was chiefly from this point of view that the political lent and the fishery Acts of the previous reign were designed. Another consideration began to excite even more attention. The trade in fish was looked upon as forming the basis of commerce and national wealth. The Dutch boasted that the herring fishery was their "gold-mine"; that "the herring

[1] Manship, *op. cit.*, 97, 120. The work was written between 1612 and 1619.

[2] Gentleman, *op. cit.*, 36; Swinden, *History of Great Yarmouth*, 465; *State Papers, Dom.*, xlvii. 112, 114.

keeps Dutch trade going, and Dutch trade sets the world's afloat";[1] and the argument that national power and wealth depended on the sea fisheries became a commonplace in the seventeenth century, and was urged as a reason why the English people should secure for themselves the fisheries in their own seas. This, it was said, would do more good to the kingdom than all the mines and the whole trade in cloth and wool; the fisheries would be more valuable to us than the Indies were to Spain, or than was the commerce with the West Indies; they were the "very goal and prize of trade and of the dominion of the sea."[2] Had not Holland, which was "not so big as one of his Majesty's shires," and where nothing "grew" save "a few hops, madder, and cheese," become a rich and powerful state, full of goodly towns, and the great mart of Europe, owing to the fish drawn from the British seas? Did not Dutch ships, in return for the fish they exported, come back laden with the riches of other lands,—with oil and wine, honey and wool, from France and Spain; with velvets, silks, and spices from the Mediterranean; with corn and wax, hemp, iron, and timber, from the Baltic? And all this great commerce was founded on their fisheries in his Majesty's seas.

Two other arguments were very commonly put forward,—that the development of the fisheries would directly increase shipping, and also give birth to many other industries. Ingenious and detailed calculations were made to show that if 20 busses were built at a seaport they would cause other 80 ships to be constructed, increase the number of mariners by 1000, and give employment to nearly 8000 people by sea and land. "It is the fish taken upon his Majesty's coasts," said Sir William Monson, the Admiral of the Narrow Sea, "that is the only cause of the increase of shipping in Europe; and he that hath the trade of fishing becomes mightier than all the world besides in number of ships."[3] Dutch ships crowded our ports; they carried away English commodities

[1] Meynert Semeyns, *Een corte beschryvinge over de Haring-visscherye in Hollandt.*

[2] Keymer, *Observations on Dutch Fishing;* Monson, *Naval Tracts*, in Churchill's *Collection*, iii. 467; H. Robinson, *Briefe Considerations concerning the Advancement of Trade*, p. 50; *England's Great Interest by encouraging the setting up of the Royal Fishery*, &c., &c.

[3] A Demonstration of the Hollanders increase in Shipping and our Decay herein. *State Papers, Dom.*, xlvii. 112.

at lower freights than English vessels could afford to do, and thus we were "eaten out of all trade and the bread taken out of our mouths in our own seas, and the great customs carried from his Majesty's coffers to foreign princes and states." The Hollanders were accused of trying "to get the whole trade of Christendom into their own hands, as well for transportation as otherwise for the command and mastery of the seas." Yet the king was "Lord Paramount of those seas" in which the foreigners caught the fish that made them so rich and powerful: surely "he would not, without question, allow strangers to eat up the food that was provided for his children!" [1]

Such was the national spirit and sentiment that had been developing during the closing years of Elizabeth's reign and the early part of the reign of James, and was well expressed by Sir Walter Raleigh when he said that "whosoever commands the sea commands the trade; whosoever commands the trade of the world commands the riches of the world, and consequently the world itself." [2] England was to become powerful and rich by shipping and maritime commerce, and the first step in the struggle was to secure the fisheries for herself. Opinions varied as to how this was to be accomplished. Some recommended the establishing of a national fishery on the plan recommended by Hitchcock in the preceding generation and tried by Charles I. in the next. Others suggested the institution of a commission of "State Merchant," which would have trade and commerce as well as fisheries under its charge. A few spoke, more faintly, of the potency of fish-days and the strict observance of Lent. But all or almost all agreed that foreigners, and in particular the Hollanders, should be either prohibited from fishing in the British seas or allowed to do so only under license and regulations and the payment of a tribute to the crown.

The proposal most commonly mooted was to build a fleet of herring-busses for ourselves, and, in short, to imitate the Dutch system in all particulars. The natural advantages we

[1] *The Trades Increase.* Keymer, *Observations on Dutch Fishing, &c. Observations touching Trade, &c.*, Raleigh's *Works*, viii. 374. *State Papers, Dom.*, xlviii. 114.

[2] *A Discourse of the Invention of Ships. Works*, viii. 325.

possessed were made the most of. The fishing-grounds were at our doors, while the Dutch had to sail long distances. We had numerous harbours and sheltered beaches for the wintering of the busses. We had all the materials for building and equipping the busses except pitch and tar, whereas the Dutch had to import everything save hemp; and abundance of men to man the vessels could be got from the "decayed towns." It was on the other hand admitted that we laboured under one disadvantage. The Dutch fishermen were more frugal, more industrious and painstaking, than the English. They were content with plain fare—with bread and butter, cheese a little pork, and fish,—while the English required beef and beer, and much of both.[1] And while the Dutch worked hard, "labouring merrily together," the English fishermen "sat day and night drinking in the ale-houses."[2]

But any scheme for establishing a great national fishery had little chance of financial support from the public unless it could be shown to be profitable, and there was no lack of calculations and computations to prove the great profits that might be made. Gentleman estimated that the clear gain from one buss, allowing for wear and tear, would amount to £565 in four months, and from a pink for cod-fishing to £158 in two months. The author of *Britaines Buss* calculated that the yearly profit from one herring-fishing and one cod-fishing of a single buss would amount to £897, after all expenses had been paid. This writer proposed that a corporation should be formed, consisting of noblemen, gentry, and citizens "of ability," each of whom should provide one buss; that the corporation should receive from the king certain powers,

[1] In one of the most elaborate and detailed of the proposals for the building of busses, the daily allowance of beer for each man was to be a gallon, as in the king's ships: the buss was to go to sea with 56 herring barrels full of beer. E. S.—*Britaines Bvsse, or a Computation as well of the Charge of a Bvsse or Herring fishing ship as also of the Gain and Profit thereby.* London, 1615.

[2] Keymer, *Observations on Dutch Fishing.* The industrious Hollander was held up as an example to the English. "If any be so weak," said one writer, "to think this mechanical fisher trade not feasible to the English people, to him I may say with Solomon, Go to the Pismire! Look upon the Dutch! Thou Sluggard! learn of them! They do it daily in the sight of all men at our own doors, upon our own coasts." "Shall we," said another, "neglect so great blessings? O slothful England, and careless Countrymen! Look but on these fellows, that we call the plump Hollanders; behold their diligence in fishing and our own careless negligence."

privileges, and immunities; and that a joint-stock should be raised like that of the East India Company, the annual profit on which was estimated at 75 per cent.

Those schemes resembled the one put forward by Hitchcock in the previous reign and frequently advocated since. Sir Walter Cope indeed told King James, in 1612, that "this royal work," within his own knowledge, had been in project for thirty years, but that in Queen Elizabeth's time it had been "ever silenced" in favour of the Netherlands, who then maintained war against a common enemy.[1]

Within two or three years of the accession of James, the project took more definite form, and was brought before the Privy Council, and it was carefully considered in 1607. An integral part of the proposal was that strangers fishing in the British seas should pay tribute to the king, while the native fishery remained untaxed, and that the tribute should be farmed out to patentees, as was done with the assize-herrings in Scotland, who would then establish a national buss fishery and pay a rent to the crown.[2] There were several schemes of the kind, but the one which received most attention was put forward by a Mr Richard Rainsford, acting on behalf of a number of London merchants, who aimed at forming an association to be called the Society of Fishing Merchants. In 1608 the proposals were referred to the Earl of Northampton, Lord Privy Seal, and the Earl of Devonshire, who commended them as being for the public good, and early next year a formal and detailed scheme was prepared.[3] In the preamble stress was laid on the fact that the Hollanders and other nations had their principal fishing on his Majesty's coasts and seas, "whose soveraignty ought therein to be acknowledged, not only to procure thereby

[1] *State Papers, Dom.*, James I., lxxi. 89. Malynes, who, as already suggested in the note on page 128, may have been the author of Cope's tract, said exactly the same thing in 1622—that there had been a continual agitation for over thirty years to make busses and fisher-boats. *The Maintenance of Free Trade*, 42.

[2] J. Bowssar to Sir Julius Cæsar, 14th October 1607, *Brit. Mus. Lansdowne MSS.*, 142, fol. 373.

[3] A Project for to restore unto the King's Majestie his Dueties of Fishing by re-establishing ye Auncient Manner of fishing for herringe, Coad, and Ling, for maintenaunce of Navigation and Marryners with greatt increase of Traffique, 22nd April 1609, *Brit. Mus. Lansdowne MSS.*, 142, fol. 371. *State Papers, Dom.*, xlviii. 95.

payment of his Majesty's duties of fishing, but also to have his kingdom provided with fish at such reasonable rates and prices as other nations have maintained thereby navigation and mariners; and setting of an infinite number of subjects on work within the realm of England and Scotland to strengthen his Majesty's dominion by sea and land, as the chief point of a most commendable Union," that is to say, a union of England and Scotland, the idea of which was still in the mind of James. The justification for imposing a tribute on foreign fishermen, which was to be in kind, was the king's right to the tithe, "grounded by ancient customs and records of his Majesty's predecessors demanding the tenth fish; whereunto three things were required: (1) how his Majesty's tithe and right can be evidently proved; (2) precedents, that other kings and princes have and do the like in their seas; (3) that it shall give no cause of offence to other princes or states to move war." The second part of the project was to build a "competent number" of ships or busses yearly, and so to re-establish the fishing trade which, it was said, one Violet Stephens and other discontented fishmongers from England had transferred to Enkhuisen and other places in Holland some ninety years earlier, teaching the Dutch to come and fish in the British seas—a false tale current in England in the reign of James.

As an alternative plan, to be put into immediate execution in connection with the truce just concluded between Spain and the United Provinces,[1] it was proposed that, his Majesty's right and tithe having been made plain as above described, the Hollanders themselves should be invited to join on reasonable terms with the English projectors in the fishing trade for one-third part, or even a half, of the fishery. This course, it was believed, would prevent any cause of offence, being, it was said, in agreement with "the known precedents of other princes." It was also thought that it would be agreeable to the Hollanders, since they would see that the Society of Fishing Merchants, being free from license or tribute, could afford to have busses built in Denmark for themselves should that be necessary. If the Hollanders could be induced to associate

[1] Treaty of Antwerp, $\frac{\text{30 March}}{\text{9 April}}$ 1609.

themselves with the Society, then, it was argued, when the time came to interfere with their "general fishery," the risk of war would be removed, and the king's tithe and right might be acknowledged and established by proclamation or otherwise.[1]

The acknowledgment of the king's "sovereignty or title annexed to the dignity of the Crown" required the contribution of the tenth or the twentieth fish, more or less, to be delivered at sea for the general good of the Society, so that they might be able to tide over bad years and maintain the fishermen. In this way, by heavily taxing the Hollanders, it was believed that "no man should be discouraged by bad successe, but might depend upon God's blessing with a quiete minde to follow his vocacion avoydinge Idlenes by ye survey of others." On the other hand, the Society would undertake to pay the king so much upon every last of fish as might be thought convenient, provided that letters patent were granted under which the Hollanders and other strangers would be "limited and ruled."

In this scheme of the London merchants it was proposed to acquire in the first year fifty fishing vessels, partly by buying them beyond the seas, and partly by building them in Denmark, Scotland, and the north of England. The busses were not to exceed fifty, or the dogger-boats thirty tons, since the Dutch in recent years had found the smaller vessels more profitable than the larger ones. It was stated that some families in Holland, the "east countries," and Hamburg, with vessels of their own, were desirous of joining the London Society,—several of them had indeed arrived in England,—and it was proposed to admit them for a few years only, in order to lay the foundations of the business, and to educate English lads in the curing of herrings, and, what was "not the least point," to make the English as industrious as themselves. When the fishery was thoroughly established, it would be easy to erect "staple towns and magazines" for the commodities of other countries; the ships of the Society would bring back merchandise for the fish exported, and a great commerce would be created. In all this prosperity "the King's Majesty might be made a partaker, as a Royal Merchant," while the stock required would easily be found among the merchants. On the

[1] A rubric in the copy at the Record Office says, "By Proclamation first, most convenient to all the world."

other hand, if the king confined his action to the issuing of licenses to foreigners, without giving means for establishing a society of merchants for the fishing, then his subjects would be entirely dependent for their fish on these foreign fishermen, who would charge higher prices to recoup themselves for the cost of the licenses. The country, moreover, would suffer from the loss of the commerce that sprung from the trade in fish; the transportation of money and bullion for fish and other commodities brought into the realm would continue unchecked; and the king would lose the great strength of shipping and mariners that otherwise would be available for the defence of the kingdom.

Objections were raised to the project on the ground that it was unlikely that the Society, even with the advantages which they desired, would be able to compete with the Hollanders. The Hamburgers and other peoples who had previously made the attempt had failed, for the Dutch were very industrious and frugal, their fish always brought the highest price, often 25 per cent above that of other nations, because they were thoroughly skilled and experienced in the industry. The freights of the Hollanders were, moreover, far lower than in English ships, as they took barrelled herrings for ballast, or even for "drink money."

A more serious difficulty was the principle that lay at the root of the scheme—the taxation of the Dutch fishermen for the benefit of the Society. It was evidently admitted that the project would fail, even if the busses were manned by Dutchmen and the herrings cured and exported by them, unless some form of subsidy was provided. But on the threshold lay the question of the king's right to impose a tribute on foreign fishermen. Rainsford endeavoured to help the solution by submitting a memorandum, "Touching his Majesty's Tythe."[1] It has some interest from the circumstance that it was the first attempt made in the reign of James to furnish historical and legal precedents for interfering with the liberty of fishing. In substance it is little more than a collection of the stories current at the time concerning the sovereignty of the sea, such as those about King Edgar, Queen Mary and Philip, and

[1] *State Papers, Dom.*, xlviii. 94. It is written on parchment and imperfect, and endorsed, "Mr Rainsford's Answeares."

Camden's statement about Scarborough.[1] It was also said that fishermen were compelled to pay taxes for liberty to fish in Russia, at the "Shoffland" islands and other islands belonging to the King of Sweden, in Denmark, and in Spain, where the Duke of Medina Sidonia derived a large revenue from the taxes on the tunny fishery. Rainsford reiterated the advantages of the scheme to the nation and the navy, and promised an annual revenue of £20,000 to the king, after the lapse of seven years, so long as he granted to the patentees the tribute on foreign fishermen.

About this time, whether by arrangement with the London merchants or independently, some influential persons addressed the king in denunciation of the Dutch. Sir Nicholas Hales in 1608, and again in 1609, strongly advised the king to take action against them. Their fisheries in his Majesty's seas, he said, were worth more than the mines of gold and silver in the Indies; in one year they had sold fish in England alone to the value of £1,200,000; by their means they maintained 100,000 men with their wives and families. Then their immense shipping was a menace to the security of the realm. They came into our roads and harbours with their guns and ordnance on board: sometimes three or four hundred sail of Hollanders sheltered in St George's Channel, where our fleet, if need were, could always strike them. The whole trade of Christendom appeared to be going into their hands. Sir Nicholas was afraid they might join with the "Turks" against us; there was even risk of invasion unless measures were taken to curb their growing power. The measures he proposed were the delivery of Flushing and Brill as pledges of security, and the payment of £4,000,000 for the king's license to carry on their fishery for twenty-one years on the British coasts. Otherwise they should be compelled to pay a tithe of the twentieth herring or be forbidden altogether.[2] Sir William

[1] See p. 64.

[2] To the King's Most excellent Majestie: A Declaration of the Fishing of Herring, Codd, and Ling, and how greatly the favour or disfavour of Your Royal Majesty concerneth the Hollanders. *State Papers, Dom.*, xxxii. 32. A Declaration how much the Favour or Disfavour of Your Royal Majestie doth concern the Prosperity or Adversitie of the Hollanders: and what inconvenience may ensue, and how to praevent the same to the honour and safety of your Majesty and the tranquillitie of the Netherlanders. *Ibid.*, xlv. 23.

Monson—who was a Roman Catholic, had been Admiral of the Narrow Sea, and was accused by the Dutch of antipathy to them—wrote several papers in the same strain. He dwelt upon the danger to England of their increase in shipping commerce and power, all derived from the fisheries in the British seas. They had already got the Irish and Russian trade, as well as that to the Mediterranean, so that while twelve years before there were twelve English ships to one Hollander in that sea, there were now ten Hollanders to one English; they even transported the red-herrings from Yarmouth and the pilchards from Cornwall and Ireland, which was previously done by English vessels. Monson's remedy was to obtain possession of the fisheries and build a fleet of English busses.[1]

There is no doubt James was inclined to listen with a favourable ear to the proposals to establish a native herring fishery at the expense of the Dutch. A year or two earlier he had, indeed, induced the Parliament of Scotland to pass an Act providing, among other things, that the royal burghs should equip busses for the herring fishery,—a suggestion frequently made and never well received. When the burghs were called upon to state the number of busses they were prepared to set forth, they declared that some of the coast towns already had vessels engaged in this fishery, especially in summer, "att the back of the Isles besyid the Flemeingis"; that on the coast there was more shipping for fishing than "substance" to furnish them with or mariners to serve in them; and that the most profitable and "easy" fishing was at the Isles and lochs on the west coast, though they were hindered there by the barbarous conduct of the natives. It was therefore, they said, "in vain" to ask them to fish "in the mayne sea" when they could get this easy and profitable fishing at the lochs and near the shore at all seasons, in great abundance, both summer and winter.[2]

At the time the fishery scheme was under consideration

[1] A Demonstration of the Hollanders Increase in Shipping and our Decay herein. *Ibid.*, xlvii. 112. Particulars of the Lawes observed by other Nations touching fishing, and the Advantages that would accrue from establishing an English Fishing fleet. *Ibid.*, 114.

[2] *Records of the Convention of the Royal Burghs of Scotland*, ii. 203, July 2, 1605.

some events occurred which favoured the plans, if not of the London merchants, at least of those who were preaching hostility to the Dutch. A chorus of complaints came from Scotland and England as to the encroachments of the Hollanders near the shore on the east coast, not only interfering with the operations of the native fishermen, but breaking up and scattering the shoals of herrings. Whereas they had been prescribed "in ancient times" in Scotland from fishing nearer the land than they might see the shore from the main-tops of their vessels, they now came as near as they pleased, and would not suffer any others, whether subjects or strangers, to fish within the bounds of their fleet, which, it was said, extended over a space "at least forty Scottish miles in length and twenty broad," thus "breaking and killing" the shoals before they could reach the mainland. They were also accused of drawing "the great fish" (by which was meant cod, saithe, &c.) from the grounds along the shore, by casting into the sea the guts of the herrings they cured on board their busses. By reason of all this the Scottish fishermen, who used to get abundant supplies at "yair awn dooris" to supply the whole country, were now scarcely able, with great pains, to supply their own families, and there was in consequence a general clamour in the country, the people affirming that "the Hollanderis fishes the meait out of thir mouthis." The evil was felt all the more by the Scottish fishermen because they paid three "assizes" every year for their several fishings, each consisting of 1000 herrings, while the Hollanders paid nothing.[1]

Early in 1609 the fishermen of the Cinque Ports, who frequented the Yarmouth fishing in large numbers, sent a petition to the king, in which they recited their grievances. They alleged that the laws prohibiting the purchase from foreigners of fish unless sufficiently salted and casked (laws which, they pointed out, had done great good in the past, and had increased shipping and mariners) were not properly enforced. This complaint was aimed against the Dutch, who sold large quantities of fresh herrings at Yarmouth, and supplied London and other towns with fresh cod. They also complained that fishermen from the Low Countries, with a few from France, came before the fishing season and "preoccupied and environed" the best

[1] *State Papers, Dom.*, xxxii. 31.

places with their shipping, enclosing, as in a circle, the shoals of herrings, and preventing the native fishermen from fishing among them. They were thus deprived of one of the best commodities of the land, and the herrings which they were prevented from catching were taken by the Hollanders and sold fresh on the English coast in contravention of the statutes. They said they were threatened with utter decay and impoverishment, and were discouraged from building barks for the Iceland fishing, which had in the past produced numbers of good mariners, to the great honour and defence of the realm. They pointed to the "ingenious dexterity of the Netherlanders, who in the care and pollicy of their State, and for the maintenance of their navigation and fishing," had imposed a tax of fifteen shillings on every last of herrings imported by foreigners into their country; and they begged the king, by the justice of *lex talionis*, to do likewise, and thus to save the poor fishermen from the multitude of foreigners who oppressed them.[1] About this time complaints began to be made of cruel and harsh treatment of the native fishermen by the Dutch, but they appear to have rested on very slender grounds.[2]

The complaints against the Hollanders gave James his opportunity. The policy of issuing a proclamation to forbid unlicensed fishing by foreigners on the British coasts was discussed by the Privy Council early in the year. Doubts, however, were expressed whether such action would be in conformity with the provisions of the "Burgundy" treaties, which granted liberty of fishing to the Low Countries. In the "qualification" of Rainsford's fishery scheme the question as to how the king's title and rights could be proved had been answered in a lofty spirit—"By prerogative royall, without any accompt to be rendered to other nations; yet

[1] *State Papers, Dom.*, xlv. 22. The petition was signed by fishermen of Yarmouth, Dover, Hastings, Rye, Hythe, and Folkestone. It is said in the petition that they had previously craved both the king and the Council for redress, without avail.

[2] The author of *Britaines Buss* had heard, but did not believe, stories of the "very foul and insolent dealing of their bussmen with our poor weak fishermen upon our coasts." Tobias Gentleman, who admired the Dutch for their industry, said they scorned us only "for being so negligent of our profit, and careless of our fishing; and they do daily flout us that be the poor fishermen of England, to our faces at sea, calling to us and saying, 'Ya English, ya zall, or oud scoue dragien,' which in English is this: 'You English, we will make you glad for to wear our old shoes.'" *Englands Way to Win Wealth*, p. 44.

others to declare the reasons thereof." But the Privy Council had to consider the matter more carefully. They remitted the draft proclamation to a committee consisting of Sir John Herbert, the second Secretary, Sir Julius Cæsar, now Chancellor of the Exchequer, Sir Daniel Dunn, Sir Thomas Crompton, and Sir Christopher Perkins, instructing them, after perusing all the Burgundy treaties, to report as to the lawfulness or unlawfulness of the proposed action.[1]

A fortnight later the report of the committee was sent to the Council. They had, they said, considered of the liberty

[1] *Brit. Mus. Lansdowne MSS.*, 142, fol. 375. A copy of the letter of the Lords of the Council, in the handwriting of Sir Julius Cæsar, is as follows: "After our very hearty recommendations. Whereas his Majesty hath of late been moved vpon many consyderations arising from the complayntes of his subiects, to take some course of restraynt of many inconveniences depending vpon the excesse of libertie, wch is taken by the subiectes of forraigne princes and states to fish vppon his coast; By which, not onlie his owne ffishermen receive wrong in their fishing, but the verie Coast-Townes themselves are much decayed for lack of meanes to sett their people on work. To wch end hee had resolved to set forth a proclamation to th'effect of that wch is hereinclosed:

Fforasmuch as vppon perusall of some Treaties from King Henry 7ths tyme till this daye betweene the Crowne of England and the house of Burgundy, we fynde certeyne clauses, by which there maye arise some question how farre any such Prohibition maye concurre with the practice of the same for so much as shall concerne the subiects of that Estate; Of wch particulars it is necessary that some deliberation were taken, beefore his Matie proceeded to a generall execution of the same: We have thought good to requyre yow ioyntly and severally to peruse all those Treaties, and to consyder of them, and all other thinges, by wch the lawfullnes or vnlawfulnes maye appeare of this proceeding; Which being don wee shall expect some report from you for his Maties better satisfaction.

Wherein wee doubt not but yow will proceede wth all convenient expedition. And so will bid yow hartelie farewell.

Ffrome the Court at
Whitehall
first of Ffebruarie, 1606.

Yor Verie loving friendes,
Subscribed by the
1. L. Chancellor.
2. L. Treasour.
3. L. Admirall.
4. The Earle of Worcester.
5. The Earle of Salisbury.
6. The Earle of Marr.
7. The L. Stanhop.

Mr Secretary Herbert.
Mr Chancellor of the Exchequer.
Sr. Daniel Dun.
Sr. Thomas Crompton.
Sr. Christopher Perkins.

This copy is dated 1st February 1606, and the copy of the report of the Committee is also dated 1606, which would imply that the matter had been before the Privy Council in that year. It appears, however, from other evidence that Sir Julius Cæsar made a mistake in dating the copies.

taken by the subjects of foreign princes and states to fish upon the coasts of the King's Majesty, by which not only the English fishermen received wrong in their fishing, but the very coast towns were decayed; they had also considered the proclamation for the restraint of fishing, and had perused the Burgundy treaties as required, and they were "of opinion that the King's Majesty may without breach of any treaty now in force, or of the law, upon the reasons specified in the proclamation sent unto us, restrain all strangers from fishing upon his coasts without license, in such moderation and after such convenient notice given thereof by public proclamation, as his Majesty shall think fit."[1]

It was on this extremely important deliverance that the new policy of interfering with the liberty of foreigners fishing on the British coasts was based. The cautious language of the Privy Council indicates that they were conscious of the strength of the case against them from the existence of the Burgundy treaties; but the committee professed to find that those treaties were no longer in force,—an argument which was made the most of in the subsequent negotiations with the Dutch Re-

[1] *Brit. Mus. Lansdowne MSS.*, 142, fol. 377. In Sir Julius Cæsar's handwriting, and endorsed, "A copy of a letter from Mr Secretary Herbert, myself, and others to the Lds of the King's P. Councell, touching the prohibition of strangers fishing on the coasts of England," &c. This important paper reads as follows: "Our humble duties dewe to yr good LLps. We have according to yr commandement, considered of the liberty wch is taken by the Subiectes of forreine Princes and States to fish vppon the kings Maties coasts by wch not onely the English fishermen receive wrong in their fishing but the very coast townes themselves are much decayed for want of meanes to set their people on work; and we have considered likewise of the proclamation for the restraint of those many inconveniences depending vppon the excesse of such strangers fishing: We haue also pervsed the treaties frõ Henry the 7th time till this day betweene the Crowne of England and the House of Burgundy, and we have considered of them, and of all other thinges by wch (as wee conceave) the lawfulness or vnlawfulness may appeare of this proceeding. And are of opinion, that the Ks Maty may wthout breach of any treatyie nowe in force, or of the lawe, vppon the reasons specified in the proclamation sent vnto vs, restreine all strangers frõ fishing vppon his coasts wthout license, in such moderation and after such convenient notice given thereof by publik proclamation, as his Maty shall think fit.

And so we most humbly take our leaves. 14 febr. 1606.

Yor Ldships humbly at commandment,

J. Herbert. Jul. Cæsar. Daniel Dun. Christoph. Parkins. Tho. Crompton.

From the erasures and corrections (see Fig. 6) there seems little doubt that the paper is the original draft.

public. The report was submitted to the Council in February; in March Grotius published his *Mare Liberum*, in which he branded as "insanely cupid" any one who attempted to interfere with the common liberty of fishing in the sea; and within a week or two thereafter the Truce of Antwerp was signed by Spain and the States-General, by which the long war between those Powers was brought to a close, and James was free to begin his policy against the Dutch fishermen. On 12th April 1609 a memorandum was drawn up for the Council, in which it was stated (1) that a conference having been held with the fishermen concerning the seasons of all the fishings on the coast, it was thought fit that the proclamation should take effect from 1st August ensuing; (2) that from that day forward it should be unlawful for any stranger to fish "upon those his Majesty's coasts and seas of Great Britain and Ireland and the Isles adjacent," where the fishing was usually carried on, until they had obtained license for the same from the king; (3) that commissioners should be appointed by the king, at London, for England and Ireland, and for Scotland at such place as the king should select, to give out licenses on such conditions as he might think fit; and (4) that the licenses should be apportionable to the number and tonnage of the ships.[1]

These provisions were embodied in the proclamation, which was issued on 6th May 1609.[2] "Whereas," said James, in his wordy style, "we have been contented since our coming to the crown, to tolerate an indifferent and promiscuous kind of liberty to all our friends whatsoever, to fish within our streams, and upon any of our coasts of Great Britain, Ireland, and other adjacent islands, so far forth as the permission or use thereof might not redound to the impeachment of our prerogative royal, nor to the hurt and damage of our loving subjects, whose preservation and flourishing estate we hold ourself principally bound to advance before all worldly respects: so finding that our connivance therein hath not only given occasion to over great encroachments upon our regalities, or rather questioning for our right,[3] but hath been a means of much daily wrongs to our own people that exercise the trade

[1] *Brit. Mus. Lansdowne MSS.*, 142, fol. 379. In Cæsar's handwriting.

[2] See Appendix F. [3] Perhaps an oblique reference to *Mare Liberum*.

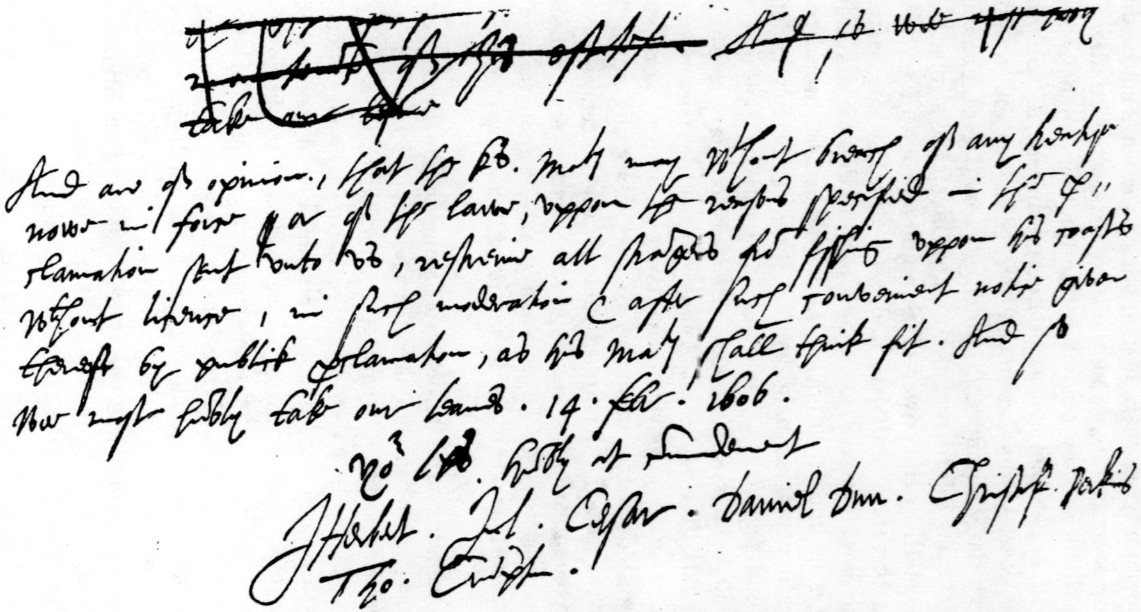

Fig. 6.—*Facsimile of the concluding part of the Draft of Committee's Report to Privy Council regarding the restraint of foreigners fishing on the British coasts.*

of fishing, as (either by the multitude of strangers, which do preoccupy those places, or by the injuries which they receive most commonly at their hands) our subjects are constrained to abandon their fishing, or at the least are become so discouraged in the same, as they hold it better for them to betake themselves to some other course of living, whereby not only divers of our coast-towns are much decayed, but the number of mariners daily diminished, which is a matter of great consequence to our estate, considering how much the strength thereof consisteth in the power of shipping and use of navigation." It was therefore both just and necessary, the king continued, to take lawful means to put an end to these inconveniences, although he had no intention, as he desired the world to take notice, to deny his neighbours "those fruits and benefits of peace and friendship" which might justly be expected at his hands in honour and reason. He therefore gave notice to all the world, that after 1st August 1609, "no person of what nation or quality soever, being not our natural born subject, be permitted to fish upon any of our coasts and seas," "until they have orderly demanded and obtained licenses from us," or the commissioners appointed at London and Edinburgh. The licenses were to be renewed yearly, "upon pain of such chastisement as shall be fit to be inflicted upon such wilful offenders.[1]

The prohibition of unlicensed fishing in the British or Irish seas was general in its character, and applied to all foreigners indifferently. But it was well understood to be aimed at the Dutch. There is no evidence to show that any steps were taken to induce the hundred or so of French boats that took part in the herring-fishing on the east coast to obtain licenses; and though the Earl of Salisbury wrote a long letter to the English ambassador at Madrid, explaining the reasons that had induced the king to issue the proclamation, it does not appear that the numerous Spanish fishermen who caught mackerel off the coast of Ireland and the south-west coast of England were ever interfered with, or asked to apply for licenses.[2]

In the United Provinces the important step taken by the King

[1] *State Papers, Dom.*, xlv. 24. *Proc. Coll.*, No. 11.

[2] Salisbury to Cornwallis, 8th June 1609. Winwood's *Memorials of Affairs of State in the Reigns of Q. Elizabeth and K. James I.*, iii. 49.

of England was regarded with much concern. Early in June the proclamation was discussed by the States of Holland, and it was resolved that as the interference with the liberty of fishing was contrary to the treaties between England and the Netherlands, the States-General should maintain their right to fish off the British and Irish coasts.[1] This resolution was confirmed on the same day by the States-General, and it was decided to make representations against putting the proclamation into force. The herring-fishing, as previously described, began in June at Shetland, and was prosecuted down the east coast to Yarmouth, where the busses were usually to be found in September. There was therefore not much time to lose. Sir Noel Caron, the Dutch ambassador in London, had several interviews on the subject with the Earl of Salisbury and with James himself. Lord Salisbury, who was believed by Caron to be the real author of the scheme, held out little hope of an amicable settlement. But the good-natured king, who loved peace even more than he loved his prerogative, was more conciliatory. He explained to Sir Noel that the proclamation was for the purpose of introducing better order into the fishery, and to make manifest to the world the authority and power which he had on the sea,[2] and was not meant in any way to wrong the States, either by hostile force or otherwise. The French Government had in the meantime moved in the matter. At first nothing was said to our ambassador at Paris about the proclamation, and he thought it "no wisdom" to speak about it to them unless they raised the question. This they did later, either on account of the French fishermen or at the instigation of the Dutch, and a year's respite was granted.[3]

[1] Muller, *Mare Clausum, Bijdrage tot de Geschiedenis der Rivaliteit van Engeland en Nederland in de Zeventiende Eeuw*, p. 52. Bosgoed, *Bib. Piso.*, 347. Resolutiën . . . van Vergaderinge van de Heeren Staten van Hollandt ende West-Vrieslandt, $\frac{2}{12}$ June 1609. "Ter Generaliteyt 's lands recht voorstaan ter saake van het Engelsch placaat op het visschen op de kusten en zeeën van Groot Brittannien en Yrland."

[2] "Ende oic Sijne authoriteyt eñ macht die hy in die See heeft voir de werelt manifest te maecken."

[3] Sir George Carew to Salisbury, 20th June 1609. Acknowledges his lordship's letter, "according the request made by the ffr. Ambr for one year's Respite longer for the ffishers of this nation," and expressing his pleasure that other considerations of state so fell out as to give his Majesty cause to grant them that favour, "for it is like to increase the amity of the two crowns."

Caron learned the welcome intelligence from the French ambassador in London, that a promise had been made to him that the project would proceed no further until after mutual negotiations, which would occupy the whole of that year.[1] Sir Ralph Winwood, who was appointed English ambassador at The Hague in August 1609, also had conferences about the proclamation with Barnevelt, whose authority in Holland was then supreme. He was told that the States would send special ambassadors to the king, "to acknowledge those many royal favours they had received from him," and to treat of the liberty of fishing. Meantime their ambassador in London had been instructed to beseech the king to have patience with their people "trading" on his coasts, and that "without impeachment they might use their accustomed liberty and ancient privileges." [2]

Sir Noel Caron had also discussions in London with respect to the legality of imposing any tax on Dutch fishermen, the principle of which he could not well understand. As previously mentioned, one of the precedents upon which James founded his claim to impose tribute was the payment by Scottish fishermen of the so-called "assize-herrings." This was an ancient tax or custom of a thousand herrings levied from each fishing-boat employed at the herring fishery, and they belonged to the king as part of the crown revenues.[3] From the extent of the

[1] Caron to the States-General, $\frac{13}{23}$ July 1609. *Brit. Mus. Add. MSS.*, 17,677.

[2] Winwood to Salisbury, 6th September 1609. *Memorials*, iii. 64.

[3] The assize-herring was thus described by Skene, in *De Verborum Significatione*, annexed to the laws of Scotland, printed in 1597. "Assisa Halecum. The assise herring signifies ane certain measure and quantity of herring, quilk perteinis to the king as ane part of his custumes and annexed propriety, *Jac.* 6, p. 15, c. 237, for it is manifest that Hee shuld have of everie Boat that passis to the drave, and slayis herring, ane thousand herring of ilk tak that halds, viz. of Lambmes tak, of the Winter tak, and the Lentrone tak"—that is, of the summer, winter, and spring fishings. The assize-herrings appear to have been originally a contribution to the king's kitchen. In 1526 James V. granted assize-herrings to Stuart of Ardgowane (*Origines Parochiales Scotiæ*, ii. 83). In 1593, in an Act of the Parliament of Scotland, entitled "Annexatioun of the Propertie of the Croun that wes nocht annext of befoir," the assize-herrings were included (Jac. VI., 1593, c. 32. *Acta*, iv. 28), and an Act of 1597, entitled "Assysis hering may nocht be disponit," ordained that no infeftment or alienation in few ferm or otherwise, and all rentals and dispositions whatsoever, past or to come, were to be null and void, because they pertained to the king as part of his customs and annexed property (*Acta*, iv. 131). Later the assize-herring was commuted into a money payment. An Act of Charles I. in 1641 (cap. 117), entitled "Act anent the Excise of Herring,"

Dutch herring fishery it is evident that a similar tax imposed on it would have brought in a goodly sum annually to the king's coffers. A few years later, when James did attempt to collect the tax from the Dutch fishermen, each buss was to be charged an "assize duty" of 10,000 herrings, or £66, 13s. 4d. Scots, which was equal to about £5, 11s. 1d. sterling; so that if the duty had been exacted from the 2000 herring-boats fishing on the coast the crown would have benefited to the extent of about £11,000 a year, and the Hollanders would have been all that the poorer.

When the principle of the assize-herring was explained to the Dutch ambassador, he appears to have devoted some attention to it. He argued that although the Scots Acts showed that the assize-herrings had been exacted from the Scottish fishermen in the firths on the east and west coasts, the tax had never been imposed in the north seas and at the Isles (Shetlands) where the Hollander busses fished; it would therefore be an "innovation" to enforce the payment there now. He further averred that treaties between King James and the United Provinces existed by which Dutch fishermen were freed from any payment to the king for fishing on his coasts and seas. Moreover, he declared the sea was free to all, *mare est liberum*, and consequently there was no king nor lord to be acknowledged upon the sea, "but every stranger may fish over all the

on the ground that the collection of the herrings was "very hard and difficult," commuted the thousand herrings in the Firth of Lothian into a money payment of £6 Scots. In the eighteenth century, when it had been for the most part granted to individuals, or farmed, it took the form of a tax ranging from £4 Scots to £10 Scots per boat or per net, and was felt as a grievous burden. In the Firth of Forth each boat that was "size-worthy" (viz., that caught 3000 herrings during the whole season) had to pay ten shillings as "size-duty." On the west coast it amounted to £10 Scots, or sixteen shillings and eightpence sterling, whether herrings were caught or not. With regard to the gross value of the tax, those of the great Dunbar fishings were leased in 1614 for five years for £1000 Scots, and a yearly rent of 2000 merks (*Reg. Privy Council Scot.*, x. 282). In 1613 the value of the "duty of the tack of the assize-herrings," amounting to fourteen lasts, which the Earl of Argyle rendered for Lochfyne, was estimated to be about £36 or £38 sterling (*Melrose Papers*, i. 124). In 1598 the assize-herring from the "east seas" was estimated to amount to 1120 dry "killing" (cod), which shows it was sometimes paid in other fish; in 1656-57 it was equal to £130 sterling (Chalmers, *Caledonia*, ii. 497); in 1629 Captain Mason claimed no less than £12,489, 7s. sterling as the value, with interest, of the assize-herrings of the Hebrides and North Isles granted to him by James for the years 1610-11, and not paid (*State Papers, Dom.*, cliv. 13).

seas where he pleases, without asking license, or paying any toll or duty whatsoever." It was moreover apparent, apart from considerations of principle as to the freedom of the sea, that no certainty existed that the king, or a successor, would not raise the tax, if once imposed, as the King of Denmark had done with the dues at the Sound, until they became a heavy burden.

A Scottish lawyer, probably in the service of the crown, in reply to the objections of Sir Noel Caron, argued that it could not be called an "innovation" to exact the tribute, if the herrings swam from the ancient places of their resort and appeared in new places in his Majesty's seas, where the tax was not previously levied, or because there was an "oversight" in levying it in olden times when, he said, there was little fishing in the north seas and about the Isles, and the cost of collecting it would have been great. As for treaties, it was most improbable that any stranger would ask or king grant that strangers should be more free to fish "within the seas of the king's dominions" than the native subjects of the kingdom. But even if such grant had been made, it could not stand good in law, because it was "repugnant to reason." By negligence, he said, the Hollanders had been allowed two advantages. In ancient times they were "appointed" to fish no nearer the land than they could see the shore from their main-tops; but now they fished as near as they pleased, excluding the natives and breaking up the shoals. Then, while the natives had to pay three assizes yearly, the Dutch were "as yet" asked to pay only one, though many of the busses made three voyages in a year. And if the sea was free to all, why had the Netherlanders entered into treaties for freedom of fishing? By making covenants with the kings of Scotland, "and taking liberty of them to fish within the Scottish seas," they had "disclaimed *mare liberum* and acknowledged the Kings of Scotland to be Lords of these Seas." Why should the Dutch alone object, if the natives, the French, and all other foreigners willingly pay the assize-herring?[1] It was, however, untrue to say that the tax was paid by the French or

[1] Arguments for Collecting the Assyze herring from all Strangers fishing in the North Seas of Scotland, and Answers to some objections proponet be Sir Noel Caron. *State Papers, Dom.*, xxxii. 31.

other foreign fishermen. Even Scottish fishermen who fished at the North Isles were exempt; and when an attempt was made some years later to force them to pay, the burghs obtained a decree of *absolvitor* from the court and the Privy Council, on the ground that the tax could only be levied on "green" or fresh fish landed, and not on herrings cured on board (see p. 166).

In the spring of 1610 James's proclamation was again taken into consideration by the States of Holland and the States-General, and it was resolved to send an embassy to London, primarily to thank the king for his friendly offices in connection with the conclusion of the truce with Spain, but in reality to deal with the fishery question and some other matters. One of the ambassadors was Joachimi, who afterwards represented the States at the English Court for over twenty-five years. Another was Elias van Oldenbarnevelt, a brother of the great statesman who was then at the head of affairs in the Netherlands, and to him the business of the fishing was specially committed. They arrived in England on 14th April, and had an audience with the king a few days later and another with the Privy Council. They asked for an assurance that the king's proclamation was not meant to extend to the United Provinces, since he was in alliance with them, and treaties existed between the two countries. But the Earl of Salisbury plainly told them that the principal motive of the proclamation arose from the multitude and disorder of their fishermen, "who had wholly drawn the fishing to themselves, to the destruction of his Majesty's people and coast-towns"; and they were invited to further conference.[1]

On the 6th May, exactly a year after the publication of the proclamation, the ambassadors had a formal conference with Sir Julius Cæsar, Sir Thomas Parry, Sir Daniel Dunn, Sir Christopher Perkins, Dr Henry Marten (Advocate-General), and Levinus Muncke, a Fleming, and "clerk to his Majesty's Signet." The English commissioners began the discussion by justifying the proclamation on the grounds previously indicated. The Dutch contended for complete freedom of fishing, resting their case on arguments drawn from the civil law, on immemorial possession, on the existence of treaties, and on

[1] Winwood, *Memorials*, iii. 105, 135, 146, 162. Muller, *op. cit.*, 56.

political considerations. They said the United Provinces had always been in peaceful possession of free fishing, and that from time immemorial they had enjoyed complete liberty to fish over the whole sea, both as a matter of usage and of right. To disturb them by force in the enjoyment of that right would be unjust. Besides, by the Law of Nations the boundless and rolling sea was as common to all people as the air, "which no prince could prohibit." No prince, they said, could "challenge

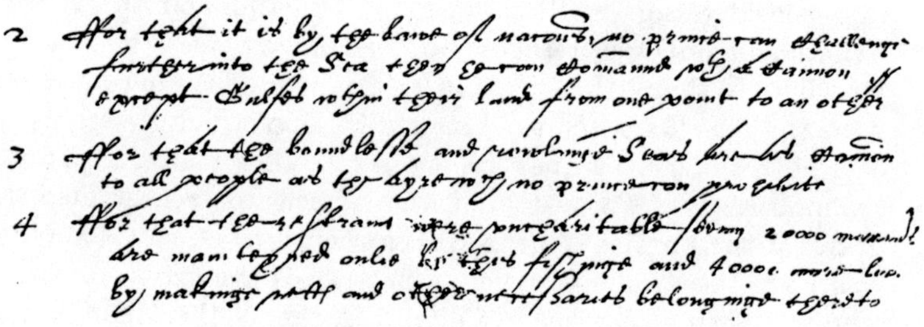

Fig. 7.—*Facsimile of Minute of the Declaration of the Dutch Envoys as to the range of guns.*

further into the sea than he can command with a cannon, except gulfs within their land from one point to another,"—the first occasion on which this principle for delimiting territorial waters, afterwards so celebrated, appears to have been advanced.[1]

[1] *State Papers, Dom.*, xlvii. 111. "2. For that it is by the Lawe of nacions, no prince can Challenge further into the Sea then he can Com̃and wth a Cannon except Gulfes wthin their Land from one point to an other. 3. For that the boundlesse and rowlinge Seas are as Com̃on to all people as the ayre wch no prince can prohibite." The paper is endorsed "Reasons vsed by the Hollanders for the Continuance of Fishing Contrarie to the proclamation made in May 1609 forbidding of strangers to fish," and there is a note, apparently in Cæsar's writing, saying, "This note was sent by Emanuell Demetrius who was present att the discourse." It is misdated "Aug. 1609." The endorsements appear to have been made after 1612, because at the end it is said, "It was answered by the *late* Lord Treasr. Salisburie att a hearing," &c. A list is given of those present at the conference—viz., the Earls of Salisbury, Northampton, Nottingham, Suffolk, Shrewsbury, and Worcester, Mr Secretary Herbert and Sir Julius Cæsar, the "Standers by" being Sir T. Edmondes, Sir Daniel Dunn, Sir Christopher Perkins, Sir William Wade, and Mr Levinus Emanuell Demetrius,—probably the Levinus Muncke of the Dutch and other records. It is to be noted that the argument as to the limitation of the territorial sea by the range of guns was not contained in the instructions to the Dutch, as printed by Aitzema (*Saken van Staet en Oorlogh*, ii. 406) and Vreede (*Vrijheid van Haringvaart*, 6; compare Muller, *Mare Clausum*,

Besides these more or less abstract arguments, the ambassadors made a strong case by reason of the treaties in which liberty of fishing was stipulated. It is noteworthy that they referred to only one of the treaties with England, the Intercursus Magnus of 1496, while they laid stress on the treaties with Scotland in 1541, 1550, and especially in 1594, when James himself was on the throne of the northern kingdom (see p. 81). They further declared that there were reasons of state which forbade the United Provinces from allowing the free use of the sea to be disputed. More than 20,000 mariners were maintained by the herring fishery alone, besides other 40,000 people who gained their livelihood by making nets, packing the fish, and in other industries depending upon the fishery. The power and security of the country and much of its commerce rested on the fishery. As for the complaint that the decay of English coast-towns was caused by their fishing off the coast, it was explained that they only fished there for herrings which were cured on board, and that this industry had been discovered by themselves, which gave them a prior claim to it. The English were free to carry on the herring fishery themselves, though, they dexterously added, it was a business that required much experience, and it would be a long time before they succeeded, especially as heavy losses sometimes occurred, which the Dutch

58, 91), and is not referred to by them in their Journal, where, however, they say they put forward "other reasons" than those they recite (Muller, *Mare Clausum*, 59). Van Meteren, whose work was published in 1614 (*Historie der Nederlandscher ende haerder Naburen Oorlogen, &c.*, fol. 650), reports, however, that there was a great dispute as to how far a country's limit might extend into the open sea, and the brief note of Levinus seems to be the only record of it. ("Sy seyden mede, dat het een groote dispute ware, hoeverre elcx Landts Custen ofte Limiten inde groote wijde Zee Oceane mochte strecken.") The document is of interest not only from the clear enunciation of the doctrine at so early a period, but because there are grounds for thinking that the idea may have originated in the fertile brain of Grotius. Competent Dutch authorities believe that Grotius either himself drew up the instructions dealing with the fishery question or was consulted in their preparation; and the fact that the argument is not contained in the official instructions scarcely weakens the supposition. It was of so drastic and novel a character to be urged against the pretensions of King James that the Dutch, anxious to conciliate him, may have followed a practice not uncommon in diplomacy, and kept it in the background only to be made use of if a suitable occasion arose. It is, moreover, known that Grotius had a close personal relationship with Elias van Oldenbarnevelt, the envoy to whom the fishery negotiations were specially entrusted.

were able to bear, since they lived cheaply and each of the 60,000 people mentioned were "adventurers," the losses being thus spread over a great number. They suggested that the English had given up the fishery because they had found a more comfortable livelihood in other ways.[1]

On the other side, the English commissioners argued that by the custom of nations the king had a right to the whole of the seas around his coasts; and this right was exercised by other countries, as Spain, France, Denmark, Sweden, Venice, Genoa, and Russia, and generally by all maritime states; and it was not opposed to the Roman law or the teachings of the Civilians. They admitted that the sea was free for navigation, but denied that it was free for fishing. All the kings of England since Edgar had the adjoining seas under their jurisdiction, and had always received "consideration" for the fishing within them. The commissioners evidently felt that the treaties offered the greatest difficulty to the policy of James, and they contended that all the Burgundy treaties had become obsolete for a variety of reasons. The great treaty of 1496 had lost its effect, inasmuch as a later treaty in 1520 (which, however, dealt with quite other things) did not confirm it. The treaties, moreover, had been made with the House of Burgundy, and concerned only the subjects of that house; but there were now no subjects of the Duke of Burgundy; and the Dutch at least could not found upon those treaties, because they had themselves broken and transgressed them. Even if those old treaties could be supposed to be in force and provided liberty of fishing without license, that could not mean without the payment of the usual dues, customs, and taxes. Besides, when the treaties were made the circumstances were different. The fishing of the Netherlanders was not then so disagreeable to this country as it was now; then about 100 vessels came to fish, while now they sent 2000. The king was therefore not bound to tolerate them any longer.

[1] Vreede, *Vrijheid van Haringvaart en Visscherij. Nota, in den Jare* 1610, *door de Nederlandsche Gezanten aan de Engelsche Regering ingediend* (*Bijdragen voor Vaderlandsche Geschiedenis en Oudheidkunde, Derde Deel.* Arnhem, 1842). Muller, *op. cit.*, 57; *State Papers, Dom.*, xlvii. 111; *Brit. Mus. Lansdowne MSS.*, 142, fol. 362. Vreede thinks it probable that the instructions were drawn up by Grotius; Muller believes that he was at all events consulted on the matter.

The negotiations between the English and Dutch commissioners went on for a short time, the arguments on either side being elaborated without much hope of agreement, when an event occurred that brought them to a sudden end. This was the assassination of King Henry IV. of France, the head of the Protestant League, which made James anxious to retain the goodwill and alliance of the Dutch Republic, in view of his relations with Spain. On 14th May the ambassadors were told by the Earl of Salisbury that while the king held his right to forbid the Netherlanders to fish on his coasts to be indubitable, he, "out of his great love to the Low Countries, would forbear to proceed according to the proclamation." [1] At the farewell audience James used very kind expressions. He made the remarkable but characteristic statement to the ambassadors that he had issued the proclamation owing to the just complaints of his subjects, not from the solicitation of courtesans or courtiers.[2] He assured them of his affection towards them and the preservation of their state, "which next unto his own he held most dear above all other respects in the world." As for the business of the fishing, he thought it was not fit now to spend more time on it, but to refer it to some better season, and in the meantime, he said, things would remain as they were.[3] This termination to the negotiations was naturally gratifying to the Dutch. Barnevelt and the States-General had become somewhat anxious as to the issue, and the ambassadors had been instructed to try to get the matter shelved for a little. Although James had suspended the operation of the proclamation, however, he had not withdrawn it. The question was merely postponed to a more convenient season.

The failure to carry out the policy of exacting tribute from the Dutch fishermen was fatal to the scheme of the London merchants to form a Society of Fishing Merchants. Rainsford wrote to Lord Salisbury in October 1609 expressing his fears that the Earl disapproved of the project to raise a great

[1] *State Papers, Dom.*, xlvii. 111. Vreede, *op. cit.* Muller, *op. cit.* *Brit. Mus. Lansdowne MSS.*, 142, fol. 362. "Answers for prohibiting of strangers fishing upon the English coastes without the King's license, 5th May 1610"—in the writing of Sir Julius Cæsar.

[2] "Niet door sollicitatiën van eenige courtisanen ofte hovelingen."

[3] The Lords of the Council to Winwood, *Memorials*, iii. 166.

revenue to the king for the fishing in his seas;[1] and in 1611 he again addressed a memorandum to the Earl, answering various objections that had been raised to the scheme, and renewing the offer for farming the tribute.

The plans to form a national herring fishery founded on taxation of the Dutch having failed, others were brought forward on the basis of receiving special privileges and immunities from the crown. One proceeded so far towards realisation, that in December 1611 a corporation was formed, consisting of a governor, deputy-governor, a treasurer, twenty-four "consuls," with "searchers" (cure-masters), gaugers, and other officials, in imitation of the Dutch system. The administration was to be general "for matter of order, and particular for matter of adventure," leaving every town at liberty to venture for itself; and laws and ordinances were drawn up for the central body in London and the affiliated societies throughout the country. Since the money necessary was to be found by private individuals, a number of privileges were asked from the Government. One of these, which made it lawful for the corporation to carry their fish abroad and to bring back commodities in exchange, "from all parts wheresoever, notwithstanding any former privileges to the contrary," was strenuously opposed by all the trading companies, and in particular by the Merchant Adventurers, who objected that it would be most injurious to their great trade in cloth.[2] This opposition killed the "business of the busses," as the fishing project was popularly called. Writing ten years later, Gerard Malynes, a London merchant and author, who appears to have been one of the promoters and to have spent both time and money on it, deplored the failure of this society, which he said was due to the opposition of the Merchant Adventurers, the Russia Company, and the East-land Merchants.[3]

Within a year or two another project came from an unexpected quarter. No less a personage than the queen became a suppliant for a royal patent empowering her to compound

[1] *State Papers, Dom.*, xlviii. 92.

[2] Sir Walter Cope to the king, *State Papers, Dom.*, lxxi. 89. See note, p. 128.

[3] *The Maintenance of Free Trade*, 42 (1622). He mentions the reasons given by the powerful companies for their action, but it was caused by their fears for their monopolies.

with strangers for licenses to fish on the British coasts. The arguments adduced from the point of view of benefit to the nation were of the usual kind; but others of a more or less domestic nature were added, which must have appealed to the heart of her consort. "It is desired by the Queene," proceeds the petition, "that the King's Majesty will be pleased to graunt unto her a Pattent of theis fishings under his Majesty's great Seales of England and Scotland, whereby her Majesty may have power to graunt lycense and to compound with these strangers for an yearly revenue to be paid unto her Majestie for theis fishings." By this means a great revenue would be drawn into the country, which would be sufficient to support and maintain her estate, "and so his Majesty's coffers will be spared." She promised besides that she would give him a full fifth of the amount she obtained; and another advantage would be that the king would be "royally invested in possession of his undoubted right, which," she naïvely added, "hath never ben yet obtayned by anie of his royall progenitors." The petition was brought before the Privy Council, who decided that the proposal was not feasible, as it depended upon "so many points of question and circumstance between us and the House of Burgundy in former times, and the States of the Low Countries and us for the present."[1]

In her petition the queen referred to the proposal to build a number of busses. While explaining that her project would not prevent the king or any of his subjects from building busses if they so desired, she questioned whether that plan would be successful. Some men, indeed, of great judgment, she said, were of opinion that the king would reap no benefit at all in that way, for 1000 busses was "the least number that could be thought to doe any good upon this fishing," and each would cost £1000 at least, while £100 a-year would be required for repairs, and 20,000 men would be needed to man them.

About this time several works were published giving details

[1] *State Papers, Dom.*, lxxvii. 79. The Earl of Northampton to Sir Thomas Lake, 4th July 1613. *Ibid.*, lxxiv. 23. The queen, who was fond of the banquet and the masque, was often in financial straits. Chamberlain wrote to Winwood in 1609 that she had been melancholy about her jointure, and that £3000 a-year had been added to it out of the customs, with a gift of £20,000 to pay her debts. *Memorials*, iii. 117.

as to the cost and equipment of herring-busses,[1] but little was accomplished. The net result in 1614 was that one Richard Godsdue, Esquire, of Bucknam Ferry, in Norfolk, had five busses on the stocks at Yarmouth, and Sir William Harvey had built a large one at Limehouse. But all the efforts made in the reign of James, and indeed throughout the whole century, to form a great national fishery on the model of the Dutch completely failed. It required nearly two centuries of experience, and the squandering of vast sums of money, to teach the people that a great industry could not be suddenly created in this way by servile imitation of a system not suited to the natural circumstances of the case. It was chiefly by the gradual evolution of the Scottish herring-boat, and not by the building of busses, that the herring industry was wrested from the Dutch.

James was doubtless privy to the queen's petition before it was officially considered,[2] and he appears not to have been satisfied with the decision of the Council. At all events, the question of the fisheries was still kept alive. In the spring of 1614 we find Wotton writing from The Hague to Secretary Winwood, saying that he still had his Majesty's commission regarding the fishings, and that it was, as Winwood said, "a tender and dainty piece," adding that though he had seen Mr Barnevelt on several occasions he had not mentioned the matter to him, and was waiting for a suitable time to speak of this "dainty and delicate business."[3] Later in the year, the Keeper of the State Papers was requested by the Lord Chancellor and the Archbishop of Canterbury to search the records in his custody relating to the king's jurisdiction on the sea and his right to the fishing. "Whereas," they said, "there is occasion for his Majesty's special service to look out such precedents and records as concern his Majesty's power, right, and sovereign jurisdiction of the seas and fishing upon the coast; and that we are informed there are many

[1] Gentleman, *Englands Way to Win Wealth, &c.*; E. S., *Britaines Buss*; *The Trades Increase.*

[2] In 1609 Sir Nicholas Hales told the king that he had been informed "the Hollanders were petitioners to the Queen to grant them a term of years in the seas for the fishing of herring, cod, and ling." *State Papers, Dom.*, xlv. 23.

[3] Wotton to Sec. Winwood, Hague, 20th March 1614.

of that kind among the records in your custody, we do hereby require you to make your personal repair hither to seek out all such precedents and papers as are remaining there and do any way concern that business," and to hold them ready for inspection.[1]

This search was doubtless in connection with the subject of the assize-herrings mentioned in the next chapter, but that the queen's scheme had been revived is evident from the action of Sir Noel Caron. As soon as he got wind of it, he wrote hurriedly to the States-General stating that the king had assigned to the queen for twenty-one years the revenue to be derived from taxing the herring-busses, and that no one would be allowed to fish on the coasts of England or Scotland without her consent.[2] This letter was at once considered by the Dutch Government. A committee was appointed to look into the treaties bearing on the question and the instructions which had been given to the ambassadors in 1610, and to report as to what action should be taken; but it was finally resolved to await further developments in England before interfering, and at the beginning of November Caron was able to announce that the danger had passed.[3]

At this period there were other disputes with England that caused apprehension in Holland. One referred to the trade in cloth, and in a proclamation which prohibited the export of wool[4] James took the opportunity to extol the commanding situation of the British Isles for navigation and trade, and to draw a parallel between the commodities of wool on land and fish in the sea, "which," he said, "are the Adamants that draw and govern all other Trade and

[1] Archbishop Abbot and Lord Chancellor Ellesmere to Thomas Wilson, 24th August 1614. *State Papers, Dom.*, lxxvii. 80. It is endorsed, "The letter to me, 24th Aug. 1614, sending for me from Harford and for the transcribing an abstract of all things out of my papers which might concern his Majesty's jurisdiction on the sea, which I did and delivered it to Mr Attorney-General, Sir Francis Bacon, by the commandment of the Lord Chancellor and the Archbishop of Canterbury."

[2] Caron to States-General, $\frac{\text{27 Aug.}}{\text{6 Sept.}}$ 1614. *Brit. Mus. Add. MSS.*, 17,677, H.

[3] Muller, *op. cit.*, 91, 92.

[4] 26th September 1614.

Merchandizing" — language which led the Dutch to think the proclamation anent unlicensed fishing was about to be renewed. Another referred to the whale fishery at Spitzbergen, which was claimed both by the Dutch and the British, and was regarded by James as being within his maritime dominion. It led, as shall be seen, to an interesting contest for *mare clausum* in the Arctic Seas.

CHAPTER V.

JAMES I.—*continued*. DISPUTES WITH THE DUTCH.

It would probably be too flattering to James to suppose that he had any well-considered plan for extending his authority over the foreign fishermen frequenting his coasts, or for extracting from them a tribute for their liberty of fishing. But the existence of the tax of the assize-herrings in Scotland clearly offered the best means for bringing that about if it was to be brought about at all. It has been explained that in the negotiations which followed the issue of the proclamation of 1609, Sir Noel Caron laid his finger on a weak spot in the English case, by pointing out that the assize-herring had never been levied on the native fishermen who fished where the Dutch fished at the North Isles. The special ambassadors in 1610 also mentioned that their fishermen had never been asked to pay it, though they naturally did not lay stress on the point. James resolved that those omissions should be remedied. In 1610 he granted the assize-herrings to Captain John Mason, who was employed with two ships of war in that and in the following year on the coast of Scotland. Mason accordingly made strenuous efforts to collect the tribute. The fishermen of Fifeshire, who carried on a herring fishery at Orkney and Shetland, resisted the unaccustomed tax, and in 1612 raised an action of *absolvitor* before the Lords of the Privy Council and gained their case.[1] The Lords of the Council decided that the "adventure" of the fishermen at the Northern Isles was of

[1] *Records of the Convention of the Royal Burghs of Scotland*, ii. 455. Anstruther Easter, one of the Fife villages, asked that the costs (£400 Scots) should be reimbursed to them for obtaining the decree against Mason "for exacting of thame certane excyse hering and fishes at the fishing in Orknay and Zetland."

the nature of a merchant voyage, and that the fishermen had no right to pay any such assize, which had never been craved of them before.[1]

Notwithstanding this decision of the Privy Council of Scotland, James in 1614 again granted the assize-herrings of the North Isles, on this occasion to the Duke of Lennox, who was his Admiral in Scotland and one of the chief noblemen of the time. In ordinary course the grant came before the Privy Council for confirmation, and the Council at once informed the Convention of Burghs, requesting them to make it known to the burghs that the Duke of Lennox had obtained a gift from the king of "ane excyse to be tayne of all heyring to be tayne be north of Buqhan Nes" (Buchan Ness, Aberdeenshire), so that they might lodge their defences. The commissioners for Dundee, St Andrews, Dunbar, and the burghs on the coast of Fife, were accordingly appointed to proceed to Edinburgh to give reasons to the Council against the "gift."[2] After hearing the representatives of the burghs and the agents of the Duke (one of whom was "Maister Johnne Browne," the central figure in the dramatic episode in 1617, referred to later), the Lords of the Council indited a long letter to the king. They cited the decision in Mason's case two years before, and the reasons for it. They expatiated on the great decay which had occurred in all trades and commerce in Scotland, and stated that the fishings would also decay if the duty was levied. In plain words they told the king that the fisheries should rather be encouraged—for the general welfare of the country, the increase of customs, the inbringing of bullion, and providing work for the poor. In face of the decree in Mason's case, the Duke's agents had to admit that they could not levy the tax from the burghs, but they craved leave to exact them from the native fishermen of Orkney and Shetland, and from the foreign fishermen who fished there. On the former point the opinion of the Council was clear. They upheld the contention of the burghs that the native fishermen were only their servants, since they paid wages to them for their labour, and that the herrings, being cured and barrelled on the sea, were exempt from assize duty, which could be exacted only on herrings brought fresh and

[1] *State Papers and Correspondence of Thomas, Earl of Melros*, i. 130.

[2] *Reg. Privy Council Scot.*, x. 231. *Rec. Convent. Roy. Burghs Scot.*, ii. 540.

"green" to land.[1] The Council evaded giving an opinion on the point of chief importance, the proposal to levy the tax on the foreign fishermen, all of whom cured their fish on board their vessels. There were, they said, according to information supplied by the burghs, "some strangers, especially of Holland," who claimed the liberty and privilege of fishing "by his Majesty's patent granted in their favour to fish in his Majesty's waters"; but the tenour of this patent was obscure and not known to them, and they had no record of it. They suggested that the king should ask his ambassador at The Hague to procure an authentic copy of it, to be sent to Scotland for inspection and consideration.[2]

Evidently the Council in Scotland were at this time as cautious as the Council in England in doing anything contrary to the treaties with the Netherlands. Had they sanctioned offhand the request of the Duke to exact the assize-herrings from the Hollanders, they would have taken the responsibility, without direct authority from the king, of an act which they knew might have serious consequences. They had no sympathy with the foreign fishermen, for complaints regarding them from the burghs were frequent. In 1611 the city of Edinburgh represented to them the "inconvenience" which was sustained

[1] The Lords of the Council to the king, 17th May 1614. *Melrose Papers*, i. 130. "It wes fundin," wrote the Lords, "by vniforme voices and consent, without ony kynd of contradictioun, that the assise dewytie aucht onlie to be payit for the hering brought freshe and greene to land, and that the hering whilkis ar maid, saltit, and barrellit vpoun the sea, and maid reddye for the transporte, hes nevir bene in vse to pay ony dewytie."

[2] *Loc. cit.* The "patent" was the treaty of 1594. See p. 81. It may be mentioned that Mason, in his petition to Charles I. (see p. 153 *note*), stated that in 1611 he collected "some part" of the assize-herrings, but that upon the marriage of the Princess Elizabeth (February 1613) "the States ambassador made suit to the king for the remission of the said assize-herrings due by their nation, which was granted." We have discovered no other evidence of this. Loose statements were often made on the subject by English writers and certain foreign authors, as Rapin (*Hist. d'Anglet.*, vii. 58), and Wagenaar (*Vaderl. Hist.*, ix. 318) following him, that the Dutch agreed to pay an annual sum for liberty to fish on the British coasts. The error was elaborated by others, as by Lediard in his great work (*Naval History of England*, i. 420), who says: "In the year 1608 (*sic*) King James published a proclamation prohibiting all foreign nations to fish on the coast of Great Britain. This prohibition, though general, was designed against the Dutch; and it occasioned the Treaty the year following whereby they engaged to pay an annual sum for leave to fish—an evident acknowledgment of the English Dominion of the Seas."

by the whole realm and by the merchants in particular through the non-observance of the Act of 1581, "anent the comming of schippis to burrowis in the west and north Isles be Flemings and uther nations"; and in the following year the "mater of the fischeing of the Flemins in the West and North Isles" was again brought up, and it was remitted to the burghs of Edinburgh and Dundee to draw up a supplication to the Privy Council to have the fishing by the Flemings in those places repressed.[1]

In view of the decision of the Privy Council, the Duke of Lennox did not at this time attempt to collect the tribute from the foreign fishermen at the North Isles. But two years later the political relations between this country and the Netherlands having become strained, the opportunity was seized to raise once more the question of the fishery and the exaction of the assize-herrings. Serious disputes involving retaliatory measures had broken out respecting the trade in cloth. In England strong resentment was aroused by an edict of the States prohibiting the importation of English dyed cloth. Winwood, now Secretary of State, wrote to Sir Dudley Carleton, who had taken his place at The Hague, that it was the opinion of "every true-hearted Englishman" that the king "ought to forbid all manner of intercourse between the Kingdoms and the United Provinces, and forbid the Hollanders, by a fresh reviving of former proclamations, to continue their yearly fishing upon our coasts."[2] The influence of this feeling was soon apparent. The Duke of Lennox was now instructed by the king to levy the assize-herrings from foreigners fishing at the North Isles, the grant, under the great seal of Scotland, being dated in June 1616; and to render his task more easy he obtained from Sir Noel Caron in the same month a letter of recommendation ("aanbevelingsbrief") to the captains of the Dutch convoying-ships. This letter was innocently given by Caron in the belief that it concerned the payment of dues on land at Shetland, which the busses had been accustomed to

[1] *Rec. Conv. Roy. Burghs Scot.*, ii. 323, 350, 354, 374.

[2] Winwood to Carleton, $\frac{14}{24}$ September 1616. *Letters from and to Sir Dudley Carleton, Knt., during his Embassy in Holland; from January* 161$\frac{5}{6}$ *to December* 1620, p. 52.

pay, and which were then payable to the Duke,[1] but it was made use of by the Duke's agent to cover the collection of the assize-herrings. The duty of collecting the tax was assigned to Mr John Brown, one of the Duke's deputies. The detailed instructions he received in 1616 do not appear to have been preserved, but they were probably similar to those issued a year or two later (see Appendix G). He was to proceed to the North Isles in one of the king's pinnaces and there to demand the assize duty from the foreign fishermen.

At the end of July 1616 Brown, in one of the king's vessels, appeared among the Dutch busses at work off the Scottish coast, and began to carry out his instructions, offering a "quittance or receipt" for the tax claimed. Probably to his surprise, it was peaceably paid by the busses, amounting for each to one angel or a barrel of herrings and twelve cod-fish. The fishermen were told that if they did not pay it the amount would be doubled in the following year; and that the king had a right to levy this tax for a distance of 100 miles from the coast in virtue of the agreement made with the States at the baptism of Prince Henry.[2] Although the toll was paid by most of the busses, it was without the consent of the captains of the convoying men-of-war. They came to Brown and demanded to see his commission; and it is said that he showed them the letter which the Duke of Lennox had obtained from Sir Noel Caron. Since no force had been used in collecting the tax, the

[1] Caron to the States-General, $\frac{\text{25 Aug.}}{\text{4 Sept.}}$ 1616. *Brit. Mus. Add. MSS.*, 17,677, J, fol. 152. In an account of the oppressions of Lord Robert Stewart in the Orkneys and Shetlands in the sixteenth century, it is stated that that nobleman laid heavy tolls upon the Dutch fishermen and the Norwegian traders. In 1575 the inhabitants complained that he compelled "the dogger boats and other fishers of this realm to pay to him great toll and taxis bye auld use and wont, to wit, ilk boat ane angel noble, ane hundreth fish, and twa bolls salt" (*Oppressions of the Sixteenth Century in the Islands of Orkney and Zetland*, xlviii. 4). It appears from a complaint of merchants of Bremen, in 1614, that it had been a custom "past memory of man" for each ship arriving at the Orkneys to pay six angels and one dollar for ground-leave and water-leave (*Reg. Privy Counc. Scot.*, x. 247); and the Dutch are said to have given to the agent of the Earl of Orkney a barrel of salt for his "oversight" of each ship, and to have offered the Earl for each ship "an angell and ane barrell of birskate (biscuit) bread," while he demanded "no less than ane double angell or ane Rose noble at the least" (*MSS. Advoc. Lib.*, 31. 2. 16).

[2] See p. 81. The treaty did not contain any stipulation of the kind; and, moreover, the Scottish copy was then amissing.

States' officers contented themselves with forbidding any further proceedings, and Brown then departed.[1]

The success of the mission was gratifying to James, and the payment willingly made on this occasion by the Dutch fishermen was often afterwards cited as an argument that they had acknowledged the king's rights in the fishery. In the United Provinces the matter was naturally viewed in another light. The Dutch officers promptly reported the occurrence to the directors of the Enkhuisen branch of the fishery; the authorities of the town complained to Barnevelt in energetic terms, and the matter was brought before a meeting of the States-General, who characterised the proceeding of Brown as an "unheard of and intolerable innovation, contrary to the existing treaties," and instructed their ambassador in London to make a strong protest against it. Orders were, moreover, issued to the commanders of the convoying ships of war to put a stop to any further payments, and even to refuse to give their names. Caron, who was indignant at the use to which his friendly letter had been put, complained to the king and to the Duke of Lennox. James explained that it was merely a small tribute or tax which was levied in Scotland on all foreign fishermen, and even on his own subjects, and had been leased to the Duke of Lennox, who paid an annual rent for it into the Exchequer. He had, he said, arranged that one of his ships of war should be stationed on the fishing-ground for the security of the fishermen and to protect them from pirates. Caron declared that their High Mightinesses were exempt from all imposts or taxes for their fishery, both by the treaties "and otherwise," and he begged the king to give other instructions, as the matter had occasioned great disquiet and alarm in Holland. Lennox also tried to minimise the importance of the measure. It was, he said, a small matter; a mere "acknowledgment" of a barrel of herrings or ten shillings from each buss, which had to be paid thrice a year by all the king's subjects who fished at the North Isles, and was willingly paid by the English, French, German, and all other foreign fishermen. The ambassador says he was shown a printed book in which it was stated that the Scottish Parliament had

[1] Muller, *Mare Clausum*, 107. *Brit. Mus. Add. MSS.*, 17,677, J, fol. 153 *et seq.* *Lansdowne MSS.*, 142, fol. 410. *Reg. Privy Counc. Scot.*, xi. 605, 608.

decreed that the assize-herrings should be paid not only by the native fishermen but by foreigners who came to fish on their coasts.[1] The latter were furthermore prohibited from approaching the coast nearer than they could see the land from the top of their masts, whereas of late they came within ten, eight, six, and even four miles of the shore, which had caused much murmuring in the country, particularly as in that year between 1500 and 1000 of their busses were there in June. Sir Noel Caron, however, continued to protest against what he said was an unjust innovation, and he closed the interview with the important declaration that, be the consequences what they might, the States would not allow a single herring to be paid in future, as it might be regarded as a precedent for further demands.[2]

Notwithstanding this strong protest from the Dutch ambassador, and a request he made to the king to forbear the right he claimed pending the appointment of a special embassy to treat of the matter, Brown was again sent to the North Isles in the next year to collect the king's dues from the herring fishers. This he attempted to do as quietly and inoffensively as possible, but his mission had an abrupt and dramatic termination. Immediately on his arrival among the busses, Captain Andrees Tlieff, the commander of one of the convoying ships from Rotterdam, formally refused the payment in the name of all the Netherland fishermen, handing to Brown a declaration to that effect in writing. Brown professed himself satisfied, and was about to leave Tlieff's vessel to proceed, as he said, among the fishermen of other countries, when the captain of the convoyer from Enkhuisen, Jan Albertsz by name, who had spoken to Brown in the previous year, came on board. He asked Brown if he was the person who had levied the tax in

[1] By the Scots Act, 1 James I., May 1424, regarding the "custome of horse, nolt, scheepe, had furth of the realm, and of herring," it was ordained that the following should be paid: "of ilk thousand of fresche herring sauld, of the Sellar one penny, and of ilk last of herring, tane be Scottis-men barrelled, foure schillinges, of ilk last be strangeris taken, sexe schillinges."

[2] Caron to the States-General, $\frac{25 \text{ Aug.}}{4 \text{ Sept.}}$, $\frac{12}{22}$ Sept., $\frac{19}{29}$ Sept. 1616. *Brit. Mus. Add. MSS.*, 17,677, J, fol. 152-166. The statement of Lennox that the tax was a barrel of herrings or ten shillings agrees with the statements of the Dutch skippers, who, however, added twelve cod-fish ("Een tonne harinck van elcke buÿsse oft een Angelott daervooren met twelff cabillauwen").

the year before, and on receiving a reply in the affirmative he at once arrested him, saying he had orders to that effect; and notwithstanding Brown's warning as to the consequences, and the exhibition of his commission, he was made prisoner by the irate Dutchman and carried off to Holland. Whether the king's pinnace had on this occasion, as two years later, more than "two small guns and ten muscattis" to represent the power and majesty of the British navy, does not appear. But Brown, meek and peaceful, was seemingly quite contented with his position. He wrote from the Dutch ship to Captain Murray, in charge of the king's pinnace, telling him of his arrest and advising him to make no attempt at rescue, but to return to Scotland and report the matter to the king.[1]

James received the news of the capture of Brown at Dumfries while on a visit to Scotland. He felt that the arrest of an officer of the state, discharging business of the state and with his Admiral's commission in his pocket, was an "insolent" personal affront to himself. The members of the Privy Council who were with him—and the Duke of Lennox was one of them—immediately wrote to the Council in London requesting them in the name of the king to arrest the masters of two or three Dutch ships in the Thames by way of reprisal, and to retain them as hostages; to inform Sir Noel Caron that reparation must be made by the States; and to instruct the British ambassador at The Hague to "demand satisfaction from them for this insolence offered to his Majesty." Winwood at once sent for Caron, and informed him of the "disgraceful affront" which had been put upon the king while his Majesty himself was in Scotland. The king, he said, was very sensible of their "injurious and scornful carriage," and immediate satisfaction and redress were demanded. Sir Dudley Carleton used even stronger language in addressing the States-General at The Hague. What, he asked, would the world say when they knew that a public officer and Minister of the King of England had been seized by them in Scotland, in sight of the ships of other nations and while the king himself was in that country? That the outrage was committed by the orders of the States

[1] Carleton, *Letters*, 156, 157. Muller, *op. cit.*, 110. *Brit. Mus. Add. MSS.*, 17,677, J, fol. 213*b*. *Lansdowne MSS.*, 142, fol. 410. *State Papers, Dom.* Collection, Charles II., vol. 339.

he did not believe; but the captains pretended they had a commission for what they did, and produced certain letters patent containing, as they said, an express commission from their masters. The ambassador concluded by requiring instant reparation and satisfaction.[1]

Meanwhile Brown himself had, perhaps, little cause for regret. He spent two days on board the Dutch man-of-war, and was then landed at Enkhuisen. The authorities of the town at once perceived the rashness of the step that had been taken by Captain Albertsz. Brown was immediately liberated, treated with the greatest courtesy, and conducted by one of the chief magistrates, with profuse apologies, to the British ambassador at The Hague. All his expenses were defrayed; he was presented with seventy "double Jacobus pieces" as a personal gift, and he left for home on 13th September. Count Maurice and Barnevelt promptly disavowed the act of Albertsz, and when the matter was brought before the States-General by Carleton, it fell to the lot of Grotius, in the absence of Barnevelt, to express the regret of the assembly for the "accident," and to request the British ambassador to put the case in writing for inquiry. In their reply later, the States-General threw the whole blame on the captains, Albertsz and Tlieff, who had, they said, acted without authority, and would be punished on their return from the fishing. They renewed their regrets, said that Brown had been immediately released, and begged that the Dutch merchant captains who had been thrown into prison in England and Scotland might be set free, and their "ancient accustomed liberty of fishing maintained." In preferring this request the States relied on their treaty with James in 1594, and the gracious answer he had given to their ambassadors in 1610 concerning the proclamation of the year before.[2]

If the States-General thought they were to get so easily out of the awkward position in which the precipitate action of their officers had placed them, they were disappointed. James not

[1] Carleton, *Letters*, 156. Caron to the States-General, $\frac{3}{13}$ Aug. 1617; Carleton to the States-General, $\frac{\text{27 Aug.}}{\text{6 Sept.}}$ *Brit. Mus. Add. MSS.*, 17,677, J, fol. 210, 213. *State Papers, Dom.* Collection, Charles II., vol. 339.

[2] Carleton, *Letters*, 168, 169, 172, 176, 186. Muller, *op. cit.*, 111.

only refused to release the Dutch ships, but said their masters would be detained in prison until the offending commanders had been sent as prisoners to England, there to receive such justice as their case merited. This request was most unpalatable to the States, and they raised various objections to it, founded both on law and privilege; and although they were assured by Carleton that the only punishment the offenders would receive would be "the crossing and re-crossing the seas," they begged that some other means might be found of settling the matter. James, however, who had submitted the case to counsel as to the legality of his demand, remained obdurate.[1] Finally, after much negotiation and debate, the States, in February 1618, resolved to send over the two captains to receive the personal rebuke of the king. Albertsz, the chief offender, fell ill and died, but Tlieff did actually come to England in April. Notwithstanding letters of recommendation from the States-General, Sir Noel Caron, and Sir Dudley Carleton (with whom Grotius had interceded), he was "very

[1] *Brit. Mus. Lansdowne MSS.*, 142, fol. 398, 400. "The State of the Case between his Majesty and the States of the United Provinces, touching the remanding to his Majesty of a Delinquent," 19th November 1617. In Cæsar's handwriting. It describes the circumstances of Brown's capture. The counsel whose opinion was obtained were "W. Byrde (? Sir Wm. Bird, Dean of the Arches), H. Marten, and Hy. Styward." "Brown, his Majesty's subject of the Kingdom of Scotland, was by authority from that State sent in a pinnace of the King to the subjects of the United Provinces, who were then fishing for herrings upon the coasts of Scotland, to demand a certain acknowledgment claimed by his Majesty, as due unto him in the right of that crown;" that "while delivering his errand he was arrested and carried prisoner to Holland by the Dutch commander, who pretended he had warrant and commission from the Lords the States so to do; that his Majesty (having represented this indignity by his ambassador there to the Lords the States, the latter disavowed the act of the captain) requireth the offender there, to be remanded unto himself here to receive as to justice shall appertain. *The Question*—Whether this offender ought to be sent herein to his Majesty as is required. *Answer*—There are good authorities that if a subject of one State commit a heinous crime within the territory of another State (though against a private person), the subject so offending ought to be remitted to the place where the crime was committed, if it be required." There were also opinions to the contrary, but "two very particular circumstances about this offence seem necessarily to enforce the remission of the Dutch captain to his Majesty (1) taken from the person of Brown, who was a public messenger sent by the State of Scotland on the affairs of the Prince, and ought to have been inviolable by the Law of Nations, and therefore a wrong and abuse done to him was *contra jus gentium;* (2) taken from the manner of the wrong done, which was *nomine publico*—viz., by a pretended commission from the Lords the States."

wrathfully" received by James, who scolded and rebuked him severely for the enormity of his offence, and then dismissed him without further punishment.[1] Thus ended an incident in the claims to *mare clausum* which almost led to a rupture between the two countries.

It would appear that James, though thus foiled in his attempt to levy the assize-herrings from the Hollander fishermen in 1617, did not intend to let the matter rest in the following season, and circumstances occurred which brought up the question of the "land-kenning" in another quarter. Early in 1618 the King of Denmark complained to him that Scottish fishermen were in the habit of fishing "within the waters of Faeröe," which was part of the dominions of Denmark, and that the native fishermen had been so much injured by their encroachments that they were unable to pay their dues and taxes. Here was a complaint against Scottish fishermen like that which they so commonly made against the Dutch. The complaint was brought before the Privy Council of Scotland, who summoned the burghs concerned[2] to appear and explain their conduct. They admitted that for some years they had gone to the Faeröe Isles to fish, but they said that they had been "driven thereto upon necessity, and by the violence and oppression of the Hollanders, who came yearly with two thousand sail and above within his Majesty's waters, and within a mile of the 'continent' of Orkney and Shetland, and not contented with the benefit that the liberty of their fishing within the said bounds affords yearly unto them, they do very heavily oppress his Majesty's poor subjects and fishers." They said that the Hollanders "stoppis thame, houndis and chaisis thame frome thair fischeing, cuttis thair nettis, threatnis thair lyveis, and thairby compellis thame, who ar a nomber of poore people haveing no other trade quhairby to manteene thair families, to seeke thair fischeing elsquhair and far frome thair awne coist, with grite tormoyll, travell, trouble, and chargeis."[3] The Lords of the Council, however, held that the oppression committed by the Hollanders on them was no warrant for their oppressing the

[1] Carleton, *Letters*, 219-263. Muller, *op. cit.*, 113.

[2] Crail, Anstruther, and Pittenweem, in Fife, and Musselburgh and Fisherrow, on the opposite side of the Firth of Forth.

[3] 12th March 1618. *Reg. Privy Counc. Scot.*, xi. 329.

subjects of other princes, and "that they ought not to have fished in the said waters without some license and oversight." A proclamation was thereupon issued by the king and Council forbidding Scottish fishermen "to fish within sight of the land of the Isle of Faeröe, but to reserve the [fishings there[1]] to the inhabitants of the said Isle, and to other" subjects of the King of Denmark, "conform to the law of nations," under a penalty of confiscation of the ships, vessels, and goods of the persons offending. At the same time the Council wrote to the king acquainting him with the oppressions committed by the Hollanders on the Scottish fishermen, and suggesting that his ambassador at The Hague should demand reparation and "instant prohibition" by the States to their people, "that they fish not within sight of his Majesty's land, but reserve these bounds to his Majesty's own subjects, conform to the law of nations."[2]

Sir Dudley Carleton accordingly made a strong representation to the States-General on the subject in April. They asked for particulars as to the persons who were alleged to have been ill-treated in Scotland, and the nature of the wrongs done to them; while with respect to the limit proposed to be set them in their fishery—namely, not to come within sight of land—they said they had never heard of any such custom, and did not understand how it could be put into practice.[3] On reporting this home, Carleton was told by the king to raise the question of the fishing again before he came away, and he explained to him that the custom of the land-kenning was that no stranger should fish either within the creeks of the land or within a kenning of the land, "as seamen do take a kenning." He asked Carleton to ascertain whether the Dutch claimed to fish wherever they liked, or were willing to accept reasonable bounds, adding that the resolution that might be taken on the subject would depend largely on this.[4]

[1] Record imperfect.

[2] *Reg. Privy Counc. Scot.*, xi. 328, 330.

[3] Carleton, *Letters*, 259.

[4] King James to Sir D. Carleton, 4th May 1618. "For the other part, which is y[e] ancient custom alleadged by O[r] Subjects that they (the Dutch) should not fish within Kenning of Land, of which they make shew to be ignorant, and would understand what is meant by it: you may say that O[r] Subjects do conceave that Custom to be that no strangers should fish either within the Creeks of O[r] Land or within a Kenning of the Land as Seamen do take a kenning, and insisting upon this interpretation of O[r] Subjects' meaning, you shall observe curiously their reply, and what scope and liberty they do limit to

A few months before this Carleton had brought similar complaints to the notice of the States-General, declaring that the Hollanders were daily guilty of "great outrages and insolencies on the Scottish fishermen." It was even said to be the opinion in London that the prosecution of the herring fishery by the Dutch under the protection of ships of war was a direct challenge to and defiance of the king.[1]

The authorities in Scotland lost no time in preparing statements recounting in detail the outrages and insolences committed by the Dutch fishermen; but an impartial perusal of the complaints leaves little doubt that they were greatly exaggerated. The Dutch fishermen were accused of going ashore in large numbers and chasing, taking, and slaying sheep; they "intromitted" with growing timber, trod down all the corn they could find, induced the best and ablest of the native fishermen to join them, or even took them by force; entered the kirks, where they broke down the seats and polluted the pulpits; carved their names on the green pastures; took uninvited rides on the horses in the fields, "to the great hurt of the owners"; and made free with the eggs and young of seafowl on the uninhabited isles, to the hurt of the proprietors. In the long catalogue of their supposed outrages on land, two were more important. It was alleged that they gave refuge to thieves and malefactors, so that justice could not reach them; and that some years before they seized an honest young woman who was selling stockings among them and held her head-downwards on an eminence in sight of the whole fleet, owing to which she died later. Among their offences at sea they were charged with shooting at native fishermen, "catching of their small netts and lynes

themselves in their fishing, and whether they understand that they may fish where they list, near or far off, or that they may be confined to any reasonable bounds, for thereupon will depend a great part of that resolution which may be taken hereafter in a matter of so great moment as this is, and the answer you shall receive you may either advertise by writing, or bring with you, as you shall find Or service to require." *State Papers, Dom.* Collections, Chas. II., vol. 339. In a later communication to the States-General Carleton described the land-kenning thus: "Ce qui est une limite bien entendue par gens de Marine, et appellée en ces quartiers là *The Kenning of the Land*, et icy *de kennis vant landt*." Dr P. P. C. Hoek informs me that "het land verkennen" is even now the technical Dutch expression when a sailor comes near the coast without knowing at what point he approaches it.

[1] Muller, *Mare Clausum*, 114.

within those huge long netts" that they used, and which they laid hard by the shore, "whereas before they approached not nearer the coasts than fourty (*sic*) myles." By fishing near the shore they had impoverished the whole trade of fishing; before they began to do so the herrings came close in, so that the poorest fisherman could enrich himself, while the shoals were now broken up and dispersed. So near did the busses come in stormy weather that they fished "hard by gentlemen's doors," where the fishing was "appropriate to the owners of the land nearest adjacent for their own fishing in the time of storms when they could not go to sea for the entertaining of their houses."[1]

Since the States-General appeared to be tardy in admitting the offences with which their fishermen were charged, the king wished strong measures to be taken by the Council in Scotland, and he instructed Lord Binning, his Secretary there, to take steps "for interrupting and staying the Hollanders to fish in his seas within sight of the land." The Council, however, pointed out in a very humble tone that inasmuch as it was a matter which concerned not only "thir Hollanders, who ar your Maiesties confederatis, pretending thair awne interes thairin, ather be right or lang possessioun," but also the whole of the kingdom, it would be better if the king's proposals were first imparted to the Privy Council in England. They requested, further, that the ambassador in Holland should again expostulate with the States as to the injuries caused to the king's subjects by their "unjust usurpation to fish within sight of his Majesty's land," and to urge them to issue a proclamation to prohibit, under heavy penalties, their people from all further fishing within his Majesty's seas, which, they said, ought by the Law of Nations to be exclusively reserved for his own subjects. They advised the king to make the States clearly understand that if they continued any longer in their "oppression," he would so provide for the maintenance of his right and the freeing of his people as his honour and justice

[1] Ane True Relatione of the Greifs and Wrangs qlks the Inhabitants of the Isles of Orknay and Schetland and Others his Maties Subjects Fishars within ye Kingdome of Scotland sustains be the Hollanders and Hamburghgers and wha within these few Zears are associat to the Hollanders in the Fishing within his Maties Seas in Scotland." *MSS. Advoc.*, 31. 2. 16. It may be noted that the custom referred to in the last paragraph was of Scandinavian origin.

required; and if the answer was not satisfactory he might then resolve upon the "next expedient," and the Council would be ready to obey whatever he should command.[1]

The States-General, while they did not go so far as the Council desired in prohibiting their fishermen from approaching near to the land, did all that they reasonably could do to prevent injuries being committed on the Scottish people. After an inquiry was made among those taking part in the great herring fishery, without any evidence being forthcoming in support of the Scottish complaints, they published an edict forbidding their subjects, under pain of severe punishment "as pirates and malefactors," from interfering with the Scottish fishermen, with whom they were enjoined to maintain "true friendship, neighbourliness, and good correspondence."[2] In forwarding a copy of this proclamation to the king, the States said that they had issued it for his satisfaction, and had given strict orders to their captains to apprehend any one who acted contrary to it. But they expressed the hope that he would not permit the fishermen of the United Provinces to be disturbed or troubled in the liberty and freedom of taking herrings throughout the whole sea, of which liberty they were in immemorial possession, and it had been confirmed to them by several treaties, in particular by that made in 1551 between the king's predecessor and Charles V. The prosperity of their country, it was added, depended on navigation, traffic, and fisheries, and the freedom of these had been provided for in treaties.[3] James, however, was far from satisfied. He sent on the missive to the Privy Council in Scotland, with the request that the rolls and registers should be searched to see if any record existed of any such treaty, whether "with the said Emperor or any other potentate of the Low Countries." The States, he said, had promised to send a copy of it, but they

[1] The Council to the king, 4th April 1618. *Melrose Papers*, i. 306, 307.

[2] 5th June 1618, *Groot Placaet-Boeck, inhoudende de Placaten ende Ordonnantien van de H.M. Heeren Staten Generael der Vereenighde Nederlanden, &c.*, i. 707. In Fraser's *Memorials of the Earls of Haddington* (ii. 66) there is printed the copy which King James sent to Lord Binning. Sir Thomas Hamilton became Lord Binning in 1613, the Earl of Melrose in 1619, and the Earl of Haddington in 1627.

[3] Answer by the States-General of the United Provinces to the Propositions of the Ambassador of James VI. relative to the Herring Fishery on the Coast of Scotland, 5th June 1618. Fraser, *Memorials*, ii. 65. *Resol.*, *St.-Gen.*, 5th, 6th June. Muller, *op. cit.*, 115.

had not done so, and in the meantime he would cause the rolls in London to be searched.[1]

The negotiations with the States-General dragged on throughout the summer without much result, and in August James took the sudden resolution again to demand from the Dutch fishermen the payment of the assize-herrings. This was doubtless caused by the receipt of a letter from Sir Dudley Carleton, informing him that the herring-fishers had gone that year to the coast of Scotland with extraordinary convoy, the number of their men-of-war having been doubled, and expressing the hope that notwithstanding this the king would send some one to make the usual demand in a peaceable manner; otherwise, said Carleton, the Hollanders "will think his Majesty has laid aside his pretension."[2] James accordingly wrote hurriedly to the Council at Edinburgh, saying it was necessary to make requisition of his duties from the Hollanders fishing on the coasts of Orkney and Shetland, in order both to keep possession of the fishing and to foil any plea from the States-General that no such duties had been demanded of them. He had intended, he said, to send a ship of war, but those which were ready were otherwise engaged, and there would not be time to equip a vessel in England before the Hollanders returned from the fishing. The Council were therefore instructed to fit out with all expedition either his own pinnace or any other ship which could conveniently be procured, and to send it to the North Isles with such person as the deputy of the Duke of Lennox should choose, who was to be instructed "in fair tearmes and calme and peciable maner to crave oure said dewties, and accept of any suche answer as they sall gif him, without making any furder questioun or dispute in the mater."[3] Here was another Brown mission over again; but James forgot, if indeed he ever knew, that at that time of year the Dutch herring

[1] The king to Lord Binning, 11th June 1618. Fraser, *Memorials*, ii. 85. Nothing seemed to be known of this treaty. James complained that the States were not explicit. "This pointe" about the treaty, he wrote, "they leave obscure, seeing they neyther expresse which of our predecessouris it was, neyther whether he were our predecessour in Scotlande or Englande."

[2] Carleton to Naunton, 19th August 1618.

[3] The king to the Privy Council, 29th August 1618. *Reg. Privy Counc. Scot.*, xi. 440.

fishermen would be very far from the North Isles, and fishing along the English coast.[1] The fact was well known at Edinburgh, but, for whatever reason, it was not pointed out to the king; and the Council, urged to use "exceeding great haste," chartered a Leith vessel, the *Restore*, put Mr Patrick Bruce on board to demand the tax from the Hollanders, along with a notary "to give instruments thereupon," and despatched it on its bootless errand to the Shetlands. No Hollanders could be discovered, and the *Restore* came back to Leith.

The reason of the king's action, as well as of Carleton's advice, is doubtless to be sought in the desire to strengthen the case against the Dutch in view of an expected special embassy from The Hague, whose appointment was now mooted, and which was designed to settle various differences between the two countries that had become acute. Besides the herring fishery, which was a never-failing subject of dispute, there was the trade in cloth, the East Indies, and the "Greenland" whale fishery, about which it is necessary to say something here.

Allusion has already been made to this phase of the controversy respecting *mare clausum* which sprang up in the Arctic seas, and was now mixed up with the question of the liberty of fishing on the British coasts. Towards the end of the previous century English whalers, for the most part in the service of the Russia or Muscovy Company, frequented the coasts of Greenland, and the northern seas which had been opened up to English enterprise by the voyages of Willoughby and Chancellor;[2] and early in the next century they also began to catch whales at Spitzbergen, where they were found in enormous numbers.[3] The whalers of other nations followed in their wake, and in 1612 two Dutch vessels arrived at Spitzbergen to take part in the fishery, and although from their ignorance of the methods they failed of success that year, a company (*Noordsche Compagnie*) was formed at Amsterdam to continue the venture under better conditions.[4] The Muscovy Company, whose

[1] P. 131.

[2] Hakluyt's *Voyages*, i. 246.

[3] M'Pherson, *Annals of Commerce*, ii. 213.

[4] Muller, *op. cit.*, 118. In a memorandum drawn up by Sir John Coke in 1625, the Dutch are said to have first "intruded" in 1613. *State Papers, Dom.*, Chas. I., dxxii. 136. See also *Brit. Mus. Lansdowne MSS.*, 142, fol. 387 *et seq.*

whalers in 1612 got within nine degrees of the North Pole, sighting 700 whales and bringing back 17,[1] became jealous of competitors. In 1613 they procured from King James a charter by which they were entitled to exclude all others, foreigners as well as subjects, from sailing to Spitzbergen; and in that year they dispatched thither a fleet of seven armed vessels to defend their rights by force as well as

Fig. 8.—*Dutch Whalers at Spitzbergen.* After Van der Meulen.

to catch whales.[2] In the seas at Spitzbergen they found a number of other whalers from Spain and France, as well as two Dutch ships which had returned to the fishery. The English vessels immediately attacked them, and drove most

[1] Earl of Northampton to King James, August 2, 1612. *State Papers, Dom.*, lxx. 23.

[2] Chamberlain to Carleton, 27th October 1613. *Ibid.*, lxxiv. 89. M'Pherson, *Annals*, ii. 273.

of the intruders away.[1] The Englishmen then set up a cross on the shore with the king's arms on it, and they called the land "King James's Newland." It is noteworthy as indicating the attitude and practice towards France throughout almost the whole of the disputes about *mare clausum*, that the French whalers were allowed to continue their operations, subject, however, to the payment of a tribute of whales or train-oil, while the two Dutch ships were despoiled of their catches and fishing-gear and were sent home empty. On their arrival at Amsterdam the ill-treatment to which they had been subjected was naturally resented, and representations to King James were made through the ordinary channels, but without success. The Dutch founded their case partly on the general principle "that according to the practice of all times and peoples, navigation, fishery, and the use of the shore were free and common to all," and partly on the claim of prior discovery. Spitzbergen, they said, was discovered by Jakob van Heemskerk, a Dutchman, in 1596; they had therefore at least as good a right as the English or any other nation to the fisheries there. On the other hand, the powerful Muscovy Company argued that Spitzbergen was discovered by Willoughby in 1553, and accordingly belonged to England; and the king adopted this view, notwithstanding the elaborate case drawn up by the famous cosmographer, Plancius, on the other side, which was submitted to him.[2] The seas around Spitzbergen were held to pertain to the British seas, and to be under the maritime dominion of the King of England,—a claim which Selden attempted to vindicate later.

[1] M'Pherson, *Annals*, ii. 274. Winwood, *Memorials*, iii. 480. M'Pherson speaks of fifteen Dutch, French, and Biscay whalers and four English "interlopers." Muller (*Mare Clausum*, 120), quoting from a contemporary Dutch account, mentions three Biscayers, three Spaniards, two French, one Dunkirker, and two Hollanders. Both the Spanish and French Governments protested against the action of the English vessels. Digby wrote from Madrid (4th September 1613) that the English merchants at St Sebastian were threatened in person and goods on the return of the Spanish ships which had been prevented from fishing at "Greenland," and they were forced to remain indoors.

[2] A Trew Declaracion of the Discoverie of the mayne Landes, Islandes, Seas, Ports, Havens, and Creekes, lyenge in the North-West, North, and North-East partes of the World, *State Papers, Dom.*, lxxvi. 51. Muller, *op. cit.*, 121, 123. Carleton, *Letters*, 7.

Having failed by diplomacy to obtain recognition of what they believed to be their plain rights, the States resolved to oppose force by force. Early in 1614 a new Dutch company was formed, and exclusive privileges were conferred on it "to navigate, trade, and fish, from the Netherlands on or to the coasts of the lands between Nova Zembla and Davis' Straits," including therefore Greenland and Spitzbergen.[1] A tax of "last-money" was established, and in the same year eighteen Dutch whalers, armed, and convoyed by three States' men-of-war, left Holland for the Arctic seas, prepared to maintain their right to freedom of fishery by fighting for it if necessary. The English whalers did not venture to attack so powerful a squadron, and as the Hollanders came in 1615 and 1616 in even greater force, they were for these three years enabled to carry on their whale-fishing without molestation. In 1617, however, their convoyers having been reduced in numbers, they were again assailed by the English; one of the Dutch vessels was despoiled, and their "cookeries," or the buildings on shore in which the oil was made, were destroyed. Then in 1618 the Dutch reappeared, and in strength sufficient not only to maintain the right they claimed, but to make reprisals. They attacked, despoiled, and drove off thirteen English ships, most of which returned to England empty, and the Muscovy Company were loud in their complaints to the king. They put their loss at £66,436, 15s., besides the spoiling of the ships and the killing of the men.[2]

At this time, as we have seen, James was pressing more than ever for the recognition of his claims to the herring fishery in the British seas, and it may be easily imagined how he was moved by the news of this fresh "outrage" at Spitzbergen. At a meeting of the States-General in October, the British ambassador used strong language in animadverting on these "violencies, robberies, and murders" committed by the Dutch on the king's subjects in the Arctic seas, on the injuries inflicted on the English in the East Indies, and on other matters in dispute; and he demanded that the embassy so

[1] *Groot Placaet-Boeck*, i. 670. Aitzema, *Saken van Staet en Oorlogh*, ii. 336. *State Papers*, *Dom.*, xcix. 36.

[2] *Ibid.*, xcix. 36-41. M'Pherson, *Annals*, ii. 287. Muller, *op. cit.*, 131.

repeatedly promised by the States should be sent to England without any further delay. The embassy in question had been originally proposed by the Dutch with the view of arranging the differences as to the trade in cloth and the herring fishery. Their diplomacy through the ordinary channels had, however, been so successful in preserving their freedom of fishing, notwithstanding the harassing efforts of the king, whom they invariably foiled, that they preferred to procrastinate, and the proposed embassy had from time to time been put off. But now the minatory demands of Sir Dudley Carleton were reinforced by the insistence of the Dutch East India Company, for it had been proposed in England to arrest the vessels of that company in the Channel in reprisal for the wrongs done to the English in the East Indies, and one of their ships had just narrowly escaped capture.[1]

The Dutch ambassadors arrived in England on 27th November;[2] but notwithstanding the earnest exhortations of Carleton, their instructions were confined to the "Greenland" (Spitzbergen) and East Indian questions, and did not contain what the king most desired—full powers to treat on the herring fishery.

James had been looking forward to this embassy as providing an opportunity for the final settlement of the fishery dispute. Sir Dudley Carleton had informed the States-General that the king wished to go into the matter of the treaties on which their claim to liberty of fishing was in great measure based, adding jesuitically that it was probably with the view of confirming them. The king in reality felt that owing to the dissensions in the Low Countries and the general political state of Europe, the time was specially opportune for negotiating a treaty in his favour.[3] He had accordingly made

[1] Carleton, *Letters*, 312.

[2] They were Johan van Goch, Ewout van der Dussen for Gelderland and Holland, and Joachim Liens for Zealand. Holland had at first intended to send Grotius. *Ibid.*, 306.

[3] Among the Cæsar papers in the British Museum (*Lansd. MSS.*, 142, fol. 383) there is one dated 23rd December 1618, containing extracts "noted out of a book called *Mare Liberum sive de Jure quod Batavia, &c.*, Lugd. Bat., 1609," together with notes from Welwood's *De Dominio Maris*, answering the assertions in that book. It was doubtless a memorandum to be used in the conferences with the Dutch ambassadors; and on the back of it are scrawled jottings difficult to decipher, headed, "The Kinges Speeche touching the Dutchemen's fishing upon

considerable preparations to meet their arguments both with reference to the treaties and the Law of Nations. Early in November he wrote to the Council at Edinburgh, saying that the wrongs suffered by his Scottish subjects from the fishing of the Hollanders in the seas of Scotland had caused him to bring the matter before the States, and to acquaint them of his "resolution to have them duly repaired." The States had signified their desire to have their rights and the actions of their subjects "orderly tried and determined," and they were therefore about to send over commissioners "sufficiently authorised" for that purpose. As commissioners to meet them, he had chosen the Duke of Lennox, the Marquis of Hamilton, Lord Binning (Secretary), and Sir George Hay (Clerk of Register), and he asked the Council to expedite the issue of their commission under the great seal. He also desired them to send him, in writing, the most perfect information they could procure as to his right to exclude the States from their pretended right or alleged possession of the herring-fishing, with full particulars of the wrongs committed by the Dutch on the Scottish people, either by scattering the shoals of herrings or by "usurpation of farder libertie to themselves nor hes bene formerlie granted or tolerated be us or our prediceesoris to them."[1]

The commissioners named were accordingly authorised to treat with the Dutch commissioners "anent the trial and verification of the rights, immunities, and privileges alleged to have been granted by his Majesty or any of his most noble progenitors, Kings of Scotland, to the said States-General of the United Provinces, or any others from whom they deduce and derive their claim to fish in the seas of the said kingdom of Scotland, or any part or place thereof." They were further instructed to treat as to the redress required for the injuries

the coasts of Great Britain and Ireland," to the following effect: "1. The treaty never so opportune as now when they fearest it most and their State least settled; in ill terms with France and Spain. 2. In the East Indies we can match them, and so in the north voyage (Greenland?). The French King taketh part with Barnevelt. The King of Spain prepareth against Venice. What the King of Denmark, the Princes of the Union, the . . . and the rest of the Protestants think of any falling out with the Low Countries." It may be noted that this memorandum contains no reference to Selden's *Mare Clausum*, which the author stated was submitted to the king this year (see p. 366).

[1] The king to the Council, 7th November 1618. *Reg. Privy Counc. Scot.*, xi. 631.

committed by the Dutch fishermen, and for preventing in future any unlawful proceeding by the States, "either by fishing in his Majesty's Scottish seas" or by doing wrong to the inhabitants. They were, moreover, "to concur" with the English commissioners to be appointed as to the "friendly behaviour" of British subjects and the subjects of the United Provinces in all other seas, fishings, voyages, and other foreign intercourse, necessary for the continuance of peace and amity.[1] The business of the herring fishery was thus placed in charge of the Scottish commissioners, while the English had specially to deal with the other subjects in dispute—the East Indian trade, the whale fishery, the coinage, and the trade in cloth. Towards the end of November Lord Binning informed the king that the Council had sent off the commission, together with a statement of the injury sustained by the whole kingdom by the daily increase of the Dutch usurpation in his seas.[2]

With regard to the other matter about which James had desired "the most perfect information,"—his right to exclude foreigners from fishing on his coasts,—the Council had the greatest difficulty in discovering anything whatever pertaining to it. It was the most important part of the question to come before the commissioners, because the States had already issued a strongly-worded edict forbidding their people from committing any wrongs upon the Scottish people (p. 179), and the king could scarcely make out a just case for prohibiting the Hollanders from fishing on this ground alone. He desired to show, what he no doubt fully believed, that his claims were supported by historical precedents and the laws of Scotland, and that none of the treaties on which the Dutch always relied in such negotiations were contrary to his claims. In his letter to the Council he therefore repeated the request that the public records should be searched, and desired that Lords Lauderdale and Balmerino,

[1] *Reg. Privy Counc. Scot.*, xi. 462.

[2] Lord Binning to the king, 27th November 1618. *Melrose Papers*, ii. 631. The statement was to the same effect as that previously referred to. A Mr Bruce of Shetland stated that while of old the Hollanders used to carry on the greater part of their fishery forty miles and more from the land, yet they came usually within fourteen miles before shooting their nets; that in the time of the late Earl of Orkney they came still nearer, within six or seven miles; while now they came so close that their nets were sometimes torn on the rocks. Sir Gideon Murray to Lord Binning, 26th November 1618. *MSS. Advoc.*, 31. 2. 16.

the Laird of Lundy, and others into whose hands such documents might have come, "from their ancestors, Chancellors, secretaries, clerks of register, ambassadors, or councillors of state," should try to find any which bore upon the matter, and to have them forwarded to him without delay. The terms of the king's letter show plainly enough the confusion and imperfection of the Scottish state records at that time; and the Lords of the Council sought high and low to discover copies of the treaties or any other official papers relating to the subject, but for a long time without any success. Copies of some of the treaties were afterwards found, but nothing to establish the king's right to exclude the Hollanders from the fishery. In these circumstances the Council advised the commissioners "to proceed warily," and to make the Dutch ambassadors produce what they had to show for their claim to the fishing, and then to answer that.[1]

But as things turned out, it was of no immediate importance whether or not the Scottish commissioners were armed with documentary proofs of the king's claims to the fishery. The Dutch ambassadors, as has been said, came without any powers to treat on that subject. In their private instructions, indeed, they were enjoined to avoid carefully any discussion about the herring fishery. If it was forced upon them, they were to point out that the States had already issued a proclamation to prevent wrongs being done to Scottish fishermen, which would be strictly enforced. If this was not sufficient, they were to fall back on general arguments as to the natural freedom of the sea, their

[1] Earl of Dunfermline to Lord Binning, 27th November 1618. *MSS. Ibid.* "Concerning the Hollanders fishing in our seas," he said, "for all the search and tryall I have made, whilk has been my uttermost, I can wryte or send to you little more nor before, in effect nothing." The Constable of Dundee searched all his records, the records of the Admiralty were explored, and all those in Edinburgh Castle and in the city archives, as well as many in the keeping of private persons, and every one likely to know anything about the matter was communicated with; but "nothing to the purpose" was found, "nor no recorde of any wryte made for the Hollanders' use in 1594 or any other time." The "wryte" of 1594, it is to be remembered, was a long treaty made by James himself. Copies were ultimately discovered of the treaties of 1531 and 1541, but nothing to the point. Copies of the treaty and of other documents referring to it were obtained, apparently from Holland, in 1619, and were ordered to be preserved in his Majesty's Register in Edinburgh Castle (*Reg. Privy Counc. Scot.*, xii. 22); but in 1630 and 1631, when they were again wanted, they could not be found. *State Papers, Dom.*, Chas. I., ccvi. 46.

immemorial possession of the fishery and its paramount importance to their country, and to plead for delay on account of the confusion and difficulties of their home affairs.

On their arrival in London they were met by two high Scottish personages, who had been awaiting their coming for some weeks. They took this for a bad sign, concluding from it that the king was resolved to raise the fishery question. They had several interviews with the Council and the king. On finding that their instructions limited them to the discussion of the two points on which there was least anxiety in England, the East India business and the whale-fishing, the Council received them coldly, Bacon indeed rating them soundly for coming without adequate powers. James himself was very angry, and made no effort to conceal his disappointment. He expressed astonishment that after all the complaints that had been made, and after all the negotiations that had gone on through the ambassadors at London and The Hague, they had ventured to come unprepared to deal with the principal matter in dispute. "The fishing," he told them, "on the coasts of England, Scotland, and Ireland, as a regality and point of sovereignty, was possessed by him alone, to the exclusion of all others." Spain, he said, had asked leave to negotiate about freedom of fishing, while France enjoyed the privilege only under great limitations, a few small vessels being allowed to fish for the use of the Court and the king's family.[1] How little becoming was it therefore, continued James with heat, that a Republic which had only been recognised for a few years should be the first to contest his sovereign rights! It was useless for them to plead unprofitable years and immemorial possession. He was king of the greatest islands in the world, and he knew very well the rights he had on the coasts of his three kingdoms.[2] He further informed them that he was bound by oath at his coronation to maintain the rights, liberties, and privileges of his crown, and that he would rather lose all that he had than give

1 This referred to the licenses to certain French boats to fish on the Sowe in the Channel. See p. 65.

2 "Zijne mat was een coninck van de grootste insulen van de werelt ende seer wel wiste het rechte dat hij hadde opte custen van sijne drij coninckrijcken." Commissioners to States-General, $\frac{\text{24 Dec. 1618}}{\text{3 Jan. 1619}}$. *Brit. Mus. Add. MSS.*, 17,677, J, fol. 372.

up his right to the fishings.[1] Declarations equally strong were expressed in despatches to the British ambassador at The Hague. The king, it was said, would not be taught the laws of nations "by them nor their Grotius." [2] It would be to their advantage to ask the king's leave for the fishing and to acknowledge his right as other princes had done, or it might well come to pass "that they that will needs bear all the world before them with their *Mare Liberum*, may soon come to have neither *Terram et solum* nor *Rempublicam Liberam*,"—phrases which lead one to think that James penned the missive himself.[2] The Council intimated to the ambassadors that the king declined to discuss only the two points mentioned in their instructions, and that they must get powers from the States-General to deal with the question of the herring fishery.

Language of this kind from the king and Council disturbed and perplexed the envoys. They were anxious that the friendly relations between the two countries should be strengthened, and yet it appeared not unlikely that they would have to return home without having been heard on any of the matters in dispute. They began to think that after all it would be better if the fishery question were taken up and settled, and they advised the States-General in that sense. The British ambassador at The Hague was using pressure with the same object. But the Prince of Orange told him that in his opinion the States of Holland would refuse to give authority for the fishery question to be opened, "for fear of the people," because the livelihood of 50,000 of the inhabitants of that province depended on the herring-fishing, and they feared that the same thing would happen with the tribute the king claimed as had happened with the dues at the Sound, which had been gradually raised until they had become an intolerable burden. He threw out the suggestion at the same time that perhaps the freedom of fishing might be purchased by a lump sum. A little later Carleton proposed to the States-General that the three subjects omitted from the ambassadors' instructions should also be brought into the negotiations — viz., the trade in cloth, the coinage, and especially the herring fishery. In a minatory

[1] Note of Treatie with the Commissioners of the Estates annent the Fishing. Dec. 1618. *MSS. Advoc.*, 31. 2. 16.

[2] Naunton to Carleton, 21st December 1618.

speech he declared that the king, who had "a legitimate title and the exclusive sovereign right and propriety to the fishery on the coasts of his three kingdoms," would not any longer permit the subjects of the United Provinces to encroach on his rights, which were recognised by all other princes and states. The condition of affairs, he said, had been brought to extremities by the extravagant discourses of one of their politicians and the violent conduct of the commanders of their ships.[1] Sweeping aside the treaties and the claim to immemorial possession, and using much the same language as the king had done as to the hardihood of a young republic flouting the sovereign rights of princes, he ended a long harangue by declaring that if there was any further delay in dealing with the fishery question, England would take measures to provide for her rights by force of arms, "for such," he said, "was the demand of the people, the advice of the Council, and the resolution of the king."

But all those strong speeches and brave words came to nothing. The leaders in the States knew the character and difficulties of James, and felt that the warlike threats of a monarch whose greatest desire was that he should be known as *Rex pacificus*[2] were not likely to be carried to the extremity of the sword. A little more delay brought about a change in the English attitude. In the Privy Council there were signs of wavering and evident hesitation to recommend extreme measures against an allied and Protestant state. In the political condition of Europe—troubles in Bohemia, the King of Spain threatening the overthrow of Venice, &c.—it was urged that harsh measures might drive the Dutch to have recourse to France, which supported Barnevelt, the king's enemy. Above all, it was feared that the Protestants throughout the world would be unable to understand how the king could attack the Dutch at that critical time over so small a matter. On the whole, "for the sake of the peace of Christendom," it might be better to "continue" the question to another time, and thus avoid an immediate rupture. The faltering in the Council coincided with a humbler tone on the part of the Dutch

[1] In apprehending Brown, p. 171. Grotius was then in prison, and known to be the author of *Mare Liberum.*

[2] *State Papers, Dom.*, xc. 65.

ambassadors. They strove to convince James that it was by no means the desire of the States to refuse to treat of the fishery, or absolutely to deny his right to regulate it on his own coasts. All they asked was that the matter might be delayed a little owing to the religious troubles which were raging in the Netherlands, and because as all the provinces were concerned and the records and treaties would have to be searched, it would take some time before they would be in a position to deal with it in an equitable way. The States-General used language equally conciliatory to Sir Dudley Carleton, and promised to send other ambassadors later, fully empowered to treat of the herring fishery and the trade in cloth. James was appeased and agreed to the delay, but he told the ambassadors that unless the States gave an undertaking in writing to send commissioners sufficiently authorised to settle the matter before a year had expired, he would take it as "a plain and perpetual declining of the treaty."[1]

Thus James was again baffled in his endeavour to force the United Provinces to acknowledge his rights in the fishery. But scarcely had the arrangement been completed when he brought forward another proposal. Pending the conclusion of the final treaty, he wished the States to issue a provisional edict forbidding their fishermen from approaching within fourteen miles of the British coasts, to which they had been coming closer and closer in recent years, a proceeding which was the principal cause of the complaints from Scotland.[2] The distance mentioned was that embodied in the Draft Treaty of Union in 1604, and was supposed to be equivalent to a "land-kenning."[3]

1 The Dutch Commissioners to the States-General, $\frac{\text{29 Nov.,}}{\text{9 Dec.,}}$ $\frac{17}{27}$ Dec. 1618; $\frac{\text{24 Dec. 1618,}}{\text{3 Jan. 1619,}}$ $\frac{3}{13}$ Jan., $\frac{\text{23 Jan.}}{\text{2 Feb.}}$ 1619. *Brit. Mus. Add. MSS.*, 17,677, J, fol. 364, 367, 370, 374, 380. Muller, *op. cit.*, 140, 147, 148, 153. Aitzema, *Saken van Staet*, ii. 402. Carleton, *Letters*, 326. *MSS. Advoc.*, 31. 2. 16. *State Papers, Dom.* Collection, Chas. II., vol. 339, p. 351, 361, 369, &c.

2 The Dutch Commissioners to the States-General, $\frac{\text{30 Jan.}}{\text{9 Feb.}}$ 1619. *Ibid.*, 387. Naunton to Carleton, 21st January 1619. Carleton, *Letters.* Justice, *A General Treatise of the Dominion and Laws of the Sea*, 179. The States were desired "to cause proclamation to be made, prohibiting any of their subjects to fish within fourteen miles of his Majesty's coasts this year, or in any time hereafter, until order be taken by commissioners to be authorised on both sides, for a final settling of the main business."

3 P. 223.

Carleton, however, thought the States would not immediately agree to this,—their cumbersome system of government would alone cause great delay,—and he counselled the king "to begin with the fishers themselves," by publishing a proclamation fixing the distance at which they would be permitted to fish.[1] But the States were disposed to go so far to meet the wishes of the king. They objected, indeed, that fourteen miles was a greater distance than that at which a person could see the coast from the sea, and thus exceeded a "land-kenning" or the range of vision, but they promised to issue orders to their fishermen to keep so far from the land as to be out of sight of people on the shore, and to strongly prohibit them from going nearer.[2]

The business of the herring fishery having thus been shelved, the negotiators took up the other matters in dispute. The East Indian question was settled by a treaty,[3] but the differences as to the whale fishery were not so easily adjusted. The English case was founded on the contention that Spitzbergen belonged to King James, on their prior fishing in those seas, and on the depredations committed by the Dutch in 1618 on English vessels. The Dutch claimed a right to the fishery from their discovery of the island, and they proposed three alternatives: (1) that both nations should fish at Spitzbergen with an equal number of ships, the bays to be divided by drawing lots;[4] (2) that fishing should be carried on by both parties everywhere with an equal number of ships of equal size, disputes to be settled by regulations; (3) that the island should be divided by an imaginary line into two equal parts, the Dutch to have one part and the English the other. The English declined all these proposals, and James informed the ambassadors that even if the island had been discovered by their nation the English had the right to the fishery because they were the first to practise it,—an argument which, it may be remarked, if applied to the herring fishery, would have been unfortunate for the king's claim to it. But while maintaining his abstract right to the sea at

[1] Carleton to the king, 6th February 1619.

[2] Muller, *op. cit.*, 156. "So verre van 't Lant souden blijven als men met oogen konde afsien."

[3] 2nd June 1619. Dumont, *Corps Diplomatique*, V. ii. 333.

[4] The English, who were the first to carry on the whale-fishing at Spitzbergen, had taken possession of the best fishing-places: whales then abounded in the bays close to the shore, where the "cookeries" were erected.

Spitzbergen, James gave way on the immediately practical point, consenting that the Dutch should continue their fishery at the island for three years longer.[1]

We have mentioned that late in 1618 James caused the Scottish Council to send a vessel (the *Restore*) to the Shetlands to demand the assize-herrings from the Dutchmen, and that it arrived on the scene too late. Next year he resolved to be in time, and while the Dutch ambassadors were still in London he wrote to the Council saying it was necessary "for divers imperative reasons" that the duties should still be craved, and requesting them to send a ship that summer with some discreet person on board, "who in fair terms may require our duties of the said Hollanders and report their answer"; and the Council were desired to take special care that the business should not fail through negligence.[2] At a meeting of the Council at Holyrood House on 29th June, arrangements were made to carry out the king's wishes. Mr John Fenton was appointed "his Majesty's commissioner" for "craving his Majesty's rent of assize and teind from the Hollanders and other strangers fishing in his Majesty's seas," and a Mr James Brown was instructed to accompany him as notary.[3] Fenton's commission, under the

[1] Muller, *op. cit.*, 160. *State Papers, Dom.*, cv. 9. The Muscovy Company, now supported by the East India Company, fitted out nine ships and two pinnaces for the Spitzbergen fishery in 1619, but the voyage was unfortunate. After carrying on the fishing for a few years longer the company abandoned it, though it was carried on on a small scale by other English vessels, mostly from Hull. The Dutch, on the other hand, prosecuted the fishing with great vigour and success under the protection of men-of-war, and they rapidly made it one of the most profitable industries of the Low Countries. A full account is given by Zorgdrager, an old whaling captain, who wrote in the early part of the eighteenth century (*Bloeijende opkomst der aloude en hedendaagsche Groenlandsche Visscherij*). The Dutch factory on Amsterdam island grew to a village called Smeerenburg or Oil-town, which was fortified in 1636. In those early years the whales were taken by the ships' boats, which lay moored in the bays; later, as the whales got scarce, they were flensed at sea and the blubber carried home. This was the case before F. Martens visited the island in 1671.

[2] The king to the Privy Council of Scotland, 16th June 1619. *Reg. Privy Counc. Scot.*, xi. 607.

[3] Since the records of the Scottish Council are silent as to the steps taken to collect the assize-herrings in 1616 and 1617 and the capture of John Brown in the latter year, while the Dutch and English records are equally mute as to the proceedings in 1618 and 1619, it at first appeared that a mistake might have been made in the dates of the former, a view that seemed to be supported by the remark in the first letter of the king to the Council, "to the intent that the

great seal, commanded him to repair to the north seas, and there "in his Majesty's name to ask, crave, receive, intromit with, and uplift from those of Holland, Zealand, Hamburg, Embden, and Rostock, and from all other strangers following the trade of fishing in his Majesty's said seas this present year, his Majesty's rent of assize and teind of the whole fishes taken, or to be taken by them in his Majesty's said seas and waters this present year." The tribute levied by John Brown, in 1616, on behalf of the Duke of Lennox, amounted to only one angel (about ten shillings) or a barrel of herrings from each buss, or twelve cod from a line-boat. But that claimed by the king was now considerably greater. The "assize" was to be computed at ten thousand herrings (which would be fully ten barrels) for every buss that fished for herrings, and a last of white fish for every buss that fished for white fish, that is to say, cod and ling; or, if the fishermen preferred to pay in money, they were to pay at the rate of £6, 13s. 4d. Scots for every thousand of the assize-herrings, and at the rate of £50 Scots for every last of the assize white fish; and the same equivalents were to be asked for each thousand "teind herrings," and for each last of "teind white fish,"—a new duty now first mentioned, "teinds" being the Scottish term for ecclesiastical tithes. The value of the assize-herrings to be levied from each buss was thus about £5, 11s. 1d. sterling, and the value of the assize white fish from each dogger about £4, 3s. 4d. On the basis of two thousand Dutch herring vessels the total duty would amount to the respectable sum of about £11,000, while the dogger-boats would yield some £1500 additional. On receiving payment Fenton was to give an "aquittance and discharge," which would be as valid and sufficient as if given

Estaitis may not alledge that no suche dewteis had bene demandit"—a curious statement in face of the fact that Brown had been carried to Holland the year before. But the late Professor Masson, who was the editor of the *Register of the Privy Council*, obligingly informed me that the documents are the original *Acta* and not copies; and among the English State Papers is a letter dated from Holyrood House, on 10th July 1619, in which it is stated that Captain Murray had been sent to claim the assize-herrings from the "Flemings" fishing in the northern seas, and that he was well equipped to secure his safety if his demands were refused (Raith to Abercromby, *State Papers, Dom.*, cix. 127). The phrase in the king's letter may be explained by the fact that the duty in 1616 and 1617 was demanded by the Duke of Lennox, to whom the assize-herrings had been granted.

by his Majesty's comptrollers or ordinary receivers of his Majesty's rents.[1]

In the particular instructions given to Fenton,[2] and which, there are reasons for thinking, were essentially the same as those previously given to Brown, he was enjoined to proceed to the north seas in H.M.S. *Charles*, under the command of Captain David Murray, and in the first place to inquire the names of the admirals and vice-admirals of the Dutch fleet, the names of their ships, to what towns and provinces they belonged, and also the number of the convoys and busses sent out to the fishing by every town, province, and state. This having been done, he was "in fair and gentle terms and with modesty and discretion" to demand from the admirals or vice-admirals, and from two or three of the convoyers and busses of each state, "his Majesty's rent of assize and teind" as specified. He was not to dispute with them as to the amount of the duty. If they offered a smaller amount, "although it were only an angel for every buss," he was to accept it, but not less; so also if he were offered fish instead of money. It was left to his discretion to make a differential duty according to the size of the busses, if that point was raised, and also to compound with the admiral for the whole of the busses of a town, state, or province. If payment of the duties were refused, Fenton was merely "to take instruments upon the said refusal without further contestation," and to report the result. He was also to inform the Dutch of the oppressions made by those landing from the fleet at Shetland, and to demand redress and a promise that such conduct would not be repeated.[3]

A short time before this the Council, for the sake of economy, had ordered the *Charles* to be disfurnished, but now, in view of her important mission, they judged it to be "no ways meet or expedient" that she should be made altogether empty of her furniture and munitions of war, so that she might be able to resist any sudden or secret onslaught by the Hollanders or others. They therefore instructed that there should be left

[1] *Reg. Privy Counc. Scot.*, xi. 605, 608.

[2] See Appendix G. Fenton was one of those who were on intimate terms with Ben Jonson during the poet's visit to Scotland. *Reg. Privy Counc. Scot.*, xi. p. clxvii.

[3] *Op. cit.*, 606.

on board "twa of the smallest pecceis of hir ordinance and ten muscattis, with some few bullets ansuerable thairto, and a litill quantitie of poulder, yf ony be within the schip."[1] Orders were given for the manning of the vessel, which was to be ready to sail before 1st July. It was with this scrimp and penurious armament, and in this attorney-like manner, that James prepared to obtain an acknowledgment from the Dutch of his rights in his seas, whereas Charles I., as we shall see, employed his great ship-money fleet for the same purpose. But apparently the king would be almost as satisfied with a refusal as with the payment of the tribute, either of which he would be able to make use of in the negotiations for the "final treaty" on which he had set his heart. It is therefore unfortunate that we can discover no further information as to the expedition of Fenton. That the *Charles* left on its mission we know,[2] but the records are silent as to the result. It may perhaps be inferred from this circumstance alone that the *Charles* was no more successful than the *Restore* in the year before.

Early in 1620 the States, which had taken no steps to redeem their promise to send another embassy to deal with the question of the herring fishery, were reminded of it, and Carleton urged this course as a point both of policy and honour. But they were as reluctant as ever to handle the matter. The increased duty which Fenton was commanded to ask—of which very probably they had heard—was not likely to make them more willing, and they continued to procrastinate, alleging the unsettled state of their affairs at home and the troubles in Bohemia and Germany as reasons for further delay. Some prominent men in Holland indeed began now to assume a firmer tone. Hints were thrown out to the British ambassador that there was really little difference between forcing on the matter and declaring war, since freedom of fishing was of fundamental importance to the people of the United Provinces. The Prince of Orange gave it as his opinion that the seaport towns of Holland would never be brought to consent to "any innovation" in the herring fishery, even if it were urged at the cannon's mouth. Still more significant was the action of the States in now voting large additional sums for

[1] *Op. cit.*, 593, 603.

[2] Footnote, p. 195.

the equipment of a greater number of men-of-war to guard the herring-busses from molestation.[1]

To all appearance, therefore, the Dutch had now stiffened their backs and were prepared to fight for their liberty to fish on the British coasts, as they had done at Spitzbergen, instead of sending commissioners to London to haggle over it. But their uncompromising attitude was soon modified owing to certain political events, which taught them the need of caution in flouting the wishes of the King of England. In the autumn of 1619, Frederick, the Elector Palatine, who had married Elizabeth, the daughter of James, was offered and accepted the crown of Bohemia under circumstances pregnant with troubles. In consequence of this, Spain, in alliance with the Emperor, attacked and took possession of the Palatinate. The strengthening of the Spanish power in Germany was by itself inimical to the United Provinces, and the sense of danger was intensified when it was found that the occupation of the Lower Palatinate was part of a plan for marching the Catholic troops overland from Lombardy to the Spanish Netherlands. In view of an impending conflict with their hereditary enemies, it became a matter of grave anxiety to the States to retain the goodwill of England. Accordingly, after many discussions, the States-General at the end of 1620 appointed another embassy to go to London; but it was rather with the view of meeting the political dangers with which they were threatened than of dealing effectually with the subjects in dispute. The ambassadors' official instructions, which were most carefully considered, referred in general terms to the affairs of Germany and the approaching expiry of the truce with Spain, and more particularly to the cloth trade, the coinage, and the East Indies. On the all-important subject of the herring fishery they were mute. In their private instructions the envoys were enjoined to avoid all discussion about it; if pressed, they were to assure the king that the States would be glad to consider it "later"; and in any discussion that did arise, they were to bear in mind that they always had been in undisturbed possession of it, and that the profit they derived from it had been greatly ex-

[1] Carleton, *Letters*, 437, 447, 448, 451. Bosgoed, *Bib. Pisc.*, 352. The sum voted in 1620 was 22,000 gulden; in the following years it varied between 23,000 and 36,000 gulden.

aggerated and was far less than the king supposed—so little indeed that they would be quite unable to carry it on if any "innovation" were made.[1]

The embassy of six persons arrived in London towards the end of January 1621. At their first audience with the king they spoke only of the affairs in Germany and the seizure of the Palatinate, desiring it to be understood that this was the principal matter to be considered; and when they met the Council they raised the question of a warlike alliance between the two countries against Spain. But the herring fishery had not been forgotten by the English, and when the subject was mooted the Dutch begged that it might be allowed to rest for a time, pleading in particular that the expiry of the truce with Spain would leave them face to face with a powerful foe. The Council reminded them of the promise given, and James bluntly expressed the hope that they had come on this occasion fully empowered to treat of the business of the fishery, which had been suspended at the conferences two years before. While disclaiming any wish to diminish their legitimate profits from the fishery, he warned them that the question touched his honour and sovereignty so closely that it could not be always left undecided and in dispute; and that he would only agree to further delay when he was informed at what time it would suit the States to conclude an agreement both about the fishing on the coasts of Great Britain and at "Greenland."[2] After many conferences and much negotiation it was arranged that another embassy should be sent by the States before the lapse of a year, and the Dutch commissioners quitted London on 16th April.

In accordance with this understanding, still another embassy came to London, in November 1621. On this occasion the ambassadors were provided with full powers to settle the East Indian disputes, and with less ample authority to deal with the Spitzbergen fishery question. But, astonishing as it appears, they were again sent without any power to negotiate any treaty about the herring fishery. That the States, after so many delays and evasions, in the face of so many protests from the king, should again break their promise, shows both the great

[1] Muller, *op. cit.*, 172, 173. Aitzema, *Saken van Staet*, i. 13, 17.
[2] Muller, *op. cit.*, 174, 178.

importance they attached to the matter and their belief that James would not force on a quarrel about it. In their secret instructions the old injunctions were repeated. They were to beg that as a year had not yet elapsed a little further delay might be granted, laying stress on the danger to the Protestant cause, in view of the relations with Spain, if anything were done to lessen the sea-power of the Netherlands, which depended so much on their fisheries. At this time the East Indian question had become important and pressing in England, and the early conferences were confined to it. But later the king broached the subject of the herring-fishing; and after listening to the ambassadors for a while, he peevishly asked them to make an end of their long harangue, called them leeches and blood-suckers, who sucked the blood from his subjects and tried to ruin him,[1] and then treated them to the same sort of disquisition as on former occasions. To the king's railing and reproaches the ambassadors made such answer as they could, and the upshot was that they were allowed to go on with the conferences on the East Indian question. This embassy, at the head of which was François Van Aerssen, Lord of Sommelsdijck, remained in England until the spring of 1623, engaged in negotiations, often interrupted, on political affairs, and on the East Indian and Greenland fishery questions. James did not harass them further about the herring fishery. At the farewell audience he spoke of it in a good-natured way. He must, he said, resume his old song, *veterem cantilenam*, but not at that time. But whenever the condition of the Netherlands was favourable, he would, he said, be glad to resume the negotiations.[2]

During their long stay in England the ambassadors had an opportunity of learning what was thought about the fishery question. On their return to the Netherlands they earnestly counselled the States-General to come to some agreement with England both on the herring fishery on the British coasts and the whale-fishing at Spitzbergen. These matters, they said,

[1] "Ghy sijt sangsues, bloetsuygers van mijn rijck, ghy treckt het bloet van mijne Ondersaeten ende souckt mij te ruineren."

[2] Muller, *op. cit.*, 191, 194, 203. Aitzema, i. 191, 193. Journal van de Ambassade van den Heere van Sommelsdyck naer Engelant, 1621-1623, *Brit. Mus. Add. MSS.*, 22,866.

were close to the king's heart, and many people whom they had met had shown much irritation in speaking of them, and had even advised forcible measures against the Dutch. By this time the Republic was again at war with Spain, while Prince Charles and Buckingham had gone to Madrid to woo the Infanta: it would be prudent to do all that could reasonably be done to cultivate good relations with England. The States therefore wrote to Sir Noel Caron telling him they had resolved to take the fishery matter into serious consideration, and their efforts were directed to the removal of all cause of complaint in Scotland. Two edicts had already been issued—one, in 1618, prohibiting any wrong from being committed on Scottish subjects; the other, in 1620, ordering their fishermen to refrain from taking herrings within the rocks and reefs of Shetland, Ireland, and Norway, on the ground that such herrings were inferior in quality and unfit for curing.[1] The technical reason given in the latter for keeping away from the coast had some foundation, but the real motive was probably to redeem the pledge which the States had given in the year before (see p. 193). What the States now did was to renew the edict of 1618, and, after a conference between the ambassadors who had returned from England and the College or Board of Fisheries, to issue orders that the herring-busses were not to go too near the coast of Scotland, which had, indeed, been agreed upon some years earlier, so as to avoid causing inconvenience to the native fishermen.[2]

There is evidence that the warning which the ambassadors gave to the States-General as to the feeling in England was well founded, and there occurred at this time, both in England and Scotland, a revival of proposals aimed against the Hollanders. The Scottish burghs complained of the "heavie hurt" they sustained owing to the English and the "Fleymings," who had lately taken up the "trade of fishing" in the North and West Isles, by which was probably meant the curing of herrings and other fish. The Council accordingly ordained that the Islesmen should "suffer no strangers to come within their

[1] $\frac{2}{12}$ May 1620. Verboth van Haringh binnen de Klippen van Yerlandt, Hitlandt, oft Noorwegen te vangen. *Groot Placaet-Boeck*, i. 752.

[2] $\frac{2}{12}$ June 1623, *Groot Placaet-Boeck*, i. 708. Muller, *op. cit.*, 206.

bounds to the fishing," and that none of the country people should sell fish to them; and they issued a proclamation forbidding "all and sundry strangers" to "slay or take any fish within the Isles, lochs and bays of the kingdom, and that they buy no fish but salted and barrelled, and at free burghs."[1]

In England fresh attempts were made to establish a great national herring fishery which might rival that of the Dutch. Within a month of the departure of the ambassadors, Lord George Carew, Master of the Ordnance, was busy with a project. Along with Lord Hervey and Sir William Monson—who was perhaps the prime mover in the matter—he had several conferences with "skilful fishermen," and then he sent for the city merchants to consider how the scheme might be floated. To them he proposed that six busses and four doggers should be bought or built at a cost not exceeding £10,000, explaining, after the usual manner, how the return from the first year's fishing would repay the whole of that sum and encourage "all men" to adventure. The city merchants, one of whom was Sir William Cockaine, were loud in their praises of the scheme,—"it was the best work for the public and the most profitable that the wit of man could imagine,"—but as for the money required, they were afraid that it could not be raised. Then the promoters asked the Lord Mayor to propound the plan to the Court of Aldermen. But the Lord Mayor curtly replied that the Aldermen were engaged in other adventures, and were "utterly unwilling" to enter into the project of building busses, while the Merchant Companies were too much in debt to undertake it. On a second appeal being made to him, he said the Court of Aldermen "absolutely declined" to entertain either the general project for fishing-busses or the lesser scheme of building six busses and four doggers. They would have nothing to do with it;[2] and this scheme was therefore nipped in the bud.

Fresh proposals were now brought forward by others, based

[1] *Rec. Convent. Roy. Burghs*, iii. 142. *Reg. Privy Counc. Scot.*, xiii. 308, 317.

[2] George Lord Carew to the Secretary of State, Calvert, 8th March 1623. *State Papers, Dom.*, cxxxix. 66. The Lord Mayor to Lords Grandison, Carew, and Chichester, 27th March, 3rd April 1623. *Ibid.*, cxl. 47, cxlii. 21.

on Government support, and a plan was propounded similar to the old one of Hitchcock and Dee in the reign of Elizabeth, but to be carried out under an Act of Parliament. Each city, county, and seaport town was to be encouraged to equip fishing-busses at their common charge and for their common benefit, with power to employ their idle inhabitants in manning them. For the security of the fishing fleet the king was to provide twenty ships of war, five of which were to belong to the royal navy, and they were to continue at sea from the beginning of April till the end of September. To meet the cost of this guard the king was to receive the tenth fish taken both by English and foreign fishermen, the promoters thinking that the latter would be quite willing to be taxed when the tax was demanded by an "Act of the King and Kingdom," and when they knew they would be protected by a squadron of men-of-war.[1] It was a pretty scheme, well-intentioned, but innocent of information as to the actual state of affairs.

Scarcely anything more was heard about the herring fishery or the taxation of Dutch fishermen during the brief remainder of James's reign. Another embassy came from the Netherlands in 1624, but it was to conclude a defensive alliance against Spain, and in the shadow of this new alliance the Dutch fishermen quietly reaped the harvest of the sea without fear of English interference. James's policy of the assize-herring had thus completely failed. All his efforts to induce or to force the Netherlands' fishermen to acknowledge his right were baffled by the superior diplomacy of the States,—their "artificial delays, pretences, shifts, dilatory addresses, and evasive answers." The only immediately practical result of the king's policy was that the herring-busses kept for a time farther from the coast of Scotland. But a new weapon had been forged for the contest with the United Provinces for supremacy at sea, and one which was to be used by his successors with much more skill, if with little greater ultimate success.

[1] A Project for the Encouragement of Fishing by passing an Act of Parliament for Building fishing-vessels, to be protected by a Fleet Royall of 20 ships, the expense to be defrayed by a Tribute of every Tenth Fish. *Ibid.*, clvii. 46.

Of one symbol of this sovereignty of the sea comparatively little was heard during James's reign—namely, the salute or homage to his flag. This traditional custom of the narrow seas, while maintained on important occasions, was not enforced with the vigour and arrogance which characterised it later, perhaps less rigorously than under the Great Queen. "I myself remember," said Raleigh a few years before his execution, "when one ship of her Majesty's would have made forty Hollanders strike sail and come to anchor. They did not then dispute *de mari libero,* but readily acknowledged the English to be *domini maris Britannici.*"[1] Sir William Monson, too, who was Admiral of the Narrow Seas in the earlier part of James's reign, tells us that the Hollanders were very "stubborn" about striking their top-sails and performing the duty due to the king's prerogative, and that he earned their lasting ill-will by compelling them to do it.[2]

But the English commanders were punctilious in enforcing the salute in the narrow seas on state occasions. A notable instance occurred in 1603, when King Henry IV. of France sent over the famous Sieur de Rosny, afterwards Duke of Sully, to congratulate James on his accession to the throne of England. With a numerous retinue he went on board an English man-of-war at Calais, which then made sail for Dover accompanied by a French warship under the command of M. de Vic, the Vice-Admiral of France. The English captain observed with displeasure that the French vessel bore the arms of France at his top, "contrary to the custom of the narrow seas"; but on account of the important personage on board and the nature of his mission, he restrained himself from challenging the "indignity" until they approached Dover Road. Unable to brook the affront any longer, he fired at the French ship, and so "constrained her to strike her flag." The shot did no harm, but M. de Vic at once turned round his vessel and went back to France in high dudgeon. Cecil thought it necessary to send a despatch to the English ambassador at Paris explaining the circumstances, and while saying that the English captain "rashly discharged" his gun, he thought that if the matter was "well looked into, and the

[1] A Discourse of the Invention of Ships. *Collected Works*, viii. 326.

[2] Naval Tracts, in Churchill's *Collection of Voyages*, iii. 220, 224.

former customs observed, there would be reason found for us to stand upon."[1]

A somewhat similar incident happened two years later, when Sir William Monson was bringing over an ambassador of the Emperor from Calais to Dover. In Dover Road he found a number of States' men-of-war, and their admiral, as Monson drew near, struck his flag thrice, but then "advanced" it again and kept it flying in the presence of the king's ship. Monson believed the Dutch admiral had come in on purpose to put this "affront" on him, so that the ambassador, as well as the Spaniards then at Dover, might "spread it abroad throughout all Europe" that the Dutch, "by their wearing their flags, might be imputed kings of the sea as well as his Majesty," and so lessen the esteem of the king's prerogative in the narrow seas. Instead of firing upon the Dutch ship, he sent to invite the admiral to dinner, and to tell him that he must take in his flag. To this request the admiral demurred, saying that he had struck it thrice, and that no former admirals of the narrow seas had required more at his hands. Monson rejoined that "times were altered"; that when the mere striking of the flag as he had done was sufficient, England and Holland were both at war with Spain and it was tolerated; but now, since the war was ended so far as England was concerned, his Majesty required "such rights and duties as have formerly belonged to his progenitors." On the Dutch admiral still refusing, Monson threatened to weigh anchor and come near him, and that the force of their ships should determine the question; "for," said the English admiral, "rather than I would suffer his flag to be worn in view of so many nations as were to behold it, I resolved to bury myself in the sea." The flag was then struck, and the Dutch ships stood out to sea. Monson tells us that he was congratulated by a Spanish general who had been watching the proceedings, who said that if the Hollanders had worn their flag times had been strangely altered in England, since his old master King Philip II. was shot at by the Lord Admiral of England

[1] Cecil to Parry, 10th June 1603. *Foreign Papers, France*, vol. 129. It is endorsed "Souverainty of ye Seas, 1603. Monsr. de Vicque beares ye armes of france in Dover road." See also Sully, *Memoires des Sages et royales Oeconomies d'Estat*, ii. 173, and Kermaingant, *Le Droit des Gens Maritimes*, 3.

for wearing his flag in the narrow seas when he came to marry Queen Mary.[1]

Sometimes, however, the zeal of the naval officers led them too far in their resolution to compel the salute. Thus in 1613, when the Count of Gondomar, the Spanish ambassador, was returning to England accompanied by two galleons, an English man-of-war forced the Spanish ships to take in their flags off Stokes Bay. The ambassador complained to the Lord Admiral (the Earl of Nottingham), who decided that the captain had exceeded his authority, for the Spaniards were not bound to strike their flag unless to the admiral of the narrow seas, and the captain was neither admiral of the narrow seas nor employed under his commission. The rules or etiquette regarding this ceremony were indeed somewhat complicated, occasionally changed, and not always well understood, and as a good deal will be heard of the striking of the flag in the following chapters, it may be well to say something here about the practice. It appears that it was customary from a remote period for merchant vessels to lower their sails on meeting a ship of war in seas under the dominion of the state to which the latter belonged,[2] but the ceremony only attained to international notoriety in connection with the claims of England to the sovereignty of the narrow seas. The practice varied at different times. Generally speaking, by the custom of the narrow seas as interpreted in this country, any foreign man-of-war meeting with an English man-of-war in those seas had to take in her flag and strike her top-sails as soon as she came within sight or within range of the English guns, and she had to keep in the flag until she had passed out of range. A merchant vessel had to strike in the same way. Further, no vessel in the narrow seas was to pass to windward of an English ship of war, but must "come by the lee"; the inferior had to make way for the superior.[3] In an English port or

[1] Monson's Naval Tracts, *ibid.*, 222. The Spaniards to whom Monson refers were no doubt the troops which Don Louis Fajardo had attempted to carry to Flanders when he was attacked by the Dutch and took refuge in Dover. Monson, it may be said, was in receipt of a secret pension of £350 per annum from Spain. Gardiner, *Hist.*, i. 215.

[2] Loccenius, *De Jure Maritimo et Navali*, 48.

[3] Thus in the Earl of Warwick's voyage, in 1627, four vessels "stood with their forefoot and very earnestly" tried to weather the king's ships off Falmouth, among

road no foreign ship or English merchant vessel could wear her flag in the presence of a king's ship. This custom was also sometimes enforced in foreign ports and roads, but usually only when out of range of forts on shore. If a foreign vessel, whether man-of-war or merchant ship, did not thus "do her duty" or "perform the homage of the sea," the English ship of war might hail her or send a boat to command her to strike. Or they might at once, without any parley, fire a shot across her bows, and after an interval another, also across her bows or over her poop, and if this was ineffective, then a third between her masts or at her flag. If the foreigner still refused to strike, a broadside was usually poured in, and the vessel might be carried into port and the offender punished. In the reign of Charles II., Spaniards, Dunkirkers, Frenchmen, and other foreigners, were not infrequently brought before the courts and fined for refusing to strike. If a merchant vessel refused to strike until she was shot at, she was compelled to pay to the king's ship twice the value of the gunpowder and shot expended.

In England the custom, no doubt, originated in the Channel, probably in the time of the early Angevin kings, when the opposite coasts were under the same rule; and it is most probable, as formerly said, that it arose in connection with the exercise of jurisdiction over pirates and for securing peaceful commerce. In early times the utmost lawlessness prevailed on the sea: it would be a common duty of the king's ships to satisfy themselves as to the character of the vessels they encountered, and the lowering of the sails and the coming under the lee, for "visit and search," might well be a relic of a duty enforced for that purpose. With regard to ships of war, the

them being a French man-of-war. The English then shot at the latter, and "soo brought him by ye lee" (*State Papers, Dom.*, lxxix. 17). In 1637 Captain Straddling explained how he compelled Dutch vessels to take in their flags, lower their top-sails, and "lie by the lee" (*Ibid.*, ccclxi. 41). In the historic encounters with the Dutch in 1652 the same rule was shown. When Captain Young met the Dutchmen on 12th May (see p. 402), their admiral came under his lee and took down his flag, but their vice-admiral, "contrary to navigation with us in the narrow seas, came to the windward of us" (*French Occurrences, Brit. Mus.*, E, 665, 6). So also when Blake met Tromp, he "fired two shots thwart Tromp's forefoot for him to strike his flag and bear down to leeward, and he taking no notice of it, the general ordered the third shot at Tromp's flag, which went through his main top-sails" (*Brit. Mus. Add. MSS.*, 11,684, fol. 5*b*).

ceremony appears to have been first confined to the Channel, and was held to be peculiarly a privilege of the admiral of the narrow seas. Thus, when Captain Plumleigh was appointed admiral of a squadron for service in Ireland in 1632, he was ordered by the Admiralty if he met "in any part of the narrow seas with the *Convertive,* in which Captain Pennington commands as admiral of those seas," to take in his flag, and to "continue it furled whilst in sight of that ship, it being an ancient honour and privilege belonging only to that admiral to carry the flag in the maintop in those seas."[1] Monson also tells us, in referring to the decision of the Lord High Admiral in Gondomar's case, above alluded to, that every ship of the king's serving under an admiral could not demand the striking of the flag when out of sight of the admiral; but the foreign ship, "be he admiral or no, is to strike his top-sail and hoist it again, to any one ship of the king's that shall meet him." He further states that any foreign ship or fleet arriving in an English port, or passing by a fort or castle, had to take in their flag three times, and advance it again, unless the English admiral's ship was in the same harbour, in which case they were to keep it in so long as the admiral was present; "but if any other ship of his Majesty's be there but the admiral's, they are not bound to keep in their flag, but only to strike it thrice as aforesaid." Monson added that he wished, in these later times (the reign of Charles I.), "that his Majesty's ships would take more authority upon them than is due," in order to curb the insolence of the French and the Hollander—a wish which, as we shall see, must have been fully gratified. It was against the Dutch that the striking of the flag was most thoroughly enforced, and one cannot but admire the patience and restraint they exhibited under great provocation. The French and Swedes avoided giving the salute as much as they could. As the century wore on, the English exaction on this point grew more outrageous. Foreign ships of war were forced to strike on their own coast even to our royal yachts, and the Hollanders were asked to strike not merely in the British seas, but wherever they were encountered. To the old sea-dogs all seas were "British" where their fleets were strongest.

[1] The Lords of the Admiralty to Plumleigh. *State Papers, Dom.*, clvii. fol. 121.

CHAPTER VI.

CHARLES I. FISHERIES AND RESERVED WATERS.

It was during the reign of Charles, into whose hands the sceptre passed in the spring of 1625, that the English pretensions to the sovereignty of the sea attained their most extravagant proportions,—a circumstance which was owing in great measure to the condition of domestic affairs and the king's assumption of personal government. James had been content to limit his assertion of sovereignty to the question of the rights of fishing and the preservation of the "King's Chambers" from the hostile acts of belligerents. But Charles, while vigorously pursuing this policy so long as he was able, combined with it the most extreme claims to dominion on the neighbouring seas that had ever been put forward by an English king. The sovereign rights of jurisdiction over the "Sea of England" which were supposed to have been exercised by the early Plantagenets, were now roused from the slumber of centuries and revived in their most aggressive form. The King of England was to be lord of the surrounding seas, and to rule over them as a part of his territory. A beneficent and universal peace was to reign over the waters of the German Ocean and the Channel, unbroken by the sound of an angry shot. No other fleets or men-of-war—be they Spanish, or Dutch, or French—were to be allowed "to keep any guard" there, to offer any violence, to take prize or booty, or to search the merchant vessels of other nations. The blockade of the opposite coasts of the Continent by an enemy's fleet, as that of Flanders by the Dutch or French, was to be interdicted, because those coasts were washed by the British seas and blockading was a warlike operation. On the other hand the king was to protect the commerce and navigation of his friends and allies. Foreign merchantmen might go on their way in security, undisturbed by fears of pirates or enemies, for "all men trading or sailing within those his Majesty's seas do justly take themselves to be *in pace Domini Regis*,"—under the peace of our Lord the King. And as an external symbol and acknowledgment of this absolute dominion, foreign vessels were "to perform their duty and homage" on meeting his Majesty's ships by striking their flag and lowering their top-sails. If they refused to do so, they were to be attacked and taken or sunk; the vessel was liable to forfeiture as "good prize," and the offenders carried into port to be tried for their high contempt. Moreover—and it looks but a small thing by comparison,—no foreigners were to be permitted to fish in British waters without first receiving the king's license so to do, and paying to him a tax in acknowledgment of the permission. In this way Charles hoped to restore the sovereignty of the King of England in the British seas—that "fairest flower of the imperial crown," as he described it—to "its ancient style and lustre."

That a scheme so preposterous was seriously entertained and for a time attempted to be realised showed the inherent incapacity of the king for rational government. He was no more able to gauge his strength in relation to foreign Powers than he was to foresee that the contest he had entered into with his own subjects would end in rebellion and the scaffold. It was ridiculous to suppose that other nations would tamely surrender their sovereign rights in the seas off their own coasts and ports, abandon the protection of their commerce and shipping and their rights as belligerents, simply because the King of England wished to be lord of the sea. Had Charles been able to give effect to his selfish and ambitious scheme, he would soon have been confronted with an overwhelming coalition of maritime Powers, to whom the free use of the sea was as necessary as it was to England. As it happened, war was averted by the dexterity of Richelieu and the prudence and patience of the Dutch; and also, it must be added, by the vacillation of Charles himself, who was always trying to arrange some new combination with Continental Governments to carry out the only policy to which he was true—the recovery of the Palatinate for his nephew.

It may be supposed that the splendour of the *rôle* attributed to the early kings of England as lords of the sea, would by itself appeal to the narrow imagination of one so deeply imbued as Charles was with a belief in the divine prerogative of kings; and the dominion of the seas was claimed as peculiarly a prerogative of the crown. But there were other more practical and less exalted inducements. The assumption of the *rôle* of the Plantagenet kings was intimately related to the state of home affairs and the means taken for the equipment of a fleet. Parliament having refused supply and been dissolved, recourse was ultimately had to the famous ship-money writs, by which it was possible to obtain the necessary ships independently of Parliament, as had been done by the early kings. To declare that these measures were indispensable for the maintenance of the sovereignty of the sea in its ancient style and lustre was well adapted to lessen their unpopularity, if anything could. It was a declaration "exactly calculated for the meridian of England,"[1] for the English people in all ages have been prone to maritime glory and willing and anxious to make sacrifices for the sake of the navy, upon which their national safety depends.

It was in connection with the policy of the ship-money writs that the old doctrine of the Plantagenets came again into being. In the writs themselves the very words were copied that Edward III. had used in 1336 in his mandate to the admirals; but some years before they were issued one may trace the growth of the idea. In the period from 1631 to 1633 there was much searching of records with the view of establishing the king's rights in his seas. Negotiations had been proceeding with Scotland, described below, with reference to a great fishery scheme, and the Scots had been very troublesome and persistent about their "reserved waters," which the scheme threatened, the "land-kenning," and the encroachments of the Dutch. They only agreed to give up their exclusive claim to the "reserved waters" for the benefit of the fishery association, provided that Charles would free the Scottish seas of the Hollander busses. In the long series of papers respecting the fishery project, mostly prepared by the indefatigable Secretary Coke, the change referred to may be perceived. In those of 1629 and 1630 there is no

[1] Meadows, *Observations concerning the Dominion and Sovereignty of the Seas*, 2.

suggestion of the sovereignty of the seas, but in 1631 instances become numerous. Coke claims the sea fishings as belonging to the crown; he begins to speak of the king's "undoubted right of sovereignty in all the seas of his dominions," and plainly says it will be necessary to exclude foreign fishermen from the British seas once the fishing society is a success. In the next year he goes further. He begins a long and formal document —also on fisheries—in the following words: "The greatnesse and glorie of this Kingdom of Great Britaine consisteth not so much in the extent of his Majesty's territories by land, as in the souerantie and command of the seas. This command is in peace over trade and fishing: and for warre in the power of his Majesty's Navie to incounter the sea-forces of anie foren prince." And he goes on to say that while Spain alone used to oppose it, it was now opposed by France and the Low Countries.[1] Still more to the point were the words of Charles himself. A few months after the fishery negotiations with Scotland were concluded, he wrote to the Clerk-Register in Edinburgh saying that, as the fishing business was now completed, he was desirous that it should be known abroad by his neighbours through some "public writing," and asking him to search the records of the kingdom for authentic evidence to show his rights to the fishings, and to send such evidence to him.[2]

At this time also the English records were being subjected to search and scrutiny with the same object, but for other reasons. The "homage" of the flag was being hotly enforced in the Channel and disputed by France. Pennington, the Admiral of the Narrow Seas, reported cases in which the French demanded the salute from English merchant vessels, and rumours that it was the intention of the French admirals to wrest the regality of those seas from England on the ground that the Pope had given it to France.[3] This news caused Viscount Dorchester—the Sir Dudley Carleton who had represented King James at The Hague, now a peer and Secretary of State—to write to Boswell, Clerk of the Privy Council (soon also to be ambassador at The Hague) for some information, however little, concerning the

[1] *State Papers, Dom.*, Chas. I. ccxxix. 79.

[2] 17th October 1632. *The Earl of Stirling's Register of Royal Letters*, ii. 627.

[3] *State Papers, Dom.*, cxcix. 51.

King's admiralty in the narrow seas. Boswell sent a few brief notes of little relevancy about the jurisdiction of the admiral and the Cinque Ports; but he added the interesting information that he believed Sir John Boroughs, the Keeper of the Records in the Tower, was able to produce an "original" concerning the first institution of "La Rool d'Oleron" by Edward I., in which the sovereignty of the kings of England in those seas appeared. This, said Boswell, was therefore before the kings of France could pretend to any sovereignty there, having "neither right nor possession of any part, or part of Britany, Normandy, or Aquitaine."[1] This, then, was the famous roll of 26 Edward I. now brought to light, or at least into use in the sphere of practical affairs. The discovery of Boroughs led Nicholas, the Secretary of the Admiralty, to draw up a note about the roll, "by which," he said, "it is apparent that in those tymes ye soueraignty of those (Narrow) Seas was acknowledged by those princes (of Denmark, Sweden, &c., as mentioned in the roll): and justly, though no man can be said to have ye property of the sea, because a man cannot say this water is myne which runs, yet it is manifest that ye Kings of England have and had ye soueraignty and jurisdiction of those seas; that is, power to give laws and redresse injuries done on the same."[2]

The germ of the new pretension of Charles to play the part of Plantagenet on the adjoining seas appears to have been this disclosing by Boroughs of the ancient roll. All the later writers on the English side of the controversy about *mare clausum* and *mare liberum*, as Selden, Coke, Prynne, as well as Boroughs himself, laid great stress on it.

It was, however, as we have already hinted, in connection with the fisheries that Charles's first actions were concerned. He earnestly believed in the common opinion of the age that sea fisheries formed a principal means of developing commerce and navigation and maintaining a powerful navy, and early in his reign, before the new idea of maritime sovereignty dawned upon his mind, he did what he could to promote and foster them. The old laws for the preservation of the spawn and brood of fish, which had fallen into disuse, were put into force; proclamations appeared prohibiting wasteful fishing; a vigorous

[1] *State Papers, Dom.*, cc. 5.

[2] *Ibid.*, ccviii. 27.

effort was made to suppress the use of injurious appliances; the strict observance of Lent was repeatedly enjoined. But what proved most attractive was the notion which had haunted men's minds since the time of the Great Queen, and had always eluded realisation. Charles became convinced that the formation of a grand national fishery association would wrest from the Dutch their predominance in the fisheries, drive their busses from our seas, and transfer to the English people the herring-fishing, with all the blessings which flowed from it—commerce, wealth, and maritime power. The last attempt which had been made in this direction, in 1623, had, as we saw, signally failed, the Lord Mayor and the opulent aldermen of London "absolutely refusing" to have anything to do with it. The scheme was now, however, to be launched by the king himself, who undertook to favour it with important privileges and immunities, and intended at a suitable time to aid it by prohibiting foreigners from fishing on the British coasts.

Shortly after Charles began to reign, the old proposals to tax the Dutch were renewed. In 1626 a petition was presented to the House of Commons praying that a duty of 10 per cent might be laid upon all Dutch or foreign ships fishing in the narrow seas; with what result the records are silent. Two years later the proposal got a step further, for in 1628 a Bill was drafted to empower the king to levy two shillings in the pound on all herrings or fish exported in foreign vessels, and the tenth of the fish taken by foreigners in the British seas, the revenue so obtained to be employed for the king's use. The latter suggestion looks almost satirical in view of the failure of the many attempts of James to get revenue from that source, and in the midst, too, of the squabbles then occurring between Charles and the Parliament, which refused supplies and was abruptly prorogued; especially as the House "humbly beseeched" him, "in recompense of the great sums which your Commons have thus cheerfully granted," "yearly to provide and maintain a strong fleet of able ships upon the Narrow Seas."[1]

The original plan of the new fishery association was drawn

[1] *State Papers, Dom.*, dxxiii. 74, dxxix. 73. The proposal to utilise the tenth herring for maintaining a navy had been long before put forward by Dr Dee. See p. 101.

up by Secretary Coke and was submitted to a meeting held at Suffolk House on 29th November 1629. The two main points for consideration were: how they should obtain command of the fishery and be able to supply both themselves and foreign people, and how to find a "vent" for the fish taken and encourage merchants to purchase and export them. With regard to the first point, Coke said that to command and govern the whole fishing so as to make it a foundation of wealth to the kingdom, "equal to the Indies," as it was then to the Hollanders, would require not fewer than 1000 busses, the cost of which would exceed £800,000. This, he admitted, would be a work of time, and he proposed, for a beginning, that timber should be felled in England, Scotland, and Ireland so as to be seasoned for the construction of 200 busses in the following year—40 in Scotland, 40 in Ireland, and 120 in England. Meanwhile, for the year beginning in January 1630, he recommended that ten or twelve busses should be bought in Holland, six Dutchmen to serve in each for the year; and that the necessary salt and timber for casks for curing the herrings should be got at Dunkirk from the prizes taken from the Dutch. As the cost of ten new busses built in England, fully equipped, would amount to £8390, including the cost of maintenance for four months, the plan suggested would be the best, and it was proposed to raise the money required by the "contributions of such adventurers as may be persuaded upon hope of the gains and by privileges from his Majesty." It was intended that the busses should fish along with the Dutch on the east coast, beginning like them at Bressay Sound, Shetland, on 23rd June, and the herrings were to be put ashore to be repacked, after the Dutch method, at Aberdeen, Tynemouth, and Yarmouth. Supplementary to the busses, it was proposed to have six "doggers" to fish for cod and ling at Orkney and Shetland in the spring.

With respect to the second head, the prospect of obtaining markets for the produce, Coke said that English fishermen did not catch above 2000 lasts of herrings in a year, of which not more than 1000 lasts were consumed in England;[1] and he

[1] The other half were exported as red-herrings.

calculated that the ten busses would catch another thousand lasts, which he thought might be mostly exported to Prussia and along the German coast. The first step in carrying out the scheme was to form a company to raise a capital of about £11,000 or £12,000, and a committee was appointed for the purpose.[1]

Coke's scheme, which, like all the others, was based upon a close imitation of the Dutch system, met with great favour from the king and the court. Further consideration, moreover, led the promoters to believe that the success of the enterprise would be increased if operations were also undertaken at the Lewes instead of being confined to the east coast, and various schemes were propounded with this end in view. The suggestion appears to have emanated from Captain John Mason, and it was made at a time when the island was a bone of contention between the royal burghs of Scotland and the Earl of Seaforth, who had obtained from the king a charter to "erect" Stornoway into a royal burgh.[2] The burghs strenuously resisted the confirmation of this charter and refused to give effect to it, all the more since Seaforth had settled at Stornoway a number of Dutch people who were engaged in the fisheries there. From an interesting report by a Captain John Dymes, who visited Lewis in 1630 at the request of certain members of the Privy Council, and apparently in the interest of the proposed fishery society, we learn that the Dutch had been fishing there with great success. Their four busses, each with twenty-five nets and a crew of sixteen men, caught 300 lasts of herrings in three months, which were sold at Dantzic for 400 guilders or about £38 a last, which Dymes calculated would total £11,400, showing, after charges had been met, a gain for the

[1] *State Papers, Dom.*, 1629, clii. 57.

[2] Mason, who was intimately associated with the fishery scheme, proposed that the island should be purchased by a company of naturalised Scotsmen, and fishing stations established; and later he recommended the purchase of the island by the king, leaving complete freedom of fishery to all Scotsmen. Sir William Monson urged that a "government" should be established in the island as well as in Orkney and Shetland, and also a principal town; and that the children of the islanders should be taught English, and "correspondence" between the inhabitants and the Highlanders hindered, "considering the danger of their too great friendship." *State Papers, Dom.*, 1629, clii. 66, 67, 68. The subject of the Earl of Seaforth's lease and the fishings is dealt with by Mackenzie, *History of the Outer Hebrides*, 290 *et seq*.

three months' work of £7500.[1] The Scottish burghs protested against the introduction of the Hollanders, which they said would ruin the whole trade and navigation of the kingdom and completely destroy the native fisheries. They petitioned the Privy Council to restrain strangers from resorting to the North and West Isles, pointing out that from the numbers of the Hollanders, their numerous ships and great commerce, they would draw the whole trade of the country into their hands, as they had done everywhere they had gone; and in a petition to the king they accused them of "great oppressions" in the Isles and on the coasts of the kingdom, and declared that by a "pretendit libertie obtenit of his father" they were "the overthrowes of the haill fischeing of this cuntry."[2]

Mr John Hay, the Town-Clerk of Edinburgh, was despatched to London to the king, to ask that the country might be freed of the objectionable Hollanders and the Seaforth charter withdrawn; and to declare that the Scottish burghs would themselves undertake the whole of the fishings at the Lewes and erect a burgh there. Secretary Coke, full of the fishery scheme, took advantage of Hay's presence to obtain from him a detailed account of Lewis and its fisheries, and of the Dutch fishings on the coast of Scotland, which, it was said, sometimes employed a fleet of 3000 busses; and from the information acquired an "estimate of the charge of a fishing to be established in the island of Lewes in Scotland" was prepared. This document showed that ten Scottish fisher-boats, of from twenty-five to thirty tons each, might be bought for £1200, and other ten boats, of twelve to fourteen tons, for a proportionately smaller sum. Each of the large boats was to be equipped with 120 nets of twenty yards in length, and the smaller boats with forty nets of the same dimensions; and it was calculated that

[1] *State Papers, Dom.*, clii. 63, 71; clxxx. 97. Dymes' report is printed in full by Mackenzie (*op. cit.*, 591). The master of one of the Dutch busses, who transported Dymes from Lewis to the mainland, told him that the herrings were in such great abundance that they were sometimes constrained to cast them into the sea again, they having more in half their nets than they were able to save, "and he was of opinion that if there had bene a thousand Busses more there was fish enough for them all."

[2] *Rec. Convent. Roy. Burghs Scot.*, iii. 257, 259, 291. The arguments against the Dutch were elaborated in a long document, which concluded thus: "Lastly, theis Netherlanders greatnes, strength, wealth, arts, and every happines doe originally proceede from their fishing in his Majesty's seas of England, Scotland, and Ireland."

with a stock of £6743, 6s. 8d. a clear profit of £18,270 might be earned in one year.

This alluring prospect was no doubt encouraging to Coke and his friends; but he learned from Hay some further information which must have been disquieting. He was told that the Scottish people would not permit any foreigners to fish within twenty-eight miles of their coast, or within the lochs, the fishings there being reserved for the natives; that by the laws of Scotland any stranger found fishing within these limits was liable to confiscation of goods and loss of life, citing as an example the story of the barbarous treatment by James V. of the Dutch fishermen who had transgressed the "reserved waters" by fishing in the Firth of Forth.[1] This point about the reserved waters was indeed the main difficulty which soon confronted the fishery scheme. To be successful, the fishing must be carried on along the Scottish coast and at the Isles, for it was there the great shoals of herrings resorted, but the objections of the Scottish Parliament, Council, and burghs had first to be overcome.[2]

The first important step was a declaration by the king of his intentions. On 12th July he wrote to the Privy Council of Scotland, laying before them his scheme for a great fishery association. With the advice of his Privy Council in England, he said, he had maturely considered that "als weill in thankfulnesse to Almighty God as for the benefite of all our loving subjects we ought no longer to neglect that great blessing offered unto us in the great abundance of fishe upon all the coasts of these Yllands. To the end we may at lenth injoy with more honnour these rights whiche properlie belong to our imperiall crowne and ar vsurped by strangers, We have considered of a way whiche in tyme by God's favour may produce this good effect and also increasse our navigatioun and trade. And becaus this worke concerneth equallie all our three Kingdomes and must thairfoir be vndertakin and ordered by commoun counsell and assistance," he had taken the opportunity of a meeting of the Scottish Parliament to send his

[1] P. 77.

[2] *State Papers, Dom.*, clii. 63; clxv. 201; clxxx. 100. *Rec. Conv. Roy. Burghs*, iii. 300 *et seq.*

"instructions" on the subject by his Secretary for Scotland, Sir William Alexander.[1]

In his instructions the king, after a preamble reciting the abundance of fish on our coasts, the benefit which was reaped by strangers, "to the great disparagement and prejudice" of his loving subjects, declared his "firm resolution" to set up a "commoun fishing to be a nurserie of seamen and to increase the shipping and trade in all parts of his dominions," and added—what must have been unwelcome news to the Scottish burghs and people—that as it was to be a "common benefit" to all the three kingdoms, so it could not be "dividedly enjoyed" by any one nation in particular. The Council were enjoined to take the matter into serious consideration, and to give their advice and assistance in bringing it to a successful issue, and as it was necessary to raise a "great stock" from adventurers, who would not be drawn into the scheme except by hope of great and immediate gains, an estimate of the outlays and profits was submitted to the Council, showing that 200 busses would earn a clear profit of £165,414 in a single year, after paying all costs.[2]

[1] *Acta Parl. Scot.*, v. 220*b*. Captain John Mason, who was afterwards appointed "Admiral" of the busses belonging to the society, was apparently originally intended to lay the matter before the Council. The draft, in Coke's handwriting, is entitled, "Instructions for Captain John Mason employed by his Majesty to treat with the Lordes of the Privie Council of Scotland about the erection of a general fishing," and is among the *State Papers, Dom.*, clxxx. 101.

[2] *Acta Parl. Scot.*, v. 221. This ambitious scheme included the building of 200 busses of from 30 to 50 tons each, "for a considerable beginning," besides the employment of the fishing vessels already engaged on the coast which were of suitable size. These were computed to number about 100 in Scotland and 200 in England (employed at Newfoundland and the north seas), while at least 300 "coasters" from Berwick to the Thames might also be made available; and it was suggested that more might be built by the company "in every town," or bought from the Dutch. It was estimated that the cost of building and equipping the 200 busses, including casks, salt, wages, &c., would be £222,586, and that the total return the first year would amount to £388,000, made up as follows: (1) summer herring fishing, 20,000 lasts at £10, equal to £200,000; (2) winter herring fishing, 12,000 lasts at £12, equal to £144,000; (3) cod and ling fishing in spring, 1,200,000 fish at £30 a thousand, and 600 tuns of oil at £13, 6s. 8d., equal to £44,000. Several calculations were made about this time as to the cost of equipping herring-busses, the profits to be derived from their use, and the loss to the realm by the transport of cured fish by the Dutch; Monson put the latter loss at £621,750 per annum. *State Papers, Dom.*, clii. 70, clxxx. 99, ccvi. 52; *MSS. Advoc. Lib.*, 31. 2. 16; *Brit. Mus. Sloane MSS.*, 26. The latter is a "Discourse on the Hollanders' Trade of Fishing," by Sir Robert Mansel, of the usual type.

Sir William Alexander was also requested to ascertain how many busses and how much money might be contributed in Scotland, and he was to urge the Council to confer on the subject with the nobility and gentry, and especially with the burghs. Moreover, as it was not thought to be feasible to manage the whole project by one common joint-stock, the king advised that subsidiary companies should be formed in the principal town or burgh of each province, to be related to one central body or corporation. No foreigners were to be admitted as members of the company, although they might be employed as servants. All the adventurers, whether English, Irish, or Scottish, were to be allowed to fish freely "in all places and at all times"; and the king signified that as the Lewes was "the most proper seate for a continuall fishing along the westerne coasts," it was his resolve to take it from the Earl of Seaforth into his own hands, as "adherent" to the crown, and to erect one or more free burghs in the Isles. If difficulties arose in the acceptance of the scheme, the Lords of Council were to be asked to appoint commissioners to treat with those he would nominate to act on behalf of England and Ireland.

The king's proposals were brought before the Scottish Parliament on 29th July 1630, and remitted to a large committee to report upon them.[1] They were ill-received in Scotland. The free burghs in particular opposed the scheme with great energy. They had brought about the withdrawal of the charter obtained by the Earl of Seaforth, and were negotiating among themselves for the formation of a company to carry on the fishing at the Lewes and establish a free burgh there. But the charter of the Highland Earl was a small thing to the scheme of the king. They saw in it an invasion of their special rights and privileges in trading and fish-curing, which had been conferred on them and confirmed by many Acts of Parliament, not merely at the Lewes but throughout the country. The "reserved waters," more-

[1] *Acta Parl. Scot.*, v. 225. The committee consisted of fifteen peers, several bishops, and a large number of commoners. Mason, who had accompanied Sir William Alexander to Scotland, reported to Coke that the Council gathered in the Lord Chancellor's chamber, "he lying sick of the gout," to hear the king's letter read, and that Mr John Hay "violently opposed" the scheme and attacked the Earl of Seaforth for bringing in the Hollanders. *State Papers, Dom.*, clxxii. 19.

over, sacredly preserved for the industry and sustenance of their own people, were to be thrown open to Englishmen and Irish, whereby the nation would suffer greatly.[1]

On 9th August a statement was drawn up by the Convention and circulated to all the burghs, in which their opinion was asked as to whether any association with England in the fishings was expedient; whether the English should be suffered to "plant" or settle in any part of the Isles; whether, if the burghs undertook the fishing themselves, they should allow the nobility and gentry to "stock" with them, and if so on what conditions; and if not, whether the burghs should undertake it themselves by a company or by burgesses, and what sums might be subscribed for an exclusive company. On the following day it was complained in the Convention that, though the king had cancelled the patent to the Earl of Seaforth, the "Flemings" still remained in the Lewes; and the burghs thereupon decided that as the Privy Council had appointed commissioners from each of the Estates of Parliament to treat on the king's proposals, their own commissioner, Mr John Hay, should be empowered to deal with the king in order to have the "Flemings" removed and the fishing "devolvit in thair hands"; to "stay" the proposed association with the English, or the plantation of strangers at any part of the kingdom where fishing was carried on; and to cause the "Flemings" to forbear from fishing on the Scottish coasts, "or not to cum neirer to the schoire of anie pairt of this kingdome than ane land kenning of the said schoire."

Meantime a smaller committee which had been appointed

[1] At this time the herring-fishing on the west coast of Scotland, which began on 1st July and continued till Christmas, employed from 800 to 1500 fishing-boats of from 5 to 6 tons each, besides about 200 "cooper" boats of about 12 tons, which carried casks and salt and brought back cured herrings to the burghs: about 6000 "seamen" were employed in this industry. The herring-fishing on the east coast was for the most part carried on at Dunbar—as many as 20,000 people sometimes congregating there—and in the deep water where the Dutch fished in July, August, and September. There was also an important winter fishing for herrings in the Firth of Forth in November, and at the North Isles from 1st October till Christmas. The "keeling" or cod-fishing at the mouth of the Clyde in February, March, and April employed about 120 of the largest boats; on the east coast this method of fishing was carried on from 1st April till 24th June.

by Parliament, no doubt under the inspiration of the opposition of the burghs, reported against the association with England in the fishings. Such a course, they said, would be "verie inconvenient to the estait; and tuiching the land fishing, whilk consists in fishing within loches and yles and twenty aucht myles frome the land, and whilk is proper to the natives, and whairof they have been in continuall possessioun and neuer interrupted thairin be the Hollanders,"—a statement inconsistent with the frequent complaints made by the burghs in the reign of James. The burghs, they said, were able and content to undertake the "said land fishing" by themselves, without "communicating" therein with any other nation; and as for the buss-fishing, to which the king's proposals specially referred, they stated that the season for it that year was passed, and that as it was a matter of great importance, it required time for consideration. The burghs reported to Parliament in the same sense.[1]

Thus Charles, in endeavouring to carry out his laudable desire to create a great national fishery to oust the Hollander from his seas, had suddenly raised against him a Scottish claim of *mare clausum*, which he found very provoking. Not only did the Scottish Parliament declare that a great extent of the sea around Scotland pertained exclusively to the natives so far as concerned fishing, but they coupled this with the request that the king should exclude foreigners from fishing within that area. It must be said that, apart al-

[1] *Acta Parl. Scot.*, v. 226. *Rec. Conv. Roy. Burghs*, iii. 322, 323. The Earl of Seaforth, writing to the Earl of Carlisle on August 17th, said that the Lord Chancellor and the Lord Treasurer had left no argument unuttered which might induce their countrymen, and especially the burghs, to concur in the king's desire about the fishing. The burghs would not admit any association either with countrymen or strangers; "they like not," he said, "that noblemen or gentry should understand matters of industry," and they would do what they could to move the king to delay. *State Papers, Dom.*, clxxii. 78. In another account of the proceedings of the Convention, it is said the burghs claimed as "absolutely theirs" the fishing within bays and lochs, and at sea for a distance of "two kennings" from the shore, and stated that they would admit no partners, either natives or strangers; that buss-fishing was distinguished by them to be "without two kennings from the land"; and they would not "on any condition" allow any busses to participate in the "land fishing" within two kennings, or to land at all, but only to "make" their fish (cure them) on shipboard, as the "Flemings" did. It is added that those who would have hazarded some means in the project were "absolutely discouraged" by the attitude of the burghs. *Ibid.*, ccvi. 45.

together from the unwritten law as to the "reserved" waters pertaining to Scotland, the Scottish people had some ground of complaint against the king for his sudden proposal to open up the whole of their seas and lochs to the English; for it was well known that in the Draft Treaty of Union which James had caused to be prepared in 1604, and which would also have conferred important privileges on Scotland in matters of trade, words had been inserted reserving to each nation the fishings within all lochs, firths, and bays within land and up to a distance of fourteen miles from the coast. This treaty was drawn up by commissioners appointed by the respective Parliaments, the most active of whom were Secretary Lord Cecil (afterwards Earl of Salisbury) and the illustrious Sir Francis (afterwards Lord) Bacon on the English side, and Lord President Fyvie and Sir Thomas Hamilton (later Earls of Dunfermline and Haddington) on the part of the Scots. It was signed by thirty-nine of the forty-four English and by twenty-eight of the thirty Scottish commissioners; it was approved by the king and adopted by the Scottish Parliament, and it was thus an instrument of high authority with respect to the delimitation of the waters of exclusive fishing. The clause in the treaty dealing with freedom of commerce contained the reservation referred to, which was as follows: "Exceptand also and reserveand to Scottishmen thair trade of fisheing within thair loches, ffirthis, and bayis within land, and in the seas within fourtene mylis of the costis of the realme of Scotland, wheir nather Englishmen nor ony stranger or forinaris haue use to fishe, and soe reciprocally in the point of fisheing on the behalfe of England."

Unfortunately, the treaty was never ratified by the English Parliament, and therefore did not come into force. But the objection of the English members was not in the least degree founded upon the reservation of fishing rights, but upon the nationalisation clauses, which caused them to dread the influx of an army of "hungry Scots" into England, Scotsmen being at the time very unpopular in London.[1]

[1] *Acta Parl. Scot.*, iv. 369. *Statutes of the Realm*, 1 Jac. I., c. 2. *Reg. Privy Counc. Scot.*, vi. *Nat. MSS. of Scot.*, iii. No. 85. *State Papers, Dom.*, 1604, x.

The stipulation in the treaty of 1604 was now brought to mind in the negotiations on Charles's fishing scheme. These negotiations, which were carried on for more than two years, were conducted on the part of Scotland with an ingenuity and refinement of procrastination scarcely surpassed by the Dutch in the previous reign.

After the report above mentioned, a large committee was appointed to discuss the business with the English authorities, and to report to the meeting of Parliament in November. Accordingly, on 3rd November the committee submitted the report of their proceedings with the English commissioners, which was signed by the Earl of Monteith, the President of the Council. They understood, they said, that the general fishing proposed by the king referred only to those fishings of which the benefit was exclusively reaped by strangers (that is to say, to deep-sea buss-fishing), and did not in any way touch the fishings which were enjoyed by the natives of any of the three kingdoms, so that the laws and freedom of every kingdom might be preserved, as indeed was "contained in the said instructions." It was therefore necessary, they said, in the first place, that such fishings "in everie kingdom whiche ar onely injoyed be the natives be made known," and that it should be clearly determined what those fishings were which were called "common benefits" that could not be "dividedly enjoyed." With their eyes probably on the fate of the nationalisation clauses in the Draft Treaty of 1604, they declared it to be desirable that Scottish adventurers in the proposed association should be naturalised in England; and with reference to the commodities brought back for exported fish, they said it was necessary to inquire how the return for the fishes exported out of each kingdom should be made to the kingdom in which they were actually taken. As to founding a burgh in the Lewes, that, they said, would be an infraction of the rights of the existing burghs.

The reply of the English commissioners was somewhat vague

No. 1. It is unfortunate that the reasonable delimitation of the territorial fishing waters proposed in the treaty was not carried out, for there can be little doubt that had it been it would have become recognised by other nations, and would have continued to the present day.

and general. It was, however, made clear that the king's intention was that every member, or "brother," of the company should be free to fish "in places near and remote, where common fishing is, or may be, used by any of his people," this "mutual participation being the bond of union and sole means to recover his Majesty's right and power at sea, and to enrich all his subjects, and those chiefly where the greatest fishings are." On the other points they said, in effect, that the king would do what was best.

A letter from the king to the Parliament was also read, expressing his desire that the business should be advanced, as it would be "a worke of great consequence for the generall good of our whole kingdome, and more particularlie for the benefite of that our ancient kingdome" by the improvement of its trade and shipping. So anxious was Charles for the success of his enterprise, that he added a postscript in his own hand, in which he said: "This is a worke of so great good to both my kingdomes that I have thought good by these few lynes of my owne hand seriouslie to recommend it unto yow. The furthering or hindering of whiche will ather oblige me or disoblige me more then anie one business that hes happened in my tyme." He also sent a letter to the burghs to mollify them, saying that it was in no ways intended that they should be wronged in their ancient privileges or benefits; and he requested Parliament to appoint commissioners charged with absolute powers to settle the matter with the English commissioners, so that there should not be undue delay.[1]

The Parliament thereupon appointed commissioners, on 11th November 1630, to treat with those of England.[2] Nominally they were given full powers to treat, but their instructions, dated 23rd December, were so detailed and remarkable that it must have been obvious to every one that rapid progress was not intended. Nothing was to be done prejudicial or derogatory to the liberties and privileges of the kingdom, the crown,

[1] *Acta Parl. Scot.*, v. 228, 230. *The Earl of Stirling's Register of Royal Letters*, ii. 478.

[2] The commissioners were the Earl of Morton (Lord High Treasurer), the Earl of Monteith (President of the Privy Council), the Marquis of Hamilton, the Earls of Roxburgh and Carrick, Sir William Alexander, Mr John Hay, and Mr George Fletcher.

or the laws of Scotland; special care was to be taken that the natives of Scotland were to be preferred in the choice of the best places for establishing "magazines" for the fishery, and that the places appointed for the English should be such as would not prejudice the "land fishing" of the Scotch; the Scottish members of the association were to have the same privileges and immunities, with power to erect magazines, in England and Ireland; English members who settled in Scotland were to be debarred from fishing in the reserved waters, or from buying fish from the natives, except for their own sustenance, as well as from any trade or commerce, unless for the same purpose; they were to be prohibited from importing or exporting commodities except fishes taken by their own vessels, and they were to pay customs and other duties for the fish they cured in Scotland and exported—and many other conditions were laid down which showed how little the Parliament had been moved by the personal appeal of the king.[1]

With respect to the fundamental question, the limits of the territorial seas pertaining to Scotland, the demands of the Parliament went much further than any previous claim. The old principle of division by the mid-line, which was held by some lawyers in the reign of Elizabeth, was now put forward. The commissioners were instructed to take care that a clause was inserted in the treaty to make it clear, "that the seas foreanent the coasts of this kingdome and about the Yles thairof and all that is interjected betuix thame and that midlyne in the seas whilk is equallie distant and divyding frome the opposite land, ar the Scotish Seas properlie belonging to the crowne of Scotland, and that the English hes no right nor libertie to fishe thairin, nor in no part thairof, bot be vertew of the association and not otherwayes." But while these were the Scottish seas ideally regarded, English members of the

[1] Among other things, the commissioners were instructed to represent to the king the prejudice which Scotland sustained by the use of the name "Great Britain" in the royal patents, writs, and records relating to Scotland, for, they reminded him, "there was no union as yet with England"; and Charles was to be requested to renew his seals under the terms *Carolus Dei gratia Scotiæ, Angliæ, Franciæ, et Hiberniæ Rex.* It must be remembered that at this time the Scottish aristocracy were smarting under the defeat which the king had recently inflicted on them in connection with the Act of Revocation, by which most of the church property in the hands of laymen was re-annexed to the crown.

association were to be permitted to fish in them, except in the waters which were reserved to the Scottish people in the Draft Treaty of Union of 1604—namely, bays, firths, and lochs within land, and a belt of fourteen miles along the coast. These waters were to be strictly preserved for the native fishermen.[1]

The instructions which the burghs gave to their representative, Mr John Hay, although less ample, were equally to the point. He was to agree to the proposal for the establishment of an English settlement at the Lewes, provided they did not fish in the reserved waters, and had no magazines or settlements in any of the other West or North Isles, or north of Buchan Ness or Cromarty, and not at Aberdeen if they wished any south of Buchan Ness; and the burghs were also to have the right to establish colonies at the Lewes. In "retribution," as they said, for those privileges to be granted to the English in Scotland, they required the "liberty" of the pilchard-fishing in England and Ireland, with equal privileges regarding it. The king was also to remove the "Flemings" from the Isles, and to prohibit them and all other strangers from fishing within a "land-kenning" (that is, within a distance at which the land was visible from the sea), and power was to be conferred upon the burghs, with the assistance of the Sheriffs and other officers to prevent their fishing nearer. "Hamburgers, Bremeners," and all other strangers, were also to be removed furth of Shetland, Orkney, Caithness, and other places.[2]

A week or two before the Scottish commissioners were selected, Charles issued a commission appointing Lord Weston (High Treasurer of England), the Earl of Arundel and Surrey (Earl Marshal), the Earl of Pembroke (Lord Chamberlain), the Earl of Suffolk (Lord Warden of the Cinque Ports), and eight others as commissioners on behalf of England and Ireland.[3] His object, he said, was to establish a "common" fishing, both to be a nursery of seamen and for the increase of navigation,

[1] *Acta Parl. Scot.*, v. 232.

[2] *Rec. Conv. Roy. Burghs*, iii. 325. The foreigners from Hamburg and Bremen were chiefly engaged in trade and barter.

[3] *Fœdera*, xix. 211. *State Papers, Dom.*, clxxxvii. 46. The commission was dated 8th December 1630, and the other commissioners were the Earls of Salisbury, Dorset, and Carlisle, Viscounts Wimbledon and Wentworth, Sir John Coke, Sir Francis Cottingham, and Sir William Alexander, who was Secretary for Scotland.

and "to make the store of fish of all kinds, being a necessary food for the people on fish-days, to be had at reasonable prices, and the overplus thereof to be a principal addition to the staple commodities of our kingdom for the increase of trade." In order that this common fishing might be extended and freely exercised in "all places by his subjects of each of the three kingdoms," he appointed them "with full power and authority to confer severally and jointly, and to consider, treat, propose, determine and conclude what they concurrently found fit and expedient for the ordering, establishing, and advancing of the said common fishing." Power was also given to them to call for any of the records in the Tower or elsewhere which might bear upon their labours.

The commissioners from both countries met early in 1631. In March the Privy Council of Scotland received a report from the Scottish commissioners in London, stating that several meetings with the English commissioners had been held, and that the extent of the waters proposed to be reserved "was thought too much," unless it could be shown that "the intention was only to reserve so much without which the natives could not subsist, and not to hinder the good public work," and they craved full and particular instructions on this point. The Privy Council at once summoned the Lord Provost and Bailies of Edinburgh before them to furnish the information required, but they replied that it was a subject which concerned all the burghs, and that time must be given to consult them. After some further delay the burghs submitted an elaborate and interesting report to the Council on 21st April, in which, after citing the clause in the Draft Treaty of Union, they proceeded to define the bounds of the waters "without the whiche the countrie can not subsist," and "whiche trewlie is the bounds whairupon if anie stranger sall resort this countrie sall suffer utter ruine." These bounds were as follows:—

"Vpon the east side of Scotland, frome Sanct Tabsheid [St Abb's Head] in the shiredom of Beruick directlie north to the Reidhead in Angus whiche comprehends the coast of the Merce, Lothiane, the Firth, Fyfe and ane part of the coast of Angus, and 14 myles without the course frome the said Sanct Tabsheid to the Reidheid. Frome the Reidhead north north-east alongs the coast of Angus, Mernes, Mar and Buchan to Buchannesse, northwards and be north to Dungisbeyheid [Duncansby Head] in Caithnes, comprehending thairin the coast of Bamf and Murrey upon the south side, Murrey firth and the coast of Rosse, Sutherland and ane part of Caithnes vpon the north, and fourtene myles without the course frome the said Buchannesse to the said Dungisbiehead, and frome the same Dungsbie in Caithnes west alongs the coast of Caithnes and Strathnauer to Farrayheid in Stranauer [Cape Wrath], and fourteine myles aff the said coast, with fourtene myles round about the yles of Orkney and Yetland. Frome the Farrayheid alongs the coast of Stranauer to the head of Stoir of Assint [Stoir Head] and 14 myles aff the said coast, and frome the said heid of Stoir Assint directlie west north-west to the eastmost point of the yle of the Lewes, comprehending thairin the haill seas interjected betuixt the said heid of Stoir of Assint and eastmost point of the said yle of the Lewes, with all the yles and loches within the same, and 14 myles without the course frome the said heid of the Stoir of Assint to the said east point of the Lewes; frome the said eastmost point of the Lewes south about the haill yles of the Lewes to the westmost part of Barra, and 14 myles without the samine; frome the said westmost part of Barra n-west, south, south-east to southmost part of the yle of Yla [Islay], frome the said southmost part of yla south-east to the mull of Kintyre, frome the said mull of Kintyre n-west, south-east, to the mull of Gallouay: Whiche bounds frome the said heid of Stoir Assint west north-west to the eastmost point of the Lewes and frome thence south to Bara be Yla, and mull of Kintyre to the mull of Gallouay, comprehends the haill west yles and loches within the samine with the loches vpon the mayne of Stranauer, Tarbet, Lochaber, Kintyre, Argyle, Renfrew, Cuninghame, Kyle, Carrick, Gallouay, Quhithorne; alongs the coast of Gallouay eastward to Solloway [Solway] sands and 14 myles aff the said coast. Quhilk bounds above designed being so necessar both for the haill lieges living vpon the saids coasts and yles, as if these sould be exhausted be strangers of fishes, they sould be depryved of all benefite of living and so be tyme bring ane vtter desolatioun vpon the land, as lykeways so necessar for ws of the borrowes [burghs] as without the said fishing the most part of our inhabitants sould be brought to extreem miserie. Quhairfoir we of the burrowes doe humbelie beseeke your Lordships to recommend the bounds abone designed to the saids commissioners in suche maner as they give not way that strangers be permitted to fishe within the saids bounds vpon anie conditioune."[1]

---

[1] *Acta Parl. Scot.*, v. 235. *Rec. Conv. Roy. Burghs*, iv. 526. *State Papers, Dom.*, clxxxviii. 72. In the record of the burghs the distance from the shore on the east coast, at the Orkneys and Shetlands, and on the north coast, is given as forty miles; but as the original records of the Convention between 1631 and 1649 were lost, and that printed is from an abstract prepared in 1700, it appears that an error was made in the transcribing.

A glance at the accompanying chart, indicating the boundary of the "reserved" waters as claimed by the burghs, will show how large an extent of the neighbouring seas was considered to be necessary for the subsistence of the people. Not only were all the great firths included, and the waters of the Minch and within the Isles, but it will be observed that the fourteen-mile limit around a very great part of the coast was drawn, not from the shore, but from an ideal straight line uniting the headlands.

When this report from the burghs was submitted to the Privy Council, they professed to find it "to be of too large an extent"; and they therefore, as they said, "out of their desire to his Majesty's contentment and for the advancement of the great work," proceeded to "retrench and restrict the universality of the exceptions" made by the burghs. The true spirit of the Council was, however, shown by the fact that their alternative scheme was practically the same. They rearranged the description of the lines at the Orkneys and Shetlands without diminishing the extent of the enclosed sea, and they carried the boundary down the east instead of the west side of the Hebrides, and so on to Islay. They thus reduced the area of the waters proposed to be reserved by omitting only the strip of fourteen miles to the west of the Hebrides. The Council declared that they had reserved an area of fourteen miles off such coasts as were well peopled, and where the inhabitants lived mostly by fishing, and could not possibly subsist and pay their rents and duties without it. They also stated that if a buss-fishing had been established in Scotland,[1] the fishing would have been reserved for the use and benefit of the country people, "seeing it cannot be qualified that ever any Hollanders or other strangers fished in these waters."

In transmitting the two schemes to the commissioners in London, on 31st April 1631, the Council observed that at first the burghs had "stood very punctually" on the instructions at first issued to the commissioners, saying there was no need to particularise the reserved waters, since they had been included in the Act of Union, but that they had been persuaded to abandon this attitude and condescend to particulars. If this was not a stroke of Scotch humour, it would indicate that the

[1] The Duke of Lennox had some time before this proposed the formation of a fishery society for the purpose.

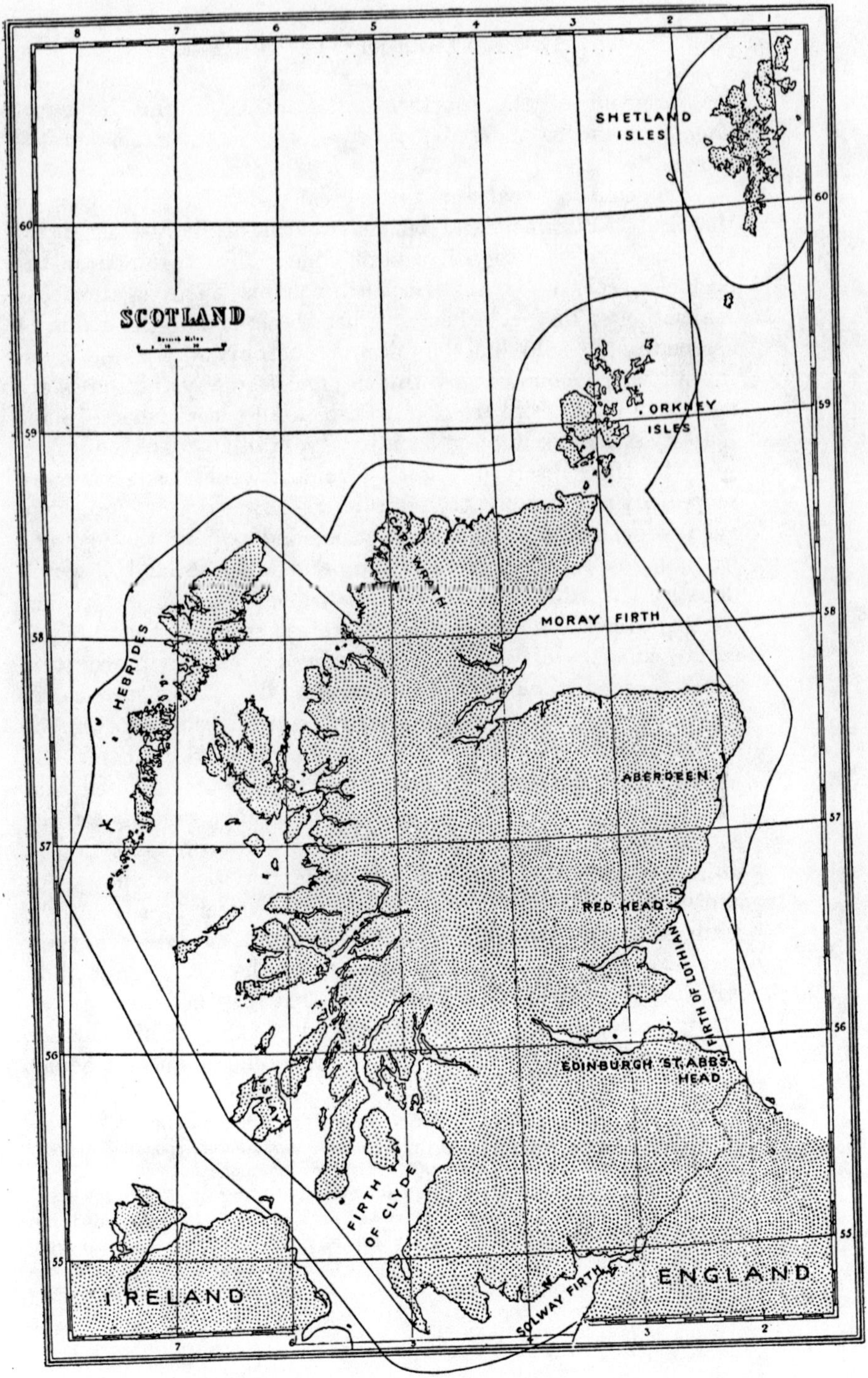

Fig. 9.—*Showing the limits of the "Reserved Waters" claimed by Scotland.*

measurement of the fourteen miles mentioned in the Draft Treaty was to be understood as expressed in the report of the burghs.[1]

This kind of zeal for the "great work" on the part of the Scottish Council and burghs was naturally displeasing to the king and the English commissioners. Coke fumed at the obstacles raised by the Scottish commissioners against the realisation of his pet scheme. They disclaim not the name of association, he said, but they decline the only way of establishing it; we propound a government, and they say their laws are against it; we desire freedom to fish in all places where, by his Majesty's license, it may be lawfully granted to us, and they reply by the "reserved waters," which "would leave no more scope to the company than strangers now enjoy." Nay, they even propound a further limitation, and request that bounds may now be set to the seas of England and Scotland; "which debates," he adds, "tending to division, we labour to avoid." At this time the minds of English statesmen had not yet become saturated with lofty ideas of the king's sovereign prerogative in his seas, and Coke did not then, as he did a little later, make use of high arguments of that kind. But he believed that the opposition of Scotland would be prejudicial to the scheme, and that further negotiations would be vain; and he proposed that an English company should be formed without waiting for the concurrence of Scotland.[2] But Charles was more patient. In June he again sent Sir William Alexander, the Secretary for Scotland, to Edinburgh, and despatched a letter to the burghs assuring them that he would be careful to preserve their privileges and liberties, and another to the Privy Council in which he expressed his astonishment that they had reserved so many places, and likewise "fyftene myles [*sic*] within the sea distant frome everie shoarr, where it would seeme expedient

[1] *Acta Parl. Scot.*, v. 236. The Act referred to was passed in 1607 by the Scottish Parliament, but it was to be inoperative until a corresponding Act was passed by the Parliament of England, which was not done.

[2] *State Papers, Dom.*, cxci. 7. Memorandum, dated 11th May 1631, by Secretary Coke, on "Matters in difference betwixt the English and Scottish Commissioners concerning the fishing." From this paper it appears that the Scottish commissioners made the most of points relating to naturalisation; they objected to the natives being employed as fishermen by the association, and they would say nothing about the proportion of busses that might be set forth in Scotland.

that these of the association for this generall fishing, as they have libertie to land in any place, paying the ordinarie dewteis, sould lykewayes be free to fish where ever they ar to passe." He plainly told the Council that while he was willing to reserve for the natives all such fishings without which they could not well subsist, and which they of themselves "have and doe fullie fishe," he would not allow anything to be reserved which might hinder the general work which was so important for all the kingdoms; and he enjoined them to give their best attention to everything that would conduce to the accomplishment of his desire. In a later letter to the President of the Council, Charles expressed his fears that if the places proposed were reserved the great business of the fishing would be put in hazard.[1] On receipt of the king's letter, the Council, on 28th July, summoned before them the representatives of the burghs, who on being asked if they were yet resolved on their answer, said they were not; they were thereupon requested to consider the matter and to report at the meeting on 21st September.

The resolute attitude of the king was not without its effect. The burghs now modified their demands, but they still declared that it was necessary to reserve the "Firth of Lothian" within a line between St Abb's Head and Red Head; the Moray Firth within a line between Buchan Ness and Duncansby Head; the Firth of Clyde between the Mulls of Galloway and Cantyre, and also the waters within fourteen miles along the coast between Red Head and Buchan Ness. They further desired that a space of fourteen miles outside the boundary lines of the Firths should be reserved, but on this point they stated their willingness to submit themselves to the king.[2]

The modified proposals of the burghs were submitted to the Privy Council on 22nd September by certain noblemen, gentry, and commissioners of the burghs, and an additional reason for reserving the fourteen miles along the coast between Red Head and Buchan Ness was now brought forward. If this space were opened to buss-fishing, it would, they said, ruin the salmon-fish-

[1] *Stirling Letters*, ii. 538, 544. *Acta Parl. Scot.*, v. 236. Charles, it will be observed, mentions 15 miles. The miles stated in the Scottish documents were Scots miles of 5929·5 imperial feet, 10 Scots miles being equal to nearly 11¼ imperial miles; the extent of the reserved waters was therefore very nearly 15¾ imperial miles (15·72).

[2] *Rec. Conv. Roy. Burghs*, iv. 534.

ings of the Dee, Don, Ythan, and the two Esks, "to the great prejudice of the whole kingdom." The question of the reserved waters at the Isles and on the west coast had not been dealt with by the burghs, and the Council asked them to report on these. The burghs thereupon modified their original demands, specifying certain places that should be reserved, where the fishings had been continually carried on by Scottish fishermen and merchants, who were able, they said, to undertake and fish the same "to the full," and within which no stranger had ever been admitted to fish. These places were as follows: (1) all lochs on the mainland between Farryhead (Cape Wrath) and the Kyle, together with Loch Hourn on the south side of Kyle; (2) the east side of Lewes, Uist, Barra, and "Muggersland" (? Mull), and the lochs of the same, together with the Broad Loch and the "Bybleheid" on the north-east part of the Lewes; (3) "Lochusherd" (? Loch Eishort) in Skye; (4) between the islands and the mainland, from "Farayhead" to the north-east point of Lewis, and for fourteen miles without the line between them it was "absolutely necessary," for the good of the fishings in the lochs above mentioned, that no buss-fishing should be permitted. All the salmon-fishings were to be wholly reserved for the natives, and the burghs expressed the wish that fourteen miles around the Orkneys and Shetlands should also be reserved, but they referred this to the king. The question of the remaining lochs on the mainland between the Kyle and the Mull of Cantyre, and of the waters on the "backside" of Lewis, Uist, Barra, "Muggersland," and Skye, except those previously mentioned, was to be "remitted" to the king's consideration.[1]

The Council forwarded these propositions to London, and the burghs instructed their own commissioner in a like sense, but with an important qualification as to the Hollanders fishing on the coast of Scotland. The king was to be informed of the great oppressions and wrongs suffered by his subjects from the encroachment of the Dutch on the seas and coasts of the kingdom, at Shetland and Orkney, and lately at the Lewes. If these encroachments were allowed to continue, the burghs declared that the rich fishings would be made quite unprofitable, and they appealed to the king "to free the seas of Scotland and the Isles of the busses of the said Northlands (Nether-

[1] *Acta Parl. Scot.*, v. 238.

lands)," and of other strangers, from Hamburg and Bremen, resorting to Orkney and Shetland. At the very least, they said, he ought to free the seas of the Dutch busses or fishing-boats "for the space of twenty-eight or fourteen miles, and to discharge them to have any fishing near the coasts of the said mainland or isles." If the king would do this, the burghs promised to further to the utmost of their power "his Majesty's most royal work of fishing," to supply the proportional number of busses that might fall to their part, and to consent that liberty should be granted to Englishmen and Irishmen to fish in all the waters around Scotland, except the Firths of Lothian, Moray, and Clyde, and those reserved for salmon-fishing; but they would only agree to this on the condition stated and not otherwise. They also asked that the buss-fishing should not be allowed at the Lewes, that it should begin on the east coast on 24th June and the fishing at the Isles on 1st September, and that they should receive equal liberty to fish in the seas of England and Ireland for pilchards and white fish.[1]

In the debates between the Scottish and English commissioners in London, at most of which the king was present,[2] Coke exerted himself to reconcile the differences that existed. He adroitly pointed out that, as the complaints from Scotland showed, strangers now possessed their fishings, and said they would be able to oust them only by degrees and by making the most of the natural advantages on the sea which both nations had. And while claiming that all the fisheries in the British seas (and even in America) belonged to the crown, and that there could not therefore be, strictly considered, any right to "reserve" certain of them, still the king, by the undoubted right of sovereignty he had in all his seas, had power to give license of fishing within them, either to subjects or foreigners as he might think fit, and by his royal prerogative alone he could establish the proposed company "whereby all his subjects which are brethren thereof may enjoy that fishing by right which strangers have by usurpation in our seas.[3] By this time the Scottish commissioners were becoming reconciled

[1] *Rec. Conv. Roy. Burghs*, iv. 534, 535.

[2] "Whereat we ourselff for the most part were present,"—king to Council, 15th July 1632. *Stirling Letters*, ii. 604.

[3] *State Papers, Dom.*, ccvi. 46.

to the proposal of forming the society on very much the original plan, and their opposition, perhaps partly from the presence of Charles at the conferences, was beginning to give way. They had been told, too, in answer to some of their objections, that while it was the king's intention to maintain existing rights, all their liberties depended wholly upon the king's grace, and he had expressed his purpose that his Council in both kingdoms should advise them in anything that required further consideration. It was much to be desired, they were told, that his Majesty's clear intentions should prevail with them as they had done with the English commissioners, not to question, but to advance and settle so needful a work.[1]

Charles himself came forward to help them with an alternative plan to that of the "reserved waters." The ground upon which the claim to the latter was based had gradually shifted. The initial argument that the surrounding seas pertained to Scotland as an independent kingdom—that they were the "seas of Scotland"—had been disposed of by the declaration that the right to the sea and to its fisheries was a prerogative of the crown; and it could not be denied that though no union of the kingdoms had taken place, there certainly had been union of the crowns. The question of the prerogative was a thorny one, which the Scottish commissioners had to avoid; and the claim to the reserved waters was now made solely on behalf of the poor inhabitants of certain parts of the coast, who subsisted mainly by their fishing in the sea, and would, it was said, be reduced to poverty and indigence unless these waters were reserved for their exclusive use. To meet this objection, Coke proposed a resolution at one of the meetings that the king should be asked to lay down a regulation to guard against interference with the poor fishermen at the places where the fishing of the company would be carried on, and at the next meeting a draft in the king's handwriting, perhaps laid on the table by Charles himself, was read as follows: "The English commissioners desire to take away all showes of wordes that may show diffidence between the two nations, and hauing heard that the Scots commissioners are to desire some places to be reserved from the company or association, it is conceived this to be the fitter way:—That

[1] *State Papers, Dom.*, ccvi. 50.

instead of those reservations, that the association should appoint the same fishermen that now fishe in them, [so that they] may continue as particular company of the said association, and to be subject [to] the law of the same, and are willing that no others should fish in those places, [unless] it be found upon examination that those places may admit more fishermen than those that now fish in them, and in that case the great committee of the association shall add such to them as they shall think fit, desiring them always to remember that the said committee is compounded equally of both nations."[1] The king's proposition was in keeping with the intention of Coke, "to bring all private fishing vessels under the company," and though it was obviously impracticable, it furnished a plausible argument against the claim to reserved waters.

After further conferences a number of articles were agreed to: That an association should be established, with no joint-stock except that received from those who voluntarily joined the undertaking; that a standing committee of the two nations in equal numbers should be formed, some of whom were to be appointed, also equally from both nations, to judge of controversies amongst the busses according to regulations to be made, with the right of appeal to the standing committee. Two hundred busses were "propounded" for the first year; "whereof," said the Scots commissioners, "wee gott to advise what number we would undertake, but our answer was never yet sought; always we intend, God willing, to sett out 100 busses." The main point, in regard to the reserved waters or fishing-places, was left for the king's consideration. Finally, the king was to be asked to give order for drawing up the charter of association.[2]

In July 1632 Charles was able to announce that the difficulties were overcome and the negotiations completed, to his "great contentment," and with the mutual consent of both parties. Desirous of removing as soon as possible the causes of the complaints which had been made by the burghs, he wrote to the Privy Council at Edinburgh about the great wrongs done by the Dutch inhabiting the Lewes and fishing

[1] *State Papers, Dom.*, cciii. 53, 54, 19th November 1631. The draft appears to have been prepared and altered entirely by the king himself.

[2] *State Papers, Dom.*, ccxxix. 78, 83, 87, 89.

there "against the laws of that our kingdom," instructing them to put in force a decree which had been previously issued at the request of the burghs, to prevent all strangers from trading or fishing there or at Shetland.[1] He also requested the Council to prohibit unseasonable fishing for herrings at Ballantrae Bank near the mouth of the Clyde, which, he had been informed, was very injurious to the herring fisheries on the west coast of Scotland, the Isles, and the neighbouring coast of Ireland, by destroying the fry of herrings at unseasonable times, which, he was informed, if they were spared, might produce such plenty in all these coasts as might very much advance the intended work of fishing. At the same time he declared that it was necessary to establish settlements for the fishings at the Isles, and the Council were asked to take sureties from the landlords of the Isles, and of the lochs of the mainland, against violations or oppressions on those of the association engaged in fishing there, and from exacting any duties or impositions from them. The Council was also invited to take into serious consideration the Act of the Scottish Parliament "of 4 James IV." respecting the building of busses by the noblemen, and to use their best means to put it into execution.[2] The nobility and gentry of Scotland were apparently expected to build forty busses for fishing on both coasts, at an estimated cost of £10,960; and in addition to equip them with nets, salt, casks, and victuals.[3]

On the all-important question of the reserved waters the king did not grant the "irreducible minimum" of the burghs.

[1] The king to the Council, 15th July 1632. *Stirling Letters*, ii. 605, 606, 617. *Acta Parl. Scot.*, v. 245.

[2] The Act specified by the king was passed in 1491, but he seems rather to have been referring to the Act 6 James III., c. 48, "That Lordes, Barrones and Burrowes gar make Schippes, Busches, and greate Pinck-boates with Nettes," which was passed in 1471, "for the common good of the realm and the great increase of riches," to be brought from other countries in exchange for fish exported. The Act of James IV., "Anent the makeing of Schippes and Busches on the quhilk all Idle Men suld Laboure," was an early attempt to carry out the policy advocated by English writers in the sixteenth, seventeenth, and eighteenth centuries. It enacted that ships and busses, not under twenty tons burden, should be built in all the burghs and towns of Scotland, provided with mariners and nets: and power was given to compel "idle men" to man them.

[3] *State Papers, Dom.*, ccvi. 47. "What is required from the Lords and Gentry of Scotland towards the fishing."

The condition which the burghs attached to their surrender of everything except the three great Firths, that is, the exclusion of the Hollanders from fishing on the coasts of Scotland, was in the meantime nominally met by the instructions to the Council mentioned above. In two or three years, as we shall see, when his naval power was greater, he would attempt to carry out their desire in quite a forcible and dramatic way. Charles would not concede the Moray Firth as an exclusive preserve for the Scottish fishermen, but he gave up to them the Firth of Lothian within a straight line from St Abb's Head to Red Head in Forfarshire, and also the Firth of Clyde within a line drawn between the Mulls of Galloway and Cantyre; because, as he said, the inhabitants of the coasts of these parts were chiefly maintained by the fishing within them and could not well subsist otherwise. These waters were therefore to be reserved to Scottish fishermen, "according to ancient custom."[1]

Everything having been arranged to the king's satisfaction, he issued a commission providing for the establishment of a Fishery Society under the great seal of both kingdoms, which was approved by the Scottish Parliament on 7th September 1632.[2] The Society was to consist of twelve councillors appointed by the king, six of them to be English or Irish and six to be Scots,[3] and also a "commonalty" composed of a large number of noblemen and other persons. They were empowered to appoint officers, to make laws, and to punish transgressions. In every "province" of the kingdom and in the towns most convenient, "judges" were to be elected by the resident members to settle disputes and make regulations. The members, their servants and fishermen, were favoured by certain immunities and privileges; they and their vessels were exempt from impressment for the king's service and relieved

[1] *Acta Parl. Scot.*, v. 236.

[2] *State Papers, Dom.*, ccxxi. 1; *Acta Parl. Scot.*, v. 239.

[3] The councillors nominated by Charles were, for England and Ireland, Lord Weston, the High Treasurer (created Earl of Portland in February of the following year), the Earl of Arundel, the Earl of Pembroke, Viscount Savage, Lord Cottingham, and Secretary Coke; for Scotland, the Earl of Morton, the High Treasurer, the Earl of Stratherne and Monteith, President of the Privy Council, the Earl of Roxburgh, Viscount Stirling, Mr John Hay, and Mr George Fletcher.

of certain civil obligations. They were to be free to fish for sea-fish wherever they pleased "within his Majesty's seas" and dominions, and at the isles pertaining thereto, as well as in the "lochs, creeks, bays and estuaries" wherever herrings or sea-fish were or might be taken, except in such creeks or firths as might be reserved in a proclamation of the king. On the trading side of the enterprise, they were to be at liberty to carry the fish to any place within the kingdom, "as well within free burghs as without them," to salt, dry, and barrel them, to erect the necessary buildings and magazines, and to dispose of the fish as they thought best, within the realm, or to export them either in their own vessels or in others. Other clauses prohibited any person not a member of the Society from exporting, or causing to be exported, abroad any sea-fish taken within, or brought within, his Majesty's dominions. Charles and his advisers aimed at no less a thing than to bring the whole of the sea fisheries and fish-curing industries of the country, as well as the foreign exports, under the control of the Council of the Society. The whole business was then to be organised and developed in such a manner that the Dutch fishermen would be driven from the British seas, and the nation to which they belonged deprived of the commanding position which, it was believed, their fisheries had been the chief means of conferring.

But the patience and perseverance of Charles in wearing out the opposition of Scotland to his scheme, and in giving it the semblance of a national design, were most inadequately rewarded. Like almost everything to which he put his hand, the fishery association failed miserably. The Scottish burghs promised to equip sixty busses for the fishing in the following year, but in point of fact the Scottish people took scarcely any part in the operations of the Society. The London merchants, canvassed personally by Sir Thomas Roe and appealed to by Pembroke, also held aloof. They gave "fair answers," but kept their money. The subscriptions, or stock, came almost exclusively from persons about the Court, from naval officers and others desirous of preferment. The first meeting of the Council was called for 24th January, but so few members attended that the meeting had to be adjourned until 19th February, when it took place in the Star Chamber. Oaths were administered, two silver seals were ordered (and never paid for) at a cost of £12, and Captain John Mason was made "Admiral of their fleet" of busses. Differences of opinion soon arose in the Council, and the Society split up into two branches or associations, one under Weston (now Earl of Portland),—that "man of big looks and of a mean and abject spirit," as Clarendon describes him,—and after his death, under the Earl of Arundel; the other branch under the Earl of Pembroke, the Lord Chamberlain, who appears to have been almost the only one, besides the king and Coke, who took a sincere personal interest in the Society. Portland's society had its headquarters at Lewis, while Pembroke's was more particularly designed to carry on operations at Shetland and the east coast, but also had a station in the Lewes. The total amount of the subscriptions to the Society up to 3rd February 1636 was £22,682, 10s., of which only £9914, 10s. was paid up, and the company had been forced to borrow £3550 at interest to set the scheme afloat. The stock of Portland's association amounted altogether to £16,975 up to and including the year 1637, while the losses in the same period reached £21,071, 5s. 7d.

Ground was acquired and houses and magazines for salt and casks erected at the Lewes,[1] and several busses were purchased in Holland by both associations, ready for fishing and manned entirely by Dutchmen. Agents despatched to Shetland and Lewis sent favourable reports of the prospects. "We hope," said the one at Lewis, "to furnish London with some plenty against the hard times of winter"; yet the total quantity of herrings cured at the island in that the first year of the Society's fishing was only 386 lasts, and the price obtained for them was so low that the loss amounted to £4261. This, according to the agents, was due to want of proper means of curing them (salt, casks, hoops, &c.), otherwise they said they might have obtained 1000 lasts or more. A great effort

[1] Martin, who visited the Hebrides about the year 1695, saw the foundation of a house, which, the natives told him, had been built by the Society as a store for salt and casks, on Hermetra, a small island in the Sound of Harris; and he saw a similar relic on a small island called Vacksay, in Loch Maddy. He was informed by the natives that "in the memory of some yet alive," as many as 400 sail had been loaded with herrings in Loch Maddy in one season: at the time of his visit the fishing had been abandoned, though herrings were plentiful. *A Description of the Westerne Islands of Scotland*, pp. 51, 54, 55.

was therefore put forth in the following year. Preparations were made to deal with 1500 lasts, and vessels were chartered to carry them from Stornoway to various Continental markets. But less than 443 lasts were cured in the second year; some were sent to Dantzic and fetched "mean prices," the rest reached London "when Lent was wellnigh over," and were sent on to Dunkirk and Dantzic, the vessels coming back in ballast, and the loss in this year was £8163, 19s. 4d.[1] In this way the operations of the Society went on. The herrings then failed to come into the lochs, and the Society turned its attention to the salting and exportation of beef, salmon, cod, and coal-fish,—a course fraught with less disastrous financial results, but not well calculated to carry out the objects for which it was founded.

Ill-fortune was encountered in other directions. Both the islanders and the Scots from the east coast treated the English adventurers badly. The Bishop of the Isles and the heritors insisted on their tithes and dues in spite of the king's charter. The busses were attacked by bands of Highlanders, armed with "swords and bows and arrows and other warlike weapons," who took various articles from them in lieu of dues. The Lowlanders, under the leadership of "one Thomas Lindsay, a fisherman of Crail," who pretended to be the deputy to the deputy of the Vice-Admiral of Scotland, were still less considerate. Lindsay "villified" their certificates, declared that King Charles had nothing to do with the Lewes, and vowed that "he would be the death of every Englishman on the island." He forcibly seized one of the vessels laden with

[1] Simon Smith, who was latterly Secretary to Pembroke's association, afterwards stated that the Society had attained to the proper cure of herrings, and was likely to have been ultimately successful. This opinion was not shared by Dutch writers. The author of *The True Interest and Political Maxims of the Republic of Holland*, published under the name of De Witt, says the herrings the Society sent to Dantzic in 1637 and 1638, though caught at the same time and place as the Hollanders' herrings, were "esteemed naught to the very last barrel"; and a contemporary author, Meynert Semeyns, a skipper of Enkhuisen, in a work written in 1639 (*Een corte beschryvinge over de Haring-visscherye in Hollandt*), says the same thing. "The Dutch," he boasted, "catch more herrings and prepare them better than any other nation ever will; and the Lord has, by means of the herring, made Holland an exchange and staple-market for the whole of Europe." No other nation, he added, ever tried the industry but to their loss, and the example adduced was the Society's herrings sent to Dantzic.

herrings which had gone ashore, on the ground that it was wreck, and wreck belonged to the Admiral of Scotland, and committed other hostile actions. The grievances of the Society became so acute, and redress from the Privy Council and the Admiralty Court so tardy and imperfect, that Charles in May 1635 appointed a commission, consisting of Archbishop Laud, the Earl of Pembroke, Sir Thomas Edmonds, and Secretaries Coke and Windebank, as judges, according to the charter, to deal with cases as they thought fit.

Disasters at sea were even more injurious to the Society than the troubles ashore. Again and again the busses were taken by Dunkirk privateers, who threw the crews into prison and held them for ransom. When those freebooters came across a Dutch-built buss, with a Dutch crew on board, they did not quite see why they should relinquish it because they were told it belonged to an English society; and the letters of "denization" which were provided by the king did not avail them much.[1] Notwithstanding strong protests, prolonged negotiations with the Cardinal Infanta, and reprisals made by English men-of-war on Dunkirk shipping, the Society suffered great loss in this way.

The misfortunes of the Society caused many of those who had promised subscriptions to withhold them. Then followed drastic measures: summonses before the Star Chamber, warrants for apprehension, threats of imprisonment, and most of the subscriptions were squeezed from the unwilling adventurers. On the other hand, creditors sued the Society for goods supplied and money lent; seamen sued it for wages; even the clerks had to petition the king for theirs, appropriately suggesting that they might be paid from the license-money that Northumberland's fleet had extorted from the Dutch herring-busses.[2] As

[1] In August and September 1633, before the Council had met (busses having been purchased on the strength of subscriptions promised), two busses were taken by Dutch men-of-war and one by a Dunkirker. The former captures were doubtless made because the Dutch fishermen were acting contrary to the fishery laws of the United Provinces in taking service with aliens, and they were promptly disavowed by the States-General and the busses restored. The Dunkirkers made prize of some of the busses (there were ten or twelve of them) almost every year: one, the *Salisbury*, was taken twice, and in 1639 four were captured. Spain was then at war with the United Provinces, and the Dutch buss was a natural prey of the Dunkirk privateer.

[2] P. 309.

Charles's domestic troubles thickened and his power on the sea began to wane, Pembroke and his associates became more and more importunate for help. Petitions were conveyed to him, and then "remonstrances." He was pointedly reminded that he was the originator and "Protector" of the Society; unless he "really" helped them the work must stop. But Charles was then unable either to compel the restitution of the captured busses or to induce his subjects to subscribe to the Society's funds. He did what he could. Pennington and the Warden of the Cinque Ports were ordered to seize Dunkirk ships to be sold for the benefit of the Society; he granted them a standing lottery, and issued a proclamation enjoining the strict observance of Lent, which might possibly help them by increasing the consumption of fish, and could at least do them no harm. Almost his last act in connection with the fishery association was to issue an Order in Council in which, somewhat irritably, he blamed the Dutch for the failure, and remitted to an influential committee to consider some means by which the fishery in the north seas might be "advanced and settled," and particularly whether the Dutch should not be deprived of English lampreys for bait, which were necessary for their cod-fishing.[1] It was a great fall for Charles as Lord of the Seas, with a policy as sketched at the beginning of this chapter, to use the lampreys of the Thames as a weapon against the Dutch rather than a

[1] *State Papers, Dom.*, ccccxxix. 48. Order of the King in Council, 29th September 1639. "Taking into consideration of what great importance it is and may be to the good of this kingdom to plant, increase and cherish the fishery in the North seas, and understanding that the Dutch, who reap an annual great benefit thereby, have and do not only privately underhand, but too manifestly also oppose the endeavours of his Majesty's good subjects, who have of late years employed their industry that way," it was ordered that the Lord Treasurer, the Earl Marshal, the Lord Admiral, the Lord Chamberlain, the Earl of Dorset, and one of the Secretaries of State, calling to their aid Sir Henry Marten (Judge of the Court of Admiralty), should forthwith "consult and advise what fitting course may be taken to advance and settle the said fishery, and particularly to consider whether it may not be fit to debar the exportation of lampreys, without which the Dutch cannot well, as is informed, continue their fishing for cod and ling, until his Majesty's subjects be quietly settled in the herring fishing." The Dutch obtained their lampreys for bait almost exclusively from England, and chiefly from the Thames. The above account of the proceedings of the Fishery Society is summarised (for the most part) from numerous State Papers. It was stated by Simon Smith, who was latterly Secretary to Pembroke's association, that £10,000 was lost through the Dunkirkers.

powerful armada. But by this time his power at sea had vanished. The Dutch lorded it in the Channel.

When the Order in Council was penned, Tromp had hemmed in the Spanish fleet in the Downs and was ready to pounce on it the moment it quitted English waters, or to destroy it there if he only could get a plausible excuse. Charles and his Council were trembling with fear lest the best known of all the "King's Chambers" should be flagrantly violated by the impatient Dutchman, with all the world looking on. And twelve days after the Council meeting this is just what Tromp did, and Charles's sovereignty of the seas vanished for ever. And the fishery scheme, "the Royal Fishery of Great Britain and Ireland," set agoing after so much patient labour, heralded by so many promises of profit and success, designed to be a great instrument for the development of naval power and commerce, was extinguished in the following year, with no tangible result save that those who had given their money to it were left "great losers."

CHAPTER VII.

CHARLES I.—*continued*. THE NAVY.

SINCE Charles had resolved to assert his claims to the sovereignty of the sea by force if necessary, it was obviously essential that he should have a strong and capable fleet. During the peaceful reign of James the navy had greatly deteriorated from what it had been under Queen Elizabeth.[1] The expedition to Cadiz in 1625, and that to Rhé two years later, revealed startling inefficiency and disorganisation, and efforts were soon made to bring it into a better state. When he assumed the crown, his fleet consisted of thirty ships; in 1633 it numbered fifty, including the ten small vessels called the "Lion's Whelps"; and when the Civil War broke out there were forty-two, the difference being due to the shedding of the smaller ones.[2]

There were many reasons why a strong fleet should be provided, apart from any question of enforcing a new political sovereignty over the North Sea and the Channel. The maritime strength of the United Provinces was growing quickly, and France, under the wise and energetic guidance of Richelieu, was rapidly becoming a formidable naval power. Within the space of about five years before 1631, as Charles knew, the Cardinal had created a fleet of thirty-nine ships, of which eighteen were of 500 tons or over, and no less than twenty-seven had been built in French ports.[3] These two states were drawing closer together, and while it was known that their alliance, which was then mooted and was soon realised, would

[1] Oppenheim, *A History of the Administration of the Royal Navy*, i. 215, 217, 221.

[2] *Ibid.*; Hannay, *A Short History of the Royal Navy*.

[3] Oppenheim, *op. cit.*, 265.

be chiefly directed against Spain, it was nevertheless a danger to England unless she was strong enough to defend her rights on the sea.

Other reasons were the insecurity of the seas from the prevalence of piracy, and the violation of the "King's Chambers," and even of English ports, by the Dunkirkers and the Dutch. Moorish pirates swarmed in the Channel and made havoc amongst English shipping. So bold and successful were they, that in 1631 they seized and sacked Baltimore, on the coast of Munster, and carried off over 200 English subjects into slavery. Within a space of ten days they captured twenty-seven ships and 200 men.[1] The Dunkirkers played a corresponding *rôle* in the North Sea. In a petition to the king in 1627, the shipowners of Ipswich complained that within a year the Dunkirkers had captured five of their ships, valued with their cargoes at £5000, and carried the crews to Dunkirk. No ship, they said, could go to sea, and the livelihood of seafaring men was taken from them, and the king's service would thus suffer. The Mayor and burgesses of King's Lynn put the losses of the town at twenty-five ships, worth £9000, and complained that they were unable to carry on the Iceland fishery. The Cinque Ports also complained that the Dunkirkers had taken their goods, imprisoned their mariners, and rifled and sunk their ships on the English shore; and they asked for a guard to enable them to go to the fishing in the north and at Scarborough and Yarmouth. The alarm was general all along the coast. In February 1629 the bailiffs of Yarmouth reported that the sea was overrun with Dunkirkers, who had even rifled and fired one of their ships close under the cliffs at Mundesley, notwithstanding the efforts of the sheriff and posse of the county; they said 250 fishing vessels were ready to go to the northern fishing and awaited convoy. In the next year they and other towns of Norfolk and Suffolk stated their intention of sending out two fishing fleets of "ships, barks, and crayers,"—one of 160 sail to Iceland and Westmony, and the other of 230 sail for the north seas,—and they begged for ships of war to guard them, as the livelihood or "utter ruin" of 10,000 people and their families depended on these fleets. Two years later they repeated their request to the Admiralty, saying they

[1] Oppenheim, *op. cit.*, 275.

usually sent out a fleet of about 300 sail, with 5000 persons, to the fishings mentioned, but the fishermen were now so terrified by the Dunkirkers that they refused to go. The Mayor of Newcastle also informed the Council that they had been despoiled to the extent of £7000; he said there were 300 sail in port which dared not venture out; and the Council were asked to take means to secure safe passage on the sea. At this time there were said to be forty Dunkirk privateers scouring the North Sea, many of them with English sailors on board.[1] We have already seen how successfully these freebooters preyed upon the busses of the Fishery Society.

Here then was a clear case for a navy, when an effective navy did not exist. The Council and the Admiralty took such isolated measures as they could; but the Dunkirkers were almost always too nimble to be caught. "They take ships," wrote the commander of a man-of-war convoying the Iceland fishing fleet, "and we in sight and cannot come up to help it." The duty and expense of providing convoys to protect the fishermen were thrown on the fishing ports and the counties. In 1627 the Council ordered four Newcastle ships to be taken up for eight months, to convoy the Iceland fleet, at a cost of £1768, to be paid out of the "loans" in Suffolk. The estimate in the following year for a guard of four merchant ships, of 400 tons each, with 120 men for one month in harbour and 240 men for six months at sea, was £4399; and the Council in authorising the Admiralty to "press, victual, arm, and man" the ships, instructed that if Yarmouth and the other towns wanted convoy in future they should first consult together as to some mode of levying monies for it, either upon the coast towns or upon the counties of Norfolk and Suffolk. This was done, in part at least, by levying a contribution of twenty shillings from each fisherman; and fishermen also protected themselves by insuring their vessels in London against the risks of capture by the Dunkirk privateers. The owners and masters of the merchant ships thus pressed to act as guards to the fishing fleets were usually most unwilling to serve, and sometimes "utterly refused," and the Admiralty had

[1] *State Papers, Dom.*, lvi. 66; lxi. 81; lxx. 8, 9; liv. 56; xc. 70, 119; clxii. 82, 45.

to get an Order in Council to compel them.[1] Provision of a guard for the east coast generally was attempted by levying a duty of two and five shillings a ton on all coal laden at Newcastle or Sunderland for English and foreign ports respectively.[2]

Equally impressive evidence of the lawlessness that then reigned on the sea, and of the inability to deal with it effectively, was furnished by the flagrant violation of English ports and roadsteads, by the Dutch as well as the Dunkirkers, who waged incessant war with one another. The herring-busses and merchant vessels of the former were frequently captured, rifled, and burned by the privateers, and when the commander of a Dutch man-of-war had a chance of destroying one of the pests, he was not always deterred from vengeance by the Dunkirker taking refuge in English waters; and in like manner the privateer did not scruple to pursue his prey into English ports and anchorages. Sometimes, indeed, the warfare was continued on English soil and the lives of the king's lieges endangered. In 1634, for example, a Dunkirker chased a Hollander vessel into Yarmouth harbour and robbed her, and a lively fusilade went on between the Dutchmen, who had taken refuge on the pier, and the crew of the privateer, and one of the former was killed. As the Dunkirkers refused to stop their "furious assault," the bailiffs ordered two of the town's guns to be fired at them, "which they only scoffed at"; and when the marshal called upon them in the king's name to desist and begone, they only "answered with unseemly gestures and scorn," and they did not make off until a company of musketeers went down to them. But next day as the privateer was hovering off the coast, two States' men-of-war bore down upon her and she ran for shelter to the beach near Lowestoft; but the Dutch followed, seized her, and carried

[1] *State Papers, Dom.*, lix. 79; xci. 30, 45; xcii. 62; xciii. 82; xcv. 39; clxiii. 65; clxxx. 94. In 1630 a Yarmouth fisherman, owner of one of the Iceland smacks under convoy, petitioned the Council for relief from the payment of the twenty shillings, on the grounds that before the Order was made he had paid £5 for the assurance of his boat during that season to the assurance office in London, and that three boats belonging to him had been previously taken by Dunkirkers.

[2] Oppenheim, *op. cit.*, 276.

her off, the crew escaping to shore, where they were promptly arrested and lodged in Yarmouth jail.

A still more outrageous transgression of the neutrality of an English port took place in the following year, at the very time that Lindsey's fleet was cruising in the Channel. A Dunkirker brought a Hollander buss into Scarborough harbour, and she was followed by a States' man-of-war, which opened fire, and a fight both with cannon and muskets took place. The bullets, flying into the town, hit several of the citizens, and some strangers on the sands were also hurt, "to the amazement and discouragement of the whole town." Twelve Dunkirkers were slain, and the rest only saved themselves by swimming ashore, while the man-of-war went off with both the privateer and the buss. A fortnight later another privateer was chased into the harbour by a Hollander man-of-war, which landed three or four score of men, armed with muskets and pikes, to set upon the Dunkirkers when the ship lay dry; and the Dutch captain only consented to re-embark them, on condition that the bailiffs of the town would themselves place a guard of fifty men to watch the privateer, so as to prevent any of the crew escaping.[1]

This glaring outrage on English soil caused the Council to arrest a Dutch man-of-war, to be held until the one that had committed the misdeed should be delivered up; for, said Windebank, it was a matter that concerned the king himself in point of honour and the safety of the kingdom, as an act of hostility, "little less than an invasion," had been committed in landing armed men on his Majesty's territories, "violating his imperial chamber and threatening his subjects." Nevertheless, in the next month a like offence was committed at Blyth, when a Dutch man-of-war not only attacked a Dunkirk privateer lying in the harbour, but landed fifty men armed with muskets, who marched in military order nearly half a mile, "to the great terror of the inhabitants," and by seizing the fishing-boats, captured the Dunkirker and took her away. Not only so, but thirty of the Hollanders, armed, and with trumpets, pursued the crew of the privateer on land for a distance of

[1] *State Papers, Dom.*, cclxviii. 31, 88; cclxiv. fol. 20*a*; ccxciii. 107; ccxciv. 46.

two miles.[1] There was a natural excuse for the violence of the Hollanders in these proceedings. They were exasperated by the immense havoc which the privateers had just committed on their herring-busses, by sinking or burning over 100 of them, the remainder of the fishing fleet escaping into Scottish and English harbours.[2]

This insecurity of the sea and the open and daring violation of English ports remind one of the conditions that too frequently prevailed in earlier centuries. The misdeeds must have been galling to Charles, for only a short time before he had issued a public proclamation with the object of putting a stop to them. In February 1633 Sir H. Marten, Judge of the High Court of Admiralty, along with the Attorney-General, had been instructed, in view of the war between Spain and the United Provinces, to draw up a regulation whereby "his Majesty's ancient rights, honours, and sovereignty in the narrow seas and in the chambers and ports may be preserved, and the trade of the kingdom of England and Ireland secured."[3] In this regulation (which is printed in Appendix H) a claim to absolute dominion over the Four Seas was made. The king spoke of "that sovereignty and especial and peculiar interest and property which he and his predecessors, time out of mind, have had and enjoyed in the said seas, and so approved not only by the fundamental laws of this his kingdom, but by the acknowledgment and assent of the bordering princes and nations, as appeareth by undoubted records"—language which seems like an echo of Selden's *Mare Clausum*. Moreover, in referring to the limits of the "King's Chambers," he continued: "Albeit his Majesty doth justly challenge sovereignty and property in all those his seas, far beyond the limits hereafter to be described, and might with like justice require

[1] *State Papers, Dom.*, ccxciii. 107; ccxciv. 46; ccxcv. 31, 69, 71; cclxiv. fol. 164. Many of the crew of the man-of-war were English, Scottish, or Irish. It was probably owing in part to the considerable numbers of British subjects serving on the Dutch men-of-war that they were always favoured by the country people.

[2] *Ibid.*, ccxcvi. 5, 14, 30. Joachimi to States-General, $\frac{\text{26 Aug.}}{\text{4 Sept.}}$, *Brit. Mus. Add. MSS.*, 17,677, O, fol. 380.

[3] *Brit. Mus. Add. MSS.*, 30,221, fol. 43*b*.

from all persons using those his seas a forbearance from injuries and all hostile actions, yet (in and through all the same) suddenly to tie the hands of his friends and allies in open hostility each with other, is not for some reasons held convenient at this time," and therefore he would cause the bounds to be laid down within which he would yield peace and security to his friends and neighbours.[1]

Clearly, however, something more than a proclamation was required to ensure the security of the seas and the neutrality of the chambers and ports. As early as 1627 official proposals had been made to build thirty ships of a small class to guard the narrow seas, which might compete in swiftness with the privateers and freebooters infesting them,—a plan that was partly carried out by the building of the ten "Lion's Whelps," which, however, proved complete failures. An estimate was also procured for building eighteen ships and two pinnaces, at a cost of about £43,000, the estimated expense of the crews being £6100 per month.[2] Various other schemes were considered, including one to form a fleet of forty armed Newcastle colliers, to be employed primarily in convoying the coal ships, but capable of being called off at any time for the king's service. The want of money was the great obstacle to the formation of a strong fleet. The wages of the seamen and others employed were always in arrear,—at the end of 1627 the arrears amounted to £251,361,—and the victualling and furnishing of the ships afloat were of the worst possible description.[3] The necessity of a fleet to maintain the dominion of the sea and defend the coasts was being constantly urged upon the king. The Attorney-General, Heath, in 1632, called attention to the truism that our strength and safety lay "in our walls, which is our shipping," and he strongly recommended that a powerful fleet should be maintained because of the boldness of the Hollanders, and in order to preserve

[1] Reglement for Preventing Abuses in and about the Narrow Seas and Ports, March 1633. *State Papers, Dom.*, cclx. 127, 128; cclxxix. 18. *Brit. Mus. Add. MSS.*, 30,221, fol. 44 (Pepys' collections). Copies exist in *State Papers, Dom.*, vol. 515, Nos. 38, 39 (1647), extracted from *Admiralty Book*, Liber E, and in *State Papers, Dom.*, Jas. I., vol. 11, No. 40 (1604), wrongly calendered (see p. 119).

[2] *Ibid.*, liv. 9, 33.

[3] Oppenheim, *op. cit.*

the king's prerogative in the fisheries in the British seas, as well as to secure the mastery of the narrow seas.[1]

Charles required no spur in a matter the importance of which he thoroughly understood, and he had private and personal reasons for wishing that a strong force should be placed on the sea. It was the family policy as to the restoration of the Palatinate that chiefly guided him. At the end of 1633 he entered into negotiations with Spain for an alliance against the Dutch, and in the following year a secret treaty was drafted and sent to Madrid (four days before the issue of the first ship-money writs) in which Charles undertook to provide a fleet, partly at the charge of the King of Spain, who was to advance a sum of £50,000 and help to recover the Palatinate for his nephew.[2] It was intended that the fleet should co-operate with the Spaniards against the United Provinces; the ports of Flanders were to be freed from the blockade maintained by the Dutch, and Spanish vessels carrying soldiers and money for Dunkirk were to be protected by English ships; the mastery of the Dutch at sea was to be destroyed, the Republic was to be attacked and overthrown, and the country divided between the allies. The open avowal of such a policy would have been equivalent to making it almost impossible, for an alliance with Catholic Spain against the Protestant Republic was in the highest degree unpopular in England, and the fleet, moreover, was to be created by means of the ship-money writs. The negotiations had been carried on with the greatest secrecy; only three members of the Council (Portland, Cottington, and Windebank) were in the king's confidence, the others remaining in ignorance. It was thus necessary to deceive them as well as the nation as to the object of equipping a fleet. The insecurity of the seas from the prevalence of piracy and the violations of English waters, referred to above, were put forward among the ostensible reasons to justify it. "The pretext of this arming," it was distinctly stated in 1634, "shall be to secure the coasts of Great Britain and Ireland, and to free them from pirates and others that commit hostilities and insol-

[1] *State Papers, Dom.*, lxxxvi. 73, 75; ccxxix. 102.

[2] Gardiner, *Hist.*, vii. 349 *et seq.*

encies there."[1] To deceive the people by fears of invasion, owing to the "great preparations both by sea and land of the neighbouring princes," orders were given to have the beacons along the coast examined; to muster and make ready the trained bands to join their colours at an hour's warning; to enrol all untrained men between the ages of sixteen and sixty, so that levies of them might be made "on any sudden occasion."[2]

Another reason put prominently forward to cloak the nefarious scheme was the need of maintaining the ancient sovereignty of the sea. While the Spanish negotiations were proceeding, Boroughs, as we shall see, had finished his treatise on the rights of the crown in the adjoining seas, and Selden was busy with his *Mare Clausum.* The language of the ship-money writs, sent out in October 1634, and the charge of Lord Coventry to the Judges, breathed the same spirit as these treatises. In the writs, which were founded upon extracts made by Boroughs from records of the times of Edward I., II., and III.,[3] the king described how "thieves, pirates, and robbers of the sea" were "taking by force and spoiling the ships and goods and merchandises, not only of our subjects, but also of the subjects of our friends in the sea which hath been accustomed anciently to be defended by the English nation," delivering the men into miserable captivity. The pirates, he said, were daily preparing all manner of shipping further to molest the merchants, unless a remedy was applied, and that in view also of the dangers menacing the realm "in these times of war," it was necessary to hasten the defence of the sea and kingdom. Therefore, he continued, "We willing by the help of God chiefly to provide for the defence of the kingdom, safeguard of the sea, security of our subjects, safe conduct of ships and merchandises to our kingdom of England coming, and from the same kingdom to foreign parts passing; forasmuch as we and our progenitors, Kings of England, have been always heretofore masters of the aforesaid sea, and it would be very irksome unto us if that princely honour in our time should be lost or in anything diminished," it was necessary for the sea-coast towns to furnish ships or

[1] Gardiner, *op. cit.*, 368.

[2] *State Papers, Dom.*, cclxxxvii. 55; ccxci. 14.

[3] *Ibid.*, cclxxvi. 65.

an equivalent in money.[1] In similar language Coventry told the Judges in 1635 that the dominion of the sea, "as it was an ancient and undoubted right of the crown of England," so was it the best security of the land, which was impregnable so long as the sea was well guarded; and that those subjects "whose minds are most fixed upon the honour of the king and country" would not endure that it should be either lost or diminished. The safety of the realm, he said, required the dominion of the sea to be kept and the sea guarded: "The wooden-walls are the best walls of the kingdom; and if the riches and wealth of the kingdom be respected, for that cause the dominion of the sea ought to be respected; for else what would become of our wool, lead, and the like, the price whereof would fall to nothing if others should be masters of the sea?" If the dominion of the sea was lost, trade and commerce would be lost by being placed at the mercy of the neighbouring nations, and the whole kingdom would suffer.[2]

In carrying out his Spanish policy, Charles's first task was to deceive his Council.[3] For this purpose no better agent could have been chosen than Coke, who, as we have seen, was by this time enthusiastic about the sovereignty of the seas, and was known to be hostile to Spain. He was accordingly directed to prepare a report for the king on the unsatisfactory relations between England and foreign countries, and the need of providing a fleet. In the long statement he drew up, Coke described how the credit of the country had been lowered abroad, and innumerable wrongs and insolences suffered in various parts of the world, because of the want of a sufficient navy to make our name respected. "All free trade," he wrote, "is interrupted"; within the king's own chambers squadrons of men-of-war from Biscay and Flanders took not only Hollanders, but Frenchmen, Hamburgers, and his Majesty's subjects. From the Hollanders "we suffered most by their intrusion on our fishings and pretence of *Mare*

[1] Rushworth, *Collections*, ii. 257. *State Papers, Dom.*, cclxxvi. 64. Compare the language of Edward III. in 1336, p. 36.

[2] Rushworth, ii. 294, 353. Compare Windebank's notes of the speech, *State Papers, Dom.*, ccxc. 108: "The Judges at the Assizes to let the people know his Majesty's care to preserve the ancient dominion (of the seas)."

[3] Gardiner, *op. cit.*

Liberum," and they pursued and took prizes in our ports and rivers. But our trade and rights were injured everywhere,—from Constantinople and Morocco to Denmark and Sweden,—and Coke recommended that the navy should be reinforced in order that the king might obtain justice and "recover his undoubted right of sovereignty in all his seas."[1] Coke read his report to the Council in June 1634; the ship-money writs were issued in October; and in May next year the first of the "ship-money fleets" was ready and was placed under the command of the Earl of Lindsey, with special instructions to maintain the king's sovereignty of the sea.

On the Continent the naval preparations of England were followed with close attention. As early as 1633, Joachimi, the States' ambassador in London, informed his Government that the English were putting forth pretensions to be sole lords and masters of the narrow seas, and he earnestly advised the States to avoid everything which might give the English offence in their excitable condition, on a matter which they had so much at heart.[2] An indication of the feeling prevailing in England was observed by the ambassador early in the year, for when he complained that Dutch vessels had been fired on from Portland Castle and then detained, he was told they had presumed to put up their flags in the face of the king's colours flying on the walls.[3] Next year the repeated complaints from England as to the violation of the King's Chambers by Dutch vessels of war, and the seizure of one of them by the English in consequence of the attack at Scarborough, did not lessen the apprehensions that began to be entertained in Holland. Rumours circulated that the English fleet was being prepared for the purpose of waging war against the Republic, and the answer given by the English ambassador at The Hague to inquiries as to the

[1] *State Papers, Dom.*, cclxix. 51.

[2] *Resol. States-General*, $\frac{9}{19}$ Nov. 1633; Muller, *Mare Clausum: Bijdrage tot de Geschiedenis der Rivaliteit van Engeland en Nederland in de Zeventiende Eeuw*, 229.

[3] *State Papers, Dom.*, ccxxxiv. 87; Nicholas's *Letter Book*, Feb. 16, fol. 97. Muller thinks it was this revival of feeling about the dominion of the sea that caused the edition of Grotius' *Mare Liberum* to be published this year, with the Magnus Intercursus appended.

object of the fleet was not calculated to allay anxiety. In the spring of 1635, a little before the Earl of Lindsey hoisted his colours on the *Merhonour*, Coke wrote a long and resounding despatch to Boswell, the English ambassador at The Hague, explaining the reasons for the naval preparations. "First," he said, "we hold it a principle not to be denied, that the King of Great Britain is a monarch at land and sea to the full extent of his dominions, and that it concerneth him as much to maintain his sovereignty in all the British seas as within his three kingdoms; because without that these cannot be kept safe, nor he preserve his honour and due respect with other nations. But, commanding the seas, he may cause his neighbours and all countries to stand upon their guard whensoever he thinks fit. And this cannot be doubted, that whosoever will encroach upon him by sea, will do it by land also when they see their time. To such presumption," he added, "*Mare Liberum* gave the first warning-piece, which must be answered with a defence of *Mare Clausum:* not so much by discourses, as by the louder language of a powerful navy, to be better understood when overstrained patience seeth no hope of preserving her right by other means." The innuendo against the United Provinces was still further developed. They had impeached the king's dominion in his seas for a long course of years. They had been permitted to gather wealth and strength in our ports and on our coasts by trade and fishery, for which they had "sued to King James for license," granted under the great seal of Scotland; and when they had possessed themselves of our fishings "by leave or by connivance," and obtained a great trade by our staple, they so increased their shipping and naval power that now they would not endure to be kept at any distance. "Nay," exclaimed Coke, "to such confidence are they grown, that they keep guard upon our seas," and prohibit us free commerce within them; they take our ships and goods unless we conform to their placarts. Besides all which, "what insolencies and cruelties" they have committed against us in the past, in Ireland, in Greenland, in the Indies, as known to all the world; care would be taken to refresh their memories on these wrongs "as there should be cause." After a preamble of this sort one might expect a declaration of war to follow. But the fleet, Coke continued, was neither for revenge nor for the execution of justice for past wrongs. It was primarily to put a stop to the "violent current of the presumption" of men-of-war and freebooters, who had abused the freedom allowed by the king to friends and allies to make use of his seas and ports, by assaulting one another within his Majesty's chambers and in his rivers, "to the scorn and contempt of his dominion and power." The king intended no rupture with any prince or state; he was "resolved to continue and maintain that happy peace wherewith God hath blessed his kingdom, and to which all his actions and negotiations have hitherto tended." But that peace must be maintained by the arm of power, "which only keeps down war by keeping up dominion." Therefore the king found it necessary, even for his own defence and safety, "to re-assume and keep his ancient and undoubted right in the dominion of these seas, and to suffer no other prince or state to encroach upon him, thereby assuming to themselves or their Admirals any sovereign command; but to force them to perform due homage to his Admirals and ships, and to pay them acknowledgments, as in former times they did. He would also set open and protect the free trade both of his subjects and allies, and give them such safe conduct and convoy as they shall reasonably require. He will suffer no other fleets or men-of-war to keep any guard upon these seas, or there to offer violence, or take prizes or booties, or to give interruption to any lawful intercourse. In a word," Coke concluded, "his Majesty is resolved, as to do no wrong, so to do justice, both to his subjects and friends within the limits of his seas."[1]

The substance of this bombastic despatch, in which Charles was fully displayed in his new figure as a Plantagenet, was communicated by Boswell in a memoir to the States-General, and their High Mightinesses must have rubbed their eyes as

[1] Coke to Boswell, $\frac{16}{26}$ April 1635. Needham, *Additional Evidences concerning the Right of Soveraigntie and Dominion of England in the Sea;* Justice, *A General Treatise of the Dominion and Laws of the Sea*, 181; Entick, *A New Naval History*, xvii. If, as is probable, the mention of discourses concerning *Mare Clausum* referred to Selden's work, it would show that the author was then known to be engaged in writing it.

they read it.[1] But it at least removed their fears of immediate war. Explanations of similar tenour, but couched in more moderate language, were made to other Courts. The intentions of the king were declared to be quite peaceful, and stress was laid on the violations of the King's Chambers, "to the great derogation of that dominion at sea which has always of right belonged to the Imperial crown of this kingdom"; the fleet was to free his coasts and seas from such disturbances, to secure free trade to his subjects and allies, and "to reduce his dominion upon the British seas to the ancient style and lustre."[2]

Let us now turn to the fleet which was to carry out this grand programme and see what it actually accomplished. The ships began to assemble in the Downs in May, the Earl of Lindsey being appointed "Admiral, Custos Maris, Captain-General and Governor" of the fleet, with the veteran Sir William Monson as Vice-Admiral, and Sir John Pennington as Rear-Admiral. It consisted of nineteen of the king's ships and five armed merchant vessels, making twenty-four in all;[3] and though other ten royal ships which were being prepared to reinforce it were ultimately discharged, it was said by the common people that "never before had such a fleet been set out by England." In the king's commission appointing the Earl of Lindsey it was stated that he had thought fit, by the advice of his Council, to set forth to sea a navy as well for the defence and safety of his own territories and dominions as for the guard and safe-keeping of his seas, and of the persons, ships, and goods of his own subjects and of his friends and allies "trading by sea to and fro our dominions for commerce and trade, and other their just and necessary occasions, from those spoyles and

[1] "Dessein de Sa Mate de la grande Bretagne p̄ sa flotte p̄rente," $\frac{15}{25}$ May 1635. Aitzema, *Saken van Staet en Oorlogh*, ii. 164; Muller, *op. cit.*, 230. Boswell suppressed the reference to the Dutch fisheries and to the old troubles at Greenland and in the East Indies, and he toned down the part prohibiting the warships of other nations from keeping guard in the British seas.

[2] *State Papers, Dom.*, cclxxxvi. 100.

[3] They were as follow: *Merhonour*, admiral, 44 guns; *James*, vice-admiral, 48 guns; *Swiftsure*, rear-admiral, 42 guns; *St George*, 42 guns; *St Andrew*, 42 guns; *Henrietta Maria*, 42 guns; *Vanguard*, 40 guns; *Rainbow*, 40 guns; *Red Lion*, 38 guns; *Constant Reformation*, 42 guns; *Antelope*, 34 guns; *Leopard*, 34 guns; *Swallow*, 34 guns; *Mary Rose*, 26 guns; *Bonaventure*, 34 guns; and the First, Third, Eighth, and Tenth *Lion's Whelps*, of 14 guns each. The merchant ships were the *Sampson*, *Freeman*, *Royal Exchange*, *William Thomas*, and *Pleiades*.

depredations committed at sea . . . and for sundry reasons and considerations of state best known to ourselves."[1]

In the official instructions from the Lords of the Admiralty, issued on the day after the secret agreement with Spain had been drawn up, the Earl was ordered principally to guard the narrow seas and the king's subjects and allies trading through them, and so to dispose his ships that "all parts of the seas, as well from the Start westward as the rest of the Sleeve from the Start to the Downs, and from thence northward, might be secured from men-of-war, pirates and sea-rovers and of picaroons that interrupt the trade and commerce of his Majesty's dominions." It was to be his principal care to preserve the king's honour, coasts, jurisdiction, territories, and subjects within the extent of his employment, "that no nation or people whatsoever intrude thereon or injure any of them." If he met "in his Majesty's seas" any fleet or ships belonging to any foreign prince or state, he was to expect that the admiral or chief of them, in acknowledgment of his Majesty's sovereignty there, should perform "their duty and homage in passing by"; if they refused and offered to resist, he was "to force them thereunto, and to bring them in to answer this their high contempt and presumption according to law." He was to suffer no dishonour to be done to the king or derogation to his power or sovereignty in those seas. If English ships so far forgot their duty as not to strike their top-sails in passing, the commanders were either to be punished on the spot or reported to the Admiralty, who would punish them exemplarily. When he met with foreign men-of-war or merchant vessels, either at sea or in any road "or other place," he was to send to them to discover if any English subjects were serving on board; and if so he was "to cause them to be taken forth and committed," to answer their contempt of the king's proclamation forbidding such service, and also to caution the commander of the vessel in which they were found not to receive English subjects again; but the Earl was expressly forbidden to send any of his men on board the foreign vessels to search for English subjects.

The most remarkable part of the instructions issued to the first ship-money fleet referred to the hostilities between the ships of other nations, not merely in the King's Chambers, but

[1] The king to the Earl of Lindsey, *State Papers, Dom.*, cclxxxviii. 84.

throughout the narrow seas. "In this your Lordship's employment," wrote the Lords of the Admiralty, "you are not to permit or suffer any men-of-war to fight with each other, or men-of-war with merchant, or merchant with merchant, in the presence of his Majesty's ships in any part of the Narrow Seas. But you are to do your best to keep peace in those seas for the freer and better maintenance of trade and commerce through the same, so that all men trading or sailing within those his Majesty's seas do justly take themselves to be *in pace Domini Regis*. And therefore his Majesty in honour and justice is to protect them from injury and violence."[1]

It is interesting to compare these instructions to Lindsey with those given earlier to Pennington as admiral of the fleet for the guard of the narrow seas. His private instructions from the Lords of the Admiralty in 1631 contained a clause regarding the homage of foreign vessels on meeting the king's ships. He was to expect the admiral or chief, in acknowledgment of the king's sovereignty in the narrow seas, "to strike their toppe sayles in passing by," and if they refused he was to force them to do so; and in no wise suffer any dishonour to be done to his Majesty, or derogation to his sovereign power in those seas. At that time the efforts of Richelieu to create a French navy had caused some disquiet in England, and Pennington was also ordered to do his utmost, by spies and otherwise, to discover whether any considerable preparations were being made abroad.[2] The instructions in 1631 appear to have represented the English pretensions so far as they were understood at the time. There was nothing about forbidding the hostilities of belligerents, as in Lindsey's instructions. On the contrary, Pennington was told that if he saw any Hollanders and Dunkirkers in fight at sea he was to take no part with either, "but to pass by and leave them to their fortunes"; and he issued orders to his subordinates to that effect.[3] In his

[1] Instructions for our very good Lord, the Earle of Lindsey, Admirall of his Majesties' ffiete, in his Majesty's shippe the *Merhonour*, prepared for this present Expedĩcon for Guard of the Narrow Seas. 2nd May 1635. *State Papers, Dom.*, clvii. fol. 135*b et seq.*

[2] *Ibid.*, cxcii. 3, 21st May 1631; clvii. fol. 117*b*. It was found that the French had a fleet of thirty-nine men-of-war, and two additional ships were building. *Ibid.*, cxcviii. 84.

[3] 20th May 1631. *Ibid.*, cxci. 80.

instructions in 1633 this clause was repeated, but in other respects they resembled those of Lindsey.[1] The same duties were allotted to him in 1634, and he was specially charged to free the narrow seas of pirates and sea-rovers, and to prevent hostilities in the King's Chambers. "If," he was told, "any man-of-war, or other, *in any of his Majesty's roads, harbours, or coasts*, shall offer any violence by unduly taking out any ships, vessels, goods or merchandise, of what nation soever, or commit any other insolency, you shall do your best to recover the same again from them, and reform the abuses, either by due admonition, or (if that will not serve) by bringing the offender to answer to justice, preserving by all means the honour of his Majesty from such insolencies (as much as in you lieth), having always a due regard to the amity between his Majesty, his friends and allies."[2]

But a change took place, as we have seen, in the following year. Among the suggestions made by Pennington to the king, and repeated to the Admiralty, was one that any foreign ship attacked by another foreigner in the narrow seas might put herself under the protection of any of the king's ships by coming under its lee, "in the same manner as under a castle on shore."[3] It was certainly a proposal as bold as it was brilliant. Ships of war have long been regarded by certain writers on international law as being essentially an extension of the territory of the state to which they belong; but no writer ever suggested that the water around them on the high sea should be looked upon as partaking of the same character. The sea round a king's ship, within range of the guns on board, was to be a sanctuary like the waters of the King's Chambers,—a sort of territorial girdle which it carried about with it like an aureole round the head of a saint. Pennington's suggestion was considered by the Admiralty early in April 1634, and Nicholas, the Secretary, was instructed to confer with Sir

[1] *State Papers, Dom.*, ccxxxvii. 1.

[2] *Ibid.*, clvii. fol. 132, 26th April 1634.

[3] In the memorandum which Pennington submitted to the Admiralty, he said: "Sixtly, that if any stranger bee oprest by another stranger yt is stronger than hee, within the jurisdicion of ye Narrow Seas, and yt hee flyes for succor or refuge to any of his Majesty's shippes imployed for the guard of the sayd Seas, and come under his lee, and craves protection, whether his Majesty's ffloatinge ffortes shall not have ye same privelege in succoringe and defendinge them as ffortes a Land hath." *Ibid.*, cclxv. 23.

Henry Marten, the Judge of the Admiralty Court, with regard to it. Nicholas summed up his own views oracularly in the sentence, "If a merchant fly from men-of-war, it concerns the king's ships to preserve trade." Sir Henry Marten gave a clear opinion. "It is not fit," he said, "nor honourable for the king's ships appointed to guard the Narrow Seas to suffer any men-of-war to fight with each other, or men-of-war with merchants, or merchant with merchant, in the presence of the king's ships within the Narrow Seas, for that the king's ships are set forth to keep peace in those seas for the freer and better maintenance of trade and commerce through the same: and all men trading or sailing within the king's seas do justly take themselves to be *in pace Domini Regis;* and since such are *in pace Domini Regis,* it doth concern the king in honour and justice to protect them from injury and violence." The language of the first part of this statement is the same as in the regulation prepared a little before with respect to hostilities within the King's Chambers (p. 251); but its purport went much further than the recommendation of Pennington, and in effect extended the protection afforded by the King's Chambers, and the regulation applying to them, to the whole of the narrow seas.

The Admiralty approved of the opinion of Sir Henry Marten, and Nicholas was directed to embody it in Pennington's instructions. Before doing so, however, it was deemed desirable to get the king's own opinion, and he was asked by Windebank, at the instance of the Admiralty, whether Pennington should be instructed not to permit any man-of-war to fight in the narrow seas in the sight of his Majesty's ships, while he commanded there as Admiral. Pennington had then only two ships and two "Whelps" under his command,—a force quite inadequate to enforce an innovation so revolutionary,—and Charles apparently did not think the time or circumstances fitting for it, for the Admiral's instructions in 1634 were virtually the same as in 1633, except that the clause about passing by Dutch and Dunkirkers in fight and leaving them to their fortunes was omitted at the special request of Lord Cottington.[1] But next year, when the imposing ship-money

[1] Windebank and Cottington were two of the three in the confidence of the king as to the secret negotiations with Spain. *State Papers, Dom.*, cclxv. 23, 25, 26, 41, 49, 78, 89; clvii. fol. 132.

fleet was ready, Sir H. Marten's memorandum was inserted, almost verbatim, in the Earl of Lindsey's official instructions.

In addition to the official instructions, the Earl received private commands from the king. In these the new doctrine as to the sovereignty of the seas received a new gloss, corresponding to the tenour of Coke's despatch to Boswell, and they were clearly intended to embroil us with the Dutch Republic, as well as with France, and thus enable Charles to carry out his clandestine agreement with Spain. He was not to permit the warships of other states to keep guard, or commit acts of hostility, or take spoil or booty, "within his Majesty's seas"; and it was also resolved that the fleet should be employed in forcing the Dutch herring-busses to take the king's licenses for permission to fish, or in interrupting them in their fishing. It was a common practice for orders of this kind given to naval officers to be expressed in general or indefinite language, leaving to them the responsibility of applying them to specific cases according to their judgment and discretion. Both Pennington in the previous year, and the Earl of Northumberland in the following year, had to ask for further and more precise directions. So also did Lindsey now. He wrote to Charles on receipt of the royal commands, asking a number of questions. In the first place, he asked that the "bounds of his Majesty's seas might be expressed"—a reasonable request, and one frequently made by naval officers. He was loftily told by Coke, who replied, that "his Majesty's seas are all about his dominions, and to the largest extent of those seas,"—an answer not very illuminating, and of little use to the Admiral.[1] His second question was whether the ships of the King of France, or the Archduke, or the Dutch States, might not "lie to and again" upon their own

[1] An equally obscure answer of Coke's is recorded in the collection of papers for the ambassadors to Cologne in 1673 (*State Papers, Dom.*, Chas. II., vol. 339, p. 513). "1636. Ea Leicester (*sic*) Query—What answer shall I give if I be asked what I mean by the seas of ye King my master, or our seas? The Answer returned by Mr Secretary Coke in his own hand: By the King's or our seas you are not to understand or condescend to any restrictive sense but to answer ye Brittish Seas: and that the 4 seas mentioned in our laws are thereby meant, which you must not otherwise circumscribe or limitt; besides they are the same which in all antiquity have been acknowledged to belong unto us, as is sufficiently proved by authentic records."

coasts, as they have anciently done?" To this the reply was that they might stay in their harbours or roads, or pass "to and again for trade," but not otherwise. Then he asked whether the Dutch men-of-war might not lie before Dunkirk, "as they have been accustomed to do"? (in blockading the port, which belonged to Spain). For answer, he was curtly referred to his instructions. Then there was another disturbing suggestion: If no men-of-war were to be permitted "to lie in the King's seas," notice, he said, should be given of the fact by proclamation or otherwise. He was told that this was already done—the remark having reference, no doubt, to the despatches sent to foreign Governments. Finally, he inquired what he should "do with the herring fishers." But the patience of Coke appears to have been exhausted, and no answer at all was given.[1]

It was obviously the intention of Charles to force a quarrel with France and the Dutch Republic on a point or points connected with the sovereignty of the sea, which might rouse popular enthusiasm in England and enable him to attempt to recover the Palatinate for his nephew, while ostensibly defending the national honour. But the punctilios and hesitation of Lindsey about the duties before him must have raised misgivings at Court as to whether the right man had been chosen for the job. It was not long before this feeling deepened into mortification and disgust.

The fleet was ready at the beginning of June. Before its setting off one or two incidents happened which might have seemed ominous to the superstitious. A shot fired from the Admiral's ship, in answer to the salutation of the rest of the fleet as he sailed into the Downs, hit a poor woman on shore and broke her leg; the same day, during musketry exercise, a seaman nearly killed a master of the navy,—and these, as it turned out, were the sole effective warlike operations of the fleet. On the very day of departure a couple of Dunkirk privateers "were so insolent" as to set upon a Dutch merchantman in Dover Road, under the Admiral's nose and in sight of the fleet, battering the ship, slaying the gunner, and wounding the men. As an offset, the fleet captured a small prize from a Dunkirker, which was to be

[1] *State Papers, Dom.*, cclxxxviii. 84, 85.

sold for the benefit of the Fishery Society. Then the Earl himself had been snubbed by the Admiralty, and left with a flea in his ear. He wanted a vessel to serve as a "kitchen" to accompany the fleet, and a salary for a secretary; but there being no precedents, the requests were refused. Then he complained that he had not enough flags, and above all that he lacked a standard, which made him "not a little wonder, considering his commission gave him as much power as a Lord Admiral of England—or rather more by being General, who is always a representative person of his prince"; he said he was "a little maimed" without it.[1]

The fleet weighed anchor early on the morning of the 7th June, and steered down Channel on its mission. At that time a combined Dutch and French squadron blockaded Dunkirk—France, which in January had entered into a treaty with the States for an invasion and partition of the Spanish Netherlands, having declared war against Spain a month before Lindsey left the Downs. There was thus every prospect of a collision if the English Admiral carried out the king's wishes, and both the Court and the capital were on the tiptoe of expectation of stirring news. The fleet had scarcely quitted its anchorage when London was full of rumours. The *Swallow* got credit for having sent to the bottom a Dutch man-of-war before she had even left Deptford. A few days later it was reported that a fight had taken place in the Channel, a violent cannonade having been heard on the English coast, whereat Charles looked anxious and moody.[2] But it was only a peaceful salutation between the English fleet and a Danish man-of-war, "who did their duty" in passing by. On 12th June "certain news" arrived by express from Dungeness that a great battle had been fought off Calais, in which the Hollanders were totally defeated. Authentic despatches from the fleet soon put an end to such rumours. Very bad weather had been experienced, which

[1] *State Papers, Dom.*, cclxxxviii. 4; cclxxxix. 75. He had "no more than two blue and two white flags with six pendants to each of them; there are wanting two red flags and six pendants, one blue flag and one white." The office of Lord High Admiral was in commission from the death of the Duke of Buckingham in 1628 until the appointment of the Earl of Northumberland in 1638.

[2] Gardiner, *Hist.*, vii. 385.

forced them to take shelter at the Isle of Wight; thereafter they sailed for Portland, having received intelligence that a French squadron of fourteen sail and a Dutch one of the same number were there, each flying its national flag.

At a council held on board the Admiral's ship, it was resolved that if the Dutch struck when they came up with them and the French did not, a message was to be sent to the Dutch Admiral "that we did not expect to see the friends of the king our master in company of them that do affront him, therefore we desire them, like friends, to stand by and see the sport." But there was no "sport," for when the English fleet got to Portland on 20th June, the allies had gone; "the same wind," wrote Lindsey, "which brought me thither carried them out to sea" the day before. Learning from the Mayor of Dartmouth that a fleet of fifty-six sail had been seen off Falmouth on the 19th, the fleet went off westwards, calling at Plymouth, where it stayed for a few days. On one occasion they thought they had come up with their quarry. They espied a great number of ships at a distance, dimly visible in the morning mist, which made them "provide their guns" and get ready for action. But they turned out to be only peaceful salt-ships from Rochelle. Despatches were sent to the Court from Plymouth on 23rd June, in which Lindsey stated he was going on to Land's End, "and so to make a short return from thence." He also defended himself from complaints that seem to have been made against him from Dunkirk, apparently owing to his seizure of the prize for the Fishery Society. He told Windebank that two or three more Dunkirk men had been brought to him who had taken prizes from the French, but that he had dismissed them without meddling with their prizes. And then he added—what must have been unpleasant reading to Charles—that the king's instructions had bound him to carry an equal hand between the subjects of his allies, and from that "compass" he would not vary. He would perform as friendly offices to the Dunkirkers as to either the French or the Hollander.

Neither the impartial sentiments of the Admiral nor his proceedings were approved at Court, where the king was getting impatient. The summer was passing, and the opportunity of forcing a conflict was passing with it. He soon learned how his conduct was regarded from despatches from Coke. Since the Earl went to sea, wrote the bustling Secretary, the account he had been able to give the king out of his despatches had been only of a fall from his coach, and of the stay his fleet had made in the Downs, then near St Helens, and thence of his plying along the coast to Plymouth, where the Mayor had advised him he was on Sunday, five days earlier. All this, he said, gave his Majesty little satisfaction, who expected to hear the fame of his acts in the open sea, whereof he had committed the custody to his trust. And though the civil answer sent by the French Vice-Admiral to the Mayor of Weymouth[1] had been well taken, yet it would have been more for the king's honour and the Earl's also if this office had been done with due homage to the Earl. And this all the more because there was a common report that the French had forced some English merchant vessels to strike sail to them, and that the French and Dutch had visited English ships,—an act, said Coke, of direct pretence to equal rights in our seas which the Earl must not suffer; he must not allow English ships to be visited by the men-of-war of any nation whatsoever, and he must be careful to protect them from all wrongs. In particular—and the request should have opened his eyes,—if any English merchant ships came from the Straits, Spain, or Portugal, with Spanish coin or other commodities (for Dunkirk), he must take care that no man go on board or interrupt them. He should convoy English ships in the same way, and for the honourable execution of his employment he should "strive to keep the open sea." Coke concluded by telling him that he "thus freely enlarged himself" chiefly by the direction of the king, out of his own honour and interest. In another letter to Viscount Conway, who was on board the Admiral's ship and had written a note to Coke of their proceedings, he used similar language. He did not want to hear of "misinformations," but of "noble effects"; he had written to the Admiral whereby he would "perceive that neither spending time in harbour, nor at anchor, nor coasting along our shore, would

[1] The inhabitants of the coast were apprehensive of the French fleet, and the Admiral sent a message to the Mayor offering to show his orders from the King of France, which bound him to honour and respect everything that belonged to his Majesty of Great Britain. *State Papers, Dom.*, ccxci. 23.

answer the expectation they had of the fleet." "You must command the seas or be commanded," said Coke in his pompous vein. "Wisdom seeks not danger when with honour it may be shunned; but where honour and dominion lie at stake, brave men will set up their rests."[1]

All which, when he came to know of it, very naturally nettled the Admiral. He had obtained the information about the allied fleet on 9th June, three days after he left the Downs, and he had gone in pursuit as speedily as the weather and the heavy-sailing English vessels would allow. He was now away at the Scilly Isles, but he failed to see any French ships, and was duly honoured in the matter of the flag by the few Dutch men-of-war encountered. He sent further despatches from off the Lizard on 28th June, explaining his movements, stating that his ship was leaking, grumbling again about the want of a standard,—"his commission making him equal to a Lord High Admiral of England," &c., &c.,—and complaining that his letters were not answered. Coke's letter awaited him at Plymouth, and in reply to it he said, on 5th July, that he neither deserved his scorn for a fall in a coach nor his blame for negligence. Was it his fault that the French sought to avoid him? They had left the English seas, and they could have done no more if he had fought with them; but if they came again he should meet and fight them, time enough. Sir Henry Vane had also written to Conway of the discontent about the fleet. It was not well taken, he said, that they did not put over to the coasts of Flanders, Holland, and France,—not indeed that they should go into the harbours and force them to salute and strike, but to keep at sea upon these coasts and act according to their instructions.

Lindsey then stood to sea and plied about in the middle of the Channel, off the coast between the Lizard and Plymouth, and sometimes standing over to the coast of France, until the beginning of August, without finding any trace of the French and Dutch fleet, which was supposed—and rightly—to be to the southward on the Biscay coast. No glimpse of the lilies of France could be obtained; not even a pirate was seen, the presence of the fleet no doubt having scared them from their haunts in the Channel. On 3rd August Lindsey's fleet re-

[1] *State Papers, Dom.*, ccxci. 58, 59.

turned to the Downs for revictualling, what remained of the victuals on board being very bad,—"the beef is so extremely tainted," he had written on 21st July, "that when the shifter stirs it, the scent over all the ship is enough to breed a contagion." No sooner was he in the Downs than news came that the French squadron had come back to the English coast, twenty-six sail of them having been seen about the Lizard. "They haunt us like a shadow," murmured the Admiral from his anchorage, "flying when we pursue, and following when we retreat."

Lindsey was not far wrong on this occasion, for the withdrawal of the French ships from the narrow seas on the approach of the English fleet was due to the sagacious plan of Richelieu. He appears to have been well aware of the pretext and design of Charles, and endeavoured to outwit him. At war with Spain, he desired to avert an open rupture with England. At the same time, it was not fitting that he should break the tradition of France, or check the maritime ambitions which aimed at rivalling England on the seas, by lowering the French flag to the English Admiral. While the Earl was still at the Isle of Wight, Richelieu ordered the French Admiral to retire with three of his smallest vessels round Cape Finisterre to Belle Isle, off the coast of Brittany and well out of the Channel, and to put the rest of the French squadron under the command of the Dutch Admiral. The French ships left in the narrow seas were to carry no flags at all, and therefore could not strike them; and if the combined fleet met the English, the Admiral of the States would, in his accustomed manner, strike, without the dignity of France being compromised or Charles being given the rebuff for which he was seeking.[1] When on the following day Richelieu learned that the Spanish transports for the relief of Dunkirk had entered that port, he ordered the

[1] Gardiner, *op. cit.*, 385; *State Papers, Dom.*, ccxcv. 61. The English agent in France reported in August that two squadrons under French admirals, and bearing the French flag, were to ply, one along the coast of France from Belle Isle to Bayonne, the other at the mouth of the Channel. The remainder of the fleet, half French and half Hollander (which guarded the coast up to Calais and to the north of it), bore the States' colours, and were under the command of the Hollander Admiral,—"an expedient to avoid acknowledging his Majesty's right in the Channel, in case this squadron should meet his Majesty's fleet and be constrained to vail the bonnet."

combined fleet to withdraw altogether from the Channel, as their further presence there was useless and might give occasion for a conflict.[1] Thus it was that Lindsey could not find them. While Richelieu's strategy succeeded, the course adopted was somewhat pusillanimous and not calculated to add to the laurels of France. He therefore took advantage of an incident to raise the question of the flag diplomatically with England, in the hope of having the respective rights of the two nations settled, and no doubt for other reasons. He complained to Charles that the Earl of Lindsey—who denied the story—told a Dutch captain of whom he inquired the whereabouts of the French fleet, that he was "going to make them lower their colours";[2] he inquired as to the intentions of the king, and he proposed that in future the French should salute the English on the coast of England, and, reciprocally, that the English should salute the French on the coast of France; while if the fleets were in the middle of the sea they should either pass one another without saluting, or the weaker fleet should first salute the stronger. If Charles did not like these proposals, he was invited to suggest others.[3] It appears indeed that instructions of a similar tenour had been actually given to the French Admiral, except that they might strike to the English when out of sight of the French coast.[4]

Richelieu's proposals for equality and reciprocity in the narrow seas were instantly rejected. Coke, in a despatch to the English agents at Paris, the draft of which was revised by the king, expressed astonishment that the French ambassador, instead of the negotiation of a treaty for a confederation between England, France, and the States-General for the restitution of the Elector Palatine, should raise "impertinent questions" about the king's dominion at sea. The king could enter into no such debate with the French ambassador. But Coke had assured that personage that the instructions given to the Earl of Lindsey were no other than had been given in effect in all former times, and "for near forty years within his

[1] Gardiner, *loc. cit.*

[2] It was from this Hollander, met off Beachy Head on 9th June, that Lindsey learned that the French fleet was at Portland.

[3] *State Papers, Dom.*, ccxci. 80, 27th June 1635.

[4] *Ibid.*, ccxcvi. 14.

own knowledge,"—that the Admiral should defend and maintain the ancient known rights of the crown; guard the seas, secure freedom of commerce, suppress pirates, and oppose hostile acts in prejudice thereof; assist his Majesty's friends and allies, attempt no innovation, nor do anything contrary to his treaties,—and so he presumed that no one would do anything to impeach his Majesty's ancient and undoubted rights. But instead of being satisfied with this "fair answer," the French ambassador put into Coke's hands a regulation he had drawn up, prescribing to both kings "when and where the one shall vail his bonnet to the other." Coke informed the agents that it was hoped this proceeding would be disavowed; and he instructed them, pending the arrival of the new English ambassador (Lord Scudamore), to refrain from all discussion with the French king or his Ministers as to the king's right to the dominion of the sea, or about the extent thereof, and to say nothing further as to the designs of the fleet.[1] Richelieu, who had quite enough to concern him in the failure of his attack on the Spanish Netherlands, was content to leave alone the dispute about the flag, and the French ambassador was requested to say as little as possible concerning it.[2]

The Earl of Lindsey, failing to find the French fleet and coming to revictual in the Downs, now bethought himself of the other part of the king's private instructions, about the Dutch herring-busses. If he had been baffled in the attempt to lower the lilies of France, might he not yet force the herring-boats to take his Majesty's license before they cast their nets in his Majesty's seas? But here, too, obstacles arose. He wrote to Charles on 2nd August that he had consulted the ablest men in the fleet, the captains and masters, and they were of opinion that "his Majesty's great ships would run much hazard" upon the northern coasts. Moreover, if the fleet went north, would it not encourage the French to quit their retreat and "embolden them perhaps to do that which now standing in awe they forbear to do?" Still, he was willing to do whatever the king thought best. The king agreed that it might be better to stay, especially as he thought that before the Earl could apply himself to that service the fishing season would be past. Besides, said Coke, who penned the despatch, the fleets his Lordship

1 *State Papers, Dom.*, ccxciii. 12.

2 Gardiner, *op. cit.*, 386.

had left behind him—"pressing after him," as he said—were of more consideration. The king therefore ordered that when the victualling was completed the fleet should again keep the sea to the westward.[1]

This decision probably saved the Earl of Lindsey, as well as the king, from further humiliation and disappointment. Even had he at once sailed to the north, he would have found no Dutch herring-busses to deal with, any more than he had found the French fleet. For the Dunkirk privateers, swiftly taking advantage of Richelieu's withdrawal of the blockading squadron from their port, had made a bold dash into the North Sea and overwhelmed the Hollanders off the coast of Northumberland. More than 100 busses had been sunk or burnt, and 1000 fishermen carried prisoners to Flanders; the rest were in full flight homewards or pent up in British ports, and the herring-fishing was ruined for that year.[2]

The calamity soon brought over the Dutch fleet to protect the remaining busses. Van Dorp, with fourteen French and Dutch men-of-war, arrived in Calais Road about the middle of August and sailed thence northwards, thirsting for vengeance on the freebooters. Lindsey detached some of the ships from his fleet, which lay victualling in the Downs, for convoys, as well as to punish the "contempt" of the Dutch at Scarborough (see p. 250), and a few of the smaller vessels were engaged in looking for "picaroons" in the Straits of Dover. For during the absence of the fleet, the post-boat between Dover and Dunkirk had been attacked and pillaged five times within seven

[1] Lindsey to the king, 2nd August; Coke to Lindsey, 4th August. *State Papers, Dom.*, ccxcv. 9, 42. The rumour that two of the king's ships were to go north to the busses reached the ears of the States' ambassador. *Brit. Mus. Add. MSS.*, 17,677, O, fol. 376.

[2] *State Papers, Dom.*, ccxcvi. 5, 14, 16, 30. *Brit. Mus. Add. MSS.*, 17,677, O, fol. 380. *Res. Holl.*, 7th September, Bosgoed, *op. cit.*, p. 358. Twelve busses and three of the convoys took refuge at Newcastle; others in the Firth of Forth. The skipper of a coasting vessel from Scotland to Scarborough saw seven busses in flames; the sky was red from the conflagration. The *Leopard*, one of Lindsey's fleet, convoying merchantmen to Dunkirk, met eighteen of the privateers returning in triumph. The Dutch busses were the natural prey of the Dunkirkers, and the States were put to great expense and pains in guarding them. In 1625 a Spanish agent, Egidio Ouwers, submitted to Cardinal de Ceva, at Brussels, an elaborate plan for destroying the Dutch herring fishery, so as to "spoil their chiefest mine by which they maintained their wars." *State Papers, Dom.*, dxxi. 30.

weeks, and the packages containing the king's letters opened.[1] A French man-of-war, too, had taken an English ship off Harwich and carried her off to Boulogne. Such occurrences, and the presence of Van Dorp in the north, delayed Lindsey's departure. But on 4th September he again left the Downs with most of his ships, stood over to Calais and ranged the French coast for some distance southwards, and then out to sea. Heavy weather coming on, he had to run for shelter to the Isle of Wight, where the fleet lay weather-bound, and with much sickness on board, from the 12th till the 29th September. The Admiral then made for the Downs, where he arrived on 4th October, and on the 8th he struck his flag.[2]

Pennington was left with seven ships for the winter guard of the narrow seas; and with "private" instructions from the Earl not to suffer any breach of the peace to be done to any of his Majesty's allies, nor to permit his sovereignty to be infringed upon; to give convoys to merchants when they wished it; to clear his Majesty's seas of pirates, and to compel the "due homage of the sea." Finally, he was to assist the farmers of the customs, particularly in preventing the smuggling of tobacco.

It was a fitting close to the first ship-money fleet. The great armada by which Charles expected to recover the Palatinate, and restore his sovereignty of the seas to its ancient style and lustre, upon which the eyes of Europe had been fixed, accomplished practically nothing. It had snatched a petty prize from a Dunkirk privateer and seized a Dutch man-of-war in reparation for the "contempt" at Scarborough; it had convoyed a few vessels, English and Spanish, to Dunkirk, and as its greatest achievement had caused the blockade of that port to be raised. No wonder that that tough sea-dog, Sir John Pennington, when he heard that a still stronger fleet was

[1] *State Papers*, *Dom.*, ccxcv. 44.

[2] The facts as to the movements, &c., of the fleet are mostly taken from the Earl of Lindsey's Journal, written for the king's information, and preserved in the Record Office. "A Relation of the passages that daily happened in this late expedition under my conduct, being by Your Majesty's gratious appointment Admiral and General of your Majesty's ffleet sett forthe for guard of your Narrow Seas, from the time that the ships mett all together in the Downes, 28° May, untill the 8° of October following, I making my first entrance aboard yor Royall ship the *Merhonor*, 16° May, in Tilbury Hope." *Ibid.*, ccxcix. 28.

preparing for the next year, should exclaim, "God grant they may do more than the present fleet has done, or the money were as well saved as spent."[1] No doubt the fleet had a moral value, if that term can be used about it, the naval demonstration being an intimation to France and to the Dutch Republic that Charles was resolved to assert command of the sea. Whether England could have proved herself mistress of the seas in 1635, had Lindsey's fleet been opposed, is problematical. But, at all events, Charles attained none of his special objects. The sudden and successful uprising of the Spanish Netherlands against the armies of France dispelled the fears of Spain, and that power having no further immediate need of England, the nearly completed alliance came to naught, and the recovery of the Palatinate was further off than ever.[2] On the other hand, the Dutch were much irritated. Charles had denied their right to blockade the Flemish ports against free commerce,[3] and it was through his action that the privateers had been able to work such havoc and destruction among the herring-busses.

Something more must be said about one of the duties imposed on Lindsey, in regard to which it was expected the English fleet would shine—namely, the homage of the flag. Apart from forcing a number of merchant vessels, English and foreign, to lower their top-sails, and some Dutch men-of-war and Dunkirkers, and even one or two of the French (on the English coast) to strike their flag to the king's ships, nothing was accomplished. The politic arrangement of Richelieu foiled Lindsey and Charles alike, and the great spectacle of the Admiral of France lowering his flag to the Admiral of England,

[1] Pennington to Nicholas, 3rd August 1635. *State Papers, Dom.*, ccxcv. 18. Pennington, it may be said, lost no chance of sneering privately at the Earl of Lindsey, especially in his correspondence with his friend, Nicholas, the Secretary to the Admiralty. When Lindsey finally reached the Downs in October, and Pennington was appointed to command the winter fleet, he told Nicholas that he had hoped that "they" who had had the "sweet of the summer should have had a little of the sour sauce of the winter"; he had spent "twice as much as he, and more every way for the king's honour." Nicholas shared the feeling. On hearing that Lindsey had appointed a French cook on board the *Henrietta Maria* he refused to believe it, "as it was never since his time known that any Frenchman was admitted scarce to go aboard, much less to be an officer in any of the king's ships"; and he foretold great evils from it. *Ibid.*, ccxcix. 19; ccxci. 61.

[2] Gardiner, *op. cit.*

[3] *Brit. Mus. Add. MSS.*, 17,677, O, fol. 364.

or giving battle and refusal, was not witnessed. The disappointment at the English Court was all the more keen, inasmuch as France, in the treaty of confederation with the States-General in the beginning of the year, had stipulated that the Dutch men-of-war should salute the French flag in the same way as they saluted the flag of England, thus "challenging a dominion," as Sir Thomas Roe said, "where anciently they durst not fish for gurnets without license."[1]

By this time the question of the striking of the flag had been forced into great prominence: even the "footpads" of the Channel, the humble picaroons and shallops, hailed the English ketches which they pillaged with the cry of "Strike, you English dogs!" It has been shown in a previous chapter that though the ceremony was enforced in the narrow seas in the reign of James, it did not then become a burning political question, and the same is true of the early part of the reign of Charles. The English commanders were then satisfied with a moderate acknowledgment of the "honour," and the Dutch at least rarely ever contested it. That it was enforced in 1627 appears from the narrative of the Earl of Warwick's voyage in that year, when a French man-of-war was compelled off Falmouth "to come up by the lee," though nothing is said about the flag itself.[2] But when France openly aspired to become a great naval Power, England began to force the salute with a high hand. It is from the year 1631 that we may date the marked development of this symbol, as it was claimed to be, of the sovereignty of the sea. We have already seen Pennington's instructions in that year, which, however, only mention the

[1] *State Papers, Dom.*, cclxxviii. 3. Roe's reference was to the fishings at the Zowe or Sowe, where great numbers of gurnards were caught (see p. 65). The stipulation of Richelieu concerned the allied squadrons which were to blockade Dunkirk, as arranged by Article viii. of the treaty. Article xii., after providing for the size of the squadrons, continues, "Et au cas que lesdites esquadres viennent à s'assembler, comme il peut arriver qu'il sera necessaire pour le bien commun, l'Admiral desdits Seigneurs les Estats abaissera à l'abord son pavillon du grand mast, et le saluëra de son canon, et celui du Roi le resaluëre comme de coustume, et comme il en a esté use par le Roi de la Grande Bretagne." Dumont, *Corps Diplomatique*, 83 (?).

[2] *State Papers, Dom.*, lxxix. 17. "Athwart ye opening of Falmouth four sailes stood with their forefoot," and very earnestly tried to weather the English ships. Among them was a French man-of-war of Rochelle, but they shot four or five pieces of ordnance at him, and "soo brought him by ye lee." See p. 207.

striking of the top-sail; and although the omission of the flag may have been only verbal, there are reasons for thinking that the custom and etiquette of the ceremony were not well understood at the Admiralty. Thus on Pennington reporting that French men-of-war were trying to force English merchant vessels to strike to the French flag,[1] he was ordered by the Admiralty "to see that no one presumes to carry the flag in the Narrow Seas"; all the more since "some" pretended to have an interest in the sovereignty of these seas.[2] When Pennington pointed out that this "was more than ever was done, for our own merchants' ships and all other nations ever have and do wear their flags, till they come within shot of the king's ships: if they take them in and keep them in till they are out of shot again, it is as much as has ever been expected," —when he told the Admiralty this, he was informed that the "Lords would not expect impossibilities"—the main business he was to take care of was to see that no foreigner carried the flag where his Majesty's ships were present in the Narrow Seas.[3] Then Captain Plumleigh in the *Antelope* reported that on meeting two States' men-of-war guarding the herring-fishers off Orfordness, the Admiral had "stood" with the *Antelope* with his flag aloft, and did not take it in till several shots had been fired at him; and when requested to come on board and explain his conduct, he refused. How, asked Plumleigh, was he to comport himself in such cases? The matter was brought before the Admiralty, but no answer appears to have been

[1] He reported, 16th September 1631, that two English merchantmen had met five French men-of-war, bearing the French king's colours on the main-top, and the Malta colours on the poop, who saluted them with, "Amain, rogues, for the King of France"; but as the English ships refused to strike and prepared to fight, the French sheered off. He added that he had learned, through an interview between one of his lieutenants and one of the French commanders, that the latter had a commission to compel any English ships he could master to take in their flags and dowse their top-sails, and that three French admirals had been appointed for regaining the regality of the Narrow Seas, because, as the French officer said, the Pope had taken it from France and given it to England, but now that we had fallen from their religion it had been reassigned. *State Papers, Dom.*, cxcix. 51.

[2] Nicholas to Pennington, 29th September 1631. *Ibid.*, cc. 45.

[3] Pennington to Nicholas, 2nd October (*ibid.*, cci. 7). Pennington, whose information about the French trying to make the English strike had given the Admiralty and the king "good content" (*ibid.*, cc. 27), had been ordered westwards to retaliate, but "he hoped the Lords would not think that his two ships half-manned were able to encounter with twenty well manned. *Ibid.*, cci. 29.

then given.[1] Two or three years later Pennington put the same and other queries to the king. He had been appointed in April 1633 Admiral of the Narrow Seas, with general instructions already quoted (see p. 262), to preserve the king's honour, coasts, and jurisdiction, and to compel homage to the flag. Pennington asked whether, when a stranger refused to take in his flag till forced, he should not be "brought in as a delinquent"; whether, if he met a foreign fleet of far greater strength than his own, and they refused to take in their flags, he should fight with them about it "upon so great disadvantage," or make "a fair retreat"; whether on going into Calais, Dunkirk, or the Briel—that is to say, ports in France, Flanders, and Holland—and finding strangers riding there with their flags aloft, he should force them to take them in?[2] He also wrote to the Admiralty in 1634 substantially repeating these inquiries, and asking for a positive or negative expression in regard to them in his instructions. The Admiralty remitted Pennington's letter to Nicholas and Sir Henry Marten to frame answers. The final opinion on the first point was that by the law of the Admiralty both in England and France, the ships were forfeited—that is to say, the same penalty applied as was prescribed in King John's ordinance. It was, however, rarely, if ever, carried into effect. The instructions on this matter usually ran that punishment was to be inflicted at the place, or the commander brought in to answer his contempt. When the Earl of Northumberland asked a similar question in 1636, he was told the offender should be "punished on the place."[3] In Nicholas' opinion much more than the forfeiture of the ship was required; the offender, he thought, should be brought in as a delinquent, and if he resisted he should be tried as a pirate; but this absurd interpretation was overruled.

On the other points it is not quite clear what the final official answers were. Nicholas thought that when a superior fleet was encountered, the English Admiral ought not to engage rashly about the flag; but if he once commanded the foreigners to strike, then "the ships were better to be lost than his (the king's) honour and sovereignty yielded." The opinion he gave with regard to forcing foreign vessels to strike in foreign ports

[1] 14th October, 12th November 1631. *State Papers, Dom.*, cci. 54; cciii. 32.

[2] *Ibid.*, cclxiii. 75.

[3] *Ibid.*, cccxvii. 102.

was in these words: "For ye French roades," he said, "ye king of England's ships should suffer none to wear ye flag but themselves: but in other roades after salutes both may weare ye flag without dishonour." The exceptional treatment proposed for ships in French roads may have been in part owing to the political circumstances of the time, but probably chiefly had reference to ancient custom and the old claims of England to the soil of France. Charles still styled himself King of France; and later Selden argued that though English dominion had been lost in France itself, it nevertheless extended over the sea up to the very shores. It became the common practice to enforce the homage on the coast of the Continent, but not within harbours, ports, rivers, or within buoys, or at any place under the command of the guns of forts or castles.[1] The Earl of Northumberland, on repeating Pennington's question in 1636 as to Calais, Dunkirk, and the Briel, was told that the homage was to be exacted "in the roads out of command of any forts."[2]

There was always some doubt as to the etiquette of the salutation between ships and forts or castles. Dutch vessels were fired on and detained at Portland Castle in 1633 for putting up their flags in the presence of the king's colours, which were flying on the walls; and the act was justified to the States' ambassador when he complained about it. In the year before, the commanders of the Castles at Deal and Walmer fired upon a French man-of-war that came in with his flag in the maintop, because after taking it down when requested, he hoisted it again on going away. "I gave him five shots," said the Captain of Deal, "without hitting him," and he added that the Council on a previous occasion approved of a like action against the Dutch, who had never since offended, but he had never heard of the French attempting it before. The Admiralty asked Pennington's opinion as to the proper course, and he said he thought that all the ships of his Majesty's subjects and of foreigners and strangers should strike their flags and top-sails as they passed by any of his Majesty's castles; such, he said, was the custom in all parts of Christendom, "which, being done, they may ride under the castles with their colours flying abroad if there be none of the king's own ships present." The king's

[1] *State Papers, Dom.*, cclxv. 23, 25, 41, 49. [2] *Ibid.*, cccxvii. 102.

castles had thus not so high a status as the king's ship; but the military officers were not less zealous than those of the navy. Pennington himself had an amusing illustration of their zeal, for in 1631 Sir William Killigrew, the Captain of Pendennis Castle, persisted in "spending the king's powder" in shooting at the *Bonaventure*, Pennington's ship, for not striking its flag to the castle,—"a thing," said the Admiral, "never used by a king's ship, nor would he be the beginner of it." Fortunately, the gunnery of the time was wild; but Killigrew had to be summoned before the Admiralty, rebuked, and, "upon submission, discharged with strict command never more to offend in that kind," before the practice ceased. The Admiralty also issued an order to the notorious Sir James Bagg, the Governor of Plymouth and the Vice-Admiral for South Devon, strictly forbidding that any castle or fort under his command should fire upon the king's ship, even if passing near with their flags on the top of any of their masts, "for," he was told, "they are as absolutely his Majesty's castles or forts, though floating, as that under your command."[1]

As was to be expected from the attempted maritime rivalry openly displayed by France, and from English policy at the time, our naval officers vied with one another in compelling homage to the flag. The Dutch, bòth merchant vessels and men-of-war, more particularly the latter, usually struck at once to the English ships. If they showed reluctance, or hoisted their flag again too soon, they were fired at. The English captains insisted on the right off Continental ports. Thus Captain Richard Plumleigh, having gone to Calais in 1632 to bring over the corpse of Sir Richard Walker, late British ambassador, in his ship—well named the *Assurance*,—"bestowed some powder on the French flags," and caused all the French shipping in Calais Road to take in their colours, "at which," he said, "they repined heavily." Some of the States' men-of-war also riding in the Road took the side of the French, and sent to Plumleigh to say that they knew no reason why he should demand superiority on that side of the sea, and "threatening" to wear their flags there as well as he. But Plumleigh boldly returned a message—what he called "a cooling card"—to their Admiral, saying that if he showed a Dutch flag there, he "would sink

[1] *State Papers, Dom.*, cci. 59; ccii. 17; ccciii. 71, 79; ccx. 58; ccxxxiv. 37; ccxlviii. 81.

him or be sunk by him," which caused him to keep his colours close.[1] In the following year, Captain Ketelby, of the *Bonaventure*, was sent to Boulogne to bring over another ambassador (Lord Weston), and finding the Admiral of Amsterdam in the Road with his flag up, he "gave her a shot," when she struck it and presently hoisted it again. Ketelby then sent his lieutenant to command him to take in his flag or prepare to defend it. The Dutch Admiral argued, and kept it up till Ketelby was preparing to shoot again, when he took it in. Two days later another Dutch admiral, this time the Admiral of Holland, came into the Road with ten or twelve ships of war; within a reasonable distance he struck his flag twice and saluted with seven pieces, and then he also hoisted it again. Ketelby "conceived this homage not sufficient," and notwithstanding the disparity of force, sent him a command to take in his flag, which he did, and kept it in till the *Bonaventure* departed. Such incidents show both the domineering conduct of the English captains and the forbearance and good sense of the Dutch, who acted in obedience to the strict orders they had received to strike to the English ships. But nearer home Ketelby had not so much glory. On returning with the ambassador he met ten sail of Hollanders on the English coast between Dover and Folkestone, one, a States' man-of-war, bearing his flag on the main-top, while a merchant vessel had his top-sails "a-trip." Both were obdurate as to rendering the accustomed homage, and in spite of the fact that Ketelby sent twenty shot "in and through" the sides of the merchantman, she would not lower her sails in the least.[2]

[1] *State Papers, Dom.*, ccxx. 25, 26.

[2] *Ibid.*, ccxxxiv. 5, 32. "The Ambassador and the other Lords being at dinner in the great cabin, the gunner sent word that a Hollander was passing with his top-sails a-trip, to whom he gave order to make a shot. The Lords and gentlemen left the table to see the event, but the Hollander, neither for that shot nor two or three others, would lower the same one foot; whereupon he gave order to shoot him through, which was done, with as much speed as they could bring ordnance to bear, so as before she passed she had twenty shot in and through her sides, which they heard to crash in the same. They could perceive but one piece she had forth; to that fire was given twice. The shot came not near, but they might well hear the same. After her came the Admiral with his flag on the main-top." Ketelby cleared for action and was giving orders for a broadside; but the ambassador twice desired him to give over and stand for Dover, and he submitted. If it had not been for his passengers, Ketelby did not doubt he would have brought them in to answer the contempt.

In many instances peaceful merchant vessels suffered greatly over this question of striking. During the cruise of Lindsey's fleet, Dutch men-of-war, and also a Danish warship, struck without hesitation, even at Calais. So also as a rule did the merchant vessels; but sometimes they transgressed the rule, it might be from ignorance, and then they were exposed to harsh treatment. Thus, three great ships of Amsterdam bound for Pernambuco, on meeting the *Constant Reformation* off Plymouth, did everything required of them; but hoisting their sails before they got clear of the *Vanguard*, the latter gave them six pieces of ordnance, twice sending a cannon-ball through the hull of one of them. Then for a similar reason, too great an alacrity in re-hoisting her flag, another Hollander was shot through with five pieces by the *Rainbow*. So anxious were the English officers to compel the homage that they sometimes demanded it at night. The *Freeman*, returning from convoying merchant-ships to Dunkirk, met in the night-time a fleet of Dutch merchantmen with one convoy accompanying them, and shot to make them strike. In the darkness the traders took the English ship for a Dunkirk privateer and made what haste they could away. The States' man-of-war, coming up to the rescue, approached so near the *Freeman* before she discovered what she was (and then immediately struck) that a collision occurred, the bowsprit of the English ship being broken, while her anchor carried away the Dutchman's chains and stays. The Dutch captain then came on board, humbly asked pardon for what had happened, excused himself by the night and the mistake, offered to go before the Lord Admiral, and paid for the bowsprit and the shot.[1]

While the Dutch were thus forbearing, the Dunkirkers, the *protégés* of Spain, for whom Charles was supposed to be making sacrifices, were refractory. They refused to strike to the *Vanguard* lying at anchor off Gravelines, although it fired many times at them: before the anchor could be got up they were off, and it was useless to follow. They sent a message that they did not care for the English now, and would not strike. On the other hand, just as Lindsey reached the Downs at the beginning of October, Captain Stradling in the *Swallow*

[1] *State Papers, Dom.*, ccxcv. 13; ccxcvii. 28; ccxcviii. 16. It was the usual practice to make the offender pay for the shot.

met the French Admiral, for whom the Earl had been searching all summer, off Falmouth with two ships. He immediately shot at him, and he struck his top-sails and saluted. But this was on the English coast, and was not contrary to Richelieu's instructions. The French, on their part, a week or two afterwards forced an English merchant vessel to strike "for the king of France."[1]

Perhaps the worst offenders of all were the British merchantmen. Again and again the naval commanders complained to the Admiralty of their remissness or neglect to strike, which they said set a very bad example to foreigners. Pennington reported to the king that they passed his ships in the narrow seas, not only without speaking, but even "presumptuously wearing their flag at the topmast head" until forced to take it in; and he recommended the king to issue a proclamation commanding all ships to speak with the king's ships and give an account of themselves, or be subject to fine and punishment. Pennington asked what he was to do if any of the king's subjects were so stubborn as not to strike their flag and top-sails in due time: "I meane," he said, "soe soone as they come within distance of our ordynaunce." On this Sir Henry Marten recommended that when an English ship did not strike in time, the naval captain should complain to his Admiral or to the Admiralty. He was strongly of opinion that too much discretion should not be left to the naval officers in this matter. It was, he said, too much to hazard an English ship being sunk or English lives lost on a point on which a mistake might easily be made.[2] The official instruction given to the officers was either to punish the offenders themselves or to report them to the Admiral or to the Admiralty. Neglectful merchant vessels were sometimes severely punished. In April 1632, when Lady Strange and a large party of Lords, with a great retinue, went on board Pennington's ship, the *Convertive*, lying in Tilbury Hope, a merchant ship, the *Matthew* of London, passed up the river "in an insolent manner," not striking his flag until he had come up with the *Convertive*, and soon hoisting it again notwithstanding the shots Pennington fired at him. For this the master was lodged in jail, and was only released on expressing his contrition to the Lords of the

[1] *State Papers, Dom.*, ccc. 43; ccci. 28; ccxcix. 21.

[2] *Ibid.*, cclxv. 49.

Admiralty. The Earl of Lindsey took a sharper course in a similar case. On returning to the Downs, no doubt irritated from his failure and smarting under Coke's gibes, he pounced upon two English merchantmen who had presumed to wear their flags within full view of the fleet, "almost within command of shot," and in the presence of nearly 200 sail of British and foreign ships. The masters were at once seized, brought on board and put in custody, and a day or two later, a council of war having been called and Sir H. Marten consulted, one of them, William Bushell of Limehouse, captain of the *Neptune*, was fined £500, and the other, Thomas Scott of Ratcliffe, was fined £100, for so gross a misdemeanour.[1]

From the foregoing it is evident that in those days peaceful merchant vessels traversing the narrow seas had not a very happy time. It must often have been irksome in the extreme to the masters, probably not always understanding the minutiæ of the rules,—which, indeed, the naval captains themselves sometimes failed fully to comprehend,—to render due and proper homage to the English flag. To compel foreign men-of-war to salute the king's ships was a different matter. It flattered the national vanity and kept alive the national aspiration for power on the sea, and it did not interfere with the duties of the men-of-war which gave the salute. But to the merchantman anxious for his voyage, often undermanned and contending with turbulent seas, it must have been vexatious to be called upon every now and again to lower his top-sails to a king's ship, or take the risk of a shot through his sides or a heavy fine. The inconvenience led later to a modification in the practice, so far as concerned English vessels, it being insisted on only "when it could be done without loss of the

[1] Ketelby and Viscount Conway explained that it was necessary to punish them in a public manner, since imprisonment in the bilboes and such corporal punishments were not effective. Conway recommended Scott's fine to be remitted, owing to his worth and poverty, as well as from the fact that he had recently been taken captive by the "Turkish" pirates, and his ransom was not all paid. Bushell, as we learn from a petition "of divers poor men, women, and children, whose kindred are now in slavery at Argier and Sallee," had redeemed and brought home thirty of the captives; and it is probable that neither of the fines was exacted. It is doubtful if Lindsey's action was regular, for the vessels, according to his statement, had not come within gunshot. The *Neptune* was one of the three ships fitted out by London for Northumberland's fleet. *State Papers, Dom.*, ccxv. 28, 65, 67; cclxv. 50; cclxiii. 75; ccxcvi. 30, 34, 37; ccci. 31.

voyage";[1] but it may be said here that the regulation with regard to merchant vessels striking to a man-of-war was always afterwards embodied in the Admiralty instructions, offenders being reported to the Admiralty, and proceedings often taken against them in the Admiralty Court.[2]

[1] Molloy, *De Jure Maritimo et Navalis*, 149.

[2] *Regulations and Instructions relating to his Majesty's Service at Sea*, 1734, 1766, 1790, Art. xi.; 1808, Art. xxiv. A case of the kind occurred in 1829. Phillimore, *Commentaries upon International Law*, ii. 58.

CHAPTER VIII.

CHARLES I. NAVY—*continued.*

CONSIDERING the failure of his foreign policy and the inglorious fiasco of the first ship-money fleet, it might be supposed that Charles would pause in the unusual method he had adopted of wringing money from the country for empty displays. While the Earl of Lindsey was still cruising at sea, and before the issue of the second ship-money writs, he knew that his schemes had miscarried. He was left drifting about without any definite policy, but still clinging to the plan of the restoration of his nephew to the Palatinate as the one thing before him. He was equally ready to ally himself with France against Spain, or with Spain against France, whichever would be most likely to aid him in realising that object;[1] and as he had neither money nor troops to attract a Continental alliance, his only pawn lay in the navy. In the summer of 1635, while Selden was busy in the Temple at his book, it was resolved to equip a fleet far more formidable than Lindsey's for the following year. Coventry made his speech to the Judges in June, and in August the second writs for ship-money were sent out. In this case, as is well known, they were addressed not only to the coast towns but to the whole of England, with consequences notorious in English history. The number of ships it was at first intended to set out was forty-five, totalling 21,850 tons, and with 8650 men, the estimated cost being £218,000.[2] At the beginning of December the Admiralty considered what number should be set out in the spring; and by an Order of the King in Council on December

[1] Gardiner, *op. cit.*, viii. 84. [2] *State Papers, Dom.*, ccxcvi. 69; cci. 26, 97.

27th, it was decreed that twenty-four should be prepared "for guarding the narrow seas," while ten other ships should be got ready as a second fleet to reinforce the first, or to take its place later.[1]

The second ship-money fleet was placed under the command of the Earl of Northumberland, an able, accomplished, and high-spirited young nobleman, much better fitted than Lindsey was for the office of Admiral. This fleet is usually said to have been the most powerful ever set out by England up to that time.[2] According to Northumberland's Journal, it consisted of twenty-seven vessels, all of which were king's ships, except three which had been fitted out by London. Sir John Pennington was appointed Vice-Admiral and Sir Henry Mervin, Rear-Admiral.[3]

But what was to be done with the fleet? That was a question put by Windebank in the autumn of the previous year. The king had remitted to the Foreign Committee two inquiries: what answer he should make to the French ambassador concerning "a nearer conjunction" with France; and whether he should declare his neutrality. Windebank argued against either a French alliance or a declaration of neutrality. Against the former proposition he urged four reasons, one being that the French "had challenged a joint sovereignty on the sea with his Majesty"; and against the latter that the French and Hollanders would besiege Dunkirk or some part of Flanders, and the king would have to sit still and suffer it to be lost, or break his neutrality. "Besides," said Winde-

[1] *State Papers, Dom.*, ccciii. 74; cccv. 36, 38; cccxi. 1. The total number of men in the first fleet, which included five of the "Whelps" and two pinnaces then building, was to be 4580; in the second, in which were included two "Whelps," it was to be 1890.

[2] Hume (*Hist. Engl.*, ch. lii. an. 1636), following earlier writers, places the number at sixty. Thus Frankland (*Annals of King James and King Charles the First*, 477 (1681)) speaks of "sixty gallant ships." Baker (*A Chronicle of the Kings of England*, 455 (1679)) and others, including most of the naval historians of the eighteenth century, give the same number.

[3] Northumberland's Journal, *State Papers, Dom.*, cccxliii. 72. Pennington, on hearing of the appointment of the Earl of Northumberland, wrote in February 1636 to the Council expressing his satisfaction; verily believed he would carry himself like a general in all respects, unless led away, "as the last was, by such as neither knew the honour of the place nor the way of managing the service for the honour and safety of the kingdom."

bank, clinching his arguments, "what was to be done with the fleet next year if his Majesty declared his neutrality? it must lie still and do nothing."[1] Apparently the problem of what was to be done with the fleet was not quite solved until the February following, though there had been several tolerably clear indications that one part of its duty at least would be the suppression of unlicensed fishing on the British coasts. Selden's *Mare Clausum* was issued from the press in December 1635, and it was with great satisfaction that Charles welcomed it (see p. 368). The idea of playing the more distinguished *rôle* of Lord of the Sea was not therefore likely to be abandoned because Lindsey's fleet had been able to do nothing.

At the same time Charles thought he might get some money as well as honour by means of his fleet, and he submitted two propositions to the Lords of the Admiralty for their consideration in employing the fleet "for his honour and profit": first, in "wafting and securing" foreign merchant vessels passing through his seas; second, in protecting all such fishermen as should fish under his license upon his seas and coasts. With reference to the latter suggestion, Sir Henry Marten delivered an elaborate opinion to the Admiralty. He recited how King James, after long and mature deliberation, had satisfied himself and resolved that the fishing "in his seas and upon the coasts of his dominions, did justly appertain unto him as a right incident to his crowns," and had issued a proclamation declaring his title and forbidding unlicensed fishing by foreigners. He also explained that the United Provinces had then sent over commissioners who alleged continued custom and present possession of the fishings, "mentioning withall some treaties that had been heretofore between the Kings of England and the Dukes of Burgundy" in favour of their liberty of fishing. After hearing Sir Henry, the Admiralty expressed a unanimous opinion that "the right and royalty of that fishing upon your Majesty's coasts doth undoubtedly belong unto your Majesty by inheritance, so as you may justly prohibit or license all strangers at your royal will and pleasure." They further declared that by reason of his strength at sea, the time was then most fitting to put his claim into execution; and they

[1] *State Papers, Dom.*, ccxcviii. 63.

recommended that the States' ambassador should be informed that the king had not relinquished his right to the "royal fishing," but was "resolved to defend it as the hereditary right and possession of any other of his dominions." This intimation was to be wrapped up in sophistries, lest the Dutch should think the king challenged it at a time when they had most need of his favour and grace. James had offered them a bare license for liberty to fish; Charles was to offer them safety and security as well, and the depredations which the Dunkirk privateers had committed on the herring-busses were to be used as an impressive argument to convince them of the benefits they would receive from his protection. The privateers had driven them from the fishing, even in sight of English harbours, by which the king was prejudiced both in honour and interest; but if they accepted his licenses he might feel justified in drawing his sword in their defence, in spite of any league or treaty. If, however, the Hollanders should be so wanting in discretion as to refuse the royal licenses, the Lords of the Admiralty were "all clear of opinion that his Majesty should renew and publish the like proclamation to that of the King his father, and prosecute the settling of that his right as a thing so highly concerning him in honour, dominion and profit."

As to the second proposition, the convoying of foreign merchant vessels, the Admiralty were more guarded in their opinion. They all agreed that the king was entitled to have profit by it, but not by way of a general imposition on all ships passing through his seas, as Charles, fresh from the perusal of *Mare Clausum*, apparently had proposed. That, they said, would doubtless "draw a just complaint and clamour" from the neighbouring princes and their subjects. The best course, they thought, was for a tribute to be taken from such vessels as desired convoy, in proportion to the value of the ship and the length of the waftage. The King of England was thus to hire out his ships of war when any foreign vessels were willing to pay for their employment.[1]

The instructions to the Earl of Northumberland were issued by the Admiralty on 7th April, and they were substantially the

[1] The Lords of the Admiralty to the king, 24th February 1636. *State Papers, Dom.*, cccxiii. 24, 25. The documents are in Windebank's writing; the first is endorsed "Fishing. Waftage. An excellent Piece." See Appendix I.

same as those given to Lindsey in the previous year. In the clause referring to hostilities in the presence of the king's ships, the phrase, "in any part of the Narrow Seas," in Lindsey's instructions, was replaced by the words "in any part of his Majesty's seas,"—an alteration of some importance in view of Coke's description of the extent of them; and the same change was made in the title of his instructions.[1] The king also gave the Earl private and verbal commands, particularly as to the operations to be conducted against the Dutch herring-busses.

The fleet mustered in the Downs, the Earl embarking in the *Triumph* on 14th May. Leaving some of the ships to convoy merchant vessels and guard the Straits of Dover, he hoisted sails on the 20th, and stood away westwards in search of the French fleet. It was known that a large number of ships had been equipped by France and lay at Rochelle; and Pennington had reported at the end of February that twenty-four States' men-of-war were at Amsterdam, ready to come out and join the French, and that they were to wear French colours. It was believed that the intention of the allies was to lay siege to and blockade Dunkirk, and Northumberland was ordered to keep a watch on them and to force them to strike. On leaving the Downs he passed over to the French coast, sailing along it within sight of Calais, Boulogne, and Dieppe, and then stood over for the English coast. On 26th May he was at Portland; thence he passed westwards to the Lizard, and cruised between it and Ushant and within sight of the French coast till 11th June, when the fleet put into Plymouth. During all this time they got no glimpse of the fleet for which they were seeking, but they had frequent reports from passing vessels that it was at the Isle de Rhé, and numbered between forty and fifty sail, most of which were small and unprepared to put to sea. Within ten days of leaving the Downs, Northumberland had apparently satisfied himself that they would see nothing of the French that summer; he thereupon reminded the Admiralty that the fishing season was approaching, and requested to know the king's pleasure as to whether he should go northwards. On the 14th, the Admiralty informed him that as the season

[1] "Instructions for our very good Lord, the Earle of Northumberland, Admirall of his Majesty's ffleete in his Majesty's ship the *Triumph*, prepared for this present Expedičion for guard of his Majesty's Seas." *State Papers*, *Dom.*, clvii. fol. 141.

for fishing began about the 20th June, he was to repair to the northwards as soon as his other business would permit. Northumberland received this letter at Plymouth on the 22nd, together with other information that the French fleet had passed towards Dunkirk. He thereupon hurried eastwards, arriving at the Downs on 24th June, and finding that the report as to the movement of the French fleet was false, prepared for the campaign against the Dutch fishermen.

The Channel cruise of Northumberland's fleet was thus as barren of result as had been Lindsey's in the year before. He fell in with a few Dunkirk privateers, far too nimble to be caught up by the "great unwieldy" English ships. When in Portland Road, a glimpse was got of eight large ships at a great distance, which were thought to be States' men-of-war. Northumberland stood towards them, but as soon as they perceived the movement they tacked about and were speedily out of sight. "They are so well built and fitted for sailing," remarked the Earl, "that I can never come near when they have a mind to avoid, unless by chance." It has indeed been well said that whether Charles was sovereign of the seas or not, he could not build ships that would sail.[1] For the same reason the English vessels were unable to find the "Turkish" pirates, which, when the Earl put into Plymouth, came out of the Irish seas, and carried off about thirty English fishermen into captivity. During Northumberland's cruise, Captain Carteret with six ships was busily employed in convoying such trading vessels "as desired it" from the English coast to Dunkirk or Ostend, "taking an acknowledgment in money of strangers."[2]

But if Northumberland was foiled by the Fabian tactics of Richelieu, as they had foiled Lindsey, with regard to the striking of the flag, he succeeded in forcing the Dutch fishermen to take the king's license, a policy which Charles had contemplated long before even the first ship-money fleet was equipped. We have already seen how the Scottish burghs

[1] Gardiner, viii. 157. The English ships were "clogged with timber," which, however, served them well in the first Dutch war when they were pitted against the slighter-built ships of the States. (Oppenheim, *op. cit.*, 254.)

[2] *State Papers, Dom.*, clvii. fol. 141*b*; ccxiv. 107. The Earl of Northumberland to the Lords of the Admiralty, cccxxi. 44, 45, 65, 78, 87; cccxxii. 16, 40; cccxxv. 78, 79; cccxxvi. 16, 38; cccxxvii. 42, 73. The Lords of the Admiralty to Northumberland, 14th June, cccxxvi. 32.

in the course of the negotiations about the Fishery Society, repeatedly insisted that the unwelcome Hollander should be driven from their seas (see pp. 227, 234). As early indeed as 1630 rumours were rife in Paris that a fleet of fifteen English ships, under the command of Sir Kenelm Digby, was to be equipped for this purpose;[1] and there were signs from other quarters of what was impending. In 1634 Sir Nicholas Halse addressed a treatise to the king on Dutch trade and fisheries, like those so profusely bestowed on James, in which he drew a lively picture of the ills which arose from their predominance. The yearly profit derived by the Hollanders from their fishing in the British seas he placed at £6,000,000 sterling, which enabled them to maintain their wars; and yet they were so ungrateful as to say that England would never be well governed until they had the governing of it. He recommended that the Hollanders should be licensed to enjoy half the fishings, a course which he said would make Charles the most powerful sovereign in Christendom,—superlatives and hyperbole never being stinted in such forecastings.[2] Then a very influential body, the Merchant Adventurers, exasperated by certain measures taken by Holland and the States-General with respect to their staple at Amsterdam, petitioned the Council to retaliate, and among their retributory suggestions was the prohibition of the Hollanders from fishing on the British coasts or drying their nets on the English shore.[3] It would appear indeed that originally one of the principal ostensible objects of the fleet of 1635 was to force licenses on the Dutch. Thus Nicholas, the Secretary to the Admiralty, who was not in the secret of the Spanish negotiations, in a memorandum drawn up in that year, suggested that the duties of the fleet should be the suppression of piracy about the mouth of the Straits, and the establishment of the king's rights to the fishings in the eastern and northern seas.[4]

The course upon which Charles had now embarked in refer-

[1] Rowland Woodward to Francis Windebank, 16th December 1630. *State Papers, Dom.*, clxxvii. 13. The writer said he "much feared the event if it should be put in execution."

[2] *Ibid.*, cclxxix. 67.

[3] Petition of the Governor, Assistants, and Fellowship of the Merchant Adventurers of England to the Council. *Ibid.*, cclxxxix. 91.

[4] *Ibid.*, cclxxxv. 84.

ence to foreign fishermen was a revival of the policy of the "assize-herring" of James. No foreigner was to be allowed to fish in the British seas without obtaining, and paying for, a license from the king. James, as we have seen, demanded his right in a pettifogging way, sending a scarcely-armed and half-dismantled pinnace among the busses, with a lawyer on board, to ask the tribute in fair and gentle words, and if refused "to take out instruments upon the said refusal." Charles sent his Admiral with a powerful fleet, and with instructions to force the fishermen to take the licenses in spite of all opposition. The first step was to issue a formal proclamation like that issued by James in 1609, forbidding unlicensed fishing by foreigners. The opinion of the Lords of the Admiralty and their legal adviser (to whom appertained the jurisdiction of the fisheries) being emphatically in favour of the king's claims, the draft proclamation was drawn up and submitted to them on 3rd May.[1] It was approved, and published to the world on May 10th, four days before Northumberland joined the fleet.

In this proclamation Charles recited the provisions contained in the earlier one of 1609, "since which time," he said, "neither Our said father nor Our Self have made any considerable execution of the said Proclamation, but have with much patience expected a voluntary conformity of our neighbours and allies to so just and reasonable prohibitions and directions as are contained in the same." But finding by experience that all the inconveniences which occasioned the previous proclamation had rather increased than abated, being "very sensible of the premises, and well knowing how far we are obliged in honour and conscience to maintain the rights of our Crown, especially of so great consequence," he thought it necessary, by the advice of his Privy Council, "to renew the aforesaid restraint of fishing upon our aforesaid coasts and seas, without license first obtained from Us, and by these presents to make public declaration that Our resolution is (at times convenient) to keep such a competent strength of shipping upon Our Seas, as may (by God's blessing) be sufficient, both to hinder such further encroachments upon Our regalities, and assist and protect those our good friends and

[1] *State Papers, Dom.*, cccviii. 48; cccxx. 14.

allies, who shall henceforth, by virtue of our license (to be first obtained) endeavour to take the benefit of fishing upon our coasts and seas, in the places accustomed."[1]

In connection with the proclamation several hundred licenses were prepared, the precise form of which appears to have occasioned some trouble.[2] The duty of drawing them up had

[1] A Proclamation for Restraint of Fishing upon His Maiesties Seas and Coasts without License. *State Papers, Dom.*, cccxx. 62. *Fœdera*, xx. 15.

[2] The form annexed to the Earl of Northumberland's instructions, sent to him on 14th June from Hampton Court, and which he received at Plymouth on the 22nd, is as follows :—

"CHARLES R.

"We are gratiously pleased by these Presents to grant Lycense to . . . to fish with the Men and Company belonging to a Ship or Vessel called the . . . being of the Burthen of . . . Tonnes, upon any of Our Coasts or Seas of Great Brittaine and Ireland, and the rest of our Islands adjacent, where usually heretofore any fishing hath been. And this Our Lycense to continue for one whole Year from ye Date hereof : Willing and requiring as well all Our subjects as others of what Nation, quality or condition soever that they give no Impeachment or molestation to ye said . . . or his company in the said Vessell in the Execution of this Our Lycense, upon such Paines and Punishments, as are to be inflicted upon the Violators of Our Royall Protection, and the wilful Breakers of Our Peace, in Our aforesaid Dominions and Jurisdictions, further requiring and Commanding all Our Admiralls, Vice-Admiralls, Rere-Admiralls and Captaines of Our Ships, Castles, and Forts to protect and assist the said . . . in ye quiet enjoying the benefit of this Our Lycense."

Another form, dated in July, was as follows :—

"Charles by the Grace of God King of Great Brittaine, France and Ireland, Defender of the Faith, &c. To all his Admiralls, Vice-Admiralls, Rere-Admiralls, and Captaines of oure Shippes, Castles and fforts, and to all and every other our Officers, Ministers and subjects to whome it shall apperteyne, Greeting. Whereas Wee are gratiously pleased by these presents to grant License to . . . Master of a Busse or Vessell called the . . . beinge of the burthen of . . . Tonnes, To fishe with the Men and Company belonging to the said Busse or Vessell upon anie of our Coastes and Seas of Great Brittaine, Ireland and the rest of our Islands adiacent where usually fishing hath bene, from the date hereof, to the last of December next. These are to will and require as well Yow our said Officers and Subjects, as others of what Nacion, quality, or condition soever That yow not onely give noe impeachment or molestacion to the said . . . or his Company in the said Vessell in the Execucion of this Our License, upon such paynes and punishments, as are to be inflicted upon the Violaters of oure Royall Protecion and the wilfull Breakers of our Peace in oure aforesaid dominions and jurisdictions : But that yow protect and assist the said . . . and his Company in the quiet enioying the benefitt of this oure License during the time before limitted : Given . . ." *Ibid.*, cccxxvi. 32 ; cccxxix. 77, 78, 79. It appears from copies without the names and particulars filled in, which are preserved at The Hague, that the first form was used in July, a certain Joost Bouwensz of Delfshaven having accepted one on the 24th (N.S.) of that month.

been remitted in April to Nicholas and Sir Henry Marten, and on June 14th a hundred of them were sent to Deal Castle for the Earl of Northumberland, with instructions from the Lords of the Admiralty. The king, they said, had told them he had already verbally given the Earl directions to charge the busses which took the licenses at the rate of twelvepence a ton; with respect to such as might refuse to accept the license, he was "to take order that they may not fish in the said seas; and in case they shall fish without license, he is to send their vessels and fish into some of his Majesty's ports till further order." The Admiralty left to his own discretion what ships he should take with him, but they said he would require the bigger ships to repel such force as he might encounter, and the smaller ships to apprehend the fisher-boats.

The fleet remained at the Downs, victualling, taking in stores, and waiting for pilots acquainted with the northern coasts, from 24th June to 19th July. The masters of the ships were unwilling to risk the large vessels among "the sands and flats" of the east coast, or where there were no good harbours; and they were all of opinion that if they went at all, they ought to leave before 12th July, in order to fall in with the herring fleet north of Buchan Ness. In any case they declined to go unless pilots were provided, and these had to be obtained from the Cinque Ports and Yarmouth. There was obviously much reluctance in the fleet to go on this expedition. The objections and difficulties were brought to the notice of the king, but Charles stood firm, and expressed his "pleasure" that the northern voyage should be undertaken; and Northumberland before leaving wrote to Windebank to assure him that the fleet would decide the business they had in hand, for either the Dutch would take the licenses and pay the acknowledgment, or else the fleet "would put an end to that work." There could be no doubt of success, because the men, he assured Windebank, were full of resolution to do the king's service and gain credit to themselves. At the same time, he asked for further instructions with regard to his stay among the busses—those he had received, he said, being like oracles.[1]

[1] *State Papers, Dom.*, cccxix. 81; cccxxii. 40; cccxxvi. 32; cccxvii. 93; cccxxviii. 11, 41, 69.

On July 19 the English fleet weighed anchor and shaped its course northwards in its expedition against the Dutch herring-boats. It consisted of sixteen ships, one Whelp, and a frigate; and both Vice-Admiral Sir John Pennington and Rear-Admiral Sir Henry Mervin accompanied the Earl. Contrary winds compelled them to come again to anchor, but on the 22nd a fair breeze carried them to the north of Cromer, on the Norfolk coast. On Sunday, 24th, when at Tynemouth, the Admiral called all his captains together and gave them precise instructions in the event of their meeting with any considerable opposition from the States' men-of-war guarding the busses. On the 25th, 26th, and 27th, foul and misty weather caused them to ride at anchor ten leagues off the coast. About noon on the 28th they descried sixteen sail of herring-busses accompanied by one man-of-war; and immediately the Dutch skippers observed the English fleet they made off "with all the sails they could pack on." Northumberland's unwieldy ships started in pursuit—"but in vain," wrote the Earl, "for none of our ships could come near them." The States' man-of-war was less fortunate or more courageous. It was from the first far astern of the busses, and it was soon overtaken by the *Swan*—which, it may be noted, was a Dunkirk privateer that had been captured and converted into an English warship. Northumberland kept the Dutch captain on board his own ship, the *Triumph*, all night, expecting, as he said, that the busses would not go far without him—for of course they were liable to be swooped upon by the privateers. But the fishermen now feared the Dunkirkers less than they feared the English fleet, and the Earl's ruse failed. After dark he sent off four ships to try to surprise them at their nets, but "they plied away all night without making any stop."[1] They were well aware of the mission of the fleet, but they had no mind either for the license or the protection of the King of England. Next day Northumberland, finding that the busses "trusted only to their good sailing" and did not return, and that the convoying men-of-war were not likely to be

[1] The herring-busses in ordinary course fished all night in fleets, with their drift-nets floating in the water; during the day the crews were employed in curing and packing the herrings caught.

able to oppose him,—two or three "very meane ships only able to defend them from the Dunkirk frigates" accompanying each fleet of busses,—and hearing, moreover, that the principal fishing was past and most of the busses gone home, resolved to divide his fleet into three squadrons, the better to meet in with those which remained. Sir John Pennington was sent to the north as far as Buchan Ness,

Fig. 10.—*Dutch Herring-busses under sail.* After Van der Meulen.

and Sir H. Mervin to the south as low down as Flamborough Head, each with instructions to use his best endeavours to get the Dutchmen to take the king's licenses, while the Earl himself plied "to and again" between them. Next day—Saturday, 30th July—being misty and calm, Northumberland's squadron lay at anchor. About noon they espied four or five sail at a distance, and as there was not a breath of wind, the boats were ordered to take the frigate in tow and go towards them; but a breeze soon springing up, all the ships weighed anchor and stood after them. On getting up to them they proved to be a Hollander man-of-war and a few busses; but the fog was so great that they were unable that night to get more than three of the busses, the skippers of which, as well as the commander of the man-of-war, were brought on board the *Triumph*. On Sunday four other busses were captured, and having been manned with English sailors and threats made that their nets would be taken from them, they at last consented to receive licenses and pay the acknowledgment, and Northumberland sent them away "very well satisfied."[1]

On August 1 the Admiral stood into the Firth of Forth and despatched to Edinburgh a missive for the Court, telling the good news. Then the squadron from the 2nd to the 8th of August beat off and on the coast, going as far north as Aberdeen (5th August) and reaching twenty to thirty leagues off without seeing any busses. It then turned southwards, and on the 9th gave chase to two men-of-war guarding a fleet of busses, the latter, as before, making all haste away. The Dutch men-of-war coming up to the English squadron, no doubt to inquire and protest, were promptly manned with English sailors and sent in hot haste after the busses that had fled. "Yet," said the Earl, "with all the wayes we could use, we gott not above 20 of them, though wee spent divers shott to make them come in."[2] On the same afternoon Pennington's squadron came up from the northwards, where they had succeeded in distributing only three licenses; and on this day three of the ships were sent

[1] "Next day wee fetched in 4 more of them, and having caused their busses to be manned with English, and threatened the takeing away their nettes, they at last consented to take Licenses, and paying the acknowledgment I sent them all away very well satisfied." These busses belonged to the Enkhuisen herring fleet, which was convoyed by a warship under Captain Gerrit Claesz. Ruyter, to whom Northumberland, after the licenses had been accepted, gave a written certificate and safe-conduct for bringing in the busses. Muller, *Mare Clausum*, 269, 377.

[2] These were the Delfshaven busses, the skipper of one being Joust Bouwensz, previously referred to. According to the Dutch accounts, money was scarce on the busses, but the English very willingly took herrings instead, a barrel of herrings being reckoned at from four to four and a-half florins.

back to port by reason of "divers desertes," which made them unfit to keep the sea longer.[1]

Passing to the southward of the Firth of Forth on 10th

Fig. 11.—*Dutch Herring-busses hauling their nets, with convoying ship-of-war.* After Van der Meulen.

August, the English squadron, before the day broke on the 11th, had the good luck to sail into a great fleet of about two hundred busses, which were guarded by five States' men-of-war. To thirty-five of these fishing-boats Rear-Admiral

[1] These were the *Victory, Repulse, and Swallow.* From a report of the Officers of the Navy to the Admiralty, on 20th August, we learn that the *Repulse* had a great many sick on board—"some three or four having died within these two days; some thirty sick were landed at Margate and eight are ill on board. The surgeon is dead, as is said of the spotted fever, full of spots, and it is much doubted that the pestilence is amongst them." The plague in this and the following year made great ravages in London and at the naval ports, partly from the want of simple precautions—*e.g.*, in this case the sick men were to be discharged "for fear of infection (of the ship) and to cease a needlesse charge." *State Papers, Dom.*, cccxxx. 61.

Mervin, whose squadron was found here, had given licenses on the previous day, and Northumberland now distributed about a hundred more amongst them, and left the *Convertive*, the *Bonaventure*, and the *Fifth Whelp* to act as a guard to them on behalf of the King of England, with spare licenses for any other busses that might require them. Next day Northumberland disposed of a few more licenses and came to anchor, lest the ships should damage the long drifting-nets of the fishermen. But a heavy gale coming on and threatening to increase, the Admiral fired a warning gun and weighed at break of day on the 13th: so furious was the wind and sea that two of the vessels broke loose, and others had the greatest difficulty in getting up their anchors, and the English fleet was dispersed. The *Triumph* made for Scarborough, where it was joined during the next few days by the rest of the fleet, and then they all left for the Downs. On the morning of the 20th they descried twenty sail of good ships, and on filling sails and standing to them they found they were Dutch men-of-war, under Van Dorp, who, as we shall see, had been sent by the States-General to protect the busses and prevent the acceptance of the English licenses. The Dutch ships, as the Earl carefully recorded in his Journal, "tooke in all their flaggs, strucke their topsails, and every ship one after another saluted us with their guns, which we answered." Van Dorp went on board the *Triumph* to explain to the English Admiral the reason of the presence there of the Hollander squadron, and when they departed they again saluted. On 22nd August the English fleet cast anchor in the Downs, and Van Dorp, having arrived too late to carry out the instructions of his Government, returned to the Flemish coast.[1]

From the foregoing narrative it is clear that the Dutch fishermen evaded as much as they could the acceptance of the king's licenses. They endeavoured to escape when escape was possible, and only yielded when they were threatened with the loss of their nets and the interruption of their fishing; and it would have shown little wisdom for the

[1] The account of the movements of Northumberland's fleet is extracted from his "Journall of oure Summer's Voyage in the yeare 1636." *State Papers, Dom.*, cccxliii. 72.

few small men-of-war guarding them to have attempted resistance to a force so superior. Northumberland, however, in his report, while explaining that from the lateness of the season they had encountered fewer busses than they expected, said that "those we could come to speak with, when they were made to understand the business, have been very willing to take licenses, and are most desirous of the King's protection." About two hundred licenses, he stated, had been distributed among the busses, and others were left with the ships he had appointed as their guard.[1]

As was to be expected, the revival in England of the policy of James as to unlicensed fishing by foreigners on the British coasts occasioned serious concern in the United Provinces. Since Charles came to the throne the Dutch had been careful to repress as much as they could any cause of further complaints from Scotland. In 1628, when they were informed of the continued "insolencies" of their fishermen, the States-General renewed their previous edict (see p. 179), and gave instructions that extracts from it should be sent to the Chancellor of Scotland; and they issued peremptory orders to the captains of the convoying ships and the masters of the busses and others to obey it strictly.[2] When the Fishery Society was instituted, the States were kept advised by their ambassador in London of its progress and of the measures proposed to be taken at the Hebrides and on the east coast; and although they soon perceived that they had very little to fear from it in the sphere of commercial competition, they rightly suspected that the project foreshadowed the revival of exclusive claims to the fishery, such as had given them so much trouble under James.[3] We have noted also how anxiety was aroused in Holland over the equipment of Lindsey's fleet, and that Joachimi, their ambassador,

1 Northumberland to Windebank, 16th August 1636 (from Scarborough). *State Papers, Dom.*, cccxxx. 41. About 400 licenses in all, each signed by the king, had been furnished to the Earl.

2 20th Dec. 1628. "Clachten van de insolentien van 't bootsvolk en de visschers deser landen in Schotlandt." Muller, *op. cit.*, 232.

3 The English Company and the king's relation to it were considered by the States in January 1631, 25th Oct. 1632, 19th Nov. 1633, and 15th Sept. 1634. (Bosgoed, *Bib. Pisc.*, 357. Oprichting eener Engelsche compagnie voor de Haringvisscherij, Muller, *op. cit.*, 235.)

had got wind of the intention to send some of the ships northwards among the busses. But the proclamation of 10th May as to "restraint of fishing" removed any lingering doubts they had of the king's intentions, especially as it appeared so soon after the publication of *Mare Clausum.* At that time the policy of the Dutch was earnestly directed towards detaching England from the side of Spain and bringing her into line with France and the Republic, and a special ambassador, Van Beveren, was sent over to the English Court to help Joachimi in bringing this about. He arrived in London in March 1636, and in April Coke and Windebank explained to him that the intention of the king in setting forth the fleet was to preserve and maintain his sovereignty and hereditary right over the sea, as well as to furnish convoys for the protection of traffic; and further, that no one could be allowed to fish in the British seas without express license from the king, and the rendering of a proper acknowledgment for the liberty. They told him that the Dutch fishermen would find the king's protection against the Dunkirk privateers both advantageous and profitable. On asking for a statement in writing of the king's claims, the Dutch ambassadors were coldly referred to Selden's *Mare Clausum.*

In notifying the States-General of this conversation, Van Beveren asked for prompt and precise instructions how to deal with what he described as an important, dangerous, and far-reaching business. He was told by De Seneterre, the French ambassador, that he had received a similar notification, and that he had expressed the opinion that it was inopportune to raise at that time a prickly question that had been sleeping for five-and-twenty years, and which was equivalent to a tacit declaration of war against the United Provinces. At an interview which Van Beveren had with Charles on April 25th, he explained that the main object of his coming was to arrange for open and combined action against Spain and help to the young Elector to recover the Palatinate; but the king in a few words put the proposed alliance aside, and began to speak of the herring fishery. The States-General, always anxious to burk discussion of this matter, had postponed giving Van Beveren definite instructions about it, in the hope and expectation that it would be submerged in the more important business of the alliance.[1] There were other circumstances which led them to think the king would not press his claim to the fishery. One was that the publication of the proclamation for restraint of fishing had been delayed, and even its promulgation denied. It seems, indeed, that the opinions of Charles as to his policy on this question were constantly fluctuating, and that he could scarcely make up his mind as to what it were best for him to do. Both the young Elector, his nephew, whom Van Beveren had gained over to his views, and his sister, the Elector's mother and Queen of Bohemia, were against any interference with the Dutch fishermen at that time. It was doubtless with some knowledge of the state of affairs, that the Earl of Northumberland inquired in May if the king was still desirous that he should go north against the busses. But in June all scruples had vanished: the instructions were sent to Northumberland and the proclamation was widely disseminated. In the States of Holland the king's edict was discussed at the beginning of June, and it was remitted to a committee, with Joachimi (then in Holland) and the Prince of Orange, for consideration, and to report as to what measures should be taken to protect the interests of the fishermen. The States finally resolved to do two things—first, to endeavour by all diplomatic means to get the proposed action of the king delayed, and second, to equip a strong fleet to protect the fishermen by force lest diplomacy failed.

In these anxious days Van Beveren kept a tireless eye on the English fleet lying in the Downs, and reported to the States-General from time to time anything he learned of its movements or the rumours he heard concerning it.[2] Twelve days before it sailed for the north, he informed them that the general opinion was that it would return to the westwards to look for the French fleet. A few days later he discovered its real destination, and at once demanded an audience of the king. Charles received him very courteously at Windsor on the 17th July; assured him that he would treat the Dutch "as friends"; and explained that the measures to be taken by the fleet were of a peaceful nature, and were intended to benefit

[1] *Verbaal van Beveren*, 1636-37. Muller, *op. cit.*, 246.
[2] *Brit. Mus. Add. MSS.*, 17,677, P, fol. 67 *et seq.*

the fishermen by extending to them the protection of England against the Dunkirk privateers, from whom they had suffered so much in the previous year. The payment of a small acknowledgment would in reality, he said, be very profitable to them. Van Beveren had accordingly to content himself as well as he could with these assurances. He received the condolences of the French ambassador, with whom he had frequent interviews, and who pointed out to him that the circumstances of the time were such that the wisest course would be to deprive the king of every pretext for open hostility. If the matter could only be prolonged under the pretence of negotiations until peace was concluded with Spain, then indeed France —ay, and even Spain too, he added—would join with the States in bringing the King of England speedily to reason. When Northumberland actually departed for the north, Van Beveren immediately informed the States-General of the important fact; but it was not long until the king was able to tell him that the fishermen had accepted the licenses and paid the acknowledgment "with good contentment."[1]

The ambassador's reports, and still more the accounts which soon poured in from the busses and the convoys of their treatment by the English fleet, raised a storm of indignation in the United Provinces. Captain Ruyter sent on, for visual inspection, the safe-conduct or passport which the Earl of Northumberland had forced upon him; and Joost Bouwensz, and some of the other skippers who had taken the licenses, were loud in their complaints. The unheard-of proceeding was discussed in every seaport town.

The ordinary ambassador, Joachimi, then in Holland, was hurried back to England—at such a pace, indeed, that two of the horses in his carriage dropped dead in one day from exhaustion as he sped Londonwards. He was to express to the king the regret of their High Mightinesses that he should send his powerful "armada" among the poor herring fishermen, who had been so much scared and frightened that many had withdrawn from the fishing altogether and returned home; and the king was to be urged to suspend further action until the matter

[1] Van Beveren to the States-General, $\frac{15}{25}$ Aug. *MSS. Add.*, 17,677, P, fol. 88. In his letter he says the tax on each ton was "twee sixpenningen," or an English shilling. Others placed it at two shillings a last.

had been considered by commissioners to be appointed by both sides.[1] In his audience with Charles, Joachimi avoided the long juridical arguments which used to tire the patience of King James. He laid stress on the close connection of the fishery question, so dear to the United Provinces, and the restoration of the Palatinate, in which the States might be able to afford valuable aid; expatiated on the long and close friendship that had existed between England and the Netherlands; and depicted in moving terms the poverty and hard life of the poor fishermen. But it was all in vain. Charles declared that to ask him to abdicate his sovereignty of the sea was as absurd as if Spain should ask him to give up Ireland; and he added—probably with the knowledge that the States-General had commissioned Graswinckel to answer Selden (see p. 375)—that the publication of books in France, Spain, and the Netherlands, contesting his rights, made it necessary for him to vindicate his sovereignty with all the more strength. The same attitude was maintained in a formal paper handed to Joachimi a little later, in reply to his proposals and representations. In this Charles announced his firm intention to control the fisheries in his own seas. He would only permit foreigners to fish there if they accepted his license and "acknowledged" his right, that is, paid tribute. The request for a conference of commissioners to consider the question was rejected. The king could not with honour, it was said, listen to such a proposal. His right had already been publicly confirmed before the whole world, and was sustained and recognised by all the great kings in performing homage to the fleet at sea, as well as by the Dutch themselves, who were very glad of the protection afforded to them.[2] Joachimi had to return to The Hague without having accomplished anything.

By another channel influence was brought to bear on the king to induce him to suspend the campaign against the Dutch fishermen. Elizabeth, the widowed Queen of Bohemia and the sister of Charles, resided at The Hague, patiently waiting for some lucky turn in the wheel of fortune which might replace

[1] Aitzema, *Saken van Staet en Oorlogh*, ii. 409. Muller, *op. cit.*, 263.

[2] Joachimi to the States-General, $\frac{\text{31 Aug.}}{\text{10 Sept.}}$, $\frac{9}{19}$ Sept. 1636. *Brit. Mus. Add. MSS.*, 17,677, P, fol. 99, 100. *Verbael van Joachimi*, 1636. Muller, *op. cit.*, 264.

her son in possession of the Palatinate. She was led to believe that the States would aid in this project, and in her correspondence with Sir Thomas Roe and Archbishop Laud she often murmured gently against her brother's policy. When Joachimi was hustled back to London, she wrote to Roe that the Dutch were in great alarm about the herring-busses, and she breathed the wish that "all might be laid aside at that time" when they had so much need of the States; "the king," she said, "might do it upon that consideration, and keep his claim still good, to take it up again when he would."[1] Roe argued on the other side. He thought it would show wisdom on the part of Holland, and be greatly to her advantage, if, avoiding an open breach with England, she acknowledged the right of the king and accepted his protection for her fishermen. In this way the States would reap all the advantages they already had, and be relieved of the expense of maintaining a fleet to protect the busses. The king, he felt sure, could not now recede "without weakening or blemishing his right, or his power, to all posterity"; he was prepared to guard the Dutch fishermen and to fight for them as his own subjects; and as for the "acknowledgment," that would be really only a small thing and would not burden the fishing—which would never be thought of. "I doe confidently affirme to your Majesty," continued Roe, "that this affair of ye king is a safetye, an honour, an happines, and utilitye to them, and will, if they know how to use it as a medicine, heale all ulcerations and discontents that have beene bred, or aggravated, by enemies of our mutuall and necessarye amitye. . . . Therefore I beseech your Majestie to inform the Prince of Orange clearely, there is noe other way, if they desire to reconcile, and to oblige the king at once; and if our amity be to them of any value, lett them beginn to doe right and honour to his Majestie,"—and they would get more than they hoped for in other things. At all events, he said, Joachimi had failed to get any satisfaction of his request to have the "execution" on the second fishing suspended, for a new command had been sent to the Admiral to visit the busses again.[2]

This was indeed the case. Northumberland's success had gratified the king, and yet it was felt it had fallen short of

[1] Elizabeth to Sir Thomas Roe, $\frac{15}{25}$ Aug. 1636. *State Papers, Dom.*, cccxxx. 38.

[2] Roe to Elizabeth, 19th Aug., 20th Sept. *Ibid.*, cccxxx. 50; cccxxxii. 1.

what it might have been if they only had got among the busses in time. It was therefore resolved to send the fleet among the Dutch fishermen who came to the Yarmouth fishing in September and October, and to continue the process of forcing licenses upon them. The Earl of Northumberland left the Downs for Yarmouth on 16th September, taking with him eight ships and a pinnace; another ship was to follow later. He felt that his task at Yarmouth would be more difficult than his first had been. Then, the only advantage the busses had was their good sailing; now they would have others owing to the season and the place—shoal waters; and if they avoided the king's ships, he said, as they did in the north, it would be impossible to bring any numbers of them into "conformity." He also requested fresh licenses, because some words in those he had would require to be blotted out, which "would not be so handsome to be seen abroad."[1]

The weather being stormy, they had to anchor one night off the North Foreland and the next off Lowestoft, reaching Yarmouth Roads on the 18th, where they lay for a few days getting pilots and gathering information about the Dutch fishermen. Hearing that some Holland men-of-war were cruising outside, the Earl guessed that the herring-boats would not be far off, and the wind being fair, the fleet weighed anchor on the morning of the 22nd and stood out to sea. When clear of the sands they again anchored, and the ketch was sent out during the night to discover the whereabouts of the busses, but without success. Next day the fleet stood off farther to sea, but failed to see or to hear anything of the Hollanders, and being joined by a ninth ship, the *Swallow*, the fleet lay at anchor in "blowing weather" about ten leagues from the coast until Monday, September 26. Two of the ships, the *James* and the *Nonsuch*, had been driven out of sight by the gale; two, the pinnace and the *Fortune* pinck, had to run nearer shore for fear of foundering; and the Admiral sent the two London ships, the *Jonas* and the *Neptune*, into port, because they were insufficiently victualled. On this day news was brought from Yarmouth, received from a Scottish ship which had arrived from Zealand, that the Dutch had forbidden any more busses to go to the fishing that year, and the Earl advised

[1] Northumberland to the Admiralty and to Secretary Coke, Sept. 16. *State Papers, Dom.*, cccxxxi. 55, 56.

Windebank to this effect.[1] The rumour, however, was false, for on the 28th a fleet of fifty sail of busses and two or three men-of-war was descried to windward, but Northumberland was able to speak to only three of them that "wanted licenses." On the next day, as they were following the busses that "would not come near them," they caught sight of another fleet of about sixty sail, with three men-of-war, and the English ships went amongst them and cast anchor, and made the convoyers anchor also; "then," said the Earl, "all the busses of both fleets came about us; most of them had formerly taken licenses, and such as were unprovided were then furnished by us." Next day, finding no more of the herring-boats "that wanted licenses," the English squadron weighed anchor and shortly afterwards perceived a third large fleet of busses, guarded this time by ten men-of-war. To this fleet they gave chase, plying up to windward all night, and on October 1, as the wind prevented the boats being sent out, they anchored in sight of them. All Sunday it also "overblew," but as the weather grew calmer at night the squadron again got under way, and by daybreak was among the busses, which were, no doubt, busily engaged in hauling their nets. Northumberland stayed amongst them until October 5, the ships' boats being kept occupied each day in distributing the licenses; but they "found it a very troublesome business," as the busses dispersed, and it became difficult to distinguish those that had taken licenses from those that had not. The weather growing misty and unsettled, and the Admiral being "out of all hope to give out any more licenses," the squadron quitted the herring fleet and made for Yarmouth, where the Earl landed on October 9 and journeyed to the Court. Altogether, at the Yarmouth fishing, more than 200 licenses were distributed among over 400 busses which were present, and no opposition was offered by any of the fifteen men-of-war which were guarding them. "The unwillingnesse of the busses to come neere us," wrote Northumberland to the Admiralty, "hath found us intertainement for 8 dayes together in following them, but now we have left verie few of them unprovided of his Majesty's licenses."[2]

[1] *State Papers, Dom.*, cccxxxii. 39.

[2] Northumberland's Journal, *Ibid.*, cccxliii. 72; Northumberland to Nicholas, 6th October 1636. *Ibid.*, cccxxxiii. 26. Dutch accounts vary somewhat from

Thus ended the campaign against the Dutch herring-boats, from which, as we have seen, Charles desired to reap profit as well as honour. So far as the profit went, it did not amount to much. Appended to the official journal of the voyage of the fleet is a statement of the sums received for convoying shipping,—which, in accordance with the advice of the Admiralty, was voluntary,—and also of the "acknowledgment money" taken from the fishing-busses. The former amounted to £999, nearly all of which was earned by the convoying of merchantmen and small traders to Dunkirk and Ostend.[1] Small as the amount was, it greatly exceeded what was exacted from the Dutch busses for king's license and protection, the total being £501, 15s. 2d., collected in a variety of coins.[2] The detailed schedule is as follows:—

"In Rix Dollo^{rs}	878	103	10	00
In halfe Crownes	145	018	02	06
In pieces of 3^{s}	40	006	00	00
In Kunnings Dollo^{rs}	100	025	00	00
In Ryalls of 8	134½	029	02	10
English money		018	12	08
English Gold		119	13	00
Dutch and Scotch Angells		015	15	00
Hungare Duckats	7	002	09	00
Dutch and French money		001	05	00
Dutch shillings		066	00	00
Double Stivers		030	00	06
Single Stivers		005	06	00
In Silver		000	18	00
		501	15	02"

that given by the Earl of Northumberland. According to them, seven English men-of-war fell in with a hundred busses convoyed by five States' warships, and the busses paid the tax and took the licenses. But when thirteen Dutch men-of-war, convoying a great herring fleet, arrived on the scene and put themselves in a position for battle, the English ships did not interfere any further and soon sheered off.

[1] An Accompt of the Convoy money, as it was delivered unto me by the Captaines emploied in that Service, vizt.: Captain Carteret, £657, Captaine Lindsey, £200, Captain Slingsby, £42, Captain Johnson, £20, Mr Skinner, £80.

[2] An Account of the Acknowledgment Money taken of the Holland Fishermen. The partiality for English gold is shown by the fact that £119, 13s. of the total was thus paid.

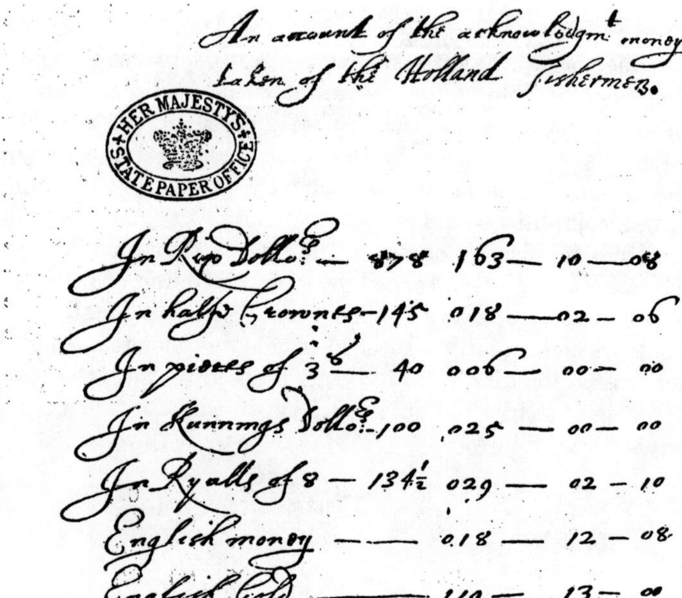
An account of the acknowledgm^t money taken of the Holland fishermen.

HER MAJESTY'S STATE PAPER OFFICE

In Rix Dollers	878	163	10	08
In halfe crownes	145	018	02	06
In peeces of 3^s	40	006	00	00
In Runnings Dollers	100	025	00	00
In Ryalls of 8	134½	029	02	10
English money		018	12	08
English Gold		119	13	00
Dutch & Scotch Angells		015	15	00
Hungary Dukatts	7	002	09	00
Dutch & French money		001	05	00
Dutch shillings		066	00	00
Double stivers		030	00	06
Single stivers		005	06	00
In silver		000	18	00
		501	15	02

Fig. 12.—*Facsimile of the official account of the monies received from the Dutch herring fishermen for the king's licenses.*

There is probably no circumstance connected with the English claims to the sovereignty of the seas that has been more frequently misrepresented by historians, pamphleteers, and writers on international law than the operations of Northumberland's fleet, and in particular the amount paid by the Dutch herring fishermen for the king's licenses; and so far as appears, the account given here is the first that is authentic and correct. Although Northumberland's Journal is preserved among the national records, only one author seems to have quoted from it, namely, Evelyn, and he deliberately misrepresented it. Under the hands of various authors the sum of money gradually became swelled to £30,000, or even to £100,000, and it was represented as a rent paid by the Dutch for permission to fish, and played an important part in all later controversies and negotiations.[1]

[1] The Dutch themselves appear to have acknowledged a payment of 20,000 florins (Muller, *Mare Clausum*, 274). Rapin (*Hist. d'Angleterre*, vii. 455) and Wagenaar (*Vaderlandsche Historie*, xi. 260) placed it at 30,000 florins; Larrey (*Hist. d'Angleterre, d'Ecosse et d'Irlande*, iv. 126) states that the Dutch concluded a treaty with Charles by which they agreed to pay him "dix mille ecus par an," which is equivalent to the same thing; Hume (*Hist. of England*, ch. lii. an. 1636) says: "The Dutch were content to pay £30,000 for a license during this year." The error is found in the earlier English historical writers. Rushworth (*Collections*, V. ii. 322) also states the sum as £30,000, and adds that the Dutch were willing to pay a yearly tribute for a like liberty in future. Frankland (*Annals of King James and King Charles the First*, 477 (1681)) says that Northumberland with his "sixty gallant ships" "commanded the Dutch busses to cease fishing until they had obtained permission from the King, which they seeming not willing and ready to do, he fired amongst them, sunk some and seized others, until they were forced to fly into his Majesty's harbours, and desired the Lord Admiral to mediate to his Majesty for his leave for this summer, and they would pay unto his Majesty's treasury therefor the sum of £30,000, which they did accordingly, and professed their readiness to become suppliants to his Majesty for a grant, under the condition of a yearly payment therefor for the future." This writer seems to have confused Northumberland's operations with those of Blake's fleet in 1652 (see p. 406) or with the onslaught of the Dunkirkers in 1635. Kennet (*A Complete Hist. of England*, iii. 85 (1719)) repeats the mistake and puts the sum at £30,000, and so with almost all the historians, as well as the naval writers. Thus, Burchett (*A Complete Hist. of the Most Remarkable Transactions at Sea*, 379 (1720)) and Lediard (*The Naval History of England*, 526 (1735)) give the statement of Frankland; Entick (*A New Naval History*, 438 (1757)) drops one of the ciphers and makes the sum £3000, but otherwise retains the false account. Admiral Colomb, in his recent excellent work on *Naval Warfare* (p. 33), no doubt founding on these naval authors, also refers to the "non-payment of the £30,000 annually, which had been fixed by Charles as license dues." The writers of minor books embellished the error. In a mendacious treatise published in 1664 (*The Dutch drawn to the Life*, 146) it is said that Northumberland "scoured the seas of the Dutch busses, seizing some, sinking others, and enforcing the rest to flee; so reducing all to the precarious condition of entreating the favour of fishing by the King's commission, which he was the readier to indulge them, because he looked upon them as the

The doings of Northumberland's fleet at the Yarmouth fishing caused increased excitement in Holland. Van Beveren knowing, as he said, that the English ships had not gone northwards "to catch flies," immediately sent intelligence of its departure to Admiral Van Dorp, so that he might extend his protection to the Dutch fishermen. Early in August the Admiral had been expressly instructed to guard the fishermen "from the Spanish and all others inclined to molest them"; and he had a fleet of fifty-seven sail under his command for this purpose.[1] But Van

most likely instruments for his nephew's restauration to the Palatinate." John Smith, writing in 1670 (*England's Improvement Reviv'd*, 257), said that "the composition of the Hollanders (for liberty to fish) was an annual rent of £100,000, and £100,000 in hand; and never having been paid or brought into the Exchequer, as I could hear of, there is an arrearages of above £2,500,000; an acceptable sum," he adds, "and which would come very happily for the present occasions of his Majesty"—Charles II. would have been very glad of much less; he quite failed to induce the Dutch to pay him £12,000 a-year for a like liberty. Evelyn in 1674 (*Navigation and Commerce*) put the "arrears" at over half a million sterling, and he said that in 1636 the Hollanders paid £1500, 15s. 2d. for licenses; but this was only, as he explained later, "the sophism of a mercenary pen," since he slumped the convoy and the "acknowledgment" money together (having had access to Northumberland's Journal), and eight years later he wrote to Pepys his remarkable letter of recantation, in which he stated, "Nor did I find that any rent (whereoff in my 108 page I calculate the arrears) for permission to fish was ever fixed by both parties" (*Diary and Correspondence*, iii.)

The writers on international law have copied the erroneous statements from the historians and from one another. Wharton (*Hist. of the Law of Nations*, 154) says, "The exclusive rights to the fisheries within these seas (the Four Seas) and near the coasts of the British Islands had been occasionally acknowledged by the Dutch in the form of annual payments and taking out licenses to fish; and was again suspended by treaties between the sovereigns of England and the Princes of the House of Burgundy." This statement, which outrages chronology as well as fact, is repeated (without acknowledgment) by Phillimore (*Commentaries upon International Law*, I., Part ii., c. vi. s. clxxxiv.), and by Travers Twiss (*The Law of Nations in Time of Peace*, 254), Hall (*Treatise on International Law*, 145), and others. Hall quotes Hume's statement that the Dutch had to pay £30,000 for leave to remain, and a more recent author supposes that the great fishing of the Dutch on our coasts originated in the reign of Elizabeth, and that, growing strong, they refused to pay the "duties levied without question for generations within the British Seas" (Walker, *A History of the Law of Nations*, i. 167). As has been shown in the text, the Dutch herring-boats resisted the payment of the "acknowledgment" money as far as they could; the States-General equipped a fleet to prevent by force their molestation by the English men-of-war, and they dismissed their Admiral because he failed in 1636 to protect them.

[1] Aitzema, *op. cit.*, ii. 408. "Op de bewaringhe ende bescherminghe van de groote ende kleyne Visscherij deser Landen tegen de Spaansche ende allen anderen die hun souden willen beschadigen," August $\frac{5}{15}$, 1636.

Dorp was too late. As we have seen, he met the Earl of Northumberland on the 20th August returning triumphantly to the Downs. On asking the English Admiral why he was among the busses, he was politely told "to protect the fishermen," and when Northumberland asked the reason of the presence of the Dutch fleet, he received the same answer, "to protect the fishermen." It was a perplexing position for Van Dorp. His instructions were to guard the busses from molestation, but they contained no article which covered the case as it now presented itself, and to attack the English squadron under the circumstances would have been foolish. He therefore sailed back to the coast of Flanders to watch the Spanish ships. He returned to the English coast in September, and on the very day that Northumberland left the Downs for Yarmouth the Dutch fleet was actually lying at that port. Van Dorp again missed both the English squadron and the herring-busses, and resumed "plying to and again" between Dover and Calais.[1] The States-General were much incensed at this failure of their Admiral to prevent the distribution of the licenses. As they well knew, it furnished Charles with a precedent, and with the argument that the Dutch fishermen desired his protection and were willing to accept and pay for his licenses. When a suitable opportunity occurred in the following year, they forced Van Dorp to resign his office.[2]

As the herring-fishing was now over for the year, the States had time to consider what they ought to do in the following season if Charles persisted in his attempts. On two occasions it was resolved to issue an edict forbidding the fishermen to accept licenses from any foreign prince;[3] and this would certainly have been done had Charles adhered to his policy. But the States naturally hesitated, until it should be absolutely necessary, to take a step which would at once have placed them in direct antagonism to England in the eyes of the whole world, and the publication of the edict was from time to time delayed. This cautious conduct served their purpose much better, for before the fishing season of 1637 arrived, the kaleidoscope of Charles's foreign relations had taken another turn, and he was

[1] *State Papers, Dom.*, cccxxxiii. 13. [2] Muller, *op. cit.*, 273.

[3] *Res. Holl.*, 19th September; *Res. St.-Gen.*, 8th November 1636; Bosgoed, *Bib. Pisc.*, 360.

anxious to avoid further trouble with the Dutch. The Earl of Arundel, who had been sent to Vienna on one of the king's wild-goose missions, to negotiate a treaty with the Emperor for the restoration of the Palatinate, returned unsuccessful to England at the close of the year. He came back full of bitterness at the perfidy of Spain, and persistently urged a French alliance, even if it should lead to war with the former Power. The strenuous arguments of Arundel, as well as the treatment of his mission, caused Charles to turn again to France, the ally of the Dutch Republic; and Richelieu promptly proposed an alliance against Spain and the Emperor, one result of which would have been to range England and the States on the same side in a maritime war.[1]

At such a conjuncture the promulgation of the edict of the States-General would have been unfortunate, and Arundel requested George Goring, who had gone to The Hague, to see the Prince of Orange in order to get it suppressed. But the Prince of Orange, while anxious enough to avoid further trouble with England, desired, before he consented, to receive an assurance that the king would cease from molesting the Dutch fishermen in the ensuing season. The Queen of Bohemia urged the same course. She "humbly besought" her royal brother to suspend further execution of his right, which, she said, he might take up again when he would, without any prejudice, "as the king, our father, did." Charles was loth to give an assurance so wounding to his vanity, and so opposed to what he conceived to be a chief prerogative of his crown. In the autumn Sir Thomas Roe had declared that the difficulty in the way for the benefit of the Prince Elector arose from the fishery dispute, and that upon nothing was the will of the king more firmly bent: if the Dutch did not yield, he feared "another procedure" next season. Even in February, Archbishop Laud told Elizabeth that the king was "so set to maintain the dominion of the sea" that he durst not speak to him any more about it. At the same time he gave a broad hint that nothing further would be attempted against the Dutch fishermen in the approaching season. He much wondered, he said, that the Prince of Orange and the States should trouble themselves to gain an overt concession from his Majesty to leave their fishing that year, since

[1] Gardiner, *Hist. England*, viii. 160, 163, 202, 205.

it was "more than manifest" there would be so much other work for his navy that the business of the fishing must needs fall asleep of itself. He would advise a silence on all hands in regard to it, and not to interrupt "business with moving a question about that which would necessarily do itself (*sic*) without questioning." Sir Thomas Roe also sent the queen assurances in the same sense. The king, he said, would never retract his declaration of the dominion of the sea, but "only for this year, and at the request of the Prince (her son) and in contemplation of concurrence expected with him, he will not trouble their fishing." These assurances seemed so far satisfactory to the States that the edicts were suppressed. They would be well content, they informed Elizabeth, if the king "forgot it and spoke no more of it," which she told them she was confident he would not, having things of greater importance on hand.[1]

The young Elector, Prince Charles Louis, took a considerable part in the conversion of the king; or rather, he was made use of by the Dutch ambassador for this purpose. When Van Beveren first arrived in London, he let it be known that the States were desirous of doing something for the Prince; but

[1] Roe to Ferentz, Oct. 15, 1636. *State Papers, Dom.*, cccxxxiv. 15. Goring to his father, Lord Goring, Feb. $\frac{4}{14}$, 1637. *Ibid.*, cccxlvi. 33. Goffe to Archbishop Laud, Feb. 2. *Ibid.*, cccxlvi. 23. The Queen of Bohemia to Archbishop Laud, Feb. $\frac{4}{14}$. *Ibid.*, cccxlvi. 34. Laud to the Queen, Feb. 28. *Ibid.*, cccxlviii. 62. Roe to the Queen, Mar. 17. *Ibid.*, cccl. 16. The Queen to Laud, $\frac{\text{Mar. 25}}{\text{April 4}}$. *Ibid.*, cccli. 1. Goffe's letter to Laud was as follows: "Your Grace will receive intelligence from other hands that certain edicts which were ready to be published by the States against paying any acknowledgment for leave to fish are now suppressed upon the hopes of his Majesty's relinquishing that business for the present. But the Prince of Orange, not willing to content himself with probabilities, hath been very pressing with the Queen of Bohemia to have some assurance given him that the king would not interrupt their fishing this year. And if no other way might be afforded, he is very urgent at least that the Elector (the son of Elizabeth) would write to him and assure him so much. How much such an assurance would be prejudicial to the honour of his sacred Majesty your Grace can best judge. But I thought it my duty to add that though their edicts are suppressed, yet their book in answer to Mr Selden's *Mare Clausum* is ready to come forth: and the author is neither so modest nor discreet that the Elector should trust him [? the Prince of Orange] with any written assurance in that kind. The Prince of Orange hath been so much upon this that it hath given others cause to believe that the Elector will be moved in it."

his hint was not then taken up, since hopes were entertained that Arundel's mission to Vienna would make other aid unnecessary.[1] Arundel was recalled in September; it was known that his mission had failed, and early in October Van Beveren saw his opportunity. Through a trustworthy friend[2] the suggestion was made to the Elector that if some arrangement could be come to about the fishery question, negotiations might be begun for a treaty between the States and England relating to the recovery of the Palatinate. The ambassador learned that the Prince had already taken steps in the same direction. Through the intermediary of Laud, the proposal had been made to Charles that the Dutch, instead of paying license-money for liberty to fish in the British seas, should place at the disposal of the Elector some ships and soldiers, the king's proclamation for restraint of fishing being meanwhile suspended. Charles would not agree to this. The ambassador, he said, had offered assistance when he arrived without any hope of an equivalent on his part, and he could not give up his claim to an acknowledgment of his rights. Van Beveren, on the other hand, informed his confidant that it was a question of principle with the States, and that it would be better to break off all negotiations if the "acknowledgment" was insisted on. Nevertheless, these private negotiations continued, and finally a draft treaty was prepared embodying two proposals. The first agreed well enough with Van Beveren's instructions. It was to the effect that a fleet should be equipped to which England should contribute thirty ships and 8000 men, and the States fifteen ships and 4000 men; and France was to be asked to furnish the same force as England. The combined fleet was to attack Spain by sea and effect a landing. The second proposal related to the fishery, and it provided that while these operations were going on, the Dutch herring fishermen would be allowed to fish freely and in security, as they had always done from the time of Queen Elizabeth and King James, approaching the coasts near enough to carry on their fishing profitably, and to dry

[1] Roe to Ferentz. *State Papers, Dom.*, cccxxxiv. 15.

[2] The "confident vrundt" was probably Roe, who was the confidential adviser of Elizabeth, and at this time had interviews with the Dutch ambassador in the Prince's interests, which he "feared would come to nothing." *Ibid.*

their nets on shore, without the king interfering with them in any way.[1]

This proposition, at first sight apparently favourable to the States, was rejected by Van Beveren. Although it got rid of the difficulty for the time, the question was sure to be raised at a later period when the naval and military operations were concluded; its acceptance would, moreover, be equivalent to a tacit acknowledgment that the king had the right to exclude them from the fishery. The ambassador was afraid of a precedent which bargained as a *quid pro quo* for what was claimed as a right; and the negotiations went no further.

But Charles, although unwilling to risk the success of the treaty with France, from which great things were expected, by openly insisting upon the acceptance of his licenses by the Dutch fishermen, was reluctant to abandon his policy. From the readiness with which the fishermen had taken the licenses after they "understood" them (as Northumberland reported), he was apparently led to believe that they really desired his protection, and that the only obstacle in his way was the opposition of the States' Government. He therefore decided that instead of trying—or at least before trying—to enforce the licenses by means of the fleet in the ensuing summer, the attempt might be made secretly to induce the fishermen to accept them in Holland before they left for the fishing. Boswell, the English ambassador at The Hague, was instructed to try what could be done in this way, and so anxious was Charles for such acknowledgment of his sovereignty of the sea as acceptance of the licenses implied, that the ambassador was authorised to reinforce his persuasion by bribing those who were most influential among the fishermen. The fishermen, according to Boswell, were not averse to the proposal, but they very naturally wished to know, first of all, how the licenses of the King of England would protect them from the Dunkirk

1 "Que durant le même temps les Pescheurs et preneurs d'hareng, subjects de leurs Seigneuries, pescheront librement et franchement, cōme ils ont tousiours faict du temps de la Royne Elysabeth et du grand Roy Jacques tous deux de très-glorieuse mémoire, s'approchants si près des bords de mer, et rivages des royaulmes, terres et ysles de sa Maté, que leur mestier, la course de poisson et hareng, et leur proffit portera, voire jusques à seicher leurs filets sur terre, sans que sa Maté directement ou indirectement leur fera ou fera faire aucun dommage, destourbier, ou empeschement en cela." *Verbaal van Beveren.* Muller, *op. cit.*, 279.

privateers. If the Government at Brussels would acknowledge the validity of the licenses, or if the Cardinal Infant agreed to back them with passports of his own, the offer, they said, would be worth considering; but they could scarcely depend on the protection of the English fleet alone. As a sign that they were in earnest, they offered to place £2000 at Boswell's disposal if he could get the matter settled in this way. This sum, with the king's approval, was forwarded to the English representative at Brussels, to be used in gaining over the Spanish authorities.[1] The Dutch fishermen were a practical race of men. They cared little for abstract questions about the sovereignty of the sea. But they suffered much from the Dunkirk privateers, and the burden of maintaining convoys was a heavy one. Any reasonable scheme which promised to free them from the attacks of their relentless enemy at small cost was bound to be attractive. That the proposal was seriously considered was also shown by a spontaneous application made to the Secretary of the English Admiralty on behalf of the fishermen of Schiedam. The agent in London, Mr Brames, who supplied them with lampreys for bait, wrote to Nicholas for a copy of the license granted in the previous year, with a statement of the rates charged. If the fishermen were pleased with the license and the price, they would, he said, come themselves for them. Charles instructed Nicholas to give the information wanted, but only "as from himself."[2]

An unexpected obstacle intervened to prevent the plan being carried out. Gerbier, the British agent at Brussels, chiefly by bribing the mistress of the Cardinal Infant, had secured a promise that the passports would be granted; but the Spanish Admiral absolutely refused to be bound by them. He declared he would not spare a single herring-boat, even if the Cardinal went down on his knees to him. He would pay attention to no passport that did not come direct from Madrid.[3] Thereupon the Dutch fishermen refused to have anything to do with the licenses which had been sent to Boswell "under the King's hand and signet."[4]

[1] Gardiner, *op. cit.*, 218. *State Papers, Holland*, Jan., Feb. 1637.

[2] March 19, 1637. *State Papers, Dom.*, cccl. 34.

[3] Gardiner, *op. cit.* *State Papers, Holland, Flanders*.

[4] Windebank to Northumberland, July 3. *State Papers, Dom.*, ccclxiii. 21.

Still, the peculiar resources of Charles were not exhausted. He might yet, he thought, be able to distribute the licenses among the fishermen when they came to fish off the British coast, without employing his fleet for the purpose, or running the risk of war with the Republic. The third ship-money fleet had assembled in the Downs in April and May; it consisted of twenty-eight ships, of which nine were merchant vessels, and the Earl of Northumberland was again appointed Admiral, his instructions, dated 15th April, being identical with those of the previous year.[1] The state of the negotiations with France, and other causes, prevented the king from renewing his enterprise against either the French for the honour of the flag or the Dutch in connection with the fishery. The fleet, therefore, to the wonder and discontentment of the officers, was kept for the most part lying at anchor, ships being occasionally detached for special purposes.

On 3rd July, Windebank wrote to the Earl of Northumberland telling him of the failure of the secret treaty with the Cardinal Infant, and saying that it was the intention of the Hollanders, who had refused the king's licenses sent to Boswell, to fish in his Majesty's seas as heretofore, many of the busses having already left Holland under strong convoys. By the king's commands he sent him about 200 licenses, "and withal his pleasure is," said Windebank, "that you dispatch immediately one of the merchant ships under your charge (being not willing to employ any of his own until it appear what the success will be) toward the north with these licenses, with order to make offer of them to the fishers, and if they accept them to distribute them at the same rates they were taken the last year. And if such as take them," he continued, "desire to be safe-conducted in their return, your Lordship is to assure them his Majesty will take them into his protection, and cause some of his fleet to accompany them homewards for their defence." But if the fishermen refused to take the licenses, then the Earl was to notify the fact to the king, who would "take further resolution." Sir William Boswell, added the Secretary, had been informed of the king's intentions, and told to assure the fishermen willing to take the licenses of his Majesty's protection. The Cardinal Infant and

[1] *State Papers, Dom.*, clvii. 151*b*.

the Spanish Ministers had also been informed, and did not well relish it.[1]

This despatch, sent by express messenger, appears to have somewhat surprised the Earl. His clear intelligence must have told him that a tortuous and fatuous proceeding of this kind could only end by making the king ridiculous. He apparently wished Charles to reconsider the matter, and asked for further directions. Ignoring part of Windebank's letter, he inquired how Captain Fielding, whom he intended to send, should behave himself if the fishermen proved obstinate and refused the licenses; and he pointed out that if they accepted them and the king resolved they should be convoyed home, it would need a large number of ships, as the busses returned in small fleets.[2] Windebank two days later repeated the instruction that, if they refused, the fact was to be immediately notified, when the king would take further resolution. "The truth is," he said, "his Majesty in this present conjuncture is not willing to proceed so roundly with them as he hath done heretofore, and therefore thinks fit to hold this way of inviting them fairly to acknowledge his right without sending his whole fleet, which would be a manifest engagement and obligation to him in honour to perfect the work upon any conditions, and notwithstanding any opposition whatsoever, and might be of dangerous consequence, and destructive to the present condition of his affairs. And therefore he chooses rather to attempt it with as little noise as may be, that if the business take not in this way it may receive the less blow, and in case of their refusal he may have time deliberately to consider what resolution to settle."[3]

At this time Charles was very anxious to be on good terms with the States. Van Beveren, the special Dutch ambassador, who was returning home, was very cordially received by him on taking his leave on 16th July. The king then insisted on the States entering the alliance, and he expressed his pleasure at the courtesies which had been shown to the Prince Elector. Besides the usual gifts on such occasions, Van Beveren tells us

[1] Windebank to the Earl of Northumberland, 3rd July 1637. *State Papers, Dom.*, ccclxiii. 21.

[2] Northumberland to Windebank, 4th July. *Ibid.*, ccclxiii. 28.

[3] Windebank to Northumberland, 6th July. *Ibid.*, ccclxiii. 41.

he sent him a few days later a handsome diamond ring.[1] But even if Charles had been moved by no special desire to conciliate the Republic, the preparations which were being made in Holland to guard the fishermen from molestation might have given pause to the attempt to repeat the operations of the year before. The Dutch Government were perfectly aware of Boswell's intrigues about the licenses, and they put little faith in the assurances received through the Queen of Bohemia. They resolved to err on the safe side by equipping a powerful fleet to protect the busses. In April and May, Pennington reported to the Admiralty that Van Dorp (not yet cashiered) was cruising between the Downs and Dunkirk with twenty sail of stout men-of-war, and that he heard that six French warships were bound for the north to aid in guarding the fishermen.[2]

Fielding departed on his mission in the *Unicorn*, one of the ships furnished by London, and on the morning of 18th July he came among the busses fishing off Buchan Ness, Aberdeenshire. They numbered between six and seven hundred, and were convoyed by twenty-three men-of-war. Fielding, according to his account, "found the busses very willing" to take the licenses, and two did so. Then one of the Dutch warships came up and lay by him, and the captain asked him to speak to his Admiral before sending for the busses; "but it blew hard that day and the next, so that no boat could pass." On the 20th he spoke with the Admiral of South Holland and the Commander of North Holland, and explained his mission; but they would not then give their answer. On the following day all the commanders of North and South Holland and of Zealand, with three other captains, told him "that they durst not let his boat pass among the busses to give out his Majesty's licenses before they had orders from their Masters." This was their answer, but they declined to give it in writing. The *Unicorn* then made sail for England to report the rebuff.[3]

The result of his manœuvre was mortifying to the king. Fielding, sailor-like, did not conceal the outcome of his mission in diplomatic reserve. The story soon spread through-

[1] "Diamentenring van tamelijcke groote," *Verbaal van Beveren.* Muller, *op. cit.*, 297.

[2] *State Papers, Dom.*, cccliv. 16; ccclv. 22.

[3] Report of Fielding, 24th July. *Ibid.*, ccclxiv. 45.

out the fleet, and occasioned both hilarity and indignation. When Fielding left, Pennington expressed the opinion to his friend Nicholas that the attempt would fail and would bring greater inconveniences in its train. On his return, Northumberland said it would have been much better if the king had absolutely forborne his request to the Dutch than have demanded it in the manner he did. After the successful campaign of the year before, Charles was now practically warned off his own seas, "as he is pleased," said Pennington, "to call them."[1] It was a pitiful position for the Sovereign of the Seas, with a great armada lying idle at the Downs and his bombastic declarations still echoing in the ears of Europe.

As soon as it was known at Court that the story had got out, Windebank was commanded to take such measures as he could to contradict it. To duplicity was added mendacity. Fielding in his report had described an occurrence he witnessed on returning along the coast to Scarborough. Thirteen Dunkirkers had attacked a Dutch man-of-war, and as the *Unicorn* came upon the scene the latter sank, and the English captain unsuccessfully endeavoured to save the drowning men. Windebank seized upon this incident. He wrote to Captain Fogg, who was in command of the ships in the Downs in the absence of the Admiral, that the report spread about that the Hollanders had refused his Majesty's licenses to fish in his seas was "utterly mistaken." Fielding had not been sent to offer licenses to the busses, but to tender the king's protection. His Majesty, hearing "that the Dunkirkers had prepared a great strength to intercept them in their return from the fishing," had sent Fielding, "in love to them," to give them notice of it, and to offer them safe-conduct. "This," said Windebank, "you are publicly to advow whensoever there shall be occasion, and to cry down the other discourse as scandalous and derogatory to his Majesty's honour."[2] Similar directions were sent to the Earl of Northumberland.

[1] Pennington to Nicholas, 10th July, *State Papers, Dom.*, ccclxiii. 99; Northumberland to Sir Thomas Roe, 6th August, *ibid.*, ccclxv. 28; Pennington to Northumberland, 20th May, *ibid.*, ccclvii. 15, ii.

[2] Windebank to Fogg, Aug. 10. *Ibid.*, ccclxv. 51. With reference to this letter of Windebank's, the following note by Secretary Williamson was made on the copy

At the beginning of August 1637, Charles, conscious of the ridicule that would ensue if the third ship-money fleet lay at anchor all the year, and yet having nothing for it to do, sent it to the west—"to make one turn in an honourable procession, to continue the boundaries of our master's dominion in the sea," as Roe, with gentle sarcasm, described it. It got as far as the Land's End, and returned to the Downs on 5th September, having "scarce seen a ship stirring on the sea, except the poor fishers that dwell upon the shore."[1] Windebank told Northumberland that the king was "very sensible" of the story which was being told about the licenses, and that he had been specially commanded to give the refutation of it in charge of the Earl, "and that you should do it in the same way that I have directed him (Fogg), namely, that his being sent to the busses was to give them notice of the forces prepared by the Dunkirkers to intercept them in their return, and to offer them his Majesty's protection, but no licenses; that of the licenses to be cried down and the other to be advowed and reported through the whole fleet." Fielding was to be admonished to be more reserved in future "in such great services," and in the meantime to "make reparation by divulging this and suppressing the former report."[2] Captain Fogg readily agreed to suppress "the false report," as he called it; but what Northumberland's answer was does not appear. He seems to have received the king's commands only on returning to the Downs, and he left the *Triumph* a few days thereafter. What he thought is not doubtful: he was getting disgusted

in the volume prepared for the ambassadors going to Cologne in 1673 (*State Papers, Dom.*, Chas. II., 339, p. 519): "This mentioned report appears by other letters and passages of that time to have been really the truth, but of that disadvantage to his Matys right and title, as it was thought fitt by all means to stiffle it, and give out Captain Fielding went to ye Holland Busses onely wth notice of ye Dunquerqrs preparations to intercept them in their return and to offer his Maties protection."

[1] Windebank to Northumberland, 1st Aug., *State Papers, Dom.*, Chas. I., ccclxv. 5; Roe to Countess of Northumberland, 20th July, *ibid.*, ccclxiv. 22; Northumberland to Windebank, 1st Sept., *ibid.*, ccclxviii. 1; Same to Admiralty, 6th Sept., *ibid.*, ccclxviii. 43.

[2] Aug. 10. *Ibid.*, ccclxv. 53. The king's real feelings were shown in the instructions given to the Earl when he was ordered to the west on 1st August. "If any of the fishers of Holland which have refused his Majesty's licenses shall be assaulted by the Dunkirkers, his Majesty will in no wise that you protect them." *Ibid.*, ccclxv. 5.

at his employment. "No man," he wrote to Roe, "was ever more desirous of a charge than I am to be quit of mine, being in a condition where I see I can neither do service nor gain credit." [1]

There is clear evidence indeed that by this time the naval officers, as well as the people generally, were becoming tired of the king's great pretensions and small performance. Even Pennington, a simple, loyal, unimaginative man, always ready to obey orders, had begun to joke, as we have seen, at the king's seas, "as he is pleased to call them." Throughout the country discontent was deepening. The opposition to the collection of ship-money was growing formidable, and the declaration of the Judges in favour of the king's right to levy it only postponed the inevitable for a little.[2] In his letter to the Judges, Charles based his case on the necessity of maintaining his sovereignty of the sea. The honour and safety of the realm of England, he said, "was and is now more neerely concerned then in late former tymes, as well by divers councells and attempts to take from Us the dominion of the seas (of which we are sole Lord, and rightfull owner and proprietour, and the losse whereof would bee of greatest danger and perill to this kingdome and other our Domynions) as many other waies." [3]

The king's dominion on the sea was rapidly waning. Fielding's ignoble mission was the last attempt that fate permitted Charles to make in actively asserting it. The shadow of the coming revolution was already upon him. The trial of Hampden for refusing to pay the ship-money focussed the attention of England, and it was followed by complaints of other grievances arising from the personal government of the king. The popular tumult in Edinburgh in the summer about the new Liturgy had as a sequence the National

[1] Aug. 6. *State Papers, Dom.*, ccclxv. 28.

[2] An example of the feeling is to be found in an incident of this summer. One, Richard Rose, a justice of the peace, on hearing that the fleet was going forth to maintain the king's title of being Lord of the Narrow Seas, exclaimed: "What a foolery is this; that the country in general shall be thus much taxed with great sums to maintain the king's titles and honours! For my part, I am £10 the worse for it already." When information of this remark was laid before the Council, the Lords "thought it not fit to question these words." *Ibid.*, ccclxx. 1.

[3] The king to the Twelve Judges, 2nd Feb. 1637. *Ibid.*, ccclxvi. 11.

Fig. 13.—*The "Sovereign of the Seas."* After Vandevelde.

Covenant and insurrection. Charles found another use for his fleet than the enforcement of his sovereignty of the sea in the expedition to Scotland to subdue his rebellious subjects; and the British seas, even the King's Chambers, were soon again the scenes of flagrant acts in violation of his authority. By a strange irony it was at this time that the king's "Great Ship," the famous *Sovereign of the Seas*, whose praises were sung by Thomas Heywood, the dramatist, was launched at Woolwich. Its construction had been under consideration for several years; it was begun in January 1636 and launched early in October 1637. Charles took a keen personal interest in his great ship, and supervised its details. He selected a scutcheon and motto to be engraved on each of its 102 brass guns—the rose and crown, sceptre and trident, and anchor and cable, with the inscription, *Carolus Edgari sceptrum stabilivit aquarum*—Charles established the dominion of Edgar over the seas; and on the "beak-head" sat the effigy of King Edgar, trampling on seven kings.[1] As its name implied, it was meant to be a symbol as well as an instrument of the king's sovereignty of the seas; and it was symbolical of it in a sense undreamt of by Charles. It was costly, highly decorated and begilt, but useless until it was cut down and made serviceable under the Commonwealth. He inserted it in the list of ships to serve in the fleet that

[1] The *Sovereign of the Seas* was the largest ship hitherto built for the navy; it was 127 feet long in the keel, 46½ feet in breadth (inside measurement), and 19 feet 4 inches in depth; the tonnage was by the "new rule" 1552 tons, by the "old rule" 1823 tons. She was also by far the most expensive. Her cost was £40,833, 8s. 1½d., besides her guns, which were estimated to cost, with engraving, £25,059, 8s. 8d. *State Papers, Dom.*, ccclxi. 71; ccclxix. 44; ccclxxiv. 30; ccclxxxvii. 87. See also Oppenheim, *Hist. Administration Royal Navy*, 260. In 1637 a "description" of the ship was published by Thomas Heywood, dedicated to the king, and with a frontispiece representation of it: "*A True description of his Majestie's Royall Ship Built this yeare* 1637 *at Wool-witch in Kent. To the great glory of our English Nation and not paraleld in the whole Christian World.* Published by Authoritie, London, 1637." The description, apart from the verse, occupies a few pages at the end, the work dealing chiefly with the ships of the ancients. A second edition was published in 1638: "*A True Discription of his Majestie's royall and most stately ship called the Soveraign of the Seas, built at Wolwitch in Kent* 1637 *with the names of all the prime officers in her*," &c. Prynne (*Brief Animadversions*, &c., p. 123) says that Charles claimed and maintained the dominion of the seas by increasing the navy, &c., and "by giving the name of the *Edgar* (with this motto engraven on it, *Ego ab Edgaro quatuor maria vendico*) and of the *Soveraign of the Sea* to the Admiral of his fleet."

assembled in the Downs in 1638, but it was not ready to join.

This fleet consisted of twenty-four king's ships and seven merchant vessels, and, owing to the illness of the Earl of Northumberland, it was placed under the command of Sir John Pennington.[1] It did still less than the fleet of the previous year. Two ships were sent to the westwards on an alarm that "Turkish" pirates were in the Channel; it convoyed two vessels laden with gunpowder into Dunkirk, notwithstanding the blockade by the Dutch, and returned to the Downs; and two ships were despatched to the north to intercept supplies of arms and munitions of war from Rotterdam and Bremen to the Scots. There was not even the "one turn in an honourable procession" to the westwards as in the previous year, and the fleet rode idly at its anchorage.

The question of the "homage of the flag" had by this time also fallen somewhat into the background. In the two preceding years it had been enforced with much zeal. In 1636, when Northumberland's fleet was among the herring-busses, Captain Carteret, in the *Happy Entrance*, forced a Spanish fleet of twenty-six sail to strike to him off Calais, though they tried their best to avoid it. A Dunkirker was also made to strike and "lie by the lee" off Nieuport by Captain Slingsby. But the French still refused to lower their flag when on the other side of the Narrow Sea. Sir Henry Mervin, on meeting two French men-of-war off Gravelines with their colours in the main-top, fired some twenty shots at them without causing them to strike. In the Mediterranean the French retaliated. An English vessel on the coast of Barbary was forced to lower its flag to French ships of war, and because the captain refused to go on board them when requested, the ship was attacked and captured. In the following year Captain Straddling of the *Dreadnought* used drastic measures against some Hollander merchant-ships. Falling in with four of them off the Lizard, homeward bound from Brazil, with their flags abroad, he commanded them to strike. One refused till many shots were fired, excusing himself afterwards by saying he thought the English ships were Dunkirkers. Straddling took him into custody, and lodged him in Plymouth fort "to answer his

[1] *State Papers, Dom.*, ccclxxx. 61; ccclxxxix. 86; cccxc. 39.

insolence and contempt of his Majesty's regality in these seas," and he remained a prisoner there for a fortnight before he was released by order of the Admiralty.[1] But in 1638 there were few incidents of this kind, probably because of the fleet lying at anchor so long, though it may be supposed that the general condition of public affairs did not whet the zeal of the naval officers.

It was not long before advantage was taken abroad of Charles's troubles in Scotland. In the early part of 1638 Pennington reported that there were many Hollander, French, and Dunkirk ships at sea, and that they were pillaging English vessels;[2] but the king was unable to protect even the herring-busses of the Fishery Society that he had taken under his peculiar care. The Dunkirkers, emboldened by immunity, took four of them in 1639, and then daringly anchored in the Downs. The Dutch men-of-war became bold, and then insolent. They began by protecting a Calais vessel that had rifled an English ship, their Admiral refusing to surrender her. Soon their fleets visited the English coasts in menacing strength, and although they "performed their duty" in the matter of the flag, they insisted on their right to stop and search English vessels, even in the King's Chambers. "The Hollanders' ships," wrote Northumberland's secretary to Pennington in June 1639, "begin to be very bold in our seas, and lie about Portland with fifty sail, examining and searching all English ships and others which pass by them, so that in effect they command where the King challenges sovereignty." The English merchants, he said, made great complaint that their trade was likely to be destroyed; they were "much perplexed, and called to mind tonnage and poundage, for which his Majesty was pleased to promise thirty sail of his ships to secure trade in the Narrow Sea."[3]

The truth was that English ships had been engaged in transporting Spanish troops and bullion to Dunkirk, and that the Dutch were merely exercising their rights as belligerents. Their action was nevertheless a plain flouting of the high

[1] *State Papers, Dom.*, cccxxv. 21; cccxxxviii. 15; cccxli. 6; ccclxi. 41; cccliii. fol. 34. *Brit. Mus. Add. MSS.*, 17,677, O, fol. 364.

[2] *State Papers, Dom.*, ccclxxxii. 44; ccclxxxiii. 29.

[3] Smith to Pennington, 8th June 1639. *Ibid.*, ccccxxiii. 56.

pretensions of the king, and it was the more disagreeable because Charles had now again veered round to the side of Spain. He was much moved at the "insolencies" of the Hollanders, which "concerned his honour" and "put his sovereignty in hazard"; and the Earl of Northumberland, who had been created Lord High Admiral in the preceding year, also expressed himself as much afflicted that such affronts were put on the nation in his time. It was, said Windebank, a very high disorder that any of the king's neighbours should presume to lie with a fleet in his Majesty's Channel, near his ports, and where he justly claimed sovereignty, and arrest and search English ships, taking out of them "such persons, being passengers, as they please"; "especially"—and this no doubt was a potent reason of the king's displeasure—"since the merchants and others took occasion by such pretences of interruption of their trade to make difficulty to pay their ship-money, which his Majesty is resolved to maintain." The king therefore commanded Pennington to put a stop to these affronts and to preserve the sovereignty of the narrow seas, so "that trade may be free and open, as well to his Majesty's subjects as to others in league and amity with his Majesty, and that peace be kept and the merchants secured according to his Majesty's proclamations and declarations published heretofore to that effect."[1]

It was one thing to indite imperious commands in London as to the necessity of maintaining the king's sovereignty of the seas; it was quite another thing to carry them out in the Channel in the presence of a powerful Dutch fleet under the new Admiral, Maarten Harpentz Tromp. Pennington, conscious of his impotency, tried at first to justify, or at least to extenuate, the action of the Dutch men-of-war. They only took out of the English ships the Spanish soldiers, he said, who were being carried to Flanders; they were most civil and courteous while doing so; in reality, it was the English captains who had committed the greater insolency. At all events, before attempting any reparation, it would be only prudent to have an overmastering force, lest greater loss and dishonour should happen, because, he said, the Dutch were in great strength, and it was

[1] Windebank to Pennington, 10th, 15th, 16th July, *State Papers, Dom.*, ccccxxv. 45, 72, 81; Northumberland to Pennington, *ibid.*, ccccxxv. 76; Windebank to Hopton, 16th August, *Clarendon State Papers*, i. 1283.

reported that the French fleet was about to put to sea. Pennington was nevertheless ordered to prevent the affronts as best he could. He then said he would do his best; but he had only four ships available, and he asked for express orders how far he should proceed if he were resisted with overmastering strength.[1]

But the question of the right of search was for the moment relegated to diplomatic channels, and before anything could be done, either by peaceful agreement or by Pennington's ships, another event put an end to it, and dissipated the king's dreams of the dominion of the seas. The battle of the Downs was fought between the Dutch and the Spaniards on 11th October 1639, in spite of Charles's express prohibition, and in spite of his helpless fleet. So glaring a violation of one of the King's Chambers within three years of the appearance of Selden's *Mare Clausum*—an injury which he was as unable to prevent as to redress—proclaimed to Europe that he was no longer sovereign over the sea that was incontestably his own.

At the end of August a large Spanish fleet, consisting of some thirty great galleons and thirty-six transports with troops for Flanders, set sail from Corunna. On 6th September it was attacked in the Channel by a Dutch squadron of seventeen ships, and a running fight was kept up, the Spaniards passing eastwards off the English coast. Tromp, engaged in blockading Dunkirk, heard the cannonading, and on the 8th he joined the Dutch squadron with fifteen sail, when a fierce battle took place in the Straits of Dover.[2] The Spanish Admiral, Don Antonio de Oquendo, having expended all his powder, took refuge with his shattered galleons in the Downs on 9th September, whither Tromp followed him. Great anxiety was felt in London, first of all lest the powerful foreign fleets should refuse to strike to the small English squadron under Sir John Pennington, and then lest they should begin hostilities in the King's Chamber. On the former point doubts were soon set at rest. Tromp at once took in his flag in the presence of the English ships, a "civility" with which Charles was pleased. So also did the proud Spaniard, but only after preliminary refusal and demur; and Pennington's insistence that the

[1] Pennington to Windebank, 13th July. *State Papers, Dom.*, ccccxxv. 61, 68.

[2] Gardiner, *Hist.*, ix. 69; *State Papers, Dom.*, ccccxxviii. 52.

standard of Spain should be lowered was made a subject of complaint at Madrid.[1] Anxiety on the second point was protracted, and it was not diminished by the reports that were received that the French fleet was coming to reinforce their allies the Dutch. Pennington, in the most emphatic manner, had forbidden hostilities within the King's Chambers, and he assigned the northern part of the anchorage to the Spaniards and the southern part to the Dutch. For several weeks the belligerent squadrons remained in the Downs facing one another. The Spanish Admiral, a few days after his arrival, succeeded under cover of night in despatching to Dunkirk some of his smaller vessels laden with soldiers. Tromp and Oquendo appealed to Charles through their respective ambassadors, "and then ensued an auction, the strangest in the annals of diplomacy, in which Charles's protection was offered as a prize to the highest bidder."[2] On the one hand, he demanded £150,000 from Spain, and better treatment in the business of the Palatinate, as the price of securing the safety of the Spanish fleet.[3] On the other hand, he declared himself ready to abandon the Spaniards to Tromp, if France would come under a binding promise to place Charles Louis at the head of the army which had been commanded by Bernard of Weimar—as a means, of course, to recover the Palatinate.[4]

While waiting the highest bid from one or the other, the king's commands regarding the fleet were puzzling and contradictory. Smith, Northumberland's secretary, who carried on a confidential correspondence with Pennington, wrote to him that the king, when the difficult situation of the English fleet was explained to him and he was asked for explicit instructions as to how the Admiral should act, "would not give any express declaration." "I earnestly pressed his Lordship [the Earl of Northumberland] to prevail with his Majesty," he said, "that you might have some justifiable instructions how you

[1] Northumberland to Pennington, 12th September, *State Papers, Dom.*, ccccxxviii. 92; Windebank to Hopton, 29th September, *Clarendon State Papers*, ii. 71; Hopton to Windebank, October $\frac{12}{22}$, *Cal. Clar. State Papers*, i. 1311.

[2] Gardiner, *op. cit.*, 61.

[3] Windebank to Colonel Gage and Count Leslie, $\frac{\text{28 Sept.}}{\text{8 Oct.}}$. *Cal. Clar. State Papers*, i. 1296.

[4] Gardiner, *op. cit.*, 63.

should demean yourself. . . . To all this he told me that he had often pressed his Majesty to declare his resolution, but never could get any." Smith privately advised Pennington to make a show of assisting the Spaniards if there was a fight, but not to run himself or the king's ships into danger where there was no hope of victory and "the only expectation was hard blows and hazard."[1]

Desperate efforts were hurriedly made to strengthen the English fleet. Ten additional ships were being got ready, and Northumberland intended to take command himself as soon as they reached the Downs, but of the 3000 men which the Admiralty were "labouring" to procure for them, only 300 could be obtained; they did not join Pennington till some days after the battle. Pennington had been ordered to press into his service all English ships he could lay his hands on, and to employ them "in any warlike manner against any that shall presume to affront his Majesty, or derogate from his sovereignty in these parts."[2] Ten vessels were thus pressed; but it was impossible to find seamen to man them properly, and by command of the king some of them were dispensed with. In presence of the powerful States' fleet, to say nothing of the Spaniards, Pennington's instructions to the masters of the merchantmen must have sounded somewhat ironical. If either of the "great fleets," he said, should presume to attempt anything in the King's Chambers "contrary to the laws and customs of nations and to the dishonour of our king and kingdom, you are to fall upon the assailants, and to do your best to take, sink, or destroy them." Moreover, if any ships of the hostile fleets assembled, "or any others that may come," should put out a flag, they were to cause them to be taken in; if refused, they were to do their best to sink the offending ship.[3] The "any others" meant the French, who were expected daily in the Downs, and whose arrival there was regarded with apprehension. The general opinion was that they would refuse to strike when they came, and, in that event, what would happen? "That," said Smith, "will set us all in combustion,

[1] Smith to Pennington, 30th Sept. *State Papers, Dom.*, ccccxxix. 70.

[2] Northumberland to Pennington, 16th September. *Ibid.*, ccccxxviii. 92.

[3] Pennington to the Master of the *Luke*, of London, 23rd Sept. *Ibid.*, ccccxxix. 15.

for then we must *strike* them, although peradventure to our own prejudice. But this punctilio of honour," added the secretary to the Lord High Admiral, with prophetic instinct, "will one day cause more blood to be drawn than ere it will bring profit or honour to our king."[1]

Meanwhile Tromp and his resolute men were getting impatient. Since they had cooped up the hated Spaniard in the English roadstead, they had been reinforced from Holland, so that the Dutch fleet was soon in the overwhelming strength of a hundred sail. Tromp also knew that Charles had arranged (for a substantial consideration) to supply the Spanish Admiral with gunpowder, of which he stood in dire need, and that thirty Dunkirk sloops had succeeded in joining Oquendo. Above all, he had in his pocket the express orders, just issued by the States-General, "to destroy the Spanish fleet, without paying any regard to the harbours, roads, or bays of the kingdom where it might be found."[2] He promptly seized an opportunity to carry out his orders. Information reached London on 8th and 9th October that the Dutch were preparing to attack. Commands were at once sent to warn them to desist, and they were informed that the king was going to fix a short period for the departure of both fleets: and this message was conveyed to the Dutch Admiral. On the evening of the 10th, the gunpowder for the Spanish fleet came alongside, and the accidental discharge of a gun on one of the Spanish ships killed a Dutch sailor. This was enough. Before the fog lifted next morning Tromp's fleet was under sail; the roar of cannon announced that the attack had begun; and within a few hours the Spanish galleons were driven ashore, burnt, sunk, or in flight for Flanders, with Tromp in hot pursuit. The English Admiral acted on the prudent advice which had been given to him by Smith. He made a show of resenting the violation of the King's Chambers by firing at the Dutch. In Madrid it was afterwards said he had fired his guns into the air, but Pennington himself tells us that

[1] Smith to Pennington, 19th Sept. *State Papers, Dom.*, ccccxxviii. 111.

[2] "De Spaansche Vloot te vernielen sonder eenige aanschouw of reguard te nemen op de Havenen, Reeden, of Baayen van de Coningryken, waar de zelve zoude zyn te bekomen." *Resol. Stat.-Gen.*, $\frac{11}{21}$, $\frac{20}{30}$ Sept. 1639. Aitzema, *Saken van Staet en Oorlogh.* Bynkershoek, *Quæstiones Juris Publici*, lib. i.

(although he affected to believe the Spaniards had begun the combat) he "chased and shot at the Hollanders" until they were all beyond the South Foreland; but the Hollanders took no notice of him. On the morning of the battle Tromp sent a letter to Pennington which was more than tinged with irony. Since the Spaniards, he said, had infringed the conditions fixed by firing at him first, the English Admiral should assist him in fighting them, "according to his Majesty's orders." At all events he—Tromp—was resolved, by instructions from his masters, to fall upon his enemies, and to defend themselves "against those that shall resist them." The Dutch would rather die as soldiers, he said, "with his Majesty's leave in clearing his Majesty's Road," than fail to carry out their orders; and he hoped that this would be "acceptable to his Majesty, but if his Majesty should take any distaste we hope he will graciously forgive us."

After pursuing the remnant of the Spanish fleet to Dunkirk, the Dutch Admiral returned triumphant to the Downs, and saluted the English squadron by striking his flag and firing nineteen guns,—"as a token," says an ironical observer, "that his Majesty was Sovereign of these his seas!"[1] Tromp indeed, in those years, was most punctiliously respectful to this symbol of the king's sovereignty. Even during the height of the battle, when he was violating not merely the sovereignty claimed by Charles but the well-understood Law of Nations, he kept his flag down until he was a good way off from the Downs,—a circumstance which Pennington reported with satisfaction. Had the Dutch Admiral shown the same willingness to strike to the flag of the Commonwealth when he encountered Blake thirteen years later, the war that followed might, perhaps, have been averted, or at least postponed.

Charles was very naturally highly incensed at this open flouting of his authority. It was an ugly blot on the lustre of his ancient prerogative, and a painful proof of the contempt in which his much-vaunted naval power was held by the

[1] Northumberland to Pennington, 8th Oct., *State Papers, Dom.*, ccccxxx. 47; Same to Windebank, 9th Oct., *ibid.*, ccccxxx. 55; Pennington to Northumberland, 11th Oct., *ibid.*, 77; Suffolk to Windebank, 11th Oct., *ibid.*, 66, 68; Pennington's report, 11th Oct., *ibid.*, 74; Hopton to Windebank, $\frac{20}{30}$ Nov., *Cal. Clar. State Papers*, i. 1323; Tromp to Pennington, $\frac{11}{21}$ Oct., *State Papers, Dom.*, *ibid.*, 80 (translation in Windebank's writing); *ibid.*, ccccxxxi. 4.

Dutch Republic, and—what perhaps he felt quite as much at the time—it robbed him of all chance of blackmailing Spain. When that Power was asked to pay the great sum above mentioned, the Cardinal Infant put the proposal aside, considering that it was the king's own interest to protect the Spanish fleet; and when Tromp's precipitation broke in on the negotiations, it was decided to withhold any payment at all until it was seen how Charles would resent the injury done to Spain.[1] At first he resolved to punish the affront. Pennington was ordered to cause the Dutch fleet, which had returned to the Downs, and was suspected of meditating further "insolency" by falling upon the stranded galleons, to immediately quit the road. The king, he was told, had made up his mind not to allow them the liberty of his ports or roads "until he shall have received satisfaction for the insolency already committed." If they refused to leave, Pennington, immediately the other ten ships had reinforced him, was to drive them out with all his power and strength, or answer the contrary at his uttermost peril. Before these orders could be executed, Tromp voluntarily departed.[2] Copies of the letter to Pennington were sent to Brussels and Madrid to show the Spaniards that the king was full of resolution. They were told he was very sensible of the affront and insolence of the Hollanders, and "would make such demonstration of it, and demand and expect such reparation as in honour he is obliged." But he was quite unable to carry out his good intention. It was in vain that he was urged from Madrid to take strong measures against the Dutch; to seize their property; even to invade Normandy as a punishment to their ally.[3] He had no fleet and no money to enable him to cope with the Dutch Republic, even if the condition of home affairs had permitted the attempt. On the contrary, to such a level had he fallen by his stubborn ineptitude that the English Minister at The Hague was ordered to avoid even a

[1] Leslie to Windebank, 11th Oct.; Gage to Windebank, $\frac{19}{29}$ Oct. *Cal. Clar. State Papers*, i. 1309, 1313.

[2] Northumberland to Pennington, 15th Oct. *State Papers, Dom.*, ccccxxxi. 18, 30; *Cal. Clar. State Papers*, i. 1324.

[3] Windebank to Gerbier, 18th Oct. *State Papers, Dom.*, ccccxxxi. 35. Gage to Windebank, $\frac{9}{19}$ Nov. Paper delivered by Hopton to King of Spain, 24th Nov. *Cal. Clar. State Papers*, i. 1321, 1324.

remonstrance about Tromp's high-handed action in the Downs. If the States-General mentioned the matter to him, he was to say that he had received no instructions, "and so to refuse any conference on that particular.[1]

The Dutch Government had expected that Charles would raise loud complaints, and they decided to take a bold attitude. On the day that they received news of Tromp's victory the proposal was made to send over an ambassador, and Aerssen Van Sommelsdijck, who was chosen for the mission, reached London early in November. There was to be no attempt made on this occasion to appease the king with soft phrases and show of submission. Aerssen was to complain of the action which England had for a long time taken in favouring the Spaniards. The violation of the King's Chamber was to be passed over, and the battle in the Downs represented as having been merely a continuation of the first fight in the Channel, which forced the Spaniards to take refuge in the English roadstead. But the pains taken by the States-General were hardly necessary. Charles in his perplexity did not know to which side to lean. He received the Dutch ambassador in a very friendly way, and began to speak again of an alliance with the Republic.[2] In another direction he was flouted by the Dutch. On the 1st October, while the belligerent fleets were at anchor in the Downs, his representative at the conference at Hamburg proposed that if the Republic joined the projected alliance with France, Charles would grant them liberty to carry on their herring fishery in the narrow seas. At the very time that Tromp was battering the Spanish galleons in the King's Chamber, the States-General were engaged in passing the resolution "that they did not intend to ask for the right of fishing in the North Sea from any one."[3]

A year later, the Long Parliament began its sittings at West-

[1] *State Papers, Dom.*, dxxxviii. 106. The paper is endorsed "Soverainty of the Seas: the Dutch attempt on the Spaniards in the Downs."

[2] *Resol. St.-Gen.*, $\frac{16}{26}$, $\frac{20}{30}$ Oct., $\frac{26 \text{ Oct.}}{5 \text{ Nov.}}$ 1639. Instructie van Sommelsdijck, Muller, *Mare Clausum*, 309; Aitzema, *Saken van Staet*, ii. 618.

[3] *Secrete Resol. St.-Gen.*, $\frac{11}{21}$ Oct., "Dat hunne meeninge gantsch niet was, het recht van Visscherie in de Noortzee van ijemant te stipuleren, versoecken ofte reveleren." Muller, *op. cit.*, 312. In the following year Vice-Admiral De With refused to lower his flag to an English ship-of-war off Hellevoetsluis.

minster, and Charles was rapidly stripped of sovereign power within his own kingdom. The Dutch, conscious that they and not the King of England were the real masters of the sea, became overbearing in their conduct. More than ever their fishermen indulged in the bad treatment of British subjects, which this country was unable to prevent. But their triumph was short-lived. A decade later they were smitten by the heavy hand of Cromwell, who resumed the sovereignty of the sea. It is to the period beginning about this time that the Dutch trace the decadence which set in in their great fisheries as well as the decline of their trade. It is, however, a satisfaction to think that the part played by this country in causing the misfortunes of Holland—a country to which civilisation is indebted for immense advances, both material and intellectual—was comparatively small. From about the middle of the seventeenth century to the peace of Utrecht, in 1713, the Dutch Republic was involved in almost constant wars with its Continental neighbours, and the herring-fishery and the trade in general suffered severely, and never afterwards regained the prosperity they formerly enjoyed.

CHAPTER IX.

THE JURIDICAL CONTROVERSIES.

THE great juridical controversies respecting *mare liberum* and *mare clausum*—the sea open to all, or that under the dominion of a particular Power — which enlivened the international politics of the seventeenth century, reached their highest pitch in the reign of Charles I., and may be conveniently considered here. The writers who touched upon the question in the previous century took it for granted that the seas were capable of appropriation, and that they were almost wholly under the dominion of one Power or another. It is true that now and again a slender voice was raised in protest, on abstract legal grounds, against the exclusive maritime sovereignty arrogated by Venice, Portugal, or Spain. Queen Elizabeth too, as we have seen, not only protested against these claims in certain cases, but actively opposed them. Her action, however, pertained rather to the sphere of diplomacy and politics than to legal controversy; and the protests of the few jurists alluded to were too feeble to have practical effect on the course of events or on the prevalent opinion.

It is noteworthy that the birth of modern international law was associated with the origin of these juridical controversies as to the freedom of the sea.[1] It was the appearance of *Mare Liberum* in 1609 that heralded the dawn of the new epoch. The little book of Grotius was at once a reasoned appeal for the freedom of the seas in the general interest of mankind, and the source from which the principles of the Law of Nations have come. The main reasons why the controversy broke out at

[1] Maine, *International Law*, 13, 75. Phillimore, *Commentaries upon International Law*, I. xxi. Wheaton, *History of the Law of Nations*, 54.

that time and the pleas of Grotius had so much success are not difficult to discover. The period was characterised by a great expansion of commercial enterprise. The Western Powers of Europe, and above all the United Provinces, were pushing into every sea for the sake of traffic and gain. In some directions the trading adventurers found their way barred by claims to *mare clausum* and monopoly of trade; in other directions it was open to them only under heavy burdens and aggravating restrictions. The northern seas, in theory at least, were closed to the whaling vessels engaged in what was then a most valuable business; and commerce and fishing within them were permitted only under irksome conditions. The passage through the Sound into the Baltic was subjected to high dues by Denmark; Venice claimed dominion in the Adriatic and levied imposts for the right of navigation there, and Genoa followed her example in the Ligurian Sea. But it was not so much the claim of Denmark to the sovereignty of the northern seas, or the rights asserted by Venice in the Adriatic, that led to the outburst for the freedom of the sea and of commercial intercourse at the beginning of the seventeenth century. Except with regard to English traffic with Iceland and Norway and the fishing there, more or less regulated by treaties, the Scandinavian claim at this time was not of great practical importance; and the dominion of Venice over the Adriatic was generally regarded as beneficial on the whole, by interposing a powerful barrier to the further extension of the Turkish empire in Europe, and by facilitating the suppression of pirates and Saracens.[1] It was the extravagant pretensions of Spain and Portugal to a monopoly of navigation and commerce with the New World and the East Indies that constituted the great obstacle to the new spirit of commercial enterprise. Founding their title on the Bulls of the Pope, and the right of discovery, conquest, and prior occupation, they arrogated to themselves the exclusive sovereignty of the great oceans which were the pathways to these immense regions,—the Atlantic, the Indian Ocean, and parts of the Pacific. Thus, as Grotius remarked, the whole Ocean except a little was to remain under the control of two nations, and all the other nations of the earth were to content themselves with the remnant.

[1] Meadows, *Observations*, p. 3. Raleigh, *A Discourse on the Invention of Ships*.

The commerce with the East Indies was of special value and importance. The discovery of the Cape route by Vasco di Gama, in 1497, led to the great stream of traffic between Europe and the East being diverted in the next century from its old channel in the Mediterranean and Levant to the Atlantic. The lucrative trade with the Indies was transferred from the Venetians and the Italian Republics to the Portuguese, who then became for a time the chief trading people of the world,[1] and strove to keep it entirely in their own hands. It was particularly with reference to this monopoly that the disputes about the freedom of the sea began. The *Mare Liberum* of Grotius was specially directed against the prohibition by the Portuguese for any other nation to navigate round the Cape of Good Hope or to trade with the Indies. It has been well said by Calvo that the historical antecedents of the controversy about *mare clausum* are to be found in the voyages of Columbus and Vasco di Gama.[2]

Very soon, however, the claims of other Powers to maritime sovereignty—of Denmark, Venice, England—were similarly assailed, and the controversy became general. It may be noted that those who took part in it on the one side or the other, including some of the most learned men of their age, were in large measure inspired by patriotic motives. National interests as much as lofty ethics or legal principles were at its root. Even Grotius, notwithstanding his impassioned appeal to the conscience of the world for the liberty of the sea and the freedom of commerce, was not exempt from this weakness. It was his happy fortune that the cause he publicly advocated was equally in conformity with the growing spirit of liberty and the immediate interests of the United Provinces. Only four years later, when the Dutch had obtained a footing in the East Indies in spite of the Portuguese, they in turn wished to exclude the English from any share in the trade with that opulent region: they did not want any freedom of commerce that might tell against themselves. And then we find Grotius arguing, in London, against his own declarations in *Mare Liberum*, and in favour of commercial monopoly for his native land—a

[1] Cunningham, *The Growth of English Industry and Commerce during the Early and Middle Ages*, p. 418.

[2] *Le Droit International*, i. 20.

task, which, we are told, he performed "with uncommon ability."

This charge cannot be made against the two authors whose voices were raised in opposition to the prevailing opinions as to the appropriation of the sea before the work of Grotius appeared, and of whose writings he made considerable use. One of these was a Spanish monk, Francis Alphonso de Castro, who wrote about the middle of the sixteenth century, protesting against the Genoese and Venetians prohibiting other peoples from freely navigating the Ligurian and Adriatic Seas, as being contrary to the imperial law, the primitive right of mankind, and the law of nature; and also against the Spanish and Portuguese claims for exclusive rights to the navigation to the East and West Indies.[1] The other author, also a Spaniard, was Ferdinand Vasquez or Vasquius, who expressed the same opinions as de Castro, and for the same reasons. He held that the sea could not be appropriated, but had remained common to mankind since the beginning of the world; that the claim of the Portuguese to forbid to others the navigation to the East Indies, and that of the Spaniards to a similar prohibition to sail through "the spacious and immense sea" to the West Indies, were no less vain and foolish (*non minus insanæ*) than the pretensions of the Venetians and Genoese. The law of prescription, he said, was purely civil, and could have no force in controversies between princes and peoples who acknowledged no superior, because the peculiar civil laws of any country were of no more value with respect to foreign nations than as if they did not exist; to decide such controversies recourse must be had to the law of nations, primitive or secondary, which it was evident could never admit of such a usurpation of a title to the sea. With regard to the right of fishery, Vasquius drew a distinction between fishing in the sea and in rivers or lakes. He held that the sea had been from the first, and still remained, by the primitive right of mankind, free both for navigation and fishing, and that its use could not be exhausted by fishing, while lakes and rivers may be so exhausted.[2]

[1] *De Potestate Legis Pœnalis*, lib. ii. c. 14. Quoted by Nys, *Les Origines du Droit International*, p. 382, and by Grotius, *Mare Liberum*, c. vii.

[2] D. Fernandus Vasquius, *Controversiæ Illustres*, Venice, 1564, lib. ii. c. lxxxix. s. 30 (p. 356, ed. Frankfurt, 1668).

From the foregoing, it will be seen that Grotius had ready to his hand many of the legal arguments of which he made so much use; but the strength of his work lay rather in its appeal to the sense of justice and the conscience of the free peoples of Christendom, to whom it was dedicated. The Spanish authors, moreover, were not in a position to assail the validity of the Papal Bulls, upon which the Spanish and Portuguese claims were partly founded, whereas it was against them that the Protestant writer levelled some of his most powerful philippics.

The *Mare Liberum* of Grotius was published anonymously at Leyden, Holland, in March 1609.[1] As the title declares, the author's object was to assert the right of the Dutch to trade with the Indies, and to combat the pretensions of the Portuguese to a monopoly of navigation and commerce in those regions; but the genesis of the book has only been recently made known. At the end of the sixteenth century, when the commerce of the United Provinces was expanding in all directions, the Dutch merchants resolved to share in the lucrative

[1] *Mare Libervm sive de Jvre qvod Batavis competit ad Indicana Commercia Dissertatio.* Lugdvni Batauorvm. Ex officinâ Ludovici Elzevirij Anno 1609. The name of Grotius did not appear on the title-page until the second edition in 1618 (*Hvgonis Groti Mare Libervm sive* . . . vltima editio. Lvgdvni Batavorum, anno 1618), the year in which he was arrested; and that he was not generally known to be the author until this time is shown by Welwood referring to *Mare Liberum* in 1613 as written by "an unknown author," and by an English State Paper, prepared for the negotiations with the Dutch ambassadors in 1618, which contains excerpts "out of a book called *Mare Liberum* (*Brit. Mus. MSS. Lansd.*, 142, fol. 383). Grotius was then one of the most prominent men in Holland. Another edition was published, also at Leyden, in 1633, together with Paul Merula's *Dissertatio de Maribus* and Boxhorn's *Apologia pro Navigationibus Hollandorum adversus Pontem Hevtervm*, under the title, Hugo Grotius, *De Mare Libero.* It was also included in Hagemeier's *De Imperio Maris, variorum Dissertationes*, published in 1663. A translation in the vernacular appeared at Haarlem in 1636,—no doubt in consequence of the publication of Selden's *Mare Clausum*,—H. Groti, *Vrye Zeevaert, ofte Bewys van het Recht dat de Inghesetenen deser gheunicerde Landen toekomt over de Oost ende West-Indische Koophandel.* Hugo de Groot was born at Delft in 1583; he was appointed Advocate-General before he was twenty-four years of age, and settled at Rotterdam in 1613, where he became Pensionary of that town; he was sent to England as one of the Dutch envoys in that year. In 1618 he was arrested in connection with the Barnevelt troubles, and in the following year condemned to perpetual imprisonment; but he escaped to Paris, where he lived for eleven years, and then entering the service of the Queen of Sweden, he was employed as her ambassador at the Court of France. He died at Rostock in 1645. Some of his works were translated into almost all European languages, and even into Persian, Greek, and Arabic.

trade with the far east. Having failed to open up a passage to the Indies by the north-east, they boldly sailed thither by the Cape of Good Hope, in 1595, through the seas and to the regions which Portugal claimed for herself. Encouraged by success, other trading voyages by the same route were undertaken almost every year. A United Dutch East India Company was formed in 1602, and the States-General decided to maintain their rights to the trade by force. The disputes and conflicts with the Portuguese which followed were soon brought to a head by the action of the redoubtable Jacob van Heemskerk in attacking and seizing Portuguese ships.[1] The valuable booty taken from the Portuguese was brought to Holland in 1604 and 1605, and caused much searching of heart among the shareholders of the company. Many were gratified by the spoil, but others of much influence, moved by conscientious scruples or good policy, refused to share in it, and they threatened to separate themselves from the company and form a rival association to carry on peaceful trade under the protection of the King of France. It was about this time that Grotius, incited by the condition of affairs, began to write a treatise with the object of encouraging his countrymen to resist the claims of the Portuguese by force. In a tract written about 1614 to vindicate *Mare Liberum* against the attack of the Scotch lawyer, Welwood—which was not published, and the existence of which was unknown till about forty years ago—he says that some years earlier, perceiving the great importance of the East Indian trade for the Netherlands, and that it could only be made secure by armed resistance to the Portuguese, he had written a book in which he explained the law of war and spoil; and in order to rouse the popular mind he gave an account of the ill-treatment of the Dutch in the East Indies at the hands of the Portuguese.[2] Grotius was then only a little

[1] Tiele, *Opkomst van het Nederlandsch Gezag in Oost-Indie;* Fruin, *Een onuitgegeven werk van Hugo de Groot*, in *De Gids*, Derde ser. zesde Jaargang, 1868, vierde del; M'Pherson, *Annals of Commerce*, ii. 209, 226.

[2] "Ante annos aliquot, cum viderem ingentis esse momenti ad patriæ securitatem Indiæ quæ Orientalis dicitur commercium, id vero commercium satis appareret obsistentibus per vim atque insidias Lusitanis sine armis retineri non posse, operam dedi ut ad tuenda fortiter quæ tam feliciter cœpissent nostrorum animos inflammarem, proposita ob oculos causæ ipsius iustitia et æquitate, unde nasci τὸ εὐελπι recte a ueteribus traditum existimabam. Igitur et universa belli

over twenty years of age, and it enhances our sense of the precocity and fertility of his genius to learn that *Mare Liberum* was only one chapter (the twelfth) of this treatise. The treatise itself was not published by Grotius; but in 1608, during the negotiations with Spain which ended in the truce of Antwerp, on $\frac{\text{March 30}}{\text{April 9}}$, 1609, the Spaniards demanded that the Dutch should relinquish the trade with the West Indies and also with the East Indies (Portugal being then united to Spain), and, probably at the request of the directors of the East India Company, Grotius then detached the part of his work which dealt with the freedom of commerce and navigation and published it in March 1609, under the title of *Mare Liberum.*

In dealing with his theme Grotius attacked in succession all the arguments put forward by the Portuguese to justify their claim. Their titles from prior discovery of the Cape route, under Papal Bulls, by the right of war or conquest, or from occupancy and prescription, were all, he maintained, invalid; by the Law of Nations navigation and commerce were free to all mankind. The action of the Portuguese in attempting to restrain the trade with India furnished a just cause of war; and the Dutch were resolved to assert their rights by force. But *Mare Liberum* was much more than a pleading in a particular case. An earnest and powerful appeal was made to the civilised world for complete freedom of the high seas for the innocent use and mutual benefit of all. Grotius spoke in the name of humanity as against the selfish interests of a few; and while he made full use of arguments founded on Roman law, on the law of nature and of nations, it was principally the lofty moral

prædæque iura, et historiam eorum quæ Lusitani in nostros sæue atque crudeliter perpetrassent, multaque alia ad hoc argumentum pertinentia eram persecutus amplo satis commentario, quem edere hactenus supersedi." *Hugonis Grotii Defensio Capitis quinti Maris liberi oppugnati a Gulielmo Welwodo Iuris Civilis professore capite XXVII. eius libri scripti Anglico sermone cui titulum fecit Compendium legum Maritimaram.* This manuscript of Grotius was discovered in 1864, along with the work *De Jure Prædæ*, to which he refers, in a collection of MSS. brought to auction, which belonged to the family of Cornets de Groot of Bergen-op-Zoom, who had descended in a direct line from the great publicist (Fruin, *op. cit.*) It was printed by Muller in 1872 (*Mare Clausum*, p. 331). The greater work, edited by Hamaker, was published in 1868, *Hugo Grotius de Jure Prædæ Commentarius.*

ideas which inspired his work that gave it its reputation and charm. He entered into a subtle and learned disquisition as to the origin of the idea of property from the primitive times when all things were held in common; the conditions under which private property is possible or lawful, and the distinction between what is private, what is public, and what is common. Much of the argument appears to us now to be of the nature of hair-splitting and word-play; but inasmuch as it was made use of subsequently in the numerous controversies regarding the freedom or the sovereignty of the sea, as well as in diplomatic negotiations, it is necessary to summarise it here. All property, he says, is based upon possession or occupation (*occupatio*), which requires that all movable things shall be seized and all immovable things enclosed; things that can neither be seized nor enclosed cannot become property: they are common to all, and their use pertains not to any particular people but to the whole human race. The distinction is also made between things which are exhausted by promiscuous use and those which are not: the latter are common, and their free use belongs to all men. Thus the air is common, because it cannot be occupied and because it cannot be exhausted by promiscuous use; it therefore belongs to all mankind. And in the same way the sea is common to all; it is clearly so infinite that it is not capable of being possessed, and is fitted for the use of all both for navigation and fishing.[1] It is also among those things which cannot be bought and sold—that is, which cannot be lawfully acquired; whence it is, strictly speaking, impossible to look upon any part of it as belonging to the territory of a people. The sea is under no one's dominion except God's; it cannot by its very nature be appropriated; it is common to all, and its use, by the general consent of mankind, is common, and what belongs to all cannot be appropriated by one; nor can prescription or custom justify any claim of the kind,

1 "Hujus generis est Aër, duplici ratione, tum quia occupari non potest, tum quia usum promiscuum hominibus debet. Et eisdem de causis commune est omnium Maris Elementum, infinitum scilicet, ita, ut possideri non queat, et omnium usibus accommodatum: sive navigationem respicimus, sive etiam piscaturum." Cap. v.

because no one has power to grant a privilege adverse to mankind in general.

Grotius places navigation and fishing in the sea on the same footing, or rather he looked upon interference with the freedom of fishing as a greater offence than interference with navigation. With regard to imposing tribute on fishermen, he said that such as are reckoned among the Regalia are imposed not on the thing, that is the sea and the fishing, but on the person; and while it may be levied by a prince on his own subjects, it is not to be levied on foreigners, for the right of fishing everywhere should be free to foreigners, lest a servitude be imposed on the sea which it cannot bear. An action of this kind would be worse than the prohibition of navigation; it would be barbarous and inhuman. If any one, says Grotius, claimed jurisdiction and sovereignty on the great seas for himself alone against promiscuous use, he would be looked upon as one who was aiming at extravagant dominion; if any one was to keep others from fishing, he would not escape the brand of insane cupidity.[1]

It is hardly possible to escape the suspicion, which was apparently shared by King James, as it was by many others, that Grotius in these sentences was aiming obliquely at England. Such strength of language about the right of free fishing in the sea was scarcely pertinent to his theme, for neither the Portuguese nor the Spaniards contested that right, and the Dutch did not fish in waters under their control. It would, on the other hand, be explicable if Grotius had got a hint of James's intention with regard to the "assize-herring" (see p. 152), and we know that as early as the beginning of 1606 proposals were made for the formation of an English fishery society, with taxation of foreign

[1] Cap. v. "Similiter reditus qui in piscationes maritimas constituti Regalium numero censenter, non rem, hoc est mare, aut piscationem, sed personas non obligant. Quare subditi, in quos legem ferendi potestas Reipublicæ aut Principi ex consensu competit, ad onera ista compelli forte poterunt: sed exteris jus piscandi ubique immune esse debet, ne servitus imponatur mari quod servire non potest. . . . Quod in aliis difficile videtur, in hac omnino fieri non potest: quod in aliis iniquum judicamus, in hac summe barbarum est, atque inhumanum. . . . In tanto mari si quis usu promiscuo solum sibi imperium et ditionem exciperet, tamen immodicæ dominationis affectator haberetur: si quis piscatu arceret alios, insanæ cupiditatis notam non effugeret."

fishermen, and that in the beginning of 1608 negotiations were on foot between the English Government and the Dutch Ambassador as to the "assize-herring."[1]

It is important to note—what many of his followers too often forgot—that Grotius restricts the application of his general argument for *mare liberum* to the open sea. He does not, he says, deal with an inland sea (*mare interiore*) which, surrounded on all sides by land, did not exceed the breadth of a river; the question concerned the ocean, which the ancients called immense, infinite, the parent of things, co-terminous with the air. The controversy, he continues, was not about a bay or a strait in this ocean, *nor concerning so much of it as might be seen from the shore:* the Portuguese claim for themselves whatever lies between the two worlds.[2] Again, referring to the Italian publicists, he says their opinion cannot be applied to the matter in question, for they speak of the Mediterranean, he of the ocean; they of bays or gulfs, he of the vast sea, which differ very much in respect of occupation.[3]

The opinions and reasonings of Grotius in *Mare Liberum* as to the free use of the sea were repeated more concisely and with some modification in his greatest work, *The Rights of War and Peace*, which was published in 1625.[4] No one, he affirmed, can have property in the sea, either as to the whole or its principal parts; and as some people admit this in respect to private persons but not in regard to countries or states, he proceeds to prove its truth by both a "moral

[1] Not improbably James had *Mare Liberum* in view in the following sentence in his Proclamation of 1609: "Finding that our connivance therein hath not only given occasion of over great encroachment upon our regalities, or rather questioning for our right." That it was believed in England that Grotius had James in view is shown by the following *précis* contained in the volume of official records prepared for the ambassadors to the Congress at Cologne in 1673: "K. James coming in, the Dutch put out *Mare Liberum*, made as if aimed at mortifying the Spaniards' usurpation in the W. and E. Indyes, but indeed at England. K. James resents it, bids his Ambr Sr D. Carleton complaine of it." *State Papers, Dom.*, cccxxxix. p. 99. Chas. II., 1673-75.

[2] Cap. v. p. 29. "In hoc autem Oceano non de sinu aut fretu, nec de omni quidem eo quod e littore conspici potest controversia est. Vindicant sibi Lusitani quicquid duos Orbes interjacet."

[3] Cap. vii.

[4] Hvgonis Grotii De Ivre Belli ac Pacis, Libri Tres.

reason and a natural reason." The moral reason is the vast extent and inexhaustibility of the sea, whether for navigation or fishing; the natural reason is that it cannot be occupied or possessed because of its fluidity, since liquids having no bounds of their own cannot be possessed unless enclosed by something else, as a river by its banks; but the sea is not contained in the earth, as it is equal to it or even greater.[1] Grotius, however, admits that his argument that rivers and lakes may be appropriated because their banks could be appropriated, may be logically applied also to certain parts of the sea. From the example of rivers he says, "It appears that the sea may be occupied by him who is in possession of the lands on both sides, although it be open either above, as a bay or gulf, or both above and below, as a strait, provided that it be not so great a part of the sea that when compared with the lands on each side it cannot be supposed to be some part of them"; and what is lawful to one king or people may be also lawful to two or three, if they have a mind to take possession of the sea thus enclosed within their land.[2] He also admits by another train of reasoning —concerning property in the marine vivaria of the Romans —that if it is not repugnant to the law of nature for a private person to appropriate a small enclosed part of the sea, one or more nations possessing the shores might in like manner appropriate a part of the sea, if it be small compared with the land; and that might happen although the sea was not enclosed on all sides. But this admission that the law of nature does not preclude appropriation of a relatively small part of the sea by the neighbouring state, he qualifies in a general way by saying that there are many things tolerated by the law of nature which the law of nations, by common consent, might prohibit; and where this law of nations was in force and is not repealed

[1] Lib. ii. cap. ii. s. iii. 1, 2.

[2] Lib. ii. cap. iii. s. viii. "Ad hoc exemplum videtur et mare occupari potuisse ab eo qui terras ad latus utrumque possideat, etiamsi aut supra pateat ut sinus, aut supra et infra ut fretum, dummodo non ita magna sit pars maris ut non cum terris comparata portio earum videri possit. Et quod uni populo aut Regi licet, idem licere videtur et duobus aut tribus, si pariter mare intersitum occupare voluerint, nam sic flumina quæ duos populos interluunt ab utroque occupata sunt, ac deinde divisa."

by common consent, the most inconsiderable part of the sea, although almost enclosed by the shores, can never be the property of a particular people. And in places where the law of nations was not received, or was afterwards abolished, it does not follow that the people merely because they possess the lands also possess the sea enclosed by them; the taking possession must be made by an overt act, and signified and made known. And if the possession thus gained by the right of prior occupation is afterwards abandoned, the sea returns to its original nature—namely, to the common use of mankind. Further, he who possesses any part of the sea cannot lawfully hinder unarmed ships, giving no room to apprehend danger, from sailing there, in the same way that he cannot justly prohibit innocent passage through his lands. Grotius goes on to explain that it is more easy to take possession of the jurisdiction (*imperium*) alone over part of the sea than of the right of property, and that it is not contradicted by the law of nations; and he points to a number of instances among the ancients.[1] He admits that sovereignty or jurisdiction may be acquired on the sea either in regard to persons or in regard to territory (*ratione personarum et ratione territorii*),—in regard to persons, as when a fleet, which is a maritime army, is maintained in any part of the sea; in regard to territory, as when those who sail along the coasts may be compelled from the land, as if they were actually on the land.[2]

The latter statement of Grotius contains the germ of the idea subsequently adopted by almost all the writers on international law, that the extent of the adjoining sea over which the neighbouring state is entitled to exercise dominion is limited by the range of guns from the land. Grotius does not mention the means by which compulsion was to be made effective, but there is little or no doubt of what was

[1] Lib. ii. cap. iii. ss. ix.-xii.

[2] Lib. ii. cap. iii. s. xiii. 2. "Videtur autem imperium in maris portionem eadem ratione acquiri qua imperia alia, id est, ut supra diximus, ratione personarum et ratione territorii. Ratione personarum, ut si classis, qui maritimus est exercitus, aliquo in loco maris se habeat: ratione territorii, quatenus ex terra cogi possunt qui in proxima maris parte versantur, nec minus quam si in ipsa terra reperirentur."

in his mind.[1] It remained for Bynkershoek, at the beginning of the next century, to give the doctrine precise expression.

It is obvious from the foregoing that the opinions expressed by Grotius as to the appropriation of the sea were not always consistent, and were sometimes self-destructive. If the fluidity and physical nature of the sea made it impossible to occupy or appropriate it, the objection applied as much to one part of it as to another, since it is everywhere fluid; and the admissions in his later book stultify many of the statements in the earlier one. It seems to be indisputable that Grotius was to some extent influenced by his environment, and expanded or contracted his argument to meet the conditions at the time—that he was, in short, like all the others, more or less of an advocate. When he published his greater work he was in the service of the Queen of Sweden, who claimed a somewhat extensive maritime sovereignty in the Baltic, and it is not unlikely that this influenced him in making the admissions referred to.

The immediate object for which *Mare Liberum* was published —the recognition of the right of the Dutch to sail to the East Indies and to trade there—was achieved by the treaty of Antwerp in the month following its appearance,[2] and no reply from the Portuguese or Spaniards to the arguments of Grotius was published till sixteen years later. Grotius tells us that a work in refutation of *Mare Liberum* had been prepared by a scholar of Salamanca, but it was suppressed by Philip III.;[3] but in 1625, when Philip IV. was on the throne, an elaborate defence of the rights of Portugal in the Indies and a reply to Grotius was published by Franciscus Seraphinus de Freiras, a Spaniard, who dedicated his book to the king.[4] The Venetians also, whose power had by this time declined, began to defend with the pen their rights in the Adriatic. These rights had been

[1] Calvo, *Le Droit Internat.*, i. 348; Ortolan, *Règles Internationales et Diplomatie de la Mer*, i. c. v. See p. 156 referring to a State Paper of 1610, which seems to be misdated "August 1609."

[2] Dumont, *Corps Diplomatique*, vol. V. ii. p. 99. The treaty was signed on $\frac{\text{30 March}}{\text{9 April}}$ 1609.

[3] *Defensio*, 332 (*circa* 1614); Letter to his brother, 1st April 1617. *Epistolæ*, 759.

[4] *De Justo Imperio Lusitanorum Asiatico adversus Grotii Mare Liberum.*

indirectly assailed by the general argument of *Mare Liberum*, and directly in the writings of de Castro and Vasquius, from which Grotius had quoted liberally; and now at the beginning of the seventeenth century they were actively contested by other Powers, and in particular by Spain. Hence quite a number of works defending the claims of Venice appeared at this period, the best of which was that of Pacius, who relied on the opinions of numerous early jurists, as Bartolus, Baldus, and Angelus; on immemorial possession and prescription, and stated that the rights of the Venetians consisted in jurisdiction, the imposition of taxes, the prohibition or regulation of navigation, the protection of subjects, and the suppression of pirates.[1]

But it is probable that *Mare Liberum* received as much attention in England as it did in any other country. Grotius, as we have seen, condemned any interference with the liberty of fishing or the imposition of taxes on foreign fishermen in very severe language, and his book appeared just at the time when King James had resolved on both these courses, and within less than two months of the issue of the famous proclamation forbidding unlicensed fishing by foreigners on the British coasts. To be by implication branded as "insanely cupid" by an anonymous Dutch writer, because he had decided to levy the "assize-herring" from Dutch fishermen, must have irritated James; and the irritation would not be lessened when he found the envoys from the Netherlands in the following year vindicating their right to liberty of fishing by just such arguments as were contained in *Mare Liberum*. James, indeed, showed a somewhat bitter feeling towards the great Dutch publicist when the authorship was revealed and the author lay in prison; and Carleton, the English ambassador at The Hague, in a speech to the States-General, held him up to opprobrium and stated that the disgrace into which he had fallen should deter others from adopting his opinions.

[1] *Ivlii Pacii De Dominio Maris Hadriatici Disceptatio*, Lvgdvni M.D.C.XIX. Other works were Angelus Mattheacius, *De Jure Venetorum et Jurisdictione Maris Adriatici*, Venezia, 1617; Cornelio Francipane, *Alegazion in Jure, per il Dominio, della Republica Veneta, del suo Golfo, contra alcune Scritture di Napolitani*, 1618; Franciscus de Ingenuis, *Epistola de Jurisdictione Venetæ Reipublicæ in Mare Adriaticum*, 1619; P. Zambono, *Del Dominio del Mare Adriatico overo Golfo di Venezia*, Venice, 1620.

The task of replying to Grotius was taken up by a Scottish lawyer, William Welwod or Welwood, a professor of the civil law. Welwood was Professor of Mathematics at St Andrews University, but exchanged the Mathematical for the Juridical Chair about the year 1587; at the royal visitation in 1597 he was deprived of his office, on the ground that the profession of the law was in no wise necessary at that time in the University, but probably because his profession as a teacher of jurisprudence was obnoxious in the eyes of James.[1] In 1590 he had published at Edinburgh a treatise on the Sea Laws of Scotland, which is believed to be the earliest regular work on maritime jurisprudence printed in Britain, and which was dedicated to James;[2] but it contains nothing bearing on the question of the fishery or "assize-herring." In 1613 he published at London a new and enlarged edition of his early work, and in one of the chapters on "The Community and Proprietie of the Seas," he endeavoured to refute the arguments advanced in *Mare Liberum*, which he seems to have looked upon as a reply to James's proclamation of 1609.[3] This

[1] M'Crie, *Life of Andrew Melville*, 206, &c. Selden describes him as *Jurisconsultus Scotus;* and Prynne "A Scot, Professor of the Civil Law" (*Animadversions*, 113).

[2] There is a copy in the Library of the University, Cambridge (Aldis, *A List of Books printed in Scotland before* 1700; Dickson and Edmond, *Annals of Scottish Printing*, 415), and I have found a MS. copy among the State Papers, entitled "The Sea Law of Scotland, shortly gathered and plainly dressed for the ready vse of all seafaring men. Dedicated to James VI. of Scotland by William Welvod. At Edinborough, A° 1590, by Robert Walgrave." (*State Papers, Dom.*, Jas. I., ccviii. No. xvi.) It was printed at Edinburgh by Waldegrave in 1590. There are fifteen chapters dealing with the freighting of ships, the powers and duties of the master, the relations between the master and the merchants, &c. In his preface to the *Abridgement*, Welwood refers to this earlier work as follows: "It pleased your M. some yeeres past most graciously to accept of this birth, in the great weaknes and infancie thereof. Therefore it is, that now being strong, and by all warrants inarmed, it most thankefully returnes, offring seruice to your M. euen for all the coasts of your Highnes dominions, vpon hope to merit your former grace." His last work is dated 1622. It is probable that, like so many of his countrymen, he followed King James to London, where all his later works were published. He was of an ingenious mind, and, while teaching mathematics at St Andrews, obtained a patent for a new mode of raising water from wells, &c., on the principle of the syphon. M'Crie, *op. cit.*

[3] *An Abridgement of all Sea-Lawes, gathered forth of all Writings and Monuments, which are to be found among any people or Nation vpon the coasts of the greate Ocean and Mediterranean Sea: And specially ordered and disposed for the vse and benefit of all beneuolent Sea-farers, within his Maiesties Dominions of Great*

work was also dedicated to the king, and in a prefatory address to the three High Admirals—the Duke of Lennox, the Earl of Northampton, and the Earl of Nottingham—he impressed upon them the importance of the "conservacie" of the sea, especially for the fisheries, and urged that strangers should be stayed from scattering and breaking the shoals of fish on the coast of Scotland, a duty on which some of his Majesty's ships might well be employed.

Welwood was scarcely fitted either by knowledge or capacity to be a formidable antagonist to a giant like Grotius; and although his writings contain quite a number of arguments which were later used and expanded by Selden, it can hardly be said that they had a great influence on the controversy. He looked upon *Mare Liberum* as an attack on the rights of King James and his subjects to the fisheries "on this side the seas," veiled under the pretext of asserting the liberty to sail to the Indies. As befitted his nationality and his time, many of his arguments were drawn from Holy Writ, and he had no difficulty in placing Providence on the side of James and in opposition to the Dutch. Others were more pertinent. He urged that the injunctions of the Roman law applied only to the subjects of Rome, and not internationally as between state and state,—an opinion also pressed, as we have seen, by Vasquius; that the fluidity of the sea was no bar to its occupation, and that it could be, and had been in certain cases, divided up into marches and boundaries, by the ordinary methods used by navigators, "so farre as is expedient for the certain reach and bounds of seas, properlie pertaining to any prince or people," —what these bounds are or should be he does not say, though he quotes the Italian limit of 100 miles with approval. He held that the liberty of navigation was beyond all controversy, and agreed to the principle of the complete freedom of the sea so far as concerned the "main Sea or great Ocean," which was "farre removed from the just and due bounds above mentioned properlie perteyning to the neerest Lands of euerie

Britanne, Ireland, and the adiacent Isles thereof. London, 1613. Tit. xxvii. deals with the "community" of seas. He refers to the work of Grotius as "a verie learned, but a subtle Treatise (*incerto authore*) intituled *Mare Liberum.*" Welwood's *Abridgement* was republished in 1636, without alteration; also in the edition of 1686 of Malyne's *Consuetudo vel Lex Mercatoria*, but without his name.

Nation." To Grotius' statement that it was worse to prohibit promiscuous fishing than to forbid navigation, Welwood justly replied that if the free use of the sea is interfered with for any purpose, it ought to be chiefly for the sake of the fishings, if the fishes become exhausted and scarce, as he says was the condition at that time on the east coast of Scotland, from the "neere and dailie approaching of the busse fishers" scattering and breaking the shoals, so that no fish "worthy of anie paines and travels" could now be found.

Two years later Welwood returned to the theme, and published a formal little book on the dominion of the seas.[1] It was dedicated to Queen Anne, who had just been endeavouring to set up a fishery society with power to tax foreign fishermen (p. 161), and, as explained in the dedication, the book was specially directed against the freedom unlawfully usurped by foreigners of fishing in the British seas. It may be regarded as an amplification of his chapter in the *Abridgement*, but is much superior and more logically arranged; and being written in Latin, it attained, if not a reputation, at least considerable recognition on the Continent. He urges strongly that the sea as well as the land is capable of distinction and dominion, both by human and by divine law, and explains the contrary opinion of many publicists, poets, and orators (so copiously quoted by Grotius) by saying they were ignorant of the true law of nature, and had infected the minds of later generations with "a preposterous notion concerning some universal community of things." The adjacent sea is claimed for the neighbouring state, because it is as necessary there as it is on land that some one should have jurisdiction, and this jurisdiction ought to be exercised by the neighbouring prince, so that both the land and the sea should be under the same sovereignty. The part of the sea next the land is, moreover, so joined to and, as it were, incorporated with it, that the ruler of the land is not permitted to alienate either a part of it, or the use of it, or to let it out (*locare*) any more than his kingdom or the patrimony of his kingdom. He held that it was incontestable that the vast and boundless waters beyond the

[1] *De Dominio Maris Ivribvsque ad Dominivm praecipve spectantibvs Assertio brevis et methodica.* Cosmopoli, 16th January 1615. It was republished at The Hague in 1653, and replied to by Graswinckel. See p. 412.

mare proximum were open to all nations indifferently for all uses, but that in the adjacent sea the neighbouring prince had in particular two primary rights besides jurisdiction—namely, the right of navigation and the right of fishing, with the power to impose taxes for either. He maintained that fishing in the sea was for the most part appropriated, and for a clear reason. God had appointed the fishes (herrings) to swarm along the coasts of Britain and the surrounding isles at seasons and places which He had pre-arranged, and for the benefit of the inhabitants: why, then, should the people be hindered from possessing as their own this benefit which God had granted them? He would be unwilling to deny the communication of this natural advantage to other nations, "but only by the same law by which they possess their own, that is by a just price." Yet, notwithstanding this special blessing which had been granted to the British people, they were despoiled of it and of their just rights, owing to their seas being taken possession of, as it were, by a continual inundation of foreign fishermen, so that the shoals were scattered and the fishery exhausted. Welwood then refers to the alleged old agreement between the Scotch and the Dutch, whereby the latter were not to fish within eighty miles of the coast of Scotland (p. 84), but which they of late totally disregarded, fishing close to the shore, in front of the houses. And while they were permitted to carry away their fish from our seas without paying any tribute, the poor Scottish fishermen had to pay tithes to the Church and the assize-herring to the crown, as well as having their livelihood damaged by the action of the foreigners.

The treatises of Welwood were composed to support the claim of James to the assize-herring, and the project of the queen to monopolise the fishings, as much as to demonstrate the law as to the dominion of the sea. On one account if on no other his works deserve to be remembered. He was the first author who clearly enunciated, and insisted on, the principle that the inhabitants of a country had a primary and exclusive right to the fisheries along their coasts—that the usufruct of the adjacent sea belonged to them; and that one of the main reasons why that portion of the sea should pertain to the neighbouring state was the risk of the exhaustion of its fisheries from promiscuous use.

But they will be remembered in the history of international law for another reason. The first of them called forth from Grotius the only reply he ever vouchsafed to the numerous writers who attacked *Mare Liberum.* In the year in which the work was published, he was in London as one of the Dutch ambassadors, engaged in the somewhat ironical task of defending a Dutch *mare clausum* in the East Indies, and probably the book then fell into his hands. In his *Defensio* (see p. 344) Grotius reaffirmed the position he took in *Mare Liberum,* with the old arguments, and with some new ones to meet the criticism of Welwood, and not without some of the customary logic-chopping and wire-drawn reasoning. He held that the Roman law as to the sea being common applied not merely among the citizens of one state, but among mankind in general, because *communis* was a different thing from *publicus.*[1] While admitting the possibility of marking out the sea by imaginary lines, he said this was not relevant to the question of appropriation, since appropriation could not take place without possession, and possession cannot be established merely by the mind or intellect, but requires a corporeal act; otherwise the astronomer might lay claim to the heavens or the geometrician to the earth. Concerning the rights of fishery, with which the *Defensio* largely deals, he asserts that as the use of the sea is common to all, no one can prohibit fishing in it or justly impose taxes on it. With respect to the right of the Dutch to fish on the British coasts, he cites the Burgundy treaties and uses the same arguments as the Dutch ambassadors did in 1610 (p. 155). They had the right by treaties, immemorial usage, prescription, and the Law of Nations. It is noteworthy that in the *Defensio,* Grotius, no doubt owing to the polemical spirit inciting him above all to refute the arguments of Welwood concerning the *mare proximum,* as well as to demolish the claims of King James, denies the existence of sovereignty or property in any part of the sea, whereas it appears to be allowed by implication in *Mare Liberum,* and is expressly admitted in his later and larger work. Here he says, and more

[1] In Roman law a distinction was made between the sea and rivers in regard to propriety. The sea is "*communis omnium naturali jure,*" but the rivers are "*publicæ res, quarum proprietas est populi vel reipublicæ.*"

logically, that whatever applies to the whole sea applies to all its parts, even to a diverticulum, and he allows no exception for the sea washing a coast: a conclusion, however, at variance with the general practice of the time. This tract, as already stated, was not published by the author, probably because it was likely to excite still more the ire of James at finding his "rights" again "questioned."[1]

In contrast with the writings of Welwood may be cited the opinions of another and more eminent Scottish lawyer, Sir Thomas Craig, who touched upon the subject of maritime jurisdiction in a non-controversial work published before the juridical controversy had arisen.[2] He states that the sea is common to all for navigation, but that property and jurisdiction in the adjacent sea pertains to the neighbouring territory according to the current opinion—the sea washing the coast of France, England, Scotland, Ireland, &c., to the respective countries. No limits or bounds are laid down by Craig as to the partitioning of the sea in this way, but when dealing with the theoretical question of islands arising in the sea, he follows Bartolus in assigning a space of 100 miles from the coast. He admits that certain seas may be prescribed, as the Adriatic, which Venice, though not possessing the shores, claimed by prescription. With respect to fisheries, the Scottish author, as might have been expected, holds that those in the adjoining sea belong to the bordering state: they are prescribed, and fishing there may be permitted or prohibited according to custom; and he says that it was not without great injury to us that the Dutch carry on their fishery around our islands.[3]

[1] Welwood's *De Dominio Maris* is not mentioned by Grotius, whose tract appears to have been written before it was published.

[2] *Jus Feudale, Tribus Libris Comprehensum*, lib. i., Diegesis 13, p. 103. Edinburgh, 1603 and 1655. The treatise was dedicated to King James. Craig was born in 1538 and died in 1608.

[3] "Quod ad mare attinet, licet adhuc ita omnium commune sit, ut in eo navigari possit. Proprietas tamen ejus ad eos pertinere hodie creditur, ad quos proximus continens adeo ut mare Gallicum id dicatur quod littus Galliæ alluit, aut ei propius est, quam ulli alii continenti. Sic Anglicum, Scoticum, et Hybernicum, quod propius Angliæ, Scotiæ, et Hyberniæ est. Ita ut reges inter se, quasi maria omnia diviserint, et quasi ex mutua partitione alterius id mare censeatur, quod alteri propinquius et commodius est; in quo si delictum aliquod commisum fuerit, ejus sit, jurisdictio qui proximum continentem possideat. Isque suum illud mare

In the period that elapsed between the appearance of the works of Grotius and Welwood and the publication of Selden's *Mare Clausum*, a number of other books were issued which dealt with the question of the freedom of the seas and the extent to which they might be appropriated. Gerard Malynes, in treatises on commerce which had a wide circulation, re-echoed the opinions of Welwood, and of Gentleman and Keymer. The "main great seas," he said, were common to all nations for navigation and fishing, but the bordering sea was under the dominion of the prince of the adjoining country, and foreigners could only fish in it by obtaining permission and paying for the privilege; within this sea navigation was free unless it interfered with the fishings. Malynes said that this was the practice in Russia, Denmark, Sweden, and Italy; and he ascribed the decay of English fisheries and trade to the admission of foreigners to fish in "his Majesty's streames" without paying for the liberty.[1] Two other authors, each celebrated in his respective sphere, touched upon the king's dominion in the seas, and they may be regarded as representing two different aspects of the subject, both of which became of great importance—namely, the limits of neutral waters, and the rights of the crown by the Common Law of England to the propriety of the sea and its bed. One was Alberico Gentilis and the other Serjeant Callis.

Gentili, or Gentilis, who was a forerunner of Grotius in shaping the Law of Nations,[2] was an Italian of the school of Perugia, domiciled in England, where he held the Regius Professorship of Civil Law at Oxford. In 1605, after the conclusion of peace with Spain, he was appointed advocate for the Spanish embassy in London, and was frequently employed in the Admiralty Court in cases where the legality

vocat. . . . Piscationes vero quæ in proximo mari fiunt, proculdubio eorum sunt qui proximum continentem possident. Itaque non sine summa injuria nostra Belgæ circa nostras insulas piscantur. Nam licet piscationes in mari non prohibeantur, tamen et hæ præscribuntur, et traduntur permissæ aut prohibitæ secundum consuetudinem."

[1] *The Maintenance of Free Trade*, p. 42 *et seq.* *Consuetudo vel Lex Mercatoria.* The latter contains chapters on Navigation and Community of Seas, and The Distinct Dominions of the Seas. Many editions were published.

[2] Wheaton, *Hist.*, 51, 153 ; Phillimore, *Commentaries*, I. xxxix.

of the capture of Spanish vessels by the Dutch had to be determined. His pleadings and the decisions in these and similar cases were collected and published in 1613, after his death, and they form, according to Wheaton, the earliest reports of judicial decisions on maritime law published in Europe.[1]

In discharging his duties in the English Prize Courts, it often fell to the lot of Gentilis to deal with the jurisdiction of England in the seas, for while he held office war existed between Spain and the United Provinces, and Spanish ships were frequently taken by the Dutch in the neighbourhood of the British coasts. Of course, captures made in the King's Chambers after the proclamation of 1604 (see p. 119) were not good prize, and were restored.[2] But when a Spanish vessel was seized clearly outside the limits of the King's Chambers, Gentilis argued that it was not good prize, because, first, the treaty of peace[3] between Spain and England provided that the subjects of either were to be protected in all places throughout the dominions of the other; and, second, the dominion of the King of England extended far into the neighbouring seas. He seemed to stretch the joint sovereignty of Spain and England as far as America, pointing out that the southern coasts of Ireland were opposite to Spain, and the western coasts were

[1] *Alberici Gentilis Juriscons. Hispanicæ Advocationis*, Libri Duo, Hanoviæ, 1613. Gentilis was born in 1551 and died, like Craig, in 1608. His most important works were *De Jure Belli* (1588) and *De Legationibus*. Professor Holland has given an account of his life and works in *An Inaugural Lecture on Albericus Gentilis*, delivered at All Souls College, 1874. See also Alessandro de Giorgi, *Della Vita e delle opere di Alberico Gentili*, Parma, 1876.

[2] In a letter from the Earl of Salisbury to Sir Thomas Lake in 1606, referring to a dispute between the Dutch and Spanish ambassadors about prizes taken in the Narrow Sea, it is said that the king, in putting in force his proclamation about the recall of subjects in foreign service (p. 119), dealt as follows : if a prize had been taken and brought into the English limits (chambers), and Englishmen were aboard the taker, he dealt with them as having offended against his proclamation, and also released the ship as not being good prize. Even more, proceeds the Earl, "although there be no English but all Flemings, the king takes all from them and restores it [the ship] wherein, tho' in effect it undoes the end of the States warr by sea, because they have no way to come home but by the narrow seas, where the least wind that can blow them can hardly keepe themself from the English coasts, and so a partiall jugement of ½ a mile more or less in a wyde sea looseth or winneth their right." *State Papers, Dom.*, xviii. 22.

[3] In 1604, between King James and Philip III. and the Archdukes. Dumont *Corps Diplomatique*, V. ii. 34.

bounded by the Indies belonging to Spain, while the northern coasts of Britain, having no countries lying against them, were washed by an immense and open sea. He held that the proclamation of 1604, fixing the limits of the chambers in connection with acts of hostilities between the Spaniards and the Hollanders, ought not to prevail against the provisions of the treaty, for the proclamation was subsequent to the treaty, and it would be unjust to allow it to lessen the extent of the territory (sea) over which protection was to be afforded by the terms of the contract. It was not a valid argument, Gentilis continued, to say that the boundaries expressed in the proclamation—that is, the King's Chambers—had been observed long before by common usage in relation to similar cases.[1]

There is no doubt, however, that although Gentilis as an advocate took this line of pleading, the boundaries of the King's Chambers from headland to headland, as defined by James in his "plat," were received as settled law in regard to neutrality both in the English courts and on the Continent.[2] Gentilis further urged that the limit fixed by the Italian jurists for the extent of jurisdiction—viz., 100 miles from the coast, unless the proximity of another state interfered with its application—also was in force off the British coasts, a view which the court declined to accept.

Yet, although this principle of extending and limiting the territorial jurisdiction to 100 miles was not accepted in the English Courts, we find it made use of in the diplomatic correspondence of the time. The Earl of Salisbury in a letter to Cornwallis, the English ambassador at Madrid, explanatory of James's proclamation in 1609 forbidding unlicensed fishing, did not seek to defend the action of the king by reason of any intrinsic right of the crown of England to sovereignty in the neighbouring sea, but rather upon what he alleged was the practice of the civil law. A sovereign prince or state, he said, was *Mundi Dominus, Lex Maris,* both because of the protection afforded to navigation in the adjacent sea and from prescription: the adjoining sea, as Baldus said, pertained to the territory of the neighbouring

[1] "Etiam non nocet, quod objicitur et longe antehac longo usu servatos in hujusmodi quæstionibus hos esse fines qui expressi nunc sunt Edicto," p. 30.

[2] Gryphiander, *De Insulis Tractatus*, Frankfort, 1623, cap. 14, s. 46.

state, and thus the Venetians, as lords of the Adriatic, could impose taxes and penalties on navigation. "In respect of both which titles," continued the Earl, "the Kings and Princes in general fronting upon the seas, as Spayne, France, Denmark, &c., have upon occasion offered, not only made ordinances and published edicts for the ruling and better ordering of the seas, but also have put them in execution; as well civilly for deciding of contracts, as criminally for transgressions; and have raised taxes and gabells in the seas as on the land to their best benefit, as part of their regalities properly belonging unto them, in sign of their sovereignty." As to the distance to which this sovereignty extended, he said it was "generally received to be about one hundred miles at the least into the seas," unless in narrow seas only, in which case the limits are divided by the channel, "except the princes of the one shore have prescribed the whole, as it falleth out in his Majesty's narrow seas between England and France, where the whole appertayneth to him in right, and so hath been possessed tyme out of mind by his progenitors."

By another channel we may trace the course of the ideas which converged and culminated in the claims of Charles to the dominion of the surrounding seas—viz., in connection with the development of the law relating to the rights of property in the foreshore and the bed of the sea. Cases frequently occurred in which those rights were contested between private individuals and the crown; and in the course of litigation, or in writings dealing with the subject, the rights in the sea which were alleged to belong to the crown were explained. We have already seen that Plowden, in a case of the kind, argued that Queen Elizabeth possessed jurisdiction as far as the middle line in the surrounding seas,—a doctrine which the queen expressly repudiated in 1602,—but denied to her any right of property in either the sea or its bed. The claims of the crown to the ownership of the foreshores originated in the reign of Elizabeth; under James and Charles I. they were systematically pursued by the "title-hunters"; and while the legal decisions in contested cases were for a long time adverse to the crown, they began in the reign of James to be in its favour, and gradually the idea was imported into and became a part of English law that the ownership of the foreshore was *prima facie* vested in the crown in virtue of the royal prerogative.[1]

Along with the development of this idea came another, which was ultimately likewise engrafted on English law—that the crown had the exclusive right of property in the sea and in the soil beneath it. The origin of the idea is to be found in a treatise written in 1569 by Thomas Digges.[2] He argued that as many things—as wrecks, treasure-trove, waifs and strays, which were originally common by the law of nature—now belonged to the Prince, so also should the sea, which was the chief of all waters, and could not by the civil law become the property of a subject. He held that just as the owners of the soil had the property in a river and its banks, the king had the interest and property in the "great salt river" environing the island, and in its shores and bottom; and he speaks of the sea as the "King's river," the "King's streme," and the "King's water," in which he had also jurisdiction. Digges also claimed that the fishings in the sea belonged to the crown, for "although the Kings of England have benne content to suffer fishermen *Jure gentium* to enjoy to theire owen use such fishe as by theire charges travill and adventure they can in the Englishe Seas take, Yet haue the Kings of England for remembrance of this theire favoure that the memorie of theire propertie in the Seas shoulde not be extinguished, alwaie reserved to them selves the cheif fishe as Sturgeon, Whale, &c."[3]

The contention that the crown had the right of property in the sea and its bed, denied by Plowden, received in the reign of James much fuller amplification at the hands of Serjeant

[1] Moore, *A History of the Foreshore and the Law relating thereto*, 1888.

[2] "Arguments prooving the Queenes Maties propertye in the Sea Landes, and salt shores thereof, and that no subiect cann lawfully hould eny parte thereof but by the Kinges especiall graunte." It is printed by Moore (*op. cit.*, 185) from *Lansdowne MSS.*, No. 100. Various copies exist; one in *Lansd. MSS.*, No. 105, belonged to Lord Burghley, and is endorsed by him "Mr Digges. The Case of Lands left by ye Seas." A copy is in *State Papers, Dom.*, cccxxxix. 1.

[3] It may be said that this claim to "royal fish," made also by Bracton, was not peculiar to the English crown. It was made on the Continent from an early period, as is shown by the ancient laws of Jutland and of Scania, and the practice in many parts of France and among the Normans. It may have been introduced into England by William the Conqueror, who granted Dengey Marsh to Battle Abbey, with the right to wreck and royal fish.

Callis, whose well-known lectures on the Statute of Sewers were delivered in 1622.[1] Callis argued that in "our *Mare Anglicanum* the king had, by the common law of England, four "powers and properties": sovereignty (*imperium regale*), legal jurisdiction for the administration of justice, property in the soil under the sea and in the water, and possession and profits both real and personal. He cites in proof a number of authorities, legal and historical, such as were cited later by Selden. The statement in a case decided in the reign of Richard II. (1377-99), that "the sea is within the legiance of the king as of his crown of England"; the charter of the Admiral giving him power in maritime cases throughout the realm of England; the phrases in certain statutes; the right to wreck and royal fishes, and so forth, "proved the King full Lord and owner of the seas, and that the seas be within the realm of England." The king rules on the sea, he held, "by the laws imperial" as by the Roole d'Oleron and others, but only in the case of shipping and for merchants and mariners; his rights of property in the bed and waters of the sea, and the personal profits (wreck, flotsam, &c.) accruing, were his by the common law. Callis did not deal with fishing, nor attempt to define the bounds of "the seas of England" in which the king had property and jurisdiction.

The interpretation of the law as to the rights of the crown in the seas, as propounded by Callis, was followed by Selden and Hale, and generally by the lawyers who came after him. Lord Chief-Justice Coke, in his *First Institute*, which was published in 1628, explains the old phrase "within the four seas" (*infra quatuor maria*) as meaning within the kingdom and dominions of England; for if a man be upon the sea of England he is "within the kingdom or realm of England, and within the ligeance of the king of England, as of his crown of England." In his *Fourth Institute*, which was not published, however, till 1644, ten years after his death, when treating of the Admiralty Court, Coke entered more fully into the question of the rights of the crown in the seas of England; and, as already mentioned, he looked upon the roll of Edward I., *De*

[1] *The Reading of the famous and learned Robert Callis, Esqr., upon the Statute of Sewers*, 23 Hen. VIII., c. 5, as it was delivered by him at Gray's Inn in August 1622. 4th ed., 1824.

Superioritate Maris, as proving that the king's right of dominion over the sea had been expressly acknowledged by neighbouring nations.

But none of the works on the rights of England in the adjoining seas, which had appeared when the new policy of Charles began to be fashioned, was sufficiently profound or authoritative to furnish reasonable justification for that policy in the eyes of the world. The king in 1632, as we have seen, desired to demonstrate his rights by means of "some public writing," founded upon the historical records of the realm,—a demonstration which was to precede the revival of the English pretension to the dominion of the seas in what Secretary Coke called its ancient style and lustre. As a result of the search made amongst the records in the Tower and elsewhere for evidence and precedents to establish the claim, several treatises and collections were compiled. Most of these were of little account,[1] but one of them attained an authority and celebrity only second to the great work of Selden. Before Charles wrote to the Clerk-Register in Edinburgh for Scottish documents to substantiate his claims (p. 212), it seems that Sir John Boroughs, the Keeper of his Majesty's Records in the Tower, had been commissioned by the king to prepare the "public writing" to which he referred. We have already seen that in 1631 Boroughs brought forward the important roll of Edward I.; he tells us in his preface that his work was composed at the request of "a great person"; it was written in Latin, the language which fitted it for foreign Courts; and it deals very largely with the Dutch and English fisheries, even recommending the construction of 250 busses for the fishery association. Boroughs' treatise, entitled "The Soveraignty of the British Seas, proved by Records, History and the Municipall Lawes of

[1] Such as "A Collection of divers particulars touching the King's Dominion and Soveraignty in the Fishings, as well in Scotland as in the British Ocean," by Captain John Mason. (*State Papers*, *Dom.*, 1590. *Admiralty*, Eliz., Jac. I., Car. I., No. 37, fol. 131.) A superior compilation, dealing with the opinions of the Civilians, as well as with the Dutch and native fisheries, and founded largely on Dee, Hitchcock, Gentleman, and Keymer, is entitled "The King's Interest in the Sea and the Commodities thereof" (*ibid.*, ccv. 92). Another treatise, also dealing with the opinions of the Civilians, the jurisdiction of the Admiral, and the rights of the crown of England to the dominion of the narrow seas, is in *State Papers*, *Dom.*, ccviii., No. x., fol. 402.

this Kingdome," was completed in 1633, but it was not published until 1651, when the question of maritime rights had been again raised between England and the United Provinces.[1] It is probable that the king discarded it for *Mare Clausum*, the incomparably superior treatise by Selden, of the existence of which he was probably made aware as early at least as 1634.

Nevertheless, Boroughs' work was the first successful attempt to bring together a great array of historical facts in favour of the English claims to the dominion of the seas. Like Selden, he begins with the Roman occupation of Britain in order to show that from the first the "British nation had the supreme power of command of their own seas"; and, moreover, he gives all the more important documents to be found in *Mare Clausum*,—the ordinance of John, the rolls of Edward I. and Edward III., the charter of Edgar, the Laws of Oleron, commissions to the admirals, safe-conducts, and extracts from the Burgundy treaties. He is very emphatic as to the king's right to the dominion of the seas and the fisheries. "That princes," he says, "may have an exclusive property in the soveraigntie of the severall parts of the sea, and in the navigation, fishing and shores thereof, is so evidently true by way of fact, as no man that is not desperately impudent can deny it"; and—no doubt for the benefit of the Dutch—he adds that "if any nation usurp our rights, the king has a good sword to defend them." He asserts that the kings of England in succession had the "sovereign guard" of the seas; had imposed taxes and tributes upon all ships navigating or fishing in them; and had closed and opened the passage through them to strangers, as they saw cause. The sovereignty of the sea he calls "the most precious jewel of his Majesty's crown, next (after God) the principal means of our wealth and safety." A considerable

[1] The original Latin copy bearing the date 1633 (confirmed by internal evidence) is in the British Museum (*Harleian MSS.*, 4314). It is entitled *Dominium Maris Britannici assertum ex Archiuis Historiis et Municipalibus Regni Legibus*, per D. Johannem de Burgo, 1633; it is dedicated to the king. Other MS. copies in the British Museum are *Harl.*, 1323; *Lansdowne*, 806, f. 40; *Sloane*, 1696; and *Harl.*, 4626, the latter being very imperfect. There is also a fine copy in English among the State Papers, dated 1637, with this addition to the title: "Also a Perticuler Relation concerning the Inastimable Riches and Commodities of the British Seas" (*State Papers, Dom.*, ccclxxvi. 68). It was republished in the third edition of Malyne's *Consuetudo vel Lex Mercatoria*, in 1686.

part of the treatise is taken up with the fisheries, the information being almost wholly derived from previous writers; the usual comparisons are drawn of the flourishing state of the fisheries of Holland and the poor condition of those of England, and the usual statements made as to the benefits that would accrue to the kingdom if the fisheries were developed.

Boroughs' treatise, however interesting from the historical documents it contained, had serious defects when considered as a formal justification to Europe of the policy of Charles. The facts were not skilfully marshalled; the deductions were bald and crude; and above all, it was destitute of arguments and reasoning founded on law. Grotius was then the Swedish ambassador at Paris, his works were well known and esteemed throughout Europe, and it would have been indiscreet to attempt to answer his elaborate arguments against such claims to *mare clausum* by saying that these claims were self-evident and that only an impudent person would deny them.

Fortunately for Charles, Selden now came upon the scene to vindicate and glorify his prerogative in the surrounding seas. The distinguished author tells us that his great work, *Mare Clausum*, was begun long before at the desire of King James, and had been lying in an incomplete and imperfect form for fully sixteen years.[1] It was presented to James in 1618, but several reasons prevented its publication, one of the chief being that the king was afraid that some passages it contained might give offence to the King of Denmark, from whom he was then endeavouring to obtain a loan of money.[2] At the request of Charles, Selden now recast his treatise, added to it, and completed it. It was dedicated to the king and published by his "express commands," as he explained a little later, "for the manifesting of the right and Dominion of Us and our Royal

[1] *Mare Clausum*, in dedication to King Charles, "Divi parentis tui jussu tentata olim adumbrataque, inter schedas sive neglectas sive disjectas per annos amplius sedecim mecum latuit; ut imperfecta nimis sic etiam ceu intermortua."

[2] *Vindiciæ Maris Clausi*, p. 25. This was the explanation which Selden gave when, in 1652, he was taunted by a Dutch writer, Graswinckel, with having written his work to get out of prison. It is surprising that James, who was loquacious and fond of displaying his knowledge, never lectured the Dutch ambassadors on the themes in *Mare Clausum*—as from the rolls of the Edwards; nor was any use made of its facts and arguments throughout the protracted negotiations in his reign.

Progenitors in the seas which encompass these our Realms and Dominions of Great Britain and Ireland."[1]

Selden, as is well known, had taken a prominent part in the Parliament of 1629, in the majority which resisted the king's wishes, and was for a time imprisoned in consequence of his share in the historic disturbances with which it had ended, when the Speaker was held down in the chair. He was released on bail under sureties for good behaviour, and he was bound to present himself, on the motion of the Attorney-General, in the Court of King's Bench, on the first day of each term, as a person under surveillance.[2] Selden was not of the stuff of which martyrs are made. After his release, we find him among the lawyers of the Inns of Court arranging for the masque which was performed before the Court, at Whitehall in February 1634, as a token of the detestation in which they held Prynne's innuendo concerning the queen in his *Histriomastix*.[3] Towards the end of the same year, in a humble petition to the king ("prostrating myself at the feet of your sacred Majesty"), he begged that the royal displeasure might be removed and the bail discharged, assuring Charles of his readiness to serve him with gladness and affection. In February 1635 the king forwarded to the Judges of the Court of King's Bench a mandate, the draft of which had been prepared by Selden himself, instructing them to discharge him of their recognisances;[4] in August we find the Dutch ambassador writing to The Hague that the book was being printed;[5] and in December of that year it was given to the world.[6] There is little doubt that Selden's petition to the

1 A Proclamation concerning a book intituled *Mare Clausum*, 15th April 1636. *Fœdera*, xx. 12.

2 *State Papers, Dom.*, cclxxiii. 30; cclxxvi. 58.

3 Gardiner, *Hist.*, vii. 330. Poor Prynne, who lost both his ears on this occasion, and had his books burned under him in the pillory, became later an ardent defender of the king's dominion in the seas in the reign of Charles II., when he held the office of Keeper of the Records.

4 *State Papers, Dom.*, cclxxvi. 58; cclxxxiii. 96-98.

5 *Brit. Mus. Add. MSS.*, 17,677, O, fol. 367. Joachimi to the States-General, $\frac{5}{15}$ Aug. 1635. "Het boeck Seldeni getituleert, soo ich hoore, *mare clausum*, is onder den druck deur ordre van den Coningh."

6 Joannis Seldeni Mare Clausum seu de Dominio Maris, Libri Duo. *Primo*, Mare, ex *Jure Naturæ* seu *Gentium*, omnium hominum non esse Commune, sed

king and its favourable reception covered the negotiations concerning the completion and publication of *Mare Clausum*, which were carried on under the auspices of certain eminent personages at Court, and probably of Laud.[1] He tells us that the early work was very imperfect, and required to be completely reconstructed, and that he was able to devote some months of leisure to the task. But even Selden's extraordinary erudition and great industry could not have produced such a book without prolonged labour; and it may be guessed that, observing the trend of the king's policy and becoming desirous of royal favour, he began to reconstruct his treatise very soon after leaving prison.

The political significance of Selden's work was instantly recognised both at home and abroad. It appeared at the time when the pretensions of Charles to the dominion of the sea were astonishing Europe. While the printers were still busy with it, the Earl of Lindsey's fleet was scouring the Channel to force the elusive squadrons of France to strike to the king's flag. The longing to compel homage to the flag burned like a fever in the breasts of naval officers; and despatches poured in from them announcing that Dutch, Danish, and even occasionally French, ships had been forced to strike, sometimes in their own waters. The supposed policy of the Plantagenets had been expounded in high-sounding despatches to foreign Courts, and formulated in Admiralty instructions. The Dutch fisheries had been threatened; and it was known everywhere that the King of England was preparing a formidable fleet to sweep the seas in the following year.

Charles did what he could to emphasise the importance of the book. When a pirated edition appeared within a few months at Amsterdam, bearing the name of the king's printers and the word London in imitation of the original edition, and with a print of the great Burgundy treaty, the Intercursus Magnus, and a tract appended by way of antidote, he com-

Dominii privata seu Proprietatis capax, pariter ac Tellurem, esse demonstratur. *Secundo*, Serenissimum Magnæ Britanniæ Regem Maris circumflui, ut individuæ atque perpetuæ Imperii Britannici appendicis, Dominum esse, asseritur. Pontus quoque Serviet Illi. Londini, excudebat Will. Stanesbeius, pro Richardo Meighen, MDCXXXV. The Preface is dated at the Temple, 4th November 1635.

[1] *Vindiciæ*, "proceres apud regem præpollentes."

plained to the Dutch ambassador, and issued a proclamation declaring that *Mare Clausum* had been published by his express commands, denouncing those who had produced the pirated copy, and banning it from the realm.[1] On 26th March, as the following record shows, he brought it before the Privy Council with high eulogy, and for a definite purpose: "His Majesty this day in Council took into consideration a book lately published by John Selden, Esquire, intituled *Mare Clausum, seu de Dominio Maris,* written by the king's command, which he had done with great industry, learning and judgment, and hath asserted the right of the Crown of England to the Dominion of the British seas. The King requires one of the said books to be kept in the Council-Chest, another in the Court of Exchequer, and a third in the Court of Admiralty, as faithful and strong evidence of the Dominion of the British seas."[2]

There was good reason for the king's eulogy of Selden's treatise. From the point of view of his policy nothing that the pen can do could have been better done. It is an elaborate and masterly exposition of the case for the sovereignty of the crown of England in the British seas, which throws into the shade all the other numerous works which were written on that side of the question. One of the most eminent lawyers of his time, a scholar, an antiquary, an historian, the author brought to his task a keen intellect, an immense erudition, and the ability of

[1] Proclamation, 15th April 1636.

[2] Rushworth, *Historical Collections*, ii. 320. Frankland, *The Annals of King James and King Charles the First*, 476. In the Exchequer Order Book, under date 5th May, the following entry occurs: "Whereas Sr William Beecher, Kt, one of the clerks of his Mats most honorable pryvy councill, did this daye deliver in Court to the Lord Treasurer, Chauncillor, and Barons of the Courte, a booke lately published by John Selden, Esqr., entituled *Mare Clausum seu de dominio maris,* to be kept in this Courte as a faithfull and stronge evidence for the undoubted right of the Crowne of England to the Dominion of the Bryttishe seas, which saide booke the said Clerke of the Councill did deliver according to an order in that behalfe made by the King's most excellent Matie and the Lords of His Highness privy councell at Whitehall, the third of Aprill last past, a coppie of which said order is alsoe delivered with the said booke: It is, therefore, nowe ordered by the said Lord Treasurer, Chauncillor, and Barons that the said booke bee receaved by his Maties Remembrancer of this Courte, and by him kypt of record amonge the Records of the Courte as his Maties evidence. And as well the said order of the third of Aprill before mentioned as this present order to bee inrolled upon Record." *Charles I. Decrees and Orders*, Series iii., No. 19, fol. 3*b*.

2 A

disposing his material and arguments to the best advantage. In learning at least he far surpassed Grotius, and he was not inferior to his illustrious contemporary in ingenuity of reasoning. It was Selden's misfortune that the cause he championed was moribund, and opposed to the growing spirit of freedom throughout the world. At the same time it must be said that, apart from its extreme doctrines as to the sovereignty of England in the seas, it more correctly represented what are now the admitted principles as to the appropriation of the adjacent sea than did most of the works written on the other side, not excepting even those of Grotius.

But in relation to the cause for which it was written, the merit of *Mare Clausum* lay not merely in the enunciation of the theoretical and legal aspects of the claim to maritime sovereignty, but also in the imposing array of historical facts and arguments by which the right of England was sought to be established. The defects of the work are scarcely less apparent. There is no ground to suppose that Selden was guilty of the offence attributed to him by some of his foreign critics, of inventing part of the evidence he cites. But the interpretation he placed upon much of it was strained or erroneous. Great conclusions were drawn from things which had in reality no connection with his case; laws and events which referred solely to English subjects were improperly extended to include foreigners; the bearing of many records was misrepresented, others were passed over in silence, or, as with the "Burgundy" treaties, referred to in such a way as to distort their plain meaning.

In the first book the author endeavours to prove that the sea is not everywhere common, but is capable of appropriation, and has been in fact in numerous cases appropriated. The objections to that opinion are classified in three groups: first, that it is contrary to the law of nature and the law of nations to forbid free commerce and navigation; second, that the physical nature of the sea, its fluidity and fluxion, renders it incapable of occupation; third, the opinions of certain learned men. He argued that the ancient law as to the community of things had become modified in certain particulars, and that the received practice and custom of many nations, ancient and modern, showed that the sea was capable of private dominion, and that such dominion or appropriation was therefore not contrary either to the law of nature or the law of nations. In support of his argument Selden drew freely upon the vast stores of his erudition. He began, like Welwood, by quoting Scriptures to show that the divine law (*jus divinum*) allowed private dominion in the sea, and that according to the opinion of those learned in the Jewish law, a great part of the sea washing the west coast of the Holy Land had been annexed to the land of Israel by the appointment of God. Among almost all the nations of antiquity, he said, it was the custom to admit private dominion in the sea, and many of them exercised maritime sovereignty.[1] Among modern nations, sovereignty was exercised by the Venetians in the Adriatic, by the Genoese in the Ligurian Sea, by the Tuscans and Pisans in the Tyrrhenian Sea, and by the Pope over a part of the sea called *Mare Ecclesiæ*. Then the sovereignty claimed by the Spaniards and Portuguese, and the maritime dominion of the Danes and Norwegians, were notorious. Even the Poles and the Turks possessed sovereignty in the Baltic and the Black Sea respectively.

How then could it be denied, with all these examples, ancient and modern, that the sea could not be appropriated? Selden indeed agreed with Grotius in repudiating the sovereignty claimed by Spain and Portugal in the great oceans,—not, however, because it was opposed to reason and nature, but because it was founded on no legitimate title, and these nations had not a sufficient naval force to assert and maintain it.[2]

As to the free use of the sea, Selden admits that to prohibit innocent navigation would be contrary to the dictates of humanity;[3] but he held that the permitting of such innocent navigation does not derogate from the dominion

[1] Besides the Romans and the Carthaginians, he mentions as among these the Cretans, Lydians, Thracians, Phœnicians, Egyptians, Lacedemonians, and a great many more; but in most cases the evidence adduced shows merely that naval power was exercised.

[2] Lib. i. cap. xvii.

[3] Lib. i. cap. xx. "Quod ad genus primum attinet (commerce, travelling, navigation); humanitatis quidem officia exigunt, ut hospitio excipiantur peregrini etiam ut innoxius non negetur transitus."

of the sea—it is comparable to the free passage on a road across another's land—and it cannot always be claimed as a right. With respect to the argument that the sea cannot be appropriated because of its physical properties, he points to the example of rivers and springs, which even by Roman law may be appropriated, as well as of lakes. It is not true that the sea has no banks or limits: it is clearly bounded by the shores; some seas, as the Caspian, are completely enclosed, and the Mediterranean is so everywhere except at the Straits of Gibraltar. Elsewhere there are islands, rocks, promontories, by which boundaries may be determined; and limits may be set in the open sea by nautical science, as in the fixing of latitude and longitude; and that was shown by the Bull of Pope Alexander VI., and the hundred-mile limit of the Italians. Selden denies that the sea is inexhaustible from promiscuous use. On the contrary he says a sea may be made worse for him that owns it by reason of other men's fishing, navigation, and commerce, and less profit accrue from it, as where pearls, corals, and other things of that kind are produced. In such cases the abundance may be diminished by promiscuous use just as readily as in the case of metals and suchlike on land; and the same argument applies to all kinds of fishing.[1]

It was, however, the second book of *Mare Clausum* which gave it its chief political importance. It was appropriate and necessary that the claims of Charles should be justified in the domain of law and custom; it was still more necessary that they should be supported by weighty precedents existing in the history of England—that some of his predecessors had been styled Lords of the Sea, and had exercised sovereign jurisdiction over foreigners even on their own coasts. After partially defining the British seas (see p. 19), Selden, as mentioned in a former chapter,

[1] Lib. i. cap. xxii. "Sed vero ex aliorum piscatione, navigatione, commerciis ipsum mare deterius Domino cæterisque ejus jure gaudentibus fieri non raro videmus. Scilicet minui, quod alias inde percipi posset, commodum. Quod manifestius cernitur in marium usu, quorum fructus sunt uniones, corallium, id genus cætera. Etiam minuitur in horas marium hujusmodi abundantia, non aliter ac sive metalli fodinarum ac lapicidinarum, sive hortorum, quando fructus eorum auferuntur. . . . Et similis sane ratio qualiscunque piscationis."

labours to show that maritime sovereignty had been continuously exercised within them by the ancient Britons, the Romans, and the Anglo-Saxons in succession, and then by the Norman and later kings. He strove to prove by a multitude of citations from records that the kings of England had perpetually enjoyed exclusive dominion and jurisdiction in the surrounding seas as part of their territory, and were hence styled Lords of the Sea; that they had always preserved the right to forbid fishing and even navigation by foreigners within the British seas, or to exact tribute for that liberty; that the rights of the crown in the seas, asserted both by kings and Parliaments, were in conformity with the common law of England, and had been in several important respects acknowledged by other nations. A great deal of the evidence adduced is, as has been said, irrelevant. The long recital of facts connected with the guarding of the sea, the disposition of fleets, the office and jurisdiction of the admirals, the raising of special taxes—as the Danegeld—for defensive purposes or the equipment of ships of war, might have been paralleled in the records of other maritime states, as France or Flanders.

The maritime sovereignty claimed by Selden for the kings of England was of the most absolute kind. Speaking particularly of the eastern and southern parts of the English sea, lying between England and the shores of France and Germany,—in which Charles was especially interested,—he declared that the powers exercised by the kings of England from the time of the Norman Conquest were as follows: (1) the custody, government, and admiralty, as if it were a territory or province of the king; (2) leave of passage granted to foreigners at their request; (3) liberty of fishing in them conceded to foreigners, and protection afforded to their fishermen; (4) the prescribing of laws and limits to foreigners in hostility with one another as to the taking of prizes.[1] It is to be noted that Selden in expounding his case expressly rejected the principle of the mid-line, the limits laid down by the Italian writers, and those prescribed by King James in defining the King's Chambers; and he disclaimed the arguments used by the English commissioners at the Bremen Conference in 1602, as to the freedom of the seas, as being contrary to English

[1] Lib. ii. cap. xiii.

rights. He concludes his famous book in the following words: "It is certainly true, according to the mass of evidence set forth above, that the very shores or ports of the neighbouring sovereigns on the other side of the sea are the bounds of the maritime dominion of Britain, to the southwards and eastwards; but in the open and vast ocean to the north and west they are to be placed at the farthest extent of the most spacious seas which are possessed by the English, Scots, and Irish."

It may be added that *Mare Clausum* became in a sense a law-book, an authoritative work to which eminent lawyers, as Lord Chief-Justice Hale and Hargrave, appealed as proving the existence and the legality of the rights of the crown of England to the dominion of the British seas. Even as late as the year 1830 this doctrine held its place in certain recognised treatises on the law of England, together with Selden's definition of the extent of those seas. (See p. 580.)

As was natural, the appearance of Selden's book created anxiety in Holland. Its very title was a challenge to the much-cherished principles in *Mare Liberum*, and the circumstances connected with its birth heightened its political importance. It was felt to be almost equivalent to a declaration of the king himself. The simultaneous measures for the formation of an English fleet of unexampled strength made the Dutch fear for even more than their herring fishery. Their interest in the book was shown by the fact that within a year of its publication no less than three editions were brought out in Holland.[1] It was promptly brought before the States of Holland, on 11th December 1635, and remitted

[1] (1) *Ioannis Seldeni Mare Clavsvm sev de Dominio Maris Libris Dvo. Quorum argumentum paginâ versâ.* Juxta exemplar Londinense. Will. Stanesbeii pro Richardo Meighen, CIↃ IↃc xxxvi. (12°); (2) with the same title and the following addition: *Accedunt Marci Zverii Boxhornii Apologia pro navigationibus Hollandorum adversus Pontvm Hevtervm et Tractatvs Mvtvi commercii et navigationis inter Henricvm VII. Regem Angliæ et Philippvm Archidvcem Austriæ.* Londini, juxta exemplar Will. Stanesbeii pro Richardo Meighen, MDCxxxvi. (8°); (3) with the title as in the original London edition, and Lvgdvni Batavorvm apud Joannem et Theodorvm Maire, 1636 (4°). The original London edition was a small folio. In all the Dutch editions the plates are badly copied. No. 1 is sometimes referred to by English writers as the original edition. No. 2 is the one alluded to by Charles in his proclamation of 15th April 1636.

to one Professor Petrus Cunæus for examination and report.[1] His report was read on 31st March 1636, and the States of Holland, after hearing it, resolved to look upon *Mare Clausum* merely as the work of a private person, which did not require any special procedure on their part.[2] The States-General, however, took another view of the book, and decided that it should be formally refuted, since they had learned that King Charles would attempt to establish his pretended rights over the so-called four seas by arguments borrowed from *Mare Clausum*. No doubt at this juncture the thoughts of men in Holland were turned towards Grotius, the one above all others most worthy of the task of refuting Selden. But Grotius was then the Swedish ambassador in France, and did not wish to offend his royal mistress by publicly opposing claims not dissimilar to those she herself made in the Baltic.[3] If we can trust Sir Kenelm Digby, Grotius was even pleased to see his works refuted. In a letter from Paris about Selden's book, which was "much esteemed" there, Digby said Selden was not to expect a reply from Grotius, "who wrote, he says, as a Hollander, and is exceeding glad to see the contrary proved."[4]

The official refutation of *Mare Clausum* was, by a resolution of the States-General on 28th April 1636, entrusted to a lawyer of Delft, called Dirck Graswinckel, who does not appear to have been very well fitted for so onerous a duty. His treatise in reply to Selden was not submitted to the States-General until 13th April in the following year, and by that time much had happened to alter the political complexion of affairs. The States-General had then reason to believe that the campaign which Charles had been carrying on against the Dutch herring-busses would be suspended (p. 315), and probably never resumed; and after remitting Graswinckel's work to a committee, it was finally set aside and was never published,

1 *Resol. Holl.*, $\frac{11}{21}$ Dec. 1635. Quoted by Arendt, *Algemeene Geschiedenis des Vaderlands*, iii., stuck 5, p. 8.

2 *Resol. Holl.*, $\frac{\text{31 March}}{\text{10 April}}$ 1636. Muller, *Mare Clausum*, 283.

3 "Ego, cum Suecia," he wrote to his brother on January 14, 1636, "multum teneat oræ maritimæ, quid aliud præstare possum quam silentium?" Grotii, *Epistolæ*, 864.

4 Digby to Lord Conway, January $\frac{21}{31}$, 1636. *State Papers, Dom.*, cccxliv. 58.

while the author was soothed by the substantial pension of 500 gulden a-year for his pains.[1]

But another Dutchman in this year assumed the task which Graswinckel had fruitlessly essayed. This was Pontanus, Professor of Philosophy and History in the College of Harderwyck in Guelderland, who also occupied the office of Historiographer to the King of Denmark. He had thus, like Grotius, to be cautious in his refutation of Selden's general arguments upon the appropriation and dominion of seas, because the claims of Denmark to such property and dominion were notorious. But he was free to contest the particular rights of England, which he did with zest. He subjected Selden's chapters, almost *seriatim*, to a rigorous criticism, beginning with the Romans and the Anglo-Saxons. He made the most of the declarations of Elizabeth as to the freedom of the seas for navigation and fishing, and of her State Paper of 1602 (see p. 110); and he dealt specially with the sovereignty over the northern seas—the *Mare Caledonium* and those flowing between the Scandinavian countries and Iceland and Greenland —which he asserted were not, and never had been, under the dominion of England, but always appertained to the Scandinavian nations. Pontanus entered very fully into the negotiations which had taken place between England and Scotland on the one hand, and Norway and Denmark on the other, concerning those seas and the rights of navigating and fishing at Iceland and Greenland—subjects on which, from his official position, he had special knowledge.[2] In the same year another author, and he a Frenchman, entered the field in defence of the appropriation and dominion of seas,[3] while a somewhat virulent

[1] The treatise was entitled, *Th. Graswinckelii, Jurisc. Delph. Maris Liberi Vindiciæ adv. virum clarissimum Johannem Seldenum.* Arendt, *loc. cit.;* Muller, *loc. cit.* Goffe, writing from Holland to Archbishop Laud on 2nd February 1637, stated that the book in answer to Selden's *Mare Clausum* was "ready to come forth, and the author is neither so modest nor discreet that the Elector should trust him with any written assurance in that kind,"—that Charles would not interrupt the Dutch fishery that year (*State Papers, Dom.*, cccxlvi. 23). We shall again find Graswinckel in the thick of the controversy during the first Dutch war, p. 411.

[2] *Joh. Isacii Pontani Discvssionvm Historicarvm Libri Duo, quibus præcipuè quatenus et quodnam mare liberum vel non liberum clausumque accipiendum dispicitur expenditurque, &c.*, Harderwick, 1637.

[3] *Jacobi Gothofredi. De Imperio Maris*, in Hagemeier, *De Imperio Maris Variorum Dissertationes.*

controversy broke out between Poland and Denmark as to the sovereignty of the Baltic Sea, which was claimed by each, as it had been shortly before by Sweden, and formed, indeed, one of the causes of the war by Gustavus Adolphus against Germany.[1]

The juridical controversies respecting the appropriation and dominion of the seas continued throughout the whole of the seventeenth century and well on into the next, and so far as this country was concerned, they were particularly vehement during the first and the third Dutch wars.

[1] *Mare Balticum* (anon.), 1638; *Ante-Mare Balticum, scilicet, an ad Reges Daniæ, an ad Reges Poloniæ, pertineat* (anon.), 1639; Azuni, *Systema dei Principii del Diritto Maritimo.*

CHAPTER X.

THE PARLIAMENT, THE COMMONWEALTH, AND THE PROTECTORATE.

THE FIRST DUTCH WAR.

On the 3rd November 1640 the Long Parliament commenced its sittings at Westminster, and within two years thereafter — on 22nd August 1642 — Charles raised the royal standard at Nottingham, and initiated the great Civil War. During the period of strife little was heard of the claim to the sovereignty of the sea, although the Parliament continued to issue the usual instructions to the naval commanders to compel homage to the flag. But under the Commonwealth and Protectorate the English pretensions were carried to as high a pitch as ever they were under the Stuarts. The stern men who then guided the destinies of England were as jealous of the symbols of the nation's greatness as had been the vacillating king they destroyed. In particular, the salutation of the flag was enforced with great vigour. A dispute on the point between Tromp and Blake occasioned the first Dutch war, and the result proved to the world that after all England possessed the actual dominion of the sea by reason of her naval power. In the negotiations with the Dutch which preceded the treaty of peace, we shall find that Cromwell put in the forefront of his conditions the recognition of England's right to the herring fishery, and to the striking of the flag within the British seas.

At first, as might have been expected from the actions of the king with regard to the ship-money collections, little sympathy was shown by the Parliament for the claim to the sovereignty of the sea. The necessity of maintaining that sovereignty had always been put forward as a principal argument for levying the money, and on that ground it was objectionable to many of those opposed to the king. In a work said to have been presented to the Parliament at its first meeting, forcible opinions were expressed against the pretension. It was doubtful, it was said, whether the sea really belonged to the crown, as the king claimed. Even if it did, it was not apparent that the fate of the land depended upon the dominion of the sea. That dominion might be considered as a right, an honour, or a profit. As a right it was a theme "fitter for scholars to fret their wits upon than for Christians to fight and spill blood about"; as an honour, by making others strike sails to our ships as they passed, it was "a glory fitter for women and children to wonder at than for statesmen to contend about"; as a matter of profit, to fence and enclose the sea, it was of moment, but not more to us than to other nations: by too insolent contentions about it we might provoke God and dishonour ourselves, and rather incense our friends than quell our enemies.[1] If such sentiments reflected the feeling of the Parliament at the beginning of their labours, they were not of long duration. Within a few years a change was wrought, which was probably in large measure due to the part taken by the fleet in the struggle with the king, as well as to the abiding spirit of the people for predominant power on the sea.

From an early stage in the conflict the control of the fleet passed into the hands of the Parliament. In the summer of 1642, when the Earl of Northumberland, the Lord High Admiral, was laid aside by illness, the Parliament succeeded, with his connivance and assistance, in placing the Earl of Warwick in actual command; Sir John Pennington, the nominee of Charles, having to stand aside.[2] Under the management of its new masters the navy rapidly became a powerful and efficient instrument for the defence of the

[1] The Case of Ship-Money briefly discussed, according to the Grounds of Law, Policy, and Conscience. Presented to the Parliament, November 3, 1640. Stubbe, *A Further Justification of the Present War against the United Netherlands*, 76.

[2] Gardiner, *Hist. Engl.*, x. 208. Clarendon, iii. 113.

realm, as was shown at the opening of the Dutch war. The general instructions given by the Parliament to its naval officers respecting the honour of the flag and the sovereignty of the sea were almost identical with those which had been issued to the Earls of Lindsey and Northumberland, but the phraseology was sometimes a little varied. On 5th April 1643 the Parliament, in view of the attempt organised by Queen Henrietta Maria to smuggle into England military supplies from the Netherlands for the use of the royalists, ordered the Earl of Warwick, if he met with "any foreign forces, ships, or vessels, as Spaniards, French, Danes, Dunkirkers, or any other whatsoever, making towards the coasts of England, Ireland, or any other of his Majesty's dominions," to command them, "according to the usual manner, to strike their flags or top-sails," and cause them to be examined and searched for soldiers or munitions of war. If they refused to strike, he was "to compel them thereunto by force of arms and surprise, and to take all such ships and vessels, or otherwise to burn, sink, or destroy them."[1] In the following year the Committee for the Admiralty instructed Vice-Admiral Batten, who was in command of the fleet, "upon all occasions, as you shall be able, to maintain *the Kingdom's* sovereignty and regality in the seas."[2]

In the spring of 1647, the Committee of the Admiralty, for some reason or other, appears to have devoted special attention to the question of the flag and the sovereignty of the sea. Collections were made from the Admiralty archives of precedents showing that all ships refusing to strike in English waters were to be reputed enemies, and were liable to forfeiture,—the examples beginning with the Ordinance of King John and ending with the instructions issued by Charles.[3] These collections were probably made in connection with the instructions which the Committee drew up at this time for the guidance of the captains and officers of the navy, and which were essentially similar to those given

[1] Rushworth, *Collections*, v. 312.

[2] Penn, *Memorials of the Professional Life and Times of Sir William Penn, Knt., from* 1640 *to* 1670, i. 224.

[3] *State Papers, Dom.*, dxv. i. 37, 38, 39. There is also in one of the collections a quotation from Selden's *Mare Clausum*, that it was treason not to acknowledge the King of England's dominion in his own seas by striking sails.

by Charles to his ship-money fleets. "It must be your principal care," they ran, "to preserve the honour of this kingdom, and the coasts, jurisdictions, territories, and subjects thereof, being in amity with the Parliament, and within the extent of your employment, as much as in you lieth; that no nation or people whatsoever intrude thereon or injure any of them. And if you chance to meet in any of the seas that are under the jurisdiction of England, Scotland, and Ireland, with any ships or fleets belonging to any foreign prince or state, you must expect that they, in acknowledgment of this kingdom's sovereignty there, shall perform their duty and homage in passing by, in striking their top-sails and taking in their flags." If they refused they were to be forced to do so in the usual way. It will be noticed that the region within which foreigners were to be compelled to strike was greatly extended by the Parliament. Up to and including the reign of James the "acknowledgment" was confined to the narrow seas, in which it had been exacted for centuries; Charles in 1635 ordered Lindsey to compel it "in his Majesty's seas," and now the Parliament extended it specifically to all the seas under the jurisdiction of England, Scotland, and Ireland. From a clause in the instructions it is clear that the seas over which the Parliament claimed sovereignty reached to the coasts of the Continent; but a territorial limit was excepted on foreign coasts. The clause in question enjoined the naval officers "to be very careful not to meddle with any ships within the harbours, or ports, or under the command of any of the castles of any foreign prince or state, or within any buoys (Buoyes) or rivers, that they may have no just cause of offence." Another feature of these instructions is of interest. The clause which was inserted in the instructions to Lindsey and Northumberland in 1635, 1636, and 1637, commanding them to prevent all hostilities between men-of-war or merchant vessels in the presence of the king's ships, was repeated.[1]

[1] Instructions given by the Committee of Lords and Commons for the Admiralty and Cinque Ports, to be observed by all captains, officers, and common men respectively in this fleet, provided to the glory of God, the honour and service of the Parliament, and the safety of the three Kingdoms, March 30, 1647. *Ibid.*, dxv. 40.

The Parliament clearly intended to abate no jot of the pretensions which had been put forward by the king.

An opportunity soon came for putting the instructions regarding the flag into force. In May of the same year a Swedish fleet of fifteen sail, consisting of ten merchantmen bound for the Mediterranean and five ships of war convoying them, was met by Captain Owen in the *Henrietta Maria* off the Isle of Wight. On being called upon to strike, the Swedes refused, declaring that they had been commanded by the Queen of Sweden "not to strike to any whatsoever." Owen, reinforced by Batten, thereupon attacked them, the fight continuing till night. The Swedes suffered much loss; the colours of their vice-admiral and rear-admiral were shot away, a "great breach" was made in the vice-admiral's ship, and their vessels were captured and taken into Portsmouth. They were afterwards released, but the Admiralty Committee expressed the opinion that the proceedings of their officers "in order to the maintenance of the kingdom's sovereignty at sea" were to be commended, and this resolution was reported to both Houses of Parliament.[1] The question of the salute between ships of war of different nations had been brought to the front in most other maritime countries by the forcible measures taken by Charles in 1633 and later. Two years before the encounter with the Swedes in the Channel, Denmark and Sweden had regulated the ceremony, as affecting their own ships of war, in the treaty of peace then concluded between them.[2]

From this time until shortly before the war with the Dutch there is little to record about the claims to the dominion of the sea. In 1649, the instructions issued to Popham, Blake, and Dean, the commanders of the fleet, included the guarding of the North Sea and the mackerel-fishing, as well as the maintenance "of the sovereignty of the Commonwealth in the sea," all in the prescribed form.[3] In the following year the Council of State issued express commands to Blake on the subject when he was ordered to proceed against Prince Rupert and the revolted ships at Lisbon. The dominion of "these seas," they said, had anciently and time out of mind belonged to the Eng-

[1] Rushworth's *Collections;* Penn, *op. cit.*, i. 242.

[2] Loccenius, *De Jure Maritimo*, x. s. 10.

[3] *State Papers, Dom.*, 27th Feb. 1649.

lish nation, and the ships of all other nations in acknowledgment of that dominion had been accustomed to take down their flags "upon sight" of the Admiral of England, and not to bear them in his presence. Blake was therefore, to the best of his powers, and "as he found himself and the fleet of strength and ability," to do his utmost endeavours to preserve the dominion of the sea, and to cause the ships of all other nations to strike their flags and keep them in in his presence, and to compel such as were refractory, by seizing their ships and sending them into port, to be punished according to the "laws of the sea," unless they submitted and made such reparation as he required. At the same time, although the dominion of the sea was so ancient and indubitable, and it concerned the honour and reputation of the nation to uphold it, Blake was not to imperil his fleet over it in the expedition on which he was employed. If he was opposed in the question of the flag by a force so consider able as to prove dangerous, he was not to press it, but to note who they were that refused, so that they might be forced to strike at some better opportunity.[1]

Such were the instructions of the Government to the English naval commanders, and they were soon to bear bitter fruit. At this period the Dutch men-of-war apparently did not show unwillingness to salute the English flag, even sometimes in distant seas. Penn notes in his journal, on 13th September 1651, that on meeting with the Dutch Admiral with his vice- and rear-admirals between Cape Trafalgar and Cape Sprat, they struck their flags to him and saluted; but they then hoisted them, which would have been contrary to the custom in the narrow sea, and Penn thereupon called his captains together for advice, but they said the Dutch "had done enough." A little later he records that young Tromp, convoying thirteen merchantmen, came into Gibraltar Road, where Penn was lying, with his flag in the main-top. The English Admiral, however, did nothing, since Tromp was in a port of the King of Spain. Shortly afterwards in the same place eight sail of Hollanders, four of which were men-of-war, all struck their flags and saluted the English fleet.[2]

The claims of England to the sovereignty of the seas were

[1] 17th January 1650. *A Collection of the State Papers of John Thurloe*, i. 134.

[2] Penn, *Memorials*, i. 365, 379.

now about to enter on a new phase, which culminated in the first Dutch war. So long as the ambitious and energetic Prince William II. of Orange was alive, the relations between the United Provinces and the Parliament were strained and menacing. The States-General, under Orange influence, refused to enter into diplomatic communication with the English Government, or to admit their ambassador, Strickland, to audience. The execution of Charles I. had raised strong feelings of reprobation and horror in the Netherlands, even amongst the Hollanders and Zealanders, who sympathised with the Puritans; and it was believed in England that the Prince of Orange was contemplating war against them for the restoration of his brother-in-law, Charles II., to the throne. The death of the Prince, on 27th October 1650, produced a great change. It was followed by a political revolution in the United Provinces, the chief outcome of which was the predominance of the States of Holland and of the party opposed to the Orange faction, and most favourably inclined to maintain good relations with the English Commonwealth.[1] It was therefore agreed at The Hague to send back Joachimi, who had been dismissed by the Parliament in the previous year, with credentials as ambassador from the States-General to the Parliament.

In London the accession to power of the republican party in the Netherlands had been watched with keen interest. The time, it was believed, was come for a close alliance between the two great Protestant Republics for safeguarding their religious and political liberties; perhaps, it was thought by some, for even a closer union than was implied in the strictest alliance known to diplomacy. The Parliament accordingly lost no time in opening negotiations with the States-General. On 17th March, 1651, Lord Chief-Justice St John and Walter Strickland entered The Hague with great pomp and splendour as ambassadors from the Commonwealth, attended by an imposing retinue of 246 persons. They were greeted in the street with insulting cries from Orange partisans and royalist refugees. On the following days their suite only ventured abroad in parties, and with their rapiers in their hands. The

[1] Geddes, *History of the Administration of John de Witt*, i. 102, 106, 150-157. Gardiner, *History of the Commonwealth and Protectorate*, i. 353, 356.

ambassadors themselves were openly jeered at, and threatened by Prince Edward, son of Elizabeth, Queen of Bohemia; and though the States-General received them with ostentatious courtesy, and prompt measures were taken to suppress the disorders and insults, the conditions of their surroundings produced irritation and impatience in their minds, with important results in the sequel.[1] The principal object of the Parliament was to make use of the Dutch Republic to help them to maintain the Commonwealth, and to resist any attempt to place Charles II. on the throne. In return they were willing to aid the Republic against the House of Orange or any other inclined to disturb it.

St John had with him two series of propositions,—one relating to a strict alliance and union; the other, private and never fully disclosed, included a novel scheme for the coalescence and fusion of the two states and peoples, on the lines propounded by the Council of State in the following year. He brought out his propositions one by one, requiring categorical acceptance of each before dealing with the next, the design being to lead step by step to the proposals for coalescence and fusion. His first proposition was in substance for "a more strict and intimate alliance and union" than any before, by which there might be "a more intrinsical and mutual interest of each in other" for the good of both.[2] After some fencing and much hesitation and delay—the Dutch proferring a qualified acceptance, which the ambassadors rejected—a guarded assent was

1 Geddes, *op. cit.*, 157, 159, 165. Gardiner, *op. cit.*, 359. *The Nicholas Papers*, i. 230.

2 "Wee doe tender the ffriendshipp of the Cofïonwealth of England unto the High and Mighty Lords the States Generall of the Vnited Provinces, and doe propound that the Amitye, and good Correspondency which hath aunciently beene betweene the English Nation and the Vnited Provinces, be not only renewed, and preserved inviolably, But that a more strict, and intimate Allyance, and Vnion, be entred into by them, whereby there may be a more intrinsicall, and mutuall interest of each in other then hath hitherto beene for the good of both." Submitted $\frac{\text{25 March}}{\text{6 April}}$. "A briefe Narrative of the Treatie at the Hague betweene the honoble Oliver St John, Lord Chiefe Justice of the Court of Cofïon Pleas, and Walter Strickland, Esq., Embassadors extraordinary of the Parliament of the Cofïonwealth of England, to the great Assembly of the States Generall of the Vnited Provinces begun upon the 20th of March 1651 and continued vntill the 20th of June 1651 and then broke of *re infectâ.*" *State Papers, Foreign, Treaty Papers* (*Holland*), No. 46, 1651.

given. St John, though not satisfied, thinking the "manner of penning the answer was dark and doubtful," "determined to proceed into some further thing which might come nearer to make a discovery of their temper and inclination in point of their neutrality, than stay any longer upon general terms," and he accordingly at the same meeting submitted another proposition requiring the confederation of the two states for the defence and preservation of the freedom and liberty of the people of each against all that might attempt to disturb them, or that were declared to be enemies to the freedom and liberty of the people living under either Government.[1] The Dutch commissioners, however, declared that this was a general proposition, and they insisted on a request they had made from the first, to be furnished with the "particulars"—they wanted the particulars, *simul et semel*, that were intended to be insisted upon.

The negotiations had been protracted. By this time a month had elapsed since the ambassadors arrived, and St John, now conscious that his mission for coalescence would fail, and irritated by the indignities to which he had been subjected, obtained an order from the Parliament for his recall. At the urgent entreaty of the States of Holland the Parliament allowed their ambassadors to stay for other forty days, and also gave them authority to treat on the basis of the old Intercursus Magnus of 1496, which the Dutch had suddenly proposed. The States, in truth, had totally different aims from the Commonwealth. They were thinking about their commerce, their navigation, and their fisheries, rather than about the repression of "rebels"; and they desired that their alliance with England should confirm and extend the benefits conferred upon them in these respects by the old treaty. The Intercursus Magnus had for generations been the sheet-anchor of Dutch policy towards England. It gave them the utmost freedom of commercial intercourse, and complete liberty of

[1] "We propound, That the two Coñonwealths may be confederated friends, ioyned, and allyed togeather for the defence and Preservation of the Libertyes, and ffredomes of the people of each, against all whomsoever that shall attempt the disturbance of either State, by Sea or Land, or be declared enemyes to the freedome and Libertie of the people liveing under either of the said Governments." Submitted, 17th April. *Ibid.*, p. 7.

fishing on the English coasts. But it contained other clauses appropriate in spirit to the political conditions of 1651. The treaty had been concluded by Henry VII. in the year in which apprehensions were entertained that Perkin Warbeck would effect a landing in England; it provided for mutual military aid against the enemies of either country, and the expulsion of rebels and fugitives from the territories of the other. St John naturally took the clauses embodying these stipulations as the basis of his new draft articles, which he submitted to the Dutch commissioners on 10th May. They were seven in number. The first required that the proposition made on 17th April for mutual defence of the freedom and liberty of each people should be an article of the treaty. The second provided that neither party should afford any aid or favour to any one whomsoever to the injury or prejudice of the other, but should expressly oppose "and really hinder all whomsoever," abiding in either commonwealth or under its power, that should do or attempt anything against the other; and the remaining articles were of similar tenour, relating to "rebels" and enemies. They were, in short, political articles of the most comprehensive scope, aimed against the royalists; so comprehensive and thorough that the English Commonwealth might, by declaring the Prince of Orange himself its enemy, demand his expulsion from the Provinces.[1] St John's articles were by no means to the liking of the Dutch; and though he pointed out that they were "but a translation of the old treaty, only enlarged for the better assurance of performance,"—the treaty which they themselves had proposed as the basis for the new one,—they insisted on sending the articles to the various Provinces for their opinion. For a full month the English ambassadors waited without an answer to their articles—a delay which they believed was meant "to spin out the treaty until the Scotch mist was over" and the result of the struggle in Scotland apparent. But the Dutch, though slow, had not been idle. On 14th June, when

[1] *Narrative of the Ambassadors* (ibid.) Geddes, *op. cit.*, 157, 159, 165, 171. Gardiner, *op. cit.*, 359, 362, 363. Tideman, *De Zee Betwist: Geschiedenis der Onderhandelingen over de Zeeheerschappij tusschen de Engelsche Republiek en de Vereenigde Provinciën vóór den ersten Zee-Oorlog*, 39-47. Thurloe's *Collections*, i. 176, 179, 181-186, 188, 193. Aitzema, *Saken van Staet en Oorlogh*, 657-660.

only four of the forty days allotted by the Parliament remained, the Dutch produced counter-proposals in the form of draft articles, thirty-six in number, which were paraphrased from the Intercursus Magnus, the treaty with King James VI. of Scotland in 1594, the treaty of Southampton with Charles in 1625, and the marine treaty with Spain in 1650.

These articles had been submitted by Holland to the convocation of the States-General on 15th May, and were under the consideration of the provincial states for nearly a month. They provided for a "perpetual friendship, unity, correspondence, and a further and nearer alliance, confederation, and union" against all who should attempt anything derogatory to the liberties of the two peoples, their commerce, and common interests; mutual defence and mutual assistance with men and ships against "notorious or known" enemies of the other, and the prohibition of assisting rebels. But there was no article under which the royalists could be expelled from the United Provinces, or which prevented the House of Orange from aiding or harbouring declared rebels of England; and it was expressly stipulated that the States should in no way be drawn into the disputes and war between Scotland and the Parliament. Having thus whittled down the proposals of the Parliament for a close alliance directed against the royalists, the Dutch propounded a whole series of articles providing for the freest commercial intercourse between the two countries, for freedom of navigation and of fishing. The trade to Virginia and the Caribbean Islands, which had been closed by the Parliament, was to be thrown open to both nations; ships were to be free to anchor without seizure of goods; the subjects of one state were not to be taxed higher in the territories of the other than the natives, and they were to be free to carry on their business or profession with the same liberty. A number of articles dealt with questions relative to the sovereignty of the seas, in such a way as to show clearly that the design of the Dutch was to render harmless a pretension which had caused them so much trouble. They had not forgotten the declarations of Charles sixteen years before, or the forceful operations of Northumberland against their herring-busses. With regard to fishing, they wished the subjects of either state to be at liberty to go to any part of the sea to fish for herrings and all other kinds of fish, great or small, without any license or pass being required. If the fishermen were forced by storms, pirates, enemies, or any other cause, to go to land, they desired that they should be courteously received and well treated in the ports of either country, and permitted to depart with their ships and cargoes, and if they had not broken their cargoes, without paying any customs or dues.[1] These stipulations paraphrased corresponding provisions in the Intercursus Magnus, and rather more favourably to the Dutch. If they had been accepted, they would have destroyed the English policy which had been pursued, though fitfully, from 1609 to the outbreak of the Civil War, of requiring foreigners to pay tribute and take out licenses for fishing on the British coasts.

Some of the other articles proposed by the Dutch were directed against the claims put forward in Selden's *Mare Clausum*, and by Charles himself, to a special dominion and jurisdiction of England in the surrounding seas. If the freedom of commerce and navigation was to be assured, it would be necessary, it was said, for both countries to equip fleets to secure the safety and liberty of the subjects of both, to purge the sea of pirates and sea-rovers, and to preserve the security of commerce and of fishing. The proposition was that each state should set forth a fleet yearly, its strength to be fixed by mutual agreement, and the ocean as well as the North Sea and the Mediterranean, with their straits and channels, were to be patrolled by the two fleets, each under its own admiral and flag. This was in effect asking the Commonwealth not only for equality of sovereignty on the sea, but for the assistance of England in protecting the immense commerce and shipping of the United Provinces. They desired that each nation should shield and defend the merchant vessels of the other, and help to recover them if taken by an enemy.

Among other proposals were that men-of-war, but only in small numbers, should be allowed freely into the ports and havens of the other, and were not to be subjected to visitation and search, the showing of the commission to be sufficient; and that no sea-rovers were to be tolerated in harbours, and no

[1] See Appendix K. *Narrative of the Ambassadors*, p. 23. Aitzema, *op. cit.*, iii. 698-700. MS. of Duke of Portland in *Hist. MSS. Com. Thirteenth Report, App. I.*, 605. Tideman, *op. cit.*, 47, 48, 49. Geddes *op. cit.* 178.

ships with letters of marque allowed to leave without first providing security that they would not exceed their commissions. One of the provisions went much further, and seems to smack of Dutch humour, when we think of the action of James and Charles. For the sake of liberty, both peoples were to use their fleets, not only against pirates, but against all and sundry, whomsoever they might be, who should attempt to molest, hinder, or—"against the right of all peoples"—impose exactions on their commerce, navigation, or their fishery. In such an event, if amicable remonstrances failed, the whole sea forces of each nation were to attack the depredators and wage war against them until complete satisfaction had been obtained.[1]

So resolved were the Dutch to have a general clearing-up with England on all points concerning the sovereignty of the sea, that they at first proposed to insert among their draft articles one relating to the striking of the flag and similar ceremonies, which frequently gave rise to differences. The States-General, however, considered the matter "too delicate" to be raised at that time, and the article was not inserted.[2] Two or three months before this, as elsewhere mentioned (p. 398), the question of striking the flag to the English had been raised and debated in the States-General in connection with Tromp's expedition to the Scilly Islands.

With the foregoing proposals before him, it is not to be wondered at that St John was dissatisfied, and longed more than ever to get away from The Hague. The Commonwealth had asked for a strict and close alliance at the very least, for the security of religious and political liberty and the common interests of both Republics, but in reality and above all for aid against the royalists. The Dutch also desired security for liberty, but it was chiefly for the liberty of commerce, navigation, and fishing; and they were anxious, if they could, to get rid of the troublesome English pretension to a sovereignty of the sea. The proposals of the two sides were incompatible, and St John left The Hague a few days

[1] Articles 17-33, *Narrative of the Ambassadors*. These articles are given in Appendix K. Tideman, *op. cit.*, 50. Aitzema, *op. cit.*, iii. 695.

[2] "Over het strijken van vlaggen ende andere Ceremonieën daeruyt meenichmael differentien in zee coomen te ontstaen." *Resol. der Groote Vergadering*, $\frac{15}{25}$ May 1651. Tideman, *op. cit.*, 52.

later with the unuttered plan for the fusion of the nations in his pocket and with bitterness in his heart. His disappointment was to cost the Dutch dear. Within a few months of his return the Navigation Act was passed, mainly by his impulse, and it dealt a serious blow to the commerce of the United Provinces.[1] It was the retort of the English Commonwealth to the rebuff of the States. If the Dutch put their commerce and fisheries above everything else, the Parliament would show them how they could injure them and at the same time foster English shipping and fisheries.

But much more than the Navigation Act, some other proceedings of the Parliament increased the tension between the two countries. In November they renewed certain letters of reprisal against the Dutch, under which a few of their vessels were captured. More serious were the actions of English men of war and of some privateers who held letters of reprisal against the French. An informal maritime war with France began in 1649 and continued till 1655, and though there was nominally peace, the English captured French vessels, and *vice versâ.* They then began to seize Dutch ships, suspected of having French goods on board, and brought them into English ports for trial in the Admiralty Court. This was an interference with freedom of commerce which the States could not tolerate, and an embassy to England, which had been decided upon after St John left The Hague, was despatched thither.[2] The three ambassadors, Cats, Schaep, and van de Perre, arrived in London on 15th December 1651.

[1] St John and Strickland left The Hague on 20th June, and the Act was recommended to the Parliament by the Council of State on 5th August, and passed on 9th October (Gardiner, *op. cit.*, ii. 82). The essence of the Act was to prohibit the importation of extra-European commodities into any territory of the Commonwealth except in English vessels, or from Europe unless in English vessels or vessels belonging to the country in which the commodities were manufactured or produced. The importation of salt-fish or fish-oil, and the exportation of salted fish, were to be permitted only in English vessels, but the importation of fresh fish was not forbidden. Early in the next year two Dutch doggers, driven into Yarmouth by contrary winds, exposed their cod and haddocks for sale and were seized by the bailiffs; their release was ordered by the Council of State.

[2] Geddes, *op. cit.*, 192, 193. Tideman, *op. cit.*, 89, 96. Gardiner, *op. cit.*, ii. 108. Gardiner, *Letters and Papers relating to the First Dutch War*, 1653-1654, Navy Records Society. In the third volume (1906) of this valuable work the papers are brought down to 10th February 1653.

They were instructed to renew negotiations for a treaty on the basis of the thirty-six articles, to endeavour to get the Navigation Act repealed, the captured vessels released, and the letters of reprisal withdrawn, with compensation for the losses suffered by reason of them. The question of adding another article to their instructions, about the striking of the flag, which had been omitted from the thirty-six articles, had again been considered. But, for the same reason as before, it was withheld. "The carrying or striking of the flags by the one side or the other" was judged to be "very delicate"; and it was decided (on 10th November 1651) that the States-General should deliberate further on the matter, and send later to the ambassadors such instructions "as should be found suitable for the removal of misunderstandings and hostilities."[1] We thus see that in 1651 the Government of the United Provinces was fully alive to the risks and difficulties about the flag. But from their proceedings at this time it would seem that they were unwilling to acknowledge unreservedly the claim of the Commonwealth to the salute, which was looked upon as a symbol of England's sovereignty of the sea. The question was only rendered "delicate" because of certain qualifications and conditions of reciprocity which they desired to attach to it, and for which they struggled hard with Cromwell during the subsequent negotiations for peace.

The ambassadors had an audience with the Parliament on 19th December,—Cats treating the members to a long and flowery oration in Latin,—and with the Council of State on 1st January 1652; but it was not until the 16th that commissioners were appointed to deal with them. The English commissioners[2] showed no anxiety to facilitate the negotiations. The spirit with which they were animated was evident from their eagerness to bring forward all imaginable reasons for dispute,—the interest taken by the Dutch in the fate of Charles I.; the partiality of some of their ambassadors at foreign Courts; their refusal to receive Strickland; and so forth. In the end, the Dutch ambassadors failed to get what they wanted. The English refused to cancel or modify the Navigation Act, to release the captured ships before the cases

[1] Tideman, *op. cit.*, 96. Aitzema, *op. cit.*, iii. 696.

[2] They were Whitelocke, John Lisle, Bond, Scott, Viscount Lisle, and Purefoy.

had been tried in the Admiralty Court, or to make reparation. They suspended the letters of direct reprisal against the Dutch, but not those against the French, which were by far the more important.

It was felt in Holland that such interference with their trade could not be endured. There were loud complaints about the seizure of the ships, and the opinion was growing in the Netherlands that it was the intention of the Commonwealth to force a war upon them. As a precautionary measure the States-General decided on 22nd February to add 150 ships to the existing fleet, "for the security of the sea and the preservation of the shipping and commerce of the United Provinces"; and the ambassadors were requested to inform the English Council of their intention, which was done on 5th March, with the explanation that it was not with the object of doing the slightest harm to any nation, and least of all to England, that the increase in the fleet was to be made, but only to preserve their freedom of navigation.[1] As this extraordinary addition to the navy of the Dutch Republic would raise it to the formidable number of 226 ships, it is not surprising that the proceeding was viewed in England as a preparation for war. The Council, on their part, put forward a series of more or less provoking claims. They demanded reparation for wrongs and losses suffered by the English at the hands of the Dutch at "Greenland" in 1618, in the East Indies since 1619, and at Brazil; and they complained of various other wrongs and affronts they had suffered. But pending an answer from the States-General to their complaints and requests, they agreed, on 3rd May, to discuss with the ambassadors the thirty-six articles.

These articles had been previously considered by the Council of State, which had prepared a commentary on them; and now both documents were taken up together. On the proposals concerning the sovereignty of the sea many differences arose. With regard to the right of the English to visit and search vessels, men-of-war as well as merchantmen, the ambassadors referred to the edicts of the States forbidding warships to take merchandise on board, and to the certificates of their Admiralty to the same effect; but it was argued on the other side that

[1] Cats' *Verbael.* Tideman, 94-108. Geddes, 198.

these measures had not stopped the abuse, and that the visitation was not prejudicial; and no agreement on this clause was reached. The commentary of the Council on the fishery article (see p. 388) was that, saving and asserting the right of the Commonwealth, they would be willing to proceed to such an agreement as should be found fit and reasonable; while the Dutch took their stand on the provision in the Intercursus Magnus, and urged that it would be unjust to deviate from an agreement which had endured for a century and a half. It was admitted by the English commissioners that the treaty gave liberty of fishing, but they asserted that long before the time of Henry VII. the right to the fisheries and to the sovereignty of the sea belonged to England. It had, moreover, been impeached by succeeding kings and especially by James, to whom, as King of Scotland, the right to the fishery pertained; while after the union of the crowns he pursued the same policy as King of England, and now that Scotland had been brought under the dominion of the English Republic, it was thought that the best course was to make a new treaty about the fisheries.[1] The ambassadors could obtain no definite information as to the nature of the treaty proposed, but it would not be difficult for them to comprehend its general tenour, for they had to listen to the recital of the "evidences" that England had constantly made use of her rights in the fishery, and of the care she had always exercised as to the sovereignty of the sea. The Dutch endeavoured to avoid mixing up these two questions, pleading that the fishery concerned the lives of a multitude of poor fishermen; but the commissioners retorted that it was a very valuable industry, the right to which belonged to England, and this, they said, had been acknowledged by neighbouring nations paying taxes for liberty to fish in their seas, adding that all peoples had been accustomed to recognise in them the masters of the sea by striking the flag to them, and that the Dutch themselves had earlier instructed their naval officers to salute English ships "*cum debita reverentia,*" and it was also expressly ordered in the commissions issued by Prince William and Maurice. From

[1] The conferences on the articles were on 3rd, 5th, 6th, 10th, and 13th May. The incorporation and union of Scotland with England was proclaimed at Edinburgh on the 21st of the preceding month.

the language of the English commissioners, it appears probable that they were acquainted with the proceedings of the States-General as to the proposed article on the striking of the flag, and with the debates in the previous year concerning Tromp's instructions (see p. 398). The negotiations on the fishery question were not carried further at this stage.

With regard to the article relating to the equipment of a fleet by each nation for the protection of commerce, the commentary of the Council of State was that "the Commonwealth of England shall take such care for the guard of their seas and defence of the freedom of trade and commerce therein as shall be fit"; and with respect to the next, which stipulated that both countries should protect commerce and fisheries from molestation or impositions, the reply was equally uncompromising. "If any person," it was said, "shall, within those seas, trouble, hinder, or unlawfully burthen any in the exercise of that freedom of trade which belongs of right unto them, this Commonwealth will use all means just and honourable to restore and preserve freedom to all lawful commerce in those seas as aforesaid."[1] The meaning of this language was unmistakable. The Commonwealth intended to adhere to the old claim to the dominion of the seas, which had been revived by Charles. And this exclusive sovereign jurisdiction, it was explained, would be of advantage to the Dutch, since they would bear no part of the cost; they must be content with freedom of navigation and commerce, and leave to the English the duty of maintaining the security of "their seas." On inquiring what means the Commonwealth proposed to take for this purpose, the ambassadors were told that the intention of the Council was "to defend the sea in their own right," and that any further explanation would be given by the Council if they applied to it.

At this stage of the proceedings William Nieuport, a member of the States-General, came to London with fresh instructions for the ambassadors. That body had been considering the English demands for reparation, above alluded to, and also the commentary of the Council on the thirty-six articles; but the refusal to liberate the captured ships, or to stop the operations of privateers against Dutch vessels, made them obdurate. The

[1] Cats' *Verbael, App.*, 21. Tideman, *op. cit.*, 117.

ambassadors were now told to insist on the articles relating to visitation and search as an essential part of the treaty. No Dutch vessel was to be visited, whether it was on the sea, in harbour, or in a roadstead. The principle of "free ship, free goods," was to be strictly enforced, and no investigation of the cargo of a merchant vessel was to be permitted; still less should they agree to the visitation of a man-of-war. The ambassadors were specially requested to avoid discussion as to any claim on the part of England to exclusive right in any portion of the sea; in any case, they were not to admit that such right existed, but were to treat only about the liberty and security of the fishery on both sides.[1] If the English protested that they would not allow themselves to be prejudiced in any of their "pretended rights," the ambassadors were then to make a formal declaration that they, on their part, could not allow the freedom of navigation and of fishery, or the free use of the sea, to be called in question, nor could they recognise the special claims of any one over the sea which might prejudice those rights. In order to avoid, if possible, directly raising the question of the dominion of the sea, they were requested when dealing with the crucial articles to speak only of commerce and fishery, and not of the "purging" of the sea of pirates; and they were also to abandon the proposal for a division of the sea into districts.[2]

So passed, peacefully enough, the early weeks of May at the conferences in London. The States' ambassadors, on the one hand, demanding freedom of navigation and fishery; above all, that the visitation and seizure of their vessels should cease. The English commissioners, on their part, putting forward incompatible claims to the sovereignty of the British seas: the right of exclusive jurisdiction, of guardianship, the right to the fishery. Whether the negotiations would have reached a happy conclusion, as the ambassadors, and apparently also the States-General, believed they would, may only

1 "De dispuyte over 't recht hetwelck de Engelsche pretenderen privative over eenigh ghedeelte van de Zee te hebben, ende in allen ghevalle aan deselve geen soodanigh recht in eenigher wijse toe te staen, ende alleen te handelen over de vryheijdt ende seeckerheijdt van wederzijts visscherije." Tideman, *op. cit.*, 119. Aitzema, *op. cit.*, iii. 708.

2 Cats' *Verbael.* Tideman, 118.

be conjectured. For an event of momentous importance now occurred which swept their labours away and embroiled the two nations in war. On the 19th May, at the very moment when the Dutch ambassadors were conveying their new instructions to the English commissioners, Tromp and Blake were engaged in furious battle in the Straits of Dover about that very matter which the States-General had found to be "so delicate"—the striking of the flag. The long-impending struggle engendered by years of mutual jealousy and commercial rivalry had now come suddenly. The claim of England to the sovereignty of the sea was to be decided, in the words of Sir Philip Meadows, by a longer weapon than a pen.

Tromp had put to sea early in May, 1652, with a fleet of forty-two sail, and bearing instructions to prevent the searching of Dutch merchantmen, to protect them against any who interfered with them, and to free them, by force if necessary, if they were captured. He was further told to refrain as far as possible from going on the English coast.[1] On one important point his instructions were defective. He received no definite orders as to how he should act if the fleet of the Commonwealth called upon him to strike his flag. The subject of the salute had been much discussed in the Netherlands, and an opinion was widely held that while their ships would suffer no loss of dignity in striking to a fleet belonging to a crowned head, it was doubtful whether the same homage should be rendered to the ships of a republic like themselves. The question had been definitely raised and fully discussed early in the previous year in connection with Tromp's expedi-

[1] Aitzema, iii. 713. Tideman, 124, 130, 132. The draft instructions were dated $\frac{\text{April 30}}{\text{May 10}}$, and were approved on May $\frac{6}{16}$. A translation of the 7th Article is as follows: "The superior officers and captains either already in command of the aforesaid squadrons or hereafter appointed, are to be charged to free the ships of this country from all search by any one whatever, and to defend them against all who try to do them injury, and to release them to the uttermost of their power from every one who may have captured them, and further to do whatever their ordinary instructions in their commission requires in a sailor-like fashion for the service of the country." By the 5th Article, fifteen men-of-war were to be sent for the protection of the "great" (herring) fishery, "which is of so great importance to the State," along with the ordinary national convoy-ships, and the ships which the towns of Enkhuizen, Delft, Rotterdam, and Schiedam were accustomed to add. Gardiner, *Letters and Papers*, i. 155.

tion to the Scilly Isles, in view of the likelihood of his falling in with the English fleet,—its consideration, indeed, delayed his departure,—but the Government hesitated in coming to a decision, and a general wish was expressed to hear Tromp's own opinion first. He accordingly prepared a memorandum describing what the States' ships had done in the past. He said that whenever their men-of-war met at sea a ship of the King of England carrying the flag of an admiral, vice-admiral, or rear-admiral, they struck their admiral's flag, lowered top-sails, and fired nine, seven, or five guns, the English answering with a like number, and the States' flag remained struck until the ships separated, when three or one adieu-shots were fired, and the flag was then hoisted. On meeting a single king's ship, he said, they did not strike their flag, but only exchanged guns; but it sometimes happened that an English ship of little power tried to compel them to strike, out of pride ("uyt hooghmoet"), but when they fired back and showed their teeth, and the English ship found it had not power to force them, it went on its way with derision; in such cases striking was a matter of discretion. When they entered a harbour or came before a castle they fired a salute, which was returned; the flag was taken in and a pennant run up in its place, and kept flying so long as they were there, particularly if a king's ship, carrying the king's flag, was present. If no king's ship was present, the governor sometimes gave his permission, out of courtesy, for the admiral to wear his flag until his departure, when it was again struck and a salute exchanged.[1]

The substance of Tromp's report was communicated to the States of Holland by De Witt on $\frac{1st}{11th}$ March 1651, stress apparently being laid on the point that it had been the custom in

[1] Tromp's memorandum was dated $\frac{\text{28 Feb.}}{\text{9 March}}$ 1651. The original is apparently lost (Tideman, *De Zee Betwist*, 68); but an account of it is given by his contemporary, Aitzema (iii. 731), and is printed in Appendix L. Tromp, in his *Rescript* of $\frac{14}{24}$ October 1652, justifying and explaining his conduct with regard to the meeting with Blake, refers to a memorandum on the subject of the flag which he presented to a committee of the States on "Jan. $\frac{6}{16}$, $\frac{1650}{1651}$," and which they considered in arranging his instructions of "$\frac{\text{Feb. 21}}{\text{March 3}}$, $\frac{1650}{1651}$" (Gardiner, *Letters and Papers*, i. 422). The dates here are those given by Tideman.

earlier times for the States' ships, "particularly when they were weakest,"[1] to salute with guns and strike their flag on meeting the English fleet.[2] The Government, however, thought that the conditions had changed; but they failed to give the admiral definite directions one way or the other as to how he should act if he met the fleet of the Parliament. He was merely told in general terms that he must so manage matters, if he met with the English fleet, that the state should suffer no affront ("geen cleynicheyt"),—a decision which left everything to his own discretion. There was the more risk in this course as the English at this time were said to be jealous of Tromp, owing to his reluctance to strike his flag to them.[3]

Later in the same year, the question was again raised by Vice-Admiral Jan Evertsen, who was placed in command of a squadron to cruise between Cape Ortegal, the Scillies, and Ushant. Before his departure he endeavoured to obtain precise orders as to how he should comport himself if called upon to strike, so that no "inconvenience" might be caused. The States thereupon merely renewed the instructions they had given to Tromp in March, and they ordered that copies of Tromp's memorandum should be distributed to the other commanders.[4]

No further directions on the matter were given to Tromp when he took command of the fleet in 1652, though it ought to have been evident to the States that in the delicate position of affairs with England, and from the nature of the duties they had laid upon their admiral, the risk of misunderstanding and collision with the English fleet was great and imminent. They hesitated to give decided orders to strike, apparently lest such action might be construed into an acknowledgment of the inferiority of the Dutch Republic to the English Commonwealth, especially at a time when they believed themselves to be superior to it in naval power;[5] and though alive to the importance of the matter, they were very reluctant to

[1] "Sonderlinge de swackste sijnde."

[2] Tideman, *op. cit.*, 68. *Resol. Holl.*, $\frac{1}{11}$ March 1651.

[3] *Hollantsche Mercurius*, April 1651, p. 49: "Seer jalours, omdat hij niet terstond gereedt was voor haar te strijcken."

[4] *Resol. St. Gen.*, $\frac{7}{17}$, $\frac{12}{22}$ Oct. 1651. Aitzema, iii. 731. Tideman, 68, 92.

[5] *Add. MSS. Brit. Mus.*, 11,684, fol. 30.

have it discussed in the negotiations in London. But if the Dutch had no clear idea as to what they were to do about the flag on meeting the English fleet, the English commanders had no doubt about their own line of action. Their instructions were explicit. They were, by force if necessary, to compel the ships of all nations to this acknowledgment of England's sovereignty of the sea.

Tromp proceeded to his cruising station off the coast of Flanders, between Dunkirk and Nieuport, and while riding at anchor there a strong north-east gale set in, which damaged some of his vessels, and on the evening of the 18th May he crossed over to the English coast for shelter and repairs. At this time Bourne was lying in the Downs with eight Parliamentary ships, and Tromp sent two of his captains to him to explain the accidental cause of his coming, the ships conveying them saluting Bourne's flag. One of the officers, according to Bourne's account, said that Tromp himself would have gone into the Downs "but that he was not willing to breed any difference about his flag, forasmuch as he had not orders to take it down"; to which Bourne replied that he "presumed there would be no new thing required of them, and neither more nor less would be expected from them but what they knew to be the ancient right of this nation"; and he added that the reality of the explanation given for their presence "would best appear by their speedy drawing off from this place."[1] According to Tromp's account of the interview, Bourne merely thanked him courteously for the message.[2]

At all events, the Dutch fleet passed along the English coast in all its bravery, the admiral's ship with his flag on the main-top-mast head, the rest with "jacks and ancients" flying, and about seven in the evening they cast anchor off Dover, within little more than gunshot of the castle. Here they remained till the following afternoon with all their flags dis-

[1] Bourne's letter in *The Answer of the Parliament of the Commonwealth of England to three Papers delivered to the Council of State by the Lords Ambassadors Extraordinary of the States-General of the United Provinces:* and also a *Narrative of the Late Engagement*, &c., *Brit. Mus.*, $\frac{517, k, 15}{36}$, p. 12.

[2] Letter to States-General, May 30. *Hollantsche Mercurius*, May 1652. *The Answer of the Parliament.* Geddes, 209. Tideman, 130.

played, and without saluting. Three times a gun was fired from Dover Castle, according to the usual practice, warning the Dutch admiral to strike his flag; but Tromp—strictly within his right if beyond gunshot—took no heed. He had probably purposely selected an anchorage beyond the range of cannon in order to avoid striking to the English flag. Not only did he not strike, but he exercised his raw musketeers in discharging volleys of small-shot for many hours together, in a way that must have been provoking to the English. On the afternoon of the 19th, Blake, who had been lying at anchor in Rye Bay a little to the westward, and who had received intimation from Bourne of the presence of the Dutch fleet, came upon the scene with fifteen ships. As he approached Tromp weighed anchor and stood off to sea towards Calais,—a movement which Blake thought to be due to a desire to avoid "the dispute of the flag."[1] So far Tromp had carried out his instructions. He had indeed, through stress of weather, gone upon the English coast, which he had been requested to avoid as far as possible. But he had preserved the States from suffering any "indignity" about the flag. Obviously there was great tension between the fleets as to the question of striking. Not unnaturally, Tromp's proceedings were regarded by the English as an attempt to brave them upon their own coast; and the English admirals, who were vigilantly watching, would not be slow to challenge any infraction of the custom of the narrow seas. They too had to take care that their country suffered no dishonour, as they understood it.

When Tromp was on his way to Calais, and about half seas over, a small Dutch vessel fired a gun and came up to him, and communicated the intelligence that a week earlier a Dutch convoy had been attacked by the English for not striking their flags; and, above all, that the seven homeward-bound merchant vessels which had been under their charge, with valuable cargoes on board, were at that moment lying at anchor off the English coast, and, it was believed, in danger from the English fleet.[2] The occurrence referred to took place on 12th May. Captain Young, in the *President*,

[1] Blake's letter, *The Answer of the Parliament*, p. 8.

[2] Tideman, 128, 129. Geddes, 210, 211.

while off the Start, accompanied by two other English men-of-war, fell in with seven Dutch merchantmen from Genoa and Leghorn, convoyed by three men-of-war, with their flags displayed. Young sent a boat to their admiral to request him to strike his flag "before any blood was shed in the controversy," which he did. But the vice-admiral, contrary to the custom in the narrow sea, came to the windward of Young, and refused to strike, telling him to come on board and strike the flag himself. The *President* then poured a broadside into the Dutch ship, together with a volley of small-shot, and several broadsides were exchanged before the vice-admiral struck, and then the rear-admiral did the same. On Young demanding the vice-admiral or his ship to carry into port to make good the damage done, he was told by the admiral that he himself had not interfered so long as it was only a question of striking the flag, but if he attempted to seize the ship he would resist him; and the matter was carried no further. "I do believe," said Young, "I gave him his bellyful of it, for he sent me word he had order from the State that if he struck he should lose his head."[1] It is probable that the Dutch vessels encountered the north-east gale that forced Tromp from his anchorage; at all events, they were brought by their convoyers along the English coast to Fairlight,[2] between Hastings and Winchelsea, where they cast anchor; then the Dutch captain who had been attacked, Joris van der Saen, went in search of Tromp to tell him of their plight.

On hearing his story, Tromp instantly turned about and made straight for the English coast, which he had left only a few hours before. In this case, at all events, his instructions were explicit. He had been ordered to prevent Dutch vessels from being visited or searched, and to recover them

[1] Young's despatch, 14th May 1652, in *The Answer of the Parliament*, p. 20. Penn's *Memorials*, i. 419. Tideman, 197. Gardiner, *Letters and Papers relating to the First Dutch War*, i. 178. *The French Occurrences*, &c., *Brit. Mus.*, E, 665, 6. It may be noted that Tromp, in his *Rescript* to the States-General (see note, p. 398), mentioned that Huyrluyt and van der Saen had received instructions to strike only to royal squadrons.

[2] In the Dutch writings the place was described as "Fairle," "Fayrleigh," "Virly," "Vierly," &c. Its position is shown, as Fairlee, in the reproduction of the chart from Selden in this book (Fig. 3, p. 121).

if captured. Blake, on seeing the Dutch fleet returning, stood off to meet it. He did not know the real reason that had made Tromp alter his course: he had passed the merchant-ships a few days after their meeting with Young, and had done nothing to them. He believed that Tromp was seeking an occasion of quarrel, and watching for an advantage to brave them on their own coast. The Dutch admiral came on with his flag at the main-top, and when he was well within range, Blake fired a gun across his bows to make him strike, and after an interval a second, and yet again a third at his flag, the ball going through the main-sail and killing a man on deck. Tromp then, still with the States' colours aloft, fired a single gun at Blake's flag, ran up a red flag,—the prearranged signal for battle,—and poured a broadside into Blake's ship, and the two fleets entered into a fierce encounter.[1] The fight lasted from four or five o'clock until nine, Blake being assisted by Bourne, who came from the Downs with his small squadron and assailed Tromp in the rear. The Dutch fleet, with the loss of two ships, gradually drew off towards the French coast, and Blake kept his position all night and anchored some leagues off Dungeness.

This was the first great fight over the striking of the flag, and it occasioned immediate war between the two countries. Encounters on a small scale had been not infrequent before, but no foreign fleet had hitherto ventured to challenge an English fleet in this way off the English coast. Tromp himself, thirteen years before, when he possessed an overwhelming force, readily struck his flag to Pennington's small squadron in the Downs. After the battle attempts were made to justify Tromp's action, but not at all on the ground that the demand for him to strike his flag to the English admiral was unjust or contrary to custom. Blake was accused of having precipitated the battle. Tromp, it was said, had men aloft ready to strike the top-sails, or had already done so; he

[1] *The Answer of the Parliament.* Gibson, Collections of Naval Affairs, *Add. MSS.*, 11,684, fol. 5*b*. Geddes, *op. cit.*, 212. Gardiner, *op. cit.*, ii. 118; *Letters and Papers*, i. 172. Tideman, *op. cit.*, 135. The Dutch accounts, which vary in certain particulars from the English and from one another, are unanimous in saying that the first broadside came from Blake's ship, the *James*, which would have been according to custom, since Tromp did not lower his flag after the third shot.

had sent a man up to strike his flag; he was preparing to send his boat to Blake after the second gun was fired to ask him the reason of his firing, and so forth. But the Dutch admiral well knew the custom of the narrow sea, and had no need to ask Blake the reason of his firing across his bows.[1] When the nature of his instructions with reference to saluting is considered, along with his memorandum and the discussions connected with it, his action before Dover Castle on the day before, and the variation in his own subsequent accounts of his intentions and proceedings, the inference is strong that he had resolved not to strike to the weaker fleet of the Commonwealth.

In London the news of the battle aroused intense indignation. It was everywhere believed that Tromp had deliberately attacked the English fleet,—an opinion confirmed by the commissioners, of whom Cromwell was one, sent to Dover to inquire into the facts. The meeting of Joris van der Saen with Tromp, which had been seen from the English fleet, was viewed in a sinister light. The little Dutch ship was thought to have carried instructions from the States for Tromp to make the attack. The Parliament thought so also: "They found too much cause," they said, "to believe that the Lords the States-General of the United Provinces have an intention by force to usurp the known rights of England in the seas, to destroy the fleets that are, under God, their walls and bulwarks, and there-

[1] See his memorandum, p. 398. Tromp wrote to Blake from Calais four days afterwards $\left(\frac{\text{23 May}}{\text{2 June}}\right)$, saying he had intended to salute him, and asking for the restoration of a ship taken. In reply Blake accused him of having sought out the English fleet, and "instead of performing those usual respects which of right belong unto them, and which yourself have often done," had attacked him. In *The Answer of the Parliament*, p. 11, it is said that one of the Dutch captains who had been taken prisoner stated that when he struck to some English men-of-war at Calais a few weeks before, Tromp asked him "why he did strike sail to them," saying, "Were you not as strong as they? And being so, why were you afraid?" As the above-mentioned letter from Tromp to Blake is given by Gardiner (*Letters and Papers*, i. 216) only as "translated from a Dutch translation of the French original," an authenticated copy of the French original is given in Appendix M, from Tideman (*De Zee Betwist*, App. C, p. 202). It is from the archives at The Hague (*Lias Engeland*, 1652 (*Copie*)), and is endorsed by Job. Corñ. Rhees, and again by N. Ruysch, as identical with the authentic copy. The original of Blake's reply is also given. It is printed by Gardiner as "retranslated from the Dutch translation" (*ibid.*, i. 257), and differs in some points from the original.

by expose this Commonwealth to invasion at their pleasure."[1] It was in vain that the States disowned responsibility for Tromp's action and sent over a copy of their instructions to him, showing that he had been commanded to avoid the English coast. The ambassadors appealed to the Council to hold their hand until the States-General had made an inquiry. Tromp was cautioned to use the greatest circumspection, so that while preserving the reputation of his country, nothing further should be done to widen the breach with England. And now, when too late, the Dutch Government came to a definite decision as to the striking of the flag. Tromp was expressly ordered to strike his flag on meeting the English fleet, according to the manner that had been customary when England was under its kings; and not to attack them, but only to defend himself if assailed.[2]

The States also sent over a special ambassador, Adrian Pauw, the Grand Pensionary of Holland, and the most venerable and influential personage in the Republic, to assure the Parliament of their pacific intentions, and to strive to maintain peace. He urged that the encounter of the fleets should be looked upon as an "accident," and that a joint inquiry should be made and the admiral found to have been in fault duly punished. He proposed, further, that regulations should be drawn up for the fleets, so that in future such disputes might be avoided,—not, he said, that it was the wish of the States to dispute the honour and the dignity of the English Republic, which they esteemed the first and greatest in Europe.[3] But the Parliament insisted that the States should first pay them the costs and compensate them for the injuries they had sustained by the Dutch naval preparations and Tromp's attack, and give security for an alliance between the two countries. Meanwhile, the Parliament had been seizing Dutch vessels and preparing for war, while in the United Provinces feeling was

[1] *The Answer of the Parliament*, p. 4.

[2] *Resol. St.-Gen.*, $\frac{25 \text{ May}}{4 \text{ June}}$, $\frac{3}{13}$ June 1652. Tideman, *De Zee Betwist*, 164. Articulen van Vreede ende Confederatie, &c. *Brit. Mus.*, 8122, ee. 12—"Dat hij aengaeñ het voeren ofte strijcken van vlagge in de Rencontre mette Engelsche Vlooten of Schepen hem bij provisie respectivelijck sal hebben te gedragen en te reguleren in sulcker voegen als bij tijden van voorgaende Coningen van Groot-Britaignen is gedaan ende gepractiseert geweest."

[3] Tideman, 171.

rising steadily and angrily against England. The ambassadors were recalled and the naval preparations on both sides pushed on with energy.

It was well understood that the most vulnerable part of the States lay in their shipping and fishery. A day or two after the news of Blake's encounter with Tromp reached London, the Council issued instructions to Major-General Dean, who commanded the troops in Scotland, that in view of the fishery carried on every year by the Dutch about Orkney and Shetland, the forces there should be increased.[1] A month later, on 26th June, before the ambassadors had left London, Blake himself sailed northwards with a fleet of about sixty ships, with a double object of putting a stop to the Dutch herring fishery and intercepting their homeward-bound East-Indiamen, which were expected to return to Holland by way of the Shetlands.[2] On 12th July he sent forward in advance eight frigates to discover the Dutch convoying men-of-war, which they soon fell in with, guarding the herring-busses, to the north of Buchan Ness. They were twelve in number, and after a stubborn fight of over three hours' duration, towards the end of which the English frigates were reinforced by other five, they were all taken, before the main fleet came up. The English wounded were sent in three of the captured ships to Inverness; other three ships were so much shattered that they were sunk. While the fight went on, most of the herring-busses escaped and made their way homewards with all speed, but about thirty were taken by the English. Blake dealt with them very leniently. He took from them "a taste and toll" of herrings, and then sent them home with this "lesson," that they "fish no more in those seas without leave from the Republick of England."[3] For this humane action Blake was subsequently

[1] *State Papers, Dom.*, xxiv. 15.

[2] Cats, Schaep, and van de Perre to the States-General, 27th June 1652. *Add. MSS.*, 17,677, U, fol. 162. Pauw was officially informed by the Council of State that the fleet had put to sea "to execute its designs." Geddes, *op. cit.*, 223. Gardiner, *Letters and Papers*, i. 301. The number of Blake's fleet was variously stated as 60, 64, 66, 68, 72 vessels: 60 were counted passing Dunbar.

[3] Letter from Leyden, $\frac{4}{14}$ August 1652. *Mercurius Politicus, Brit. Mus.*, E, 673, 1. The accounts vary somewhat. *Severall Proceedings in Parliament, Brit. Mus.*, E, 796, 11. *A Perfect Diurnall*, E, 796, 14. *French Occurrences*, E, 669, 6. *Onstelde-Zee*, p. 34, $\frac{8122, \text{ee. } 6}{11}$. *Hollantsche Mercurius*, 1652, p. 70. Gibson in his

blamed, on the ground that the busses might have been made use of in establishing a native fishery, while the detention of their crews would have helped to cripple the resources of the Dutch in manning their fleets.[1] The same generous spirit was shown towards the French boats that fished in the Channel, which were excepted from the general seizure of French shipping, unless they acted improperly.[2] In the course of the war, however, it became the rule for both the Dutch and the English vessels to bring into port all the fishing-boats captured from the enemy.

After Blake dispersed the Dutch busses, the States of Holland at first thought of calling home the rest of the herring fleet (only about 600 or 700 had returned), and for that year to put a stop to the fishing, which had just begun; but it was finally decided to continue it with twenty-four armed busses and six men-of-war as a guard,—a conclusion, no doubt, helped by the gentle way in which the English admiral had dealt with the busses that fell into his hands. When English herring-boats were seized and taken to the Netherlands, Holland, which had the greatest stake in the fishery, tried to induce the States-General to release them, and to issue orders that British fishermen were not to be molested, in the hope that such forbearance would be imitated in England. But the policy failed, and orders were given to do the English fishermen all harm possible. In the following year the States-General forbade the whaling-ships sailing for Greenland, but they did not prohibit the herring fishery, though the greater number of the busses were kept at home by the prudence of their owners. Many were captured by English cruisers. More than fifty were taken by the English fleet on the Dutch coast in May 1653, most of them being brought into Aberdeen and there sold. Some of those seized in the course of the war were handed over by the Council of State to the London Corporation for the Poor, to be used in fishing on the English coast.

narrative (*supra*) says he was on board one of the ships (the *Assurance*) that attacked the busses, and that they found them "northwards of the Dogger Bank"; but there is no doubt that the locality was far north of the Dogger, off Buchan Ness, *Brit. Mus. Add. MSS.* 11,684.

[1] *Memoirs of Edward Ludlow*, 420.

[2] *Proc. Council of State*, 20th July 1652.

On the other hand, the English fishermen suffered greatly. The Iceland and North Sea fishing came almost to a stop, and men-of-war had to guard the herring and mackerel boats. In September 1653 the Council sent a force of men and three "fit and nimble" ships to the Shetlands to ply about the islands, to intercept the enemy's trade of fishing, with what results do not appear.[1]

But the operations against the enemy's fisheries played only a small part in the war. The struggle for the command of the sea was concentrated in many fierce battles between the contending fleets in 1652 and 1653. The exploits of Blake, Dean, Monk, and Penn on the one side, and of Tromp, De Ruyter, Evertsen, and De With on the other, are famous in the naval history of the two countries; and although victory finally rested with England, there were times when the actual control of the British seas was in the hands of the Dutch. It was on one of those occasions that the Dutch admiral was said to have hoisted a broom at his mainmast-top as a sign that he would sweep the seas of all Englishmen. Tromp unexpectedly appeared in force in the Channel in the winter of 1652, and on 30th November he defeated Blake off Dungeness. From that date till the end of February in the following year no English fleet was able to oppose him. The Dutch were "lords and masters" of the sea, and English commerce suffered severely. But the popular story about the broom seems to have uncertain foundation. It was first set afloat in two English newspapers, published on 9th March 1653, after the decisive "three days' battle." In one it was said that Tromp had set forth "a flag (or standard) of Broom; and being demanded what he meant by it, reply'd, That he was once more going to sweep the Narrow Seas of all Englishmen." The other paper gave a letter from the *Nonsuch* frigate at Portsmouth, stating that the Hollanders had probably gone home after the battle, and that "their gallant Mr Trump when he was in France (we understand) wore a flagg of Broom, and being demanded what he meant by it, replied that he was going

[1] *Resol. Holl.*, 1652, pp. 343, 364, 387. *Hollantsche Mercurius*, 1652, p. 86. Beaujon, *Hist. Dutch Fisheries*, 363. *Groot Placaet-Boeck*, ii. 506. Aitzema, *Saken van Staet*, iii. 810. Penn's *Memorials*, i. 526, 527. *State Papers, Dom.*, xxv. 25; xxxii. 15; xxxvi. 15, 29, 55; xxxviii. 116; xxxix. 73; xli.

to sweep the narrow seas of all English men." The story is not mentioned by Dutch authorities, and is now generally discredited, but in an earlier century the broom had been used in this way by a Dutch admiral to signalise a victory in the Baltic;[1] and it is said that after the two days' battle in the following summer, when the Dutch had been driven from the sea, the English fleet rode triumphant off the Texel with a broom displayed at their mast-heads, perhaps in ironical parody of Tromp.

While the fleets were contending for actual dominion over the sea, the Parliament took care to keep alive the historic claims to maritime sovereignty and to place them well before the people. As early as 25th June 1652—the day before Blake sailed away to the north in quest of the herring-busses—they passed a resolution: "That it be referred to the Council of State to prepare a declaration to assert the right of this Commonwealth to the Sovereignty of the Seas, and to the fishery; to be made use of when the Parliament shall see cause."[2] No time was lost, for on the same day the Council remitted the instruction of the Parliament to the Committee for Law and Examinations, with the request that they should bring the declaration to the Council with all speed, and Bradshaw was desired to see that this was done.[3] Apparently, for the use of the Committee in drawing up this declaration, Mr William Ryley, the Keeper of the Records in the Tower, made transcripts of several of the records in his charge referring to the sovereignty of the sea, as the ordinance of King John, Edgar's charter, the mandate of Edward I. to the Bailiffs of Yarmouth, the rolls of the same king concerning Grimbald, and of Edward III. on the laws of the sea, and some others.[4]

[1] The Declaration and Speech of the Lord Admiral Vantrump, and his setting up a great Standard of Broom for the States of Holland, for the Cleering of the Narrow Seas of all Englishmen: New Broom sweepes clean, p. 4. *Brit. Mus.*, E, 689, 13. A Perfect Account of the Daily Intelligencer, *Brit. Mus.*, E, 689, 14. Gardiner, *Hist. of Commonwealth*, ii. 151. Geddes, *op. cit.*, 270, 319.

[2] *Journals of the House of Commons*, vii. 145.

[3] *State Papers, Dom., Interregnum*, xxix. 42-47.

[4] This collection is in a treatise in the British Museum (*Harleian MSS.*, 4314), entitled "The Sovereignty of the English seas vindicated and proved by some few Records (amongst many others of that kynd) remayning in the Tower of London," Collected by William Ryley, senior. Among the State Papers (*Dom.*, xxxv. 35) is a copy of the ordinance of John, in Latin, French, and English, endorsed by Brad-

It was soon apparent to the Council that the task of again attempting formally to vindicate the claims of England to the sovereignty of the seas, while Selden's *Mare Clausum* was at their disposal, would be like painting the lily. They therefore instructed the Committee for Foreign Affairs "to take order for printing the book called *Mare Clausum* and Mr Dugard to print it.[1] But simply to reprint Selden's work, with its fulsome dedication to Charles II., and in the Latin tongue, would not have served the purpose in view, and it was then resolved to translate it. This task was assigned to Marchamont Needham, who had deserted the royalist cause and placed his pen at the service of the Commonwealth, writing the *Mercurius Politicus,* in which he had latterly the assistance of Milton.[2] The translation was rapidly made, and the work was published later in the year.[3] And just as the original had been dedicated to the king, so now the translation was dedicated to "the Supreme Authority of the Nation, the Parliament of the Commonwealth of England"; and so pleased were the Council of State with it that they, on 8th November, ordered two hundred copies for their own use, and paid Needham £200 for his labours, as the book, they said, "learnedly asserted the rights and interests of the Commonwealth in the adjacent seas, and would be of good use for these and future times."[4]

The "additional evidences" brought forward by Needham

shaw, "A transcript of a record in the time of King John touching the striking of sail; brought in by Mr Ryley, Keeper of the Records in the Tower, by order of the Council of State." It contains the following note by Ryley, referring, presumably, to the *Black Book of the Admiralty:* "The French is in a very ancient and fair MS. book amongst the rest of the maritime laws, and undoubtedly was a record of the Admiralty Court, then in the possession of the registrar of that Court, the names of the Lord Admiral and registrar being written at the beginning of the book, which is now remaining with Mr Selden, and is of no less authority than antiquity."

1 *State Papers, Dom., Interregnum,* xxix. 48.

2 Masson, *Life of Milton,* iv. 149, 226.

3 *Of the Dominion or Ownership of the Sea, written at first in Latin and entituled* Mare Clausum seu De Dominio Maris *by John Selden, Esqr: translated into English and set forth with some Additional Evidences and Discourses* by Marchamont Needham. Published by special Command, London, 1652. Another edition, by "J. H. Gent," was published in 1663, "perfected and restored." It is, however, so far as Selden's text is concerned, merely Needham's translation, careful inspection showing that it was printed from the same type.

4 *State Papers, Dom., Interregnum,* xxxiv. 31-49; vol. 33, No. 14. The copy belonging to Cromwell, and bearing his autograph, was sold in 1908.

comprised the proclamation of James in 1609, and of Charles in 1636, forbidding unlicensed fishing; some of the letters that passed between the English Government and their ambassadors at The Hague; extracts from Sir John Boroughs' *Sovereignty of the British Seas,* which was first published in the previous year; and a few other papers of little importance. The purpose of the book was better served by Needham's bitter if rather frothy invective against the Dutch, and by his ranting appeals to English patriotism to conquer the foe and establish our interests on the sea beyond the possibility of future question.[1]

Selden was still alive, and the translation was doubtless made with his concurrence, whatever he may have thought of it. He was himself soon drawn into the controversy which the book evoked. Graswinckel, the Dutch lawyer who had been chosen by the States-General in 1636 to reply to Selden's *Mare Clausum*, and whose neglected treatise had ever since being lying in the secret archives at The Hague, again entered the lists. His shaft was ostensibly directed against a certain Italian writer, P. B. Burgus, who had published a work eleven years before in support of the right of Genoa to the dominion of the Ligurian Sea.[2] There was no apparent reason why the Dutch lawyer should be at the pains to attempt to refute a claim so remote and after so long an interval; but Burgus quoted largely from *Mare Clausum,* and Graswinckel seized upon the opportunity to attack Selden, and to gratify his feelings by making use of his early abortive treatise, under the guise of replying to the Italian author. And his attack on Selden was very bitter.[3] On the main question, the familiar arguments were adduced against the appropriation of seas,

[1] In some dedicatory verses Neptune thus addresses the Great Commonwealth of England :—

"Go on (great State!) and make it known
Thou never wilt forsake thine own,
Nor from thy purpose start:
But that thou wilt thy power dilate,
Since Narrow Seas are found too straight
For thy capacious heart.
So shall thy rule, and mine, have large extent:
Yet not so large, as just, and permanent."

The work appeared when Tromp was lord of the narrow seas; the preface is dated 19th November, the day before Blake's defeat.

[2] *De Dominio Serenissimæ Genvensis Reipublicæ in Mari Ligustico.* Rome, 1641.

[3] *Maris Liberi vindiciæ adversus Petrum Baptistam Burgum Ligustici Maritimi Dominii Assertorem.* Hagæ Comitum, 1652.

with the usual seasoning of Scriptural and classical quotations; the historical claims of England to the sovereignty of the sea were treated in a sarcastic and bantering spirit, and the authenticity of some of the records cited by Selden was questioned; while he said that in many respects the Hollanders were the real lords of the British seas. But he made a personal attack on Selden, accusing him of having written *Mare Clausum* in order to get out of prison.[1] Selden made a strong reply, explaining the circumstances under which his treatise was written, and entering into a minute description of the documents which Graswinckel suggested he had invented; but on the controversy as to the dominion of the seas he contributed nothing new.[2]

Stimulated by the war and the dispute which had precipitated it, a number of works were now published in Holland in defence of the freedom of the seas and the liberty of fishing, and opposing the claims of England to any special maritime jurisdiction. Among them was another dissertation by Graswinckel, published before he was aware of Selden's reply to his attack, and apparently containing further extracts from his stillborn treatise. This time the earlier Scottish lawyer, Welwood, was assailed, and his book, *De Dominio Maris,* was republished in Holland in order to serve, apparently, as a theme and target. Graswinckel was especially severe against any claim to interfere with the herring fishery or to impose tribute on the fishermen.[3] The controversy continued to rage on both sides of the North Sea, but in England it fell for the most part into the incompetent hands of ignorant pamphleteers, who vilified the Dutch in

[1] Cap. vi. p. 118. See *supra*, p. 367.

[2] *Joannis Seldeni vindiciæ secundum integritatem existimationis suæ, per convitium de Scriptione Maris Clausi, petulantissimum mendacissimumque insolentius læsæ in Vindiciis Maris Liberi adversus Petrum Baptistam Burgum, Ligustici Maritimi Dominii assertorem. Hagæ Comitum jam nunc emissis.* London, 1653.

[3] *Maris Liberi Vindiciæ adversus Gulielmum Welwodum Britannici Maritimi Dominii assertorem.* Hagæ Comitum, 1653. Other works were Mord. von der Reck, *Disputatio juridica de Piscatione*, 1652; Martin Schook, *Imperium Maritimum*, Amsterdam, 1653; Stephen S. Burman, *Mare Belli Anglicani injustissimè Belgis illata*, Helena, 1652. The latter contains a pretty full account of the old "Burgundy" treaties, and of others concluded by England with various countries in the seventeenth century, in which, as the author points out, no claim was made to the sovereignty of the seas.

pious but intemperate language without shedding much light upon the question.

But if there was a dearth of competent pens in England able to carry on a juridical controversy about the sovereignty of the sea, it was not for lack of belief in the importance of the matter. At no previous time in English history had popular feeling been more aroused or was the general resolution stronger to maintain the rights of the country in the seas. The traditional sentiment of the nation, which Charles had in large measure alienated by his ship-money exactions and his bungling and fruitless attempts to maintain those rights, was revived in full force, and it was greatly strengthened by other considerations relating to commerce and trade. Though English commerce and shipping had greatly developed since the earlier part of the century, by far the larger part of oversea traffic was still in the hands of the Dutch. It was against this predominance that the Navigation Act was aimed. The pre-eminence of the Dutch excited the emulation of the nation to outvie and outdo them, and success in this policy was believed to be closely bound up with the assertion of the sovereignty of the sea. Before the war began, the authors of works on commerce and navigation had urged the Parliament to enforce these claims, even in the Mediterranean against France, and for the same reasons that were formerly used by Sir Walter Raleigh.[1] To the national sentiment and commercial ambitions was added the zeal of religious fanaticism. The godly Barebones Parliament of 1653, who looked askance at the Dutch as carnal and worldly politicians, held it necessary that the seas should be secured and preserved as peaceable as the land, in order to prepare for the coming of Christ and the personal reign.[2]

[1] For example, Robinson, *Briefe Considerations concerning the Advancement of Trade and Navigation*, 1649.

[2] Stubbe, *A Further Justification*, 91.

CHAPTER XI.

THE PARLIAMENT, THE COMMONWEALTH, AND THE PROTECTORATE—*continued.*

THE PEACE NEGOTIATIONS.

THE importance of the questions connected with the claim to the sovereignty of the sea was revealed in the long negotiations with the Dutch which preceded the conclusion of peace. These were begun at a very early stage of the contest. From the first the war had been as distasteful to Cromwell as it was to John de Witt and the leading men in the States of Holland, and so soon as the beginning of August 1652, within three months of Tromp's encounter with Blake, clandestine negotiations were set on foot, with the approval of Cromwell, Vane, Whitelock, and other leaders in England, with the object of bringing about peace; and though nothing came of them at the time, they were resumed early in 1653. The Speaker informed the Parliament on 22nd March that he had received a formal letter from the States of Holland desiring that the negotiations might be resumed, and on 1st April the Parliament replied favourably, offering to take up the negotiations at the point at which they had been broken off when the special ambassador, Pauw, quitted London in the previous year.[1] This implied payment to the Parliament of the expense incurred in consequence of the Dutch naval preparations and of Tromp's fight with Blake, and "security" for a close alliance,—conditions unacceptable by the ruling oligarchy at The Hague.

[1] Geddes, i. 282, 289, 292. Gardiner, ii. 128, 183, 329. Aitzema, iii. 804.

In order to find some more satisfactory basis for the negotiations, the States-General in June 1653, immediately after the two days' battle, and when the English fleet was blockading the Dutch ports, sent four deputies to London. One of them, Hieronymus van Beverning, a trusty friend of De Witt's and a representative of the States of Holland, came on in advance, reaching London on June 17; the others, Nieuport, van de Perre, and Jongestal, following a few days later.[1] The deputies arrived at a time when Cromwell, having dissolved the Long Parliament and the old Council of State, was dictator, and the new Council was composed of his own nominees; and Cromwell, as is well known, had been against the war and was favourable to peace.[2] Nevertheless, a stiff attitude was adopted towards the envoys. To their request that negotiations might be resumed on the basis of the thirty-six articles the Council turned a deaf ear, putting forward the demands for reparation and security, and refusing to proceed with the negotiations until they had received a satisfactory answer.[3] Cromwell, however, sent a private message to Nieuport, on 30th June, that the Council would not insist on satisfaction and security. He suggested that Tromp should be suspended for a few months; that a binding treaty and alliance should be concluded; and that for security two or three Englishmen should sit in the States-General or Council of State in the Netherlands, and the same number of Dutchmen in the English Council. If these conditions were agreed to, little difficulty would be made about the thirty-six articles, the Dutch would be allowed to carry on their herring fishery in the British seas, and a truce probably granted.[4] But by the next day Cromwell, after discussion with the Council, had changed his mind, and the debate went on about reparation and security. The deputies were told that the

[1] Geddes, i. 315. Gardiner, ii. 340. *Verbael gehouden door de Heeren H. van Beverningk, W. Nieuport, J. van de Perre, en A. P. Jongestal, als Gedeputeerden en Extraordinaris Ambassadeurs van de Heeren Staeten Generael der Vereenigde Nederlanden, aen de Republyck van Engelandt*, i. 7, 12.

[2] Clarendon, *The History of the Rebellion and Civil Wars*, vi. 607. Gardiner, *op. cit.*, ii. 111.

[3] *Verbael of the Ambassadors*, 10, 21, 35.

[4] *Ibid.*, 84. Thurloe's *State Papers*, i. 394.

Council did not ask for a great sum, but that the "security" meant "uniting both states together in such manner as they may become one people and Commonwealth, for the good of both,"[1]—a scheme apparently much the same as St John had taken with him to The Hague.

This extraordinary proposal for a union, closer even than that which existed among the seven United Provinces themselves, astonished the envoys of the many-headed Government. They pretended at first not to understand it, and went on talking of "alliance" and the Intercursus Magnus; but the Council pointedly declared that what they meant was not the mere "establishing of a league and union between two sovereign states and neighbours, but the making of two sovereign states one," under a joint Government, all the subjects to possess equal privileges and freedom in either country "in respect of habitations, possessions, trade, ports, fishing, and all other advantages whatsoever."[2] The deputies considered such a scheme "absurd,"—nothing of the kind had ever been heard of in history; it was opposed to the constitution of the United Provinces and was impossible; and they hinted that if the proposal was pressed they would have to return home. They thought it was far better to take as a basis for the negotiations the treaty of 1496, which was a perfect, true, and sincere alliance, league, and confederation by land and sea. To this the Council replied that they had desired a coalescence of the two countries as the best security for the future of both, and especially of the United Provinces; and that the deputies offered nothing more than they did at first, by which they demanded free trade to the English colonies and the suspension of the Navigation Act; "nay," the Council continued, "they do in effect demand to share with this state in the sovereignty of the narrow seas, and in their right of fishing," whereas these advantages could only be obtained by such a coalescence as had been proposed.[3]

The negotiations had now come to such a pass that the Dutch commissioners judged it to be necessary to report verb-

[1] 21st July 1653. *Verbael*, 53.

[2] 25th July, *Verbael*, 56, 59, 62. Geddes, i. 341. Thurloe, i. 382.

[3] The Deputies to the Council, $\frac{\text{27 July}}{\text{6 August}}$; reply of the Council, $\frac{1}{11}$ August. *Verbael*, 64, 66, 70.

ally to the States, and Nieuport and Jongestal left for home with this object on 3rd August. They did not return until the end of October; and while the official conferences with the Council were suspended in the interval, the two deputies who remained in London carried on important private negotiations with Cromwell, mostly through an intermediary. At first Cromwell descanted on the advantages to the United Provinces of the proposed coalescence, including the complete liberty they would have of fishing on the British coasts. Later he put forward the extraordinary schemes which remind one of the dreams of Napoleon—a confederation of the Protestant states of Europe for the propagation of the Gospel; the partition of the rest of the world, Asia to fall to the share of the Dutch and America to England; a war of conquest against Spain and Portugal, and then there would be complete freedom of commerce and of fishery in all seas, without molestation or disturbance.[1] A less extravagant alternative offered was an alliance of the Protestant states, without the partition of the globe or the war of conquest; but this smaller scheme was not to carry with it either freedom of commerce or liberty of fishing. And now, for the first time since the negotiations began, a formal stipulation was asked that all ships of war of the Dutch Republic, on meeting "on the sea" with the ships of war of the Commonwealth, should show them the same respect and do them the same honour as had been practised in any former time.[2]

The two deputies in London could do nothing with these proposals until the States-General had decided about the original project of coalition, with reference to which Nieuport and Jongestal had gone to The Hague. But they expressed their own opinion on the twelve articles which had been submitted to them; and with regard to the striking of the flag, they thought the word "respect" conveyed the impression of too great a sovereignty on one side and of submission on the

[1] *Verbael*, 75, 142, 143, 150. Thurloe, i. 370, 417, 418. Geddes, i. 362. Gardiner, ii. 350.

[2] *Verbael*, 155. "7. Dat alle schepen onder het ressort van haer Ho. Mog. t' huys behoorende, in alle rencontres in de Zee, aen Oorloghschepen van de Republyck van Engelandt sullen draegen het selvige respect, ende deselve eere doen, als sy ooit voor desen syn gewoon geweest te doen."

other, but they agreed that another word might be chosen and a "good regulation" made. The objection was curious, because during the negotiations of 1673 the envoys of the States—and the same able Beverning was the chief of them—themselves proposed that the striking of the flag should be done "by way of respect"; and when that word, respect, was inserted in the treaty of 1674, it was said in England that the Dutch had scored a great diplomatic victory, since to show respect was not to acknowledge sovereignty.

When the two absent deputies returned to London they brought back with them the old instructions for a "close alliance and strict union," nothing being said about the proposal to fuse the two nations into one. Their memorandum was submitted to the new Council of State, on which Cromwell had a working majority; the only coalition suggested was a "coalition of interests," and a "brotherhood" of the peoples. Cromwell at once called it a mutilated coalition, and some of the Council are said to have expressed strong opinions as to the "contumelious" tactics of the Dutch. If they refused real coalition, it was our duty, they said, to make them and keep them our inferiors, so that they might never attempt this nation again; they must pay for liberty to fish on our coasts; render the usual submission at sea; give up their own wafters and pay us for convoys, since we were the proper guardians of the British sea; they must not equip many great ships, without explaining their intentions and asking leave to pass through our seas; and they must pay the costs of the war. Such were the opinions attributed to the Council by a well-informed author who wrote a little later,[1] and they indicate tolerably well the demands which were subsequently made. The Council then prepared draft articles for a treaty on the lines the Dutch desired, and Cromwell informed them that since they were averse to a coalition which would have made the privileges of both countries equal, it would be necessary first of all to define clearly their respective rights, so that disputes might be avoided in future. And in the first place, he said, they must settle their right and dominion in the narrow sea and the question of the

[1] Stubbe, *A Further Justification*, 92. Stubbe says he had an account of part of the proceedings from one of the English commissioners; he had also the use of official manuscripts.

fishery, remarking that if these points were adjusted the work in hand would be much facilitated.[1]

In putting the question of the sovereignty of the sea and the fishery in the foreground of the negotiations, Cromwell placed the envoys in a difficulty. In conformity with their traditional policy on like occasions, the States-General had expressly instructed their representatives to avoid discussion on these thorny subjects,—a circumstance no doubt well known to Cromwell. They therefore fenced with them. With regard to the "honour of the sea," they had never desired to dispute with the Parliament of the Republic of England any honour or dignity which had been rendered to former Governments, and they declared their willingness to pay the same "honour and respect" to the English flag as had been previously shown to it. They thought it would be better to defer consideration of the fishery question until the articles of a "strict union" had been adjusted, when the whole business of commerce, fishery, and the immunities on both sides might be dealt with. But Cromwell was not to be turned from his purpose. On the following day, after a long and remarkable speech on the advantages of coalition—which the Dutch once more put aside,—he again declared that the matter of the sea and the fishery must be first of all settled; and he ended the discussion by handing to the deputies the draft articles which the Council had prepared.[2] The articles were twenty-seven in number. Some of them provided for a defensive alliance and arranged details of peace. Freedom of trade was to be allowed, provided the laws in force—the Navigation Act—were observed; the rebels of the one were not to be assisted by the other, and so forth. But the Dutch were to pay a sum to be agreed upon, by way of reparation, and there were several articles dealing with the sovereignty of the sea and the fisheries.

The article[3] on the fishery was framed on the model of the

[1] *Verbael*, 189. "Syn Excellencie . . . gesyt . . . dat sy daerom voor af meenden, dat moeste vaststellen haer Reght ende Dominie in de naeuwe Zee, ende het stuck van haere Visscherye, ende . . . eyndelyck besluytende dat die pointen van de Zee ende Visscherye geadjusteert synde, het vordere werck seer souden faciliteren."

[2] *Verbael*, 189, 190, 196, 198, 214.

[3] Art. xviii. *Verbael*, 203.

proclamations of James and Charles relating to unlicensed fishing. It was as follows: "The people and inhabitants of the said United Provinces, of what condition or quality soever they be, shall with their busses and other vessels fitted to that purpose, have liberty from time to time, for the term of one and twenty years, next coming, to sail and fish as well for herrings, as all other sort of fish, great and small, upon any of the coasts or seas of Great Britain and Ireland and the rest of the Isles adjacent, where and in such manner as they have been formerly permitted to fish. In consideration whereof, the States-General of the United Provinces shall during that term pay into the public treasury of this Commonwealth at the City of London the sum of . . . at two equal payments upon every 24 day of June and 24 day of December; the first payment to begin on the 24 day of June next." When it is remembered that the Dutch in the reign of James, and again in the reign of Charles, were prepared to go to war with England rather than surrender their liberty of fishing, the objectionable nature of this article is apparent. No glimpse is obtained throughout the negotiations of the sum that was to be asked for the liberty of fishing, possibly because it was never definitely fixed by the Council. It is, however, stated by Stubbe, who had special sources of information, that it was the intention of the Council to demand £100,000, as well as payment for constant wafters or convoys,[1]—a statement which is credible only on the supposition that it was desired utterly to ruin the Dutch herring fishery.

Some of the other articles were equally or even more objectionable. That concerning the striking of the flag,[2] though not feasible in its original form, was capable of adjustment. It provided "that the ships and vessels of the said United Provinces, as well men-of-war as others, be they single ships or in fleets, meeting at sea with any of the ships of war of the State of England, or in their service, and wearing their flag, shall strike their flag and lower their top-sail, until they be passed by, and shall likewise submit themselves to be visited, if thereto required, and perform all other respects due to the said Commonwealth of England,

[1] Stubbe, *A Further Justification*, 62.

[2] Art. xv.

to whom the dominion and sovereignty of the British sea belong." By this article the whole of the Dutch fleet would be bound to strike to a single ship in the English service anywhere on the sea, and, what was a far more serious matter, to submit to be visited and searched. A stipulation of that kind was unacceptable. Tromp's fleet had been fitted out before the war expressly to prevent the visitation and search of merchant vessels; if no conflict had occurred with Blake about the flag, it would almost certainly have happened on this other point.[1] And now the States were asked to confirm in a formal treaty the right claimed by England; and above all to make it applicable to their ships of war. Another article with reference to the measures to be taken against pirates embodied the old doctrine attributed to the Plantagenets. The Commonwealth of England, it stated, had declared their resolution "to put upon these seas a convenient number of armed ships, for the defence and safeguard thereof, and to maintain and preserve all lawful navigation, trade, and commerce therein, against pirates and sea-rovers."[2] Another article which raised the strongest objections provided that the Dutch fleet passing through the British seas should be limited to a certain number, to be agreed upon in the treaty, and that if the States had occasion for a larger number to pass than that agreed to, they should first give the Commonwealth three months' notice and obtain their consent. The article also provided that Dutch merchant vessels should be allowed freely to navigate the British seas, as if the right of permitting or forbidding navigation there belonged to England.[3]

[1] Gardiner, *Letters and Papers*, i. 49, 170.

[2] Art. xvi. *Verbael*, 203.

[3] Art. xiv. "That the inhabitants and subjects of the United Provinces may, with their ships and vessels, furnished as merchantmen, freely use their navigation, sail, pass and repass in the seas of Great Britain and Ireland, and the Isles within the same, (commonly called the British Seas) without any wrong or injury to be offered to them, by the ships or people of this Commonwealth, but on the contrary shall be treated with all love and friendly offices; And may likewise with their men of war not exceeding such a number as shall be agreed upon in this treaty, sail, pass and repass through the said seas, to and from the countries and parts beyond them: but in case the States-General shall have occasion to pass the said seas with a greater number of ships of war, they shall give three months before notice of their intentions to the said Commonwealth, and obtain their consent for the passing of such fleet, before they put them forth upon these seas, for preventing all jealousies and misunderstandings between the States by means thereof." *Verbael*, 202.

Such conditions could only have been imposed on a nation hopelessly vanquished. They were conditions, the ambassadors declared, which would not be demanded from rebels or slaves. On the English side there was a strong feeling that since coalition had been rejected, the "security" for the future ought to be rigorous and complete. It was still firmly believed by the mass of men, and doubtless by many in the Council, that Tromp had attacked Blake in overwhelming force in order to destroy the English fleet; and that too by the implicit or express orders of the States. There was doubtless also a desire to cripple Dutch commerce and power as far as was possible. Commercial jealousy had long been simmering, and now that the English thought they had the power they were resolved to use it to their own advantage.[1]

The Dutch deputies were astonished and indignant at the English demands, which, as they sarcastically noted in their journal, they could scarcely reconcile with the professions of friendship and the pious words of Cromwell. Had they communicated them to the States-General all thoughts of peace would have been at an end, for it had required the most adroit diplomacy of John de Witt to induce that body to allow the negotiations to be set agoing. They therefore sent home only an imperfect official account of them, pleading that Cromwell had tied them down to the utmost secrecy,[2] and then proceeded to consider the articles themselves. Those dealing with reparation, the Prince of Orange, the visitation of ships, and the fishery, they decided absolutely to reject as inadmissible, for reasons to be given later. The one which proposed to limit their naval power in the adjacent seas they resolved indignantly to refuse, and to break off the negotiations rather than to agree even to discuss it, believing that it was a matter in which all Christian princes in Europe

[1] Sir H. Vane, who was the chief director of the war, is reported to have said that the interests of the two countries "were as irreconcilable as those of rivals, trade being to both nations what a mistress is unto lovers; that there never could intervene any durable peace, except both nations did unite by coalition, or the English subjugate the others and reduce them into a province, or by strict conditions and contrivances ensure themselves against the growth and future puissance of the Dutch." Stubbe, *op. cit.*, 119.

[2] The Ambassadors to the States-General, $\frac{18}{28}$ November. *Verbael*, 215. Geddes, i. 372.

were also interested, who would condemn the English Government for their extravagant claims to special maritime rights and to the fishery. Their conclusions were embodied in a paper which was submitted to the Council of State on 22nd November. In this they said that the visiting and searching of merchant vessels and ships of war was contrary to the practice of the United Provinces, was subject to innumerable disorders and disputes, and was injurious in point of sovereignty, since it was not reciprocal. As to the fishery, they declared that they had been in immemorial possession of complete liberty of fishing. They denounced the article concerning the limitation of the number of their ships of war, which they said they could hardly persuade themselves had been put forward seriously, since it struck at the root of their existence as an independent sovereign state, and they declined to discuss it.[1]

Cromwell throughout the whole negotiations, until he became Lord Protector, acted as spokesman for the Council at the conferences; and he now stated that the visitation of Dutch ships was an undoubted right of sovereignty possessed by the English Commonwealth. The limitation of their ships of war passing through the British seas was also a consequence of the same right of dominion; and the English had now more than ever reason to maintain it, both on account of their ancient prerogative and the recent injuries committed by the Dutch. The right to the fishery was of the same nature. No other nation in Europe had attempted to carry it on without the consent of England; the Dutch were the only people, he said, who sought a separate interest in it—a statement which was quite inaccurate. But the deputies took their stand on the obnoxious article which proposed to clip their naval power and interfere with their liberty of navigation, and threatened to return home unless it was withdrawn. After standing firm for a time Cromwell withdrew the article, asserting at the same time that England had jurisdiction on both sides of the sea, and that it was perilous to allow a fleet of sixty or eighty men-of-war to come into our rivers or ports without our knowledge or consent,—a reference, no doubt, to Tromp's action before the war.

[1] *Verbael*, 216, 219.

This concession facilitated the negotiations. Frequent conferences were held in the following week, Cromwell and his Council strongly asserting the right of the Commonwealth to the fisheries and the dominion of the sea. At this period there were four subjects chiefly in dispute—the arrangements relating to the striking of the flag, the visitation of ships of war, the preliminary part of the sixteenth article as to the guarding of the seas, and the fishery. On none of these was Cromwell inclined as yet to give way. The deputies repeated their offer as to the flag, and requested that a joint commission of old and experienced naval officers should be appointed to draw up regulations for the guidance of both sides in future. To this Cromwell replied that such a commission was unnecessary, their rights and the custom being well understood and clearly expressed in the article. There was, however, uncertainty as to the places where the right could be claimed, and the Dutch deputies said they wished to make it clear in what seas and on what coasts the flag ought to be struck, urging that it was better to be guided by a regulation than to compel it by force. But Cromwell was inflexible. To yield would be to admit that the claim was doubtful in point of right or mode, and it would stultify their whole action; he may also have thought it would open a door for some form of reciprocity. The article was therefore postponed, as was also the sixteenth article, the deputies insisting on the deletion of the introductory sentence as to a fleet to be put forth to guard the sea, which Cromwell refused to do.[1]

The keenest dispute at this time was about the herring fishery. There were two principles in the article, Cromwell said, which required attention: first, the recognition of England's right to the fishery; secondly, compensation for allowing the use of it. Unable to avoid the discussion, the envoys pleaded their immemorial possession and their treaties, and said that their liberty of fishing had never been disputed; besides, they asked, was it a friendly thing to make a proposal of the kind when they were about to conclude a strict and close alliance between the two countries? Cromwell, who had obviously been well posted up in the arguments in *Mare*

[1] *Verbael*, 229, 230, 236.

Clausum, then entered upon a lengthy disquisition on the subject. He said the English could prove by authentic documents that they had had possession of the fishery from all time, and that other nations sought their permission to fish; that the clause in the treaty of 1496 (the Intercursus Magnus) upon which the Dutch relied, was omitted in later treaties; and that the treaties had expired owing to the subsequent wars between Queen Elizabeth and Spain, and had never been since renewed; they were not the same people with whom the treaties had been made, since they were now alienated from the House of Burgundy. And they could not establish their right by prescription, for by the civil law it required a hundred years for a just prescription, and the States had not existed so long as an independent nation. Moreover, long before the treaty of 1496, licenses for fishing had been sought and granted. Even King Philip II. in Queen Mary's time had asked permission to fish for twenty-one years, and had paid £1000 a-year for the privilege. King James, too, had issued a proclamation in 1610 (*sic*) forbidding unlicensed fishing, while King Charles had demanded and received through the Earl of Northumberland an acknowledgment from their herring-busses.

To this long argument the deputies replied with arguments as long. With respect to the treaties, they said that the treaty of 1496 was not between prince and prince, but between states and towns, as specified in it; and that the article which provided for mutual liberty of fishing had been confirmed in later treaties, notably in the treaty of Binche, in 1541, between the Emperor Charles and the King of Scotland; in that of 1550 with Queen Mary of Scotland; and in that between the United Provinces and King James of Scotland in 1594.[1] Moreover, in the treaty between England and Spain in 1630, there were certain words which confirmed the ancient treaties of intercourse and commerce.[2] They expressed the opinion that Cromwell had not been well informed in saying that licenses for fishing had been granted before the Intercursus Magnus was concluded, because it was doubtful if the invention of the

[1] See pp. 78-81.

[2] Art. xviii. "Antiqui intercursus et commercii tractatus, provisionaliter pristinam vim et auctoritatem obtineant."

salting and casking of herrings was much before that date.[1] As to the alleged lease of the fishings by King Philip, there was nothing to compel him to take such a lease, and they saw no reason why he should have done so; while the proclamation of James, so far from being an argument against them, was entirely in their favour, because, as they could prove from papers in their hands, it was never put into execution, but was suspended on the representations of the States. The action of the Earl of Northumberland they described as simple extortion, since he had compelled a few defenceless fishermen, without the knowledge of the States, to pay him some money. The deputies concluded their arguments by saying they had no further instructions on the matter, and that if the Council pressed the article, they would require to return and report to their Government: there was, they said, a high and mighty Lord in heaven who knew the hearts and rights of all, and He would judge. Cromwell assured them that the article had not been inserted in the draft treaty with the object of breaking off the negotiations, but only that they might maintain their just rights. Why, he asked, should the States object to acknowledge the right of the Commonwealth to the fisheries, when other Powers like France and Sweden, who had as much claim to liberty as they, had not scrupled to acknowledge it?[2]

As Cromwell was immovable, and the deputies equally obdurate, the negotiations came to a stop, and the latter on 5th December formally requested their passports to return to The Hague. In the interval they asked the French ambassador if France had requested permission from England to fish in the sea, as Cromwell averred. He told them nothing had been said to him on the matter since he came to England, but that his papers showed that the Duke of Guise had formerly asked that certain fishermen of Treport should not be molested in their fishing.[3] They also learned that the Swedish ambassador had sought to obtain from England free commerce in general,

[1] Beukelsz, who invented the modern method of pickling herrings, is said by some to have died in 1347, by others in 1397, and by a few in 1401. Stubbe says the deputies assigned the year 1414 to the discovery, but no year is mentioned in their report.

[2] *Verbael*, 237, 238, 240-243. Stubbe, *op. cit.*, 64.

[3] The statement referred to the licenses for fishing on the Zowe. See p. 65.

free fishery, and freedom of trading to the Barbadoes. It was indeed the case that Sweden had made such proposals. In the negotiations for a treaty with the Commonwealth, the queen expressed her desire to obtain liberty for her subjects to fish for herrings in the British seas,[1] and in the preceding August the Council of State, at the request of her ambassador, had actually issued a license to four Swedish vessels to fish in the narrow seas and upon the British coasts.[2] In a treaty concluded in 1656 between the King of Sweden and the Lord Protector, the privilege, it may be said, was carried much further. The treaty provided that Swedish subjects should be free to fish for herrings and other fish in the seas and on the coasts under the dominion of the Republic, provided the number of ships so employed did not exceed a thousand; and no charges (such as the assize-herring) were to be demanded of the Swedish fishermen, who were to be treated courteously and amicably, allowed to dry their nets on the shore, and to purchase necessaries at a fair price.[3]

It may be noted as remarkable that, throughout the long discussions with Cromwell about the fishery, the Dutch deputies never made use of the argument, so frequently employed by their predecessors at the Court of James, that the English claims were opposed to the law of nations. They probably shrank from using an argument of that kind to the great dictator who had ruthlessly trampled on the laws of England; perhaps they were deterred by the abrupt intimation made earlier, that the Council had not come to listen to scholastic subtleties, but to consider the real legal rights of England. The obstinacy of Cromwell in refusing at this stage to modify the fishery article is also noteworthy. No doubt he was

[1] Whitelock to Thurloe, 10th March 1654. Thurloe's *Collection*, ii. 158.

[2] Council of State Order Book, 6th Aug. 1653. *State Papers, Dom., Interregnum.*

[3] Dumont, *Corps Diplomatique*, VI. ii. 125. "X. Subditis Serenissimi Regis Sueciæ liberum erit, per Maria atque Littora, quæ in Ditione hujus Reipublicæ sunt, piscari, atque Haleces, aliosque Pisces capere; dummodo mille Navium numerum piscantes non excedant. Neque inter piscantes ullum iis impedimentum, aut molestia asseratur Neque à Navibus præsidiariis hujus Reipublicæ, neque ab iis quibus Diplomate permissum est, res suas privatim suo marte repetere, nec a piscantibus in Boreali plagâ Britanniæ, piscationis nomine onera aliqua exigantur, immo omnes humaniter atque amice tractentur, usque retia in Littore siccare, quemque opus est commeatum ab eorum Locorum Incolis, justo pretio comparare sibi licebit."

moved by a sincere desire to benefit England. The belief was still prevalent that the herring fishery which the Dutch carried on along the British coasts was the foundation of their commerce, wealth, and naval power. It, moreover, provided them with a great "seminary of seamen" to recruit their fleets—a consideration which must have had a special force at a time when we had only the ships in the coal trade between Newcastle and London to draw upon for ours, and when the most rigorous system of pressing failed to provide sufficient men for the navy.[1] But Cromwell had other reasons for insisting on the English claims, even to the point of rupture of the negotiations. It was by this time obvious that the Barebones or nominated Parliament had only a short life before it, and it was desirable that its dissolution should be free from violence and as far as possible voluntary. The majority of the members were strongly opposed to the Dutch, and to the conclusion of peace except on humiliating terms to the enemy; and it is probable that Cromwell's insistence was partly due to his desire to conciliate them. He was now about to put on the mantle of the Lord Protector of the Commonwealth of England.

When the Dutch envoys wrote to the Council for their passports, they received no answer. On repeating their request two days later, they got a hint of what was impending,—that the Parliament which was against them would soon be dissolved, and the management of affairs placed in the hands of a council of ten or twelve.[2] Then on the 9th December they were asked by Viscount Lisle, in the name of the Council, to delay their departure, as commissioners would soon be appointed to treat with them and conclude the treaty. Cromwell took the oath as Lord Protector on the 16th; the new Council of State met on the 19th; and the conferences on the treaty were resumed four days later.[3]

[1] Stubbe, *op. cit.*, 68. Robinson, *England's Safety in Trades Encrease*, 1641. Ibid., *Considerations Concerning the Advancement of Trade and Navigation*, 1649.

[2] The Deputies to the States-General, $\frac{7}{17}$ December 1653. *Verbael*, 246.

[3] It may be noted that Philip Meadows now became Latin Secretary to the Council in place of Milton. He was afterwards an extremely able opponent of the English claims to the sovereignty of the sea, and wrote the best book against them. See p. 524.

Cromwell did not now attend the conferences, the negotiations being entrusted to four members of the Council—Viscount Lisle, Sir Charles Wolseley, Sir Anthony Ashley Cooper, and Walter Strickland, who had accompanied St John to The Hague in 1651. The discussions on the questions affecting the claim to the sovereignty of the sea were continued: the striking of the flag, the visitation of ships, and the declaration that the dominion of the sea belonged to England. The former arguments on both sides were repeated, and the Dutch proposed the following article with reference to the flag: "That the ships and vessels of the United Provinces, as well men-of-war as others, meeting with any of the ships of war of the State of England shall honour and dignify them with the striking of the flag and lowering the top-sail, in such a manner as ever under any form of government in times past they have been honoured and dignified; and to prevent all quarrels for the future the particulars thereof shall be regulated by the advice of the generals and commanders."[1] The English commissioners reiterated the objections previously made, but now stated that they had been referring only to the narrow seas;[2] and it was agreed to refer the points in dispute to the Lord Protector.

Another difficulty arose on the third article, which fixed the dates on which the peace should take effect on the sea, after which dates the capture of prizes would be illegal. The part was as follows: "Excepting such depredations as shall be committed in the British Seas (*Maria Britannica*) after the space of twelve days, and betwixt the British Seas and the Line after the space of ten weeks," &c. At the first, the phrase "British Seas" had caught the eye of the envoys; but, thinking it was merely an ordinary appellation such as might appear on a chart, and that no deep design lurked beneath it, they decided that it would not be desirable to raise "the business of the sea" on such a point.[3] They now took exception to these words, and suggested that it would be better to begin, "in the narrow sea, which was called the British Sea" after twelve days, from there to Cape St Vincent

1 *Verbael*, 260, 261. MS. Commentary, Stubbe, *op. cit.*, 60.

2 "Ende dat sy alleenlyck spraecken van de naeuwe Zee."

3 *Verbael*, 231.

after six weeks, &c. This matter also was referred to the Protector.

Cromwell, who was now settled in his new dignity, gave close attention to the peace negotiations. On 26th December the deputies were handed a paper in his name, in which he gave up the demand for a money payment in reparation for the war; agreed to the stipulation about the exclusion of the Prince of Orange—which was the corner-stone of the treaty—being put in a secret article; agreed to some new articles which the Dutch had proposed, after slight modifications; and at the same time introduced a new element of trouble and debate by formulating three additional articles requiring justice to be done for the "murder" of the English at Amboyna in 1623, and concerning the settlement of disputes and wrongs committed in the East Indies, Brazil, and Greenland. Important concessions were at the same time made on the maritime question. The article respecting the fishery was dropped. "Concerning the fishing," wrote the Protector, "the Lords Deputies having by their former papers desired that freedom of fishing in these seas might be declared in this treaty, the 17 article was thereupon propounded, whereby license is granted to the people of the United Provinces to fish freely in these seas upon the terms therein expressed, notwithstanding as in their Lordships' power either to accept or refuse, but it cannot be admitted that anything should be inserted in this treaty that may prejudice the right of this state in their fishery."[1] The Dutch thus again scored a diplomatic victory and preserved their liberty of fishing on the British coasts, just as they had done in the reigns of James and Charles. They did not succeed in getting the clause in the Intercursus Magnus inserted or confirmed, as they desired, but it still remained in force. Later writers accused Cromwell of having surrendered the rights to the fishery, and much else, as a *quid pro quo* for the stipulation regarding the exclusion of the Orange family in the Netherlands, which was his main object;[2] but

[1] *Verbael*, 272.

[2] Stubbe, *op. cit.* Geddes has shown that Beverning, acting secretly with De Witt, had clandestine communications with Cromwell as early as 8th December, clearly with reference to the exclusion of the Prince of Orange. *Op. cit.*, i. 385.

there is no doubt at all that the States-General would never have agreed to the English proposal.

Concessions were also made as to the striking of the flag. "The 15 article," said Cromwell, "to be as following: that the ships and vessels of the United Provinces, as well men-of-war as others, meeting at sea with any of the ships of war of the State of England, shall strike their flag and lower their top-sail, and perform the other respects due to this State until they be passed by"; but the request that a naval commission should draw up a "regulation" on the subject was not acceded to. On the other hand, the clauses which stipulated for a right of visitation of Dutch ships at sea, and the declaration that the dominion and sovereignty of the sea belonged to England, were entirely withdrawn; but the Protector would not yet part with the clause which provided for an English fleet to guard the seas and protect commerce. Surely, he said in effect, since the article limiting the number of warships has been withdrawn, you will not contest our dominion of the sea in this?—and at this stage it was retained, with the remark, "this article is insisted on." One of the new clauses provided that not more than eight men-of-war at a time were to enter any port of the other Power, unless constrained by force of tempest, without having obtained consent to do so; and when compelled to enter by danger of the sea, they were immediately to signify to the chief magistrate the cause of their coming, and to leave when he required them to depart.[1]

On the subject of striking the flag, the deputies were not yet satisfied. They still continued to urge that a "regulation" should be prepared; and they now raised a new point. Cromwell had always used the words "at sea," which might mean any sea or any part of the sea. They now desired that the ceremony should be restricted to the narrow seas, "which," they said, "are called the British seas."[2] To this proposal Cromwell assented in so far that the words "in the British seas" were inserted later. It is curious to notice how the

[1] *Verbael*, 273.

[2] Ad. 15. ut ad angustum mare (quod Britannicum vocant) ibique ad certas regulas cum distinctione locorum et littorum ita restringatur, ut idem ille honor eademque dignitas, quæ vexilli supremi et veli dimissione unquam delati aut observati fuerunt, in posterum adhuc deferantur, et observentur. *Verbael*, 275.

meaning of the term "British Sea" thus became confused even within the compass of a single treaty. In reference to this article, the Protector made the important admission that the narrow seas and the British seas were synonymous.[1] In the third article, as we have seen, the same term was used, and it was natural for the Dutch to suppose that it there had the same significance and meant the narrow seas or Channel. Since the clause dealt with a matter of great practical importance, namely, the restitution of vessels that might be captured after a specified date, and the term "British seas" appeared to be restricted to the Channel, they wished specifically to include in it the North Sea and the East Sea (or Baltic), both regions of great traffic. The envoys were accordingly instructed later by the States-General to have these words added, so that the clause would read, "excepting such depredations as shall be committed in the British Sea, the East Sea, and the North Sea."[2] By this addition, moreover, the objectionable phrase "the British seas" would be formally restricted to the narrow seas or Channel, with the consent of England. The proposed change was instantly rejected. When Beverning brought it forward, Thurloe resisted it with great warmth,[3] and the qualifying words confining the term British seas to the narrow seas, which the Dutch had inserted, were also deleted.[4] When it was verbally agreed that the striking of the flag should be restricted to the narrow sea,[5] the deputies made a new proposal. It was to the effect that Dutch ships, without any distinction, not only in the narrow seas but throughout the whole world, on meeting English men-of-war should give them the first salute by striking the flag and top-sails and firing guns, provided that the English ships immediately returned

[1] "Ende met eenen voortgaende tot het 15 Artikel raekende het stryken van de Vlagge, &c., syn wederom gerepeteert alle de argumenten ende redenen, die in voorige Conferentien syn geallegeert geweest, ende wierdt ten uytersten by den Heer Generael daer in gepersisteert, alleenlyck, dat hy die explicatie byvoeghde op haere laetste antwoorde, daer sonder eenige distinctie van de rencontres in zee gesprooken wordt, dat sy dat verstonden van de naeuwe Zeën die de Britannische Zeën genoemt worden." *Verbael*, 278, $\frac{\text{27 December 1653}}{\text{4 January 1654}}$.

[2] *Secrete Resol. St. Generael*, $\frac{9}{19}$ Feb. 1654. *Verbael*, 300.

[3] "Met seer scherpe woorden, ende hatelycke illatien tegensprack." *Ibid.*, 307.

[4] *Ibid.*, 320. "Angustum mare, quod vulgo Britannicum mare appellatur."

[5] "Tot de naeuwe Zee expresselyck gerestringeert." *Ibid.*, 288.

the salute in precisely the same manner. This, doubtless, was the proposition which lurked behind the reiterated suggestion for a "regulation"; but the English commissioners would not agree to any form of reciprocity. The Dutch again raised objections to the part of the sixteenth clause concerning pirates, on the ground that it contained an implication of the claim to the dominion of the seas, which they had constantly opposed, and they cited the treaties with Elizabeth in 1585, and with Charles in 1625, as having assigned to them the protection of the sea off the Flemish coast and neighbouring coasts. They declared they would prefer it to be dropped altogether unless it was amended or made reciprocal.[1]

The differences as to the sovereignty of the sea or the phraseology of the maritime articles were now, however, of little actual importance. The progress of the negotiations, secret and otherwise, had narrowed the real ground of contention to two crucial points—the exclusion of the Prince of Orange from office, and the inclusion of Denmark in the treaty. The former had been secretly agreed upon by Cromwell and Beverning, the latter acting in conjunction with De Witt;[2] but the Protector was obdurate as to the inclusion of Denmark, and the deputies decided to return home to report the state of the negotiations. They left London on 3rd (13th) January, and though a message from Cromwell overtook them at Gravesend conceding the point in dispute as to Denmark, they thought it better to continue their homeward journey. The treaty, so far as it had been officially arranged and made known, was received with approbation in Holland, the vital stipulation respecting the exclusion of the Prince of Orange being concealed. Beverning came back to London on 25th January, but was refused audience by the Protector until he had obtained proper credentials recognising the new Government. He was joined by Nieuport and Jongestal a month later, but it was not till 15th March that the conferences were resumed.[3]

By this time the Protector had in substance conceded almost everything concerning the dominion of the seas that the

[1] *Verbael*, 283, 285, 289. [2] Geddes, *op. cit.*, i. 380.

[3] *Ibid.*, 290, 293, 311, 319. Geddes, i. 378-393. Gardiner, *op. cit.*, ii. 368, 369.

Dutch had asked for, and the ambassadors—they had returned with the title of extraordinary ambassadors—were anxious to avoid any more discussion about it. For this reason Beverning disapproved of the resolution of the States-General, above referred to, for the amendment of the third article by specifying the North Sea and Baltic, and after his first interview with Cromwell he wrote to them expressing his opinion that it would occasion new disputes about the fisheries and the sovereignty of the sea. We have seen how it was received by Thurloe; and from what followed it would appear that Cromwell had either heard of the rumours going about that he had sacrificed the rights of England to the sovereignty of the seas in order to gain the exclusion of the Orange family, or that he was determined to keep the matter open until the secret arrangement for that exclusion had been officially accepted in the United Provinces—a task in which De Witt was struggling against enormous difficulties. At all events, after the treaty had been signed by the negotiators and ratified by the States-General, and when Cromwell was on the point of ratifying it, he suddenly reopened the question as to the extent of the British seas. Thurloe began by asking the ambassadors what was meant by the distinction drawn in the third article between the British seas and Cape St Vincent. Such a distinction seemed to prejudice the limits of the British seas, and might besides give rise to disputes later as to the seizure of vessels. He then treated the ambassadors to a discourse on the extent of the British seas, the particulars of which are, unfortunately, not recorded. They were, however, told that they extended to and along the coast of France, "Xaintonge" (Saintonge, an old French province) and round about there. It had not been thought, he said, to limit or define any seas in stating the districts, and he asked them for a declaration on the subject. They suspected that the design was to extract from them an explicit statement as to the southward limit of the British seas, and they said they had now no power either to alter the article or even to interpret it. The treaty had been signed on both sides and ratified by the States-General, and their instructions and commission were at an end. The proposal to alter it, they now alleged, came from themselves alone, without instructions from the

States-General, and they had willingly and immediately withdrawn it when objection was made. Cromwell then asked if it had ever been their intention to define in any way the limits of the seas by that article. They replied that they believed not, and added that they had never thought of yielding anything with regard to right or jurisdiction or limits of the seas; and they failed to see what prejudice his Highness could suffer from the extension of the article, unless it was to be maintained that the whole of the French and Portuguese coasts to Cape St Vincent were within the narrow seas, as they had defined in the fourteenth article, which was withdrawn.[1] Cromwell then angrily told them that he would not exchange the ratification of the treaty unless he got the explanation and interpretation requested.[2] It was only, the ambassadors reported home, by their earnest insistence to the Protector that the articles had been signed with perfect knowledge on both sides of their contents, that he passed from the point. Whatever the object may have been in thus raising a discussion at the last moment as to the extent of the British seas, there is little doubt that the circumstance would prove useful to De Witt in his difficult and manifold manœuvres to get the Act of exclusion of the House of Orange adopted.

The treaty of peace, which had been signed by the plenipotentiaries on 5th April, was ratified by the Protector on 19th April, and proclaimed with due solemnity on the 26th May. It was received with rejoicing both in this country and the Netherlands.[3]

[1] "Gelyk sy in 't 14 van de 27 Artikelen haere Brittannische Zën selver gedefinieert hadden." *Verbael*, 396.

[2] "Daer op syne Hoogheyt in colere seyde, dat sonder de versoghte elucidatie ende interpretatie, hy de Ratificatie niet konde uytwisselen." *Ibid.*, 397.

[3] Next day Cromwell entertained the Dutch ambassadors and their wives to a sumptuous banquet, and after dinner he passed them a paper with the remark, "We have hitherto exchanged many papers, but in my opinion this is the best." It was the first verse of Psalm cxxxiii., which they all then sang together solemnly—

"Behold, how good a thing it is,
And how becoming well,
Together such as brethren are
In unity to dwell."

Verbael, 419. Aitzema, iii. 927. Geddes, i. 422.

Comparison of the treaty as completed[1] with the original draft shows how thoroughly the Dutch plenipotentiaries had eviscerated the parts dealing with the sovereignty of the sea, and stripped it of almost all the phraseology which might imply such sovereignty. The articles imposing tribute for the liberty of fishing; stipulating for the visitation and search of vessels; restricting the number of their men-of-war in the British seas; the Plantagenet claim for the guarding of the sea; the declaration that the dominion of the British seas belonged to England,—all had been wiped out. Cromwell indeed succeeded in retaining the term "British seas" in its original ambiguity; but both he and his commissioners admitted (verbally) that it meant, in reference to the salute, only the narrow sea—a statement which was in contradiction to the instructions issued to the naval officers, and to the practice both before and afterwards. The clause providing for the striking of the flag was saved, but only in a mutilated form. It ran as follows: "That the ships and vessels of the said United Provinces, as well those of war as others which shall meet any of the men-of-war of this Commonwealth in the British Seas, shall strike their flag and lower the top-sail, in such manner as the same has ever been observed at any time heretofore under any other form of government."[2]

This, as the States-General took care to point out to their fellow-countrymen, was no more than they had voluntarily agreed to do, and had instructed Tromp to perform, previous to the declaration of war. It was, however, the first time the custom had been recognised in a treaty.

After the conclusion of peace, the English naval commanders took pleasure in vigorously enforcing their right to the "honour of the flag," and, as above stated, notwithstanding the verbal limitation made by Cromwell and Thurloe, they did not confine the demand to the narrow sea. Within a few weeks of the proclamation of the treaty, and before its details were known

[1] Dumont, *Corps Diplomatique*, VI. ii. 75. *Verbael of the Ambassadors*, 356.

[2] XIII. Item, quod naves et navigia dictarum Fœderatarum Provinciarum, tam bellica et ad hostium vim propulsandam instructa, quam alia, quæ alicui e navibus bellicis hujus Reipublicæ in maribus Britannicis obviam dederint, vexillum suum e mali vertice detrahent, et supremum velum demittent, eo modo, quo ullis retro temporibus, sub quocunque anteriori regimine, unquam observatam fuit.

to the fleet, Vice-Admiral Lawson encountered the "bellicose" De With off the north coast of Scotland. The Dutch admiral with three men-of-war was convoying seventy sail bound for Greenland, and he at once struck his flag and fired a salute, which the English returned. He also "submitted to a search," though stating that it was not customary for men-of-war to do so. "De With," wrote Lawson, "begins to know his duty, being very submissive, acknowledging the sovereignty of England in the seas, and yielding as much as could have been required of any merchant ships."[1]

In the south the Dutch were not always so compliant, and disputes with the English officers sometimes arose as to whether the place where the striking of the flag was demanded was or was not within the British seas. Thus, Captain Cockraine, in the *Old Warwick*, met a fleet of Holland merchantmen under convoy of a man-of-war between the Lizard and Ushant. The merchant vessels struck their top-sails, but the man-of-war refused to strike, on the ground that he was not in the British but in the Spanish seas. Cockraine refrained from firing, as the ship was surrounded by others and there was "much wind." Instead, he wrote to the Admiralty. "I want to know," he said, "how far is intended by the British Seas, and how far our power reaches, so that we may make no unnecessary broils." There is nothing to show what answer he got; but a week later he encountered twenty-six Dutch merchant vessels bound for the Mediterranean, who refused to strike, and he had to fire thirty guns among them before they submitted.[2] About the same time, a States' man-of-war convoying a fleet of Hollander merchantmen met Captain Heaton, in the *Sapphire*, and did not strike until a shot was fired. Heaton sent a message to the commander saying that he had not fulfilled the articles of peace, and that the keeping of his flag and top-sail aloft when within shot of one of the ships of the State of England was a great abuse, and a gross affront by the States of Holland to the Commonwealth. To which the Dutch captain replied that if he had shot back at the *Sapphire* he would have been quite justified, as,

[1] Lawson, from the *Fairfax*, at Aberdeen, to the Admiralty Committee, 13th May 1654. Same to Blackburn, 13th May. *State Papers*, *Dom.*, lxxi. 78, 79.

[2] Cockraine to the Admiralty Committee, 11th Aug. 1654. *Ibid.*, lxxiv. 39.

being on his own coast, he was not bound to strike, and had done so not out of duty, but from "brotherly love," and he then re-hoisted his top-sails and flag. Heaton deliberated whether or not he should fight the Dutchman for doing this, but refrained. He, too, wrote to the Admiralty asking how he should act in similar cases in future.[1]

The authorities at the Admiralty were always sparing in advice on such matters. They showed the same reticence as the Government in defining the extent of the British seas, and for the same reason—that they did not know themselves. This reluctance was shown, and a partial glimpse afforded, in a letter to General Montague (afterwards Earl of Sandwich) which Richard, Cromwell's son, wrote during his brief tenure of the Protectorate. Telling him to demand "the flag" of such foreign ships of war as he might encounter in the British seas, he remarked that there had been "some doubt" as to how far the British seas extend. Not unnaturally, "Tumble-down Dick" shrank from plunging into a matter which had puzzled the great Oliver and every one else. "Not being willing," he said, "to determine that in our instructions, we rather put in general terms the 'British Seas' only. We judge there is no question of all the sea on this side the Shagenriffe;[2] on the other side [the Baltic] you have need be tender, and to avoid all disputes of this nature, if it be possible, because war and peace depend on it."[3]

Disputes about the flag were not the only differences that arose on the sea. At the end of September 1654 complaints came from Yarmouth that the English fishermen were being molested by the Dutch in the herring fishery there. They had come, it was alleged, with a multitude of busses, "far above a thousand sail," and, contrary to the custom before the war, "and against the laws of this nation," shot their nets so close to the sands that the English were crowded

[1] Heaton to the Admiralty Committee, 15th Aug. 1654. *State Papers, Dom.*, lxxiv. 61, 62.

[2] The Skagerreef or Scaw, the north point of Jutland, Denmark. The ships were going to the north in connection with the war between Denmark and Sweden.

[3] Richard Cromwell, the Protector, to General Montague, 18th March 1659. Thurloe's *Collections*, vii. 633.

out and hindered in their usual fishing. The Dutch busses occupied a space of more than forty miles adjacent to the coast, and the English fishermen were afraid to use their nets lest they lost them. When they remonstrated with the foreigners for coming so near the shore, they were vilified, and muskets and "great guns" were shot at them.[1] By the direction of Cromwell and the Council, the complaints were transmitted to the ambassadors, who were still in London, and they requested the States-General and the commanders of the ships guarding the busses to make every effort to avoid giving cause for complaint. In the inquiry which followed, the Dutch fishermen denied the charges against them, and in turn accused some of the Englishmen of shooting at them, cutting their ropes, and calling them dogs, rogues, and devils. They stated that they had carried on the fishing in the old accustomed way, the English usually fishing peacefully along with them.[2]

Under the Commonwealth and Protectorate very little was heard of schemes for establishing fishery societies, such as appeared and disappeared so frequently in the preceding reigns and afterwards. That the Puritan spirit was not antagonistic to projects of the kind was shown by proposals made in 1649. One of these contemplated the employment of Dutchmen to establish "a fishing trade" in England. It was referred by the Council of State to Sir Henry Vane and Alderman Wilson, with what result does not appear. Another, briefly described, was to set up a fishing trade for the English nation;[3] and about this time the attention of some writers on commercial matters was directed to the same end. The only thing apparently effected was the gift to the Corporation of the Poor in London of some of the Dutch busses captured in the war, to be used in fishing on the English coast. During this period of our history the Government

[1] The Information of William Gunnell, and others, of Great Yarmouth, 25th September 1654. *Verbael of the Ambassadors*, 600, 601.

[2] *Ibid.*, 612, 614, 646, 689, 711. From the sworn depositions made before the Burgomasters of Enkhuisen, it appears that that town had at least 246 busses at the Yarmouth fishing in 1654.

[4] *Brit. Mus. MSS. Stowe*, 152, fol. 135.

had other things to think about than the launching of fishery schemes. Cromwell, however, at the conclusion of the war, renewed the licenses to the fishermen of Dieppe and Calais to fish in the seas between England and France, at the usual times and places.[1]

[1] Proc. Council of State, 9th June 1654. Vice-Admiral Lawson, in transmitting to the Admiralty the request from the Governor of Calais, said it had been the practice for the French and Spanish men-of-war to suffer the fishermen of each nation to fish freely, although the war between these Powers had lasted so long. *State Papers, Dom.*, xcviii. 13.

CHAPTER XII.

CHARLES II.

THE SECOND DUTCH WAR.

THE Restoration, in 1660, made no change either in the national sentiment or the national policy of England concerning the sovereignty of the sea. Charles II. encouraged the pretension with as much zeal as had been shown by his father, or by the Commonwealth and the Lord Protector; and he was more astute than any of his predecessors in taking advantage of the national feeling with regard to it in order to carry out his own selfish policy. Under the pretence of maintaining the dominion of the sea, a base and treacherous war was waged against the United Provinces in circumstances which will for ever sully the reputation of the king. The measures at first taken were, however, of a peaceful kind. Commercial jealousy of the Dutch was still a strong factor in England. As firmly as ever the opinion was held that the primary source of their great trade, shipping, and wealth lay in their fisheries, which also formed a great "nursery" of seamen for the navy.

As in the reign of Charles I., it was therefore towards the development of British fisheries that efforts were first directed. The means taken with this view were twofold: the taxation of imported fish which had been caught by foreigners, and the creation of great fishery associations like those which had been established earlier in the century. The Navigation Act, which was passed a few months after the Restoration, while more oppressive to Dutch commerce and shipping than the Act of 1651, was less stringent in this particular. The measure of the Rump Parliament prohibited the importation or exportation of fish, or its carriage coastways, unless such fish had been caught by subjects. This prohibition was ineffective,[1] and it was now replaced by the imposition of double customs on all kinds of dried or salted fish imported, if caught or brought by vessels other than English.[2] Three years later, the importation of fresh herrings, cod, haddocks, and coal-fish was absolutely prohibited unless they had been taken and imported in vessels certified to be English.[3] With the view of still further promoting the fisheries, the same prohibition was afterwards extended to cured fish and certain other fresh fish,[4] which practically restored the provision of the first Act of 1651. To a large extent these variations were due to the trade rivalries that existed in England, the party which was uppermost at the time forcing the measures that were most in its interest.

Besides protective duties and monopolies, more direct means of encouraging the fisheries were tried. The always attractive idea was revived of establishing a great national fishery society, which, on the one hand, would enrich those who supported it with their purse, and on the other hand would increase the prosperity and the power of the country. Simon Smith, who had been the agent of the Royal Fishery Society in the reign of Charles I., lost no time in presenting to the king his two books on the subject, along with a petition in which he dwelt upon the advantages that would accrue to the nation from the labours of such an association.[5] Smith recommended that all the corporations and county towns in the kingdom should con-

[1] Bills to repeal it were introduced into the Commons in 1656, 1657, and 1658. *Commons' Journals*, vii. 451, &c.

[2] *An Act for the Encouraging and Increasing of Shipping and Navigation*, 12 Car. II., c. 18, cl. v. 1660.

[3] *An Act for the Encouragement of Trade*, 15 Car. II., c. 7, ss. xiii., xiv. 1663.

[4] *An Act against importing Cattle from Ireland and other parts beyond the Seas, and Fish taken by Foreigners*, 18 & 19 Car. II., c. 2, s. ii. Any ling, herring, cod, pilchard, fresh or salted, dried or bloated, or any salmon, eels, or conger, taken by aliens and brought into the realm, were liable to be seized by any person for his own benefit and the benefit of the poor of the parish. The prohibition to import stockfish and live eels was withdrawn by 32 Car. II., c. 2, 1680.

[5] "To the High and Mighty Monarch Charles ye Second, &c., the humble petition of Simon Smith, late agent for the Royall Fishing," MS. prefixed in a copy of *The Herring-Bvsse Trade*, and *A True Narration of the Royall Fishings of Great Brittaine and Ireland*, bound together in vellum, elaborately ornamented in gold, and bearing the royal arms and the letters C. R. on both sides.

jointly raise a stock to buy hemp and other materials to equip busses, which were to be built at the seaports nearest to them and sent to the fishing at Shetland; and he calculated, after the usual fashion, that each buss would maintain twenty families in work, "breed country youths to be mariners," and cause many ships to be employed in exporting the herrings and bringing back commodities.

Charles was apparently impressed by Smith's arguments. Within two months of the Restoration he caused a letter to be written to the Lord Mayor of London, referring to the good done by the Society formed in 1632, "as by the book called the Royal Herring Busse Fishing (*sic*) presented to him, plainly appeared"; requesting particulars to be obtained of all the poor inhabitants within each ward who were in want of employment; requesting that the Lord Mayor and Aldermen should raise a stock by a free subscription to fit out a buss or fishing vessel for each ward; and that storehouses should be built in suitable places about the river Thames, provided with nets, casks, salt, and all things in readiness. The busses were to attend the fishing at Shetland, according to the "prescribed orders in the aforesaid book," and the king declared he would recommend the same course to all the cities and towns throughout the kingdom, so as to make it a national employment.[1]

The assistance of Parliament was also called in. On 8th November 1660 the House of Commons remitted "the consideration of the fisheries" to the Committee for Trade and Navigation, who were asked to inform the House "what they thought necessary for the regulation and advancement of that trade."[2] The Committee's report does not appear to have been preserved, but on 8th December a "Bill for Encouraging the Fisheries of this Kingdom" was introduced. It was remitted to a large committee, including the members for the seaport towns, and

[1] Sir Edward Nicholas to the Lord Mayor, 23rd July 1660. *Remembrancia*, p. 143. There is an undated copy among the State Papers (*Domestic*) erroneously calendared under September 1662 (vol. lix. 6: compare vol. xli. 19, under date September 1661). The original is in the Guildhall. Simon Smith was employed in the preliminary work connected with the Society, and in 1662 rendered an account of his disbursements, amounting to £456, including £150 "for setting the poor to work so as to breed up teachers for making nets, &c." *State Papers, Dom.*, liv. 77.

[2] *Commons' Journals*, viii. 179. *State Papers, Dom.*, Charles II., xxi. 27.

being read a third time on 27th December, was sent up to the Lords.[1] It was, to a large extent, directed against fishing by foreigners on the British coasts and the use of destructive methods of fishing. One of its clauses prohibited trawling, whether by subjects or foreigners, within eight miles of certain parts of the coast. The fate of this important measure was unfortunate. The Parliament was dissolved two days after it reached the Lords, and nothing further was heard of it.[2]

In the following year a measure dealing with the fisheries was passed by the Scottish Parliament.[3] The preamble contained the common declarations as to the value of the fisheries to shipping and commerce, to the navy, in the employment of the poor, and as furnishing the materials for a great native export. The Act provided for the formation of societies and companies of free-born Scotsmen, each member to supply at least 500 merks Scots as stock, and they were to receive various

[1] *Commons' Journals*, viii. 203, 215, 222, 228. *Lords' Journals*, xi. 228*b*. According to the Dutch ambassador, the Bill was not passed without much debate and opposition (De Witt's *Brieven*, iv. 68), no doubt principally owing to the provisions concerning fish-days. An amendment was carried limiting Wednesday to be a fish-day in all inns, taverns, and victualling houses.

[2] *Lords' Journals*, xi. 239. De Witt's *Brieven*, iv. 66. The preamble was of the usual kind: that the honour and greatness of the king and the power and wealth of the kingdom depended upon shipping and commerce, the fisheries being one of the greatest means thereto; and it proceeded to say that the kingdom was specially suited for fishery by reason of the number of harbours, and the sea from which foreign nations took such great wealth, set their people on work, and made their towns populous and prosperous. The foreigners were not content with a temperate and moderate exercise of the liberty of fishing on our coasts, which was permitted to them by favour of the king, but fished with illegal instruments which served to destroy the brood of fish in some places, causing the greatest poverty; and in other places they came with whole fleets among the nets and boats of subjects, to the great damage and hindrance of their lawful business. The king was therefore most humbly beseeched to establish completely and vigorously and maintain the rights of his crown over the seas, and to give such orders and instructions to the admirals and commanders at sea as might be necessary to this effect. The first clause prohibited trawling, whether by subjects or foreigners, within eight miles of the coast of Sussex and the coast to the westwards, and other clauses prohibited the use of set-nets or other nets with small meshes on the coast "or within half seas over," or the use of seines by foreigners within ten miles of any part of the coast to the hindering of subjects in their fishing. Offenders were to be brought in as prize. These provisions were in part aimed against the French.

[3] *Act for the Fishings and Erecting of Companies for promoting the same*, 12th June 1661. *Acta Parl. Scot.*, vii. 259.

privileges and immunities, including power to erect houses for the fishing trade wherever it was most convenient, a "limited allowance" to be paid for the ground. An absolute monopoly of the export of fish, fresh or cured, was granted to the companies; foreigners were prohibited from curing herrings or white fish on land, or erecting booths for the purpose,—a provision aimed against the German merchants at Shetland,—but encouragement was given to foreign fishermen to settle and become naturalised in Scotland, and even to become burgesses, and they were to be exempt from taxation for seven years. The importation of everything required for the fishery, including "Holland nets," was to be free of custom dues; the exports were to be similarly exempted, and the "teind" and "assize" herrings were to be remitted for nine years.

The provisions of this Act differed essentially from the scheme proposed by Charles I. in 1630, which aroused so much opposition, inasmuch as the companies were to be composed solely of Scotsmen. The question of the territorial or "reserved" waters belonging to Scotland was thus avoided. It appears, indeed, that the Act was due to the representations of the Royal Burghs, for in the preceding autumn they expressed a desire for the "erection of the fishing trade in Scotland," and resolved to bring the subject before the next Parliament.[1] Little was done in Scotland under this Act. A company was formed, which, however, seemed more desirous of misusing its privileges than of fostering the fisheries, if we may judge from a petition of the burghs to the Lords of the Exchequer, praying that the company might be restricted to import nothing but what was necessary for the fishing trade. The town of Musselburgh also was empowered to equip busses, and various towns in Fife applied for and received permission to fish in the northern seas. The Scottish society became an incubus, and in 1690, when its function seems to have shrunk to the mechanical exaction of a tax of £6 Scots per last

[1] *Records Convent. Roy. Burghs*, iii. 523, 15th September 1660. The commissioners, taking into consideration how advantageous it would be to the increase of trade and the common weal of the whole burghs and kingdom "that the fisching tread be erected within the samyn, and wnderstanding by thair registeris and wther paperis in thair clarkis handis that the said tread hes bein endevoured in former tymes but not takin full effect," instructed that the records be searched, and the matter represented to Parliament.

of herrings exported from Scotland, the Act under which it had been formed was repealed.[1]

In England the efforts to establish a fishery association met with but little more success, although the king showed an active interest in its promotion. On 22nd August he issued a commission under the great seal, appointing his brother, the Duke of York, and twenty-nine noblemen, including all the great officers of the Court, with six others, as the "Council of the Royal Fishery of Great Britain and Ireland," to which he assigned various privileges and monopolies. To encourage the building of busses, the king "requested" that wharfs, docks, and storehouses should be built on the Thames and in all the ports of the kingdom for their accommodation and use; all the "returns" or commodities brought back from foreign lands for the fish exported were exempted from customs for seven years; all victuallers, inns, alehouses, taverns, coffee-houses, and the like, were to be bound to take from one to four, or more, barrels of herrings from the society yearly at thirty shillings a-barrel, "until foreign vent be attained to perfection"; each barrel of pickled herrings or cod-fish brought into the realm by the Flemings, or others, was to be taxed half-a-crown, the tax to be paid into the coffers of the society, and the protection of the State was to be given to their fishing vessels and the vessels employed in exporting fish. It was further provided that the money necessary for the scheme should be obtained by a lottery, to be set up for three years, and by a collection in every parish in the kingdom.

A few days later, Charles issued letters-patent saying that he had requested a bountiful subscription from London to fit out fishing vessels, which should belong to the wards, and recommending the same to the whole country, as the Hollanders had so engrossed the fisheries that the fishing towns were greatly decayed; the local officers were to see to the collections being made, the monies to be paid to the high-sheriff and by him remitted to the Earl of Pembroke, who was appointed treasurer. Those who subscribed to the stock were to pay their money in three instalments to Mr Thomas King, a London merchant

[1] *Rec. Conv. Roy. Burghs*, iii. 626. *Acta Parl. Scot.*, vii. 64, 103, 195, &c. *Ibid.*, William and Mary, c. 103.

and member of Parliament, who became the moving spirit in the project; and the adventurers were to have the option of withdrawing after three years, on giving six months' notice.[1] Literary puffs were not neglected. A highly-coloured account of the value of the Dutch fisheries (founded mainly on the Raleigh tract) and of the rosy prospects of the society was published "by command." The cost of a buss, equipped and provisioned for four months, was set down at £835; the herrings caught in that time were calculated to fetch a round £1000, giving an immediate profit of £165 after meeting all expenses.[2]

Notwithstanding the active support of the Court and the energy of many agents, subscriptions to the fishery society filtered in but slowly. The sum collected for it in the London churches in the year 1661 amounted to the paltry total of £818, 6s. 4½d.—scarcely enough to set forth one buss,—and in the autumn of 1664 it was reported that the amount collected throughout England and Ireland was only £1076. The lottery, too, from which a great deal was hoped, gave rise to much corruption, confusion, and dispute, without notably enriching the society.[3] In these depressing circumstances recourse was again had to Parliament. On 5th March 1662 a "Bill to confirm his Majesty's letters patent concerning the fishing trade" was introduced into the House of Commons and remitted to a committee; but it ultimately became transformed into a mere local Act dealing with pilchard-fishing.[4] The king was not yet discouraged. The Masters of the Trinity House were consulted in July as to the cost of ten busses he had resolved to build, and the amount required—£9000—was actually handed over to Mr Thomas King. Charles further offered to pay £200 to every person who had a new

[1] *State Papers, Dom.*, xli. 20.

[2] ΙΧΘΨΟΘΗΡΑ, *or the Royal Trade of Fishing, Discovering the inestimable Profit the Hollanders have made thereof, with the vast Emoluments and Advantages that will redound to his Sacred Majesty and his three Kingdoms by the Improvement of it. Now seasonably published by Command for the Benefit of the Nation.* London, 1662.

[3] *State Papers, Dom.*, 1663, lxxiii. 56; lxxxvi. 104, 105, 106; xci. 53; ciii. 130; cix. 2. "But Lord!" says Pepys, "to see how superficially things are done in the business of the Lottery, which will be the disgrace of the Fishery, and without profit." *Diary*, iv. 369 (ed. 1893).

[4] *Commons' Journals*, viii. 378, 383. 14 Car. II., c. 28.

English-built fishing-buss ready for the fishing before the middle of the following year.[1] To facilitate the success of the society on the foreign markets, an Act was passed in 1663, after considerable discussion, to make the use of the Dutch system of curing and packing herrings compulsory, so as to avoid abuses, and bring the English-cured herrings into repute.[2]

At a meeting of the Privy Council a few months later, Sir William Batten, Sir Richard Chaterton, and Sir William Ryder were appointed to formulate proposals for the organisation of the Royal Herring Fishery, and, after consultation with Simon Smith and Mr Thomas King, it was resolved to adopt the Dutch system and regulations and to go on with the scheme.[3] The next step was the issue by the king in the spring of 1664 of another commission under the great seal, by which the Duke of York and thirty-six assistants were incorporated as Governors and Company of the Royal Fishery of Great Britain and Ireland; the Lord Mayor and the Chamberlain of the City of London were appointed treasurers.[4]

In spite of all efforts, such as they were, extremely little was done by the society before the outbreak of the second Dutch war. The slovenly way in which the business was managed and the corruption in regard to the finances were notorious. Pepys, who was a member of the council of the society, and had grave misgivings as to the issue of their labours, gives amusing glimpses of the proceedings in his Diary. He examined the accounts, and declared that "the loose and base manner that monies so collected are disposed of in, would make a man never part with a penny in that manner." The Duke of York and the members did not even meet to read the king's commission until July, and

[1] Lord Southampton to the Masters of the Trinity House, 31st July 1662. The Masters to the Lord Treasurer, 23rd August. The Lord Treasurer to the king, 2nd Sept. *State Papers, Dom.*, lix. 7; *Entry Book*, vii. 258. Pepys' *Diary*, ii. 403, 404.

[2] *Commons' Journals*, viii. 497, &c. *Lords' Journals*, xi. 555, &c. 15 Car. II., c. 16. All herrings, white or red, were to be "justly and truly packed, and of one time of taking, salting, saving, or drying, and equally well packed in the midst and every part of the barrel." This was to be done by a sworn packer, and the barrel branded after the Dutch method.

[3] John Collins, *Salt and Fishery*, 2. 1682.

[4] *State Papers, Dom.*, ciii. 130.

the later meetings were often futile from the want of a quorum. "A sad thing it is to see," says Pepys, "so great a work so ill followed, for at this pace it can come to nothing but disgrace to us all."[1]

The failure of the attempt to establish a great national fishery to expel the foreigner from the British seas, after five years' endeavour, was very agreeable to the Dutch, who had watched the proceedings with close attention, and had tried, openly and secretly, to hinder success whenever they had an opportunity. Immediately after the Restoration, the States-General, anxious to come to a good understanding with Charles, sent special ambassadors to London to arrange a treaty of friendship and alliance, and to renew previous treaties.[2] The negotiations which ensued dealt, among other things, with the fisheries, the flag, and the sovereignty of the sea. The object of De Witt, the great Dutch Minister, was the usual one of his countrymen on similar occasions—viz., to secure as far as possible the commercial and other privileges which had been granted by the Intercursus Magnus. Charles, on the other hand, wished at the very least to retain all the concessions that Cromwell had secured by the treaty of 1654.[3]

When the Dutch ambassadors arrived, or at all events when they began negotiations in London, the House of Commons had already taken up the question of the fisheries. Action of this kind always occasioned the Dutch anxiety. They knew it was directed against their predominance in a vital industry, and that it was usually followed by troublesome claims to the sovereignty of the sea and to an exclusive fishing on the British coasts. Here were all those questions raised in threatening fashion in the Bill passed by the Commons and

[1] *Diary*, vol. iv. 177, 192, 233, 263, &c.

[2] The ambassadors were Van Beverwaert (Louis of Nassau), Simon van Hoorn, the burgomaster of Amsterdam, Michael van Gogh, and Joachim Ripperda. Pontalis, *John de Witt*, i. 263. *Brieven, geschreven ende gewisselt tusschen de Heer Johan de Witt, Raedt-Pensionaris en Groot-Segelbewaerder van Hollandt en West-Vrieslandt, ende de Gevolmaghtigden van den Staedt der Vereenigde Nederlanden*, &c., iv. 1, 46.

[3] De Witt's *Brieven*, iv. 109, 119. Clarendon's *Memoirs*, iii. 434. There are numerous papers referring to these negotiations and the subsequent treaty, including "the articles which the States' Ambassadors Extraordinary are to procure from his Majesty of Great Britain," among *State Papers, Foreign Treaty Papers* (*Holland*), 1651-1665, Bdl. 46.

sent up to the Lords. Moreover, English privateers, sailing under Swedish colours, had lately been seizing Dutch herring-busses, and though protests were made by the ambassadors, no redress was obtained.[1] The debates and proceedings in the House of Commons attracted immediate attention in Holland.[2] De Witt at once took up a firm attitude. He declared that the new pretension of England to the dominion of the seas and for the ruin of the Great Fishery would meet with the most determined resistance of the Republic; and, while consoling himself with the thought that reason had always prevailed against it in the past, he urged the ambassadors to use every means in their power with the Peers and the king in order to frustrate it. The Marquis of Ormonde, who was an intimate friend of Beverwaert's and one of Charles's Ministers, was bribed to use his influence to the same end. This nobleman informed the ambassador that when he was asked to favour the fishery project, he had answered that while he desired the advantage of the nation as much as any man, it would be first necessary to prepare for war, as it was in reality an affair of state; and he took credit with his Dutch friend for having induced many members of Parliament to oppose the Bill.[3] Whether these intrigues had any influence in causing the fishery question to be so frequently "laid aside" in Parliament can only be surmised.

So much concerned were the States-General about the provisions of the Bill, that they despatched a special letter to be presented to the king, in the hope, as De Witt said, that the resolution of the Commons might be suspended and its execution prevented.[4] But when it became known in Holland that

[1] *Res. Holl.*, 13th Sept. 1659, 261. *Ibid.*, 1660, p. 749; 1661, p. 181.

[2] *Hollantsche Mercurius*, 1661, pp. 9, 10. De Witt's *Brieven*, iv. 48, 61, 68, &c.

[3] De Witt to Van Beuningen, $\frac{\text{27 December 1660}}{\text{6 January 1661}}$; the same to Van Beverwaert and Van Hoorn, $\frac{4}{14}$ Jan. 1661; Van Beverwaert to De Witt, $\frac{3}{13}$, $\frac{4}{14}$ Jan. 1661. *Brieven*, i. 344; iv. 65, 66, 68. Pontalis, *John De Witt*, i. 267.

[4] "Dutch Ambrs Memoriall desiring the Act of Parliament about fishing may not pass," 17th Dec. 1660. Copy in *S. P., Dom.* Collection, Chas. II., vol. 339, p. 581. It is to the effect that the extraordinary ambassadors were informed that a Bill had been introduced into the Lower Chamber regarding the herring fishery, in which foreigners were to be prohibited from fishing within eight or ten "leagues" ("huiet ou dix lieuës") from the coast, and praying the king to prevent the said Bill from becoming an Act of Parliament. It contains the usual arguments as to immemorial possession, treaty rights, &c.

the Bill had been shelved by the dissolution of Parliament, and that Charles was unlikely to summon another Parliament for a long time, the ambassadors were told to withhold it, but at the same time to make its substance known to the Ministers, so that the king might learn of it indirectly. They were also warned to say nothing, in the negotiations for the treaty on which they were engaged, that might allow it to be supposed that the right of the Dutch to fish in the seas around the coast of England was derived from any treaty or compact, or from any concession on the part of England. On the contrary, it arose *jure proprio* from the law of nature and the law of nations, the stipulation in the treaty of 1495 merely expressing this mutual right of free fishery with the view of preventing violence on either side.

The negotiations dragged on slowly. The English commissioners showed no anxiety to discuss the questions of the fishery, commerce, or navigation, about which the Dutch were most concerned. Taking their stand on the Navigation Act, which Parliament had recently passed, they declined to listen to any proposal for free fishing on the English coast. The Dutch ambassadors grew hopeless of being able to conclude a treaty satisfactory to the States, and this feeling was strengthened by the jealousy and resentment which the English began to manifest concerning the simultaneous negotiations that were going on between Paris and The Hague.[1] Foreseeing the difficulties likely to arise with England over the fishery question, De Witt had made a dexterous move. In the negotiations with France for a treaty between the two countries, he proposed that an article should be inserted reciprocally guaranteeing the right of free fishing in the sea to the subjects of each nation against any that might endeavour to interfere with it. A similar proposal had been made to France in 1653, but was rejected owing to the desire of the French Government to avoid irritating Cromwell.[2] Even now, when international conditions were more favourable for its acceptance, the French looked askance at it, and asked the States to define precisely their position as to the right of fishery. They said in reply that

[1] *Brieven*, i. 344; iv. 66, 69, 81, 87, 89, 105, 109.

[2] Boreel to De Witt, $\frac{\text{25 Nov.}}{\text{5 Dec.}}$ 1653. *Ibid.*, i. 54.

they claimed the right of fishing in the open sea by the law of nations; that it was a right independent of any treaties, which merely illustrated and explained it, and was like the liberty of commerce and navigation — free and open to all. The two countries should therefore, it was urged, agree mutually to support one another in the free exercise of this common right. In substance this was clearly a demand that France should combine with them to resist the English pretension to the sovereignty of the sea, on the point in which it chiefly affected the United Provinces—namely, the fishery. The French met it by suggesting that, as a *quid pro quo*, the States should guarantee them in the same way against the claim of the English to make French ships lower their flag to them in the narrow seas. France, as we have seen, was not troubled by England about the fishery, although many French vessels fished off the English coast. On the other hand, the Dutch had formally agreed to strike to English ships by the treaty of 1654,—a ceremony that France declined to render, and avoided as far as possible. De Witt saw that if the States gave the guarantee desired, it would place in the hands of the French the power to compel them to take up arms against England at any time they chose, and he instructed the Dutch ambassadors, if they could not evade the proposal altogether, to request a declaration, in writing, of the precise claims concerning the striking of the flag which the King of France put forward as against the King of England. He said the obligation of the States to strike was indisputable; but it was not a recognition of England's pretended dominion of the sea, but merely a formal deference that republics had always shown to monarchies. De Witt privately expressed the opinion that the French would hesitate to formulate in writing any claim of that kind, and the result proved his foresight. The French ambassador in London made certain overtures to Charles without receiving a satisfactory reply, and the French proposal for a guarantee about the flag was dropped.

A diplomatic tussle then took place as to whether the word "fishery" should appear in the treaty. The French were anxious to keep it out, and the Dutch as desirous that it should be expressly included. Later, De Witt seemed disposed to concede the point, provided other words could be found which would "clearly stipulate, in express terms, that if their subjects were molested in their fishery the French would carry out against those who molested them the guarantee promised." At this stage, however,—March 1662,—the Dutch towns insisted on the fishery guarantee being absolutely explicit. The states most concerned—Holland and West Friesland—unanimously passed a resolution that if France refused to agree to the word "fishery" being inserted, the negotiations should be broken off and the ambassadors recalled. Louis XIV. then gave way. "I must admit," he wrote to his ambassador in London, "that I have the same interest in this guarantee as the Dutch, since the right of fishing may just as well be refused by England to my subjects as to those of the States-General.[1] The treaty was signed on 27th April 1662, and in the fourth article the two contracting Powers mutually agreed to assist one another in protecting their fishermen from those who might molest them.[2]

The stipulation in the treaty with France was a notable triumph for De Witt. For the first time in their history the Dutch had succeeded in formally binding another Power to help them in resisting the English claims to the sovereignty of the sea, so far as concerned the liberty of fishing. Should Charles II. wish to emulate the exploits of his father by sending a fleet to force licenses on the Dutch herring-busses, he would now have to reckon on the combined opposition of France and the United Provinces. The triumph was,

[1] Letters from Van Beuningen to De Witt, $\frac{1}{11}$ Feb. 1661 to $\frac{20 \text{ Feb.}}{2 \text{ March}}$ 1662; from De Witt to Van Beuningen, $\frac{3}{13}$ Oct. 1661 to $\frac{12}{22}$ March 1662. *Brieven*, i. 432-514. *Secreete Resolutiën van de Staaten van Holland en West-Vriesland*, ii. 246. Pontalis, *John de Witt*, i. 276. Pontalis scarcely grasps the question of the fishery when he says: "The free right of fishing still more directly concerned the States-General; they could not prevail in England to allow them the enjoyment of it, *so long as it had not been accorded to them by France*, and they therefore made it a condition of their treaty with Louis XIV."

[2] Dumont, *Corps Diplomatique*, VI. ii. 412. Aitzema, *Saken van Staet en Oorlogh*, x. 305. The article was as follows: "IV. L'obligation reciproque de s'entr'aider et deffendre, s'entend aussi pour estre Sa Majesté et lesdits Seigneurs Estats Generaux, leurs Pays et Sujets, conservez et maintenus en tous leurs Droits, Possessions, Immunitez et Libertez, tant de Navigation, que de Commerce et Pêche, et autres quelconques par Mer et par Terre, qui se trouveront leur appartenir par le Droit commun, ou estre acquis par des Traitez faits ou à faire, en la maniere susdite, envers et contre tous Roys, Princes, Republiques, ou autres Estats Souverains," &c.

however, a barren one, and the treaty had no practical effect. Within a few years the Dutch Republic was in the throes of war, first with England, and then with England and France, and other treaties took its place. It had, however, an immediate influence upon the policy of Charles, who feared an alliance of the two Continental Powers against England. When he heard of the negotiations about the fishery guarantee he tried, both at Paris and at The Hague, to prevent an agreement being reached, and the obstacles which he interposed delayed the conclusion of the treaty. Sir George Downing, the English ambassador in Holland, who had taken a prominent part in the debates in the Commons on the Fishery Bill, and whose hostile sentiments to the Dutch were notorious, took up an unusual attitude. He assured De Witt that since the United Provinces were a republic and did not seek to encroach on England, they might freely continue their fishery without fearing the least trouble; but England could never allow that France, a monarchy, and a bold and enterprising nation, should have unrestricted liberty of fishing on the English coasts. It was feared, he said, that by its fishery the abundance of mariners and the increase in shipping which would follow would make it formidable to England, and this the English, in accordance with their political maxims, would prevent. The French had frequently requested and received licenses for a limited number of vessels to fish in English waters, sometimes for the king's table. If, therefore, he continued, the proposed guarantee were agreed to, the Republic as well as France would be *de facto* at war with England, because England would never leave the French fishermen at peace. The same language was used by Downing to many of the deputies of the States-General, in the hope of frightening them, but it made no impression. "I have declared to Downing," wrote De Witt, "that sooner than acknowledge this imaginary sovereignty over the seas, or even receive from the English, as a concession, that freedom of navigation and fishing which belongs to us by natural right and the law of nations, we would shed our last drop of blood." [1]

[1] "Herr Downingh de voorsz. antwoorde begonde te justificeren, door de gepretendeerde Souverainiteyt van de Engelschen op de Zee, . . . ende hebbe ick rondt uyt verklaert, dat eer wy die imaginaire Souverainiteyt souden erkennen, ofte by

The inflexible attitude of De Witt, and the actual conclusion of the treaty with France, extinguished for a time the hope of compelling the Dutch to acknowledge the right of England to the exclusive fishing along her coasts, and the proposal was not pressed upon the ambassadors in London during the dilatory negotiations for the Anglo-Dutch treaty. With regard to the striking of the flag, Charles received more satisfaction. The tenth article of the treaty, which was signed at Whitehall on $\frac{4}{14}$ September 1662, stipulated that Dutch ships, whether men-of-war or others, should strike their flag and lower their top-sails on meeting an English man-of-war on the British seas. It was indeed precisely the same clause as that contained in Cromwell's treaty of 1654, except that certain verbal alterations were made in accordance with the change in the form of the English government.[1]

In the earlier years of the reign of Charles II., comparatively little was heard of disputes about the flag, which afterwards became so frequent and important. One instance occurred in 1662, when a Dutch vessel that was in Yarmouth Roads without a commission was taken to the Downs for refusing to lower her sails to a king's ship.[2] A case of much greater interest happened in the previous year, when Captain R. Holmes, in command of the *Royal Charles*, allowed the ship of the Swedish ambassador to pass him on the Thames without compelling it to strike. As the English Admiralty were always punctilious in enforcing the salute on state occasions, as when a foreign ambassador was concerned, Holmes

maniere van concessie van de Engelschen ontfangen, die vryheydt tot het bevaeren ende bevisschen van de Zee, die ons van de nature, ende nae 't Volckeren-reght competeerde, wy alle den laetsten druppel bloedt daer by souden laeten." De Witt to Van Beverwaert and Van Hoorn, $\frac{14}{24}$ June 1661 (*Brieven*, iv. 144); the same to Van Beuningen, $\frac{4}{14}$ Dec. 1661 (*ibid.*, i. 471).

[1] Dumont, *op. cit.*, VI. ii. 424. "X. Item, quod naves et navigia dictarum Fœderatarum Provinciarum, tam bellica et ad hostium vim propulsandam instructa, quam alia, quæ alicui e navibus bellicis dicti Domini Regis Magnæ Britanniæ in maribus Britannicis obviam dederint, vexillum suum e mali vertice detrahent, et supremum velum demittent, eo modo quo ullis retro temporibus, unquam observatam fuit."

[2] *State Papers, Dom.*, lv. 14.

for his remissness was deprived of his command.[1] The case of Holmes had some interesting consequences. It revealed once more the want of precise knowledge at the Admiralty as to the rules which should be followed in making foreign ships strike their flag. The Duke of York, who was the Lord High Admiral, was himself ignorant on the point, and he asked the principal officials about it—Sir George Carteret, the treasurer; Coventry, his own secretary; Sir William Batten and Sir William Penn, commissioners of the navy and experienced naval officers; and lastly Mr Pepys, who was the clerk to the navy. It appears, however, that though they all "did do as much as they could," the information they possessed was of the scantiest kind. Pepys tells us that he knew nothing about it himself, and was forced "to study a lie" by fathering an improbable story on Selden, on the spur of the moment; but on the same evening the genial diarist bought a copy of Selden's *Mare Clausum* and sat up at nights diligently studying it, with the view of writing a treatise "about the business of striking sail" to present to the Duke. After nearly six weeks' inquiry and cogitation the Admiralty officials "agreed upon some things to answer to the Duke about the practice of striking of the flags," which encouraged Pepys to persevere with his treatise, but it was never completed.[2]

A case of greater international importance occurred in the Mediterranean in the following year. Vice-Admiral Sir John Lawson was co-operating with De Ruyter against the Algerine pirates, and when the fleets met, the Dutch admiral saluted the English flag with guns and by lowering his own flag. Lawson returned the guns, but he did not strike his flag, as was the custom in distant seas, and De Ruyter, indignant at the slight, resolved not to strike his flag in future either, on

[1] *State Papers, Dom.*, xliv. 64. Pepys' *Diary*, ii. 135, 151. According to Rugge (*Brit. Mus. Add. MSS.*, 10, 116), quoted by Lord Braybrooke, Holmes insisted upon the Swede's lowering his flag, and had even fired a shot to enforce the observance; but the ambassador sent a message to the English frigate to assure the captain, on the word of honour of an ambassador, that the king by a verbal order had given him leave and a dispensation, and upon this false representation he was allowed to proceed. The Swedes, it may be added, were always disinclined to strike to English ships.

[2] Pepys' *Diary*, ii. 145, 146, 148, &c.

the ground that he was not in British waters, and that he had verbal orders which authorised him in refusing. When De Witt heard of his intentions, he immediately sent instructions in the name of the States of Holland strictly to observe the treaty, and declaring that the lowering of the flag must not be confined to British waters, since that might be interpreted into subjection to English dominion of the seas. If the English admiral again declined to lower his flag in return, De Ruyter was merely to report the fact to the States.[1] The action of De Witt was not designed simply to avoid a quarrel. As will be seen later, it expressed his settled conviction and the fixed policy of the Republic on this thorny subject.

All such questions as to the flag and the fisheries were soon submerged in the second Dutch war. The causes which brought it about were at root the same as those which had led up to the first. Commercial jealousy was always a smouldering flame, ready to burst into a great conflagration. The English believed that the Dutch had juggled them out of their trade and trading rights in several quarters of the globe, and with some reason. But probably the real motive was succinctly stated by Monk, now Duke of Albemarle, when he said that the essential cause of the quarrels between the two nations was that the English wanted a larger share of the trade of the Dutch. Charles himself, like his great Minister, the Chancellor Clarendon, seems to have been disinclined to the war, which, however, was advocated strongly by the Duke of York, who supported the contention of the merchants that it would benefit English commerce. Accusations were levelled against the Dutch of having by fraud and stratagem driven English trade almost entirely from the East and West Indies, and greatly reduced it in the Mediterranean and in Africa. These complaints were echoed in Parliament, and in April 1664 a resolution was passed by the two Houses declaring that the wrongs and

[1] Pontalis, *op. cit.*, i. 313. It would appear that on a previous occasion Lawson had returned the salute with the flag, for in the controversy with France on the striking of the flag a few years later, the Dutch stated, as an instance of the custom with England, that Lawson had shown this courtesy to De Ruyter off Tangiers. De Witt's *Brieven*, ii. 474.

outrages committed by the Dutch on our merchants in India, Africa, and elsewhere were "the greatest obstruction of our foreign trade," and that the king should be asked to "take some speedy course for redress." John de Witt fruitlessly endeavoured by all honourable means to avert hostilities. The warlike and marauding expedition of Holmes (now restored to favour) against the Dutch settlements on the west coast of Africa and in America was followed, as it was bound to be, by the retaliatory expedition of De Ruyter, which gave the English the pretext for declaring war in the spring of 1665.[1]

The war was exceedingly popular in England, and large sums were willingly voted by the House of Commons. Pepys tells us that the Court were "mad" for it, and another contemporary writer says it was the universal wish of the people.[2] Thus no appeal to the national passion of Englishmen about the sovereignty of the sea was required on this occasion, and such references as were made to the subject were of a formal kind. One of the accusations which the Parliament flung at the Dutch was that they had "proclaimed themselves Lords of the South Sea; and, in contempt, shot at and use other indignities to our royall flag, thereby affronting his Majesty and this nation." Then, in the preamble of the Act granting money for the equipment of a fleet, it was declared to be "for the preservation of his Majesty's ancient and undoubted sovereignty and dominion in the seas";[3] and in his instructions to the Duke of York as Lord High Admiral, the king said the great fleet he had prepared was "to assert his right to the dominion of the Narrow Seas," and for the mastery of the sea and the security of navigation.[4] But these phrases were to be expected. For the same reason, popular literature on England's dominion of the seas was on this occasion scanty,

[1] *Commons' Journals*, viii. 548, 553; *Lords' Journals*, xi. 599, 614; *Parlt. Hist.*, iv. 291, 308; Clarendon's *Memoirs*, ii. 235-237, 288; Hume, *Hist. of England*, lxiv.; Pepys' *Diary*, iv. 31, 42, &c.; Pontalis, *John de Witt*, i. 309.

[2] *The Dutch Drawn to the Life*, 1664. "Never was anything so unanimously applauded by men of all persuasions and interest as a Dutch Warre, which is the universal Wish of the people."

[3] 16 & 17 Car. II.

[4] The king to the Duke of York, 22nd March 1665. *State Papers, Dom.*, cxv. 76.

though some attempts were made to excite national animosity by the familiar arguments.[1]

The general course of the war, in which France, and then Denmark, combined with the United Provinces against England, does not concern us here.[2] It did not add fresh laurels to the brow of Charles II. as Sovereign of the Sea. Three great sea-fights took place—off Lowestoft, on 13th June 1665; in the Straits of Dover, from 11th to 14th June 1666 (the Four Days' Battle); and off the North Foreland, on 4th August in the same year. In the first and last the English were successful; in the Four Days' Battle the advantage lay with the Dutch; but the war ended in naval disaster and national humiliation for England. In June 1667, when the plenipotentiaries were quietly sitting at Breda leisurely engaged in arranging terms of peace, De Ruyter, with Cornelius the brother of John de Witt, suddenly appeared in the mouth of the Thames, and sent up a squadron which seized Sheerness and Chatham, and might have gone to London Bridge for all the king could have done to prevent it. They burned the best ships of the great fleet which was to have "asserted England's dominion of the sea"; London was paralysed with consternation and amazement,—Pepys locked his father and wife in a bedroom to save them from the perils of a sack,—and while Monk, the one stout heart among them, posted down to Gravesend "in his shirt," the libertine monarch was engaged with his mistresses in pursuing "a poor moth" about the supper-room! For many weeks afterwards, until the peace of Breda, De Ruyter rode triumphant in the narrow seas, and England was in terror of a French invasion, not knowing of the ignoble intrigue in which Louis and Charles were now engaged.

Passing from these notorious blots on English history, and before considering the relevant business in the negotiations

[1] The author of *The Dutch Drawn to the Life* expatiated on the inestimable benefit the Dutch derived from the British seas by encroaching on our fisheries, and asserted that the only way to keep them under was "by commanding the narrow sea, their coast and ours,"—the narrow sea, according to this writer's view, or at least the "right and dominion of England," extending as far as the Mediterranean (p. 75).

[2] See Mahan, *The Influence of Sea Power upon History*; Colomb, *Naval Warfare*; Pontalis, *op. cit.*; Clarendon's *Memoirs*, ii. 111.

for peace, a word or two must be said of some of the minor events and consequences of the war. During its continuance the fisheries of England, and still more those of the United Provinces, suffered severely. In January 1665, before war was declared, but when it was obvious it might break out at any moment, the States-General laid an embargo on the fisheries and on all shipping,—a measure which, it was reported in England, furnished them with 30,000 men for their navy. The stoppage of the fishing was a heavy blow to those dependent on it, and advantage was taken of the fact by the English, who tempted the Dutch fishermen by offering licenses, for a nominal payment, which would enable them to fish notwithstanding the war. The States of Holland, however, forbade the acceptance of the obnoxious licenses, "considering that it might be of very dangerous consequence, as making the inhabitants of these countries indirectly tributary to the King of England"; and the treasurer of the herring fishery at Maassluis, who had purchased some of them, was severely censured and forbidden to make use of them. Notwithstanding this patriotic resolution, it appears that private cupidity in some cases prevailed, and a few licenses were accepted in the following year. One of these, dated 21st November 1666, was granted on the petition of one, Gisbert Petersen, of "Scheveling" (Scheveningen), the captain of the "sailing waggons" of the Prince of Orange, who "wafted" the king on board his fleet at the Restoration. It gave him authority, in his vessel, the *Young Prince of Orange*, "to fish in any part of our seas, not being within . . . leagues of land," and to carry the fish which were caught to Holland; and in certain circumstances he was to have the freedom of English ports. The Scandinavian name of the recipient, and the circumstances recited, throw doubt on the genuineness of the case. The license was renewed on 7th June 1667.[1]

A much more interesting concession for fishing in all parts of the British seas, irrespective of distance from shore, was granted by Charles in the same year, though not to subjects

[1] *Groot Placaet-Boeck, inhoudende de Placaten ende Ordonnantien van de H. M. Heeren Staten Generael der Vereenighde Nederlanden*, iii. 291-293. *Resol. Holl.*, 1665, 24, 59, 78, 210, 383. *State Papers, Dom.*, cxiv. 104. *Ibid., Warrant Book*, 18, p. 213; 23, pp. 283, 475. *Ibid.*, clxxviii. 172.

of the United Provinces. The citizens of Bruges, in Flanders, where the king had received friendly treatment when in exile, petitioned him to allow all the sworn burgers and citizens of that city to fish "freely and frankly" at all times, to the number of fifty busses or other vessels fit for fishing, on the seas and coasts of his kingdoms; to enter the ports and rivers to buy necessaries, for shelter, and to dry their nets, and to depart without molestation, on giving security not to sell fish to his enemies.[1] Charles granted them a charter under the great seals of England and Scotland, giving them liberty to fish with fifty vessels at a time for herrings or any kind of fish in the British seas, up to the coasts or shores, with the privilege of drying their nets on land, and using English or Scottish ports in security. The Duke of Lennox and Richmond, the High Admiral of Scotland, and others concerned were commanded to treat the vessels of Bruges with friendship, "in whatever part of the sea, whether near the shores, in rivers, or ports" they might be.[2] The fishermen of Bruges continued to fish near our shores, in terms of this charter, and even from our harbours, until 1850, and the charter was regarded by the English authorities as spurious.[3]

By granting this charter, it is not unlikely that Charles also hoped to strike a blow at the fisheries of the Dutch Republic. While refusing to allow their subjects to accept any compromising English license or concession for fishing, the States-General tried to bring about a mutual and equitable arrangement. Early in 1665 they issued instructions that English fishermen should not be attacked till further orders; and in October of the same year—that is, when, in peaceful times, Dutch fishermen would have been taking part in the profitable fishing at Yarmouth — one of their

[1] *S. P., Dom.* Collection, Chas. II., vol. 339, p. 591. It is a copy in English. The petition was from the "Burgomasters, Eschevins, Counsellors, and the rest of the body of Citizens."

[2] "Warrant to ye Lord Chancellor for affixing ye great seale to an instrument containing a grant of fishinge in these seas for a certain number of boates belonging to ye City of Bruges, yearely," July 17, 1666. *State Papers, Warrant Book*, 23, p. 27. "Patent in favour of the Citie of Bruges in ffianders for a libertie of fishing in the British Seas with 50 saill of ships," 29th August 1666. *Advoc. MSS.*, 25. 3. 4. The draft or copy of the Royal Letter which followed upon the Warrant is given in Appendix N.

[3] See p. 617.

naval officers delivered an official letter to the Bailiffs of that town, intimating that orders had been given to all their admirals, commanders, and captains at sea that no English fisherman was to be molested, and expressing a hope that a similar Christian forbearance (*medelijdentheyt*) might be shown to Dutch fishermen on the part of England. No answer was returned, but an emphatic response was made a week or two later when the *Sapphire* seized several Dutch fishing vessels and brought them into port,—a circumstance which also shows that the embargo had not been strictly observed.[1] In the following year the embargo was officially continued, the "small" or fresh-herring fishery carried on along the coast being excepted;[2] but after the defeat of the English fleet in the beginning of June, the deep-sea fishing appears to have been partially resumed. Early in August reports reached London from Yarmouth and Whitby that the Holland busses and doggers were fishing off the land, and had been seen by our fishermen. They were said to number 400 and to be guarded by eight convoyers, and it was rumoured the English fleet had gone in pursuit and sunk eighty busses; and a few doggers were in reality brought in. It was again reported later that a fleet of busses was fishing off the coast of Suffolk, attended by seventeen ships of war.[3] If the retaliation of the Dutch was less effective, it was because the English fishermen carried on their industry close to their own ports; to which, moreover, they were often confined by fear of the Dutch privateers, which boldly hovered about the coast, and the sight of a sail was enough to frighten them back.[4] After Van Ghent had burned the English ships in

[1] *Resol. Holl.*, $\frac{11}{21}$ Jan. 1665, p. 54. *Hollantsche Mercurius*, 15th Oct. 1665, p. 143. *State Papers, Dom.*, 4th Nov. 1665, cxxxvi. 35.

[2] *Groot Placaet-Boeck*, iii. 295, 296.

[3] *State Papers, Dom.*, clxvi. 8, 46, 77, 100; clxvii. 148; clxxv. 146; clxxxi. 113.

[4] *Ibid.*, clxxi. 30; clxxii. 7, 41. At the Yarmouth fishing this year (1666) "the sea was fuller of herrings than was ever known"; no sooner were the nets in the water than they were full of fish, and many herrings had to be thrown overboard, so that it was locally rhymed, "twelve herrings a penny fills many a hungry belly." The exceptional abundance was attributed by the fishermen to the war having practically put a stop to the Dutch fishing off our coast, so that the shoals came to the inshore grounds in a body and not broken up. The herring fishing was also unusually successful during the third Dutch war. In 1666, however, the herring fishing in Ireland was likewise uncommonly productive. *Ibid.*, clxxiv. 52, 100, 129, 156; clxxv. 49.

the Thames and the Dutch were supreme at sea, the States of Holland withdrew the embargo on the Great Fishery, and when peace was proclaimed the *schuyts* again took part in the autumn fishing at Yarmouth.[1]

It has been already mentioned that France, which had bound itself by the recent treaty to aid the United Provinces, declared war against England in January 1666, but Louis showed great reluctance to begin actual hostilities; and one of the diplomatic obstacles which served to delay the junction of the French and Dutch fleets referred to the striking of the flag. A French squadron of thirty sail had been equipped under the Duke de Beaufort, and Louis required that the Dutch admiral should salute not only the Admiral of France, but the vice- and rear-admirals; and further, that the French admiral should not be required to lower his flag in returning the salute of the Dutch. The States-General were willing that their admiral should strike to De Beaufort first, but they demanded that the latter should return the salute in a similar manner. The French, who were apparently anxious to be placed in the same position as England with respect to this ceremony, argued that the English did not re-salute the Dutch fleet by striking the flag, but only returned the guns, citing the treaty of 1662 and the actual practice; and they proudly boasted that the flag of the Admiral of France had never at any time been lowered to that of any nation. To this De Witt replied that they were willing to give the same respect to the French as they did to the English; that the re-salute was not expressly mentioned in the treaty because it was a well-understood custom on their own coast; and that in point of fact the English did return the salute, as had been done by Admiral Montague (the Earl of Sandwich) in 1661 and by Vice-Admiral Lawson on meeting De Ruyter. If on some occasions it was omitted by the English, it was on the seas they called "British," and was to be attributed to the claim they pretended to the dominion of the seas—a claim which France and the Republic had solemnly agreed by treaty to resist. If a similar claim was now advanced by France, it would argue a like pretension to maritime sovereignty by a nation which had engaged itself to preserve the liberty of the sea. Moreover, the salute at sea between

[1] *Resol. Holl.*, $\frac{\text{21 June}}{\text{1 July}}$ 1667, p. 210. *State Papers, Dom.*, ccxvi. 143; ccxvii. 77.

the fleets of two sovereign states was not an act of submission of an inferior to a superior, but one of civility, honour, and respect, and should therefore be mutual and equal. They, as a republic, offered to strike first, and to keep their flag lowered until the French admiral had struck and re-hoisted his flag. This discussion about the re-salute was prolonged, extending from June 1666 to July 1667, for De Witt was not a man lightly to agree to diminish the dignity of his country; and after the peace conference met at Breda, and De Ruyter was master of the sea, the Dutch roundly declared they would not strike to the French admiral at all, unless he agreed to return the salute by dipping his flag, but would only salute him with guns.[1]

At the conferences at Breda Charles had little right to expect that he would gain much, in view of the inglorious events at the end of the war. He retained New Amsterdam (re-named New York), which Holmes had taken in 1664, but he lost Poleroon and Surinam, and relinquished the claims which had been put forward to justify the war. An important concession was made to the Dutch by a modification of the Navigation Act, for a repeal of which they pressed, by a stipulation, in separate articles, that they might import into England in Dutch vessels all commodities produced or manufactured in Germany or Flanders, for which, it was claimed, the United Provinces were the natural outlet to the sea; and all the essential articles of the commercial treaty of 1662 were confirmed.[2] All pretensions to exclusive fishing off the British coasts were withdrawn; the old stipulations of the Burgundy treaties were not, however, renewed.

With regard to the "honour of the flag," De Witt, in the preliminary negotiations, strove to come to an arrangement with France and Denmark, who were also parties to the treaty, to compel England to relinquish her claim to pre-

[1] De Witt to Van Beuningen, $\frac{12}{22}$ July 1666 to $\frac{18}{28}$ July 1667; Van Beuningen to De Witt, $\frac{\text{21 June}}{\text{1 July}}$ 1666 to $\frac{12}{22}$ July 1667. "Raisons par lesquelles il paroît, que le contre-salut du Pavillon, aux rencontres des Flotes de Sa Majesté Très-Chrétienne et des Etats Généraux, est d'une justice toute évident." De Witt's *Brieven*, ii. 473, &c. Pontalis, *op. cit.*, i. 353.

[2] *Articles touching Navigation and Commerce, concluded at Breda*, $\frac{21}{31}$ July 1667.

eminence in this matter, especially by insisting that English vessels should return the salute by lowering their flag.[1] Charles was saved from this humiliation by the good offices of Louis, and the article in the treaty of 1662 was simply repeated in precisely the same words.[2] Another of the maritime articles gave less contentment in England. We have already seen how persistently the Dutch had struggled in deliberating on the terms of the treaty of 1654 to restrict the application of the term "British Sea" to the Channel. What they were then unable to accomplish was now conceded to them. In the usual article about the cessation of hostilities on the sea, it was specified that restitution of prizes should not be made if they were taken "in the Channel or British Sea within the space of twelve days, and the same in the North Sea; and within the space of six weeks from the mouth of the Channel unto the Cape of St Vincent."[3] In the treaty with France, signed at Breda on the same day, the French plenipotentiaries took care that the terms English Channel or British Sea in the corresponding clause were omitted, the neutral if indefinite phrase "the neighbouring seas" (*maria proxima*) being substituted.[4] In the similar treaty with Denmark, the phraseology was even less tender to English susceptibilities—namely, "in the Northern Ocean

[1] "Dat de scheepen van oorlois (*sic*) van den Coninck van Groot Brittannien door die van desen staet met het strijcken van de vlagge gesalveert werdende, van haere sijde vervolgens met het strijcken van haere vlagge contra salueren sullen." Extract from *Secret Resolution, States-General*, 11th May 1667, Instructions to Ambassadors. *Treaty Papers* (*Breda*), 1667, Bdl. 73.

[2] Art. xix. See p. 455. Van Beuningen to De Witt, $\frac{5}{15}$ April 1667. De Witt to Van Beuningen, $\frac{18}{28}$ April, $\frac{20}{30}$ June, $\frac{\text{27 June}}{\text{1 July}}$ 1667. *Brieven*, ii. 483, 487, 528, 533.

[3] *Treaty of Breda*, Art. vii. It may have been in connection with the interpretation of this clause that the High Court of Admiralty asked the Trinity House their opinion as to the end of the English Channel westwards, and got the following answer: "We shall not presume," said the Masters, on 2nd January 1668, "to determine matters that have for some ages past been controverted, and for anything that we at present know have not had a full resolution or any precedent for deciding questions relating thereunto;" but the opinion of "the past and present age," with which they concurred, was that when any commander brought Scilly N.N.W. he had entered "the Channel of England." *Brit. Mus. Add. MSS.*, 30,221.

[4] *Treaty of Peace and Alliance between Charles I. and Louis XIV., concluded at Breda*, $\frac{21}{31}$ July 1667. Article xvii.

and in the Baltic Sea and the Channel, &c."[1] However trifling such points may appear to us now, they had a real importance in the seventeenth century, and the phraseology cited caused some heart-burning in England as being derogatory to our rights to the dominion of the British seas.[2]

For some years after the conclusion of peace at Breda, and indeed up to the opening of the third Dutch war, the question of the salute was a frequent subject of international discussion. Dutch statesmen had always wished to come to a definite arrangement with England about it, for they saw that to leave it in ambiguity while the English looked upon it as touching their national honour, was fraught with danger. A whole series of points was in doubt, any one of which might furnish occasion for war unless clearly defined and mutually understood. Was a whole fleet or squadron of the States to strike to a single English ship of war? Were they to strike to a frigate, or to a still smaller ship, such as a ketch, or only to ships carrying the flag of an admiral, vice-admiral, or rear-admiral? Was the salute to be returned by the English in the same way, by dipping the flag and lowering the top-sails as well as by guns? Within what parts of the sea was the salute to be enforced, or differentiated, or the re-salute given? English statesmen purposely left many of these points undefined, in order to gain as wide a recognition

[1] *Treaty of Peace and Alliance between Charles II. and Frederick III., concluded at Breda*, $\frac{21}{31}$ July 1667. Art. ii.

[2] In the negotiation of subsequent treaties, controversy was usually occasioned about the wording of these articles relating to the date of cessation of hostilities on the sea, the United Provinces or France pointing to the treaty of Breda as a precedent, while the English took their stand on Cromwell's treaty of 1654. In the treaty of Ryswick in 1697, between the United Provinces and France, the term "British Channel" was employed in conjunction with the Baltic and North Sea (Art. ii.); and in the treaty between William III. and Louis, signed at Ryswick on the same day, the words were "in the British and North Seas, as far as the Cape St Vincent" (Art. x.) In the negotiation with France in 1712 for a suspension of hostilities, the French insisted on the words, "the seas which surround the British Isles," citing the treaty of Breda, while the British were equally obstinate to have the term *in maribus Britannicis* inserted, as in the treaty of 1654, arguing that the "error" of Breda had been rectified in the later treaty of Ryswick; the result being that in one article "the Channel, the British Sea, and the North Sea" were specified, and in another the phrase was "in the Channel and North Sea." Dumont, *Corps Diplomatique*, VIII. i. 306. Burchett, *A Complete History of the Most Remarkable Transactions at Sea, &c.*, p. 38.

of the ceremony as was possible, and when disputes did arise with other Powers, to enable them to avoid war or to make war as circumstances and policy might determine. They held that England, and England alone, was the rightful interpreter of what was due to her flag by ancient custom. On the other hand, the Dutch Republic looked upon the whole business as a troublesome affair; and as the greatest commercial nation of the time, whose chief interest was peace, they naturally desired that the dubious points about the salute should be permanently settled.

Immediately after the conclusion of the Triple Alliance against France, at the beginning of 1668,[1] De Witt, taking advantage of the good feeling existing between England and the Netherlands, and especially of the presence of Sir William Temple as English ambassador at The Hague, proposed that a formal settlement should be made of the doubtful points concerning the striking of the flag. Temple, who was a staunch friend of the Dutch and was on intimate terms with De Witt, shared this opinion. He thought that by a slight concession, or by a definite agreement, England might count with some confidence on the support of the States-General in any future quarrel with other nations about the flag. The subject was formally raised by De Witt on a proposal for a union of the Dutch and English fleets, in certain contingencies, against France. He offered to give the same honour to the king's ships at sea as their ambassadors gave to his Majesty's person, "to uncover first and cover last"; but stipulated that any agreement about the flag must not be regarded as an acknowledgment of England's pretension to the sovereignty of the sea, which the Dutch would "die rather than do." Knowing that it was a "delicate" subject to broach with the King of England, he thought the negotiations might be opened by the States-General sending a polite letter to Charles, laying stress on the good relations between the two nations, and intimating that in order to prevent sinister encounters which any new sourness might occasion, they had issued orders to all their naval officers to strike their flag with every mark of civility on meeting with the royal flag of England. The king was then (according to the scheme) to inform the States-

[1] See p. 474.

General that he had received this mark of deference to his royal dignity with singular satisfaction, and that he on his part would order his admirals and commanders to re-salute the States' flag. Temple thought the matter was so "ticklish," that it ought to be first broached verbally at a fitting opportunity; and De Witt, in advising the Dutch ambassadors in London to this effect, reminded them that the salute was merely a mark of honour and respect, and that if anything was put into writing this should be expressed. He added that he had never been able to understand how it could be conceived that the free element of the sea, or dominion over it, could belong to England or to any nation, and that in Holland the common right of sovereignty of all nations over it was held to be incontestable.

When, about a month afterwards, the ambassadors spoke to the king, he said he did not see how the question could be ambiguous, since it was provided for in the treaty. They pointed out that the re-salute was not mentioned, and then used the arguments which De Witt had put into their mouths about its being a ceremony of respect which it would be only reasonable and courteous to return, just as his Majesty would do, sitting on his throne, in response to the salutations of the ambassadors of the Republic; and they adduced one or two instances in which the English ships had returned the salute. Charles told them they were possibly thinking of the custom in the Mediterranean, which was different from all the other seas (meaning the British seas), and said he claimed nothing but the old practice; but he promised to look into the matter. The ambassadors did not press the subject further, and the important declaration they had been charged to make, that in future the States' ships would refuse to strike unless the salute was returned in the same way, remained unspoken. Shortly afterwards, when the States were asked to send some of their warships to strengthen the squadron of Sir Thomas Allin, who was ordered to enforce the restitution of some English vessels seized by the French, they refused, unless the difficulties about the flag were first settled, and the discussion continued throughout the summer.

It is interesting to note, in view of the antecedents of the next war, that the ambassadors were instructed to say that the

States' fleet would not strike, even in the Channel, to a frigate or ketch, which did not customarily carry the royal flag in the main-top, but only to an admiral's ship, or one carrying the royal flag. This contention was promptly set aside by the Duke of York and Lord Arlington (the Secretary for State); but De Witt, still clinging to the hope that a "regulation" might be arranged, asked the ambassadors to find out the instructions which were actually issued to the English captains serving in the Downs, the Channel, the North Sea, the Mediterranean, and the Ocean, as it was generally believed in Holland that outside the Channel neither side should strike the flag or lower the sails to the other, but that the States' ships should first salute with guns alone, and the English answer with guns also. In any case, if the principal fleets of the two countries were combined for any purpose, or jointly brought into action, it was to be first arranged that they should salute one another with guns only, or at all events in an equal and reciprocal manner, the Dutch always giving the salute first; and the ambassadors were to insist earnestly and finally for a settlement.

The ambassadors informed De Witt that, as was shown in the copy of the instructions found on board the *Charity*, an English man-of-war taken by the Dutch in the battle of Lowestoft, in 1665, and which was published by Aitzema, the commander of an English man-of-war was to compel every foreign ship, or ships, to strike their flag in the British seas, and that in these seas no English king's ship was to strike to any foreign ship. In all other seas the English ship was never to strike to a foreigner unless the latter struck first or at the same time. According to this, they said, a single English man-of-war could compel a whole fleet to strike their flags and lower their top-sails in the so-called British seas, and it was forbidden for it to strike in return. In all other seas, if the foreign ship did not strike, the English would not strike, and no salute would be exchanged. They said this was well known to be the regular formula in England, and no distinction was drawn between the Channel and other "pretended English seas." The "British seas," they said, according to the Admiralty instructions, extended to Cape Finisterre, in Galicia, and westwards, according to Selden, to America. It would be an excellent thing, they thought, if they could succeed in drawing a distinction between the Channel and the other seas, since their fisheries, the main object of solicitude, were carried on, not in the Channel, but in the North Sea. But as the whole subject was very delicate, they advised De Witt to pass from it for the time and to allow things to remain on their old footing; and to show the spirit in which the matter was regarded in England, they sent him specimens of the coin issued by Charles a few years before, which bore the king's effigy on one side with the inscription *Carolus a Carolo*, and on the obverse the figure of Britannia, with the proud words, *Quatuor Maria Vindico*.[1] De Witt, who had just arranged with Temple that the matter should be brought to the notice of the king, acquiesced, but with reluctance. He expressed satisfaction that they now at least knew more about the English pretension, so that fresh hostility and war could be avoided on that point; but that an English frigate or ketch should claim to compel a whole fleet to strike was, he said, intolerable. And it was this very thing that Charles selected to force war upon the United Provinces a few years later.[2]

It was not only with the Dutch that discussions arose at this time as to the rights of the English to demand the salute. The astute Dutch statesman, as was his wont, began to pull diplomatic wires at other Courts in order to have the subject raised by them. The King of Denmark in the following year

[1] This was the farthing known later as the "Lucas farthing," from the gibes of Lord Lucas in his attack on the king's policy made in the debate on the Subsidy Bill in the House of Lords in 1670. Speaking of the scarcity of money in the kingdom, he said: "What supply is preparing for it, my Lords? I hear of none, unless it be of copper farthings; and this is the metal that is to indicate, according to the inscription on it, 'The Dominion of the Four Seas.'" *Parl. Hist.*, iv. 473.

[2] "Omtrent het point van de Vlagge, saegen wy alhier seer gaerne iets seeckers gedetermineert, ten minsten dat wy moghten weten waer mede men buyten nieuwe feytelyckheydt ende Oorloge konde verblyven; dat een Fregatje ofte een Kitsje een gantsche Oorloghs-Vloote soude doen strycken, is notoirlyck intolerabel." De Witt to Meerman, $\frac{12}{22}$ June 1668. The same to the same, $\frac{29\text{ Feb.}}{9\text{ March}}$, $\frac{3}{13}$, $\frac{7}{17}$ April, $\frac{24\text{ April}}{4\text{ May}}$, $\frac{22\text{ May}}{1\text{ June}}$ 1668. De Witt to Meerman and Boreel, $\frac{17}{27}$ March, $\frac{29\text{ May}}{8\text{ June}}$ 1668. Meerman to De Witt, $\frac{28\text{ March}}{7\text{ April}}$, $\frac{6}{16}$ June 1668. De Witt's *Brieven*, iv. Sir William Temple to Lord Arlington, $\frac{2}{12}$ Feb., $\frac{6}{16}$ March 1668; the same to the Lord-Keeper Bridgeman, $\frac{25\text{ Oct.}}{4\text{ Nov.}}$ 1668. *Works*, iii. 134, 199, 348. *State Papers, Dom.*, 1668, ccxxxv. 49, 62; *ibid.*, 1665, cxxiii. 67. Aitzema, *Saken van Staet en Oorlogh*, v. 390.

proposed to Charles that new regulations should be arranged with respect to the "salutes and civilities" at sea between the men-of-war of the two nations. Charles declined the invitation. He did not think it fit, he said, to make any new regulation on the salutes at sea, "since there has never been any question made of the constant practice in that matter, which we shall always observe."[1]

A renewed attempt to convince the French that it was to their interest to curtail the English claim to the sovereignty of the sea had consequences little dreamt of by De Witt. The Dutch Minister, clinging to his principle, urged at Paris that Charles, who wished to be the supreme ruler of the sea, ought to be forced to modify his pretension and to give the salute in return. It had indeed been rumoured in London that the French king had decided to forbid his naval commanders to strike to the English, and even to compel both English and Dutch to strike to his own flag.[2] Louis certainly raised the question at the Court of St James's, but in a different way. Colbert, his ambassador there, secretly revealed to Charles the confidential negotiations which the States-General had opened at Paris, in the hope that this mark of confidence would make more easy his policy of detaching the King of England from the Triple Alliance.[3] By this time Charles and Louis were drawing closer together, and in order to prevent chance disputes about the flag, a verbal arrangement was made through Colbert, in the summer of 1669, that no salutes should be exchanged between English and French men-of-war in the Mediterranean, nor should the ship of one be expected to go to leeward of the other. Instructions of this tenour were given to Sir Thomas Allin, who was on the point of leaving with a squadron to chastise the Barbary pirates.[4]

About this time the Duke of York and the officials of the

[1] The king to the Duke of York, 31st Oct. 1669. *State Papers, Entry Book*, 31, fol. 37.

[2] Pepys' *Diary*, 20th Dec. 1668, viii. 184.

[3] Pontalis, *op. cit.*, ii. 24.

[4] The king to the Duke of York, 26th June 1669. *State Papers, Entry Book*, 31, fol. 29. Instructions by the Duke of York to Sir Thomas Allin, 6th July 1669. *Ibid.*, cclxii. 120. A marginal memorandum on the latter document says, "This rule was adjusted with Colbert, the French Ambassador here, *but nothing passed in writing but this.*"

navy began to devote close attention to the rules regulating the salute and the striking of the flag, and a number of memoranda were prepared which described recent precedents, and dealt with other points. With reference to recent practice, it was stated that the Earl of Sandwich had struck in return to De Ruyter in 1661 or 1662; that Sir John Lawson declared he would strike to none, and kept his flag aloft in Toulon harbour; while Sir William Berkeley, serving under Lawson, refused even to fire a gun on meeting De Beaufort, the Admiral of France, until he was assured that the report attributed to him that he would force the English to strike was unfounded. A statement was compiled of the number of guns fired in salute to English vessels arriving in various foreign ports, and rules were formulated with respect to the salutation of forts and on other points. The general custom was that "the sea should salute the land"—that is, the vessel first saluted the forts, except on extraordinary occasions, as when a prince or an important foreign embassy arrived. No foreign man-of-war was to be allowed to pass above the ports at Gravesend and Sheerness, or at any other harbour, without special permission from the Lord High Admiral or the governor of the fort; all vessels were to keep in their flag as long as they were in sight of the fort, and if they refused they were to be forced to comply; salutes of foreign flagships were to be answered gun for gun, and of other foreign ships with two guns less. As for the striking of the flag, the Earl of Sandwich and other naval authorities who were consulted intimated that the matter was too important for them to decide upon, and should be left to the king—a plain acknowledgment of its political character. The Duke of York, however, the Lord High Admiral, stated that the rule was that English ships were everywhere to be saluted first, and were not to strike in return, but only to answer with guns; but if a single English ship met a foreign fleet out of the British seas, it was to salute first with guns, but neither was to strike the flag.[1]

This activity at the English Admiralty may not have been wholly unconnected with the circumstances which ushered in the next war, but it was more probably due to the general revival of punctiliousness regarding the salute and similar

[1] *State Papers, Dom.*, 1669, cclxi. 82-87.

naval ceremonies which took place at this time throughout Europe. Even the petty states in the Mediterranean became infected with the spirit of their powerful neighbours, and followed their example. At Genoa and Leghorn frequent disputes, and sometimes sanguinary encounters, occurred between the authorities and Dutch and English men-of-war as to the number of guns that should be fired, or the striking of the flag. French and Dutch men-of-war lying in the Tagus were only prevented by the governor of the castle from putting to the arbitrament of force the question whether the latter should strike to the former. At Civita Vecchia, at Glückstadt, at Dover, at Dieppe, at Kronberg, similar incidents took place. The Earl of Essex, going on a special embassy to the King of Denmark, and on board the king's yacht, had a sharp dispute with the Governor of Kronberg, in the Sound, as to lowering his flag, which the Danish officer requested him to do. But Essex was well primed with precedents before he left England, and was able to maintain his refusal.[1] Though Dutch men-of-war engaged with spirit in such quarrels about the salute in foreign ports, their action was not countenanced by the policy of the States-General. On 16th May 1670 they instructed that the fort of Kronberg should be saluted by Dutch vessels in such manner as the King of Denmark might require; and on 3rd February next year the States of Holland issued a general order that their men-of-war should salute those of other sovereigns on their coasts, within the reach of the guns of batteries or forts, in the precise manner that the Government of the country might demand, leaving it entirely to the discretion of that Government to return the salute or not, just as they pleased. Every foreign Government, they added, was sovereign within its own jurisdiction, and every foreigner was a subject there.[2]

[1] *State Papers, Dom.*, 1668, ccli. 191 ; 1670, cclxxiv. 157 ; cclxxv. 43 ; cclxxvi. 206 ; cclxxxi. 15 ; 1671, ccxc. 5, &c. Temple's *Memoirs*, iii. 433. Justice, *Dominion and Laws of the Sea*, 298.

[2] Bynkershoek, *De Dominio Maris*, cap. ii. iv. As elsewhere explained (p. 557), it was this custom which helped to prepare the way for the acceptance of the principle that now determines the extent of the territorial sea on an open coast —viz., the range of guns.

CHAPTER XIII.

CHARLES II.—*continued.*

THE THIRD DUTCH WAR.

THE "honour of the flag" and the sovereignty of the sea were now about to gain a shameful notoriety in connection with the third Dutch war, which Charles, from the basest personal motives and in the most treacherous manner, suddenly sprang upon the Republic. At that time, and for long afterwards, European policy turned upon the ambitious designs of Louis XIV. Laying claim to the Spanish dominions, he overran the Low Countries in 1667 with an army of 40,000 men. The rapidity of the conquest and the display of formidable military power filled Europe with alarm; and the United Provinces, which lay nearest the scene of danger, were thrown into apprehension as to their own safety. In England popular feeling was very hostile to France, and Charles, after some hesitation, despatched Sir William Temple to The Hague to conclude an alliance against France, which he succeeded in accomplishing in a few days—in January 1668,—and it was adhered to by Sweden. The Triple Alliance thus formed was hailed with enthusiasm in England, and it abruptly and effectually checked Louis in the execution of his plans. Deeply mortified, the French king bent his energies and talents to detach Charles from the League, in order to wreak his vengeance on the Dutch Republic, and he succeeded even better than he expected. Charles was deeply in debt, and the expenses of his Court were heavy. His relations with the Parliament were becoming strained and difficult. Mistrust was growing up between him and his subjects, and, mindful of the fate of his father, he thought it prudent to secure in secret a wealthy and powerful ally lest rebellion again broke out in England. Within a year of the signing of the Triple Alliance Charles was gained over by France, and the compact was sealed in the disgraceful secret treaty of Dover in May 1670. Under the treaty Charles was to receive a large yearly pension from Louis, and aid in case of insurrection; he was to avow and re-establish the Roman Catholic religion in England when it could be done with safety; and he was to begin hostilities against the Dutch Republic when Louis required him by furnishing 4000 men and fifty ships of war, for which he was to receive a subsidy of £120,000, and to gain as his share of the spoils of conquest Walcheren, Sluys, and Cadsand. Louis crowned the dishonourable compact with the appropriate gift of a new mistress to his royal ally—Mademoiselle de Kerouaille, afterwards the Duchess of Portsmouth, who well served the interests of France.[1]

In order to carry out his part of the iniquitous bargain, it was necessary for Charles, as the vassal of France, to deceive his subjects and his Parliament as well as his public ally, the Dutch Republic. He had first to get money for the armaments, for which the subsidy from France was insufficient, and he had then to discover some pretext for the war which would make it least objectionable to the English people. For the former purpose he resorted to a bold subterfuge. The sentiment of both the Parliament and the people was hostile to France, and advantage was taken of this circumstance to obtain a subsidy under false pretences. When Parliament met in October 1670 the Lord Keeper, by the king's commands, made a speech on the state of public affairs, in which he enlarged on the king's need of supply; pointed to the great strengthening of the French navy and the decay of our own; urged the necessity of fitting out in the ensuing year a fleet of fifty sail; and dwelt upon the obligations placed upon the king by several treaties to exert himself for the good of Christendom, mentioning among others the Triple Alliance and the League with the United Provinces. The trick succeeded. Parliament, uneasy

[1] Hume, *Hist. of England*, c. lxv. Temple's *Memoirs and Letters*. Pontalis, *John de Witt.* Macaulay, *Hist.*, i. c. ii.

at the recent journey of Louis to Flanders and the naval preparations in France, voted a sum of £800,000.[1]

It was also indispensable to foment ill-feeling against the Dutch, and to devise disputes with them so as to prepare the way for a rupture. Some time before this, at Genoa, a Dutch commander, Captain Braeckel, who had led the attack on the English ships at Chatham in 1667, had hoisted under the Dutch colours some English flags which he had taken on that occasion, in derision of the English in the port. Charles demanded reparation and the punishment of Braeckel; and the States-General ultimately ordered the trophies to be given up, and sent them to London.[2] Later, the king complained that the States-General had allowed him and the English people to be insulted by lampoons, medals, &c., commemorating the exploits of the Dutch fleet in the Thames in 1667, the king suing for peace at Breda, and so forth. The States-General, when the king continued to press these complaints, seized all copies of certain lampoons and destroyed the dies of several of the medals. Charles then boldly accused the Grand Pensionary De Witt of having carried on a confidential correspondence with France with the object of inducing that Power to take up arms against England. The accusation was meant to prejudice the Dutch in the eyes of the Parliament; and the States, to prove their sincerity, sent fresh proposals for an alliance, to which Charles replied that they should first have offered him sudsidies. The apprehension of the States that the king was inclined to force a quarrel on them was not lessened by intelligence they received that he had abandoned the Triple Alliance, and especially by the recall of Sir William Temple from The Hague in 1670,—a step that followed the seizure of Lorraine by Louis.

Affairs were ripening to the wished-for crisis, and Charles now sought for a decisive pretext, which, while making war inevitable, would lessen its unpopularity in England. Such a pretext was to be found in the "honour of the flag." No cry was more likely to rouse resentment in the people than that the flag had been insulted and the sovereignty of the

[1] *Parl. Hist.*, iv. 456. Hume, *op. cit.*

[2] De Witt's *Brieven*, iv. 837. Pontalis, *op. cit.*, ii. 122.

sea threatened. To insult the flag was to insult the nation. The king was well aware from the repeated declarations of the States-General that they would never willingly acknowledge England's sovereignty of the sea: they had said they would "rather die first." He was also doubtless fully acquainted with the fixed opinion of the Grand Pensionary that to claim that the whole Dutch fleet should strike to a single frigate or a ketch was "intolerable." He contrived his measures accordingly, and decided to send one of his yachts to pass through the States' fleet, on their own coast, and to fire upon them if they did not strike their flags in the accustomed manner. The matter was deliberately considered. The clause in the treaty of Breda was not very clear as to whether a yacht, or even a man-of-war, could compel the whole Dutch fleet to strike, and on the Dutch coast. Just about the time Temple returned from The Hague, Sir Leoline Jenkins, Judge of the High Court of Admiralty, wrote a confidential letter to Sir Thomas Allin, the commander of the Blue, asking him to find out secretly, "as if for his own satisfaction," whether there were any "ancient seamen" at Trinity House or elsewhere who were on board the *Happy Entrance* when it carried the Earl of Arundel to Holland in 1636, and if so, whether they remembered that on entering the road of Goeree, in Holland, Admiral Tromp, who was at anchor there, struck his flag to it; and similar information was asked in regard to other cases of like import in 1637 and later. The question was also put to Sir Thomas, "How far the British Sea, or British Ocean, does in common reputation extend itself; and whether all that which washes the coasts of the Low Countries, as well as that which runs upon the French coast, has been anciently deemed and reputed to be British Sea?" Jenkins explained that he had been desired by the king to obtain proof of the striking of the flag as secretly as possible; and the two chief points were, (1) "Had not the French and the Dutch always struck to the king's flag even on their own coasts? and (2) that a single ship of ours, if commissioned for war, though never so inconsiderable in its strength, did make whole squadrons and fleets of the neighbouring nations to strike, and particularly the Spaniards near the Spanish Netherlands and the subjects of the United Provinces near their coasts?"[1]

The reference to the French and Spaniards was no doubt meant to conceal the real significance of the inquiry. The reply of the admiral seems not to have been preserved, but a later memorandum of Jenkins answers the questions as to the striking of the flag at Goeree, and in the other cases, in the affirmative. The Trinity House, whose opinion was also asked, said that it had been commonly received by them from their predecessors that the British seas "extend to Cape Finisterre, or the North Cape" (*sic*), and that the sea which washes the coast of the Low Countries and France had been always reputed part of the British seas. "To know how far it does extend northwards," they ingenuously added, "we desire you will please to consult those authors who have treated on that subject, it not being known to a certain by us."[2] They had been unable to meet with any persons who knew about the alleged cases of striking, so that Jenkins must have obtained the information about them from other sources.

There can be no doubt that Charles was advised by the authorities he consulted on the ambiguous points in the article of Breda that (1) any king's ship, however small, commissioned for war, was a "man-of-war" in the sense of the treaty, and could call upon the whole Dutch fleet to strike; (2) that the British seas included those washing the coasts of the United Provinces; and (3) with respect to the previous custom referred to in the treaty, that the Dutch had struck on their own coasts.

Thus fortified in law and precedent, the way was clear for Charles to pick a quarrel with the States about the striking of the flag, and he despatched, not a man-of-war, nor even a frigate, but his yacht, the *Merlin*, for the purpose. Ostensibly it was sent to bring over Lady Temple, who had, by his wish, remained in Holland since her husband's departure, but with orders to pass through the Dutch fleet then cruising in the Channel, and to fire at them until they struck their flags or fired back at the *Merlin*. As the French ambassador,

[1] Sir Leoline Jenkins to Sir Thomas Allin, Admiral of the Blue Flag, 8th Oct. 1670. *Life of Sir Leoline Jenkins*, ii. 699.

[2] *Brit. Mus. Add. MSS.*, 30,221, ff. 46*b*, 48*b*.

who was in the secret, tersely put it to his Court, "the captain is to use all his powder, so as to give good cause for a quarrel." The *Merlin* on her way to Holland passed through the Dutch fleet, but owing to a heavy gale she could not get near enough to execute the king's commands. She appears, however, to have met two Dutch men-of-war convoying the herring-busses, who exchanged guns with her but did not strike their flag.[1] But in returning, early in August, with Lady Temple on board, the *Merlin*, with the royal standard flying, came upon the States' fleet lying at anchor beyond the Goodwins, six leagues from the coast of Zealand and sixteen leagues from England. The little yacht, while still at a distance, began to fire at the Dutch flagship. De Ruyter did not reply at once, but the Lieutenant-Admiral, Van Ghent, thinking that it was merely a question of the salute, returned the guns in the usual manner, and was not a little surprised to receive for his pains a discharge of cannon-balls. He sent an officer on board the yacht for an explanation, and Captain Crow, the commander of the *Merlin*, informed him that he had been sent to bring the English ambassadress with her family from Holland, and had orders to make the Dutch fleet lower their colours wherever he met with it. On hearing this, Van Ghent, on the pretext of paying a compliment to Lady Temple, whom he had frequently met at The Hague, went himself on board the *Merlin*. He told Captain Crow that the point he had raised was one on which he had received no orders from the States, and that he could not concede the claim without express commands. He declared his willingness to pay due respect to the English flag according to the former practice, but he thought it could scarcely be contended that the admiral and the whole fleet should strike on their own coast to a single vessel, and that vessel a yacht, which was only a pleasure-boat, or at least served only for a passage, and could not pass for a

[1] *Brit. Mus. Add. MSS.*, 30,221, fol. 47*b*. The affidavits of three English sailors who witnessed the meeting of the *Merlin* and the two Dutch convoyers off Flamborough. The sailors swore "that they exchanged guns but did not strike their flags, but went away with their flags abroad." This evidence was obtained to magnify the offence; the position assigned, "off the Flamborough," makes its value doubtful.

man-of-war. It was at all events, he said, a question which should first be submitted to inquiry by the two Governments.

Captain Crow was puzzled and perplexed, and on Van Ghent's departure he appealed to Lady Temple as to what he should do. She, seeing he did not relish his job and would be glad to get out of it by her help, shrewdly told him that he knew his orders best and what he ought to do, and begged him not to mind her or her children. After firing another gun, the *Merlin* continued her voyage to England, leaving the Dutch fleet with their flags displayed, and without having fired a single angry shot in reply. Very naturally, Charles was irritated at the miscarriage of his plan. He had hoped for a sharp and unequal contest about the flag, the news of which would have rung from end to end of England and enabled him to drag the country into war to resent the affront. Crow was thrown into the Tower, "for refusing to do his duty towards the Dutch men-of-war who refused to strike to the king's flag." The Privy Council debated whether a frigate, the other class of vessel to whose status De Witt had objected, should not be hastily despatched to the Dutch fleet to draw the spark which the *Merlin* had failed to elicit, by firing on every ship that refused to take in her flag. Probably the device was deemed to be too transparent; but it was rumoured that the captain of the *Reserve*, which left Deal a few days later for Portsmouth, had received instructions to fight the Dutch fleet if he met them and they did not strike,—a rumour which, it was reported, "deads the hearts of people lest we should have war with Holland."

Meanwhile, Sir Leoline Jenkins was requested to inquire into the case of the *Merlin*, presumably to see what could be made of it. He examined Lady Temple and others, and drew up a memorandum embodying the information he had received as to the extent of the British seas and the precedents of striking to the English flag off foreign coasts.[1] After citing the precedents at Goeree and elsewhere, he expressed an opinion against calling witnesses in such cases "for fear of chicane," declaring that we had "a constant uninterrupted possession of the prerogative,

[1] "A Draft made by Sir Leoline Jenkins about the King's Sovereignty in the British Seas." *Brit. Mus. Add. MSS.*, 30,221, fol. 46*b*. Undated, but probably referring to this case.

with the highest notoriety that public immemorial reputation can give, in the British seas, and that the onus of making proof as to the non-use and enjoyment of it in some certain places or rencounters, as for instance the Dutch coast, or when a small sail of ours met a fleet of theirs, was cast by the law and by reason upon our opposers."[1] The English Government did not make any immediate protest to the States-General about Van Ghent's refusal to strike to the yacht, possibly lest they might proffer satisfaction and dispose of the episode; but Charles boldly told the Dutch ambassadors that he thought the conduct of their admiral had been premeditated.

Up to this time the Dutch had failed to discern the danger which was approaching. After the *Merlin* incident indeed, as Temple tells us, the Dutch ambassadors in London, "with as ill noses as they have, began to smell the powder after the Captain's shooting." But relying on the well-known animosity of the English people and Parliament to France, and their aversion to a rupture of the Triple Alliance, they fondly clung to the belief that the incident was one of the temporary misunderstandings about the flag which would be readily cleared up. The States-General were equally undiscerning, and perhaps a little more obtuse. They adopted a course which, however proper it might have been under other circumstances, now served only to play into the hands of Charles. A manifesto was prepared declaring that by the terms of the treaties with England the salute was to be regulated according to the custom in the past; that it could not be claimed except in British waters, where—as their High Mightinesses thought it well to remind the king—it was offered only as a mark of courtesy, and not in recognition of England's pretension to the sovereignty of the sea. And in order that their intention might be perfectly clear, they instructed De Ruyter to draw up a set of rules prescribing the salute to be given in future by the Dutch fleet to English or French men-of-war on the Dutch coast, which was to be confined to the exchange of guns without striking the flag at all.

[1] Sir William Temple to Sir John Temple, 14th Sept. 1671. *Works*, iii. 501. Pontalis, *John de Witt*, 126, 127. Hume, *Hist. of England*, cap. lxv. *State Papers, Dom.*, 1671, ccxcii. 45, 77, 78, 81, 215. Evelyn's *Diary* (ed. 1850), ii. 69. *Brit. Mus. Add. MSS.*, 30,221.

Thus, by their own maladroitness as it happened, the States were drawn into precisely the dispute that Charles had been longing for—a dispute about the flag and the sovereignty of the sea. He replied by sending Downing to The Hague, in December 1671, as ambassador extraordinary, with a sheaf of peremptory and intolerable demands. The choice of the ambassador was in itself significant of much, for Downing was known to be repugnant to the States-General, partly from his overbearing and quarrelsome disposition, still more because of his unconcealed enmity to the Dutch people. He was to demand free trade for the English in the Dutch plantations in the Indies; redress and satisfaction for the pamphlets and medals insulting to the king; above all, he was to present to the States-General a memorial requiring that they should "solemnly and clearly acknowledge, in writing, the king's right to the dominion of these seas, and that they neither do nor will dispute it, but expressly engage themselves that all ships or fleets of theirs, however numerous, shall, upon warning given by any ship or ships of war, carrying English colours, of what rate or bigness soever, strike their top-sails and lower their flags, as has been ever practised." As a pendicle to this, he was to demand that Van Ghent should be "exemplarily punished for the insolent affront done by him to a small English man-of-war [the *Merlin*] in refusing to strike." If within a fortnight no answer was received to this "memorial," Downing was to present a sharp and peremptory note demanding an immediate reply, and if he did not get it within another week, he was instantly to quit The Hague, without giving any notice of his intention to go.

While Downing was away on his explosive mission, Boreel, the Dutch ambassador in London, was beguiled with smooth words in order to lull the States-General into a feeling of security. On the eve of his departure, Downing told him he was going to The Hague with the object of strengthening the good understanding between the two countries, and Charles treated the ambassador with the most friendly courtesy. The ease with which the Dutch were being hoodwinked caused much amusement in Paris. But Charles was not yet quite ready. He needed a great deal more money than what was left of the £800,000 which the House of Commons had voted.

Afraid to summon Parliament again, or to levy taxes under the prerogative as Charles I. had levied the ship-money, he had recourse to the daring expedient of closing the Exchequer, by which he robbed the public creditors of some £1,200,000, causing widespread ruin and commercial panic. A little later, on 21st January 1672, the first quarterly instalment of the subsidy of three million livres from Louis was landed at Rye, and escorted to the Tower by forty men of the Guards and a trumpeter. Now in possession of ample supplies, Charles hastened to throw aside the mask. Downing played his arrogant part at The Hague, refusing to allow any debate as to the justice of his demands. When he suddenly called for his passports, the States-General began to awaken to a truer sense of their position, menaced as they also were by imminent peril from France. Adopting the advice of the deluded Boreel, that by yielding on the question of the flag they would remove any inclination the English people had for war with them, since England really cherished enmity against France, the States-General agreed to comply with the claims of Charles respecting the salute. The concession was still joined with the offensive proviso that they gave it only as a mark of respect to a powerful monarch: it was, moreover, to be conditional on the maintenance of the Triple Alliance. Downing told them the offer came too late, and slunk away home, reaching London on 6th February, where the king, displeased with his management of the affair, sent him to the Tower "for not having obeyed the orders sent him."

The flight of Downing threw the States-General into consternation. Meerman, previously their ambassador at the English Court, was despatched in haste to London to renew the offer about the flag, to agree to the dismissal of Van Ghent, and to tender large subsidies for the king's privy purse. At the audience with Meerman and Boreel, Charles skilfully evaded their proposals and expressed surprise that they had not submitted a formal signed paper. This they made haste to do, and they were then informed that it was ambiguous and obscure, but in what particulars they could not learn. They next submitted a draft to Arlington and Lauderdale, the English commissioners appointed to treat with them, with the request that they might amend it as they thought fit, but they were haughtily told that it was none of their business to draw up papers for the Dutch. Finally, they signed a written engagement to give satisfaction about the flag, but at the conference appointed for its reception the English refused to consider it, saying the time for negotiations was now past.[1]

The time was now obviously ripe for a declaration of war; but Charles before taking this step had resolved on an audacious and treacherous stroke, by which he hoped to gain much plunder for himself while diminishing the resources of the Dutch. In spite of the solemn obligations of treaties for the temporary security of their shipping even if war broke out, it was decided to attack and capture Dutch merchant vessels in time of peace. Here also a ready excuse might be found by contriving disputes about the striking of the flag. As early as 26th January, Sir Robert Holmes sent an express to Arlington recommending the seizure of a Dutch fleet laden with salt and wine, which lay windbound at the Isle of Wight, under the convoy of three or four States' men-of-war. He said that in Holland there was a great scarcity of salt, and that without it they could not carry on their fishery or provide for their garrisons;

[1] Pontalis, *op. cit.*, ii. 130, 134. Hume, *op. cit.*, cap. xlv. Sir William Temple to his brother, 23rd May 1672. *Works*, iii. 505. Clarendon's *Memoirs*, ii. 289. *England's Appeal*, p. 22. *State Papers, Entry Book*, 24, fol. 54. *Ibid., Dom.*, 1671, ccxciv. 127; 1672, cccii. 55, 112, 233; ccciii. 206. *Entry Book*, 34, f. 147. It was in connection with the offers of the Dutch on this occasion or a little later in the year that Sir Leoline Jenkins made the following pronouncement as to the king's rights to the dominion of the seas. He was asked by Secretary Coventry "what his Majesty, his heirs and successors, Kings of England, may reasonably pretend to be signified by these words, *en la pleine et entiere joüissance du droit de pavillon*"? Jenkins replied (1) that the King of England for the time being was Lord of these seas, where he had the right of his flag acknowledged, and that these seas were, as much as that watery element is capable of being so in its nature, no less a domain of the Crown than the Honour of Greenwich or the Manor of Eltham; (2) that the *droits souveraines* of the king in his seas against strangers had all the legal requisites of a prescription beyond the memory of man, and did not consist in one individual point, as for instance in having the flag struck to, or in having the liberty of fishing acknowledged by yearly sums of money; but in all the several rights, honours, and perquisites that a sovereignty is capable of producing, and have been enjoyed by former kings of England, with this difference from all *seigneuries* that move from a *mesne* Lord, or Lord Paramount, that our kings hold this as they do their crown, from God alone, and by their sword. *Life*, ii. 697.

the capture of the salt fleet would thus overwhelm them in ruin even greater than would the loss of their East Indian fleet. But ships were apparently not ready for this venture—and, besides, it was not salt that Charles wanted. On 18th February orders were sent to the Mediterranean to take and sell, or to destroy, all Dutch shipping. On 5th March Charles wrote to the Duke of York commanding that, as he had received many indignities from the States-General, and his demand for reparation against one of their subjects who refused to strike his flag remained unanswered, such men-of-war as were ready at Portsmouth should immediately put to sea and seize and bring into port, with their cargoes intact, any Dutch vessels they met with, and destroy those that resisted. Another royal command on the following day included Hamburg vessels in the piratical order, since Dutch ships often sailed under that flag; and in this missive, as a sort of moral salve, the king announced that he had resolved to make war on the States-General.

The first capture was made on 8th March, and when Boreel demanded restitution, he was told, boldly but incautiously, that the Dutch ships would be seized everywhere. The Cadiz fleet returning to the United Provinces had a very narrow escape, having passed up Channel on the day Holmes received his instructions. On the next day, 13th March, off the Isle of Wight, he fell in with the Smyrna fleet of fifty-six merchant vessels returning home from the Mediterranean with rich cargoes of silks, plate, cochineal, gums, &c., estimated to be worth over a million pounds. It was upon this fleet that Charles had been counting. Eleven States' men-of-war acted as convoy to the merchantmen, many of which were also heavily armed as fighting ships. To deal with this formidable force Holmes at first had only five ships, having failed to effect a junction with Spragge's squadron, from the selfish design, it was alleged, of keeping the prize-money among as few as possible. The Dutch fleet, which had been warned of their danger by Boreel, were on the alert. On the approach of the English the armed vessels moved into line to protect the defenceless merchantmen. Lord Ossory, in the *Resolution*, bore up to the Dutch vice-admiral and gave him a "warning piece" to strike his flag, and as he took no notice of it, Ossory gave him another and "placed it in him." Sir Robert Holmes, in the *St Michael*, treated Captain Adrian de Haas, who commanded the convoy, in the same way, and when the latter sent his lieutenant on board the *St Michael* to ascertain the cause of shooting, he was promptly clapped into the hold, "having, it seems," as the English official account says, "given some saucy language to Sir Robert."[1] The *St Michael* then poured in a broadside and the fight began. It continued until night, and was resumed on the following day, when Holmes was reinforced by three other ships, and on the day after that, as the Dutch fleet made its way up the Channel, defending itself with the greatest valour. The English were hopelessly outnumbered. They sank one Dutch man-of-war and captured another, with four or five of the merchant vessels, but all the others safely reached port. The English ships which were beaten off were so terribly battered and cut up that they could scarcely make their way back to the Downs. On the *St Michael* alone thirty-four men were killed and fifty-six wounded, as well as "a great many" missing.

Charles was deeply disappointed at losing the booty on which he had calculated. He was further annoyed when he found he could not confiscate the whole of the cargoes actually taken, and which Holmes with vainglorious exaggeration boasted "would give him credit for £200,000 at least." When the question came to be decided whether the captured ships were lawfully good prize, Holmes and his officers showed the greatest reluctance to be examined. Included in the cargoes were goods belonging to Spaniards and subjects of other nations, but notwithstanding this the Council wished to confiscate everything. Sir Leoline Jenkins, Judge of the High Court of Admiralty, opposed this design with great energy. The confiscation of Dutch ships and property in time of peace might be colourably made under the pretence that the owners refused to strike their flag and were the aggressors. But to condemn neutral goods on board as lawful prize would be, Sir Leoline said, to introduce "a new law of war, not so honourable for us to endure from others when

[1] The account was brought to Court by Lieutenant Churchill, afterwards the great Duke of Marlborough, who was serving under Lord Ossory.

his Majesty shall be at peace and his neighbours at war." He declared that no hostile act of the Dutch, supposing them the aggressors, could involve a stranger not party to it, before a public declaration of war; and as he threatened to resign his office if the course was persisted in, the Council gave way, and restitution was made of the property of neutrals.[1]

The iniquity of this shameful and deliberate attack on Dutch shipping in time of peace was not extenuated or obscured by the plea of the English Ministry that it had been caused by the obstinacy of the Dutch in refusing to strike the flag. The opinion of Europe was expressed in the remark of a French diplomatist at one of the German Courts, that "when the king, his master, made war on the States-General, he would not do so like a pirate." An immediate result of the onslaught on the Smyrna fleet was to convince not only the States-General, but the French Court, that Charles was in earnest, and the formal declaration of war could not be longer delayed. On 17th March 1672, the day after Churchill brought the tidings to London, an Order in Council was issued to print and publish the declaration of war against the States-General. In this long, verbose, and rhetorical document of eight pages Charles tried hard to justify his flagrant violation of treaties. The real reason of the war could not be avowed, but every complaint that had at any time been levelled against the Dutch was now dragged forth, accusation being piled on accusation. The accumulated charges connected with the East Indies, the West Indies, and Surinam were revived and aggravated; the safety of trade, upon which the wealth and prosperity of the English people depended, was in danger; the king and nation were declared to have been insulted by lampoons and caricatures. But, as was to be expected from the antecedents, a principal ground of rupture was found in the flouting by the Dutch of the right of England to the honour of the flag and the sovereignty of the sea. "The right of the flag," the king declared, "is so ancient that it was one of the first prerogatives of our royal predecessors, and ought to be the last from which this kingdom should ever depart. It was never questioned, and it was

[1] Pontalis, *op. cit.*, ii. 239. Hume, *loc. cit.* *State Papers, Dom.*, *Entry Book*, 24, f. 57; *ibid.*, 34, f. 164; cccii. 130; ccciii. 26, 72, 211-218; ccciv. 9, 11, 20, 21, 25, 36; cccvii. 169; *Foreign Entry Book*, 21, ff. 1, 9.

expressly acknowledged in the treaty of Breda; and yet this last summer it was not only violated by their commanders at sea, and that violation afterwards justified at The Hague, but it was also represented by them in most Courts of Christendom as ridiculous for us to demand. An ungrateful insolence! That they should contend with us about the dominion of these seas, who, even in the reign of our royal father, thought it an obligation to be permitted to fish in them, by taking of licenses and for a tribute." Notwithstanding all these provocations, the king continued, he had patiently waited expecting satisfaction. To the memorials sent to them they had at last replied to this effect: "That in this conjuncture they would condescend to strike to us, if we would assist them against the French; but upon condition that it should never be taken for a precedent hereafter to their prejudice." The concluding negotiations were mendaciously summarised by saying that after the return of Downing the States-General sent over an extraordinary ambassador, who declared he could give no satisfaction till he had consulted his masters. "Wherefore," said the king, "despairing now of any good effect of further treaty, we are compelled to take up arms in defence of an ancient prerogative of our crown, and the glory and safety of our kingdoms."

Louis' declaration of war, of fewer words and greater dignity, followed; arrangements were completed for the union of the English and French fleets, and no difficulty was made about the salute. Charles, while taking so high and imperial a tone in the declaration of war about the ancient and sacred rights of the English flag, immediately relinquished them to his royal ally and paymaster. For the first time in history the French fleet was put on an equality with the English in the British seas. Orders were issued that if an English squadron under a vice-admiral was sent to the Mediterranean to be commanded by a French admiral, the latter was to be saluted in the same manner as he was saluted by French vice-admirals. When an English frigate was sent to Brest with a despatch for the Comte d'Estrées, the Vice-Admiral of France, it was ordered if it met the French squadron appointed to join the English fleet to salute them as if they were English ships, and to treat the French Vice-Admiral as if he were English. Charles sent similar commands to the Governors of Portsmouth, Dartmouth,

Dover, and other places—that the French ships were to be saluted as if they were English. Thus not only in the Mediterranean, but in the Channel and in English ports, the English flag was to be lowered to that of France—a proposition that might have made the old sea-dogs turn in their graves.[1]

The junction of the allied fleets was followed, on 28th May, by the fierce and sanguinary battle of Solebay. The victory was indecisive, but the advantage lay rather with the Dutch. De Ruyter withdrew to his own coast, and the English were too much crippled to follow.[2] No other great sea-fight took place in 1672, but in September Sir Edward Spragge employed his squadron against the Dutch fishermen. Just before the declaration of war the States-General laid an embargo on their fishing vessels; but they removed it in September,[3] and towards the end of the month it was reported that a hundred Dutch busses, convoyed by twenty frigates, were fishing off the Norfolk coast. On the 22nd Spragge's squadron, showing no colours, appeared off Yarmouth, and greatly frightened the English herring fishermen, who thought the Dutch fleet was upon them. By noon on the 24th he had captured eleven Dutch doggers and 117 prisoners; two of the doggers had licenses from the English Government, and were released later. By the end of the month the prizes numbered about thirty doggers, one buss, and a privateer, with over 300 prisoners,—not a very large haul,—while about 200 others had been chased home, and many nets, which the fishermen had cut and left in the water, were destroyed. Spragge having thus, as he reported, "cleared these seas of fishermen except our own," returned to the Thames.[4]

While the Dutch maintained the contest at sea with honour and success, they were overwhelmed on land. A great French army, under Turenne, Condé, and other celebrated generals of

[1] Hume, *loc. cit.* Pontalis, *loc. cit.* Temple's *Works*, i. 175; iii. 505. *Parl. Hist.*, iv. 512. *Hollantsche Mercurius*, 1672, p. 50. Dumont, *Corps Diplomatique*, VII. i. 163. *State Papers, Dom.*, cccii. 210; ccciv. 21, 22; cccvi. 27; *Entry Book*, 31, f. 90. *Ibid.*, 34, f. 157.

[2] Mahan, *op. cit.* Colomb, *op. cit.*

[3] $\frac{9}{19}$ March, $\frac{5}{15}$ Sept. 1672. *Groot Placaet-Boeck*, iii. 292, 298. The embargo was renewed in the next year.

[4] *State Papers, Dom.*, cccxv. 108, &c.; cccxvi. 43

the age, poured into the Provinces. Town after town, fortress after fortress, surrendered to the invaders, and the Prince of Orange, with the remnant of his small army, retired into Holland. It seemed inevitable that the Republic, contending with the two most powerful states in Europe and bereft of allies,—for Sweden as well as England had been detached from the triple league,—would soon be subjugated. The States-General, in despair, sued for peace. Two ambassadors were sent to Louis and two to Charles. Louis offered them impossible terms, and allowed ten days for acceptance or rejection. Charles refused to see them at all, but sent them to Hampton Court along with Boreel, who had not yet left England; and there they remained for some weeks carrying on a sort of backstairs negotiation. Then the king, fearing they might intrigue with his own subjects, who were in sympathy with them, dismissed them early in August. But becoming apprehensive at the unexpected rapidity of the French conquests, he despatched the Duke of Buckingham and Lord Arlington, and soon also Viscount Halifax, to negotiate anew with Louis, and to inform him of the overtures for peace from the States-General. On their way they passed through Holland, where they had several interviews with the Dutch Government and the Prince of Orange. After renewing the league with Louis at Utrecht, and agreeing that neither king should conclude peace except with the consent of the other, the conditions on which Charles was willing to make peace were formulated. The States were asked to undertake, on demand, to banish perpetually any person guilty of treason against the king, or of writing seditious libels; to pay £1,000,000 sterling towards the cost of the war; to invest the Prince of Orange with the sovereignty of the United Provinces, or at least to confer upon him the highest offices; and to surrender as security to the king Walcheren, the city and castle of Sluys, as well as the isles of Cadsand, Goeree, and Voorne. With regard to the sovereignty of the sea, they were to yield the honour of the flag without the least reserve or hesitation, so that whole fleets were to lower their top-sails and strike their flags to a single English ship carrying the king's flag, in any part of the British sea up to the coasts of the United Provinces. The States-General were, moreover, to agree to pay to the King of England, for ever, the sum of £10,000 a-year for permission which the king would grant them to fish for herrings on the coasts of England, Scotland, and Ireland.[1]

The demands of Louis were even more oppressive to the Dutch, and threatened them in what they held most dear—their religious liberty, for the sake of which they had formerly fought so long and so heroically against the tyranny of Spain.

In this crisis of their history despair and fury seized upon the people. The Ministers were blamed for the misfortunes of the country; a popular tumult burst forth in favour of the Prince of Orange; and John de Witt, the clear-eyed statesman who had so long held the helm and steered the Republic through so many dangers and difficulties, was foully murdered in circumstances of great brutality—a fate which his brother shared. The young Prince infused his own invincible spirit into the people. The terms of peace were rejected, and a supreme effort was made to save the country by the method which had been adopted against Alva and Requesens just a century before: the dykes were opened and the land laid under water, causing the enemy to retreat. The steadfast

[1] Dumont, *Corps Diplomatique*, VII. i. 206. Hume, *op. cit.*, c. lxv. In *State Papers, Foreign, Treaty Papers* (*Breda*), 1667, Bdl. 73 (as at present arranged), are a number of papers belonging to these negotiations and the later ones at Cologne in 1673, consisting mostly of draft articles, with copious notes by the plenipotentiaries. In one, marked "1st project as framed," Art. xiv. refers to the flag as follows, the words in brackets being inserted here from a second copy: "That the ships and vessells of the United Provinces, as well men-of-war as others, be they single ships or in Fleets how great soever, meeting in any part within ye Brittish seas, with any one of ye ships of war (yatchs) or other vessells w'soever of ye said K. of Gr. Brittain, or in his service and wearing his flagg, colours (or Jack) shall strike their flaggs and lower their Topsailes untill they be passed by, as a Ancient and undoubted Right belonging to the said K., and which hath been payd and performed to his R^{ll} progenitors in all times." The fishery article (xxiv.) was as follows, the words within brackets being taken from another copy, to fill up a blank: "And the said States acknowledging his said Maj^{ts} ancient and undoubted Right in the Brittish Seas, as they do hereby own and acknowledge ye same, Doe further promise and agree, that they and their successors will from henceforth pay to his said Maj. his Heirs and successors, for euer, at the Receipt of his Exchequer, a yearly sum̄ of . . . (10^{mte}—as likewise ye yearly summe of 2^{mt} sterling by ye yeare at ye Receipt of his Ma^{tys} Treasury of his Kingdom of Scotland) . . . sterling by the year, in considerac̄on of his Maj^{ts} license and permission to them and their subj^{ts} to fish in the said seas and upon his Ma^{tys} coasts." Another article (xxv.) provided for the payment of £1,000,000 for the charges of the war, £400,000 in the following October, and the remainder later.

courage of the Prince of Orange and the growing alarm at the designs of France at last brought allies to the States. Spain and both branches of the house of Austria espoused their cause, and German troops came marching to the Rhine.

But the ally on which the Dutch most relied was the Parliament of England. It had now been prorogued for nearly two years, and Charles was at last forced to summon it by his need of money to carry on the war. When it met, the members were told by the king that he had been forced into a war which was just and necessary both for the honour and the interest of the nation, and he referred them to his declaration, in which the reasons were given. He also defended the Declaration of Indulgence to dissenters, which had been designed to favour the Roman Catholics, and about which the country was greatly agitated. The Earl of Shaftesbury, as Chancellor, enlarged on the same themes. Against the Dutch he levelled such charges as were contained in the declaration of war. They had broken treaties about the East Indies and Surinam, "and at last," he exclaimed, "they came to that height of insolence, as to deny the honour and right of the flag, though an undoubted jewel of this crown, never to be parted with; and by them particularly owned in the late treaty of Breda and never contested in any age." He accused them of disputing the king's title to it in all the Courts of Christendom, and of having made great offers to the King of France if he would stand by them against England. They were branded as the common enemy to all monarchies, and especially to that of England, "their only competitor for trade and power at sea," who alone stood in their way to a universal empire as great as Rome. They had, he said, slighted all negotiations and refused all cessation of hostilities; and the king, he claimed, in entering on the war had only carried out the maxims of the Parliament which had advised the last war, and had then judged it necessary to extirpate the Dutch, laying it down as an eternal maxim, "*delenda est Carthago*, that government is to be brought down." The Parliament was then asked to vote further supplies.

At first, while avoiding the least approbation of the war, Parliament passed a resolution that they would grant eighteen months' assessments, at the rate of £70,000 a-month, for the king's "extraordinary occasions"; but this was designed merely to allow them time to deal with the Declaration of Indulgence before Charles could afford to dismiss them. The contest with the king on this question ended in victory for the Parliament, which then passed the Test Act, disqualifying Catholics for all offices under the crown. The king was still resolved to pursue the war. The money voted by Parliament served to equip a fleet; and as the Duke of York was made ineligible owing to the Test Act, Prince Rupert took his place as admiral. In May 1673 the combined naval forces of France and England sought out De Ruyter on his own coast, and three battles were fought in the summer,—on 28th May, 4th June, and 11th August,—both sides claiming victory; but the Dutch prevented the projected landing of English troops, and compelled the allies to retire to their own coasts.[1]

By this time, however, the king saw he could not with safety continue to carry on the war much longer. Spain, which had already declared war against France, threatened to do the same against England unless peace was made, and this would destroy the lucrative English trade with that country. The war was intensely unpopular in England, and the seamen fought without heart. The timid conduct of the French squadrons in the various battles excited deep and widespread resentment. It was on all sides rumoured that Charles had sold his country in order to carry out the selfish designs of Louis. The subsidies, moreover, were soon exhausted, and it would be necessary to ask Parliament again for more money. It was clear that the appeal which Charles had made to the spirit or vanity of the nation with respect to the honour of the flag and the sovereignty of the sea had thoroughly failed, although inspired and mercenary pens did what they could to arouse enthusiasm. These efforts were indeed a measure of the unpopularity of the third Dutch war. Before it broke out certain authors had handled the theme. The learned Prynne, who lost his ears for opposing

[1] Hume, *loc. cit.* Temple's *Memoirs*, i. 166. *State Papers, Dom.*, cccxi. 75, 82, 206; cccxiii. 233. *Commons' Journals*, ix. 246. Dumont, *op. cit.*, VII. i. 206. *Hollantsche Mercurius*, 1672, p. 265.

Charles I., became a subservient supporter of his son; and, as Keeper of the Records in the Tower, he published an erudite, but confused, book in which the absolute right of the King of England to the dominion of the surrounding seas was maintained.[1] In a very different kind of book, one Captain John Smith repeated current arguments and misstatements on the same topic, especially with reference to the fisheries, for he had been one of the agents of the Fishery Society of Charles I. He makes a statement that must have caused the king, if he saw it, some surprise at his modesty in asking only £10,000 or £12,000 from the Dutch. He had heard, he says, that the "composition" of the Hollanders for leave to fish on our coasts was an annual rent of £100,000 and £100,000 "in hand"; and as none of it had been paid into the Exchequer, he computed the arrears then to be over £2,500,000, a sum which, he very truly remarked,—and it is the sole truth in the statement,—"would come very happily for the present occasions of his Majesty." Like many others before him and after him, he advocated the building of a fleet of busses and the prohibition of the Hollanders from fishing in the British seas.[2] Still other writers laid stress on the close connection between the sovereignty of the sea and trade, commerce, and navigation;[3] and after the war broke out more pointed attacks were made against the Dutch. They were accused of invading our fisheries without license from the king, refusing to strike sail, disputing our dominion of the seas, and by artifice supplanting us in trade and commerce.[4]

None of those works was of much account, and the Ministry felt the need of obtaining the services of an able writer to stimulate ill-feeling against the Dutch, and in particular to answer a well-reasoned pamphlet which the Dutch had widely circulated in refutation of the reasons for the war given in

[1] *Brief Animadversions on, Amendments of, and Additional Explanatory Records to the Fourth Part of the Institutes of the Lawes of England, concerning the Jurisdiction of Courts, compiled by the late famous Lawyer, Sir Edward Coke, Knight, &c.*, 1669.

[2] *England's Improvement Reviv'd: Digested into Six Books*, 1670.

[3] Roger Coke, *A Discourse of Trade*, 1670.

[4] William de Britaine, *The Dutch Usurpation, or a Brief View of the Behaviour of the States-General of the United Provinces towards the King of England*, 1672.

the king's declaration. The States-General did not reply to that document, but Wicquefort did so in the pamphlet referred to, which was entitled "Considerations on the Present State of the United Netherlands." The tone of his reply was extremely temperate. The writer insisted on the difference between the striking of the flag and the sovereignty of the sea; the former was merely a ceremony of respect which all republics paid to monarchies, and not in the least a sign of subjection or an acknowledgment of sovereignty, and as such it had been regulated in the treaty of Breda. The States had always resisted the claim that a whole fleet of theirs should strike to a single English ship. In 1654 Cromwell had abandoned a similar claim on their objecting; and as the article in the treaty of Breda was the same as the one agreed to in 1654, it was unjust to construe it now in the sense of the article which Cromwell had withdrawn. On that ground alone, therefore, it could not be maintained that Van Ghent and the whole Dutch fleet were bound to strike to the king's yacht. Moreover, the article applied only to the British seas, and the writer argued that that meant the Channel and not the North Sea, citing the seventh article of the treaty of Breda as to the cessation of hostilities. Since the Dutch fleet were lying at anchor off their own coast when the king's yacht passed, they were not obliged to strike, because they were in the North Sea, and not in the British seas at all. The conclusion was drawn, and as we have seen justly, that the king had sent his yacht for the deliberate purpose of getting a ground of quarrel. As for the sovereignty of the sea, the States attributed to God alone such dominion as the king usurped to himself. They therefore refused Downing's demands, which had been put forward to give the king a pretext for war. To admit them would ruin the United Provinces, which lived by commerce and the liberty of the sea. As for the fisheries, they had never asked for permission to fish from the King of England; and though in 1636 licenses were forced upon some of their defenceless fishermen by English men-of-war, that was an act of violence from which no right or title could be derived, and the attempt was relinquished at the demand of the States-General, and had not been repeated.

The cogent arguments of the Dutch writer were well fitted to confirm the general opinion in England as to the cause of the war, and the Court promptly secured the services of Henry Stubbe, a clever, versatile, and prolific writer, to refute them. His answer to Wicquefort was considered by the private committee on 15th May 1672,[1] and it was published anonymously in the following month.[2] The spirit in which Stubbe entered into his task is revealed in a letter he wrote to Secretary Williamson. "The rule I go by," he said, "is this: that no nation is more zealous for their honour than the English; that if they are put into a great passion they forget their particular interests and animosities."[3] He therefore tried as much as he could to inflame the public mind.

The *Justification*, though rabid in tone, is in many respects an able book. It differs from many of the controversial works of the day in that the author, however oblique may be his inferences from them, does not, so far as we have observed, pervert and misquote the documents he cites. It is unnecessary to particularise his arguments on the sovereignty of the sea. They were drawn mainly from Selden, Welwood, and other authors, and partly from certain State Papers which the Ministry placed at his disposal. The striking of the flag by foreigners was, of course, declared to be a regality, and "paramount to all treaties"; it was a "fundamental of the crown and dignity of the King of England." The attack on the Smyrna fleet, which Wicquefort denounced and made the most of, was justified by their refusal to strike their flags, the instructions issued to the admirals of England for four hundred years compelling them to seize all ships which refused. The universal dominion which the king possessed over the British seas was thus formulated: (1) the regality of fishing for pearl, coral, amber (!), &c., and the "direction

[1] *State Papers, Dom.*, cccviii. 143.

[2] *A Justification of the Present War against the United Netherlands, wherein the Declaration of his Majesty is vindicated, and the War proved to be Just, Honourable, and Necessary; the Dominion of the Sea explained, and his Majesty's Rights thereunto asserted; the Obligations of the Dutch to England, and their continual Ingratitude: Illustrated with Sculptures. In Answer to a Dutch Treatise entitled, Considerations upon the Present State of the United Netherlands.* By an English Man, 1672.

[3] 8th July 1872. *State Papers, Dom.*, cccxii. 166.

and disposal" of all fishes "as they shall seem to deserve the regards of the public"—a somewhat cryptic claim; (2) the prescribing of the laws of navigation to foreigners as well as to the king's own subjects; (3) the power of imposing customs and taxes upon those navigating or fishing in them; (4) jurisdiction in regard to maritime delinquencies; (5) the duty of foreign ships to strike their flags and lower their top-sails to the king's "floating castles," the ships of war, by which "submission they are put in remembrance that they have come into a territory wherein they are to own a sovereign power and jurisdiction, and receive protection from it." It was admitted that the sea was free for commerce and innocent passage; but both might be refused if there was suspicion of danger, and that the imposition of tribute for fishing, convoy, or the maintenance of lights and beacons did not infringe the liberty of commerce.

The work appears to have pleased his employers, for immediately after its publication Stubbe began the composition of another on the same lines—to vindicate the "honour" of his Majesty and the kingdom. In this he wished very much to deal with the lampoons and "scandalous pictures" circulated in Holland, "thereby to raise a due passion and resentment in the English," especially one which represented the English ambassadors at Breda kneeling in supplication to their High Mightinesses the States-General; and Sir Joseph Williamson, who was then in Holland with Buckingham and Arlington, was asked to bring over specimens of these. He told Williamson that in his new work, which he proposed to entitle "An Apology for the King's Majesty's Declaration, By an Old Commonwealth Man," he would represent to the English people his Majesty's "generous concern for his subjects' welfare and trade," and his admirable prudence in the noble conduct of affairs; he would excuse his stop of the Exchequer and the Declaration of Indulgence, and descant upon the growth of the Dutch by contumelies to the king and nation. Stubbe was also anxious to obtain, besides the pictures and medals, a manuscript book which he had seen, containing an account of the transactions between the Dutch and the Commonwealth. This was in the possession of Thurloe, who had been Secretary under Cromwell, and he refused to produce it, until a warrant issued by Lord Clifford compelled him to give it up.[1]

The second work was published in 1673, and Stubbe did all that he promised to do, copiously illustrating it with figures of the objectionable medals and pictures, and greatly abusing the Dutch.[2]

But all such efforts to stir up animosity against the Dutch and to convince the public and Parliament of the justness of the war completely failed, and Charles was forced to enter into negotiations for peace. Immediately after the battle of the Texel, in August 1673, a congress of the Powers which had assembled at Cologne began its deliberations to arrange terms of peace, under the mediation of Sweden. The English plenipotentiaries were Sir Leoline Jenkins and Sir Joseph Williamson, and the instructions given to them by Charles included the following:—"The principal points we shall insist upon," said the king, "beyond the particular ones relating to general amity, commerce, &c., are these following: *First*, To have the honour for the future paid to the flagg of England, which hath been practised and acknowledged by them in all former times. *Secondly*, A million of pounds sterling to reimburse us in some part the expenses we have been at in making the war. *Thirdly*, Ten thousand pounds per annum as an honorary acknowledgment for the great benefit that Republic reaps for the fishing on our coasts, and two thousand pounds more for the like liberty they enjoy upon the coast of our kingdom of Scotland."[3]

[1] Benson to Williamson, 28th June, 9th July 1672. Stubbe to Williamson, 8th July. *State Papers, Dom.*, cccxii. 45, 166, 184. The warrant was to Mr Thurloe and Mr Bish of Lincoln's Inn. Stubbe made considerable use of the book, citing it as "MSS. Commentary of the Treaty and Articles betwixt the English and the Dutch in 1653."

[2] *A Further Justification of the Present War against the United Netherlands, illustrated with several Sculptures.* By Henry Stubbe, a lover of the Honour and Welfare of Old England, &c., 1673. Unfortunately for Stubbe, he tried his hand on another line, and was arrested and imprisoned in the same year for denouncing, in his "Paris Gazette," the Duke of York's marriage with Princess Mary of Modena.

[3] *Life of Sir Leoline Jenkins*, i. 3. For the use of the plenipotentiaries a volume of transcripts of documents, mostly State Papers, and chiefly in the handwriting of Williamson's clerks, was prepared, dealing with the claims to the sovereignty of the sea in its various phases. It comprised 613 folio pages, and forms volume 339 of the Domestic series of Charles II. There is a long memorandum in regard to the striking of the flag, consisting for the most part of brief paragraphs reciting

The terms of peace now offered, it will be observed, were much less exacting than those demanded in the previous year, and the request for an express acknowledgment of the king's sovereignty of the sea was dropped. The Dutch plenipotentiaries at the outset of the proceedings said little difficulty would be raised about the question of the flag, but they demurred to the demand to pay tribute for liberty of fishing.[1] This thorny subject was threshed out on either side with all the old arguments which were used in the times of James and Cromwell. The Dutch pled possession, prescription, treaties; the English replied that the treaties had expired in subsequent wars, and were abrogated by the separation of the Provinces from the House of Burgundy, with whom the treaties were made. A new point was raised to show that no right could

precedents (and many of them are omitted), and arranged under the following heads: (1) Strikeing in Generall; (2) Whole Fleets to Single Ships and a Greater Number to a Lesser; (3) Till they be passed by to keepe downe their Flag in sight of ye English; (4) Within the Brittish Seas, What the Brittish Seas are, &c., where done, &c. What Places esteemed according to this Practice to be within ye Brittish Seas; (5) This done as a Duty and Right and not only as a Civillity. Some of the papers have notes on them, apparently penned by the ambassadors at Cologne.

[1] In one of the papers in the volume provided for the use of the ambassadors, containing a copy of the fishery article put forward by Cromwell in 1653 and afterwards withdrawn, is the following, with a sidenote referring to the "king's instructions to the special ambassadors": "Lastly, that ye subiects of ye States generall shall for ye future abstayne from fisheing vpon ye Countreys and shores of any of his Matyes Dominions wthout leaue and Passeports first obtayned. One thing more I must obserue to you relating to those six propositions particularly that of ye fishery. In his Matyes former Instructions to you vpon that Point you were bid to consent to ye leauing out that Article in case ye Dutch should be obstinate vpon it. But his Maty by progress of tyme finding that his Subiects seem fonder thereof, bids me now to direct you to insist vpon that, as vpon ye rest and to frame it as neare as you can according to ye Words set down in ye Reply." Then after Cromwell's article is the following: "Ye Art. of the Fishery as contained in ye Project, 1673." It is the same as that given in the previous year (note, p. 491),—the part referring to the contribution of £2000 for Scotland being interpolated,—except that it concludes with this sentence, "In wch fisheing ye said States shall oblidge themselues that their Subiects shall not come wthin one league of ye shoares of England and Scotland," which is the first mention of a three-mile limit that has been discovered. Sir Arnold Braems suggested to Arlington, in August 1673, that the king should insist in the treaty for an annual payment of £10,000 or £12,000 for their free fishing on his coasts, and that £3000 of this should be devoted to the bringing over of Dutch families and fishing-busses to England, a project which was then being tried by more or less surreptitious methods. *State Papers, Dom.*, vol. 336, No. 295.

now be claimed under the Burgundy treaties. If they were still in force, why had the citizens of Bruges in the Spanish Netherlands, subjects of the King of Spain, who was the successor and descendant of the Dukes of Burgundy, and the very people in whose favour the Magnus Intercursus was made, petitioned the King of England as lately as 1666 for a license to fish in the British seas, a privilege which had been granted to them?[1] To this the Dutch replied that the right to the fishery did not spring from the treaty of 1495, which had been made merely to avoid contests that previously occurred. As the result of conferences with the Dutch representatives, the Swedish mediators informed Jenkins and Williamson that the States-General would not consent to an annual payment for the right of fishery, but they suggested, as the Prince of Orange had done once before, that the matter might be compromised by the payment of a lump sum. Charles declined this proposal, but he reduced the amount of the yearly payment he asked by half—to £5000 for the English fishery and £1000 for the Scottish. The conference was at the same time informed that it was then, and always would be, the "passion" both of king and subject in England to assert and preserve the great royalty of the fishery.

Since the Dutch would not agree to the payment of an annual tribute for the liberty to fish, and Charles would not agree to a lump sum, the mediator suggested that the Dutch might be asked for a small yearly payment for the privilege of drying their nets on shore. This ingenious device roused the suspicions of the English delegates, who feared the tabling of a clause which would represent the tribute as for the use of the land and not for the liberty of fishing. Charles agreed with them in refusing the compromise, telling them that the article about the fishing was "to be barely and solely for the liberty of fishing on his Majesty's coasts," and was not to be mixed up with any question of drying nets. They were also told to make it clear that his license was to be a "successive permission" only, from his Majesty to the Dutch, for liberty to fish, and to take care not to part wholly with his right in the fishery to them. By an arrangement of this nature Charles and his successors would have been free to follow the

[1] See p. 461.

example of the kings of Denmark in dealing with the dues at the Sound—that is, in gradually raising the amount.[1]

Passing from this subject to the question of the flag, it was soon apparent that the Dutch had been too sanguine in thinking there would be little difficulty in dealing with it. The mediators, in drawing up a protocol of the English demands, had modified the article put in concerning the flag. The English had confined themselves to the bare words "the right of the flag" ("le droit du pavillon"), to which the Swedes added, "in the manner your Excellencies (the Dutch ambassadors) projected." The Dutch, in short, had expanded the meaning of the nineteenth article of the treaty of Breda so as to omit the troublesome and objectionable words "the British seas," their proposed article being "that ships of the United Provinces meeting British ships *at sea* should lower the top-sail and the flag, in such manner as the same had ever been previously observed." Jenkins and Williamson strongly opposed the omission of the phrase "the British seas." They declared that the King of England had a special right and immemorial prerogative in those particular seas, but if he grasped at the same honour in all places, not only the Dutch but all the world besides would have reason to dispute it with him. They said further that the king wished that yachts, by name, and all vessels whatsoever in his service and carrying his colours, flag, or jack, should have the same honour paid to them. They also objected to the clause "in such manner as," &c., as being vague and open to misunderstanding, and insisted that it should be set down clearly what the Dutch were to do and how they were to do it in the future. They wished, in short, to bind the Dutch by an express stipulation to the view that the meaning of the clause in the previous treaties was that whole fleets should strike to any single vessel in the king's service in the British seas, while leaving "the British seas" undetermined; and they tabled an article to that effect. Both the Dutch and the mediators objected to this clause as asserting positively that to have been the custom in former times, and saying that to admit it would be to condemn themselves in what

[1] The ambassadors to the Earl of Arlington, $\frac{8}{18}$ Aug., $\frac{26\text{ Aug.}}{5\text{ Sept.}}$, $\frac{13}{23}$ Sept., $\frac{23\text{ Sept.}}{3\text{ Oct.}}$, $\frac{3}{13}$ Oct. 1673. *Life of Sir Leoline Jenkins*, i. 68, 86, 87, 109, 126, 133.

they had done in regard to the *Merlin*. They were quite willing, they said, to do the thing for the future, but it was unreasonable to ask them to avow so openly that they had been in the wrong in not doing it hitherto. To this the English replied that it was most certainly and notoriously an ancient right of the crown of England, of which they had proofs in all ages, and that to omit the words would be to accept of the ceremony as a courtesy and not as a right.

At this stage, however, the king sent them a new article about the flag, defining in part the limits within which the Dutch were to be asked to strike, and these were from Cape Finisterre to the North Cape in Norway. These surprising boundaries had been suggested a year or two before as the limits of the British seas by the Masters of the Trinity House (p. 478), and no doubt Charles meant them to be so considered. They were derived primarily from Selden's *Mare Clausum*, and the southern limit, Cape Finisterre, had been for some time incorporated in the Admiralty instructions.[1] The Dutch were thus to be asked to strike to English ships along almost the whole extent of the western coasts of Europe, a distance exceeding two thousand miles.

The English plenipotentiaries did not like this article. They informed Lord Arlington that when they were preparing the one they had already submitted, they had wished there had been means to ascertain the bounds of our seas as well as there was for clearing up the point regarding whole fleets striking to a single ship; but they had concluded that the king and the Lords of the Committee (for foreign affairs) looked upon it as a thing so invidious and difficult as not to be attempted at that juncture. They explained that they would receive no assistance from the French ambassador or the mediators, all of whom, they clearly perceived, had difficulty in containing themselves from disputing the right of striking at all. As long as they confined the claim to the British seas they were not afraid of opposition, since they had overwhelming evidence as to the

[1] Penn was in error in supposing that "Finisterre" in the subsequent treaty was *finis terræ*, and meant the Land's End in England (Granville Penn, *Memorials of the Professional Life and Times of Sir William Penn*, ii. 255). It was described as "Finisterre, in Galicia," by the Dutch ambassadors in 1668. See p. 469.

usage. But if they insisted on the limits of Cape Finisterre and the North Cape, and supported their contention with arguments from geography or tradition, or if they were asked to produce proofs or instances as to "the matter of fact" near those limits, they foresaw that objections would be raised which they were not sufficiently instructed to answer. No doubt, they continued, it might be advantageous to fix some limits in order to lessen the chance of disputes, but even if mathematical lines could be laid down and agreed upon, it would not remove all ground of quarrel. Besides, to fix definite bounds would place upon themselves a burden which properly lay upon their adversaries; for when the king's right of the flag was established as incontrovertible within the British seas, if any one who was called upon to strike declared he was not in the British seas, he would have to prove it. This long disquisition failed to convince the king. He insisted that the previous article, in which the term "British seas" alone occurred, should be withdrawn and the new article with the specified limits substituted.[1]

The influence of certain important changes in political affairs which had taken place since the congress met now made itself strongly felt at the deliberations. The position and the prospects of the United Provinces had greatly improved. The States-General had succeeded in entering into alliances with the Emperor, the King of Spain, and the Dukes of Brandenburg and Lunenburg. In the field the movements of the Prince of Orange and his allies caused Louis to abandon his conquests with even greater rapidity than he had made them. The English Parliament, too, from which the Dutch had reason to hope for much, was about to assemble. It was thus natural that the Dutch ambassadors and the representatives of their allies at the congress should take a higher tone in dealing with the peace proposals. Some of the conditions which had been put forward by France and England were now declared to mean "utter ruin" to the Dutch, or their "eternal servitude"; and among them was the demand of Charles for a payment for liberty of fishing, which it was asserted would make them

[1] The ambassadors to Arlington, $\frac{29\text{ Aug.}}{8\text{ Sept.}}$, $\frac{2}{12}$, $\frac{13}{23}$ Sept., $\frac{23\text{ Sept.}}{3\text{ Oct.}}$, $\frac{3}{13}$ Oct. 1673. *Life of Sir Leoline Jenkins*, i. 91, 95, 109, 117, 120, 125, 133.

tributary to England. The English plenipotentiaries employed all the arguments they could discover in Selden's *Mare Clausum* and other similar works, and in the volume of State Papers with which they were provided, to convince the congress that fisheries might be "appropriated" on the high seas as well as in rivers and lakes, and that the King of England had the exclusive right to the fisheries off his own coasts. They cited the example of Genoa with the tunny fishery, the treaties between England and Denmark concerning the fisheries on the Norwegian coast and at Iceland, the licenses of the kings of Denmark, the English licenses to French fishermen and the grant to Bruges, the Act of Richard II., and the licenses forced by the Earl of Northumberland on the Hollander busses in 1636. They even displayed the original documents showing King James's expostulations with the Dutch in 1618, and the charter granted to Bruges. It was all in vain. The times had changed. The Dutch ambassadors could now afford to pass the matter off with a raillery. They told Jenkins and Williamson that they "would bait the herrings, as men do carps, to come and feed upon their coasts, and then they would be in possession of a liberty to fish"; adding that they would then allow the English to fish upon the Dutch coast without fear of molestation. More seriously, they said that since no similar stipulation had been allowed in any previous treaty, the States-General trusted to the goodness of the king to pass over the article on that occasion; and Beverning, who was one of the Dutch representatives, recalled how he had discussed the whole matter with Cromwell in 1653, who had withdrawn the claim to the fishery.

No one, neither the mediators nor even the French, the allies of Charles, gave the English ambassadors any encouragement to insist on the fishery article; and finally De Groot informed them, in language more forcible than elegant, that his countrymen would rather "burst" than submit to any acknowledgment in that matter, and that he believed the States would sooner forbid their subjects to fish at all than to ask leave to do so of the crown of England.

The English ambassadors were forced to tell the king that they had no hope of obtaining consent to the article about the fishery, unless indeed the Parliament (which had by this time strongly and boldly shown its sympathy with Holland) "should happen to stand vigorously by his Majesty in this demand which he is pleased to make." They suggested—almost, one may think, with a touch of irony—that the Dutch might be offered, as an alternative, "a Bill," like the proclamation of James in 1609, or the Act of 2 Richard II. that laid an impost of sixpence a ton on our own fishing vessels, "wherein," they added, "if strangers be not intended (as we humbly conceive they are), they may be more expressly taken in."[1]

Although it was on the fishery article that the negotiations stuck most, difficulties also continued to arise about the one on the flag. The Dutch said they were willing to do anything that had been done in former times by way of respect to the crown of England; they could not do it as a right, nor could they do anything that might be construed to be an acknowledgment of the king's claim to the dominion of the British seas. They were unable to admit, without proof, that it was the former practice for a whole fleet of theirs to strike to a single English ship; and while again affirming their willingness for this to be done in future, they declined to make any express recognition of it as a right in the treaty, saying that it would be "abundant courtesy" if they admitted the words *Maria Britannica*, as in all their other treaties; it was a term, moreover, which the French could not be brought to admit into their treaty of Breda, insisting on the term *maria proxima* instead. The English representatives would not condescend to adduce proofs as to the past usage. The king, they said, would not allow an observance so ancient and notorious to be questioned as a matter of fact, any more than that England was an ancient monarchy; and they did not ask for a fuller stipulation than in the article proposed by Cromwell. On the other side, it was pointed out that Cromwell had given up all the points raised, especially the striking of a whole fleet; and, moreover, they could not allow that all the tract of sea between the North Cape and Cape Finisterre was the British Ocean, and they hinted they were willing to strike all the world over without any limitation of places. The English ambassadors

1 The same to the same, $\frac{24 \text{ Oct.}}{3 \text{ Nov.}}$, $\frac{11}{21}$, $\frac{14}{24}$ Nov. 1673, $\frac{23 \text{ Dec. } 1673}{2 \text{ Jan. } 1674}$, $\frac{2}{12}$ Jan., $\frac{3}{13}$ Feb. 1674. *Ibid.*, i. 151, 170, 171, 223, 235, 237, 279.

wrote to Arlington that although they had not been instructed to claim as British the sea between the limits named, yet, if these limits were adhered to, the Dutch would not fail to alarm the Dane and the Swede, the French and the Spaniard. They were justly suspicious of the too generous offer of the Dutch to strike in all seas. They saw in it the design to make the special right possessed in the British seas, in virtue of the king's sovereignty there, less certain and evident in future ages, and to transform it into a mere mark of civility. Charles gave way to a slight degree. In February 1674 he sent on another article, in which the northern limit was brought down from the North Cape to the middle point of the Land-van-Staten in Norway.[1]

By this time, however, negotiations for a separate peace between England and the United Provinces had been begun in London, and the sluggish congress at Cologne, slowly evolving a general peace, broke up and dispersed. Charles was driven to negotiate separately by the action of the Parliament, which financial necessities had forced him to summon in October, and which lost little time in showing its ill-humour with his policy. In his opening speech he stated that he had hoped to be able to announce the conclusion of an honourable peace, but the Dutch, he said, had treated his ambassadors at Cologne "with the contempt of conquerors," and had other thoughts than peace; and he asked for supplies. Shaftesbury, as usual, filled in the picture. The king, he said, had expected to meet them with the olive-branch of peace, but the obstinacy of the Dutch had foiled the negotiations, although his Majesty's concessions had been so great. "He could not," he continued, "be King of Great Britain without securing the dominion and property of his own seas: the first, by an article clear, and not elusory, of the flag; the other, by

[1] The same to the same, $\frac{10}{20}$ Oct. 1673 to $\frac{3}{13}$ Feb. 1674. *Ibid.*, i. 139, &c. *State Papers, Foreign, Treaty Papers* (*Breda*, sic), Bdle. 73. There were prolonged discussions as to the extent of the British seas both in regard to the article on the flag and that on the cessation of hostilities on the sea, as shown by the very numerous notes on the draft articles. The ambassadors were of opinion with regard to the latter article that St George's Channel and the sea between England, Ireland, and Scotland were comprehended in the term "the Channel," a point which was left for the opinion of the king.

an article that preserved the right of the fishing, but gave the Dutch permission, as tenants, under a small rent, to enjoy and continue that gainful trade upon his coasts." But the Dutch, he said, would not agree to any article on the flag that was clear or plain, and they refused any article about the fishery except such a one as might convey to them the right of inheritance for an inconsiderable sum of money, "though it be a Royalty so inherent in the crown of England, that I may say (with his Majesty's pardon for the expression) he cannot sell it." "There is not," continued the Chancellor, "so lawful or commendable a jealousy in the world, as an Englishman's of the growing greatness of any Prince at sea. If you permit the sea, our British wife, to be ravished, an eternal mark of infamy will stick upon us." It was therefore the duty of Parliament to provide the king with more money.[1]

Parliament was not to be cozened by fair words or beguiled by the oratorical tropes of Shaftesbury. The Commons boldly affirmed they would vote no more money unless it appeared that the Dutch were so obstinate as to refuse all reasonable conditions of peace; and with regard to other matters they showed a bellicose spirit. The king resolved to prorogue them suddenly, and went unexpectedly to the House of Peers and sent for the Commons. When Black Rod approached to summon them the door was hastily closed, the Speaker was hurried into the chair, and the following motions were instantly put: that the alliance with France was a grievance; that the evil counsellors about the king were a grievance; that the Duke of Lauderdale was a grievance and not fit to be trusted or employed. Before the motions could be passed, Black Rod, knocking loudly in the king's name, was admitted, and the House rose in confusion. A scene so reminiscent of the days of his father could hardly be lost on Charles. It was clear that it would be impossible to continue the Dutch war if its continuance depended on Parliament voting money for it.

Shortly afterwards the king found it necessary to summon Parliament again, and, changing his attitude, he condescended to submit to them, for their opinion, certain propositions for

[1] *Commons' Journals*, ix. 282. *Lords' Journals*, xii. 588.

peace which the States-General had communicated through the Spanish ambassador. At the same time he sent privately for John Evelyn, who had been for some time engaged on a history of the second Dutch war, and asked him to write something "against the Hollanders about the duty of the flag and fishery," no doubt with the intention and object of influencing the opinion of Parliament.[1] Parliament acted with promptitude. They passed a resolution, on 27th January 1674, recommending the king to make a speedy peace. Louis, who saw how things were tending with the Parliament, having advised the same course, Sir William Temple was summoned from his orchards a few days later and requested to proceed to The Hague to conclude the treaty. On the eve of his departure, the Marquis de Frezno, the Spanish ambassador, announced that he had received full powers from the States to treat and conclude a peace. The negotiations were thereupon conducted in London between Sir William Temple and the Marquis, and they went on so smoothly and speedily that the treaty was signed at Westminster on 9th February. The two points that caused the greatest difficulty were the flag and the recalling of the English troops from the French service: the claim for tribute for liberty to fish was dropped altogether.[2]

The article relating to the flag differed from the corresponding articles in the previous treaties. It was as follows:—

"The said States-General of the United Provinces, duly acknowledging, on their part, the right of the above-mentioned most serene prince, the King of Great Britain, to have honour paid to his flag in the seas to be hereafter named, will and do declare and agree, that all and singular the ships and vessels belonging to the said United Provinces, whether ships of war or others, whether single ships or in squadrons, which shall meet with any ships or vessels whatsoever belonging to the most serene prince, the King of Great Britain, whether one or more, carrying his Britannic Majesty's ensign, or flag called the *Jack*, in any of the seas from the Cape called *Finisterre*, to the middle point of the land called *van Staten*, in Norway, the foresaid ships or vessels of the United Provinces shall strike their flag and lower their topsail, in the same manner and with the like testimony of respect, as hath been

---

[1] P. 513.

[2] Hume, *loc. cit.* *Commons' Journals*, ix. 299. Temple's *Memoirs*, i. 167-169. Temple to the Prince of Orange, Feb. 1674. The same to the Duke of Florence, 11th Feb. 1674. *Works*, iv. 13, 16.

customary in any time or place heretofore, by any ships of the States-General or their predecessors to any ships of his Britannic Majesty or his predecessors."[1]

Most writers who have dealt with the subject have followed Temple in thinking that this article was a great triumph for English diplomacy. "The point of the flag," said Temple, "was carried to all the height his Majesty could wish; and thereby a claim of the crown, the acknowledgment of its dominion in the narrow seas, allowed by treaty from the most powerful of our neighbours at sea, which had never yet been yielded to by the weakest of them, that I can remember, in the whole course of our pretence; and had served hitherto but for an occasion of quarrel, whenever we or they had a mind to it, upon other reasons or conjectures."[2]

[1] Prædicti Ordines Generales Unitarum Provinciarum debite, ex parte sua agnoscentes jus supramemorati Serenissimi Domini Magnæ Britanniæ Regis, ut vexillo suo in maribus infra nominandis honos habeatur, declarabunt et declarant, concordabunt et concordant, quod quæcunque naves et navigia ad præfatas Unitas Provincias spectantia, sive naves bellicæ, sive aliæ, eæque vel singulæ vel in classibus junctæ, in aliis maribus a Promontorio *Finis Terræ* dicto usque ad medium punctum terræ *van Staten* dictæ in Norwegia, quibuslibet navibus aut navigiis ad Serenissimum Dominum Magnæ Britanniæ Regem spectantibus, obviam dederint, sive illæ naves singulæ sint, vel in numero majori, si majestatis Britannicæ sive aplustrum, sive vexillum *Jack* appelatum gerant, prædictæ Unitarum Provinciarum naves aut navigia vexillum suum e mali vertice detrahent et supremum velum demittent, eodem modo parique honoris testimonio, quo ullo unquam tempore aut in alio loco antehac usitatum fuit, versus ullas Majestatis suæ Britannicæ aut antecessorum suorum naves ab ullis Ordinum Generalium suorumque antecessorum navibus." Art. iv. Dumont, *op. cit.*, VII. i. 253. The land *van Staten* (which is a Dutch expression) is the peninsula of Stadtland in N. Berghus, in 62° 5′ N. latitude. It is probable that the English Ministers took the advice of the Trinity House (p. 478) to consult the authors who had written on the northern boundary of the British seas, and that the substitution of *van Staten* for the North Cape, first made at the congress of Cologne (see p. 506), was based upon Selden's plate showing the British seas (*Mare Clausum*, lib. ii., cap. i., p. 122), and which is reproduced in the frontispiece of this book. Selden's plate was much less liberal to the British seas than was his text. The Dutch appellation may have been extracted from a Dutch map.

[2] *Memoirs*, i. 170. Temple added: "Nothing, I confess, had ever given me a greater pleasure, in the greatest public affairs I had run through, than this success; as having been a point I ever had at heart, and in my endeavours to gain, upon my first negotiations in Holland, but found Monsieur De Witt ever inflexible, though he agreed with me it would be a rock upon which our firmest alliances would be in danger to strike, and to split, whenever other circumstances fell in to make either of the parties content to alter the measures we had entered into upon the triple alliance."

Temple's eulogy of his own diplomacy was hardly justified. The Dutch had offered a similar article at Cologne; the striking of the flag had been provided for in previous treaties, and it was not in the least, as Temple should have known well (for De Witt often told him), and as the wording of the article shows, an acknowledgment of the dominion of England in the narrow seas. There is nothing in the article of the Westminster treaty that the Dutch were not perfectly willing to concede at Cologne. It was an improvement on the arrangement in previous treaties, inasmuch as the northern and southern limits of the seas in which the Dutch were to strike were defined, and it was made clear that the Dutch were to strike to a single English ship.

But in truth the real diplomatic victory lay with the Dutch. The striking of the flag is expressly described in the article as a ceremony of "honour" and a "testimony of respect,"—a qualification and attenuation not to be found in the previous treaties. By the introduction of these words the Dutch gained a point they had long contended for. Equally pertinent was the omission of the term "British seas," which is found in all the earlier treaties,—an omission for which Charles was in part responsible. The ceremony "of respect" was to be paid "in any of the seas" between Cape Finisterre and Van Staten; and while the Dutch refused to consider those seas British, the English plenipotentiaries at Cologne were unable to contend that they were British. The limits fixed were therefore, as Sir Philip Meadows observed, "too wide for dominion and too narrow for respect";[1] for we never claimed dominion in the Sea of Norway or the Bay of Biscay, and the Dutch offered to strike to the king's flag all over the world. There is little doubt that the part of the article in which Charles was most interested was that relating to the striking of a squadron to a single ship of his, as it furnished a sort of justification for the action of the *Merlin* before the war. Temple himself was most anxious that the "former custom" referred to in all the previous treaties should

[1] *Brit. Mus. Add. MSS.*, 30,221, fol. 59. Some writers on international law erroneously describe the boundaries mentioned in the article as the boundaries of the British seas.

be clearly defined; and Charles was entirely satisfied with the article.[1]

Notwithstanding Temple's satisfaction as to the article on the flag, it did not end disputes on the subject. In the year in which the treaty was concluded, and in the year following, several episodes occurred. One of them concerned personages no less eminent than the English ambassadors who had been at Cologne, and it formed a practical commentary on the fruitless negotiations in which they had been engaged. Sir Leoline Jenkins and Sir Joseph Williamson did not return until after the conclusion of peace, and when the king's yacht, the *Cleveland*, which had been sent to bring them over, was lying at anchor off the Briel, with Sir Leoline on board, a yacht of the States passed between it and the shore without striking its flag or firing any guns. When a message was sent from the *Cleveland* to the commander of the yacht, who was ashore, telling him he should have struck his flag, he only shrugged his shoulders and said he had the States' ambassadors bound for England aboard. The *Cleveland* then weighed anchor and went about a league seawards, where the Dutch yacht and a man-of-war were lying. Again no flag was lowered to the king's yacht, and the English captain asked Jenkins what he should do. Jenkins adduced the case of Tromp's striking to the Earl of Arundel in Goeree Road, and also of Prince Maurice's yacht, which a few days before had struck "to the kitchen-yacht in the canal of Delf-Haven, between the houses." The captain then remembered that the Dutch had struck to him in that very place as he passed up to Rotterdam, and he proceeded to take vigorous measures to compel the "duty." A shot was fired "under the forefoot" of the States' man-of-war, and after a "convenient" interval another over his poop, and then a third between his masts. This brought a boat from the man-of-war to say that the States' ambassadors were "much astonished" at the shots being fired, and that they would not strike, as they were within their own ports. But when Sir Leoline Jenkins sent a formal request to Van Beuningen, one of the Dutch ambassadors, the man-of-war

1 Temple to the Duke of Ormonde, Oct. 1673. The same to the Duke of Florence, 11th Feb. 1674. *Works*, ii. 91; iv. 19.

took in its flag, and the incident ended.[1] In the following year Sir Leoline Jenkins was again a passenger on board one of the royal yachts, the *Charles;* on reaching the Maes a Holland man-of-war saluted with five guns, but kept its pennant flying, and only took it in and repeated the guns after two shots had been fired at it by the *Charles;* the men-of-war at the Briel also saluted with their pennants struck.[2]

In the spring of the same year Captain Herbert in the *Cambridge* encountered six French ships off Dungeness which refused to strike, and returned the fire, their admiral saying it was the King of France's ship, and did not strike. They outsailed the *Cambridge,* said Herbert, which was no match for them. A few weeks later a French privateer in the same locality refused to strike to the *Garland;* and the tables were turned on the English by a Dutch privateer, which fired on a Whitby merchant vessel for not striking quick enough, and fined the master six shillings and eightpence for each shot expended, as well as beating and abusing him.[3] A case of quite a different kind, unique indeed, as it appears, occurred at the end of 1675. On the return of the *Quaker* ketch to England the officers charged the commander, Captain Joseph Harris, with having lowered his top-sails to a Spanish man-of-war, supposed to be an Ostend privateer, in the Bay of Biscay, to the great dishonour of the king. He was tried by a court-martial, found guilty, and condemned to be shot to death at such time and place as the Lords Commissioners of the Admiralty should appoint.[4] He was, however, reprieved and then pardoned.[5]

[1] *Life of Sir Leoline Jenkins,* ii. 697. [2] *State Papers, Dom.,* vol. ccclxxvi. 46.

[3] *State Papers, Dom.,* ccclxx. 238, 245, 252.

[4] *State Papers, Dom.,* ccclxxvi. 92; ccclxxix. 9. The incident occurred on 11th November 1675, between 46 and 47 degrees latitude. The Spanish ship "required him to strike for the King of Spaine, and the said Cap^n^ Harris haueing seuerell times refused to doe it, and required the said Ostender to strike for his Ma^ty^ of Greate Brittain; yet neuerthelesse he, Capt Jos. Harris, in the time of their convention (*sic*) about this matter, did order the Topsaile of the said Ketch to be Lowered, wch was accordingly done, and is proued by the depositions vpon Oath taken in Court," &c. The court found that by lowering his top-sails he struck to a foreigner in his Majesty's seas, "a great derogac̃on from his Maties Honour, contrary to the 32th Article of the General Instrucc̃ons and punishable by the Eleventh Article of War."

[5] *H. O. Warrant Book,* i. 126, 144.

Difficulties not infrequently occurred with merchant vessels, and even with fishing-boats, over this matter of the flag. We find Pepys writing to Captain Binning of the *Swan*, at Yarmouth, telling him that while he should take care that the Dutch "do their parts of civility towards his Majesty's flag," he ought not to impose upon them any "innovation," the reference being to the taking of twelve barrels of herrings from each of the offenders in lieu of carrying them into port.[1] Foreign merchant vessels, especially Spanish and French, were sometimes brought into port and their masters tried before the High Court of Admiralty for refusing to strike to English men-of-war. By the strict law of the Admiralty such vessels might have been forfeited, but this extreme course was apparently rarely or never taken, the usual punishment inflicted being fine and imprisonment. Cases of this kind were naturally apt to raise unpleasant questions with foreign Powers, and they had to be dealt with cautiously. In 1675, when two Frenchmen were brought before the court for this offence, the judge, Sir Thomas Exton, appealed for advice to Sir Leoline Jenkins, then at the Congress of Nimeguen, and was warned by him to be very careful how he dealt with the case. He advised him to meddle as little as possible with the French edicts of 1555 and 1584 (see p. 117), under which the French Admiralty claimed similar rights, and to "stick to the terms of the indictment of the Spanish Captain at the Old Bailey," adding that although much might be said plausibly on the subject of striking, that indictment had never been attacked; and he argued against the seizure and forfeiture of the ship.[2]

After the third Dutch war several works appeared in which the claims of England to the salute and to the sovereignty of the sea were maintained. It has been already mentioned that at the beginning of 1674, when the Dutch offers of peace were received in London, the king asked Evelyn to write something against the Dutch about the flag and fishery. As the occasion was pressing, Evelyn extracted the introductory part of his work on the second Dutch war (a work which was

[1] 8th Oct. 1674. Tanner, *Catalogue of Naval MSS. in Pepysian Library*, No. 1838.

[2] *Life*, ii. 716. Various other indictments are referred to in *Brit. Mus. Add. MSS.*, 30,221, fol. 62*b*.

never completed), and after submitting it to the king, published it under a rather misleading title.[1] Notwithstanding the haste shown, the book appeared too late. Peace had been concluded, and the Dutch ambassador complained about it to the king. Charles ordered it to be recalled, but with characteristic artifice he instructed that the copies which were seized publicly to pacify the ambassador should be immediately restored to the printer, by which means the sales at least were much increased.[2] About the book itself little need be said. It is an ill-digested and unveracious account of England's claim to the sovereignty of the sea and the fishery, founded on Selden, Boroughs, and less reputable writers. The author computed the arrears of "rent" due by the Dutch, and which he said they had engaged to pay for liberty of fishing, at over £500,000; and he falsified the amount of "license-money" received by Northumberland in 1636, although the Earl's journals, and many other documents, were placed at his disposal. The most severe criticism of the work was made by the author himself, in a long and remarkable letter which he sent to Pepys a few years later, in which he repudiated, *seriatim*, all the "evidences" he had adduced in favour of the English pretension.[3]

Another book of more influence than Evelyn's, because it was for a long time considered the standard work on the maritime law of England, and went through many editions, was published by Molloy two years later; and in it the English pretension received perhaps its most arrogant expression.[4] Notwithstanding the terms of the treaty of 1674, the author declared that the striking of the flag was not a mere

[1] *Navigation and Commerce; their Original and Progress*, 1674.

[2] Evelyn's *Diary and Correspondence*, ii. 90, 91 (ed. 1850).

[3] Evelyn to Pepys, 19th Sept. 1682. "To speake plaine truth," he says, "when I writ that Treatise, rather as a *philological* exercise, and to gratifie the present circumstances, I could not clearly satisfie myself in sundry of those particulars, nor find realy that euer the Dutch did pay toll or tooke license to fish in Scotland after the contest (with Spain) from any solid proofs. . . . I think they neuer payd a peny for it . . . nor did I find that any rent (wheroff in my 108 page I calculate the arrears) for permission to fish, was euer fixed by both parties."

[4] *De Jure Maritimo et Navali, or a Treatise of Affaires Maritime and of Commerce*, London, 1676. Editions were published in 1682, 1690, 1744, 1769, &c. It is still quoted by writers on international law. Molloy was the author of a work attacking the Dutch during the second Dutch war—*Holland's Ingratitude, or a Serious Expostulation with the Dutch, &c.*, 1666.

ceremony of respect, but an absolute acknowledgment of England's sovereignty of the seas, the king granting foreigners a general license to pass through his seas, "paying that obeisance and duty, like the services when Lords grant out estates, reserving a rose or peppercorn, the value of which is not regarded, but the remembrance and acknowledging their benefactor's right and dominion." Molloy held that by the treaty of 1674 the dominion of the British seas was "ascertained" to extend from Cape Finisterre to Van Staten, in Norway, and similar opinions on this and on the subject generally were expressed by other writers on naval matters, as by Godolphin[1] and Zouch,[2] and by most writers on Admiralty affairs during the remainder of the century and well into the next.

With respect to the fisheries, the failure of the previous attempt to establish a great fishery society did not deter others from being proposed. Efforts were indeed made throughout nearly the whole of the reign of Charles to keep the subject alive. An elaborate report was prepared by Dr Benjamin Worsley, who was Secretary to the Council for Trade and Plantations, on the Dutch fisheries and the best means by which a fishery could be established in this country with good hope of success. He stated that the least valuation generally placed on the Dutch herring fishery was £3,000,000, and that it was said to employ 1600 busses. Detailed reasons were given for the belief that success would not attend any attempt to establish a great fishery in England, unless it received the active support of the king and Parliament, and unless we were able to undersell the Dutch in the markets, which he thought by a change of methods we might be able to do.

Various efforts were made, openly and surreptitiously, to induce Dutchmen to settle at Yarmouth and Dover; the king even issued a declaration to encourage this in June 1672. But the schemes failed, and Sir Arnold Braems suggested that £3000 of the amount expected to be paid by the Dutch for the liberty of fishing should be devoted to bringing over

[1] *A View of the Admiral Jurisdiction, &c.*, London, 1661; 2nd edition, 1685.

[2] *The Jurisdiction of the Admiralty of England Asserted*, London, 1686.

busses and men.[1] Early in 1675 a detailed scheme was laid before Charles for the setting up of a fishery company with forty busses and a capital of £40,000, the estimated profit in the first year being placed at £31,463.[2] Among the objections urged to the setting up of the fishery by the king were the want of seamen and experienced curers; the acquaintance of the Dutch with the markets and their spare living, which would enable them to undersell us; and the laziness of English seamen. These objections were apparently answered satisfactorily,[3] and in 1677 Charles issued a commission to the Duke of York, the Earl of Danby, and others for a new society, to be called "The Company of the Royal Fishery of England," granting a number of privileges and £20 per annum from the customs of the port of London for each buss or dogger. Stock was subscribed to the amount of about £12,500, which was spent in purchasing busses; but as they were Dutch-built and manned by Dutchmen, the French, then at war with the United Provinces, seized six of the seven belonging to the company and brought the work to a stop. Although the company was reconstructed later, and an attempt to raise £60,000 to carry it on made with some success, the death of the king and the troubles which followed caused the enterprise to be suspended. Thus the endeavours of Charles II. to create a great national fishery in England were no more successful than those of Charles I.

[1] *England's Great Interest*, 38. *State Papers, Dom.*, cccxi. 86; cccxv. 196; cccxxxvi. 295.

[2] *State Papers, Dom.*, ccclxix. 263. It is endorsed by Williamson, "Herring Fishery: Given me by ye King to keepe. Sunday, 24 Ap. 75," and is unsigned. Each buss was to be of 70 tons, with a master, mate, pilot, and 12 seamen, to be all paid partly by results. The whole charge for the first year was put at £58,537, and the earnings at £90,000, on the assumption that each buss would catch 100 lasts of herrings, 15,000 cod, and 10,000 ling.

[3] *State Papers, Dom.*, *ibid.*, 264, 265.

CHAPTER XIV.

JAMES II. AND AFTER.

In the short and troubled reign of James II. little was heard of the claims of England to the sovereignty of the sea. Bad king as James was, he rescued the navy from the deplorable condition into which it had sunk in the later years of Charles,—of which Pepys has left so graphic a picture,[1]—and the naval officers continued to enforce the routine duty of the flag; but the domestic troubles with which he was surrounded prevented him from turning it to account against any of his neighbours, even if he had been so inclined. And with the Revolution of 1688 the whole aspect of the question was changed. The English pretension, as we have seen, had been specially directed against the United Provinces, but when the Prince of Orange was called to the English throne as William III., and was thus the ruler in both countries, it was not to be expected that he would show much zeal in continuing the policy of the Stuarts against his own countrymen.

It is true that in the treaty which was concluded between England and the Dutch Republic in 1689, the article on the flag in the treaty of Westminster was repeated and confirmed. This, however, was very much a matter of routine and formality, though it must be said the Dutch ambassadors in London complained that William was as obstinate and punctilious about the question of the flag as any purely English sovereign could have been.[2] But from this time until well on in the next century England and the United Provinces were united as

[1] *Memoires relating to the State of the Royal Navy of England for Ten Years, determin'd December* 1688. London, 1690.

[2] Dumont, *Corps Diplomatique*, VII. ii. 236. Wagenaar, *Vaderlandsche Historie*, c. lxi.

allies in the great wars with France. There was thus little room for serious disputes with them about the flag, the right to the herring fishery, or the sovereignty of the sea, even if the desire had existed. Against France, however, William made use of the customary language as to the English sovereignty of the sea. In the spring of 1689, after William had been proclaimed King of England, Louis XIV. foresaw the formidable coalition that would be formed against him, and he boldly issued what was virtually a challenge to England on the subject. He published an ordinance on 15th April in which he not only prohibited his officers from giving the first salute to ships of other nations carrying flags of equal rank to their own, but ordered them to demand the salute from foreign vessels on whatever seas or coasts they might encounter them, and to compel them by force if they refused.[1] That this challenge of Louis to dispute the sovereignty of the sea was not too presumptuous was shown in the following year, when the combined fleets of England and Holland were defeated by the French off Beachy Head. In the declaration of war against France, in May 1689, the ordinance of Louis was made one of the reasons for hostilities. "The right of the flag," said William, "inherent in the crown of England, has been disputed by his orders, in violation of our sovereignty of the Narrow Seas, which in all ages has been asserted by our predecessors, and which we are resolved to maintain, for the honour of our crown and of the English nation."[2] They were strange words to come from the mouth of one who was Prince of Orange as well as King of England, but the times were changing and such phrases were soon to become merely empty forms.

With respect to this ceremony of the flag, which the English professed to regard as an acknowledgment of their sovereignty on the sea, it may be said that from this time on it ceased to have much importance in international affairs. The instructions issued by the Admiralty to the naval officers continued to be explicit enough, and they indeed suffered but little change for another century. The commander of one of his Majesty's ships, on meeting with any ship or ships belonging to any foreign prince or state within his Majesty's seas (which, it was explained,

[1] Valin, *Nouveau Commentaire sur l'Ordonnance de la Marine*, &c., ii. 689.
[2] Dumont, *op. cit.*, VII. ii. 230.

extended to Cape Finisterre, Van Staten not being mentioned), was to "expect" such ship or ships to strike their top-sail and take in their flag, "in acknowledgment of his Majesty's sovereignty of those seas," and if they refused or offered to resist, they were to be compelled to do so. Within his Majesty's seas his Majesty's ships were in no wise to strike to any; and in other parts only if the foreign ship struck first or at the same time, except in a foreign harbour or in a road within gunshot of a fort or castle, in which case a salute with guns was to be given if the commander of the fort agreed to answer gun for gun. If any British ship was so far forgetful of its duty as not to salute the king's ship by striking the top-sail as it passed by, when it might be done without loss of the voyage, they were to be "brought to the Flag" to answer their contempt, or reported to the Admiralty for proceedings to be taken.[1] Sim-

[1] "Upon your meeting with any ship or ships within his Majestie's Seas, (which for your better guidance herein, you are to take notice that they extend to Cape Finisterre) belonging to any foreign Prince or State, you are to expect them in their passage by you, to strike their topsail and take in their flag, in acknowledgment of his Majestie's Sovereignty in these Seas; and if any shall refuse, or offer to resist, you are to use your utmost endeavour to compel them therto, and in no wise to suffer any dishonour to be done to his Majesty; and in case any of his Majestie's subjects shall be so far forgetful of their duty, as to omit striking their topsail as they pass by you, when it may be done without the loss of the voyage, you are to bring them to the Flag to answer their contempt, or otherwise to return the name of the ship and of the master to the Secretary of the Admiralty, or the Lord High Admiral of England, or the Commissioners for executing the office of Lord High Admiral for the time being, as also the place whence and the port to which he shall be bound. And you are to make the master of such ship pay the charge of what shot you shall make at her. And you are further to take notice that in his Majestie's Seas his Majestie's ships are in no wise to strike to any; and that in other parts no ship of his Majestie's is to strike her flag or topsail to any foreigner, unless such foreign ship shall have first struck, or at the same time strike, her flag or topsail to his Majestie's ship, except in the harbour of some foreign Prince, or in the road within shot of cannon of some fort or castle, where you are to send on shore to inform yourself what return they will make to your salute. And in case you have good assurance you shall be answered gun for gun, you are then to salute the port as is usual; but if you shall not be well assured that you shall have an equal number of guns returned you, you are in no wise to salute that place. And in case the ship in which you now command shall at the same time carry his Majestie's flag, you are, before you salute the place, carefully to inform yourself how flags of the same quality with that you carry, of other Princes, have been saluted there, and you are to insist on it being saluted with as great respect and advantage as any flag of the same quality with yours, of any other Prince, hath been saluted in that place, from which you are in no wise to depart." Art. xxxv. 1691. *State Papers, Dom., H. O. Admiralty*, 1, No. 14. Justice, *A General Treatise of the Dominion and Laws of the Sea*, 595.

ilar instructions were issued in succeeding reigns, the injunction to compel by force those who refused to strike being limited to flag officers and commanders.[1]

Disputes as to striking appear to have been much less common in the latter part of the seventeenth and in the eighteenth century than they were previously, but they sometimes occurred; and the ceremony seems to have been enforced on Dutch ships, though they were allied with the English fleet at the time. At all events, the Lords of the Admiralty in 1694 wrote to the Duke of Shrewsbury saying that the instructions required the respect of the flag from all nations whatsoever, without any distinction, and that Sir Cloudesley Shovel had been advised to that effect.[2] At this period, as indeed always, the Danes were very punctilious as to Kronberg Castle on the Sound being saluted with proper respect by foreign ships, and in 1694 Shrewsbury advised the Admiralty that the king had signified his pleasure that all ships of war sent to the Sound should salute Kronberg with three guns only, upon assurance that their salute would be returned by the castle with a like number of guns.[3]

Early in the reign of Anne, in 1704, a sanguinary encounter took place with reference to the striking of the flag that equalled if it did not surpass in brutality any case that happened under Charles. An English squadron under the command of Admiral Whestone fell in with a Swedish man-of-war convoying some merchant vessels. The Swedish commander refused to strike to the English admiral, on the ground that he had received strict injunctions not to do so to any flag whatever, even in the Channel, and thereupon the English proceeded to compel him by force. After about 150 Swedes had been killed or wounded, as well as many English, the unlucky man-of-war, with all the merchantmen, was brought into Yarmouth Roads.[4] Another case of a different kind happened in 1728, early in the reign of George II. A French man-of-war, the *Gironde*, under the command of Mons. de Joyeux, on going

[1] *Regulations and Instructions relating to His Majesty's Service at Sea. Established by His Majesty in Council.* 2nd edition, 1734, Art. xi. *Ibid.*, 10th edition, 1766. *Ibid.*, 13th edition, 1790.

[2] *State Papers, Dom.*, *H. O. Admiralty*, 5, 1108, October 19.

[3] *State Papers, Dom.*, *Petition Entry Book*, 3, 90.

[4] Justice, *op. cit.*, 193.

into Plymouth Sound on 23rd November, was hailed by an English frigate, which demanded that he should salute the fortress and the frigate. The Frenchman replied that the bad weather had prevented his sending an officer to the governor to agree about a salute, but that he owed none to the frigate, which carried a pennant only, it being usual to salute none but flags; and he passed quickly into the port, where the captain of another frigate sent to ask him if he would not salute the commodore, who carried a bare pendant, and he returned the same answer. On coming out again on the 29th the frigate called upon him to strike his pennant, and on his refusal threatened to fire upon him. M. de Joyeux, feeling that it was by no means proper to hazard his ship under the cannon of the castle and the batteries, then complied, and also saluted the fort with eleven guns, as previously arranged. This "insult" was made the subject of complaint by France, and when all the papers had been submitted to the king he instructed that the officer responsible, Lieutenant Thomas Smith of the *Gosport*, should be forthwith dismissed the service as having in this particular exceeded his instructions.[1]

In the writings of the naval historians of last century one may find expressed the views which were then prevalent in naval circles as to the striking of the flag and the sovereignty of the sea generally. They claimed for the crown of England an exclusive propriety and dominion in the British seas, both as to the right of passage and the right of fishing, and the widest limits were assigned to those seas. Thus Burchett, who was Secretary to the Admiralty, defined them as follows in 1720: On the east they extended to the shores of Norway, Denmark, Germany, and the Netherlands, so as to include the North Sea; on the south they were bounded by the shores of France and Spain to Cape Finisterre, and by a line from that Cape westwards to meet the western boundary, thus comprising the Channel, the Bay of Biscay, and part of the Atlantic Ocean; on the west they extended to an imaginary line in the Atlantic in longitude 23 degrees west from London,

[1] *State Papers, Dom., Naval*, 1769, 45. Copies of the various papers sent from the Admiralty to the Under-Secretary of State. Professor Laughton states that Lieutenant Smith was reinstated to a higher rank next day. *Fortnightly Review*, Aug. 1866, p. 721.

passing from the southern boundary to latitude 63 degrees north; and on the north they were bounded by this parallel to the middle point of Van Staten. These were declared to be the British seas proper, in which the crown had the most absolute dominion and the right to the honour of the flag from all other nations; but in addition, it was stated that on the north and west as far as America and Greenland the crown had also "most ample rights" in virtue of first discovery and occupation.[1]

No doubt much of the claim put forward by these writers on behalf of the maritime dominion of England was stereotyped, and had more form than substance. Entick, indeed, in 1757, although asserting the right of Great Britain to an absolute sovereignty of the sea, and to the striking of the flag as an acknowledgment of it, himself described this duty as "but an indifferent honorary ceremony." The changed point of view in which the matter was regarded was shown also in the declaration of war by Great Britain against the United Provinces in 1780, because they had joined the Armed Neutrality. It contained nothing referring either to the flag or to the sovereignty of the sea; and it was doubtless as a mere matter of form and precedent that a brief article relating to the striking of the flag was inserted among the preliminary articles of peace, drawn up at Paris in 1783, and in the definitive treaty of peace concluded with the United Provinces in the next year.[2] The time was approaching when this ceremony was to pass away altogether as a symbol of our maritime sovereignty, even in the eyes of Englishmen. There was little need of

[1] *A Complete History of the Most Remarkable Transactions at Sea, &c.* By Josiah Burchett, Secretary to the Admiralty, 1720. Burchett's account and definitions were adopted by later writers, as Lediard, *The Naval History of England*, 1735; Colliber, *Columna Rostrata; or a History of the English Sea Affairs*, 1727; Entick, *A New Naval History or Compleat View of the British Marine, &c.*, 1757; Campbell, *Lives of the Admirals and other Eminent British Seamen*, 1742-44. Entick claimed for the crown the right to all the fisheries in the British seas, the right to impose tribute on all merchant ships navigating them, the execution of justice for all crimes committed within them, the permitting or denial of free passage through them to foreign ships of war, and the striking of the flag.

[2] In both it was as follows: "Art. ii. À l'égard des honneurs du pavillon, et du salut en mer, par les vaisseaux de la République vis-à-vis de ceux de Sa Maj. Britannique, il en sera usé respectivement de la même manière qui a été pratiquée avant le commencement de la guerre qui vient de finir." Martens, *Recueil de Traités*, iii. 514, 561.

claiming it as an acknowledgment of our actual naval supremacy during the greater part of the eighteenth century, for it was obvious to all the world that British sea-power was supreme. From the reign of Anne onwards the naval force of Great Britain was overwhelming, and formed a determining factor in the history of Europe. This country was undisputed mistress of the seas,—or tyrant of the seas, as our enemies preferred to put it,—and our old rival, the Netherlands, was left far behind in the race for naval power as well as in commerce.[1] Nor was it longer necessary to insist on the honour of the flag in order to stimulate the valour of our seamen, to keep alive the spirit of maritime glory in the nation, or to evoke the reverence of foreign peoples. The forcing of all foreign ships to strike in the British seas became a political encumbrance unsuited to the times. It was allowed to fall into disuse when its inconvenience had long outgrown any utility it had possessed, and the battle of Trafalgar, in 1805, gave the opportunity of departing from the ancient claim. The naval power of France and Spain having been humbled, it was thought a convenient time spontaneously to abandon a pretension which "could not probably have been maintained much longer except at the cannon's mouth."[2] The Admiralty, with the approbation of the Government, accordingly omitted the arbitrary article from their instructions for the fleet.[3]

In the closing years of the seventeenth century and the earlier part of the next there were many signs that the era of claiming an exclusive sovereignty over extensive regions of the sea was passing away; and that, on the other hand, the policy of fixing exact boundaries for special purposes, either by international treaties or national laws, was taking its place. Such signs may be observed in the writings of public men, as in the letter of recantation which Evelyn indited to Pepys in

[1] Mahan, *The Influence of Sea Power upon History*, 209, 225, 510, &c.

[2] *The Life of Richard, Earl Howe*, 200 (1838).

[3] In the *Regulations and Instructions* issued in 1808, the article is as follows: "XXIV. Within his Majesty's seas his ships are not on any account to strike their topsails, nor take in their flags; nor in any way to salute any foreign ship whatever; nor are they, in any other seas, to strike their topsails, or take in their flags, to any foreign ships, unless such foreign ships shall have first struck, or shall at the same time strike, their flags and topsails to his Majesty's ships."

1682 (see p. 514), which included a long reasoned argument against the English pretensions. Still more to the point was the appearance of an extremely able work by Sir Philip Meadows in 1689, immediately after the Revolution, in which these pretensions were subjected to the most destructive criticism.[1] Meadows had considerable experience of public affairs. As Latin Secretary to Cromwell's Council—an office to which he was appointed in 1653 in order to relieve the poet Milton, whose blindness interfered with his duties—he was conversant with the negotiations then proceeding with the Dutch; and later, as ambassador to Denmark and then to Sweden, he had opportunities of acquainting himself with the claims to maritime sovereignty put forward by those countries. The keynote of Meadows' work was, that as the dominion of the seas was apt to become a specious pretence to a war between England and Holland, while the real causes of such a war were hidden and remote, nothing would conduce more effectually to preserve a lasting peace than a true knowledge and right understanding of the matter. If the claim of England as expounded by Selden was to be considered the proper standard of right and wrong between us and other nations, "if what was well written must be fought for too, not being to be gained but by a longer tool than a pen," then the King of England would be cast upon this hard dilemma—either of being involved in endless and dangerous quarrels with all his neighbours abroad, or of having his honour and reputation prostituted at home, as tamely suffering "the best jewel of his crown to be ravished from it." The English pretension, he pointed out, differed from that of Venice, inasmuch as it related not to a bay or gulf, but to a sea open on both sides which formed the passage of communi-

[1] *Observations concerning the Dominion and Sovereignty of the Seas: being an Abstract of the Marine Affairs of England.* In his preface the author says the work was presented in manuscript to Charles II., "and well accepted by him." In a letter from W. Bridgeman to Sir J. Williamson, dated from Whitehall, 13th May 1673, there was enclosed "a paper drawne up as I remember about the beginning of this Warre by S[r] Philip Meadowes, which I find amongst other papers, and showing it to My Lord he directed mee to send it to you." The enclosure is endorsed, "Soveraignity and Fishery by S[r] Phil. Meadowes, 1674," the proper date being probably 1672. It is evidently a draft of the later work, essentially the same in substance and tone. (*State Papers, Dom.*, Chas. II., vol. 335, Part II., No. 168.) Later he sent a copy to Pepys, dated January 2, 1686. *Brit. Mus. Add. MSS.*, 30,221, ff. 13-43.

cation for the northern and southern nations of Europe. Persistence in the pretension would therefore result in war between the island and the Continent, as to whether the island should have the sea to herself, or whether the Continent should have a share of it with her. No nation had ever acknowledged the claim of England, which, moreover, was not enforced, because if one foreigner did violence to another, outside the King's Chambers, but in the Channel or any part of the so-called British sea, he did not come under the jurisdiction of the King of England but under that of his own state.

While strenuously opposing the pretensions to the sovereignty of the sea, Meadows agreed with all other authors in holding that every country had an exclusive right to certain parts of the sea adjoining its coasts: the difficulty was to fix the bounds. "If there is no certain standard in nature," he says, "whereby to ascertain the precise boundaries of that peculiar Marine Territory I am now speaking to, which belongs to every prince in right of his land, yet, by treaty and agreement, they may easily be reduced to certainty. For, as to the judgment and opinion of private persons, we cannot fetch from thence any true measure; for though they all agree unanimously that there is something due of right, yet they vary in the *quantum*, or how much. Therefore the surest way is to prescribe the limits of fishing betwixt neighbouring nations by contract, and not by the less certain measure of territory. For, if no bounds be fixed, how many inconveniencies, and what a licentious extravagance, may such a liberty run into?" The Dutch, he said, unless boundaries were fixed, might dredge for oysters on the coast of Essex, as they did formerly; or fish within the mouth of the Thames, or in our creeks, havens, and rivers; and it was unreasonable not to draw a distinction as to fishing between natives and aliens. Meadows therefore, foreshadowing modern practice, urged that the boundaries of exclusive fishing should be determined by treaty, and he prepared a draft article for the consideration of those concerned.[1]

[1] *Op. cit.*, pp. 44-46. The draft article was as follows: "To maintain a due distinction betwixt natives and foreigners fishing upon the coasts of their respective sovereigns; and to prevent the manifold inconveniences which occasionally arise by a promiscuous and unlimited fishing; 'Tis mutually covenanted, concluded, and agreed, That the people and subjects of the United Netherlands shall henceforth

In a later unpublished treatise he advocated much the same method of mutual agreement with France, with respect to the striking of the flag, as had been formerly proposed by Richelieu—that in our half of the Channel they should strike to us, and that in the half next France we should strike to them.[1]

Whether or not the writings of Meadows had any influence upon the practice, or, what is more likely, merely reflected the change in opinion that had begun, it is from about this time that we find instances of definite boundaries being fixed, usually in connection with the rights of fishery, instead of the vague claims that commonly prevailed. The first case of the kind happened indeed a few years earlier. In a treaty between James II. and Louis XIV., which was concluded in 1686, concerning the rights of trading and fishing in the British and French possessions in America, it was agreed that the subjects of each were to abstain from fishing or trading "in the havens, bays, creeks, roads, shoals or places" belonging to the other, and the liberty of innocent navigation was not to be disturbed.[2] Though no definite limit was laid down in this treaty, the meaning of the terms used was well understood; they were practically the same as those used in the proclamations as to neutral waters in 1668 and 1683.

abstain from fishing within any the rivers, fryths, havens, or bays of Great Britain and Ireland, or within a distance of leagues from any point of land thereof, or of any the isles thereto belonging; under a penalty and forfeiture of all the fish that shall be found aboard any vessel doing to the contrary, and of all the nets, utensils and other instruments of fishing. The like distances, and under the same penalties, to be kept and preserved by the subjects of His Majesty of Great Britain and Ireland, from any of the coasts belonging to the United Netherlands. But beyond these precincts and limits, that the people and subjects on both sides be at freedom to use and exercise fishing, where they please, without asking or taking licenses or safe-conducts for so doing, and without the let, hindrance, or molestation one of another. Saving always the ancient rights of the crown of England, and that nothing herein contained be interpreted or extended to any diminution or impeachment thereof, But that they remain in the same force and vertue, as before this agreement." Meadows does not suggest the number of leagues within which fishing should be reserved, but he quotes with approval the proposal of James, in 1618, to fix a limit of fourteen miles—that is, one "land-kenning" of the Scotch.

[1] "Reflections upon a Passage in Sr William Temple's Memoirs, printed 1692, relating to the Right of Dominion on the British Seas." *Brit. Mus. Add. MSS.*, 30,221, fol. 55. It is dated 1693.

[2] *A Treaty of Peace, Good Correspondence and Neutrality in America, &c.*, 16th November 1686, Art. v. By Article xvi. French subjects were to be at liberty to fish for turtles in the islands of Cayman.

They are interesting as being the first definitions of the kind which apply to the coasts of America, and they do not materially differ from the terms used in the treaty of 1818, the interpretation of which has given rise to so much dispute. Another example for a different purpose is to be found in a convention between France and Algeria in 1689, which established a limit of ten leagues along the Mediterranean coasts of France in connection with the operations of the Barbary corsairs.[1]

In the treaty above referred to, between Great Britain and France, the rights of trading and fishing went together. This was a very common thing in those times, particularly in remote seas, where the two pursuits were often combined, and it was especially the case in the northern seas which were supposed to be under the sway of the King of Denmark. The disputes which occurred between Denmark and the United Provinces of the Netherlands are of interest in this regard, since they reveal the methods and the stages by which a defined boundary was eventually substituted for a general claim to maritime dominion. They show, moreover, that at the end of the disputes Great Britain stood by the side of Holland in opposing the Danish pretension to *mare clausum*, and was altogether in favour of the free sea. It was apparently the assertion of James I. to a monopoly of the whale-fishing at Spitzbergen (see p. 181) that induced Denmark to put forward a similar pretension with regard to Greenland. As early as 1615 a Danish man-of-war demanded a contribution from Dutch whalers for liberty to fish there, and the King of Denmark complained to the States-General that their subjects were carrying on the fishery without his license and contrary to his rights. The Dutch opposed this claim and sent armed ships to the scene, which kept the Danes from active interference. A little later, in 1623, Denmark raised fresh complaints in connection with the fishing at Jan Mayen, an island discovered by the Dutch, and which, therefore, according to the charter of the Dutch Arctic Company, belonged to them. In 1639 Danish men-of-war again interfered with Dutch whalers, this time at Spitzbergen, in virtue of a decree prohibiting fishing without a license from the King

[1] Rayneval, *Institutions du Droit de la Nature et des Gens*, i. c. x.

of Denmark; but the firm attitude of the States-General, whose fleets were then all-powerful, cooled the ardour of the Danes. Denmark also raised difficulties in connection with the cod-fishing in the northern seas. In 1616 foreigners were prohibited from fishing either at Færöe, Iceland, or on the coast of Norway, an injunction renewed in 1636 and 1639, and various limits were assigned with respect to the cod-fishing at Iceland. In 1636 the Norwegian Government declared that the exclusive right of fishing pertained to subjects within a distance of four to six Scandinavian leagues from the coast, which is equal to from sixteen to twenty-four geographical miles. The Danish claim to *mare clausum* also included a monopoly of trade in those remote regions, and the Hanseatic towns as well as the Dutch were forbidden to carry on traffic with the natives. But the efforts of Denmark to preserve a monopoly of fishing and trading in the Arctic seas were intermittent and ineffectual. The great Dutch Arctic Company (*Noordsche Compagnie*), by their charter granted in 1614, were entitled not only to the exclusive right, so far as concerned Dutchmen, "to trade and fish from the United Provinces on or to the coasts of the lands between Nova Zembla and Davis' Strait," including Spitzbergen, Barent's Island, and Greenland, but also to the possession and fishery of any islands they might discover in those seas. The rights granted to this powerful company were thus directly opposed to the Danish claim to *mare clausum,* and owing to the preponderating naval force of the United Provinces, which was behind them, they eventually prevailed. In February 1691, after the defeat by the French of the allied British and Dutch fleets off Beachy Head and the suspension of the Dutch whale-fishing by reason of the war, King Christian V. issued another decree prohibiting whale-fishing at Greenland to all but Danish subjects; and in the following year Hamburg was forced to conclude a treaty with Denmark to enable her citizens to carry on fishing and navigation in Davis' Strait.

It was at this time, nevertheless, that Denmark substituted a fixed limit at other parts of her dominions for her previous vague and general claim to maritime sovereignty. By a decree of 26th June 1691, the sea between the south coast of Norway and the coast of Jutland, within a straight line drawn from Cape Lindesnæs to Harboore in Rinkjobing, a distance of over a hundred geographical miles, was declared to belong to Denmark; and it was further ordained that in places where the king possessed only one of the coasts, the sea was under his dominion up to the distance at which the land was lost sight of—*i.e.*, within the range of vision. At the end of the following year (3rd December 1692) another edict was issued declaring that no one without royal authority would be allowed to carry on whale-fishing within ten Norwegian leagues, or forty geographical miles, of the coast.[1] This tendency of Denmark to formulate defined boundaries in the seas along her coasts was carried further, as we shall see, in the eighteenth century.

Within the areas above mentioned, Denmark enforced her authority with considerable vigour. In 1698 a Dutch ship was seized and confiscated for fishing at the Færöes; and in the period 1738-1740 great energy was displayed in repressing violations of the Danish decrees. Several Dutch ships were fired on by Danish men-of-war for trading at Greenland; the crews were turned adrift in open boats, and the vessels taken to Copenhagen, where they were condemned as prize in the Admiralty Court. In retaliation, a Danish ship was seized at Amsterdam, and then Danish men-of-war fell upon the Dutch doggers fishing around Iceland, about a hundred in number, captured four, and dispersed the others without, it was alleged, offering to molest the British and French smacks fishing along with them. While bringing the captured doggers to Denmark, one of them managed to escape, and carried off to Holland the prize crew on board, consisting of a Danish midshipman and three seamen—an episode that recalls John Brown's experience in 1617. These occurrences were naturally followed by diplomatic controversies. Denmark at first based her action in seizing the doggers on a decree of 1733, reserving to her own subjects the exclusive right

[1] *Resol. van de Staten-Generael*, April, May, June 1616. *Resol. d. Stat. van Holl.*, March, April 1616. *Ibid.*, 15th Dec. 1623; March, May 1635; 19th May 1637; Dec. 1639. *Res. St.-Gen.*, 18th June 1639. *Res. Holl.*, 13th April 1691. Lindemann, *Die Arktische Fischerei der Deutschen Seestadte*, p. 8. *Groot Placaet-Boeck*, iv. 235, 237. Auber, *Annuaire de l'Institut de Droit International*, xi. 144.

of fishing and navigating within four leagues of the coast of all Danish possessions in the Arctic seas; and the Dutch were accused of carrying on an extensive illicit trade at Iceland, under cover of fishing. The States-General used the familiar arguments about the freedom of the seas for fishing and navigation, urged long-continued possession, and cited an old treaty of 1447 which gave the Dutch the right to navigate "usque ad Boreæ oras." Then Denmark placed her case on its ancient basis, declaring that the kings of Denmark and Norway had enjoyed from time immemorial the dominion of the northern seas, and were therefore entitled, even according to the teaching of Grotius, to the exclusive fishing. They denied that the Dutch had ever possessed the right of fishery in these seas, alleging that clandestine acts, punished as soon as discovered, could not be construed into possession. This revival of *dominium maris* called forth an energetic protest from the States-General, and affairs took a bellicose turn. Denmark sent a squadron north to maintain her claims, and Holland provided an armed convoy for her whalers and Iceland cod-smacks, "to defend themselves against the pretensions of the Danes." Hostilities were averted by the intercession of Sweden, and of the British and French Ministers at Copenhagen, in favour of the Dutch Republic and the freedom of the seas.

Occasional disputes of the same kind occurred between Denmark and the United Provinces later in the century. In 1757 a Dutch ship was arrested—it was said in the open sea—on the ground that it had been trading in Davis' Strait, and the matter was adjusted a few years later by an undertaking that the Dutch vessels would refrain from trading within the precincts of the Danish possessions. The States-General in 1762 issued a placard to this effect, and they also sent a ship of war to enforce it. In 1776 an English brigantine and two Dutch vessels were seized for trading at Greenland, and condemned by the Danish Admiralty Court, and although on the protests of the British and Dutch Governments the vessels were released, compensation for detention was refused.[1]

[1] *Resol. St.-Gen.*, Nov., Dec. 1698, 1740, 1741. *Resol. Holl.*, July 1699; Jan., March, April, Sept., Dec. 1739; Jan., March, May 1740, 1741; Oct. 1757; Jan.

Other and later examples of the tendency alluded to, of fixing definite limits for the rights of the state in the seas washing its territories, may be found in the international treaties, which were concluded during the eighteenth century, concerning the rights of fishery on the coasts and islands of the British possessions in North America, a region of the world which has furnished numerous examples of agreements of the kind. One of these, in 1686, has been already mentioned. By the great treaty of Utrecht in 1713, following Marlborough's successful campaigns on the Continent, France ceded Newfoundland and Nova Scotia to Great Britain; but certain concessions were made to French fishermen, who, of course, previously enjoyed the right of fishing there, which subsequently for a long period formed a fertile source of trouble and dispute. In addition to certain privileges as to landing and drying fish, French subjects were to be free to fish in the seas, bays, and other places to thirty leagues from the south-east coast of Nova Scotia.[1] Half a century later, by the treaty of Paris in 1763, at the conclusion of the seven years' war, Canada was ceded to Great Britain, and the concessions to French fishermen at Newfoundland were confirmed, with some modifications. Liberty of fishing was also granted to them in the Gulf of St Lawrence, subject to the condition that they did "not exercise the said fishery, except at a distance of three leagues from all the coasts belonging to Great Britain, as well those of the continent as those of the islands situated in the said Gulf of St Lawrence." On the coasts of the island of Cape Breton, outwith the Gulf, they were not to fish within fifteen leagues of the shore.[2] These provisions concerning the fishery in the Gulf of St Lawrence and at Cape Breton were confirmed twenty years

1758; Aug. 1761; April 1762. Martens, *Causes Célèbres*, i. 359-398; ii. 122-131. Beaujon, *Hist. Dutch Fisheries*, 479. A full account of the proceedings in 1738-40 is said by Beaujon to be contained in the memorials of Mauricius, who was the Dutch ambassador at Hamburg at the time, and was closely connected with the negotiations; they are contained in the Koninklijke Bibliotheek at The Hague.

[1] Art. xii. "D'exercer la pêche dans lesd. mers, bayes, et autres endroits à trente lieues près des costes de la nouvelle Ecosse au sudest, en commençant depuis l'isle appellée vulgairement de *Sable*," &c. Dumont, *Corps Diplomatique*, VIII. i. 341.

[2] Treaty of Paris, 10th February 1763, Art. v. Hertslet, *Collection*, i. 274. Martens, *Recueil*, i. 109.

later by the treaty of Versailles in 1783, the article regarding Newfoundland being at the same time modified.[1]

In these various treaties the fisheries were dealt with in a special and exceptional manner, in connection with the cession of the adjacent territories by France to Great Britain. The French fishermen had always enjoyed the right of fishing in these seas in virtue of the ownership of the land; and though full sovereignty over the latter was acquired by Great Britain, the liberty of fishing, under certain restrictions, was continued notwithstanding the transference of territory. The fisheries of Newfoundland and Canada were of great importance. They were highly valued by France as forming nurseries of seamen for her navy, and for this reason the preliminary treaty of 1762 was severely criticised by the Opposition in the British Parliament, and especially by Pitt, who perceived that the concessions with respect to the fisheries would enable France to revive her naval power.[2]

A concession still more extensive, on the same principle, was granted by Great Britain to the newly-established United States of America in the treaty of 1783, by which their independence was recognised. The question of the rights of fishery was very fully discussed in the negotiations which preceded the treaty; and though Great Britain did not deny the right of American citizens to fish on the Great Banks of Newfoundland, or in the Gulf of St Lawrence, or elsewhere in the open sea, she denied their right to fish in British waters, or to land on British territory for the purpose of drying or curing their fish. A compromise was arrived at, and the treaty provided that the people of the United States should continue to enjoy, unmolested, the right to take fish of all kinds on the Newfoundland Banks, in the Gulf of St Lawrence, and at "all other places in the sea where the inhabitants of both countries used at any time heretofore to fish"; also on such parts of the coast of Newfoundland as British fishermen should use, and "on the coasts, bays, and creeks" of all other parts of the British-American dominions. They were further permitted to dry and cure their fish on

[1] Treaty of Versailles, 3rd Sept. 1783, Arts. v., vi., and Declaration attached. Hertslet, i. 246. Martens, iii. 522.

[2] *Parl. Hist.*, xv. 1063, 1261-1263. In the negotiations for peace in 1761, Pitt, who was then in office, most wisely insisted on an exclusive fishery.

unsettled parts of the coast of Nova Scotia, the Magdalen Islands, and Labrador, so long as these parts remained unsettled.[1] It will be observed that by this treaty the liberty of fishing in the territorial waters of the British possessions in America was conceded to the citizens of the United States, who had exercised the fishery before their independence was declared. They continued to enjoy the right which they had had as British subjects after they had ceased to be British subjects, and they did so until the war of 1812.

With regard to the fisheries at home, in whose interest James I. had originally raised the question of the sovereignty of the sea, the clamour against the Dutch gradually died out, or was only heard at intervals and received but scant attention. Pamphleteers continued to denounce the liberty allowed to foreigners to fish along the British coasts, and drew the usual picture of the great national advantage that would flow from the creation of native fisheries to rival those of the Dutch.[2] Under James II., William, Anne, and the Georges, the policy of fostering the fisheries by protective legislation and by means of organised societies or associations was continued, with but little good result. The most serious attempt was made in the middle of the eighteenth century, when an Act was passed[3] for the incorporation of "The Society of the Free British Fishery," giving power to raise a stock of £500,000, and guaranteeing 3 per cent interest on the sum raised within eighteen months, —which amounted to £104,509,—as well as conferring various privileges and immunities, including a tonnage bounty to encourage the equipment of busses. This society, which was incorporated in the autumn of 1750, with the Prince of Wales as Governor, had a chequered career. Its headquarters were pitched at Southwold, Suffolk, where docks were built and

[1] *Treaty of Peace between Great Britain and the United States of America, signed at Paris*, 3rd Sept. 1783, Art. viii. Martens, *Recueil*, iii. 556.

[2] Gander, *A Vindication of a National Fishery, wherein is asserted that the Glory, Wealth, Strength, Safety, and Happiness of this Kingdom . . . doth depend (under God) upon a National Fishery . . . to which is added the Sovereignty of the British Seas*, 1699. Puckle, *England's Way to Wealth and Honour*, 1699. *A Discourse concerning the Fishery*, 1695. *The British Fishery recommended to Parliament*, 1734. *The Wealth of Great Britain in the Ocean Exemplified*, 1749, &c., &c.

[3] 23 Geo. II., c. 24, 1750. *An Act for the Encouragement of the British White Herring Fishery.*

buildings erected. In 1756 it possessed thirty busses and six "yagers" to carry the pickled herrings to Hamburg and Bremen, the masters of the busses being Dutch or Danish, and the crews chiefly from Orkney, the fishing being carried on at the Shetlands and down the coast to Yarmouth. Financial and other difficulties were encountered, some of the vessels being taken by French privateers, and all the remaining busses and effects were sold in 1772 for £6391. Half a century later, the relics of some of the discarded busses were dug out of the mud at Southwold.

The Act above referred to was the parent of many others designed to encourage the fisheries, chiefly by providing bounties; but probably more effective than such measures in stimulating the native industry was the decay which overtook the fisheries of the Dutch. This decay was no doubt due to several causes, but among the chief must be reckoned the frequent maritime wars of the eighteenth century in which the United Provinces were engaged. Their herring-busses were often captured or destroyed, sometimes in large numbers at a time, as in 1703, when a French squadron fell upon them at Shetland and burned many of them—variously stated at from 150 to 400.[1] Not infrequently their herring fishery was entirely suspended, it might be for a series of years, owing to the inability of the States-General to protect the fishing vessels from the French or the British cruisers; and such interruptions told seriously upon a business which depended so largely on the export trade of the cured herrings. From these repeated blows the Dutch fisheries never recovered, and the fleets of busses gradually dwindled. In 1703, 500 of them fished at the Shetlands and southwards along the coast; half a century afterwards there were but little over 200; and in the later years of the century the number sank as low as 120, which scarcely exceeded the vessels from Denmark, Prussia (Emden), and Belgium. Thus the part of the pretension to the sovereignty of the sea which related to the fisheries along the British coasts was gradually solved, the British fisheries, now the greatest in the world, rising on the ruins of the Dutch.

[1] Gifford, *Historical Description of the Zetland Isles*; Edmondston, *A View of the Ancient and Present State of the Shetland Isles*; *Europische Mercurius*, 1703, ii. 107.

SECTION II.

THE TERRITORIAL WATERS

CHAPTER I.

THE HISTORICAL EVOLUTION OF THE TERRITORIAL SEA.

From what has been said in previous chapters, it is apparent that the extensive claims which were formerly made to the dominion of the English or British seas were practically abandoned in the eighteenth century, and the pretensions of other states to a similar and more effective dominion in particular seas long ago shared the same fate. It is now settled as indisputable, both by the usage of nations and the principles of international law, that the open ocean cannot be appropriated by any one Power. But it is also as firmly established that all states possess sovereign rights in those parts of the sea which wash their shores, although there is not, and has never been, universal agreement as to the precise nature of those rights, or as to the extent of the sea that may be thus appropriated. While the general movement of opinion and practice in modern times has thus been from the *mare clausum* to the *mare liberum*—from the sea held to be appropriated by particular nations to the sea under no sovereignty, but free and open to all for all purposes,—there has been another movement in the opposite direction, by which the exclusive rights of maritime states in the waters immediately adjoining their coasts have come to be more clearly recognised and definitely incorporated in international law. To this extent all maritime countries now possess a sovereignty of the sea.

It is desirable to trace the evolution of this limited sovereignty over what is now known as the territorial waters or territorial sea (also named the neighbouring, proximal, adjacent, or littoral sea—*mare proximum, mare vicinum, mer territoriale, nächstangrenzendes Meer*), and to consider in particular the two main aspects it presents,—first, the actual practice of nations on the one hand, and, second, the opinions of the accredited writers on international law.

The sovereignty over the so-called territorial sea has sometimes been regarded as the direct remnant of a sovereignty which was previously asserted by particular nations over whole seas or large parts of them.[1] This is true in a general sense, but in tracing the historical evolution of the territorial waters it is found that the steps by which the transference was effected varied in different cases. The pretensions of Denmark, for example, to a wide dominion over the Norwegian Sea and the North Atlantic, were slowly curtailed by gradual concessions to the opposition of other Powers, so that the extensive territorial waters at present pertaining to Norway may be looked upon as the residuum of the ancient claim. The exclusive rights have persisted, while the area over which they are exercised has dwindled. In like manner, the equally extensive territorial waters of Sweden may be regarded as an abridgment of her old claims in the Baltic. The same process may have operated in the case of Spain and Portugal, both of which Powers now claim maritime sovereignty to a distance of six miles from their coasts; but here the successive stages of contraction are not obvious. The territorial sea now held to pertain to Great Britain, so far as it has been defined, did not originate in this way, by direct descent from the old claim to the dominion of the British seas. That claim simply died out and vanished in the lapse of time, without apparently leaving a single juridical or international right behind it. The British territorial waters, as usually defined, are of modern origin, and were derived from the international jurisprudence of the Continent, and especially from the doctrine of Bynkershoek, to be referred to later.

Even during the time when some nations were asserting a wide maritime dominion, and other nations were opposing such pretensions, there was a general recognition that every maritime state was entitled to exercise jurisdiction over some extent of the neighbouring sea. This was admitted by the most thoroughgoing advocates of the *mare liberum*, as by Grotius himself, and it was acknowledged by the common usage of

[1] Maine, *International Law*, 77.

nations. The rights exercised by the crown of England, for instance, in the so-called King's Chambers in the seventeenth century were apparently not challenged by foreign Powers. But while the sovereign rights of a state over a part of the adjacent sea were recognised by the usage of nations and the opinions of publicists, there was no agreement as to the extent which might be appropriated, and various limits or boundaries have from time to time been proposed or adopted, by which the sea pertaining to a state might be divided off from that which was open and free to all. From an early date attempts were made by jurists to discover some general principle or to lay down rules which might be applied in all such cases. Some of these rules were of such a nature as to assign to states an extent of sea almost as great as any comprised under the widest claims to maritime sovereignty, and none of them received a general assent. The early English lawyers of the twelfth and thirteenth centuries, Glanville, Bracton, Britton, and "Fleta," merely followed the Roman law with regard to the sea—that is to say, they held that it is by its nature common, like the air, and they did not suggest any limit within which the prince of the adjoining state had exclusive jurisdiction or dominion (see p. 66).

It is in the writings of the early Italian jurists, who lived after the time when Venice by force of arms had established her sovereignty over the Adriatic, that we first meet with proposals to assign legal limits to the maritime jurisdiction of the neighbouring state. Bartolus of Saxo-Ferrato, a great Perugian jurist who died in 1357, and whose authority in the middle ages was very great, declared the law to be that jurisdiction extended to a distance of one hundred miles from the coast, or less than two days' journey from it. Within this space the ruler had power to apprehend and punish delinquents just as he had on land.[1] Baldus Ubaldus, another eminent Italian jurist, who was a pupil of Bartolus and died in 1400,

[1] *Tyberiadis, D. Bartoli de Saxoferrato, Jurisconsultorum omnium facile principis, Tractatus de Fluminibus, &c.*, Bononiæ, 1576, p. 55. "Jurisdictionem habens in territorio mari cohærenti habet etiam jurisdictionem in mari usque ad centum milliaria, . . . sicut præses provinciæ debet purgare provinciam malis hominibus per terram, ita etiam per aquam. . . . Constat autem quòd centum miliaria per mare minus est duabus dietis."

also allotted a wide limit to the maritime rights of the prince of the adjoining territory; but he reduced the space from one hundred to sixty miles, a distance which was supposed to be equal to one day's journey from the coast.[1] The boundaries assigned by these jurists, or sometimes the equivalent of one or two days' voyage from the coast, were very generally accepted by civilians later, although frequently with qualification, more particularly as to the nature of the rights to be exercised.[2] Bartolus confined the rights of the prince to jurisdiction and the appropriation of islands, and since the distance prescribed included the space within which navigation in those times was almost entirely restricted, it is probable that the primary idea was the maintenance of order and the suppression of piracy. The underlying principle was the range of navigation from the coast or from a port, just as later it was the range of guns.

Baldus seems to have gone a step further than Bartolus by including sovereignty (*potestas*) as well as jurisdiction (*jurisdictio*) among the rights of the neighbouring prince, and he declared that the proximal sea pertained to the territory of the adjoining state, which, as in the case of Venice, had power to impose taxes for the use of it.[3] Much the same opinion was expressed by Bodin, a French lawyer who wrote about the middle of the sixteenth century. When speaking of the taxes or tolls that might be imposed by a state, he said that though the sea was incapable of appropriation, it was in a measure accepted that for a distance of sixty miles from the shore the prince of the adjoining country could impose law on those who approached the coast, and that it had been so adjudged in the case of the Duke of Savoy.[4] Gentilis, writing at the beginning of the next century, stated that it was laid down by the civilians that not only jurisdiction, but dominion, pertained to

[1] *Commentaria ad Institutiones, Pandectas et Codicem*, iii. 79. Venice, 1577.

[2] Bodinus, *De Repvblica*, lib. i. c. x. § 170, Frankfort, 1591; Pacius, *De Dominio Maris Hadriatici Disceptatio*, c. i., Leyden, 1619; Welwood, *De Dominio Maris*, c. i. p. 5, 1615; Dee, *General and Rare Memorials*, p. 21, 1577; Gryphiander, *De Insulis Tractatus*, c. xiv., 1623; Gentilis, *Advocatio Hispanica*, c. viii. de marina territorio tuendo, 1613; Gothofredus, *De Imperio Maris*, 1637.

[3] "Mare dicitur esse de territorio illius civitatis cui magis appropinquat et ideo Veneti quia domini sunt maris Adriatici possunt imponere navigantibus vectigalia, et adversus contra facientus pœnam adjicere."

[4] *Loc. cit.*

the neighbouring state as far as one hundred miles from the coast, and even further unless the proximity of another state interfered.[1]

It is thus clear that long before the beginning of the seventeenth century, the original simplicity of the Roman law regarding the appropriation of the sea had undergone a change at the hands of its commentators, and that the doctrine of sovereignty or dominion over a very considerable maritime zone was widely held by jurists. But there is no evidence that either of the boundaries prescribed by Bartolus or Baldus was sanctioned by the general usage of nations. They do not appear ever to have been adopted by any state of northern or western Europe as the limits of its territorial sea or maritime sovereignty; although they were occasionally used in arguments in State Papers, as when the Earl of Salisbury justified to the Spanish Court King James's proclamation of 1609 against unlicensed fishing, on the ground that maritime jurisdiction was "generally received to be about one hundred miles at the least into the seas." The actual application of these large boundaries appears to have been confined to parts of the Mediterranean, where the doctrine took its rise, and where it survived till the eighteenth century.[2] A more recent and a curious survival of the old boundary of Bartolus is to be found in the abortive Russian Ukase of 1821, by which foreigners were prohibited from navigating in Behring Sea within one hundred Italian miles of the coast, a claim which was revived by the United States as late as 1891.[3]

Another general principle for the demarcation of the seas belonging to a state had even wider currency than the above. It consisted in the transference to the sea of the principle of the mid-channel, or *thalweg*, as applied to rivers in apportioning the waters pertaining to either bank,—a doctrine laid down in Roman law and in vogue among the Anglo-Saxons as

1 "Et dicunt doctores, quod domini Veneti, et Genuenses, et alii habentes portum, dicuntur habere jurisdictionem, et imperium in toto mari sibi propinquo per centum miliaria, vel etiam ultra, si non propinquant alteri provinciæ." *Loc. cit.*

2 Azuni, *Systema Universale dei Principii del Diritto Maritimo dell' Europa*, i. 58, 1798. Jurisdiction was conferred within certain boundaries on land, "et intus mare centum milliaria."

3 *Parl. Papers, U.S., No. I.*, 1893. *Behring Sea Arbitration, British Case*, 37, 133.

early at least as the seventh century.[1] The *thalweg* or mid-channel was not infrequently a boundary between contiguous states, and it was not a great step to transfer its application in theory from wide rivers and estuaries to intervening seas. In this way the mid-line in the sea lying between the coasts of two states was held to be the boundary of their respective maritime jurisdiction or sovereignty. The whole extent of a sea stretching between territories belonging to the same state, however far apart these territories might be, was looked upon as being under the sovereignty of that state. This principle, therefore, covered most extensive claims to maritime dominion, since it left hardly any part of the sea unappropriated. The mid-line as an international boundary was in the case of narrow seas logically derived from the tenets of the Italian lawyers, but there are grounds for believing that it may have been much older. An ancient example of its use in a limited way is to be found in King Cnut's charter, in 1023, granting the port of Sandwich, in Kent, to the Church at Canterbury, by which certain rights of wreck up to the middle of the sea were conferred on the monks. After mentioning "the great sea without the port," it provided that half of whatever was found "on this side of the middle of the sea," and brought to Sandwich, should belong to the monks and half to the finder.[2] Cnut's charter cannot be taken as expressing any direct claim to jurisdiction to the middle line, but as wreck was a prerogative of the crown—and this is the first grant of it—the limit assigned seems to imply a differentiation of authority. More pertinent is the statement in the *Mirror of Justice*, a law-book written about the end of the thirteenth century, and attributed to Andrew Horn, who was Chamberlain of London in the reign of Edward II., that the king's sovereign jurisdiction extended as far as the middle line of the sea surrounding the land.[3]

[1] In the definitions of the boundaries of lands and fisheries in Anglo-Saxon charters such descriptions occur as "up midne streame," "ūt on Temese oð midne stream," "up midne streame by halfen streame," &c. Birch, *Cartularium Saxonicum*.

[2] "Quicquid etiam ex hac parte medietatis maris inventum et dilatum ad Sandwic fuerit sive sit vestimentum sive rete arma ferrum aurum argentum, medietas monachorum erit, alia pars remanebit inventoribus." Kemble, *Codex Diplomaticus Ævi Saxonici*, iv. 21.

[3] *Le Mirroir des Justices*, c. iii., "la sovereine seignurie de tote la terre jeqes el miluieu fil de la meer environ la terre."

Plowden, the Elizabethan lawyer, believed that this work contained the law as it existed before the Norman Conquest, but it is now declared to contain much that is spurious. Whether that be so or not, there is no doubt that this principle of maritime delimitation was adopted by many of the lawyers and scholars of Elizabeth's time, as Dee and Plowden.[1] Even well on in the next century no less a personage than Lord Chief-Justice Hale, in an early unpublished treatise on the law of the customs and seaports, maintained that the king had "right of jurisdiction or dominion of so much at lest of the sea as adjoines to the British coast nearer then to any forren coast."[2] From internal evidence this tract appears to have been written about 1636, and the influence of Selden's *Mare Clausum*, which was published at this time, and in which the mid-line was repudiated as a boundary of the British seas, was shown in Hale's later treatise. In it the mid-line was abandoned, and the "narrow sea, adjoining to the coast of England," was declared to be "part of the waste and demesnes and dominions of the King of England," who had in it the double right of jurisdiction and property or ownership, "Master Selden" being referred to as authority.[3]

There is no evidence that the principle of the mid-channel as applied to the sea was ever homologated by an English sovereign or Government. Notwithstanding its currency in the reign of Elizabeth, we know that it was explicitly disavowed by the queen herself in diplomatic controversy with the King of Denmark, who, in virtue of it, claimed the whole of the sea between Norway and Iceland. Still earlier the English Parliament vainly petitioned the victorious Henry V., fresh from his conquests in France, to impose tribute on vessels passing through the Channel, on the ground that he possessed both shores, and therefore had a legal title to the intervening sea.[4] But although the mid-line appears never to have been clearly adopted, there are two circumstances, both referring like Cnut's charter to the Channel, which may point to its ancient usage there. One is that an important fishing-bank, the Zowe

[1] See p. 102.

[2] *Brit. Mus. Hargraves MSS.*, No. 98; printed by Moore, *Hist. of the Foreshore*, 362.

[3] *A Treatise relating to the Maritime Law of England*, 10.

[4] See p. 35.

or Sow, extending about one-third across the Channel between Rye and Dieppe, was recognised by France as within the English jurisdiction, and French fishermen for a very long period were in the habit of procuring licenses from the Warden of the Cinque Ports for permission to fish there (see p. 65). The other is that when the question was raised as to how far the jurisdiction of the Cinque Ports extended into the sea—in connection apparently with complaints against French fishermen towards the end of the reign of Charles II.—the Trinity House, while avowing their own ignorance, stated that the Sergeant of the Admiralty within the Cinque Ports claimed to exercise his authority "half seas over or further." [1]

The methods of delimitation hitherto mentioned consisted in drawing imaginary lines in the sea, usually at a considerable distance from the coast. Another principle, which probably originated among seafaring men and was capable of being made use of in a rough-and-ready fashion, depended on the range of vision on a fair day, seawards from the shore, or usually from the sea to the land. The space of sea between the coast and the horizon, or *vice versâ*, was regarded as belonging to the adjoining state. This was the principle adopted in Scotland, but it was not confined to that country. It was employed in olden times in England to determine whether a bay or arm of the sea was within the body of a county, *inter fauces terræ*, and therefore under common law, or part of the high sea and under the jurisdiction of the Admiral.[2] An early instance of its adoption as a boundary of international jurisdiction is to be found in the nautical laws prescribed for the Netherlands in 1563 by Philip II. of Spain, by which it

[1] *Brit. Mus. Add. MSS.*, 30,221, fol. 50. The opinion of the Trinity House was given in November 1686. In 1677 the Privy Council, on a petition of the fishermen of Hastings complaining of the French fishing on the coast, sent to the Cinque Ports for an account "of the old limitations used to be put upon the French and others in their proceedings in that fishing," and also ordered two ships to be sent "to forbid the French to fish on the coast as having no license thereto, and to drive them away from thence" (*ibid.*) On the other hand, Jeakes, in his *Charters of the Cinque Ports*, written in 1678, states with reference to the powers "by land and sea" conferred on the Ports by various charters, that *per mare* did not mean *altum mare*, the high sea, where the Admiral had jurisdiction, but only the "havens, creeks, and arms of the sea, so far as can be judged in a county, where the land is on both sides," p. 69.

[2] See p. 547.

was forbidden, on pain of death, for any violence to be done by reason of war, or for any other cause, to his subjects or allies, or to foreigners, on the sea within sight of the land.[1] Grotius also referred to the range of vision as a boundary, when he said that the controversy respecting the freedom of the sea was not about bays or straits, or "so much of the sea as might be seen from the shore."[2] We have already seen that in Scotland the fisheries within sight of the coast, or a "land-kenning," were claimed as belonging exclusively to the Scottish people. In this case the range of vision was from the sea to the land, and it was to be determined from the main-top of the fishing smack.[3] The extent of a land-kenning was stated to be fourteen miles, and this was the distance expressed in the Draft Treaty of Union in 1604, and pressed upon the Dutch by King James in 1618; but sometimes twenty-eight miles, or two land-kennings, was claimed, and it is to be noted that in the case of bays and firths the distance was measured from a base-line drawn between headland and headland. The range of vision, or land-kenning, as the boundary of the reserved fishing waters, was embodied in Scottish law as well as claimed against other nations by the Privy Council, the Parliament, and the king.[4]

It was also conceded to Denmark, for in 1618 the Privy Council prohibited Scottish fishermen from fishing within sight of land at the Færöe Isles. The King of Denmark, indeed, assigned the same limit in a decree of 1691 with regard to places where he did not possess the opposite coasts.[5]

[1] 31st Oct. 1563, tit. i. par. 27, "Ne qua in mari vis fierit vel suis subditis, vel sociis, vel peregrinis, sive belli, sive alterius rei causa intra conspectum a terra vel portu." Bynkershoek, *Quæstiones Juris Publici*, lib. i. cap. viii. *De Domini Maris*, c. ii.

[2] *Mare Liberum*, c. v. See p. 347.

[3] Foreigners were not to fish "nerer the land nor nor yai mycht see the shoir out of yair main toppis."

[4] Stair, *The Institutions of the Law of Scotland*, bk. ii. tit. i. 5 (1681). "The vast ocean is common to all mankind as to navigation and fishing, which are the only uses therof, because it is not capable of bounds; but where the sea is enclosed, in bays, creeks, or otherwise is capable of any bounds or meiths, as within the points of such lands, or within the view of such shores, there it may become proper, but with the reservation of passage for commerce, as in the land. So fishing without these bounds is common to all, and within them also, except as to certain kinds of fish, such as herrings, &c." The qualification and the "etcetera" are peculiar.

[5] See p. 528.

Although the principle was not formally acknowledged by the Dutch in determining their fishing on the British coasts, they agreed to adhere to it (see p. 193); and there is evidence to show that the British cruisers caused them to respect this limit, at all events in connection with the herring-fishing at Yarmouth.[1] A later example of the adoption of this limit is to be found in a treaty concluded in 1740 between the Porte and the King of Naples, by which it was stipulated that neither party would permit vessels to be pursued or molested on their coasts within a distance at which ships could discern the land.[2]

The method of determining the extent of the territorial sea by the range of vision was vague and open to obvious objections, even though it was ascertained only on a fair day. The distance, as Bynkershoek pointed out, would vary according to the position of the observer, the keenness of his vision, the climate, and many other circumstances, and it was inapplicable to narrow seas, such as the Channel, where the opposite coasts belonged to different states. It is, however, questionable whether, under proper rules, it would have furnished a zone much less definite than that of the range of guns. It has been proposed by some modern publicists, as Rayneval, Azuni, Heffter, and Godey, as a boundary of territorial waters; and if it had been generally adopted as a principle of delimitation, there is no doubt that the equivalent distance of fourteen miles as used in Scotland would have proved more satisfactory in several respects than the ordinary limit of three miles, which was supposed to represent the range of guns.

Still less definite was another principle, if such it can be called, which was proposed as a guide in allotting the space of sea within which exclusive rights of fishing should belong to the adjacent state. Welwood, Selden, and many others, held, in opposition to Grotius and his school, that the fisheries along a coast might be exhausted or injured by promiscuous

[1] Captain George St Lo, *England's Safety, or a Bridle to the French King*, 1693. "During the time I was convoy to our fishing there, as aforesaid (1685-6), my business was to see that no foreigner should fish in sight of the shore, because the fish draw thither to spawn; the best draughts are there."

[2] Azuni, *Sistema universale dei Principj del Diritto marittimo*, i. 78.

fishing, and that the inhabitants of the coast had a primary right to the *fructus* of the adjacent sea, as against the intrusion of foreigners—a principle which lay at the root of the Scottish claims to the "reserved waters." Sarpi, an Italian author of the early part of the seventeenth century, in a work defending the claims of Venice, formulated the opinion that the extent of territorial sea should not be fixed everywhere in an absolute manner, but should be made proportionate to the requirements of the adjoining state, without violating the just rights of other peoples. Thus a country or city which possessed large and fertile territories that provided adequate subsistence for the inhabitants, would have little need of the fisheries in the neighbouring sea, while one with small territories that drew a large part of its subsistence from the sea ought to have a much greater extent of sea for its exclusive use.[1] This doctrine, though obviously difficult of application internationally, has much to recommend it on grounds of reason and justice. It is one of the fundamental principles on which Norway claims at the present day an unusually large extent of territorial sea.

With regard to bays, straits, and arms of the sea, the general usage from the earliest times has included them within the jurisdiction of the neighbouring state. They have been always regarded as differing from the sea on an open coast, the only disputes about them referring to the size of such areas that might justly be looked upon as territorial. By the old common law of England, which Hale dates as far back at least as the reign of Edward II. (1307-1327), bays, gulfs, or estuaries, of which one shore could be "reasonably discerned" from the other shore, were regarded as *inter fauces terræ,* and within the body of the adjacent county or counties, so that offences committed there were triable at common law. But along the coast, on the open sea, the jurisdiction of the common law extended no farther than to low-water mark; beyond that it was high sea, or *altum mare,* and under the jurisdiction of the Admiral.[2] Here we see a sharp distinction

[1] *Dominio del Mar' Adriatico e sue Raggione per il Jus Belli della Serenissima Repvblica di Venetia*, Venezia, 1686.

[2] Hale, *A Treatise relating to the Maritime Law of England*, c. iv. Coke's *Fourth Institute*, c. xxii. p. 140 (ed. 1797). Blackstone, *Commentaries*, i. 110. Hale, *Pleas of the Crown*, ii. 54. An early authority is in Fitzherbert's *La Grande*

drawn between bays and the open coast, the former being included within the realm as part of the territory. It seems reasonable on many grounds that the waters lying in view between two parts of the same continuous territory should have been regarded as pertaining to that territory, and it may be noted that in early times the navigation of a vessel along a coast was conducted from headland to headland, and thus a distinction was likely to arise between the open sea lying outside a line joining the headlands, as a waterway common to all, and the sea inside the headlands as an access to the territory. The distinction was maintained from an early period with regard to international relations. Reference has already been made to the treaty arranged by Cardinal Wolsey in 1521, in which it was stipulated that English harbours, bays, rivers, and roads should be exempt from hostilities between belligerents, and to the proclamations of King James in 1604, and of succeeding sovereigns, defining the extent of the King's Chambers, or bays, according to ancient custom, for purposes of neutrality.[1] It is interesting to note that the rights exercised within the King's Chambers, or bays, on the coasts of England referred only to neutrality and had nothing to do with fishing, while in Scotland it was exactly the opposite. The large bays and firths on the Scottish coast were reserved for fishing, without any specific reference to the rights or obligations of neutrals. The differentiation of bays and arms of the sea from the territorial belt on open coasts has persisted to the present day, both in the writings of publicists and in the practice of nations, although the in-

Abridgment (1565), Corone et Plees de Corone, fol. 259, placit 399, "Nota p. Stanton justic q̃ ceo nest pas sañce demere ou hoe puit veier ceo q̃'est fait del ou part del ewe et del aut, coe a rier de lun terr tanq̃ a laut q̃ le cozon viendr' en ceo cas et fra son offic auri coe auent a vyent en vu brau del mer la ou home puit vier de lun parte tanque a lauter del auer que en cel lieu auient puyt paiis auer conisans." There are some words in this passage difficult to translate, but the following has been given as its rendering: "Nota per Stanton Justice, that that is not sance [which Lord Coke translates 'part'] of the sea where a man can see what is done from one part of the water and the other, so as to see from one land to the other; that the coroner shall come in such case and perform his office, as well as coming and going in an arm of the sea, there where a man can see from one part to the other of the [word undeciphered], that in such a place the country can have conusance."

[1] See p. 119.

troduction of another principle of delimitation has tended to keep the claims to bays within moderate bounds.

The various methods of determining the territorial waters of a state referred to above were more or less arbitrary, and did not rest upon a natural basis capable of universal application. During the seventeenth and eighteenth centuries another principle was gradually evolved, and was ultimately accepted as furnishing such a natural basis, so that it may now be regarded as an established part of international law. It was, that the maritime dominion of a state ended where its power of asserting continuous possession ended. The belt of sea along the coast which could be commanded and controlled by artillery on shore thus came to be regarded as the territorial sea belonging to the contiguous state. Beyond the range of guns on shore the sea was common.

This principle was of slow growth. It did not even receive definite expression among jurists until the beginning of the eighteenth century; but as previously stated (see p. 156), the Dutch ambassadors who came to London in 1610, to endeavour to induce King James to withdraw his proclamation against unlicensed fishing, made use of it in their conferences with the English Ministers, not improbably at the instigation of Grotius. But whether or not Grotius was the person who enunciated the principle in 1610, it is in his writings that we first meet with it, although in a veiled form. It is not mentioned in *Mare Liberum*, but in his greater work, the Law of War and Peace, which was published in 1625, he said that a state might acquire sovereignty over parts of the sea, in regard to persons by an armed fleet, and "in regard to territory, as when those who sail on the coasts of a country may be compelled from the land, just as if they were on the land."[1] The principle of compulsion from the land is clearly enough expressed, and though Grotius did not define the nature of the compulsion to be exercised, modern writers have generally held that what he meant was compulsion by artillery. If Grotius was the author of the dictum of 1610, he must have had reasons for expressing it

[1] Lib. ii. cap. iii. s. xiii. 2, "Ratione territorii, quatenus ex terra cogi possunt qui in proxima maris parte versantur, nec minus quam si in ipsa terra reperirentur." See p. 349.

in a less definite form in 1625,—perhaps owing to his employment at that time by the Queen of Sweden, to whom the naked doctrine would have been no more attractive than to James.

For a long time, however, the doctrine was equally neglected by publicists and statesmen. This may have been partly due to the somewhat obscure and incidental way in which it was advanced, but probably mainly to the fact that the time was not ripe for its acceptance. It represented much too stringent a limitation of the territorial sea to receive general assent. Selden does not refer to it, and it was passed over by the authors, such as Pontanus,[1] Burgus,[2] Shookius,[3] Conringius,[4] and Strauchius,[5] who favoured more or less extensive claims to maritime dominion, while even writers who opposed such claims, as Stypmannus[6] and Graswinckel,[7] do not adopt it.

The opinions of Grotius with respect to the appropriation of the sea had, indeed, comparatively little influence among jurists in the seventeenth century. The views which prevailed in the latter part of the period are rather represented in the works of two of the writers whose reputation was greatest, Loccenius and Puffendorf. Loccenius, a Swedish author who wrote about the middle of the century and is still quoted as an authority, declared that while a nation could not acquire a universal dominion over the sea, it might possess sovereignty in a particular sea as far as it was under its power or dominion, subject to the rights of innocent passage and navigation by others; and he cited as examples Sweden and Denmark, which exercised sovereignty in the Baltic.[8] As a general rule, however, Loccenius held that states had jurisdiction only in the waters adjacent to their coasts, for the preservation of peaceful navigation; but no attempt is made by him to lay down any fixed rule or limit as to the extent of such jurisdiction. He merely contrasts the opinions of those, as Baldus and Bodin, who contended for a wide limit of sixty miles, or two days'

1 *Discussiones Historicæ de Mari Libero*, 1637.

2 *De Dominio Seren. Genuensis Reipub. in Mari Ligustico*, 1641.

3 *Imperium Maritimum*, 1654.

4 *Dissertatio de Imperio Maris*, 1676.

5 *De Imperio Maris.*

6 *Jus Maritimum*, 1652.

7 *Maris Liberi Vind. adv. P. B. Burgum*, 1652; *Maris Liberi Vind. adv. G. Welwodum*, 1633.

8 *De Jure Maritimo et Navali*, lib. i. c. iv. Ed. 1652.

journey, with those who argue for a narrow but undefined space in the neighbouring sea.

The celebrated Puffendorf, whose authority later was only second to that of Grotius, dealt with the question in his great work on the Law of Nature and Nations, and with even less precision than Loccenius.[1] On the general question of the appropriation of the sea he discarded the objection that its fluidity rendered it incapable of possession, but held that it would be morally impossible for one nation to possess the ocean. He also set aside the moral objection in the absolute form in which it was put forward by Grotius, that the use of the sea was inexhaustible. On the contrary, he held with Selden and Welwood that fisheries in the sea might be exhausted by promiscuous use. "If all nations," he said, "should desire such a right and liberty (of fishing) near the coasts of any particular country, that country must be very much prejudiced in this respect; especially since it is very usual that some particular kind of fish, or perhaps some more precious commodity, as pearls, coral, amber, or the like, are to be found only in one part of the sea, and that of no considerable extent. In this case there is no reason why the bordering people should not rather challenge to themselves this happiness of a wealthy shore or sea, than those who are situated at a distance from it."[2] On this ground, the right of exclusive fishing, and also for the security and defence of the state, a nation was justified in claiming dominion in the neighbouring sea. The extent of this territorial sea, he says, cannot in general be accurately determined; but it is clear that he thought it might be very considerable. We had the power to abridge others of the use of the sea by forts on shore, in narrow creeks and straits, or by armed fleets; but it would, he thought, show unreasonable jealousy to claim "some hundreds of leagues." The true bounds could only be discovered either from "the right of possession" of a state, or from its treaties with its neighbours. Gulfs, channels, or arms of the sea, on the other hand, were "according to the regular course" supposed to belong to the state which had possession of the shores. If the shores belonged to several peoples, the sovereignty was distributed to the middle line, unless treaties directed otherwise, or one

[1] *De Jure Naturæ et Gentium*, 1672.

[2] Lib. iv. c. v. s. vii.

people had obtained the exclusive sovereignty by convention, conquest, or prescription.

We thus perceive that the opinion of jurists at the end of the seventeenth century with regard to the appropriation of the sea was very much what it was at the beginning. With the exception of the clear and terse declaration of the Dutch ambassadors in 1610, and the somewhat dubious dictum of Grotius in 1625, the principle that the maritime sovereignty of a state was limited by the range of guns from the shore does not appear to have been advanced throughout the century.

Nor does an examination of the usage of nations during the period show that the opinions of publicists were at variance with the actual practice. All maritime countries enforced an unquestionable jurisdiction, more or less extensive, in the neighbouring seas, and several of them exercised dominion over particular regions. The extravagant pretensions of Spain and Portugal had long since vanished; but Venice, while sadly fallen from her former greatness, still asserted her sovereignty over the Adriatic. Sweden and Denmark possessed a joint sway over the Baltic; and Denmark maintained her claim to the northern seas between Iceland, Greenland, and the coast of Europe. Moreover, the pretensions of England to the sovereignty of the so-called British seas, although in abeyance, had not been withdrawn. The striking of the flag was still enforced by English men-of-war, and there was nothing to prove that the other phases of the pretension might not be revived at any time.

With regard to the extent of neutral waters, it would appear that the boundaries were as a rule vague, and that general considerations determined jurisdiction in particular cases. In connection with the declaration of war by the United Provinces against France in 1689, a placard was issued by the States-General in which both Dutch and foreign vessels were exhorted to keep out on the high seas; and it was declared that any vessels suspected of having contraband goods on board and found "on the coast of France, or of other countries, islands, and places under the dominion of the King of France, and particularly in the bays and gulfs on the coast of the said kingdom," would be seized and brought to trial.[1] On the English coast the

[1] 7th March, 1689, Art iv.

limits of jurisdiction were better defined, but still, in many cases, without precision. Within the King's Chambers, as specified by James I. in 1604, "or other places of our dominion, or so near to any of our said ports, or havens, as may be reasonably construed to be within that title, limit, or precinct," the hostile acts of belligerents, captures of the enemy's vessels, and the hovering of foreign ships of war were forbidden. The injunction with respect to the neutral waters was renewed in 1633, 1668, and 1683, and it was in no case confined strictly to the "chambers." In the proclamations of 1668 and 1683, which were drawn up by Sir Leoline Jenkins, the definition was merely "within our ports, havens, roads, and creeks, as also in every other place or tract at sea that may be reasonably construed to be within any of these denominations, limits, or precincts."[1] These limits were upheld by the decisions of the High Court of Admiralty during the greater part of the century. Sir Leoline Jenkins, it may be noted, although in questions of international policy advocating the most extreme pretensions of the English crown to the sovereignty of the seas, was careful in his judicial decisions to restrict jurisdiction within the terms of the royal proclamations. If a capture was made in one of the chambers or beyond them by a foreign privateer which had issued from an English port and had been hovering in the neighbourhood, the vessel was ordered to be restored. So also if the prize was taken, in any case, outside a chamber, but near enough the coast to be "reasonably construed" to be within the king's jurisdiction. This usually happened on the east coast, where the chambers were small. In one such case the vessel was taken between half a league and one league off Orfordness (the headland of a chamber); in another instance the vessel was seized eight leagues at sea off Harwich, and presumably four leagues from the boundary of the nearest chamber.[2]

[1] *State Papers, Dom.*, Chas. II., ccxxxiv. 112, 113, 8th Feb. 166$\frac{7}{8}$. *Brit. Mus. Add. MSS.*, 30,221, fol. 64, 12th March 1683.

[2] Wynne, *Life of Sir Leoline Jenkins*, ii. 727, 732, 755, 780, 783. In reporting to the king in one case, in which he found the capture was made in the Channel beyond the limits of a chamber, Jenkins says: "However the truth be as to the chamber, 'tis certain the seizure was made in your Majesty's seas: but so it is, that notwithstanding your Majesty's undoubted right of dominion and protection in these seas, strangers do hold themselves, if not permitted, yet excused for such hostilities, when they are acted at a due distance from your Majesty's ports,

At the end of the seventeenth century, while the old pretensions of various nations to the appropriation of particular seas had not been withdrawn, they had in many cases become by the force of circumstances to a large extent nominal or were in abeyance. There was moreover a tendency, as we have seen (p. 526), to substitute fixed boundaries in place of a wide and vague sovereignty, and to arrange by treaty defined limits for special purposes. In the historical retrospect we can now perceive the main influences which led to the modification of the claims and practice in the century that followed. The juridical controversies on the subject between the writers of various nations were doubtless not without effect. The repeated decisions of the High Court of Admiralty in this country, going counter to the English pretension even in the Channel, and fixing limits for neutrality, must also have had an important influence. But the chief causes were probably twofold. One was the moral and material victory of the Dutch Republic in its long and persistent struggle against the exorbitant claims to maritime dominion, first, of Spain and Portugal, and then of England and Denmark. The other was the great extension of commerce and navigation, in which England secured an ever-increasing share, so that in the next century we find her taking the part of Holland in opposing the Danish claims to *mare clausum*. As maritime commerce

harbours, and chambers; grounding themselves upon what was done and observed in that long war between Spain and the Netherlands." The preamble of the proclamation of 12th March 1683 was as follows: "Whereas the safeguard and protection we owe to such of our own subjects, and to all others in league and amity with us, as pass and repass the seas belonging to these our kingdoms, has been always a principal part of our royal care and concern, and we, finding that the freedom and security of our navigation and commerce to and from our ports in time of hostility between our neighbouring princes has been much disturbed, nay, the reverence due to our ports, harbours, and other places under our immediate protection has been violated by the partial practices, depredations, and insolencies of private men-of-war and others pretending commissions for the present hostilities: We have thought fit, by the advice of our Privy Council, after an exact view first taken of the rules, ordinances, and provisions made on the like occasions by our royal progenitors and ourself, to revive, establish, ratify and publish to all the world these rules and ordinances following." The rules are similar to those in the regulations of 1633 and 1668; but it is noteworthy that the "King's Chambers" are not specifically mentioned, nor is any reference made to a "platt," and the claim to the dominion of the seas, so prominent in 1633, is omitted.

extended and the security of the sea became established, it was felt more and more that claims to a hampering sovereignty and jurisdiction were incompatible with the general welfare of nations; and as the states interested in this commerce had the greatest power, the assertion of a wide dominion was gradually abandoned, surviving only in remote regions or in enclosed seas, like the Baltic.

At the beginning of the eighteenth century the question of the appropriation of the sea was placed on another footing. The principle of delimiting the territorial sea which is now generally accepted was first expounded in 1703 by a distinguished publicist, Cornelius van Bynkershoek, who, like Grotius, was a Dutchman, and held the office of Judge in the Supreme Court of Appeal of Holland, Zealand, and West Friesland. In his early work on the dominion of the sea,[1] and in a later treatise published in 1737,[2] he dealt with the subject with much acumen. With respect to the general question as to the capability of appropriation, he agreed with Puffendorf rather than with Grotius. While holding that the open ocean could not be wholly brought under dominion, he admitted, with Selden, not only that large parts of the sea are susceptible of appropriation, but that various nations had at different times enjoyed such dominion: the fluidity of the sea was not a bar to its occupation, and by taking possession of it the same right was acquired as by taking possession of the land. But he declared there was no instance at the time he wrote of any ruler possessing maritime dominion of that kind, unless when the surrounding territory belonged to him, and that the general freedom of the seas for navigation had been established both by usage and by various treaties. He denied that England had the dominion of the so-called British seas, mainly on the ground of the want of uninterrupted possession, pointing out that all the neighbouring nations freely navigated them without paying any tribute or requiring any permission.

It was, however, with regard to the delimitation of the territorial sea immediately adjacent to the coast that Bynkershoek's teaching had its chief results. He showed how un-

[1] *De Dominio Maris Dissertatio.* Hagæ-Batavorum, 1703.

[2] *Quæstiones Juris Publici.* Lugduni-Batavorum, 1737.

certain and unsatisfactory were the limits previously proposed, and, following Grotius, he laid down the principle that the dominion of a state extended over the neighbouring sea as far, and only as far, as it was able to command and control it from the land. But he went further and showed how the principle was to be carried into practice. The dominion of the territory extended as far as projectiles could be thrown from the shore by artillery, so that exclusive possession might be taken of the part so commanded: "the dominion of the land ends where the power of arms terminates."[1] Thus Bynkershoek assigned the dominion of the adjacent sea (*mare proximum*) to the neighbouring state, within the range of a cannon-shot from the shore. Besides the general reasoning on which the limit was based, he cited in support of it an Act of state. He was apparently unaware of the clear declaration made by the Dutch ambassadors a century earlier; but he referred to an edict of the States-General in 1671, which enjoined that the commanders of their ships should give the salute on the coasts of a foreign Power when they were within the range of the guns of a town or fort, in such manner as the Government of the country should require, leaving to its discretion the return of the salute, and adding that every Government was sovereign within its own jurisdiction and every foreigner a subject there.[2]

This decree could not, of course, as Bynkershoek admitted, bind other Powers to the same opinion. Nevertheless it may be said that the almost universal practice which had grown up, regulating the salute of a vessel coming within range of a battery on a foreign coast, had prepared the way for the acceptance of the doctrine. It was a recognition that the vessel had passed within the sphere of territorial authority

[1] "Unde dominium maris proximi non ultra concedimus, quam e terra illi imperari potest, et tamen eo usque; nulla siquidem sit ratio, cur mare, quod in alicujus imperio est et potestate, minus ejusdem esse dicamus, quam fossam in ejus territorio. . . . Quare omnino videtur rectius, eo potestatem terræ extendi, quousque tormenta exploduntur, eatenus quippe cum imperare, tum possidere videmur. Loquor autem de his temporibus, quibus illis machinis utimur: alioquin generaliter dicendum esset, potestatem terræ finiri, ubi finitur armorum vis; etenim hæc, ut diximus, possessionem tuetur." *De Dom. Maris*, cap. ii. In the *Quæstiones* the phrase is "imperium terræ finitur, ubi finitur armorum potestas," and "terræ dominium finitur ubi finitur armorum vis."

[2] *Ibid.*, cap. ii.

of the particular state. It was the rule, in England at least, that "the sea should salute the land," and the range of guns determined the limit within which the salute ought to be rendered. Beyond the reach of cannon no salute was expected; within it usage, international courtesy, or the law, required it. No foreign ship with its flag aloft could come within range of an English fort or castle without exposing itself to the risk of a shot. It is indeed a curious circumstance, that it was largely through the action of England with regard to the salute that the acceptance of the cannon-range limit was facilitated. The relation of the ceremony to the sovereignty of a state was forced by her prominently into international politics. Before the time of Selden and Charles I. jurists paid little attention to the matter, but afterwards they dealt with it as a department of international law: Loccenius and Bynkershoek, for example, each devotes a chapter to it. Even when the English were most actively asserting "the honour of the flag," they recognised the rights of foreign states within the actual range of guns on their shore. In 1636 the Earl of Northumberland was instructed by the Admiralty not to enforce the salute within the command of the guns of forts on foreign coasts,—an order which was repeated by the Parliament in 1647,[1] and became the rule in the service. Molloy, a vehement supporter of the most extreme claims of England to the sovereignty of the seas, stated in 1676 that English men-of-war entering a foreign harbour, or "the road within shot of cannon of some fort or castle," were to pay such respect as was usually there expected.[2]

The gunshot limit had been long established in connection with another international relationship—namely, the right of visitation of neutral vessels in the open sea. Many treaties had been made which stipulated that the visiting ship was not to approach nearer than within cannon-shot, and was then to send one of its boats with a few men to conduct the examination necessary. It is, moreover, extremely probable that with respect to what was in those times the principal attribute of the territorial waters—viz., the rights and obligations of neutrals—the gunshot limit, at the least, was recognised where guns were actually in position. In view of the general

[1] See p. 381.

[2] *De Jure Maritimo*, p. 150.

practice, as shown for instance in the decisions of the English Admiralty Court, and the usage in connection with the salute, it can scarcely be supposed that a capture made under the guns of a neutral fortress would be held as good prize; at all events, it was not so held in the Admiralty Court in 1760. But the merit of Bynkershoek's doctrine was, that it transferred in theory to all parts of a coast this decisive property of compulsion and dominion which, strictly speaking, only existed where forts or batteries were placed. The doctrine, justly enough, has been called fictitious, because there are various coasts and districts where it would be impracticable to maintain dominion over the territorial sea by means of artillery on shore; and because in point of fact such dominion, unless in the neighbourhood of forts, is actually maintained by other means, as by coastguards and naval vessels. Nevertheless the principle, though resting largely on hypothesis, had much to recommend it, and it gradually became incorporated into international law as the rule for fixing the boundary of the territorial waters. Apart from its intrinsic merits, its acceptance was perhaps not a little facilitated by the felicity with which it was expressed. Bynkershoek gave it the form almost of an aphorism, and the phrase, *terræ dominium finitur ubi finitur armorum vis*, has been quoted by almost all later writers.

But although the doctrine of Bynkershoek was attractive, and was eventually accepted almost everywhere, it did not command immediate assent. The publicists who came after Bynkershoek in the eighteenth century, while usually referring to the cannon-range limit, or adopting it with respect to questions of prize, did not as a rule adhere to it as the sole principle for delimiting the territorial belt. The earliest notice of it after the *Quæstiones* appeared seems to have been by Casaregi, an Italian writer of authority, who was judge in the Court of the Grand Duke of Tuscany, in a work which appeared in 1740, and referred more especially to the practice in the Mediterranean.[1] Foreign ships, he said, were under the protection of the prince whose seas they sail through, when they are in his ports, or in the sea so near as to be within the

[1] *Discursus Legales de Commercio*, Venice, 1740, D, 136, 174, 211, tom. 2. An earlier edition was published at Florence in 1719.

range of guns on shore; if seized by the enemy there, they require to be restored.[1] This was the ordinary rule in regard to neutrality; but with regard to the question of sovereignty in the neighbouring sea, Casaregi followed preceding Italian jurists in assigning a space of one hundred miles from the coast for civil and criminal jurisdiction, with the power of levying tolls and dues from passing ships, and even of prohibiting or permitting navigation.

A little later a Spanish writer, Abreu y Bertodano, in a work on the law of maritime prize,[2] held that it was unlawful for cruisers to attack the enemy's vessels in the seas adjacent to the coast of a neutral within a distance of two leagues from the shore, or within the reach of a cannon-shot from it. He stated that no European Power had asserted the dominion of the sea with more heat and boldness than Great Britain, and yet by Act of Parliament the visitation of ships by the coast-guard was restricted to two leagues from the coast, which was as much as could reasonably be claimed.[3] But this author also followed the Italian rule that jurisdiction, including the levying of tolls, &c., was not limited to the coast waters, but extended for at least a hundred miles from the shore, and said that this was in agreement with the teaching of the lawyers of all nations.[4]

Wolff, who wrote on the law of nations about the same time, appears rather to have followed the opinions of Puffendorf. He argued that the use of the sea next the shore, for fishing and the collection of things that grow on it, was not inexhaustible, nor its use for navigation always innocuous; and since it served as a protection for the adjoining state, it was reasonable that it should be under the dominion of that state. The inhabitants of the shores had therefore the right to occupy

1 "Naves exteræ dicuntur esse sub protectione illius principis, cujus mare navigant, quando reperiuntur intra portus illius, aut in mari, ita vicino, ut illuc tormenta, bellica adigi possent. Et si deprædentur ab inimicis, de jure restituendæ sunt."

2 *Tratado jurídico-politico, sobre pressas de mar, y calidades, que deben concurrir para hacerse legitimamente el Corso*, Part I. c. v. Cadiz, 1746.

3 "No podrá con razon pretender mas extension de sus Costas, que las dos leguas."

4 "Y circunda en el espacio á lo menos de cien millas en recto: lo qual es una infalible, y conforme tradicion de los Letrados de todas las Naciones."

it "so far as they can maintain their dominion over it"; and the same was true of straits and bays.[1]

Some ten years later Vattel, the pupil and follower of Wolff, published a work on the law of nations, which is still of authority, and in which much the same opinions as those of Puffendorf and Wolff are expressed.[2] On the general question of the appropriation of the sea the usual statement was made; but Vattel held that a nation might acquire exclusive rights of navigation and fishery in the open sea by treaties, but not by prescription, unless in virtue of the consent or tacit agreement of other nations. Thus "when a nation that is in possession of the navigation and fishery in certain tracts of the sea claims an exclusive right of them, and forbids all participation on the part of other nations, if the others obey that prohibition with sufficient marks of acquiescence, they tacitly renounce their own right in favour of that nation, and establish for her a new right, which she may afterwards lawfully maintain against them, especially when it is confirmed by long use." On the other hand, Vattel states that the uses of the sea near the coast render it very susceptible of appropriation: it supplies fish, shells, pearls, and other things, and with respect to all these its use is not inexhaustible. A maritime people may therefore appropriate and convert to their own profit "an advantage which nature has placed within their reach as to enable them conveniently to take possession of it, in the same manner as they possessed themselves of the dominion of the land they inhabit." Vattel does not state his opinion as to the distance from the coast within which the fisheries may be appropriated, but from the examples he cites it is evident that the space might extend considerably beyond the range of guns. "Who can doubt," he asks, "that the pearl fisheries of Bahrem and Ceylon may lawfully become property?" And the same principle may be applied to floating fish, which appear less liable to be exhausted. If a people, he says, have on their coast a particular and profitable fishery of which they can become

[1] *Jus Gentium*, Halæ Magdeburgicæ, 1749, cap. i. ss. 120-132, pp. 99-107. "Partes maris a gentibus, quæ idem accolunt, occupari possunt, quousque dominium in iisdem tueri possunt."

[2] *Le Droit des Gens*, Liv. i. c. xxiii. 5, 279-295, 1758.

masters, shall they not be permitted to appropriate that bounteous gift of nature as an appendage to the country they possess, and to reserve to themselves the great advantages which their commerce may thence derive, if there is sufficient abundance of fish to furnish neighbouring nations? Thus, Vattel states, the herring fishery on the British coasts might have been appropriated by the English if they had originally taken exclusive possession of it, instead of allowing other nations to take part in it. Another reason for the extension of territorial dominion over the adjoining sea, "as far as a nation is able to protect its right," is the security and welfare of the state; but the author says it is not easy to fix upon any precise distance. Between nation and nation, "all that can reasonably be said is that, in general, the dominion of the state over the neighbouring sea extends as far as her safety renders it necessary and her power is able to assert it." At the time he wrote, "the whole extent of the sea which is within cannon-shot of the coast is considered as forming part of the territory; and for that reason a vessel taken under the cannon of a neutral fortress is not a lawful prize." The principle that applied to the adjacent sea applied with much greater force to roads, bays, and straits, since they were more capable of being possessed, and were of greater importance to the safety of the country. But such areas must be "of small extent," and not great tracts of sea—as Hudson's Bay and the Straits of Magellan: a bay "whose entrance can be defended" might clearly be appropriated.

The opinions of Vattel do not, therefore, materially differ from those of Puffendorf in the previous century, though the tendency of the earlier writer to allow a wide dominion is modified. Bynkershoek's principle of cannon range is adopted in a somewhat cautious manner, and shown to apply especially to captures under the guns of a neutral fortress. But the general argument in regard to fisheries, the security of the state, and the exercise of territorial jurisdiction—as in the King's Chambers on the English coast, which Vattel cites as an example of the practice—implies that a nation might lawfully extend its sovereignty much beyond the range of guns.

In the writings of other international jurists later in the century, the tendency to narrow the extent of the territorial sea in accordance with Bynkershoek's teaching becomes more manifest, particularly in those which treat specially of the rights of neutrals. Hübner, who was assessor in the Consistorial Court at Copenhagen, treating of this subject, said with reference to Bynkershoek's doctrine that it was evident the parts of the adjacent sea belonged to the master of the country, as accessory to the land,—first, "because it is in his power to take possession and to maintain it by means of forts and batteries which he is able to erect on the shore"; and, secondly, because the waters serve as a rampart to the land.[1]

Valin, a French writer of authority, introduced another principle in combination with that of the range of guns. In his commentary on the marine ordinance of Louis XIV., first published in 1760, he stated that the rule that the adjacent sea within the reach of guns from the coast is under the dominion of the neighbouring state was universally recognised, the alternative distance which he gave being two leagues—the same as given by Abreu. But he thought that the depth of the water ought also to be taken into account, and that the sea up to the point at which the bottom ceased to be reached by a sounding-line pertained to the adjoining coast—an idea vague and impracticable.[2]

In 1778, Moser, a councillor of state in Denmark, adopted Bynkershoek's doctrine, declaring that the sea adjacent to the coast of a country was, according to the law of nations,

[1] *De la Saisie des Bâtimens Neutres*, La Haye, 1759, tom. i. Part I. c. iii. s. 5, p. 57.

[2] *Nouveau Commentaire sur l'Ordonnance de la Marine du mois d'Août* 1681, Rochelle, 1766, t. ii. Liv. v. tit. i. pp. 687, 688. "Jusqu'à la distance de deux lieues, et avec cette restriction encore, la mer est donc du domaine du souverain de la côte voisine; et cela que l'on puisse y prendre fond avec la sonde, ou non. Il est juste au reste d'user de cette méthode en faveur des États dont les côtes sont si escarpées, que dès le bord on ne peut trouver le fond; mais cela n'empêche pas que le domaine de la mer, quant à la jurisdiction et à la pêche, ne puisse s'étendre au delà; soit en vertu des traités de navigation et de commerce, soit par la règle ci-dessus établie qui continue le domaine jusq'où la sonde peut prendre fond, ou jusqu'à la portée du canon, ce qui est aujourd'hui la règle universellement reconnue." Lawrence, in his annotated edition of Wheaton's *Elements of International Law*, Part II. c. iv. s. 6 (1864), makes a curious blunder in regard to the limit proposed by Valin, who, he says, "proposed to fix it according to the *sound of a cannon*, or as far as the ball would reach." The authority Valin gives for the statement that the rule was universally recognised is *Journal de Commerce*, Mai 1759, p. 40.

indisputably under the sovereignty of the neighbouring territory, as far as a cannon-ball could reach.[1] On the other hand, Lampredi, Professor of Public Law in the University of Pisa, writing at the same time, while allowing to a state the right of property in the adjacent sea, makes the limit of its dominion depend, not on cannon range, but upon considerations of general convenience.[2] Another contemporary Italian, Galiani, who was Sicilian Secretary of Legation at Paris, and was employed by his master, the King of the Two Sicilies, to write a book in defence of his adhesion to the Russian League of Armed Neutrality, expressed somewhat varying opinions as to the limits of the territorial sea.[3] Admitting as a received doctrine that the belt of sea washing the coasts of a country belonged to it as a part of its territory, he at first seems to extend it, in accordance with the Italian principles, as far as the authorities can cause their jurisdiction to be enforced. Later, he advances the gunshot limit for certain purposes, as the imposition of tolls and the regulation of navigation; and finally, with regard to the observance of neutrality he considers the boundary should be two leagues, or twice the distance of cannon range, and he appears to have been the first to fix upon three miles as equivalent to the range of guns.[4]

G. F. von Martens, one of the greatest authorities on international law, writing a little later, more definitely adopted the principle of the range of guns; but he gave the equivalent distance as "three leagues," and moreover admitted

[1] *Versuch des Neuesten Europäischen Völkerrechts in Friedens- und Kriegs-zeiten*, Bd. v. 486, Frankfort, 1778. "Das an die Küsten eines Landes stossende Meer stehet nach dem Völkerrecht unter der Oberherrschaft des angränzenden Landes unstreitig, so weit es mit Canonen von dem festen Land bestrichen werden kan."

[2] *Juris Publici Universalis, sive Juris Naturæ et Gentium, Theoremata*, ii. 7, 65. "Nobis visum est singulas gentes eam partem circa littus suum occupare posse, cujus usus necessarius, quamque tuendis littoribus et territorio necessarium arbitrantur."

[3] *De' Doveri de' principi neutrali verso i principi guerreggianti, e di questi verso i neutrali.* Naples, 1782.

[4] "Mi parrebbe peraltro ragionevole, che senza attendere a vedere se in atto tenga il Sovrano del territorio construtta taluna torre o batteria, e di qual calibro di cannoni la tenga montata, si determinasse fissamente, e da per tutto la distanza di tre miglia dalla terra, come quella, che sicuramente è la maggiore ove colla forza della polvere finora conosciuta si possa spingere una palla, o una bomba," p. 432.

that a nation might acquire maritime dominion beyond that limit.[1] The principle of appropriation, he says, which applies to lakes and rivers also applies to straits, which are in general not wider than great rivers and lakes, so that the middle may be reached by a cannon-ball fired from the shore; and those parts of the sea which border the land may also be regarded as the property and under the dominion of the nation possessing the coast. By a custom generally acknowledged, he continues, the authority of the possessor of the coast extends as far as the range of guns from the shore—that is to say, to a distance of three leagues;[2] and he adds that this distance is the least that a nation ought to claim as the extent of its dominion in the sea. But he also says that a nation may occupy and extend its dominion beyond that distance, and maintain it, if the security of the nation require it, by a fleet of armed vessels; and, further, that its sovereignty may extend as far as it has been acknowledged to reach by the consent of other nations, and beyond the boundary of its property—Von Martens, like many others, drawing a distinction between property in the sea and sovereignty over it. As examples of such cases, he definitely states, as well established at the time he wrote, that St George's Channel was under the sovereignty of Great Britain and the Gulf of Bothnia under that of Sweden, while the straits between Sweden and Denmark were considered to be the property of Denmark. On the other hand, the Bay of Biscay, the Mediterranean, the Straits of Gibraltar, the White Sea, and the North Sea were acknowledged to be free.

Towards the close of the century, an Italian author, Azuni,

[1] *Précis du Droit des Gens moderne de l'Europe, fondé sur les Traités et l'Usage*, Göttingen, 1789, Liv. iv. c. iv. In an earlier work, *Primæ Lineæ Juris Gentium Europæarum*, published at Göttingen in 1785, the three-league limit is omitted. After speaking of ports, bays, and straits, he says, "Neque minus in genere eæ maris partes, quæ territorio proximæ sunt (mare proximum vocant) et tormentorum in limite terræ constitutorum ictui subsunt, censentur esse in dominio gentis terræ dominæ, et pro parte territorii habentur."

[2] "Sur la mer voisine en général jusqu'à la portée du canon placé sur le rivage; c. a. d. jusqu'à trois lieues du rivage," p. 189. He also speaks elsewhere of the range of guns being equivalent to three leagues; but it would appear that the terms "miles" and "leagues" were sometimes used indifferently and carelessly (see Bluntschli, p. 682), and three leagues was far beyond the range of guns in Von Marten's time.

who was judge in the commercial court at Nice, published a work on maritime law, in which he dealt with the territorial sea; and adopting the range of guns as the principle of delimitation, he declared that the equivalent distance ought to be fixed at three miles, which, he said, was "without doubt" the farthest a cannon-shot could ever be made to reach.[1] In this Azuni followed Galiani, making the statement more definite, and thus we see the three-mile limit put forward by publicists, as the alternative to the range of guns, before the century closed. In point of fact, however, it had actually been applied in the United States a year or two before Azuni wrote;[2] and it is clear from what he says that no general agreement then existed as to the extent of the territorial sea, for he complained that the limit was still undecided,—a statement repeated in his enlarged work, published in 1805,—and he contended that it ought to be fixed by a solemn treaty between the maritime Powers, as Meadows had suggested a century before.[3] Although Azuni adopted the principle of cannon range, and, like Galiani, declared that three miles was the farthest that a ball or bomb could be thrown,[4] he was of opinion that for purposes of neutrality, as an asylum against hostilities, the territorial waters should be extended to two leagues from either shore in the case of bays and gulfs, which, he says, even when their centre was at a greater distance than three miles from either shore, were admitted to be territorial. He even strongly recommended the adoption of the range of vision as the boundary of neutral waters in time of war.

From the above review of the opinions of publicists in the latter half of the eighteenth century, it is evident that

1 *Sistema universale dei Principj del Diritto marittimo dell' Europa.* Florence, 1795-96. The work was translated into French in 1801—*Système Universel de Principes du Droit Maritime de l'Europe*—and revised, enlarged, and republished in 1805.

2 See p. 574.

3 "Giacchè essa sola è, secondo me, il giusto ed unico mezzo, che potrebbe servire di norma per fissare una volta il mare territoriale sempre combattuto, e non ancora deciso, o almeno non stabilito come si dovrebbe in un pubblico Trattato tra le Potenze marittime," i. 75.

4 "La distanza di tre miglia dalla Terra come quella, che senza dubbio è la maggiore, dove colla forza della polvere a fuoco finora cognita si possa spingere una palla o una bomba," p. 76.

there was a general agreement that the sea, at least as far as the range of guns from the coast, was accessory to the land: no one doubted that this space at all events was included within the territorial sea of the neighbouring country. Almost all the writers went further, and held that the sovereignty of a state was not confined to gunshot range, but could be extended to a greater distance from the coast, either for the security of the state or for jurisdiction, but there was not agreement as to how far this could be carried. We see, moreover, the growing tendency to assign a fixed distance as an alternative to cannon range or as a boundary to neutral waters. Abreu, Valin, and Galiani placed it at two leagues from the coast, and the same distance is given by the writer of the article "Mer" in a great French work published in 1777[1] — that is, twice the distance of cannon range, which was said to be one marine league, or three miles.

Turning from the opinions of international jurists in the eighteenth century to the practice and usage of nations in the same period, we may note certain features of prominence: (1) the continued decadence of claims to sovereignty over extensive areas; (2) the growing custom of fixing definite boundaries for special purposes by international treaties or by municipal laws; (3) legal decisions by which the limit of cannon range was recognised in certain cases. In the eighteenth century claims to the sovereignty of seas became greatly restricted and lost their previous importance. The feebleness of Venice prevented her from asserting in practice the rights which were hers by law and ancient prescription. Both Vattel and Azuni, while admitting that she possessed a limited sovereignty, questioned whether any other Power would recognise her claim to the whole of the Adriatic. "Such pretensions to empire," says the former author, "are respected so long as the nation that makes them is able to assert them by force, but they vanish, of course, on the decline of her power." In 1779, indeed, before Azuni wrote, the Republic issued a decree respecting her neutrality, in which the limit of cannon range was fixed as the boundary of her waters for that purpose.[2] Her ancient dominion over

[1] *Répertoire de Jurisprudence.*

[2] See p. 571.

the Adriatic was soon finally extinguished. When Napoleon conquered Venice in 1795 and transferred her like a chattel to Austria, her maritime sovereignty came to an end, and the picturesque and symbolic ceremony of "espousing" the Adriatic, which had been performed by the Doge every year for many centuries, terminated with it.[1]

The similar pretension of England to sovereignty of the sea, as previously mentioned, did not survive till this century, except on the point of the flag; and this ceremony fell into desuetude, and was abandoned finally in 1805. Great Britain now appeared rather as a champion of the freedom of the sea than as an advocate of *mare clausum*. This was particularly shown in connection with the rights claimed by Denmark in the northern sea, especially at Iceland and the Danish portion of Greenland. As already stated, Denmark tried in the preceding century to keep alive her ancient rights to the fisheries and trade in these remote regions, and having failed in her efforts, introduced a fixed limit of forty geographical miles from the coast, within which whale-fishing by foreigners was forbidden (see p. 529).

While Denmark was unsuccessfully endeavouring to assert exclusive rights to the fisheries within a wide extent of water in the northern seas, she was at the same time claiming a much less extensive space along her coasts for purposes of neutrality. Moreover, it may be added that just as in most European countries the cannon-range limit and then the three-mile belt—which likewise originated in connection with neutral rights—came to be applied as the boundary of the territorial seas for all purposes, so the Danish limit for neutral waters, which was a different one, was also adopted later as the general boundary of the territorial seas by the Scandinavian states. The decree in regard to neutrality was issued in 1745 by the King of Denmark and Norway, and communicated to the foreign consuls, and it forbade all foreign privateers to capture any vessel of the enemy within a distance of one league, of fifteen to a degree of latitude, from the coast or its outlying banks

[1] Daru, *Histoire de la République de Venise*, i. 445; Smedley, *Sketches of Venetian History*, i. 72. See p. 4. When Venice was conquered, the *Bucentaur* was stripped of her gilding and finery, and, under the name of *Hydra*, became a prosaic guardship, stationed at the mouth of the Lido until 1824, when she was destroyed.

or rocks.[1] This ordinance in regard to neutral waters was renewed in 1756, 1759, and 1779,—that of 1759 expressly declaring that the league was the marine league of fifteen to a degree.[2] It may be added here that early in the next century, in view of the war with Great Britain, decrees were published prohibiting either Danish or Norwegian privateers from capturing the enemy's vessels within the territorial sea of any foreign state which was friendly or neutral; and such sea, it was said, was usually supposed to extend for one marine league from the coast.[3] The same distance of four geographical miles was assigned by Sweden, in a decree of 12th April 1808, which prohibited the seizure of vessels nearer the coast of neutrals than the limit named.[4]

The various ordinances cited referred solely to the limit of the territorial sea in relation to neutrality. But as early as 1747 the same boundary was applied to a limited part of the Norwegian coast in connection with fisheries. In that year a royal decree prohibited Russian fishermen at Finmarken from fishing within one league of the land,—a measure which was not opposed by the Russian Government, and which was renewed by a Norwegian law in 1830.[5] In 1812, as we shall see (p. 653), the territorial waters of Denmark and Norway were declared to extend to four miles from the coast or its outlying isles,—that is to say, the limit which was adopted for neutrality was applied in regard to fisheries and other purposes.

Another example of the decadence of wide claims to mari-

[1] *Rescripter, Resolutioner og Collegial-Breve for Kongeriget Norge, i Tidsrummet fra* 1660-1813, i. 315, 18th June 1745. "Rescr. (til Stiftsbefalingsmændene i Norge) ang. det ikke skal være nogen fremmed Caper tilladt at opbringe noget Skib een Miil nœr de Norske Kyster og de der udenfor beliggende Grunde og Skjær," &c. The league in the Scandinavian ordinances measures fifteen to one degree of latitude, or one German mile, equal to about 7420 metres. The marine league, or three-mile limit ordinarily adopted, is of twenty to a degree of latitude, or about 5565 metres, or 3.4517 English statute miles.

[2] *Ibid.*, i. 423, 439, 602.

[3] 14th Sept. 1807, s. 5; 28th March 1810, s. 7. In the last the privateers were forbidden to capture ships in the Sound within such distance of the Swedish coast as was within the range of guns. Auber, *Ann. de l'Institut de Droit Internat.*, xi. 145.

[4] Kleen, *Neutralitetens Lagar*, ii. 865.

[5] Boeck, *Oversigt over Litteratur, Love, Forordninger, Rescripter, m.m. vedrørende de Norske Fiskerier*, p. 12.

time sovereignty is to be found in the case of Spain, which, like the Scandinavian countries, adopted a fixed limit in the eighteenth century as the boundary of her territorial waters, and, as with them also, it was placed at a greater distance than the range of guns from the coast. An eminent Spanish publicist, Abreu, as we have seen, declared in 1746 that the boundary of neutral waters should be at least two leagues from the coast, and by a royal decree of 17th December 1760 this distance was assigned, the territorial sea of Spain being declared to extend to six miles from the land. This boundary was again given in 1775 and in 1830, and it is still retained by Spain—and also, until last year, by Portugal—as the maritime frontier for customs, fishery, neutrality, and jurisdiction.[1] At various times Spain has entered into treaties with her neighbours, France and Portugal, concerning the rights of fishery within the six-mile zone, either for reciprocal liberty to fish in the whole extent of the territorial sea, or in the outer belt of three miles. A treaty of this kind was concluded with France in 1768.[2]

The uprising in America in 1775, which resulted in the independence of the United States, brought in its train a widespread maritime war, Great Britain having to meet the naval forces of France, Holland, and Spain, and at this time and throughout the remainder of the century we meet with numerous decrees and treaties bearing upon the delimitation of territorial waters, particularly in connection with the rights of neutrals. One of the first of these was a circular which the American Commissioners at the Court of Paris addressed to the commanders of American armed vessels in 1777, instructing them to abstain from capturing the enemy's vessels, or vessels of neutrals, when they were "under the protection of a port, river, or coast of a neutral country." To do so, it was said, would be contrary to the usage and customs of nations; and the proclamation issued by the American Government in

[1] Real Cédula, 17th December 1760; Real Órden, 1st May 1775; Real Decreto, 3rd May 1830; Real Decreto, 20th June 1852. Riquelme, *Elementos de Derecho Público Internacional, con esplicacion de todas las reglas que, segun los Tratados, &c., constituyen el Derecho Internacional Español*, i. 211, App., 187, 197, 200; Madrid, 1849. Negrín, *Tratado de Derecho internacional maritimo*, Madrid, 1883, p. 66.

[2] Martens, *Recueil*, i. 479.

the following year on the same subject is couched in équally general terms.[1]

We find the same want of definition in an edict of the King of the Two Sicilies in the same year, which speaks only of the accustomed rules being observed in his "ports, coasts, and adjacent seas."[2] But in corresponding proclamations issued at the same time by the Grand Duke of Tuscany, the Republic of Genoa, the Republic of Venice, and the Pope, the range of guns is expressly mentioned as determining the boundary of their territorial waters in respect to neutrality. The Grand Duke prohibited all acts of hostility in the ports or coasts of Leghorn, within certain places specified, and in the seas adjacent to all his other ports, castles, or coasts within gunshot of the shore.[3] With respect to Civita Vecchia, Ancona, and his other territories, the Pope prohibited, "according to the common usage of nations," all acts of hostility or superiority between belligerents there or in the adjacent seas, "or generally within the range of guns from the shore";[4] while the Genoese edict forbade all acts of hostility between belligerents "in the ports, gulfs, and coasts, within range of guns,"[5] and contained particular rules for carrying the prohibition into effect. Thus, if such an act of hostility should be committed within range of cannon, a shot was first to be fired into the air, or to a distance from the vessel or vessels violating the neutrality, unless there was risk of damage to other vessels, in which case a blank shot was to be fired. If this did not put a stop to the transgression, the offenders were to be assailed with shot and musketry. In places where cannon were not

[1] 21st Nov. 1777; 9th May 1778. Martens, *Recueil*, iii. 16, 18. In Kent's *Commentaries on American Law*, i. 118 (ed. 1884), it is said (apparently on the authority of Sparks' *Diplomatic Correspondence*, ii. 110) that the Commissioners, in their circular letter of 1777 to the commanders of American armed vessels, "carried very far the extension of neutral protection when they applied it indiscriminately to all captures within sight of a neutral coast." There is nothing of this in the document given by Martens.

[2] 19th Sept. 1778. *Op. cit.*, i. 47.

[3] 1st Aug. 1778. "E ne' mari adjacenti agli altri porti, scali, torri, e spiagge del Gran Ducato non potrà usarsi atto veruno di ostilità nella distanza, che potrebbe circoscriversi da un tiro di cannone." *Op. cit.*, 24.

[4] 4th March 1779. "Nè generalmente dentro la distanza di un tiro di cannone da terra." *Op. cit.*, i. 52.

[5] 1st July 1779. "Nei porti, golfi, e spiagge del nostro dominio nella distanza, che potrebbe circonscriversi da un tiro di cannone." *Op. cit.*, 64.

available, the same course was to be followed with muskets, and, it was said, the rules had to be carried out precisely as they had been ordained in a decree of 1756, when, no doubt, the gunshot limit was equally in force. The Venetian decree is couched in similar terms, and the size of the cannon whose range was to determine the limit is mentioned. All acts of force or authority between belligerents were prohibited "in the ports, roads, and coasts of our dominion, and in all the adjacent sea, at least to the distance within range of a large cannon of battery."[1] In several of the edicts, as in the two last referred to, the range of vision was also used as a limit within which no belligerent vessel was to be allowed to station itself, or cruise about waiting for the enemy's vessels: such action was prohibited within view of the ports or roads.

It will be noticed that all these edicts regarding neutral waters in which the limit of cannon range was prescribed, emanated from the small Mediterranean states; but in many of the international treaties which followed the Armed Neutrality of 1780 the gunshot limit for neutral waters was also adopted. This league, which was directed against Great Britain, had its source in a declaration by the Empress Catherine II. of Russia regarding the rights of neutrals; especially that neutral vessels should be free to carry on trade on the coasts of belligerents, and that the property of belligerents in neutral vessels, except arms, equipment, and munitions of war, should be free from capture. The seizure of enemy's goods in neutral ships by English cruisers bore hardly on the commerce of neutral countries; and for this reason, and, according to English views, because it was perceived by the other Powers that they could not directly contend against the naval force of Great Britain, a new code of international law was introduced which would have the effect of sapping it.[2] In some of the treaties referred to, the limits of neutral waters were defined in vague or general terms, as in that of 1782 between the United

[1] 9th Sept. 1779, Arts. viii., ix. "Ed in tutti mari ad essi adjacenti, limitati, almeno allo spazio circoscritto dalla portata d'un grosso cannone di batteria." *Op. cit.*, i. 78.

[2] Jenkinson (Lord Liverpool), *A Discussion on the Conduct of the Government of Great Britain in respect to Neutral Nations* (1758), ed. 1801, Pref. Phillimore, *Commentaries*, iii. 273. Wheaton's *Elements* (ed. 1864), 1024. Martens, *Recueil*, iii. 158, *seq.*

States and the United Provinces.[1] The gunshot limit, however, was specified in a treaty between the United States and Morocco in 1785, which stipulated that if a vessel of either state was engaged with that of another Christian Power within the range of guns of a castle of the other state, it was to be protected and defended;[2] in a treaty of navigation and commerce between Great Britain and France in 1786;[3] and in a treaty between France and Russia in 1787. In the latter it was stipulated that in agreement with the principles laid down in the Russian declaration regarding the navigation of neutrals, either Power, if at war, should abstain from attacking the enemy's vessels within cannon range of the coasts of the other Power, or in the ports, harbours, gulfs, and "other waters comprised under the name of closed waters."[4] Russian activity in the direction indicated was shown by the conclusion of a similar treaty in the same terms with the Two Sicilies a few days later.[5] A little later, in 1803, the range of guns was adopted by Austria as determining the extent of neutral waters, as in the treaties above referred to.[6]

In contrast to the gunshot limit in connection with neutrality, was another which Spain incorporated in a treaty with Tripoli in 1784, by which it was agreed that Tripolitan vessels of war or privateers should not capture ships of their enemy within

[1] Mutual protection was to be afforded "dans leurs ports ou rades, mers internes, passages, rivières, et aussi loin que leur jurisdiction s'etend en mer." 8th Oct. 1782, Art. v. Martens, *op. cit.*, 433.

[2] "À la portée du canon des châteaux de l'autre." *Vide* Martens and De Cussy, *Rec.*, i. 381.

[3] 26th Sept. 1786, Art. xli. "Leurs dites Majestés ne souffriront point que sur les côtes, à la portée du canon, et dans les ports et rivières de leur obéissance, des navires et des marchandises des sujets de l'autre soient pris par des vaisseaux de guerre, ou par d'autres qui seront pourvus de patentes de quelque prince, république, ou ville quelconque," &c. Martens, *Rec.*, iv. 178.

[4] 11th Jan. 1787, Art. xxviii. ". . . Hors de la portée du canon des côtes de son allié . . . dans les ports, havres, golfes et autres eaux comprises sous le nom d'eaux closes." By Article xx. the salute was abolished. *Ibid.*, 207, 210. The mention of closed waters no doubt referred to the Baltic, which was declared to be a closed sea (*une mer fermée*), into which the armed vessels of belligerents were to be refused entry, by a decree of the King of Denmark in 1780, and by conventions between Russia and Denmark and Sweden in the same year, and between Russia and the United Provinces and Prussia in the following year. *Ibid.*, iii. 175, 195, 219, 250.

[5] 17th Jan. 1787, Art. xix. *Ibid.*, iv. 237.

[6] 7th August 1803. Martens, *Recueil*, 2. viii. 105.

ten leagues of the coasts of the Spanish dominions[1]—that is to say, within the same extent of sea as was expressed in the treaty between France and Algeria a century earlier.[2] A few years later the same limit of ten leagues was agreed to in a treaty between Great Britain and Spain concerning fisheries and navigation in certain parts of the Pacific. Disputes had arisen with Spain concerning proceedings at Nootka Sound, Vancouver; and in a convention between the two Powers, signed in 1790, it was agreed, *inter alia*, that British subjects should not navigate or carry on their fishery within a distance of ten sea leagues from any part of the coast already occupied by Spain, the object being to prevent illegal trading with the Spanish settlements.[3]

We thus perceive that towards the end of the eighteenth century various maritime boundaries were assigned in particular places for particular purposes, and that many states looked upon the limit of gunshot from an open coast as fixing the extent of their neutral waters. But hitherto, with the exception of the league limit prescribed by Denmark and Norway, which had no avowed reference to the range of guns, and was in reality equivalent to much more than three miles, no Power had yet adopted one marine league as the equivalent of gunshot from the shore. It appears that this step was first taken by the United States of America, and it is of interest to note that the three-mile limit was put forward tentatively, and, in a manner, as a temporary expedient. When the war between Great Britain and France broke out in 1793, the United States found it necessary to define the extent of the line of territorial protection which they claimed on their coast, in order to give effect to their neutral rights and duties. Washington, who was then President, instructed the executive officers to consider the line restrained, for the time being, to the distance of one sea league, or three geographical miles, from the shores, a distance which was said to be not more extensive than was claimed by any other Power. This limit was adopted tentatively, since the Government "did not propose, at that time, and without amicable communication with the foreign Powers

1 Martens, *Recueil*, iii. 763, 10th Sept. 1784, Art. vi. 2 See p. 527.

3 Oct. 28, 1790, Art. iv. Martens, *ibid.* iv. 489, 497. Wheaton, *Elements*, 307 (ed. 1864).

interested in the navigation of the coast, to fix on the distance to which they might ultimately insist on the right of protection." It was stated that the greatest distance to which any "respectable assent" among nations had ever been given was the range of vision, which was estimated at upwards of twenty miles, and the smallest distance claimed by any nation was "the utmost range of a cannon-ball, usually stated at one sea league."[1] Besides the extent of sea referred to, the bays and rivers were held by usage and the law of nations to be territorial, with immunity from belligerent operations. This was well shown in the same year, when the United States claimed that the whole of Delaware Bay and New Jersey, an arm of the sea about fifty English miles in length and a little over eleven miles wide at the entrance, was under their territorial jurisdiction, and ordered the restitution of a British vessel, the *Grange*, which had been captured there by a French frigate, *L'Ambuscade;* and this was done notwithstanding the protest of the French Minister that Delaware Bay was open sea and not under the exclusive jurisdiction of the United States. The American Government rested its action on the law of nations, and declared that they were entitled to attach to their coasts an extent of sea beyond the reach of cannon-shot—a claim which showed that the three-mile limit had not been adopted as an inflexible rule.[2]

Next year the United States Congress passed a law authorising the district courts to take cognisance of all captures made within one marine league of the American shores;[3] but in the treaty concluded between Great Britain and the United States in the same year, it is interesting to observe that the less precise limit of gunshot was adopted, in the same words as in the treaty of 1786 between Great Britain

[1] Wheaton, *Elements*, 723; President's Proclamation of Neutrality, April 22, 1793; Mr Jefferson, Secretary of State, to M. Genet, 8th Nov. 1793; Wharton's *Digest of the International Law of the United States*, i. c. 2, s. 32.

[2] Opinion of Attorney-General, 14th May 1793; Letter of Sec. of State to the French Minister, 15th May 1793; Kent's *Commentaries*, i. 30. Delaware Bay, it may be said, has always been, and still is, claimed as territorial water by the United States. *Vide* reply of Government of United States to Observations of British Government on Draft Treaty, 1887. Correspondence relative to the Fisheries Question, 1887-1888. *Parl. Papers* (*Canada*), 1888, p. 70.

[3] Act of Congress, 5th June 1794, c. 50. Kent's *Commentaries*, 30.

and France. The twenty-fifth article of this treaty provided that neither Government should permit the ships or goods belonging to the citizens or subjects of the other "to be taken within cannon-shot of the coast, nor in any of the bays, ports, or rivers of their territories, by ships of war, or others, having commissions from any prince, republic, or state whatever."[1]

It may be mentioned here that the claims which have been put forward by the United States as to the extent of their territorial or jurisdictional waters have varied greatly on different occasions. The above declaration to M. Genet was, for instance, repudiated by President Jefferson as establishing a fixed limit; and it was claimed that the limit of neutrality should extend "to the Gulf Stream, which was a natural boundary (!), and within which we ought not to suffer any hostility to be committed."[2] On another occasion, in a controversy about the right of jurisdiction, they claimed that the extent of neutral immunity off the American coast ought at least to correspond with the claims maintained by Great Britain around her own territory, and that no belligerent rights should be exercised within "the chambers formed by headlands, or anywhere at sea within the distance of four leagues, or from a right line from one headland to another."[3] The American Government endeavoured to obtain from England in the same year the recognition of a territorial belt six miles in breadth, and in the draft treaty proposed in 1807 a distance of five miles was in reality specified.[4]

[1] Wheaton, *Elements*, 724.

[2] Wharton's *Digest*, i. c. 2.

[3] Mr Madison to Messrs Monroe and Pinckney, 17th May 1806. Kent, *Commentaries*, i. 31.

[4] Hall, *A Treatise on International Law*, Part II. c. ii. s. 2.

CHAPTER II.

GENERAL ADOPTION OF THE THREE-MILE LIMIT.

It is evident from the foregoing that, notwithstanding the variation in the extent of water claimed in certain cases, the principle of determining the general boundary of the territorial sea by the range of guns from the coast had become tolerably firmly established in the practice of nations before the end of the eighteenth century, with reference in particular to the rights of neutrals. Shortly before the century closed, moreover, we have seen that one of the important maritime Powers, the United States of America, had adopted a fixed distance of three miles or one marine league as equivalent to the utmost range of the cannon of those days. The range of guns naturally varied according to their size and power, and though it was specified in some of the Continental ordinances that the distance was to be determined by a large gun of battery, there was no certainty that it would be everywhere the same. It was thus clearly an advantage to have a fixed distance, which could be marked on charts, substituted for the less definite cannon range, so long as it really represented it. By the progress of the military art, however, most notably perhaps after about the middle of last century, the range of guns became enormously increased, so that long ago the three-mile limit ceased to represent it.

The new boundary of one marine league, as equivalent to the range of guns, was soon introduced into English law and practice, in the first place through the decisions of the High Court of Admiralty in questions affecting the extent of neutral waters. It is noteworthy that nothing was heard at this period about the principle of the King's Chambers in such cases. It is very doubtful whether, as the American Government implied in 1806, the boundaries of the King's Chambers had retained their validity at the beginning of last century. There seems to be no evidence that they were enforced during the eighteenth century, or even in the closing years of the seventeenth, possibly because occasions to test the point had become rare. But it is perhaps more probable that the claim to the King's Chambers was allowed gradually to die out, and that the deliberate omission of any reference to them in the later proclamations of Charles II. (see p. 554) foreshadowed this change in practice. It is clear at all events that long before the end of the eighteenth century it was well established that a vessel captured by one belligerent from another belligerent in a port of a neutral state or within the actual reach of cannon was not good prize.[1] The next step was to give effect to the same principle, whether the place was actually within the range of a fort or not.

The decisions which introduced the three-mile limit into English jurisprudence were those of Sir William Scott (afterwards Lord Stowell) at the beginning of last century. In 1800 and 1801 this great authority adopted both the gunshot limit and the distance of three miles as its equivalent for the boundary of neutral waters, in deciding the well-known cases of the *Twee Gebroeders.* It was these decisions of Lord Stowell's which introduced the three-mile limit into English jurisprudence. The cases arose from the capture of certain vessels in 1799, by the boats of a British man-of-war, in the Groningen - Watt, between East Friesland and the island of Borkum, in the belief that they were bound from Hamburg to Amsterdam, which was then blockaded by the British; and it was claimed by the King of Prussia that the capture was made within the territory of that state. In deciding the first case,[2] Lord Stowell found that the *capturing*

[1] The High Court of Admiralty, for instance, decided in 1760 that a French vessel taken by an English privateer at Hayti was not good prize, as it had been attacked while in a port belonging to the King of Spain, "within reach of his cannon and under his protection" (Marsden, *Report of Cases determined by the High Court of Admiralty,* 175).

[2] There were two cases of *Twee Gebroeders*—the first (Alberts, master) tried on 29th July 1800; the second (Northolt, master) tried on 27th November 1801.

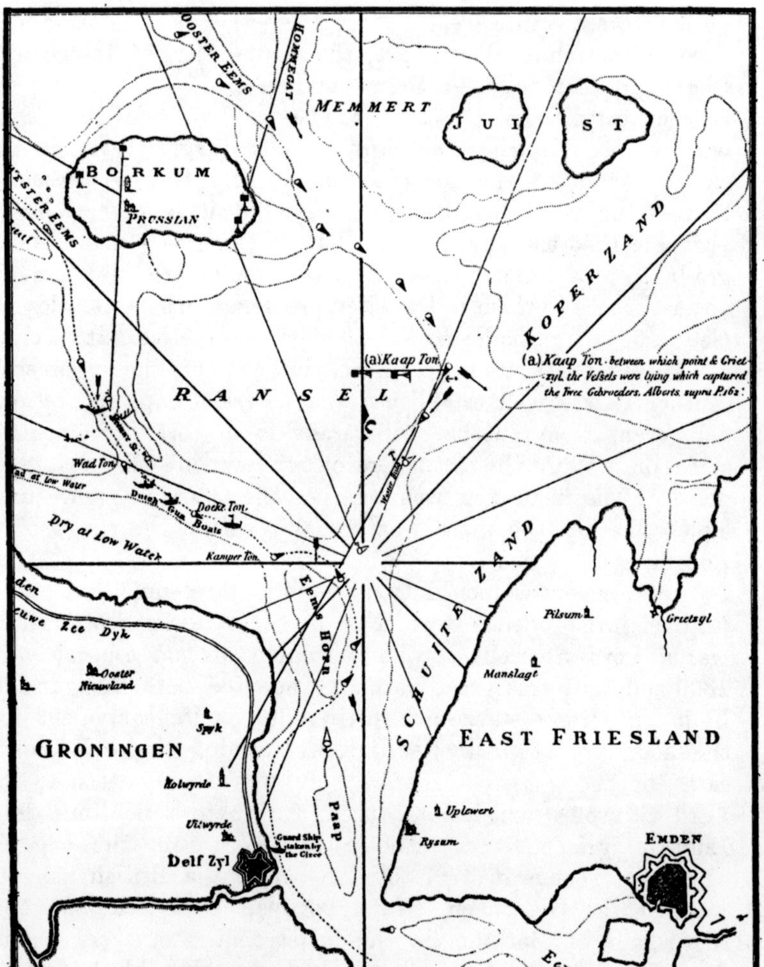

Fig. 14.—*Facsimile of part of the chart, showing where the "Twee Gebroeders" were taken.* From Robinson, Admiralty Reports.

vessel was "lying within the limits to which neutral immunity is usually conceded. She was lying in the eastern branch of the Eems, within what may, I think, be considered as a distance of three miles, at most, from East Friesland. An exact measurement cannot easily be obtained; but in a case of this nature, in which the Court would not willingly act with an unfavourable minuteness towards a neutral state, it will be disposed to calculate the distance very liberally; and more especially, as the spot in question is a sand covered with water only on the flow of the tide, but immediately connected with the land of East Friesland, and when dry, may be considered as making part of it. I am of opinion, that the ship was lying within those limits in which all direct hostile operations are by the law of nations forbidden to be exercised."[1] In this decision the three-mile limit is assumed to be, "by the law of nations," the boundary of the neutral waters. It is also to be observed that the distance was reckoned, not from low-water mark, but apparently from the land; while according to the rule apparently governing such cases now, the sand-bank itself would be a part of the territory, and the distance of three miles would be measured from its outer margin at low water (see fig. 19, p. 635).

In deciding the second case, in which the circumstances were much the same, Lord Stowell said that "in the sea, out of the reach of cannon shot universal use is presumed"; but he made no reference to three miles as an equivalent distance.[2] A few years later, in 1805, in deciding the case of the *Anna*, which was captured at the mouth of the Mississippi by a British privateer, and in which the question of the violation of American waters had to be considered, the same judge, quoting Bynkershoek, said: "We all know that the rule of law on this subject is *terræ dominium finitur, ubi finitur armorum vis;* and since the introduction of fire-arms, that distance has usually been recognised to be about three miles from shore."[3]

It is, as above stated, in these decisions of the High Court of Admiralty that the three-mile limit originated in England. They furnished the legal precedents which regulated subsequent practice. The gunshot limit was a doctrine borrowed from Continental publicists, and three miles as its equivalent from

[1] Robinson, *Reports of Cases Argued and Determined in the High Court of Admiralty*, iii. 162. London, 1802.

[2] *Ibid.*, 339.

[3] *Ibid.*, v. 373.

recent American practice. Both were previously unknown to English law.[1]

Moreover, although, as we shall see, the writers on international law had in only a few instances accepted the three-mile limit as an alternative to the range of guns from the shore, and scarcely any of the Continental publicists of repute, the actual practice of Great Britain and the United States, together with the legal decisions in the British and American courts, and the dicta of the judges, tended steadily to bring about its adoption. At first the boundary of one marine league as equivalent to the range of cannon had reference solely to questions of neutrality, as the capture of prizes, in the maritime wars that prevailed. But very soon it was applied to

[1] *Vide* Chief Justice Cockburn, *Law Reports, Excheq. Div.*, ii. 178. It is a curious circumstance that many English writers on municipal law, even after this time, adhering to a different line of inquiry, clung tenaciously to the husk of the old claims of England to the sovereignty of the sea. Hale, as we have seen, followed Selden, as did Hargrave and Blackstone, though with apparent diffidence. Chitty, in his *Treatise on the Law of the Prerogative of the Crown*, published in 1820, relying on Selden, Hale, and Molloy, declares that "the king possesses the sovereign dominion in all the narrow seas, that is, the seas which adjoin the coasts of England, and other seas within his dominions" (p. 173); and that he "has an undoubted sovereignty and jurisdiction, which he has immemorially exercised, through the medium of the admiralty courts, over the British seas, that is, the seas which encompass the four sides of the British islands; . . . the law of nations and the constitution of the country have clothed the sovereign with this power, that he may defend his people and protect their commercial interests" (p. 142). He also assigns the soil under the sea to the king. Hall, in his *Essay on the Rights of the Crown and the Privileges of the Subject in the Sea Shores of the Realm*, published in 1830, states the doctrine even more nakedly. After defining the British seas according to Selden, he says, "Over the British Seas, the King of England claims an absolute dominion and ownership, as Lord Paramount, against all the world. Whatever opinions foreign nations may entertain in regard to the validity of such claim, yet the subjects of the King of England do, by the common law of the realm, acknowledge and declare it to be his ancient and indisputable right." Hall also assigns the bottom or *fundum* of the British seas to the king, the authorities cited being Coke, Callis, Molloy, Hale, and Blackstone. Loveland, the editor of the second edition of Hall's *Essay*, which was published in 1875, does not attempt to qualify the statements. It was not, indeed, till after the decision in the case of the *Franconia* in 1876, and the Territorial Waters Jurisdiction Act of 1878, that the doctrine was abandoned in theory by English lawyers. Even Moore, the editor of the third edition of Hall's *Essay*, which appeared in 1888, while pointing out the alteration of the law by the decision in the *Franconia* case, and by the Territorial Waters Jurisdiction Act, thought it undesirable to vary Hall's text, having regard to the diversity of the opinions expressed by the judges in the case referred to. *Vide* p 590.

other purposes, and first of all by the British Government in connection with the rights of fishery. During the peace negotiations with the United States at Ghent, after the war of 1812-14, the British Government intimated that they did not intend to grant to the United States gratuitously the privileges formerly given by the treaty of 1783 "of fishing within the limits of British territory, or of using the shores of the British territories for purposes connected with the fisheries." The treaty of Ghent contained no stipulation on the subject, but shortly afterwards the British Government expressed its intention to exclude, and gave instructions to exclude, fishing vessels of the United States from fishing within the harbours, bays, rivers, and creeks, and within one marine league of the shores of the British territories in America, and from drying and curing their fish on shore. Several American vessels were seized for trespassing within British waters, and the prolonged diplomatic discussion which followed resulted in the convention of 1818, by which the fishermen of the United States were allowed the same rights as British fishermen on certain parts of the coast, but at all other parts they were forbidden to fish within a distance of three miles of the "coasts, bays, creeks, or harbours."[1] This was the first of the treaties in which the three-mile limit was specified, and it naturally formed a precedent for those which followed.

That the principle of adopting the distance in question as the proper boundary of the territorial sea had not yet become firmly incorporated in British policy in all cases was, however, shown a few years later in the negotiations with Russia concerning Behring Sea. In 1821 the Emperor of Russia issued a ukase or decree, in which he declared that the pursuit of commerce, whaling, and fishery, and of all other industry, on all islands, ports, and gulfs, including the whole of the northwest coast of America, beginning from Behring Straits to

[1] Convention, 1818, Art. i. ". . . And the United States hereby renounce for ever any liberty heretofore enjoyed or claimed by the inhabitants thereof to take, dry, or cure fish on or within three marine miles of any of the coasts, bays, creeks, or harbours of his Britannick Majesty's dominions in America not included within the above-mentioned limits." Wheaton, *Elements*, 324, 463 (ed. 1864). *Parl. Papers, North America*, No. 1 (1878). Henderson, *American Diplomatic Questions*, 497.

the 51st of northern latitude, and in other parts specified, had been exclusively granted to Russian subjects; and therefore prohibiting "all foreign vessels not only to land on the coasts and islands belonging to Russia, as stated above, but also to approach them within less than 100 Italian miles," the penalty for doing so being the confiscation of the transgressing vessel and the cargo.[1] The Russian Government claimed that the extent of sea of which the Russian possessions formed the limits "comprehended all the conditions which are ordinarily attached to closed seas (*mers fermées*), and it might consequently judge itself authorised to exercise upon this sea the right of sovereignty, and especially that of entirely interdicting the entrance of foreigners; but it preferred only asserting its essential rights without taking any advantage of localities." This, it will be perceived, was a revival in the nineteenth century of pretensions similar to those which Denmark had advanced in the seventeenth and eighteenth; and the claim was opposed by Great Britain and the United States, whose interests were threatened by it. The British Government declared that it was contrary to the law of nations, and that it could not admit the right of any Power possessing the sovereignty of a country to exclude the vessels of others from the seas on its coasts to a distance of 100 Italian miles. In its justification Russia cited, not the Italian publicists or the earlier practice in the Mediterranean, but an article in the treaty of Utrecht, which assigned thirty leagues as the distance of prohibition (see p. 531),—an argument which was sufficiently answered by the statement that the distance mentioned was a particular stipulation in a treaty to which the other party had given its deliberate consent. At an early period in the discussion the Russian Government suspended the execution of the ukase, and instructed the commanders of their ships of war to confine their surveillance as nearly as possible "to the mainland, *i.e.*, over an extent of sea within the range of cannon-shot from the shore."

An article in the draft convention subsequently arranged between Great Britain and Russia provided for an exclusive fishery, not within three miles, but within two leagues or six

[1] Martens, *Nouv. Recueil*, V. ii. 358; Behring Sea Arbitration, British Case, *Parl. Papers*, *United States*, No. 1 (1893), p. 38, App. I. No. 1.

miles, from the coasts of their respective possessions in the regions referred to; but when the British Government discovered that in the corresponding convention concluded a little earlier between Russia and the United States no limit at all had been specified, they withdrew this article. Mr George Canning, in a despatch to Mr Stratford Canning, the British plenipotentiary at St Petersburg, withdrawing the article, said that its omission was, in truth, immaterial, since "the law of nations assigns the exclusive sovereignty of one league to each Power on its own coasts, without any specific stipulation." The Russian Government raised no objection to the new article, and the distance from the coast at which the fishing was to be exercised in common passed without specification, "and consequently," added Stratford Canning, "it rests on the law of nations as generally received." A little later, before the convention was ratified, the British plenipotentiary, thinking it might be desirable to have the law of nations declared therein, jointly with the Court of Russia, in some ostensible shape, broached the subject anew and suggested that notes should be exchanged in London "declaratory of the law as fixing the distance at one marine league from the shore." The Russian Minister, however, expressed disinclination to do anything that might retard the immediate ratification of the convention; and he assured Canning that the Russian Government would be content in executing the convention to abide by the recognised law of nations, and that if any question should afterwards be raised upon the subject, he would not refuse to join in making the suggested declaration, "on being satisfied that the general rule under the law of nations was such as the English Government supposed."[1]

It is evident from these despatches that the British Government at that time held the opinion that the territorial waters of a state on an open coast extended, "by the law of nations," for one marine league from the shore. But it would not have been easy for them to adduce convincing testimony in support

[1] The Duke of Wellington to Count Nesselrode, 17th Oct. 1822; G. Canning to the Duke of Wellington, 27th Sept. 1822; Count Nesselrode to Count Lieven, 26th June 1823; G. Canning to S. Canning, 8th Dec. 1824; S. Canning to G. Canning, 3rd April 1825. *Parl. Papers, ibid.*, 41, 42, 44, 46, 56, App. II. pt. i. 14, 15, 29, 52, 57.

of that opinion from the accredited writers on the law of nations whose works were then available, or from the general usage of nations apart from Anglo-American practice. The Russian Government were obviously not satisfied on the point, and their instruction to their naval commanders to enforce the limit of cannon range, though that was a less definite boundary, was more in consonance with the law of nations as generally understood. It was natural that the British Government should give weight to the decisions of Lord Stowell in the Admiralty Court.

The Government of the United States, in discussing the Russian pretension, did not apparently lay the same stress on the principle of the three-mile limit as they did on some other occasions. The claim that the Northern Pacific might strictly be regarded as a closed sea was met by the simple statement that the opposite coasts on the parallel of 51 degrees were 4000 miles apart. The right of American subjects to navigate and fish within the prescribed distance of 100 miles from the coast was rested on continuous exercise from the earliest times. Universal usage, it was declared, which had obtained the force of law, had established for all coasts "an accessory limit of a *moderate distance*," which was sufficient for the security of the country and for the convenience of its inhabitants, but which laid no restraint upon the universal right of nations, nor upon the freedom of commerce and of navigation.[1]

In the conventions which followed, it was provided that the subjects of the contracting Powers should not be molested either in navigating or in fishing in any part of the Pacific Ocean, and they were to be at liberty for ten years to frequent without hindrance all the inland seas, gulfs, havens, and creeks, on the coasts mentioned, for the purpose of fishing and of trading with the natives, subject to certain conditions to prevent illicit commerce.[2]

It may be here stated that some years later, when American and British whalers had greatly increased in numbers in

[1] *American State Papers, Foreign Relations*, v. 452 ; *Parl. Papers, ibid.*, App. II. pt. ii. No. 5 ; Wheaton, *Elements*, 308.

[2] Treaty between Russia and the United States, April 17th, 1824, Art. i. iv. ; treaty between Great Britain and Russia, 28th Feb. 1825, Art. i. vii. Martens, *Nouv. Recueil*, vi. 684. *Parl. Papers, ibid.*, 52, 53.

Behring Sea, the Russian officials on several occasions urged their Government to preserve the sea as a *mare clausum*,[1] or to prohibit foreign whalers from approaching the coast within a distance of forty Italian miles.[2] The Russian Government pointed out in reply that to fix such a limit would be contrary to the conventions, and might lead to protests from other Powers, "since no clear and uniform agreement has yet been arrived at among nations in regard to the limit of jurisdiction at sea." In 1847 the Government repeated the objections, and expressed the opinion that "the limit of a cannon-shot, that is, about three Italian miles, would alone give rise to no dispute"; and they further observed that no Power had yet succeeded in limiting the freedom of fishing in open seas, other Powers never recognising such pretensions. Subsequently, in 1853, in consequence of continued complaints as to foreigners fishing in the sea of Okhotsk, the Russian Government were pressed by the influential Russian-American Company either to close that great stretch of waters, as an inland sea, or to prohibit whalers from approaching close to the shores and whaling in the bays and among the islands. Instructions were thereupon issued to the commanders of the Russian cruisers to prevent foreign whalers from entering bays or gulfs, or from coming "within three Italian miles of the shores" of Russian America (north of 54° 41′ lat.), the peninsula of Kamtchatka, Siberia, the Kadjak Archipelago, the Aleutin Islands, the Pribyloff and Commander Islands, and the others in Behring Sea, as well as Sakhalin and others; and at the same time it was declared that while the Sea of Okhotsk, from its geographical position, was a Russian inland sea, foreigners were to be allowed to take whales there.[3] Thus the Russian Government adopted at first the principle of the range of guns, then spoke of this or three Italian miles, and eventually accepted and enforced, on the great extent of coast referred to above, the three-mile limit.

Reference must now be made to some decisions in the courts of law and to certain provisions in particular Acts of Parliament which bear upon the question of the extent of the territorial waters. Owing to the long-continued peace on the sea since the decisions of Lord Stowell at the beginning of last

[1] In 1842. *Parl. Papers, ibid.*, 83. [2] In 1846. *Ibid.*, 84. [3] *Ibid.*, 87.

century, few occasions have occurred for the question of the boundary of neutral waters to be raised. In a number of civil cases tried in our courts the three-mile limit has, however, been referred to, either as a ground for the decision, or more usually as a dictum of the judges, as the proper boundary of the territorial sea; but this has been frequently coupled with the qualification that it is the assumed distance of the range of guns, or the smallest extent that has been claimed by publicists or states.[1] Some of these cases dealt with the vexed question of bays.[2] One of the most important was tried in 1859, and it referred to the Bristol Channel. An offence was committed on an American vessel within one mile of the coast in Penarth Roads, but where the width from shore to shore is less than ten miles, and Chief Justice Cockburn, in delivering judgment, said, "We are of opinion that, looking at the local situation of this sea, it must be taken to belong to the counties respectively by the shores of which it is bounded; and the fact of the Holms,[3] between which and the shore of the county of Glamorgan, the

[1] *E.g.*, the case of the *Leda*, in which Dr Lushington claimed that the term United Kingdom included the waters to a distance of three miles from the shore (Swa., *Adm.*, 40); General Iron Screw Company, in which Lord Hatherly said that it was "beyond question that for certain purposes every country may, by the common law of nations, legitimately exercise jurisdiction over that portion of the high seas which lies within three miles from its shores,"—whether this limit was determined by the range of cannon was not material, since it was clear it extended at any rate to that distance (1 J. and H., 180); Whitstable Fishery Case, in which it was said that the soil of the seashore to the distance of three miles from the beach was vested in the crown, and in which Lord Chelmsford observed that "the three-mile limit depends upon a rule of international law, by which every independent state is considered to have territorial property and jurisdiction in the sea which washes their coast within an assumed distance of a cannon-shot from the shore" (11 C.B. (N.S.), 387; 2 H.L.C., 192); the *Annapolis*, in which Dr Lushington said, "Within British jurisdiction, namely, within British territory, and at sea within three miles from the coast" (1 Lush., *Adm.*, 306); Rex *v.* Forty-nine Casks of Brandy, in which Sir John Nicholl said that "as between nation and nation, the territorial right may, by a sort of tacit understanding, be extended to three miles" (3 Haggard, 257); Gammell *v.* Commissioners Woods and Forests and Lord Advocate, in which Lord Wensleydale referred to the distance of three miles as belonging, by the acknowledged law of nations, to the coast of the country, and "under the dominion of the country by being within cannon range, and so capable of being kept in perpetual possession" (3 MacQueen, H.L., 419).

[2] This subject is treated of by Mr A. H. Charteris, Lecturer in International Law, University of Glasgow, in a paper read before the International Law Association at Berlin in 1906 (*Twenty-third Report*, 103).

[3] Two small islands in the Channel.

place in question, is situated, having always been treated as part of the parish of Cardiff, and as part of the county of Glamorgan, is a strong illustration of the principle on which we

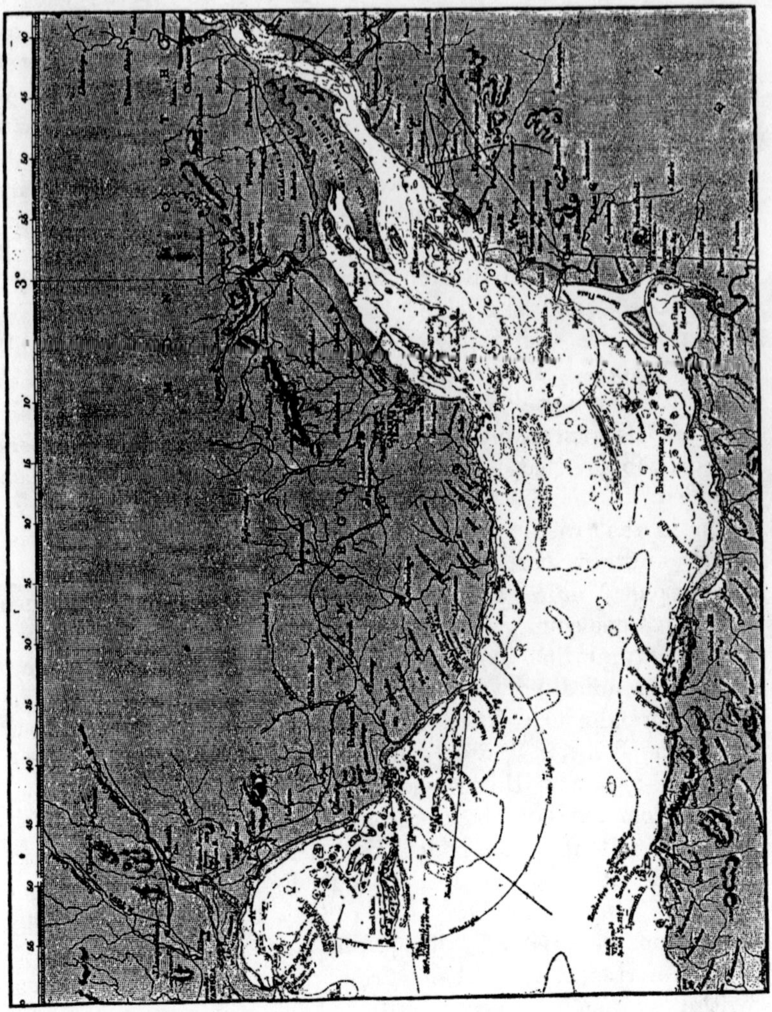

Fig. 15.—*The Bristol Channel.*

proceed, namely, that the whole of this inland sea, between the counties of Somerset and Glamorgan, is to be considered as within the counties by the shores of which its several parts are respectively bounded." A good deal of discussion has taken place as to the precise meaning of these words. It is to be noted that much farther seawards than the place in question the width of the Channel is less than ten geographical miles. On the usual rule for bays (as laid down in the fishery conventions), the ten-mile base-line would pass between Nash Point in Glamorgan and Hurtstone Point, the headland east of Porlock in Somerset, and the closing line would be three miles west of this, or about twenty geographical miles from Penarth Roads. The six-mile limit, from land to land, is, however, about twenty-seven miles farther east, between the coast near Goldcliff, in Monmouth, and that near Walton Castle, Somerset. But about midway between these two limits (and seawards of Penarth Roads) there is a part where the three-mile zone around the island, Steepholm, joins that of the coast on either side, and though eastwards of this there are small areas beyond the distance of three miles from shore, the fact that the territorial waters are continuous from side to side at this place probably confers territoriality on all the waters inside, though that is a point which has not apparently been decided. A line drawn from the western boundary of Somerset (and in that case not from a headland) to Worms Head, the most western part of Glamorgan, measures about thirty geographical miles, and it is a markedly oblique line. What is true of one county ought to be true of another, and a much more natural line would be one of about twenty-three geographical miles between Morte Point in Devon and Worms Head in Glamorgan; or one still farther seawards between Hartland Point in Devon and St Goven's Head in Pembroke, which are about thirty-eight geographical miles apart; but under common law the range of vision has to be taken into account. It may be added that the whole of the Bristol Channel within a line from Land's End to Milford was one of the "King's Chambers" (see p. 122), the closing line being nearly one hundred miles long; and that Continental publicists have referred to it, probably from this circumstance, as being within British jurisdiction.[1]

Another case of the kind decided in a British court concerned Conception Bay in Newfoundland, which is rather more

[1] Bell, *Crown Cases Reserved*, 72. See Hall, *Internat. Law*, 5th edit., p. 156; Westlake, *Internat. Law*, i. 118.

than twenty miles wide between the headlands and from forty to fifty miles in length. It was decided by the Judicial Committee of the Privy Council in 1877 that it was a British bay and part of the territorial waters of Newfoundland. The decision was based partly on the configuration of the bay, but mainly on the evidence that the British Government had for a long time exercised dominion over it, which had been acquiesced in by other nations, and the Legislature had by Acts of Parliament declared it to be British territory.[1] Lord Blackburn, in delivering judgment, said that there was a universal agreement among writers on international jurisprudence that harbours, estuaries, and bays, landlocked, belong to the territory of the nation which possesses the shores round them, but no agreement existed as to what is the rule to determine what is a "bay" for this purpose. "It seems generally agreed," he continued, "that where the configuration and dimensions of the bay are such as to show that the nation occupying the adjoining coasts also occupies the bay, it is part of the territory," most of the writers referring to defensibility from the shore as the test of occupation. But the judgment was founded on the principle above stated.

With regard to jurisdiction over foreigners in the waters along our coasts, it is surprising that until quite recently there was no statutory enactment or international agreement defining the extent of that jurisdiction. Even in certain statutes in which the territorial waters are specially mentioned their boundaries are not defined, Thus, the provisions of the Foreign Enlistment Act of 1870,[2] which was passed for purposes of neutrality in the war between France and Germany, were declared by the second section to extend "to all the dominions of Her Majesty, including the adjacent territorial waters"; and the fourteenth section provided that any ship captured during the war between other nations when Great Britain was neutral, "within the territorial jurisdiction of Her Majesty, in violation of the neutrality of this realm," &c., would be illegal; yet, in the interpretation clause no definition is given of the meaning or extent of "the

[1] The Direct United States Cable Company *v.* the Anglo-American Telegraph Company, Privy Council, 1877. *Law Reports*, Appeal Cases, ii. 394.

[2] 33 & 34 Vict., c. 90.

adjacent territorial waters." A similar reluctance apparently to fix a definite boundary to the territorial seas for all purposes has been shown by the British Government on several occasions in recent years—as, for example, in the Territorial Waters Jurisdiction Act, and in the negotiations preceding the North Sea fishery convention of 1882.[1]

The statute just referred to was the outcome of a very important case which was decided in the English courts in 1876, and raised indirectly the whole question of the extent of the territorial sea (apart from bays) and the nature of the jurisdiction over it. A German ship, the *Franconia*, bound from Hamburg to the West Indies, ran into a British ship, the *Strathclyde*, off Dover and within two and a half miles from the English coast, whereby the *Strathclyde* was sunk and a passenger drowned. The master, a German named Keyn, was convicted of manslaughter in the Central Criminal Court, according to English law, and the case was carried to the Criminal Court of Appeal. The defence was that as the defendant was a foreigner, in a foreign vessel, on a foreign voyage, sailing upon the high seas, he was not subject to the jurisdiction of any court in this country, while it was contended for the crown that inasmuch as at the time of the collision he was within three miles of the English shore, the offence was committed within the realm of England and was triable by the English court.[2] It was held by seven of the thirteen judges that in the absense of statutory enactment the Central Criminal Court had no power to try such an offence, inasmuch as the original jurisdiction of the admiral, which had been transferred to that court, did not enable him to try offences by foreigners on board foreign ships; the other six judges held the opposite, on the ground that the sea within three miles of the coast of England is part of the territory of England; that the English criminal law extends over those limits; and the admiral formerly had, and the Central Criminal Court now has, jurisdiction to try offences there committed although on board foreign ships. In referring to the limits of the territorial waters under the law of nations, the three-mile distance or the range of guns from the shore was very gener-

[1] See pp. 592, 632.

[2] Regina *v.* Keyn, *Law Reports, Excheq. Div.*, ii., 1876-7, p. 63.

ally quoted, and not infrequently the two were confused and spoken of as if they were one and the same thing. This was particularly the case with Sir Alexander Cockburn, who referred to various treaties and edicts (see p. 570) in which the range of guns alone was mentioned, as having fixed a three-mile limit for purposes of neutrality. He even gives Bynkershoek the credit of having propounded the three-mile theory.[1] His conclusion was cautiously expressed as follows: "Possibly, after these precedents and all that has been written on this subject, it may not be too much to say that, independently of treaties, the three-mile belt of sea might at this day be taken as belonging, for these purposes [in connection with fisheries and neutrality], to the local State."

It was, as we have said, in sequence to the above case of the *Franconia* that the important statute, the Territorial Waters Jurisdiction Act, was passed by the British Parliament in 1878.[2] This Act is sometimes loosely referred to as having settled the extent of the territorial waters at three miles from the shore. This is far from being the case. In the preamble it is stated that "whereas the rightful jurisdiction of Her Majesty, her heirs and successors, extends and has always extended over the *open seas* adjacent to the coasts of the United Kingdom and of all other parts of Her Majesty's dominions to such a distance as is necessary for the defence and security of such dominions. And whereas it is expedient that all offences committed on the *open sea* within a certain distance of the coasts of the United Kingdom and of all other parts of Her Majesty's dominions, by whomsoever committed, should be dealt with according to law," it was enacted that an offence committed by a person, whether or not a British subject, within the territorial waters of Her Majesty's dominions was an offence within the jurisdiction of the admiral, although committed on board, or by means of, a

[1] *E.g.*, p. 204: "There are several treaties by which nations have engaged, in the event of either of them being at war with a third, to treat the sea within three miles of each other's coasts as neutral territory," the treaties being those referred to on p. 572. "After the three-mile theory had been propounded by Bynkershoek," p. 177. Mr Justice Amphlett went further, and attributed a similar doctrine to Grotius: "All the earlier writers, including Grotius, the vigorous advocate of the free navigation of the high seas, and many of the later writers, maintained that within the zone of three miles the state had, without qualification," &c., p. 122.

[2] 41 & 42 Vict., c. 73.

foreign ship, and the person who committed the offence might be arrested, tried, and punished accordingly. The legal advisers of the Government were, however, careful to guard against the limitation of the general rights of the crown in the adjacent seas to the distance to which criminal jurisdiction was declared to extend. In the interpretation clause it is stated: "'The territorial waters of Her Majesty's dominions,' in reference to the sea, means such part of the sea adjacent to the coast of the United Kingdom, or the coast of some other part of Her Majesty's dominions, as is deemed by international law to be within the territorial sovereignty of Her Majesty: and for the purpose of any offence declared by this Act to be within the jurisdiction of the admiral, any part of the open sea within one marine league of the coast measured from low-water mark shall be deemed to be *open sea* within the territorial waters of Her Majesty's dominions." The reservation is made explicit in the fifth section, which says that "nothing in this Act contained shall be construed to be in derogation of any rightful jurisdiction of Her Majesty, her heirs or successors, under the law of nations, or to affect or prejudice any jurisdiction conferred by Act of Parliament or now by law existing in relation to foreign ships or in relation to persons on board such ships."

In the debate that took place in the House of Lords in 1895 in connection with the Sea Fisheries Regulation (Scotland) Act,[1] by which power was conferred on the Fishery Board for Scotland of regulating trawling, under certain conditions, up to thirteen miles from the coast (see p. 720), it was stated by Lord Halsbury, who had charge of the Territorial Waters Jurisdiction Act in 1878, that "in that Act they took care specially to avoid any measurements. The distance was left at such limit as was necessary for the defence of the Realm; then the exact limit was given for the particular purpose in view." Equally clear was the statement of the late Lord Salisbury in the same debate, that "Great care had been taken not to name three miles as the territorial limit. The limit depended on the distance to which a cannon-shot could go."[2]

[1] 58 & 59 Vict., c. 42.

[2] *Hansard*, xxxiii. 504. The Lord Chancellor (Lord Herschell), who followed, said: "He was far from saying that three miles was to be the limit of territorial waters for all time. Originally the distance was fixed by gunshot, and it was

It is evident from the foregoing that the territorial sea that may be claimed as belonging to this country is not restricted to a distance of three miles from the shore on an open coast, though a certain jurisdiction and certain rights may be confined to that distance by municipal law or international agreement. The determination of the extent is left to the law of nations, and there is but little doubt that by the law of nations the true principle of delimitation is the actual range of guns from the coast, where the coast is washed by the open sea. It is to be noted that in the Territorial Waters Jurisdiction Act nothing is said about bays: criminal jurisdiction is confined to "the open sea" within one marine league of the coast. Offences such as come under the Act may obviously be committed as well in territorial bays and arms of the sea as within the three-mile limit on the open coast; and the omission to include bays was no doubt deliberate, bays in England being left under the common law on the principle previously explained, the range of vision, and in Scotland presumably under Scots law—*i.e.*, "within land" (see pp. 545, 547).

Other Acts of Parliament which fix limits of jurisdiction beyond three miles from the shore include those relating to smuggling, the public health, and slave-ships. In 1736, and later, statutes were made by Parliament, known as the Hovering Acts, by which vessels with certain cargoes on board, destined for British ports, might be seized within four leagues of the British coast; and foreign vessels so taken have been brought for adjudication before British courts and forfeited for illicit trade.[1] By later Acts concerning the customs, differential limits were fixed with respect to jurisdiction over vessels having dutiable goods on board. Those belonging wholly or in part to British subjects, or having half the persons on board British subjects, found or discovered to have been within four

always said that the distance a gun could fire to was three miles. How far this principle was to be extended, and whether it was to be extended indefinitely, was a question for consideration, and it was a question which would not be without its difficulty." Lord Salisbury referred to a gun which was fired on Jubilee Day and carried twelve miles, and Lord Herschell to one which had a range of thirteen miles.

[1] 9 Geo. II., c. 35; 24 Geo. III., c. 47; Twiss, *The Law of Nations in Time of Peace*, 261; Hall, *A Treatise on the Foreign Powers and Jurisdiction of the British Crown*, 244.

leagues of the coast between the North Foreland and Beachy Head, or within eight leagues of any other part of the coast; or any foreign ship with one or more British subjects on board, found or discovered to have been within three leagues of the coast, or any foreign ship irrespective of British subjects within one league, might under certain specified conditions be forfeited; and power was conferred on the commander of a ship of the royal navy to fire on such vessel if it refused to bring to after a warning gun had been given.[1]

Other nations have also assigned boundaries for customs jurisdiction, which in nearly all cases exceed the ordinary limits of territorial waters. The United States in 1799 extended its jurisdiction for such purposes to four leagues from the coast, and in 1807, in an Act against the importation of slaves, the seizure of vessels laden with certain cargoes within that distance was also authorised.[2] In Spain the customs limit is six miles, and therefore corresponds to the territorial zone which is claimed;[3] in Sweden it is also six miles, but measured on the Scandinavian system from the outermost rocks; in Norway it is four miles, measured on the same principle, but a treaty between Norway and Mexico, concluded in 1886, places it as between these countries at three leagues from low-water mark.[4] In Italy the boundary is ten kilometres; in France two myriametres, or about four leagues; in Austria it is also four leagues; while in Canada it is three leagues.[5] Wide limits for jurisdiction have also been fixed by certain quarantine Acts. By the British Act of 1753, all vessels coming from places whence the plague might be brought were required to make signals on meeting other ships within four leagues of the coast, a distance which was reduced to two leagues by a later Act.[6]

Such extension of jurisdiction as is indicated for customs or quarantine purposes over foreign ships approaching the

[1] 16 & 17 Vict., c. 107, ss. 212, 218; 39 & 40 Vict., c. 36, s. 179.

[2] Kent, *Commentaries*, i. 31; Wheaton, *Elements*, 267, 323.

[3] Riquelme, *op. cit.* See p. 569.

[4] *Fifteenth Ann. Rep. Assoc. for Reform and Codification of the Law of Nations*, 18, 22; *Seventeenth, ibid.*, 302; *Annuaire de l'Institut*, xi. 151.

[5] *Fifteenth Rep., ibid.*, 84, 121; *Ann. de l'Institut* for 1894. Customs Act of Canada, 49 Vict., c. 32, s. 21.

[6] 26 Geo. II.; 6 Geo. IV., c. 78.

ports of a country, has only been sanctioned in a few cases by international treaties. It is now generally held to rest upon another basis than the absolute rights possessed by a state in its territorial waters proper; although it is quite in agreement with the principles laid down by the older publicists, as Puffendorf, Vattel, and Von Martens, and by several recent writers, as Latour,[1] that a nation is justified in exercising jurisdiction in the sea as far as its security or interests render it necessary. The current opinion is that such rights can only be enforced against foreigners under the comity of nations or by their tacit assent, as a matter of mutual convenience, and in practice they are acquiesced in by other Powers.[2] But it is important to observe that, as will be more apparent when we come to deal with the exclusive right of fishing, maritime nations find it necessary for the protection of their just interests to extend their jurisdiction beyond the somewhat narrow boundary at present ordinarily assigned.

The statement made above, that the true principle for determining the extent of the territorial sea on an open coast is the range of guns from the shore, is borne out by an examination of the writings of the accredited authorities on the law of nations. A review of the opinions of the leading publicists of the earlier part of last century shows that while the majority accepted Bynkershoek's principle of cannon range, comparatively few restricted it to the distance of three miles, and many logically insisted that the extent must necessarily vary with the improvements in artillery. Works of a purely polemical nature may be passed over, such as those of the worthless Barrère[3] and of Champagne.[4] They were inspired by hatred of Great Britain and the desire of flattering Napoleon rather than by love of the truth, and were written in order to show that the British were the tyrants of the sea. Another contemporary French author, of much superior merit, who

[1] *Mer Territoriale*, 222; and see pp. 551, 560, 564.

[2] Twiss, *op. cit.*, 261-264; Phillimore, *Commentaries*, i. 236; Kent, *loc. cit.;* Wheaton, *loc. cit.;* Hall, *loc. cit.* The latter author states that they "repose on an agreement which, though tacit, is universal," and that "no civilised country encourages offences against the laws of a foreign state when it sees that the laws are just and necessary."

[3] *De la Liberté des Mers, ou le Gouvernement Anglois devoilé*, 1798.

[4] *La Mer Libre, La Mer Fermée*, 1803.

dealt with the question was Rayneval, although his views were also somewhat coloured by national prejudice. In 1803 he published a treatise on international law,[1] and in 1811 another on the liberty of the sea.[2] The latter for the most part consists, like the work of Champagne, of an examination of the writings of Grotius and Selden regarding the *mare liberum* and the *mare clausum*, and also of the trenchant little book of Jenkinson (Lord Liverpool) on the conduct of the British Government in relation to neutrals. But in the earlier treatise, which is still cited as an authority, Rayneval expounded the law of nations respecting the territorial sea with marked impartiality. On the general question of the freedom of the sea and the appropriation of straits and bays the usual opinions were expressed. He held that the sea bathing the coasts of a country makes part of it; that the security and tranquillity of the state require that it should be held as a rampart against hostile surprise or violence and illicit trading; and that the fisheries form a natural appendage to this zone. With regard to the extent of sea that may be appropriated, Rayneval stated that it had not been determined by any uniform rule. Some, he said, carried it to a hundred miles, or to sixty miles, from the coast, others only to three miles, and others placed it at the distance of gunshot from the shore. On the southern coast of France it had been fixed by agreement at ten leagues with respect to the Barbary privateers. Like Meadows and several preceding writers, he held it to be desirable in the interests of the peace of nations that a general rule, or at least particular rules clearly determined, should be adopted on a matter so important and exposed to such uncertainties and disputes. Authors, he said, had usually fixed the distance at the range of cannon, but their opinion was not founded on a general regulation nor on uniform practice; and the most equitable limit according to some was the range of vision from the coast or the apparent horizon. Rayneval was of opinion that within the territorial seas the neighbouring state had the right to forbid navigation, except in cases of stress and necessity—a claim generally discarded, though still made by Norway. Any liberty to foreigners to fish along the coasts or in the bays of a country, he thought,

[1] *Institutions du Droit de la Nature et des Gens.* [2] *De la Liberté des Mers.*

was a matter of tolerance, founded principally on the supposed abundance of fish; and he held the opinion, which is at variance with that of most other writers,—unless when confined to the territorial zone,—that a state does not lose the right to forbid foreigners from fishing in the waters along its coasts because it at one time allowed them to do so.

Much more definite and restricted was the opinion of a contemporary English lawyer, Chitty, who published a work on the law of nations in 1812.[1] Quoting Vattel, that the whole extent of the sea within cannon-shot of the coast is considered as making part of the territory, and that a vessel taken under the guns of a neutral fortress is not lawful prize, he says that the same doctrine is enforced by Von Martens; and he refers to the decisions in the English Court of Admiralty in the cases of the *Twee Gebroeders* and the *Anna*, which established the principle in English law. Chitty, however, makes no allusion to the three-mile limit as an alternative to the range of guns.

Bynkershoek's principle, and also a fixed distance in place of it, were likewise accepted by Schmalz, Professor of Law in the University of Berlin. Writing in 1817,[2] he declared that the adjacent sea pertained to the neighbouring land as far as it could be defended by cannon from the shore; that this principle had been systematically adopted; and that the distance had been fixed arbitrarily at three marine leagues,[3] —an erroneous statement, no doubt derived from G. F. von Martens, which has been previously referred to,[4] and was copied from one book into another. Two years later another and a greater German authority, Klüber, also adopted the principle of the range of guns, without, however, proposing an equivalent distance in miles.[5] He allowed to the state the waters susceptible of exclusive possession, over which it had acquired, by occupation or convention, and maintained,

[1] *A Practical Treatise on the Law of Nations relative to the Legal Effect of War on the Commerce of Belligerents and Neutrals.* London, 1812.

[2] *Das Europäische Völkerrecht*, Berlin, 1817, p. 141.

[3] "So weit der Schuss des Geschützes vom Ufer es bestreichen möge; dies selbst nahm man mit noch ungebundenerer Will-Kühr auf 3 Lieues an."

[4] P. 564.

[5] *Europäisches Völkerrecht*, Stuttgart, 1821, p. 204; *Droit des Gens moderne de l'Europe*, 1819, III. ii. 130 (ed. 1831).

its sovereignty. Among the parts so comprised are (1) the sea adjoining the continental territory of a state—at all events, "according to the generally received opinion," to the extent to which it can be reached by cannon-shot from the shore; (2) parts extending into the land, as bays and gulfs, which can be commanded by guns on shore; (3) straits which are equally commanded by guns; (4) gulfs, straits, and seas adjoining the continental territory of a state, which, though not entirely under the range of guns on shore, are recognised by other Powers as closed seas—that is, under one dominion, and inaccessible to foreign vessels without permission.

Wheaton, an eminent American jurist, whose first work was published about this time, likewise accepted the principle of cannon range, or, as an alternative, a distance of three miles from the shore.[1] The territorial jurisdiction of a neutral Power, he says, "extends to the ports, harbours, bays, and chambers formed by headlands of the neutral Power. The usual addition allowed to this is a distance of three English miles, or a marine league, or as far as a cannon-shot will carry from the coasts or shore." His statement is based on the decisions in the English Admiralty Court, and on the writings of Vattel, Bynkershoek, Von Martens, and Azuni. In his great treatise on the law of nations, first published in 1836,[2] the same views are expressed, it being stated that the general usage of nations superadds "to bays, ports, &c., a distance of a marine league, or as far as a cannon shot will reach, along all the coasts of the state"; and, incorporating into his text Lord Stowell's observation, he says, "The rule of law on this subject is *terræ dominium finitur, ubi finitur armorum vis*, and since the introduction of fire-arms, that distance has usually been recognised to be about three miles from the shore." Wheaton also states that the exclusive territorial jurisdiction of the British crown over the enclosed parts of the sea along the coasts of Great Britain has immemorially extended to those bays called the "King's Chambers,"[3]

[1] *A Digest of the Law of Maritime Captures or Prizes*, New York, 1815, c. ii. p. 55.

[2] *Elements of International Law*, c. iv. ss. 6-10. London, 1836.

[3] The King's Chambers were, however, confined to the coast of England. See p. 122.

and that a similar jurisdiction is also asserted by the United States over Delaware Bay, and other bays and estuaries forming portions of their territory, and that a state had the exclusive right of fishing within its territorial waters.

Chancellor Kent, who was another high American authority, expressed somewhat different opinions from those of Wheaton, in a treatise published in 1826, and seemed inclined to extend territorial jurisdiction much farther into the sea than the latter writer.[1] The extent of such jurisdiction over the neighbouring sea is, he says, often a question of difficulty and of dubious right, but as far as a nation can conveniently occupy, and that occupancy is acquired by prior possession or treaty, the jurisdiction is exclusive. It is difficult, he states elsewhere, to draw any precise conclusion, amidst the variety of opinion, as to the distance to which a state may lawfully extend its exclusive dominion over the sea adjoining its territories, and beyond harbours, gulfs, bays, and estuaries, where its jurisdiction unquestionably extends. "All that can reasonably be asserted is, that the dominion of the sovereign of the shore over the contiguous sea extends as far as is requisite for his safety, and for some lawful end. A more extended dominion must rest entirely upon force and maritime supremacy. According to the current of modern authority," he continues, "the general territorial jurisdiction extends into the sea as far as cannon-shot will reach, and no farther; and this is generally calculated to be a marine league." These opinions do not differ materially from those of Puffendorf and Vattel, and the tendency of this writer to allow an extended maritime jurisdiction is shown by his statement regarding bays. He holds that the American Government have the right to claim for fiscal and defensive regulations an extensive jurisdiction, and that it would not be unreasonable to assume, "for domestic purposes connected with our safety and welfare," the control of the waters within lines stretching from quite distant headlands, as from Cape Ann to Cape Cod, and from Nantucket to Montauk Point, and from that point to the capes of the Delaware, and from the south cape of Florida to the Mississippi; that is to say, within areas in comparison with which the "King's Chambers" are insignificant,

[1] *Commentaries on American Law*, i. Part I. Lect. iii.

since a straight line from the south cape of Florida to the Mississippi measures about 500 miles, and encloses a tract of sea as much as 180 miles in breath. Kent adds that the Government of the United States would certainly view with uneasiness, in the case of war between other maritime Powers, the use of the waters of the American coast, far beyond the reach of cannon-shot, as cruising ground for belligerent purposes.

Manning, an English publicist, writing a little later,[1] adopts the usual opinion, stating that the distance to which the special right of jurisdiction or the qualified dominion of a state extends on the adjacent sea has been variously measured, the most prevalent distances being those of a cannon-shot or of a marine league from the shore. Heffter, a publicist of high authority, asserting as incontestable the right of all maritime nations, both for defence and for the protection of their commercial and revenue interests, to establish an active surveillance on the neighbouring sea, declares that for these purposes a state has the power of fixing, according to the particular conditions of its coasts and waters, the distance to which its rights shall extend. A common usage, he says, has established the limit at the range of guns, a principle sanctioned by the laws and regulations of many nations. But he maintains with Vattel that the dominion of the state in the adjacent sea extends as far as it is necessary for its security, and it can enforce it,—qualifying this declaration, however, by adopting Rayneval's suggestion that the horizon should be the extreme boundary of the territorial sea. In his opinion the range of guns, although the principle commonly adopted, affords no invariable basis, and the distance may be fixed, at all events provisionally, by the laws of each state: formerly, he adds, it included two leagues, and now usually three marine miles.[2]

A much more restricted view of the extent of the territorial sea was taken by Reddie, an English writer whose work

[1] *Commentaries on the Law of Nations*, p. 119. 1839.

[2] *Das Europäisches Völkerrecht der Gegenwart*, Berlin, 1844. *Le Droit International de l'Europe*, Paris, 1873, s. 75. "La ligne de la portée du canon elle-même, bien qu'elle soit regardée comme de droit commun, ne présente aucune base invariable et peut-être fixée par les lois de chaque État, du moins d'une manière provisoire."

appeared in the same year.[1] He adopted Bynkershoek's doctrine of the range of guns, but makes no mention of the three-mile limit or any other alternative distance. A certain breadth of the adjacent open sea is, he says, necessary for defence and security, and it is that portion within reach of cannon-shot, capable of being protected and commanded by artillery from the land, and thus susceptible of exclusive and permanent dominion, if not of appropriation. Beyond the range of artillery the sea is common; within that range each nation has the right of sovereignty, legislative, judicial, and executive, and the exclusive fishery. This part of the sea cannot be used by nations generally, without diminishing the use or enjoyment of others, and its produce is by no means inexhaustible.

Ortolan, a French publicist of eminence, writing about the same time, not only adopted the principle of Bynkershoek, but affirmed in a positive manner that the extent of the territorial sea should correspond to the actual range of artillery at the time.[2] Although the gunshot limit was the one recognised, there was nothing, he says, to hinder two or more states from fixing between themselves, by treaty, another limit, but such would be binding only on those who were parties to the agreement. Bays and arms of the sea whose shores belong to the same state are also territorial, provided that their width does not exceed twice the actual range of guns, or that the entrance can be commanded by artillery, or is naturally protected by islands, banks, or rocks. Within the territorial sea as thus defined the state has the power of making laws and regulations for its safety, prosperity, and interests, but it has not the right of property,—Ortolan, like so many other writers, drawing a distinction between property and jurisdiction. The opinion that the real range of guns is the true principle for the determination of the extent of the territorial sea was also affirmed by Hautefeuille, another French writer of authority.[3] According to him, it extends to the distance a ball can be actually thrown from

1 *Researches in Maritime International Law*, i. 16. 1844.

2 *Règles Internationales et Diplomatie de la Mer*, i. 177.

3 *Histoire des Origines, des Progrès, et des Variations du Droit Maritime International*, ed. 1858, p. 22.

the shore and no farther. Within the space thus commanded the rights of the state are absolute, both in regard to jurisdiction and property, and even to the prohibition of navigation. The right of fishery is exclusive, since the products of the sea are not inexhaustible, and the pursuit of them requires to be kept under proper regulation. On this view, therefore, the fisheries of right belong to the neighbouring state up to the limit of gunshot from the coast.

Other French writers of authority have maintained the same opinion as to the principle for the delimitation of the territorial waters. Thus, Pistoye and Duverdy[1] state that each Power is able, in a given zone, measured by the range of cannon, to impose its laws and enforce obedience to them. It cannot take bodily possession of the waves, but it can maintain over them direct and constant domination. While there has been much discussion, they say, as to the extent of the territorial sea, the principle upon which its appropriation rests serves also to determine its bounds, "and it must be acknowledged that the range of cannon from the shore is the only real and true boundary of the sea in question."[2] No measure, they add, has been generally agreed upon between different nations as to the distance which the range of guns may be supposed to cover; but they think the eyes of experienced officers on the coast may be trusted to judge how far a given spot is within the distance. Still another French author of repute expressed the same view as to the extent of the territorial sea. Massé, in his elaborate work on commercial law in relation to the law of nations,[3] pointed to the fact that the arbitrary opinions of the older writers had been rejected, and stated that the real basis of delimitation was the range of guns — a distance which he places at "about three miles"; but he says that this rule is not always followed in practice. Bays and gulfs are declared to be undoubtedly part of the territorial sea, even when they are not capable of being defended from the shore.

[1] *Traité des Prises maritimes*, i. 93. Paris, 1855.

[2] "La portée du canon, placé à terre, est la seule limite réelle et vraie des mers territoriales."

[3] *Le Droit commercial dans ses rapports avec le Droit des Gens et le Droit Civil*, Paris, 1844-47, tom. i. Liv. ii. tit. i. c. i. ss. 103-105.

The reasons for this opinion are the same as those advanced by Hubner—namely, that such areas form natural harbours and anchorages, sheltering vessels from tempests: the vessels are thus under the protection of the coasts, and consequently of the sovereign of the coasts. The true boundary in such cases Massé regards as the line joining the headlands, or passing between the islands that may lie off the mouth, even if the distance be greater than the range of guns, or than what has been fixed by convention for an open coast.

It is obvious from the above review of the opinions of publicists in the first half of last century that no complete agreement had been reached in theory or principle respecting the extent of the territorial sea. Many of the writers held to the opinions expressed by Puffendorf, Wolff, and Vattel, which allowed a more or less wide and vague jurisdiction in the neighbouring sea for the security of the state; and most of them refer to the cannon-range limit as the one usually adopted. Few, however, accept the three-mile boundary as an alternative to the range of guns: most of the authors indeed do not even mention it, and those who do, appear to have been guided in the main by Lord Stowell's decisions. On the other hand, the later of the French writers affirm that the boundary of the territorial waters is determined by the actual range of artillery from the shore at the time, which is a virtual repudiation of the three-mile limitation. Their view is summed up by Pistoye and Duverdy when they say that the principle on which the appropriation of the bordering sea rests serves also to determine its bounds—*i.e.*, control and command from the shore.

CHAPTER III.

THE FISHERY CONVENTIONS.

COMPARED with the eighteenth century and the earlier part of the nineteenth, the period which has elapsed since the close of the Napoleonic wars has been singularly free from occurrences raising the question of the extent of the territorial sea in connection with the rights of belligerents and neutrals. There has been no great maritime war in Europe since the enormous advance in the power of artillery rendered the three-mile limit untenable for the security of a neutral state against the operations of belligerents in the sea off its coasts, though some questions involving the inadequacy of that limit came to the front during the civil war in America. The chief questions affecting the boundary of the territorial waters were concerned with sea fisheries, and several conventions were made between European nations in which limits were fixed for exclusive fishing. They originated in the perennial disputes between British and foreign fishermen.

In previous chapters it has been shown that the intermittent efforts of the British Government to establish an exclusive right to the fisheries along the coasts of this country were without definite result, except that it came to be tacitly understood by the Dutch fishermen that they should keep out of sight of the shore. At various times during the eighteenth century complaints were made to the Government of the encroachments of Dutch, French, and Danish fishermen along our coasts and in the Channel, and representations were in several instances made to the foreign Government concerned. An examination of these complaints shows that in many cases the foreigners were alleged to fish within the bays and close to the shore, destroying the spawn and brood of fish. In other cases they were accused of fishing in British waters when they were between three and four, or even between six and seven, miles from the coast,—the real ground of complaint being that they occupied the localities where the fish were most abundant, and where the native fishermen mostly carried on their industry.[1] From causes previously described, the number of Dutch fishermen frequenting the British coasts diminished very much during the eighteenth century, while at the same time French fishermen, and on the coast of Scotland also Danes and Prussians, as well as fishermen from the Austrian Netherlands, came in increasing numbers. During the war with France and Holland the fishermen of these nations were unable to pursue their fishing on the British coasts. But shortly after the restoration of peace they returned, and complaints of their encroachments, especially on the coast of Scotland and the south coast of England, soon became prevalent. In 1819 the Board of British White Herring Fishery received numerous complaints of foreign, and more particularly Dutch, herring-busses shooting their nets too near the coasts, and committing depredations on the lines and nets of the native fishermen. The Board were urged to prevent foreigners from fishing "within a certain distance" of the shore; but they considered they had no power to do so, and forwarded copies of the petitions to the Lords of the Treasury. The clamour continued, and in 1821, and again in 1822, the Board strongly recommended the Government to take action. In the latter year the Government made representations on the subject to the Government of the Netherlands; and as a result a royal decree was issued in 1824 by the King of the Netherlands prohibiting Dutch fishermen from fishing on the main coast of Scotland, or even, in the absence of urgent necessity, from approaching it within a distance of two leagues, twenty making a degree, or twice the limit of three miles.[2]

[1] *Plans and Proposals transmitted to the Committee on the Fishery*, No. 1, &c.

[2] *Reports by the Commissioners for the British Herring Fishery* for 1819, 1821, 1822; *Staatsblad*, No. 28, 4th April 1824, for a copy of which I am indebted to Mr H. van Hall, of the Universiteits-Bibliotheek, Amsterdam. After a reference to the previous decrees prohibiting the taking of herrings "between the banks and rocks of Scotland," as being injurious to the reputation of Dutch pickled herrings (see p. 201), it is stated that the Board for the Great Fishery is of opinion that, in the

In 1827—and thus only twelve years before the Anglo-French convention fixed a three-mile limit—this Dutch ordinance was renewed, and from that time few complaints were made of the encroachments of Dutch herring-busses on the Scottish coast. They continued to conduct their herring fishery, for the most part, at distances ranging from twelve or fourteen to forty or fifty miles, as they still do at the present day.

As the disputes with the Dutch fishermen were thus amicably arranged by the recognition of a six-mile zone of reserved water, similar contentions sprang up, and continued for a long period, with fishermen from France. In 1824, some years after the peace, they began to frequent the coast of Scotland, and they came in great numbers in each succeeding year, fishing at the Shetlands, Orkneys, and along the north and east coasts from Cape Wrath to Berwick, and down the English coast as far as Flamborough Head.[1] Several circumstances connected with the French fishery tended to provoke disputes. While the Dutch fished from their busses at a distance from the coast, where the largest and best herrings were caught, and were forbidden under heavy penalties from buying or selling herrings while at sea, or even from entering any foreign port except by reason of urgent necessity, the French fished, as a rule, near the shore from small boats, which they even hired for the season, not uncommonly from Scotch fishermen. They frequented the Scottish ports; they bought herrings in large quantities surreptitiously from native boats engaged to local fish-curers, for

interest of this branch of national industry, the fishing should be carried on at a farther distance from the main coast of Scotland (*Schotsche vaste kust*), and it is determined and resolved as follows: "Art. I. Het zal aan geenen Nederlandschen visscher geoorloofd zijn, de groote of pekelharingvisscherij op eenen naderen afstand der vaste kust van Schotland uitteoefenen, dan dien van twee uren hemelsbreedte (20 zoodanige uren eenen graad uitmakende), noch onder eenig voorwendsel hoe ook genaamd (alleen met uitzondering van het geval van dringende noodzakelijkheid bij art. 22 der voormelde wet voorzien), gedurende den tijd dat hij de vangst van pekelharing bedrijft, de vermelde kust op eenen minderen afstand te naderen." The second article excepted the fishing at Shetland (Hitland) and Fair Isle (Fairhill), the autumn fishing on the English coast and off Yarmouth, and the fresh-herring fishery; but these exceptions were withdrawn by a royal decree of 5th June 1827 (*Staatscourant*, 1827, No. 278). It may be said that in 1818 the old prohibition of fishing between the sandbanks and rocks of Norway, Shetland, and Scotland had been renewed. *Staatsblad*, No. 15, 12th March 1818.

[1] *Rapport fait en Exécution des Ordres du Ministre de la Marine*, par M. L. de Montaignac, Capitaine de frégate, Commandant la Station de la Mer du Nord.

money, brandy, tobacco, biscuits, and other articles; and they were allowed to dry their nets, and even sometimes to salt their herrings, on shore for a small payment.[1] They were thus intimately associated with the native fishermen along the coast, and they carried on their fishery near the shore in the waters which were mostly used by the natives.

In the English Channel disputes between British and French fishermen were still more frequent and acrimonious. British naval supremacy during the long war had given a monopoly of the fisheries to the people of the English coast, but after peace was concluded French fishermen swarmed in the Channel, and began to fish along the English shores. Complaints became rife of the decadence of the English fisheries, owing to the alleged encroachments of the French and a general diminution in the abundance of fish. In 1833 a Select Committee of the House of Commons was appointed to inquire into the state of the British Channel fisheries and the laws affecting the fishing trade of England, with a view to their amendment. After taking evidence, the Committee reported that they found those fisheries, and the interests connected with them, to be in a very depressed and declining state; that the decline had begun with the peace in 1815; that the number of fishermen and boats had diminished; and that the fishermen and their families were indigent.[2]

The principal causes of the depression were found to be the extensive interference and aggressions of the French fishermen on the coasts of Kent and Sussex, the large quantity of foreign-caught fish illegally imported, and the great decrease and comparative scarcity of fish in the Channel. Large fleets of French fishing vessels from Calais, Boulogne, Dieppe, and other ports were in the habit of fishing along the English coasts, frequently within half a league of the shore, and occasionally nearer, as well as in the bays and shallow waters, "in which," said the Committee, "it is particularly necessary for the preservation of the brood of fish, that such as frequent those waters during the breeding season should not be dis-

[1] Montaignac, *op. cit.*; *Parl. Papers*, Sess. 1837-38; *Rep. Com. Brit. Herring Fishery*, 1834.

[2] *Report from the Select Committee on British Channel Fisheries, Parl. Papers*, Sess. 1833, No. 676.

turbed, or their young destroyed before they have attained maturity." The French fishing vessels were more numerous and larger than the English boats,—between two and three hundred coming from Boulogne alone,—and they had caused great injury to the nets and gear of the English fishermen, especially in the herring and mackerel seasons. At other times of the year it was proved that they were in the habit of coming in great numbers every morning into English bays, and dragging there for bait in the shallow waters close upon the shore, taking and destroying an immense quantity of young and unsizeable fish, at periods when they were prevented by French laws from conducting similar operations in their own bays.[1] These laws, the Committee reported, were understood to be enforced also against English fishermen within three leagues of the coast of France; on approaching nearer they were warned off by French cruisers, and told that they would not be allowed to fish within that distance.

The Committee considered it to be proved that the scarcity of fish in the Channel (with the exception of herrings and mackerel) had been occasioned by the great destruction of the spawn and brood of fish in the shallow waters. They recommended as remedies for the evil "that foreign fishermen should be prevented at all seasons of the year from fishing within one league, or such other distance of the English coast, as by the law or usage of nations is considered to belong exclusively to this country," and that they should also be required to observe, during the spawning or breeding season of fish, all such laws or regulations as might be imposed upon English fishermen for the better preservation of the spawn and brood of fish in the bays and shallow waters on the coast.[2] In order to accomplish these objects, they

[1] An ordinance of the French Marine Department, of 15th January 1829, prohibited the use of certain nets, as drag and trawl nets, within *three leagues* of the shore from 15th April to 1st September, and within two leagues from 1st September to 15th April.

[2] Some of the English fishery Acts then in force, at least nominally, extended jurisdiction beyond the distance of one league with regard to the use of certain nets, &c., and the Committee apparently desired that, besides a zone of exclusive fishery, foreigners should be bound to observe the municipal law for the protection of the spawn and brood of fish that might apply beyond such zone. The Acts referred to were 3 Jac. I., c. 12 (1605), for the better preservation of sea fish,

recommended that customs and revenue officers and the commanders of cruisers should be instructed to prevent foreign fishermen from fishing "within such prohibited distance of the shore," to enforce the observance by foreigners as well as by subjects of our fishery laws and regulations, and to protect the English fishermen from aggression at sea.

The Committee had considerable difficulty in arriving at their conclusion respecting the limit which should be fixed for exclusive fishing on the English coast. They were influenced partly by what they understood to be the usage, that the sea for one marine league from the shore was considered to be the territory of the adjoining country, partly by the practice of the Customs' authorities in connection with the prevention of smuggling, and partly by considerations affecting the preservation of the fry and brood of fish. Under the Customs' regulations, vessels and boats of certain descriptions, including fishing-boats, required a license, and the Commissioners of Customs had discretionary power[1] to prescribe within what distance of the English coast they might be employed. In some cases fishing-boats were restricted to a distance of four leagues, in other instances they were allowed to fish to within one league of a foreign coast, one league of sea being regarded by the Customs' authorities as belonging to the territory of the adjacent country. With regard to the right of fishing, however, it was generally understood among the English fishermen that the limit on the French coast reserved for French fishermen was three leagues; and they desired that the same limit should be applied on the English coast. The Committee laid great stress on the fixing of a limit of exclusive fishing in order to preserve the spawn and brood of fish. It was universally believed, and stated by all the witnesses, including Mr James Cornish, an ich-

which, *inter alia*, prohibited the use of certain nets within five miles of any harbour, haven, or creek; 14 Chas. II., c. 28 (1662), regulating the pilchard-fishing in Devon and Cornwall, which prohibited the use of any "drift, trammel, or stream net," between 1st June and 30th November, within one and a half leagues of the coasts of these counties; 1 George I., stat. 2, c. 18 (1714), which prohibited the use "at sea upon the coast of England" of certain nets, and the landing or sale of undersized fish; the Act 33 Geo. III., c. 27 (1759), prohibited the taking or knowingly possessing "any spawn, fry, or brood of fish, or any unsizeable fish, or any fish out of season."

[1] Under the Act 6 Geo. IV., c. 108, 1825.

thyologist of repute, that the fish spawned in the shallow water near the shore,—an erroneous opinion that has prevailed almost to the present day, but which was shown to be incorrect by the observations made by the Fishery Board for Scotland[1] and others.

It was deemed to be of great importance that the breeding fish, and the eggs which they were supposed to deposit near the shore, should be protected from alleged injurious modes of fishing; and the Committee recommended statutory enactments to establish close-times, and to prohibit the use of trawl or drag nets within a league from the shore or in water less than ten fathoms in depth. They inquired carefully as to the limit which would be sufficient for this purpose. Most of the fishermen were of opinion that the distance of one league would be sufficient to include the "breeding-grounds," and bring them under the protection of the law; but they held that the distance should be measured not from the shore, following its sinuosities, but from a straight line drawn from one headland to another,—an opinion with which the Committee concurred.

No immediate action was taken by the Government to establish a definite boundary for exclusive fishing, and petitions and memorials continued to pour in from various parts

[1] Mr Cornish, quoting from his MS. treatise on zoology, said: "It is generally supposed that all sea fish, the cetaceous (*sic*) and cartilaginous excepted, deposit their ova in sand-banks, in creeks, bays, and shallow water near the shores, because it is imagined that a certain, though a small, degree of the sun's action on the water and atmosphere is necessary to bring such ova to maturity. This we know to be the case with the salmon species, which always ascend to the shallow parts of rivers for that purpose, and never lay their eggs in deep water, and therefore we infer that the same influence prevails over the sea fish: this cannot, however, be proved, and rests mainly on opinion and probable conjecture, founded on such facts as we are acquainted with." It may be said that a Select Committee of the House of Commons, appointed in 1817 to inquire into the condition of the fisheries on the south coast of Devon, strongly recommended Parliamentary action for the protection of the fisheries, founding on the same erroneous assumption that the fishes spawned near the shore. A Bill was accordingly introduced in the session of 1819, and again in 1822, for the appointment of conservators or overseers of the bays, creeks, and arms of the sea, to supervise regulations for the preservation of the fish coming there to spawn, and of their brood and fry, and applying to a distance of one and a half leagues from the shore; but it did not pass the Lords. *Rep. Select Com. on the State and Condition of the Fisheries on the South Coast of Devon*, 1817; *Parl. Bills*, xxii. 587, 601. *Eighth Ann. Rep. Fishery Board for Scotland*, Part III., pp. 13, 258 (1890); *Tenth, ibid.*, pp. 19, 235; *Eleventh, ibid.*, p. 13.

of the coast complaining of the depredations of French fishermen. They were accused of interfering with British fishermen engaged in dredging for oysters fifteen miles from the shores of France; of fishing for herrings and mackerel within less than a mile of the British coasts, compelling the native fishermen to shoot their nets to the seawards of them; of maliciously destroying fishing gear, and of recklessly extirpating the spawn and brood of fish in the shallow waters along the English coast. The Government were urged to give effect to the recommendations of the Committee of 1833, and they were asked by the Commissioners for the Herring Fishery to issue instructions to the naval superintendent in Scotland to prevent the encroachments complained of.[1]

From a perusal of these petitions it is evident that much doubt existed at the time, not only in the minds of fishermen but among many in authority, as to what was the precise limit of exclusive fishery that might be claimed or enforced. As a general rule, it was believed to extend much farther than a league from the shore. Many fishermen maintained that the boundary was three leagues, an opinion strongly held in Scotland as late as 1862. The fishermen of Eyemouth, probably influenced by traditions of the extent of the "reserved waters" in earlier times, asked that foreigners should be "kept without the limits prescribed by law, and that limits (*sic*) be seven leagues," declaring that they went that distance themselves, and were annoyed and endangered by foreign vessels taking up the ground.

On the part of French fishermen there were also numerous complaints against the English, the most bitter referring to the dredging for oysters off the French coast. In 1837 a mixed commission was appointed by the British and French Governments in connection with these complaints, and especially to ascertain and define the limits within which the subjects of the two countries respectively should be at liberty to fish for oysters between Jersey and the neighbour-

[1] Memorials, &c., received by Her Majesty's Government since 1st January 1832, complaining of the Aggressions of French fishermen on the British Coasts, *Parl. Papers*, Sess. 1837-38; Supplementary Papers relative to the Complaints respecting the Aggressions of French fishermen on the British Coasts, 1838, *ibid.*, 1839; *Reports by the Commissioners for the Herring Fishery*, for 1834, 1835, 1839.

ing coast of France. The opportunity was taken at the same time "to define and regulate the limits within which the general right of fishery on all parts of the coasts of the two countries shall be exclusively reserved to the subjects of Great Britain and of France respectively," and a convention was concluded at Paris in 1839 defining these rights.[1] By its articles a very considerable stretch of water containing oyster-beds, in the Bay of Granville on the French coast, between Cape Carteret and Point Meinga, south-east of Jersey, and extending far beyond the three-mile limit, was reserved exclusively for French fishermen, the boundaries being minutely defined and laid down on a chart annexed to the convention; and British fishermen were prohibited from carrying on any kind of fishing, even for floating fish, within this area. The bay thus appropriated is over seventeen miles in breadth, and the closing line passes in some places about fourteen miles from the shore.[2] This concession to France was a recognition of the principle that fisheries of this nature—that is, for objects which are attached to or stationary on the bottom—require special treatment.

The article defining the general fishery limit on the coasts of the two countries was as follows:—

"ARTICLE IX. The subjects of Her Britannic Majesty shall enjoy the exclusive right of fishery within the distance of three miles from low-water mark, along the whole extent of the coasts of the British Islands; and the subjects of the King of the French shall enjoy the exclusive right of fishery within the distance of three miles from low-water mark, along the whole extent of the coasts of France; it being understood that upon that part of the coast of France which lies between Cape Carteret and Point Meinga, French subjects shall enjoy the exclusive right of all kinds of fishery within

---

[1] *Convention between Her Majesty and the King of the French, defining and regulating the Limits of the Exclusive Right of the Oyster and other Fishery on the Coasts of Great Britain and of France.* Signed at Paris, August 2, 1839.

[2] The line of closure, as will be seen from fig. 16, was not a single straight line, as usual, but a series of lines determined by landmarks. The area between this series and the three-mile limit, from which British fishermen were excluded, measures a little over 100 square (geographical) miles. On the other hand, all of the closing line north of 49° 3′ (and thus the greater part of it) is, curiously, *within* the three-mile zone; the area outside this line to the three-mile line is about 23 square miles.

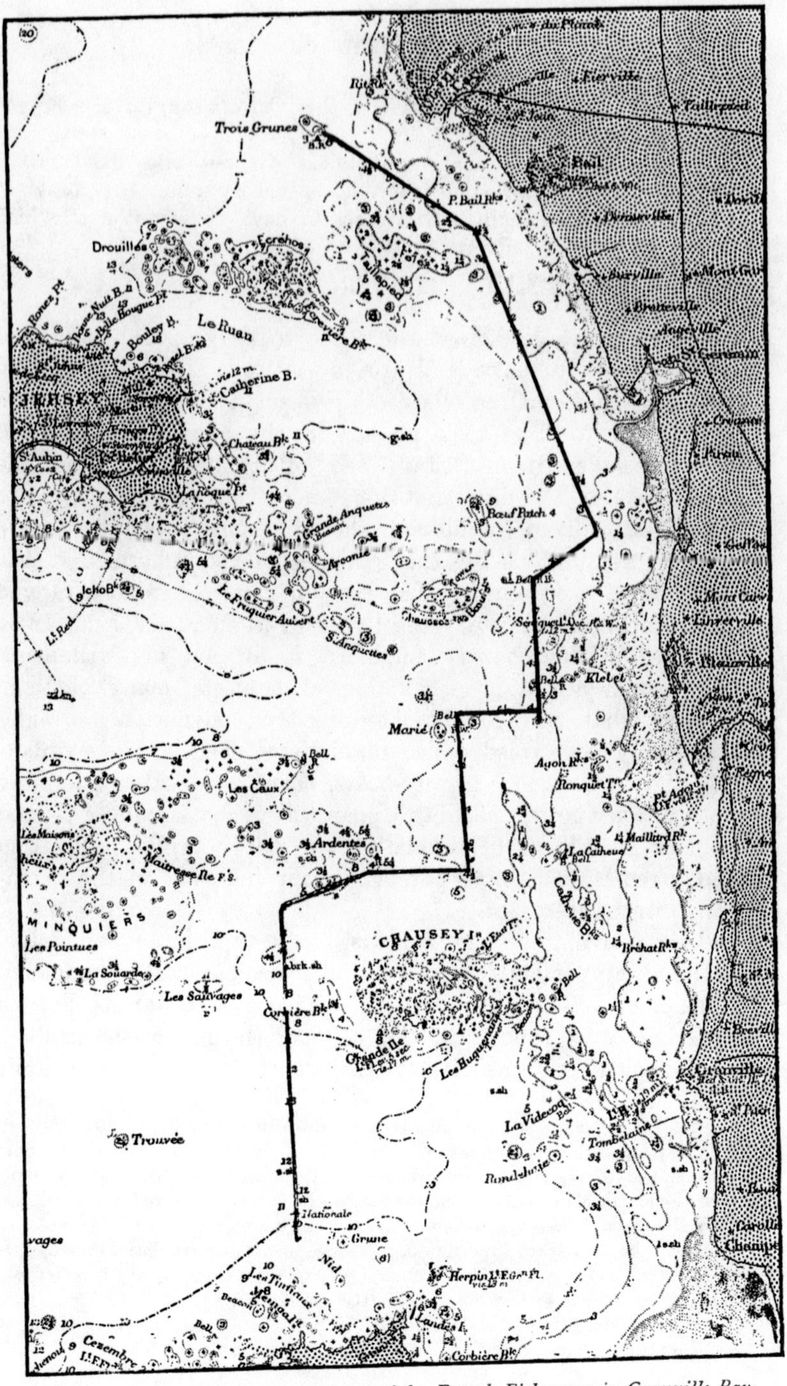

Fig. 16.—*Showing the Limits reserved for French Fishermen in Granville Bay.*

the limits assigned in Article I. of this Convention, for the French oyster fishery.

It is equally agreed, that the distance of three miles fixed as the general limit for the exclusive right of fishery upon the coasts of the two countries shall, with respect to bays, the mouths of which do not exceed ten miles in width, be measured from a straight line drawn from headland to headland."

The next article defined the miles to be geographical miles, of which sixty make a degree of latitude; and it was also provided that with a view to prevent the collisions which from time to time took place "on the seas lying between the coasts of Great Britain and of France," between the trawlers and the line and long-net fishermen of the two countries, a mixed commission should be appointed to prepare a set of regulations for the guidance of the fishermen in the seas above mentioned. The code of regulations so arranged was confirmed by the respective Governments in June 1843, and was in this country embodied in an Act of Parliament. They embraced a large number of subjects, many of them beyond what was contemplated in the convention. Besides what may be termed police regulations, such as the numbering and lettering of fishing-boats, there were others defining and restricting the fishing apparatus to be employed;[1] and all this machinery of regulation was to be applied to British and French fishermen pursuing their industry in the extra-territorial waters.

This convention was the first to establish by an international agreement the three-mile limit as the boundary of exclusive fishing on the British coasts, so far as French fishermen were concerned. In view of the numerous conflicts and disputes, it was clearly of importance that some limit

[1] 6 & 7 Vict., cap. 79. "An Act to carry into Effect the Convention between Her Majesty and the King of the French concerning the Fisheries in the Seas between the British Islands and France," 22nd August 1843. The mesh of trawl-nets, the length of the trawl-beam, the weight of the trawl-irons and of the ground-rope, the mesh of herring, mackerel, "bratt," and trammel nets, were in no case to be over or under a specified standard. A series of detailed regulations for oyster-fishing was also made, including a close-time and a minimum size. This Act was repealed by the Sea Fisheries Act, 1868 (the Convention Act), 31 & 32 Vict., c. 45, but it was revived by Parliament in 1877 (40 & 41 Vict., c. 42), the Convention of 1867 not having been ratified by France.

should be precisely fixed, but the selection of so narrow a strip of the adjacent sea was in some respects unfortunate, and has probably acted injuriously on the interests of the sea fisheries. It was imposed, no doubt, partly because it was the limit already recognised in England and America as bounding the territorial seas for the purposes of neutrality, and because it was deemed sufficient to afford protection to the breeding fishes and fish-spawn, one of the objects the Parliamentary Committee had in view in recommending it.

The disputes between the fishermen of the two nations were not set at rest by the convention. Numerous infringements of the new boundary of exclusive fishing occurred, and the difficulty of causing it to be respected was for many years considerable.[1] As many as twenty-one French vessels were seized and taken into Berwick at one time for transgressing the limit, and the convention was naturally not looked upon with favour in certain French seaports.[2] Nor was it generally regarded among the fishery classes in this country as a triumph of diplomacy. In Scotland it was thought that the British Government had made a very bad bargain in parting with the exclusive right to fish for herrings beyond a limit of only three miles instead of three leagues, the boundary maintained to be the "legal" and just distance, for the sake of obtaining, as it was supposed, some fancied advantage for the English oyster fishermen.[3]

The convention, moreover, was binding only on French and British subjects. It left unsettled the limit in relation to other nations, and the inconvenience of this was shown by the action of Belgian fishermen. While the French were excluded from the three-mile zone, the Belgians not only fished within it, but in many cases they anchored their vessels in the Scottish harbours and bays and fished in the neighbouring waters from their small boats. In 1848 the commis-

[1] *Reports of the Commissioners for the Herring Fishery*, 1839, 1840, 1841.

[2] It was denounced in the Boulogne Chamber of Commerce as the greatest blunder the French Government had ever made, and many complaints were received from French fishermen of their boats having been captured or pursued by British cruisers. Deseille, *Histoire de la Pêche à Boulogne-sur-Mer*, 229. The French cruisers were no less active in apprehending British transgressors. *Parl. Papers*, Sess. 1854-5, 459.

[3] Mitchell, *The Herring: Its Natural History and National Importance*, 243.

sioners for the British fisheries brought the question before the Board of Trade, and they were advised to enforce the boundary laid down in the Anglo-French convention with respect to Belgian and all other foreign boats also.[1] Against this procedure strong remonstrances were made by the Belgian fishermen, and these were followed by representations from the Belgian Government. The Fishery Commissioners, who were anxious that the law in regard to foreigners fishing on our coasts should be made clear, continued to press the matter. The Belgian fishermen then produced to the naval superintendent a copy of the charter that had been granted by King Charles II., in 1666, to the citizens of Bruges,[2] under which they claimed equal privileges with British subjects. That charter appears to have been generally regarded as fictitious; but, acting on the advice of the Queen's Advocate, the Board of Trade directed that for the ensuing season of 1851 Belgians should be allowed to fish on the same system as before, but that afterwards this liberty should cease, except in the case of such as had been able to prove special privileges under the asserted charter in the English courts of law. The dispute was settled by a convention between Great Britain and Belgium in 1852, in which, without mention of any specified limit, it was stipulated that

[1] The Board pointed out that the fishermen of other foreign countries were not disposed to observe the limits laid down in the Anglo-French convention, specifying Dutch as well as Belgians, and that the naval superintendents were perplexed from the want of fixed instructions on this point. The letter from the Board of Trade was as follows (*Report of the Commissioners for the year ended* 5*th January* 1849):—

"OFFICE OF COMMITTEE OF PRIVY-COUNCIL FOR TRADE,
"WHITEHALL, 14*th September* 1848.

"SIR,—With reference to your letter of 4th ultimo, requesting, on the part of the Commissioners of British Fisheries, to know whether Foreign Fishermen are permitted to fish within three miles of the Shore; I am directed by the Lords of the Committee of Privy-Council for Trade, to inform you, that it is the opinion of this Board, that no such permission is recognised by the British Government, and accordingly, that it is the duty of the Superintendents of British Fisheries, to warn Dutch, Belgian, or any other Foreigners, as well as French Fishermen, to keep outside of the limits above mentioned.—I am, sir, your obedient servant,

(Sd.) DENIS LE MARCHANT.

The Honourable B. F. PRIMROSE, Secretary,
Board of Fisheries, Edinburgh.

[2] See p. 461.

Belgian fishermen should enjoy the same rights of fishing on the coasts of the United Kingdom as the most favoured foreign nation, and, in like manner, that British subjects should enjoy corresponding rights on the coast of Belgium.[1] This convention was more beneficial to Belgium than to us, as the Fishery Commissioners pointed out, owing to the extent of the respective coasts conceded for fishing, but it was thought to be satisfactory, inasmuch as defined rights were substituted for vague and disputed privileges. Nevertheless, as the Belgian Minister remonstrated that sufficient time had not been afforded for trying in the British courts the validity of the charter "alleged" to have been granted to the fishing vessels of Bruges, the vessels of that port were allowed for one season more (namely, 1852) the privilege of using the Scottish harbours for their fishing vessels and of fishing from them with small boats.[2] When the authorities attempted in 1852 to enforce the convention against Belgian vessels other than those of Bruges, by excluding them from our harbours, so much dissatisfaction was caused that the Belgian Minister again appealed to the British Government, and the restriction was relaxed for another year for all Belgian boats, so that the enforcement of the three-mile limit against them did not come into operation till 1853.

The violations of the boundary by French vessels, above referred to, continued for many years, and the disputes were sometimes so frequent and serious as to occasion the employment of seven or eight gunboats on the east coast of Scotland to maintain the law. Yet the three-mile limit, as the Commissioners declared, was but "a slender privilege" to retain for the native fishermen. "The extent of it," they truly said, "when looked at from the sea appears small indeed,

1 Convention between Her Majesty and the King of the Belgians relative to Fishery. Signed at London, March 22, 1852. "Art. I. Belgian subjects shall enjoy, in regard to fishery along the coast of the United Kingdom of Great Britain and Ireland, the treatment of the most favoured foreign nation. In like manner, British subjects shall enjoy, in regard to fishery along the coast of the Kingdom of Belgium, the treatment of the most favoured foreign nation." The convention was to endure for seven years, and it was to remain in force thereafter until the expiry of twelve months after either party notified to the other its intention of terminating it.

2 *Reports by the Commissioners for the British Fisheries*, 1848-51. *Parl. Papers*, Sess. 1856.

seeming but a narrow slip lying close under the high cliffs of the land, and when it is taken into account that the whole sea outside is free to every comer, whether British or foreign, the slight boundary within shore ought to be strictly kept." Sometimes, however, the French were accused of infringing the limit from a common misconception on the part of our fishermen that the boundary was the traditional one of three leagues or nine miles, instead of only three miles. Upon explanation, they admitted their misapprehension, "but," said the Commissioners, "with a significant expression of their wish that it had been leagues instead of miles."

The French herring vessels swarmed chiefly about Berwick and the coast of Northumberland, and in 1853 a question of the limit at the Farne Isles was raised by the French commodore. He interpreted the words of the convention (which did not specify islands) as meaning that the three miles was to be measured from low-water mark on the mainland, which would have allowed the French to fish close to the islands. The British naval superintendent, on the other hand, held that the limit extended to three miles from low-water mark on the islands as well, but, pending a legal opinion, he released two French vessels he had seized for fishing within that distance from them. The Queen's Advocate decided in favour of the latter interpretation, and the point does not appear to have been again raised.[1] The infringement of the boundary by the French gradually became less frequent, and in 1867 it was reported that they had begun to fish at a greater distance from the coast than formerly, and even out of sight of land.

At this time it was found to be desirable to conclude another fishery convention with France. Nearly all the elaborate regulations under the convention of 1839 had turned out to be unworkable or were disregarded, and much difference of opinion existed as to what actually were "the seas lying between the British Islands and France" to which they applied.[2] In this second convention, in 1867, the ex-

[1] *Reports of the Commissioners for the British Fisheries*, 1852, 1853, 1862.

[2] *Report of the Commissioners appointed to Enquire into the Sea Fisheries of the United Kingdom*, I. lxix. (1866).

clusive fishery limits of the two countries were defined as in the convention of 1839, and the boundaries of the large area in the Bay of Granville or Cancale, reserved for French fishermen, were precisely the same as before.[1] The international "extra-territorial" regulations under this convention were much less detailed than in the previous one. Fishing beyond the reserved limits was to be entirely free, with the exception that a close-time for oysters was established for the English Channel. The police regulations were to apply to "the seas surrounding and adjoining Great Britain and Ireland," and adjoining the Atlantic coast of France, between the frontiers of Belgium and Spain. The conditions under which the fishing-boats of one nation might enter the exclusive fishery limits of the other, such as by stress of weather, were carefully specified; and each boat while there was to hoist a blue flag, and was again to leave as soon as the exceptional circumstances had ceased. The convention was to continue in force for ten years, and afterwards from year to year, terminable on twelve months' notice. But, although confirmed by an Act of the British Parliament, in 1868,[2] it was not ratified by France, and its provisions never came into practical operation, except with regard to the close-time for oysters, owing to certain objections raised by the French Government.[3] Certain of its provisions, includ-

[1] *Convention between Her Majesty and the Emperor of the French, relative to the Fisheries in the seas between Great Britain and France.* Signed at Paris, 11th November 1867. Art. I. "British fishermen shall enjoy the exclusive right of fishery within the distance of three miles from low-water mark, along the whole extent of the coasts of the British Islands; and French fishermen shall enjoy the exclusive right of fishery within the distance of three miles from low-water mark along the whole extent of the coast of France, the only exception to this rule being that part of the coast of France which lies between Cape Carteret and Point Meinga. The distance of three miles fixed as the general limit for the exclusive right of fishery upon the coasts of the two countries shall, with respect to bays, the mouths of which do not exceed ten miles in width, be measured from a straight line drawn from headland to headland. The miles mentioned in the present Convention are geographical miles, whereof sixty make a degree of latitude." In neither of the conventions was it expressly said that the ten-mile closing-line for bays was to be measured from low-water mark of the headlands, but it was so declared in the Act of 1843, 6 & 7 Vict., c. 79.

[2] 31 & 32 Vict., c. 45.

[3] *London Gazette*, 9th Feb. 1869. C. E. Fryer, *The Relation of the State with Fishermen and Fisheries. Parl. Papers, Commerc.*, 24 (1882), p. 1.

ing, amongst others, the article in the convention defining the exclusive fishery limits, were repealed by the Sea Fisheries Act, 1883.[1]

Both conventions, as we have seen, dealt with oyster fisheries in a special manner, and on the coast of France a large area, extending much beyond the three-mile limit, was reserved to French fishermen on account of the valuable oyster-grounds it contained. An interesting point was raised by the Irish authorities. It happened that Ireland also possessed productive and extensive oyster-beds on the coast of Wexford, stretching for many miles beyond the exclusive fishery limits laid down in the convention, and the Irish authorities claimed the right of control over the whole of them. They had enforced regulations there before the first convention with France, in 1839, had been entered into, and at that time they protested against its application to Ireland. Accordingly, in the Act of 1843 giving effect to the convention, a clause was inserted empowering the Board of Trade, with the sanction of the Privy Council, to suspend the operation of the convention in Ireland or any part thereof, so long as the fisheries there should be carried on exclusively by British subjects, and also to make bye-laws for enforcing the Act as soon as French boats frequented Irish waters for the purpose of fishing.[2] On the day following the passing of the Act an Order in Council was issued directing "that the said Act and articles of regulation shall be suspended with respect to the fisheries of the whole coasts of Ireland, so long as such fisheries shall be carried on exclusively by the subjects of Her Majesty."

The matter was again raised in connection with the convention of 1867, and it was associated with a recent act of jurisdiction by the Irish authorities beyond the three-mile limit. Some Welsh boats which had been dredging for oysters on the coast of Wexford, at a distance, it was said, of four or five miles from the shore, were arrested, taken to Wexford, the fishermen fined, and the oysters forfeited. The Board of Trade thereupon asked the Irish Department, with reference to an Act that had been passed in 1842 to regulate the Irish fisheries,[3] to state what were "the limits of the Act to regulate

[1] 46 & 47 Vict., c. 22, sec. 30.

[2] 6 & 7 Vict., c. 79, s. vi.

[3] 5 & 6 Vict., c. 106.

Irish fisheries" in pursuance of the provisions of which they presumed they had acted, and "whether the oysters in question were captured within those limits." The reply was that the oysters were taken two and a half miles from the shore, but that the most extensive and valuable oyster-beds on the east coast of Ireland lay at a distance of from five to ten miles from and parallel to the shore, and so far as they, or any other beds, were "within the reach of ordinary shore boats, and were habitually frequented by and afforded the means of living to a shore population, the Commissioners conceive they are justly entitled to be considered Irish beds, and to come within their control."[1]

The Irish Members of Parliament strenuously supported this contention, and they succeeded in getting a clause inserted in the Convention Act of 1868 enabling the Irish Commissioners, with the approval of the Queen in Council, to regulate the dredging for oysters on any oyster-beds situated within the distance of twenty miles seawards from a straight line between Lambay Island and Carnsore Point—an area of nearly 1300 square (geographical) miles, outside the three-mile limit, including the Arklow and Wexford banks, and stretching from twelve and a half to nineteen miles beyond the ordinary limit. All such regulations were to "apply equally to all boats and persons on whom they might be binding," and they were binding "on all British sea-fishing boats, and on any other sea-fishing boats in that behalf specified in the Order, and on the crews of such boats."[2] By an Order in Council, dated 29th April 1869, regulations were made under this section of the Act appointing a close-time; but no other boats than British boats were therein specified.[3]

In the interval between the two conventions with France, referred to above, there were some other treaties that dealt with territorial waters to which allusion may be made. The provisions of the treaty of 1818 with the United States respecting the fishery rights on the coasts of the British dominions in America (see p. 581) had given rise to disputes, and in particular the words "within three marine miles of any of the coasts,

[1] *Parl. Papers*, Sess. 1867-68, Fisheries (Ireland), 135.

[2] 31 & 32 Vict., c. 45, s. 67.

[3] *Report from the Select Committee on Oyster Fisheries*, 8, 166 (1876).

bays, creeks, or harbours." This was interpreted by the British and Colonial Governments as meaning that the boundary of three miles was to be drawn, not everywhere along the coast following all its sinuosities, but, where bays or creeks existed, from a straight line passing from one headland to another across their mouth or entrance—that is, according to the principle now known as the headland doctrine. The United States, on the other hand, generally contended that the words meant that the three-mile limit was to be measured everywhere along the coast from the line of the shore, following it in all its curves and indents, thus eliminating altogether any special treatment for inlets or bays, and dealing with all parts of the coast as if it were an open coast. There is little doubt that the British interpretation was the correct one. This is evident from the previous usage with regard to bays as shown by the rules relating to the King's Chambers and the practice of the Admiralty Court in England, and the reserved firths in Scotland, and by the claim advanced by the United States with respect to neutral rights in 1806. It is also evident from the language of previous treaties. That of 1686 between France and Great Britain referred to "havens, bays, creeks, roads, shoals, or places"; in that of 1783 between Great Britain and the United States, "coasts, bays, and creeks" are spoken of; and in that between the same Powers in 1794, with respect to neutral rights, it was agreed that ships should not be taken "within cannon-shot of the coast, nor in any of the bays, ports, or rivers of their territories." It is clear that a distinction was drawn between coasts and bays—a distinction which is now and always has been recognised in international law, which is made in the North Sea and other fishery conventions of recent times, and is claimed by the United States with regard to their own coasts.[1] If no such

[1] Had the coasts of the United States been visited by British fishermen, it is not unlikely that the Government of that country would have been more willing to admit the ordinary interpretation with regard to bays. British vessels do not, however, fish on the coasts of the United States, and the United States fishermen, having exhausted the once productive waters of their own coasts of the New England States, go to catch a large part of their fish to the waters on the coasts of British North America, and hence it is to their interest that the limit of exclusive fishing on the latter should be as small as they can get it made. The position is very similar to that of the English trawlers who, having impoverished the North Sea, now go to foreign coasts, as Iceland, to keep up the supplies. See p. 707.

distinction between coast and bays was meant in the clause of the treaty of 1818, then the words "bays, creeks, and harbours" are without meaning and superfluous, a construction which is contrary to the rule which requires that effect be given to every word in a contract or treaty. That the British construction was correct was virtually admitted by Mr Webster, the American Secretary of State, when he said in a State paper, 6th July 1852, that "it was undoubtedly an oversight in the convention of 1818 to make so large a concession to England,

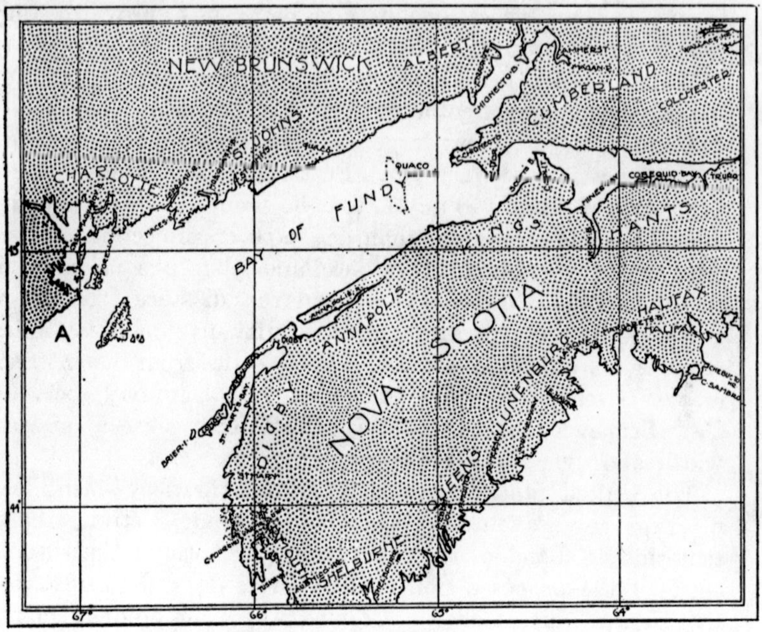

Fig. 17.—*Bay of Fundy.* A, *United States territory.*

since the United States had usually considered that those vast inlets, or recesses of the ocean, ought to be open to American fishermen as freely as the sea itself, to within three miles of the shore." He admitted, moreover, that the word bay applied equally to small and large tracts of water situated between capes or headlands.

In 1824, and again in 1838 and 1839, British cruisers seized American vessels for fishing within the Bay of Fundy, the Bay of Chaleurs, and elsewhere in contravention of the treaty of 1818; and in 1843 the schooner *Washington* was arrested for fishing in the Bay of Fundy at a distance of ten miles from shore, taken to Yarmouth, Nova Scotia, and sold. In the diplomatic correspondence which followed these seizures, the two Governments took up the position as to the interpretation of the treaty which is referred to above; but eventually, in March 1845, Lord Aberdeen intimated that the British Government, while adhering to their interpretation, would as a matter of courtesy relax the rule with regard to the Bay of Fundy, and allow "the United States fishermen to pursue their avocations in any part of it, provided they should not approach, except in cases specified in the treaty of 1818, within three miles of the entrance of any bay on the coast of Nova Scotia or New Brunswick." The Bay of Fundy (fig. 17) is a very large but typically landlocked inlet of the sea, passing between Nova Scotia and New Brunswick for a distance of about 140 miles from its mouth. As with many other bays, there is more than one cape or projection of land that might be taken as its headlands, but one of them is clearly in the United States; and the distance from it to the opposite coast is from forty to fifty-five nautical miles, while the bay itself at sixty or seventy miles from the entrance is over twenty-five miles in width. Chaleur Bay, between New Brunswick and Quebec, is a little over sixteen miles in width and over sixty miles long (fig. 18).

The United States declined to receive the above-mentioned privilege as a favour, and the colonists made a strong representation to London as to the injurious results that would ensue if the proposed policy were adopted; and in 1849 the British law officers of the Crown gave their opinion on the provisions of the treaty, "that the prescribed distance of three miles is to be measured from the headlands or extreme points of land next the sea of the coasts, or of the entrance of the bays, and not from the interior of such bays or inlets of the coast; and consequently that no right exists on the part of American citizens to enter the bays of Nova Scotia, there to take fish, although the fishing, being within the bay, may be at a greater distance than three miles from the shore of the bay."

In terms of the convention of February 8, 1853, the case of the *Washington*, above described, came before referees in

London, and on their disagreement it was decided by the umpire, Mr Joshua Bates, in favour of the United States. His conclusion was that the Bay of Fundy was not a British bay, nor a bay within the meaning of the word as used in the treaties of 1783 and 1818, but belonged rather to the class which comprised such bays as the Bay of Bengal and the Bay of Biscay, over which no nation can have the right to assume sovereignty. He also pointed out that one of its headlands was in the United States; and he thought that the doctrine of the headlands had "received a proper limit"

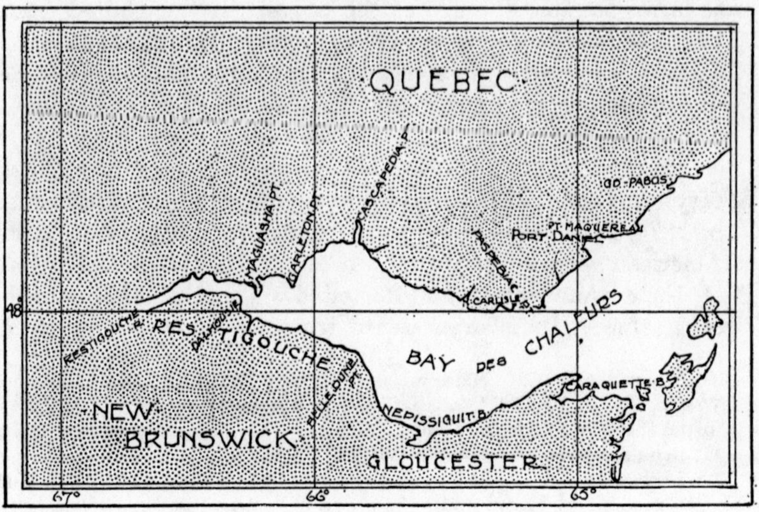

Fig. 18.—*Bay des Chaleurs.*

in the Anglo-French convention of 1839, where a ten-mile base-line was adopted.

A few years before this, negotiations had been opened between the Governments with the view of establishing reciprocal free-trade between Canada and the United States, and in June 1854 a treaty was signed at Washington, commonly known as the Reciprocity Treaty, by which certain articles of produce of the British colonies and of the United States were admitted to each country respectively free of duty, and reciprocal rights of fishery were granted. The subjects of either state were to be free to fish along the coasts and in the bays, harbours, and creeks of the other, without any restriction as to distance from the shore, in Canada, New Brunswick, Nova Scotia, and Prince Edward's Island, and on the eastern coast of the United States north of the 36th degree of north latitude. On each side salmon and shad fisheries, and the fisheries in rivers and the mouths of rivers, were reserved.[1] This treaty was to endure for ten years, and it was terminated by the United States and came to an end on 17th March 1866, when, in consequence, the provisions of the treaty of 1818 again came into force. The British Government, however, being very desirous to prevent, as far as possible, the loss to the citizens of the United States by a sudden withdrawal of the privileges which they had enjoyed for twelve years, decided to allow American fishermen to continue to fish in all provincial waters upon the payment of a small fee.[2] From the neglect of American fishermen to obtain the licenses, the fee for which had been raised from fifty cents to two dollars per ton, the system was discontinued in 1870, and orders were given to British cruisers to exclude American vessels from fishing in territorial waters, and several of them were seized and forfeited. The Canadian Minister of Marine and Fisheries issued instructions, in May 1870, for

[1] Treaty between Her Majesty and the United States of America, signed at Washington, 1st June 1854, Art. i., ii. I. "It is agreed by the high contracting parties that in addition to the liberty secured to the United States' fishermen by the above-mentioned convention of October 20, 1818, of taking, curing, and drying fish on certain coasts of the British North American Colonies therein defined, the inhabitants of the United States shall have, in common with the subjects of Her Britannic Majesty, the liberty to take fish of every kind, except shell-fish, on the sea coasts and shores, and in the bays, harbours, and creeks of Canada, New Brunswick, Nova Scotia, Prince Edward's Island, and of the several islands thereunto adjacent, without being restricted to any distance from the shore, with permission to land upon the coasts and shores of those Colonies and the islands thereof, and also upon the Magdalen Islands, for the purpose of drying their nets and curing their fish; provided that, in so doing, they do not interfere with the rights of private property, or with British fishermen, in the peaceable use of any part of the said coast in their occupancy for the same purpose." The second article accorded to Canadian fishermen similar privileges in the waters of the United States, north of 36 degrees N. latitude.

[2] Before this arrangement was made, the British Government, on 12th April 1866, instructed the Admiralty "that American fishermen should not be interfered with, either by notice or otherwise, unless they are found within three miles of a line drawn across the mouth of a bay or creek, which is less than ten geographical miles in width, in conformity with the arrangement made with France in 1839.'

the same limits as are contained in the Anglo-French convention of 1839 to be put in force against American fishermen; but, on representations from London, these were withdrawn and other instructions issued to the commanders of the cruisers, in which bays of six miles or less in width at the mouth were alone reserved.[1]

Further negotiations between the Governments ended in the treaty of Washington in 1871, in which reciprocal rights of fishing were re-established in much the same way as in the treaty of 1854, but the liberty to British subjects to fish on the coast of the United States was restricted to the part north of the 39th degree of north latitude.[2] Under this treaty it was agreed to appoint joint commissioners to determine the amount of compensation, if any, which should be paid by the United States for the greater privileges granted to American citizens by the treaty; and this commission met at Halifax in 1877, the sum of 5,500,000 dollars being so awarded. The award was not received with favour in the United States, and notice was given at the end of the stipulated ten years for the abrogation of the treaty, and the articles referring to the fisheries were so terminated on July 1, 1885, the provisions of the convention of 1818 again, for the third time, coming into force. Further troubles and disputes occurred, not so much in relation to fishing within territorial waters, as to American vessels frequenting colonial ports for the purchase of bait, salt, &c., a liberty which was

[1] 27th June 1870. "The limits within which you will, if necessary, exercise the power to exclude United States' fishermen, or to detain American fishing vessels or boats, are for the present to be exceptional. . . . Her Majesty's Government are clearly of opinion that, by the Convention of 1818, the United States have renounced the right of fishing, not only within three miles of the Colonial shores, but within three miles of a line drawn across the mouth of any British bay or creek. It is, however, the wish of Her Majesty's Government neither to concede, nor for the present to enforce, any rights in this respect which are in their nature open to any serious question. Until further instructed, therefore, you will not interfere with any American fishermen, unless found within three miles of the shore, or within three miles of a line drawn across the mouth of a bay or creek, which, though in parts more than six miles wide, is less than six geographical miles in width at its mouth. In the case of any other bay—as Bay des Chaleurs, for example—you will not interfere with any United States' fishing vessel or boat, or any American fishermen, unless they are found within three miles of the shore."

[2] Treaty between Her Majesty and the United States of America, signed at Washington, 8th May 1871, Art. xviii., xix.

not granted by the treaty of 1818, and several of them having been seized, retaliatory measures were threatened by the United States. After negotiations between the two Governments another treaty was signed at Washington, on February 15, 1888, the principal British plenipotentiary being Mr Joseph Chamberlain. This treaty provided for the appointment of a mixed commission to delimit "the British waters, bays, creeks, and harbours of the coasts of Canada and of Newfoundland, as to which the United States, by Article I. of the Convention of 20th October 1818, between Great Britain and the United States, renounced for ever any liberty to take, dry, or cure fish." The delimitation was to be marked upon charts by a series of lines regularly numbered and described, the three marine miles being measured from low-water mark, "but at every bay, creek, or harbour, not otherwise specially provided for in this treaty, such three marine miles shall be measured seaward from a straight line drawn across the bay, creek, or harbour, in the part nearest the entrance at the first point where the width does not exceed ten marine miles." A large number of bays were specially dealt with by lines specified, that of Chaleurs being closed, or by other special lines from which the three miles was to be measured; and other articles in the treaty regulated the entry of American fishing vessels into colonial ports. It was further provided that whenever the United States removed the duties on fish and fish-oils from Canada and Newfoundland, United States' vessels would be licensed, free of charge, to enter the colonial ports and harbours to purchase provisions, bait, ice, seines, and all other supplies and outfits, to tranship their catch, or for the shipping of crews.

But, inasmuch as the above treaty could not possibly be ratified before the commencement of the next fishing season, the British plenipotentiaries, in order to avoid a recrudescence of the usual friction and irritation, and to afford evidence of their anxious desire to promote good feeling, agreed, in a protocol of the same date, to a "temporary arrangement for a period not exceeding two years, in order to afford a *modus vivendi* pending the ratification of the Treaty." This arrangement granted the privilege to American fishing vessels of entering the bays and harbours, on payment for an annual license of a fee at the rate of one and a half dollars per ton, in order to purchase bait, ice, and all other supplies and outfits, to tranship their catch and ship crews, and gave them some other privileges, declaring also that forfeiture was to be exacted only for the offence of fishing or preparing to fish in territorial waters.[1]

Unfortunately, this treaty failed to pass the Senate of the United States and was never ratified, and the system temporarily adopted as a *modus vivendi* has been regularly renewed since, and is still in force.[2]

It is to be noted that the arrangement in the treaty, both as to drawing lines on charts to separate the common from the exclusive fishing waters and for the adoption of a ten-mile base-line for bays, was proposed, not by the British Government, but by that of the United States. The British Government, indeed, strongly objected to a ten-mile line as involving "a surrender of fishing rights" and making "common fishing-grounds of the territorial waters which, by the law of nations, have been invariably regarded, both in Great Britain and the United States, as belonging to the adjacent country," and they cited the Bay of Chaleurs as an example. They argued that in the convention with France in 1839, and in other similar conventions, the boundary-lines selected were due to special configuration of the coast, and could not be well settled "by reference to the law of nations"; and attention was called to the claims of the United States to Delaware Bay and other bays on their coasts. In reply to these observations of the British Government, the United States said they had proposed the width of ten miles not only because it had been adopted in fishery conventions, but also because it was deemed reasonable and just in the case in question; "while they might have claimed a width of six miles as a basis of settlement, fishing within bays and harbours only slightly wider would be confined to areas so narrow as to render it practically valueless, and almost certainly expose the fishermen to constant danger of carrying their operations into forbidden waters; a width of

1 *Parl. Papers*, No. 1 (1888), (C.—5262).

2 The number of American fishing vessels which take the licenses for Canadian waters is usually about 100, the fees aggregating 10,000 or 12,000 dollars per annum. *Ann. Reports, Marine and Fisheries*, Ottawa.

more than ten miles[1] would give room for safe fishing more than three miles from either shore, and thus prevent the constant disputes which this Government's proposal, following the conventions above noticed, was designed to avert."[2]

Nevertheless, notwithstanding this proposal by the United States' Government, the limit now enforced for bays on the coasts of British North America is that of six miles, with the exception of the Bay of Chaleurs.[3] It was apparently found that the attitude adopted by the British Government in 1870, then stated to be temporary and exceptional, of allowing the United States' fishermen to fish "except within three miles of land, or in bays which are less than six miles broad at the mouth," ought to be adhered to, during the existence of the *modus vivendi* and pending the ratification of the treaty of 1888. If a recent statement of the Under-Secretary for Foreign Affairs, made in the House of Lords, represents the policy of the British Government at the present day, this six-mile limit for bays is to be regarded as established not alone for British North America, but for every part of the British dominions unless specially provided for otherwise. (See p. 730.)

From the foregoing summary of the disputes, negotiations, and treaties, concerning the rights of Americans to fish on the coasts of the British possessions in North America, it is evident that the British Government has gradually given way to the pressure exerted by the United States. In allowing a six-mile line for bays they have, indeed, as just shown, gone further than was demanded, and have departed from the terms of the fishery conventions which they have concluded with European Powers. The basis of the delimitation adopted in the treaty of 1888 was, as Mr Chamberlain intimated to Lord Salisbury, derived from the North Sea Convention of 1882, to which important treaty we must now turn our attention.

It has been already said that the fishery convention with France in 1867 was not ratified by that country, and never came into operation in the general police regulation of the fisheries in extra-territorial waters. The desirability of inter-

[1] The three-mile limit is measured from the ten-mile arc.

[2] Mr Phelps to the Marquis of Salisbury, 3rd August 1887, enclosing *ad interim* arrangement proposed by the United States' Government, with "Observations" by the British Government and Reply of the Government of the United States.

[3] Gordon, 15*th Ann. Rep. Assoc. for Reform of Law of Nations* (8). 1893.

national regulations to preserve the peace between the fishermen of various countries frequenting the neighbouring seas, and particularly the North Sea, soon became apparent. Complaints of malicious interference with one another increased in number. The Belgians and French were accused of cutting and stealing the lines of Scottish fishermen, and the Dutch of taking their derelict nets, and the Fishery Board for Scotland accordingly pressed upon the Government, as early as 1876, the advantage of negotiating a fishery convention with Holland.[1] A little later the free use by foreign trawlers of a destructive implement known as "the devil," or "the Belgian devil," aroused a strong feeling among British drift-net fishermen. The instrument consisted of a shank and sharpened flukes, which was hung overboard and was designed for the sole purpose of cutting fishing-nets in the sea which might impede the movement of the boat making use of it. It was a product of the disputes and difficulties that occurred in carrying on trawling and drift-net fishing in the same localities at the same time. The British Government in January 1880 appointed Mr W. H. Higgin, Q.C., to make an inquiry on the subject. His report[2] showed that the state of things with regard to fishing operations in the North Sea by British, Belgian, French, and Dutch boats was unsatisfactory. He found that grievous injury and damage had been done to the drift-nets and tackle of English fishermen in the North Sea by trawlers belonging to France, Belgium, and Holland;[3] that there was no international law or convention between England and France, England and Belgium, or England and Holland, affecting the fisheries in the North Sea,—the convention with France in 1867 never having been ratified, while that of 1839 was, he said, confined to the English Channel and referred only to French fishermen; and he stated that some international law of the kind was urgently required, as it would be impossible otherwise to put a stop to the outrages described. In conse-

[1] *Report by the Commissioners for the Herring Fishery, Scotland*, 1869, p. 4; *Report by the Commissioners of the Fishery Board, Scotland*, 1876, p. 7.

[2] Report of W. H. Higgin, Esq., Q.C., on the Outrages committed by Foreign upon English Fishermen in the North Sea. *Parl. Papers* (C.—2878), 1881.

[3] After all, however, the damage from the monetary point of view was not very great, amounting, according to the detailed information collected by Mr Higgin, to £4372, 3s. over the years 1870-1880, or at the rate of about £400 per annum.

quence of this report the Government invited the co-operation of France, Belgium, Holland, Sweden and Norway, and Denmark in devising a remedy, suggesting that separate agreements might be made for the purpose. At the instance of Holland, it was agreed to have one joint convention, and a conference of the North Sea Powers was convened at The Hague, in 1881, to negotiate it, Germany, at her own request, being included.[1]

In the proceedings at the conference the question that caused the greatest difficulty and discussion was the definition of the territorial waters or exclusive fishery limits. The British Government, in curious contrast to their action earlier in the century, desired to avoid any definition at all. The memorandum prepared by them as the basis of the deliberations, stipulated that the convention should "apply to the high seas generally outside the fishery limits of the countries joining in the convention." This somewhat vague, not to say illogical, phraseology did not meet with the approval of the other Governments. It was objected to by France in particular. That Power had accepted the invitation to the conference on condition that the regulation to be agreed upon should be restricted to police rules intended to prevent conflicts between fishermen of different nationalities, "and to secure to them the free practice of their calling in the common waters of the North Sea." In making a special convention dealing with the open sea which was common to all, it seemed to it impossible to do otherwise than begin by defining the limits within which it was intended to operate.[2] The French delegates at the conference therefore proposed that the extent of the territorial waters should, for fishery purposes, be defined in precise terms, and they endeavoured further to get the limit made as contracted as possible. They urged that the boundary should be fixed everywhere at three geographical miles from low-water mark, whatever might be the configuration of the coast. As to fixing a larger measurement for bays, as in the Anglo-French con-

[1] Correspondence respecting the Conference at The Hague and the Convention of the 6th May 1882, relative to the Police of the Fisheries in the North Sea. *Parl. Papers, Commercial,* No. 24, 1882.

[2] M. Barthélemy St Hilaire to Lord Lyons, 2nd July 1881; M. de Freycinet to M. Challemel-Lacour, 2nd March 1882.

vention of 1867, they argued that the rules laid down on this subject in the convention in question ought not to apply to the North Sea; in many instances these rules had reference only to the interests of oyster fisheries, which, they said, did not exist in the North Sea. The French contention regarding bays was thus similar to that of the United States in the negotiations concerning the treaty of 1818; and it was of course to the interest of France, whose own coast would be but little affected, and whose fisheries along the British coast in the North Sea were of great importance, to have the exclusive fishery limit made as narrow as possible.

The proposal that the territorial waters for fishery purposes ought to be precisely defined, and that the limit on the open coast should be fixed at three geographical miles from low-water mark, was generally accepted, Belgium alone supporting the British view that it was better not to define them in the convention. But as regards bays, objection was taken to the French scheme on the part of Germany, with special reference to the mouth of the Elbe, which was declared to be a part of the sea belonging exclusively to Germany; and on the part of Norway, on the ground that that country could not agree to fix the limit at three miles, particularly with respect to bays. The rights which particular states might have acquired, it was urged, ought not to be prejudiced, and "bays should continue to belong to the State to which they at present belonged." The French delegates then formulated their proposition in the following terms: "In the North Sea the limit of the part known as territorial waters (*mer territoriale*) is fixed, whatever may be the configuration of the country, at three miles from low-water mark, along the whole length of the shores of . . . It is, however, understood that this shall not be taken to modify in any way the rights acquired on certain parts of their coasts by the different Powers to whom the shore belongs;" or else, "It is, however, understood that the present convention shall not be taken to modify in any way the rights which any Government may possess outside the three-mile limit in bays."

As the British and French delegates could not agree on this subject, further discussion was postponed until the former had consulted their Government. When this was done, they announced that their instructions did not permit them to adopt the French proposals; and they continued to press the draft article for acceptance, declaring that the question of defining the limits of the maritime jurisdiction of the various countries did not fall within the province of the convention. The other delegates, however, did not share this view, and when a complete definition was insisted on, the British representatives ultimately agreed to accept the terms employed in the first article of the Anglo-French convention of 1867, and they submitted the following article: "The fishermen of each country shall enjoy the exclusive right of fishery within the distance of three miles from low-water mark along the whole extent of the coasts of their respective countries. As regards bays, the entrances of which do not exceed ten miles in width, the distance of three miles shall be measured from a straight line drawn from headland to headland." The counter-proposal on the part of France did not materially differ from this, except by the inclusion of islands, by the better definition regarding bays, and by the insertion of a clause providing for the right of free navigation and anchorage in territorial waters.[1] The German delegate, anxious about the waters at the mouths of German rivers, urged that flats or banks uncovered at low water should also be included, as well as islands. This proposal had been agreed to by the British Government in 1868, after correspondence between the Foreign Office and the German Embassy in London, and though apparently not now desired by Great Britain, it was formally adopted.[2]

The article as finally agreed upon was as follows: "The

[1] "The fishermen of each country shall enjoy the exclusive right of fishery within the distance of three miles from low-water mark along the whole extent of the coasts of their respective countries and of the dependent islands. As regards bays, the entrances of which do not exceed ten miles in width, the distance of three miles shall be measured from a straight line joining the two extreme points of the bay. The present article shall not in any way prejudice the right of free navigation and anchorage in territorial waters accorded to vessels of all sizes, provided they conform to the special police regulations enacted by the Powers to whom the shore belongs."

[2] Messrs Kennedy and Trevor to Mr Farrer, Oct. 31, 1881. In the Anglo-French convention of 1867 the British negotiators unsuccessfully pressed for the insertion of the words, "the islands . . . and their dependencies." M. de Freycinet to M. Challemel-Lacour, 2nd March 1882.

fishermen of each country shall enjoy the exclusive right of fishery within the distance of three miles from low-water mark along the whole extent of the coasts of their respective countries, as well as of the dependent islands and banks. As regards bays, the distance of three miles shall be measured from a straight line drawn across the bay, in the part nearest the entrance, at the first point where the width does not exceed ten miles. The present Article shall not in any way

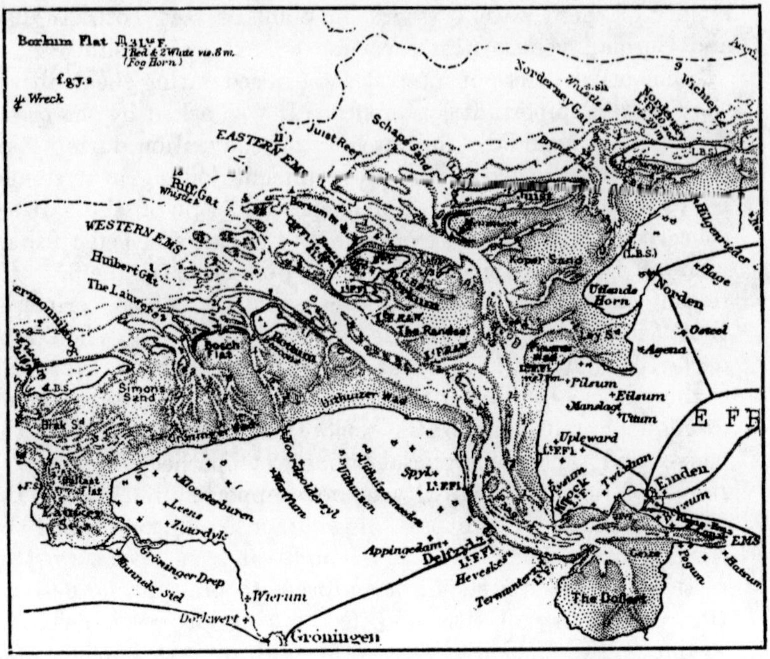

Fig. 19.—*Showing the Sandbanks at the mouth of the Ems.*

prejudice the freedom of navigation and anchorage in territorial waters accorded to fishing-boats, provided they conform to the special police regulations enacted by the Powers to whom the shore belongs."

It is interesting to note that, at the instance of the Dutch president, the conference agreed that the provisions of the convention would not be applicable to the Zuiderzee; and that in deliberating on the boundaries of the North Sea within which they would apply, it was agreed to exclude the Skagerrack, the fisheries of which, it was stated by the president, were not international, but were "essentially within the jurisdiction of the States to which the shores belong." The greater part of the Zuiderzee, however, would have been excluded by the definition of bays in the convention, and the rest of it by the inclusion of "banks"; but the Skagerrack, on the other hand, is nowhere less than sixty geographical miles from shore to shore. Neither Norway nor Denmark has asserted since the convention exclusive jurisdiction in its moiety of these waters, where, in point of fact, both English and German vessels now carry on an extensive fishing.[1]

Some other points of interest were raised during the deliberations of this important conference. It was asked by the president: What would be the fate of the convention during war, in which one or two of the Governments joining in it should be belligerents? Would the fishery cruisers of the Powers concerned merely retire from the North Sea and leave fishermen of their nationality without protection or help? He recommended that the conference should adopt the principle that fishing-boats, *bonâ fide* engaged in fishing, should be declared neutral. This was to revive a subject that had earlier, especially during the time of Napoleon I., caused much discussion, and which was remote from the object of the convention; and the proposal, though sympathetically received by the French delegates, was not supported by any of the Governments. A proposal of another kind was made by the German delegate. He thought it was necessary that restrictive measures should be enforced to prevent the destruction of the fry of fish and the taking of small fish; for example, by forbidding trawling within a certain distance of the shore, so as to provide a shelter for the free development of fish, and by regulating the construction of trawl-nets. The British and French delegates were opposed to any system of restriction, relying on the results of the inquiry which had been then recently made by Messrs Buckland and Walpole,[2] and on the part of France the

[1] Vide *Fiskeri-Beretning for Finansaaret*, 1907-1908, p. 178. Kjobenhavn, 1908.

[2] *Report on the Sea Fisheries of England and Wales*, 1879. The British delegate laid stress on one of the conclusions reached by Mr Buckland, to the effect that "nothing that man has done, and nothing that man can do, can affect the supply

following draft clause was formulated for insertion in the convention: "In the extra-territorial part of the North Sea, fishery shall be free at all seasons, and with all kinds of implements, without any sort of distinction." The clause was not adopted, and it was generally agreed that the question was not ripe for decision by that conference, which was moreover concerned with the police of the fisheries, and not with the reproduction of fish, in the North Sea.

The North Sea Convention was concluded in 1882, the signatory Powers being Great Britain, Germany, France, Belgium, Denmark, and the Netherlands.[1] Although the delegates of the United Kingdom of Sweden and Norway signed the protocol and were present at the final deliberations, those Powers did not join in the convention, objections being raised as to the definition of the territorial waters and on some other points.[2] An additional article was inserted providing that the King of Sweden and Norway might adhere later, for both or either country; but this has not been done, though the coast of Norway forms a not inconsiderable part of the boundary of the North Sea as defined in the convention. The reasons which induced these countries to abstain from joining in a friendly agreement with the neighbouring Powers of western Europe, after having accepted the invitation to the conference and taken part in its deliberations, must have appeared to them strong; and from the delay that occurred in coming to a decision it is evident that the matter received full consideration. They believed, however, that to agree to so restricted a boundary for their territorial waters in respect to fishery would be disadvantageous to them: it is probable, moreover, that the raising of the question was not foreseen, since the object of the conference was to consider the police of the fisheries in extra-territorial waters in the North Sea. It is curious, indeed, that

of herrings in the seas." Even if this were proved for the herring in the absolute form in which it is expressed,—and it is clearly illogical and unwarrantable to pledge the future in this loose way,—it obviously might not, and in point of fact does not, apply to the great bulk of the fishes that would have been affected by the German suggestion.

1 *International Convention for the Purpose of Regulating the Police of the Fisheries in the North Sea outside Territorial Waters.* Signed at The Hague, 6th May 1882.

2 Sir H. Rumbold to Earl Granville, 16th March 1882; H.M. Plenipotentiaries to the same, 8th May 1882.

the limits for exclusive fishery, both in the convention with France in 1839 and with the other North Sea Powers in 1882, were fixed as it were incidentally.

The duration of the convention was to be for five years from the date at which it came into operation, unless one year's notice to terminate it were given by any of the contracting Powers; and it was to continue in force from year to year subject to similar notice. That none of the signatory Powers have withdrawn from the convention is the best proof of its general utility. From the number and influential position of these states, and from the character of the sea to which it applies,—one of the most productive in the world,—this convention is an international document of high importance to the sea fisheries, and deserves careful consideration. The first article declares that the provisions shall apply to the subjects of the high-contracting parties, the object being "to regulate the police of the fisheries in the North Sea outside territorial waters"; and the limits of the North Sea were carefully defined.[1] The provisions of the convention relate to the registration, lettering, and numbering of boats, the operations of fishermen pursuing different methods of fishing at the same place at the same time, the malicious use of instruments for cutting nets, the salvage of derelict fishing-gear, and the superintendence by cruisers. It was put in force in this country in 1883 by an Act of Parliament,[2] which also extended its application, so far as British sea-fishing boats were concerned, to the whole of the seas around the British Islands, whether within or without the

[1] The boundaries specified are, on the north, the parallel of the 61st degree of latitude; on the east and south, the coast of Norway between the above parallel and Lindesnæs Lighthouse, a straight line thence across the Skagerrack to Hantsholm Lighthouse in Denmark, the coasts of Denmark, Germany, the Netherlands, Belgium, and France, as far as Cape Gris Nez Lighthouse; on the west, a straight line from Gris Nez Lighthouse to the easternmost lighthouse at the North Foreland in Kent, the eastern coasts of England and Scotland, a line from Duncansby Head in Caithness to the southern point of South Ronaldsha in the Orkneys, the eastern coasts of the Orkney Islands, a straight line from North Ronaldsha Lighthouse to Sumburgh Head Lighthouse in the Shetland Islands, the eastern coasts of these islands, and the meridian of the North Unst Lighthouse as far as the parallel of the 61st degree of latitude. The Dutch proposed the 60th degree of latitude as the northern limit, and the British the 62nd degree.

[2] 46 & 47 Vict., c. 22. An Act to carry into effect an International Convention concerning the Fisheries in the North Sea, and to amend the laws relating to British Sea Fisheries.

exclusive fishery limits. In this Act the stipulation in the second article of the convention, as to the freedom of navigation and anchorage in territorial waters on the part of foreign fishing-boats, received a limiting definition. The clause in question was inserted in the convention at the instance of France, and was accepted with some reluctance by the British delegates, who agreed to it in general terms only, without the recognition of a right.[1] By the Act foreign fishing-boats were prohibited from entering the exclusive fishery limits of the British Islands except for purposes recognised by international law, or by any treaty or arrangement in force between this country and any foreign state, or for any lawful purpose. If a foreign boat did enter, it was to return outside the limits as soon as the purpose for which it entered had been answered, and fishing or attempting to fish within the limits was, of course, forbidden under penalties.

The definition of the exclusive fishery limits in the North Sea Convention differed in two respects from that contained in the previous conventions with France. The rule for the measurement of bays was modified, and the dependent islands and banks were expressly included as part of the coast from which the limit should be measured. In the Anglo-French conventions of 1839 and 1867 bays which did not exceed ten miles in width at the mouths were comprised in the reserved waters, and the three-mile limit was measured from the line joining the "headlands." Thus some bays whose width at the mouth, or between their headlands, exceeded ten miles were deprived of the benefit of the principle applied to bays and came under the three-mile rule, even although at a small distance within the entrance the width might not exceed ten miles. Since all bays have not headlands, the French proposal at The Hague conference to substitute "the two extreme points of the bay" for that term was an improvement. Still better was the definition finally adopted, to place the base-line at the first point nearest the entrance where the width did not exceed ten miles. The specific inclusion of islands removed such difficulties as were raised in 1853 by a French commodore at the Farne Islands (see p. 618), though it had long been established in connection with the rights of neutrals that islands

[1] Messrs Kennedy and Trevor to Mr Farrer, 31st Oct. 1881. *Doc. cit.*

carried with them, no less than the mainland, the belt of territorial sea. The inclusion of banks was, however, novel, and was not received with favour by the British Government. It was feared that it would lead to difficulties and complications in future if such banks as the Goodwin Sands, which were situated beyond the three-mile limit, and the similar banks on the German and Dutch coasts, were held to be territorial dependencies of the coast; and so strong was the objection of the British Government to their inclusion, that they instructed their ambassadors abroad, if an objection was raised by any Power, to have this definition reconsidered.[1] The objection is theoretically well founded. Sand-banks of this character may be not permanent, and usually vary in extent, configuration, and position with lapse of time and even after a single tempest; and the extent of sea appendent will vary likewise. It would thus be difficult to fix a precise and permanent limit in connection with them. Moreover, since the banks may be covered by the sea except at low-water without losing their territorial value, it would sometimes require more than ordinary care on the part of foreign fishing-boats to avoid infringing the limit around them. On the other hand, for the purpose of regulations designed to protect fish life, such as are referred to in the sequel, banks of this nature are of especial value; and, in point of fact, few difficulties in practice appear to have arisen on this score in carrying out the convention.[2]

[1] Dispatch to Hon. E. Ashley, 17th Nov. 1881; Earl Granville to Her Majesty's Representatives at Paris, Brussels, The Hague, Berlin, Copenhagen, and Stockholm, 6th December 1881.

[2] A case occurred in 1908 in which the master of an English trawler, the *Taurus*, was convicted in a German court for trawling within the three-mile limit on the German coast, and the case was appealed on the ground that the place was outside the territorial waters, and was so shown on the English fishery charts. It was found, however, that the three-mile line on these charts did not take into account the dependent banks, whereas the German charts did take them into account, the limit running in some cases six or seven miles from the coast. It may be mentioned that as considerable parts of the Goodwin Sands are visible at low-water of neap tides, such parts are entitled to a three-mile limit in the same way as the dependent banks on the German coast. Recently, also, it has been found that the three-mile limit in the neighbourhood of the Scaw fluctuates considerably owing to the shifting of the shoals, and the Danish authorities, early in 1907, intimated that any case of alleged infraction of the limit by foreign fishing vessels would be judged of by the actual position of the line at the time, and not by what may be shown on any chart in use. The point in regard to banks was

On one or two points, however, the definitions in the convention might have been improved. Nothing is said as to the tides at which low-water mark is to be taken for measurements, though on certain coasts the extent of territorial water will vary much according to whether it is a neap or a high spring tide; and the question whether certain banks are or are not territorial and entitled to the limit may vary in the same way. It is to be presumed that the tide is an ordinary neap tide, as in English law. More important is the fact that "rocks" are not included along with islands. Quite recently the omission has given rise to difficulties in regard to three places on our coast—viz., the Eddystone, the Bell Rock, and the Seven Stones Rocks, off the Scilly Islands.

raised a century ago in connection with neutral rights in a case in which a British privateer captured a French corvette, the *Africaine*, on the coast of the United States, six miles from shore. It was argued that the capture was unlawful, because the place was within the neutral waters of the United States, the extent of which had been defined by Congress in 1794 as one marine league from the coast (see p. 574). It was contended that "coasts" included all the shoals or banks which, in Florida, extended to a distance of twenty miles from the land, and were therefore within territorial jurisdiction, and that the distance of protection should be reckoned from the outermost shoal. The American judge overruled the argument, because, although in a maritime sense this interpretation of "coasts" might be correct, it was too vague for juridical purposes, since the shoals vary, and there would be no fixed rule by which the boundary could be ascertained; and that the district courts would have to apply different rules at different places, instead of the one marine league everywhere. A somewhat similar question was argued in 1805 in the English Admiralty Court in the case of an American ship, the *Anna*, captured by a British privateer off the mouth of the Mississippi, at a point claimed to be within the neutral waters of the United States—viz., 1½ mile from an island, and "within view" of a fort, which was, however, five miles distant. A question raised was whether certain small mud-islands, formed of earth and drifted logs, and covered with reeds, where people occasionally went to shoot wild-fowl, was United States territory from which the marine league could be measured. It was argued that the islands had not sufficient consistency to support the purposes of life, and were sometimes scarcely distinguishable, and that since the distance of neutral protection "is reckoned according to the efficacy of protection, that is, within the range of firearms," the land from which the extension is measured should be a place from which this protection could be in reality afforded. Lord Stowell, in deciding that they were United States territory, stated that the right of dominion did not depend upon the texture of the soil; and he quoted Bynkershoek's formula as the rule of law, saying that the distance "has usually been recognised to be about three miles from the shore." It may be said here that in the earlier writings and decisions about the limit of territorial waters, low-water mark is not specified, and in the case of the *Twee Gebroeders* (see p. 577) it is clear that sand-banks uncovered at low-water were not regarded as entitled to an independent zone, the distance being measured from *terra firma*.

The Seven Stones Rocks are a reef near the south-west extremity of Cornwall, about seven miles from Land's End, and about a mile in length, and with a lightship at it; but it does not appear that any portion is above the sea-level at low-water of neap tides. Complaints were made to the Government by the Cornwall Sea Fisheries Committee that French fishing-boats fished within three miles from the rocks, and close to them; but it was stated by the Admiralty, and also by the Foreign Office, that these rocks could not be claimed as being within British territorial waters.[1] In this case, presumably, the decision might rest on the fact that the rocks do not appear at low-water of ordinary tides. The Eddystone is somewhat different. The rock or reef on which the lighthouse is placed lies about fourteen miles south-west of Plymouth, and while covered by the sea at high tide, is exposed to the extent of an area of about 500 yards at low-water of neaps. French fishermen also fish around it and close to it, a practice which caused the Devon Sea Fisheries Committee to complain. The gunboat *Circe*, in August 1905, seized and took into Plymouth two French "crabbers" for fishing within three miles from the Eddystone, but after communicating with the Board of Trade, instructions were sent to release the boats; and the Board of Agriculture and Fisheries, while saying that they were not in a position to express an authoritative opinion on the matter, called attention to the decision in 1902 regarding the somewhat similar case at the Seven Stones. Here, no doubt, the decision rested on the absence of the specific inclusion of "rocks," as distinguished from islands, in the conventions, and one can understand the expression of surprise by the Devon Sea Fisheries Committee that a rock which was recognised as British, and was inhabited by lighthouse-keepers, was not considered as within the territorial limit for fishing purposes.

Similar complaints have been made concerning the Bell Rock, which lies about ten miles east-south-east of Arbroath, Forfarshire, and has a lighthouse upon it. It is entirely covered at high-water; at the ebb of spring tides it is uncovered to a depth of four feet, while at low-water of neap tides the top of the rock is just visible, and would then

[1] *Fish Trades Gazette*, May 31st, 1902, p. 8; *ibid.*, April 4th, 1903, p. 21.

probably acquire validity for the measurement of three miles from it and around it, if rocks had been included in the conventions, as they are now included in the recent convention between this country and Denmark concerning Iceland and the Faroës (p. 647). The case of the Seven Stones and the Eddystone is, however, on a different footing; for while the limit of exclusive fishery along the coasts of the North Sea, with the exception of the part formed by Norway, was settled by the convention of 1882 (so far as concerns the fishermen of the signatory Powers), there appears to be some obscurity as to how far the three-mile limit operates on the coasts that lie outwith the boundaries of the North Sea,—such, for example, as the west coasts of England and Scotland and the coasts of Ireland. The second article of the convention declares, without qualification, that the three-mile limit shall apply "along the *whole extent* of the coasts" of the respective countries,—it does not say merely to the North Sea coasts,—and the view that this stipulation operates on all the coasts appears to be widely prevalent, and is expressed, for example, in the Belgian law which put the convention in force in that country.[1] It is, however, held by legal authorities that since the special object of the convention was "for the purpose of regulating the police of the fisheries in the North Sea outside territorial waters," and as the boundaries of the North Sea are defined "for the purpose of applying the provisions of the present Convention," the definition of the exclusive fishery limits applies only within the area specified, and not to the other coasts of the signatory Powers.[2] In the Convention Act, as in the Territorial Waters

[1] "Les articles 2 et 3 de ce contrat stipulent que les pêcheurs nationaux jouiront du droit exclusif de pêche dans le rayon de trois milles géographiques de 60 au degré de latitude, à partir de la laisse de basse mer, le long de toute l'étendue des côtes de leurs pays respectifs, ainsi que des îles et des bancs qui en dépendent." *Loi relative à la pêche maritime dans les eaux territoriales. Exposé des motifs.* Sess. 1890-91.

[2] The Marquis of Lothian, Secretary for Scotland, in introducing the Bill which became the Herring Fishery (Scotland) Act, 1889, said: "With regard to the east coast there is no very great difficulty in fixing the limits of territorial waters, because between Her Majesty's Government and what I may call the riparian powers of the North Sea there is a Fisheries Convention; but on the west coast there is no such convention, and therefore it has been thought desirable to attach a schedule to this Bill in order to show exactly what are the waters closed against

Jurisdiction Act, we accordingly find a distinction drawn between the exclusive fishery limits under international law and those under specific treaties or conventions. In the definition clause, the expression "British Islands" is explained to mean the United Kingdom of Great Britain and Ireland, the Isle of Man, the Channel Islands, and their dependencies, and it is declared that "the expression 'exclusive fishery limits of the British Islands' means that portion of the seas surrounding the British Islands within which Her Majesty's subjects have, by international law, the exclusive right of fishing, and where such portion is defined by the terms of any convention, treaty, or arrangement for the time being in force between Her Majesty and any Foreign State, includes, as regards the sea-fishing boats and officers and subjects of that State, the portion so defined."[1]

From all this it would appear that, notwithstanding the ambiguity introduced by the unqualified phrase "the whole extent of the coasts of their respective countries," the definition of the exclusive fishery limits in the convention of 1882 applies only to the coasts of the North Sea. In the convention of 1839 with France, on the other hand, there seems no reason to doubt that the three-mile limit was applied to all parts of the coasts of Great Britain and France respectively. By Article ix. it was declared that the exclusive right of fishing was reserved for subjects within that distance "along the whole extent of the coasts" of each country; and the British Act of Parliament to carry into effect this convention, and the international regulations agreed upon under it, so far from expressing any qualification or reservation as in the Act of 1883, made it clear that the limit applied generally. In the preamble it is stated that "Whereas a Convention was concluded between Her Majesty and the King of the French . . . defining the limits of the oyster fishery between the island of Jersey and the neighbouring coast of France, and also defining the limits of the exclusive right of fishery on all other parts of the coasts of the British Islands and France"; and Article 85 of the regulations enacted that the fishing-boats of the one country,

trawlers apart altogether from the general international rule as to the three-mile limit." June 28th, 1889. Hansard, vol. 337, p. 975.

[1] 46 & 47 Vict., c. 22, s. 28.

except under certain circumstances, "shall not approach nearer to any part of the coasts of the other country than the limit of three miles specified in Article ix. of the convention." [1]

In the convention of 1852 between Great Britain and Belgium, which was simply entitled "relative to fishery," without any particular purpose, seas, or regions being specified, it was stipulated that "Belgian subjects shall enjoy, in regard to fishery along the coast of the United Kingdom of Great Britain and Ireland, the treatment of the most favoured foreign nation." The most favoured foreign nation at that time was France, and although no distance was fixed in the Belgian treaty, there is no doubt the three-mile limit applied, and was indeed, as stated above, enforced, on the east coast of Scotland against the Belgians as well as against the French.

In the convention of 1867 the same limit was assigned "along the whole extent of the coasts" of the two countries; and the provisions of the convention were expressly stated to apply beyond the exclusive fishery limits, in the one case "to the seas surrounding and adjoining Great Britain and Ireland," and in the case of France to the seas adjoining the coast of that country between the frontiers of Belgium and Spain; and the object of the convention was "relative to fisheries in the seas between Great Britain and France." As already stated, this treaty, with an unimportant exception, did not come into effect, and the convention of 1839 remained in force.[2]

As no other treaties exist defining the exclusive fishery limits along our coasts than those referred to, the position in

[1] 6 & 7 Vict., c. 79 (1843). The international regulations agreed upon in virtue of the eleventh article of the convention were to apply to "the seas lying between the coasts of Great Britain and of France"; and differences of interpretation arose in this country as to the extent of the seas coming under this denomination—*e.g.*, whether those on the west coast of Scotland were included. The power given to the crown to suspend the operation of the Act on the Irish coasts, and the obvious intention of the Act and articles, seemed to the Royal Commissioners of 1863 to warrant the opinion that these extra-territorial regulations applied to all the seas around the British Isles (*Report, Royal Commission on Sea Fisheries*, i. p. lxiii). On the other hand, it was contended that the words quoted must be construed strictly, and included only those seas which were situated geographically between the two countries. This difference of opinion as to the interpretation of the phrase in question does not, however, affect the validity of Article ix. of the convention, one of the principal objects of which was to determine the limits of exclusive fishery.

[2] *Vide* 46 & 47 Vict., c. 22, s. 24.

relation to conventional law appears to be as follows. With respect to France and Belgium, the three-mile limit, with the ten-mile line for bays, seems to be in force along the whole extent of the British and Irish coasts. With respect to the other Powers which were parties to the North Sea Convention of 1882,—namely, Germany, Denmark, and the Netherlands,—this limit is in force only on the eastern, or North Sea, coasts of England and Scotland. On the north and west coasts of Scotland, the south and west coasts of England, and the whole of the coast of Ireland, the limits of exclusive fishery as regards these countries, and as regards all countries except France and Belgium, fall to be determined by the principles of international law. With respect to all other nations, as, for example, the Norwegians, Swedes, and Spaniards, the limits on all parts of our coasts also fall to be determined under international law. The principles of international law, as expounded by the accredited writers, do not, as will be shown later, and as is implied in the quotations from the Acts above cited, support the view that the right of exclusive fishing, apart from treaty, must necessarily be restricted to the three-mile limit. The preponderance of opinion is that the boundary of the territorial sea, including, therefore, the exclusive right of fishery, coincides with the range of guns from the shore; and it is evident that as against such nations as claim for themselves a greater extent than three miles on their own coasts—viz., Norway, Sweden, and Spain—a larger limit than that contained in the conventions could be rightfully enforced on the British coasts.

There are many things to show that the unsatisfactory state of affairs, not to say confusion, with respect to the limits of exclusive fishing to which we are entitled on various parts of our coast, has been brought about partly by a widespread belief that the boundary under international law is three miles, partly also by what must be characterised as a want of knowledge and care on the part of those dealing with the question. Mr T. H. Farrer, the permanent Secretary of the Board of Trade, told a Committee of the House of Commons in 1876 that the convention and regulations with France were "hastily and recklessly" made,[1] and the record of the proceed-

[1] *Report from the Select Committee on Oyster Fisheries*, p. 1. 1876.

ings at the conference at The Hague in 1881 shows that it would not have been a difficult matter to clear up some of the obscurity that exists. One point of importance is that, notwithstanding the absence of any treaty or agreement defining the extent of the limits of exclusive fishery with certain nations, the three-mile limit alone has been enforced against the vessels of such nations fishing on our coasts. This has been the case, except for a brief period, with respect to Norwegian and Swedish trawlers in the Moray Firth in Scotland, which is "closed" to British trawlers, and the vessels of these two nations are thus put on the same footing as those of other countries with which a convention has been made. It is also the case on the west coast of Scotland, where the limit of three miles is enforced against foreign trawlers, apparently irrespective of nationality, and certainly against Dutch and German vessels as well as against Belgians in the Clyde, from which British trawlers are excluded.[1] How far this undoubted usage may modify the position under international law it would be of importance to determine.

A more recent convention must be referred to, which, however, does not relate to the coasts of this country, but to those of the Danish islands, the Faröes, and Iceland, where British trawling vessels carry on extensive operations. The Icelanders, who depend so much upon their fisheries, were desirous of having a considerable extent of the waters around their coasts reserved to themselves, and wished to have a limit of seven miles to protect the grounds from the action of foreign fishing-boats.[2] As a result of negotiations, however, with Great Britain, Denmark agreed to the usual limit of three miles. The treaty was signed at London on 24th June 1901, and after

[1] 19th, 22nd, and 23rd *Reports Fishery Board for Scotland*, Part I. Corresponding particulars are not given in the English or Irish fishery reports.

[2] The preceding laws, however, left the territorial limits indefinite, under the law of nations, or subject to any special international agreement, as that of 12th February 1872, concerning foreign fishermen at Iceland. ("1. Drive fremmede Nationers Fiskere nogetsomhelst Fiskeri under Islands Kyster indenfor Søterritoriets Grænse, saaledes som denne er bestemt ved den almindelige Folkeret, eller ved særlige internationale Overenskomster for Islands Vedkommende maatte blive fastsat, straffes de med Bøder fra 10 til 200 Rd." C. F. Drechsel, *Samling af Islandske Love, Forordninger, m.m. gældende for Fiskeriet paa Søterritoriet ved Island*, 1892.) Later laws, both for the Faröes and Iceland, merely referred to the "territorial sea."

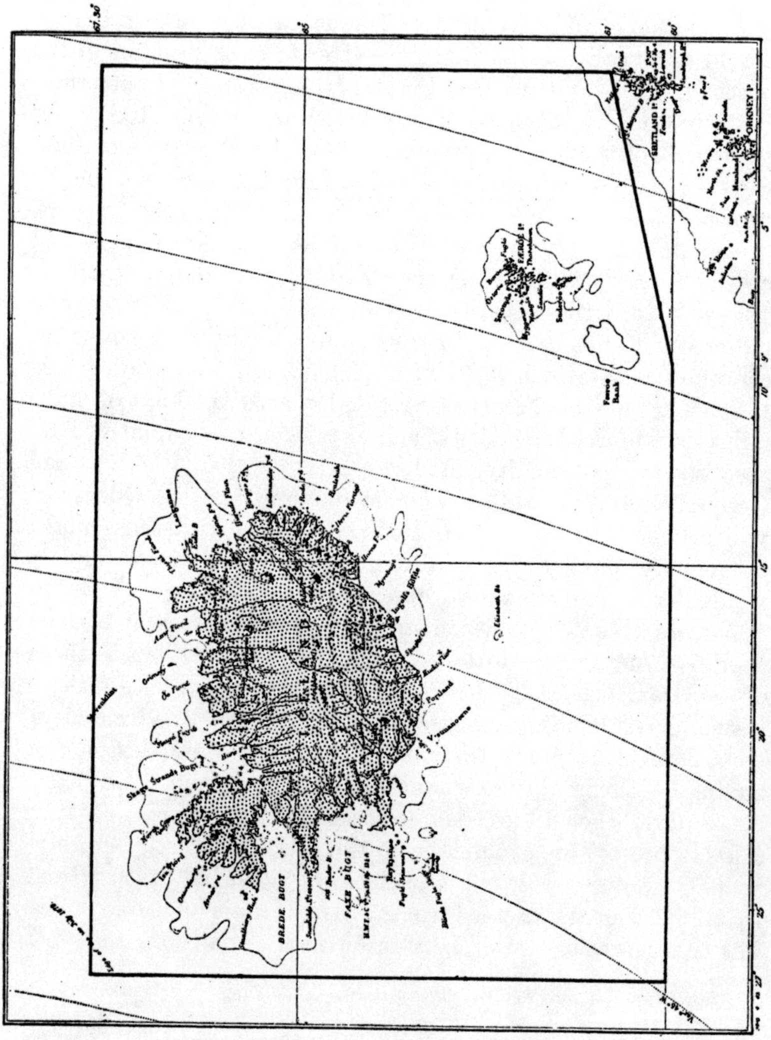

Fig. 20.—Showing the Limits for the Anglo-Danish Fishery Convention of 1901.

ratification was brought into force on 31st March 1903 by an Order in Council of the 12th of that month. Its main object, apparently, was to regulate the fisheries of the subjects of the two countries outside territorial waters in a large part of the ocean surrounding the Faröe Isles and Iceland, in a small part of which extensive fisheries are now carried on by foreigners, especially by English and German trawlers; but its immediate effect was to impose the three-mile limit on the coasts in question. The article defining the territorial waters is the same as in the North Sea Convention, except that islets and rocks are included, which thus gets rid of some possible difficulties in interpretation, such as have arisen in connection with the Eddystone and Bell Rock.[1]

[1] Convention between His Majesty the King of the United Kingdom of Great Britain and Ireland and His Majesty the King of Denmark for regulating the Fisheries of their respective Subjects outside Territorial Waters in the Ocean surrounding the Faröe Islands and Iceland. Art. ii. "The subjects of His Majesty the King of Denmark shall enjoy the exclusive right of fishery within the distance of three miles from low-water mark, along the whole extent of the coasts of the said islands, as well as of the dependent islets, rocks, and banks.

"As regards bays, the distance of three miles shall be measured from a straight line drawn across the bay, in the part nearest the entrance, at the first point where the width does not exceed ten miles." The geographical limits for the application of the convention, which embodies practically the same regulations as in the North Sea Convention, are as follows: on the south, by a line commencing from where the meridian of North Unst Lighthouse (Shetland Islands) meets the parallel of 61st degree of north latitude to a point where the 9th meridian of west longitude meets the parallel of 60° north latitude, and from thence westward along that parallel to the meridian of 27° west longitude; on the west, by the meridian of 27° west longitude; on the north, by the parallel of 67° 30′ of north latitude; on the east, by the meridian of the North Unst Lighthouse (which is about 50′ west longitude). The area is thus very large, much larger than the North Sea. The convention continues in force until the expiration of two years from notice by either party for its termination, and a clause is inserted providing for the adhesion of any other Government whose subjects fish in the ocean surrounding the Faröe Islands and Iceland.

CHAPTER IV.

THE MODERN PRACTICE OF STATES AND THE OPINIONS OF RECENT PUBLICISTS.

We may now pass to the consideration of the modern practice of states with respect to the extent of territorial sea which is claimed or allowed by them, and of the opinions of the later writers on the law of nations as to the extent that may be rightfully conceded or appropriated. It will be found that there is apparently a very considerable discrepancy between the one and the other. For while the opinions of publicists have on the whole become more decided and definite as to Bynkershoek's principle being the true principle for the delimitation of territorial waters, and the inadequacy of the three-mile limit has been formally declared, the general usage of states is indicated by the common adoption of the latter limit for several purposes. As elsewhere stated, this general use of the one marine league is in large measure owing to the example, or the pressure, of Great Britain and the United States of America, and perhaps chiefly, if indirectly, to the influence of the latter. Although the United States more than any other Power has varied her principles and claims as to the extent of territorial waters, according to her policy at the time —now claiming the vague and wandering "boundary" of the Gulf Stream or the whole of Behring Sea, and now the liberty to fish right up to the shores of the Falkland Islands,—she has been consistent in this, that she has steadily and constantly pressed for the narrowest limit she could get in favour of her own fishermen on the coasts of the British North American Colonies. The unhappy heritage of the British Foreign Office that came from the abnegation of territorial dominion over large parts of the waters in question by Great Britain in former times, has been as fruitful of trouble as Lear's renunciation of his sovereignty. The numerous negotiations as to the rights of fishing on the coasts of British North America have always resulted in concessions to the United States, and appear to have been conducted, as they were almost bound to be, rather in the light of the general political relationship of the two Powers than on the intrinsic merits of the particular question at issue; and thus in Canada and Newfoundland British diplomacy on this subject has often been criticised. Obviously, when British policy takes this course in regard to North America, one must expect for the sake of consistency, if on no other ground, that it will tend to take the same course elsewhere. An example of this was quite recently shown, when a concession of the kind referred to, as to the rule for bays, which was granted during a *modus vivendi* as a temporary act of grace, was spoken of as if it were now definitely incorporated in British international policy (see p. 730).

The discrepancy alluded to between the authorities on the law of nations and the common usage is perhaps more apparent than real. The international treaties and municipal laws in which a limit is fixed refer to a few subjects, and in particular to fisheries, and they relate to times of peace. The most vital attributes of the territorial sea relate to the security, the obligations, and the rights of neutral states in time of war; and there has happily been no great maritime war in Europe for a long time to put the principles to the test. But when such a war does come, there is little doubt that during hostilities the three-mile limit will be set aside by the neutral states concerned, and another and greater limit fixed for security, in closer correspondence with the actual range of guns. It is to be further noted, that notwithstanding the numerous municipal enactments and the international conventions in which the three-mile limit is fixed for certain purposes, no state seems to have formally and deliberately defined the absolute extent of the neighbouring sea which it claims as pertaining to it under all circumstances. Many states—and Great Britain is one of them—have taken pains to make it clear that in adopting a three-mile limit for particular purposes they do not abrogate their right to the farther extent of sea that may be necessary for other purposes.

Though Germany has not defined the extent of her territorial waters by municipal law,[1] she has entered into agreements with various Powers respecting the limits of exclusive fishery. The first of these was made with Great Britain in 1868, and the rules for the guidance of British fishermen, issued by the Board of Trade in accordance with it, stated that,—"The exclusive fishery limits of North Germany are designated by the North German Government as follows: that tract of the sea which extends to a distance of three sea-miles from the extremest limit which the ebb leaves dry of the German North Sea coast, of the German Islands or Flats lying before it, as well as those bays and incurvations of the coast which are ten sea-miles or less in breadth, reckoned from the extremest points of the land and the flats, must be considered as under the territorial sovereignty of the North German Confederation;" and it is further said that the exclusive rights of fishery in the above spaces are reserved to Germans, and English fishermen are not at liberty to enter these limits except under certain specified circumstances, as of wind and weather.[2] These limits were again formally recognised by Great Britain in July 1880, and, according to Perels, were further confirmed by the North Sea Convention of 1882. It is obvious that "the extremest limit which the ebb leaves dry," both for the open coast and for bays, will differ considerably on such a coast as that of Germany from the low-water mark of ordinary tides, and that the space included in the measurement will be correspondingly enlarged. Germany also agreed with Denmark, in 1880, to the three-mile limit for the adjacent coasts of the two countries in the Baltic, with a ten-mile base-line for bays, the mid-line or *thalweg* applying where the waters between the respective coasts were less than six miles in width. More recently, an agreement has been concluded

[1] "Das positive deutsche Recht enthält keinerlei ausdrückliche Bestimmung über die Grenze der Küstengewässer landwärts. . . . Auch für die Grenze seewärts hat das deutsche Recht keine ausdrückliche Bestimmung, und adoptiert in dieser Richtung lediglich die Regeln des Völkerrechts." Harburger, *Fifteenth Ann. Rep. Internat. Law Assoc.*, 73. 1893.

[2] Herstlet, *Commercial Treaties*, xiv. 1055. Perels, *Das Internationale öffentlichs Seerecht der Gegenwart*, 38.

precisely defining on charts the exclusive fishing waters of the two countries in the Little Belt.[1]

Denmark is one of the Scandinavian countries which, as previously mentioned, claimed a wide extent of territorial sea. In 1812 the limits, both for Norway and Denmark, were defined as follows in a royal ordinance: "We will that it be established as a rule in all cases where it is a question of determining the maritime boundary of our territory, that that territory shall be reckoned to the ordinary distance of one marine league from the outermost islands or islets which are not overflowed by the sea."[2] The league in these Scandinavian ordinances, as previously mentioned, is one-fifteenth of a degree, or four geographical miles, and therefore one mile more than the ordinary three-mile limit. But, in point of fact, owing to the method of measurement adopted, the space of sea included as territorial is much greater. Instead of computing the four miles from low-water mark on the shore, which is the base usually taken, it is measured from an imaginary straight line connecting the outermost points of the permanently visible isles or rocks lying farthest from the coast. In some places the extent of water thus cut off as territorial is very considerable. Though the other Scandinavian countries, Norway and Sweden, have maintained this limit to the present day, it has been in practice abandoned by Denmark, which has adopted the three-mile limit in certain agreements with Germany, in the North Sea Convention of 1882, and in the recent treaty with Great Britain with respect to Iceland and the Faröes. In the Skagerrack and Cattegat she concedes the three-mile limit to German and British fishermen, and no doubt also to the fishermen of the other nations which were parties to the North Sea Convention; and it is of

1 *Mittheilungen des deutschen Seefischerei-vereins*, Bd. xiii. 61. 1897.

2 "Vi ville have fastsat som Regel i alle de Tilfælde hvor Spørgsmaal er om Bestemmelse af Vor Territorial-Hoiheds Grændse udi Søen, at denne skal regnes indtil den sædvanlige Sø-Miils Afstand fra den yderste øe eller Holme fra Landet, som ikke overskylles af Søen." *Rescripter Resolutioner*, &c., i. 626, 22 (25), Feb. 1812. A circular of the Royal Danish Chancellory of 18th August 1810 made an exception for the territorial waters near the fortress of Kronberg, on the Sound, and of Glückstadt, on the Elbe, where the distance was to be computed only up to the range of the guns of the fortress. Auber, *Annuaire de l'Institut de Droit International*, xi. 146 (1894).

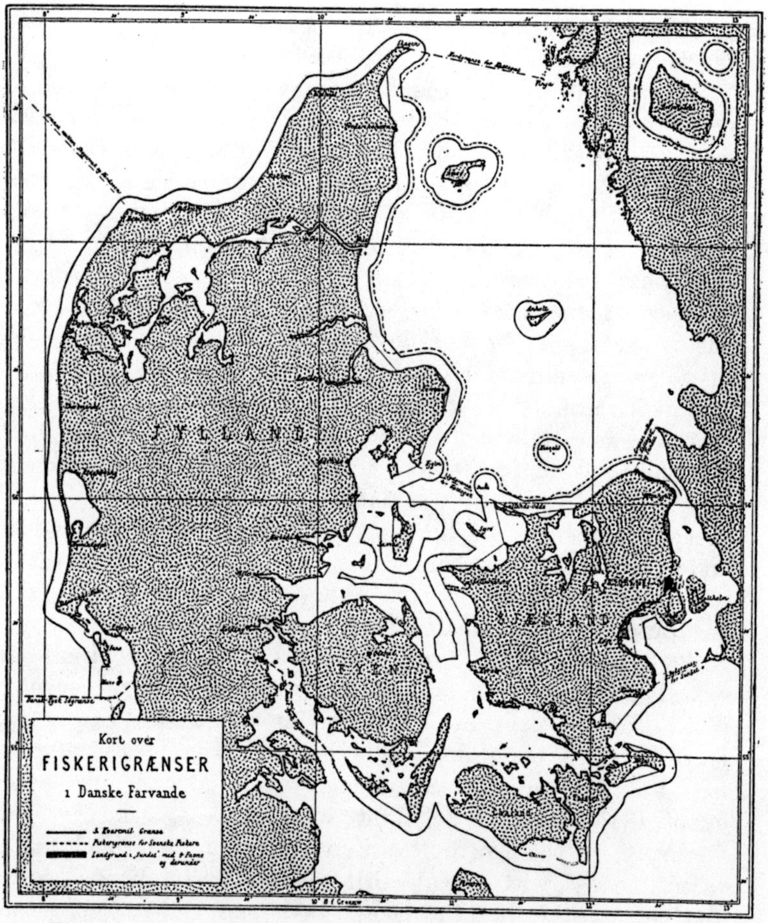

Fig. 21.—*Showing the two Limits in Danish Waters; the dotted line shows the Scandinavian Limit.* From 'Dansk-Fiskeritidende.'

interest to note, with reference to the discussion on a former page as to the extent of coast really comprised in the North Sea Convention, that it is in virtue of this convention that the old boundary of four miles has been abandoned there.[1] But while Denmark has taken up this attitude with reference

[1] *Svensk Fiskeri Tidskrift* 9e Årg., 78. Stockholm, 1900. "Danmark räknar på grund af konvention samma [with Sweden] fyra mils gräns mot oss, men däremot på grund af Nordsjötraktaten blott tre mil gentemot de i denna deltagande makterna, t. ex. engelsmän och tyskar." Instruks for det ved Fiskerikontrollen ansatte Personale, Landbrugsministeriet, den 20 Marts 1908, *Fiskeri-Beretning for Aaret* 1908-9.

to English and German fishermen, it is claimed on her behalf by an eminent Danish authority that it is within her right still to maintain the old geographical league as the boundary of her territorial sea,[1] and this has indeed been recently done in a fishery convention with Sweden, which claims the same limit with regard to the fisheries in the Cattegat, the Sound, the Baltic along the Swedish coast from Falsterbo to Simbrishamn, and around the islands Bornholm and Kristiansö.[2]

It is to be noted that the terms used in this treaty in defining the limit differ from those in the ordinance of 1812. The ordinance speaks of islands and islets which are not submerged or overflowed by the sea, while the treaty mentions the outermost islets or rocks which are not *constantly* submerged or overflowed by the sea, — a distinction which might make a very considerable difference in the extent of the waters reserved.

We thus see that Denmark enforces two limits in connection with fishery—one of four miles, measured according to the Scandinavian method, in the Baltic, &c., as against Sweden (and doubtless also against Norway); and the ordinary one of three miles in the Baltic, &c., as against Great Britain and Germany at least, and also in the North Sea and at the Faröes and Iceland. The various limits are shown in the accompanying figure, which is a reproduction of the official chart. It also

1 Natzen, *Den Danske Statsforfatningsret*, i. 36. 1888.

2 Fiskerikonventionen mellem Danmark og Sverig, 14*de* July 1899. *Fiskeri-Beretning for Finansaaret*, 1898-1899, Copenhagen, 1900. "Art. I. I de til Kongerigerne Danmark og Sverig grænsende Farvande skal, med de i Art. II. nævnte Undtagelser, det Omraade, hvor Fiskeriet udelukkende er forbeholdt hvert Lands egne Undersaatter, udgøre en Strækning af en geografisk Mil ($\frac{1}{15}$ Breddegrad) fra Kysten eller yderste der udfor liggende Holme og Skær, som ikke til Stadighed overskylles af Vandet," &c. The definition in the Swedish is "en geografisk mil ($\frac{1}{15}$ breddgrad) från kusten eller ytterst därutanför liggande holmar och skär, som icke ständigt af vattnet öfversköljas." (*Svensk Fiskeri Tidskrift*, 16*e* Årg., Häft 6, p. 189.) Article II. makes the fishery in the Sound, including Kioge Bay, common to the subjects of each state, except that on either side, *within a depth of seven metres* (four fathoms), subjects of the other country shall be allowed to fish for herrings only, with nets; and mutual liberty of herring-fishing with drift-nets is conceded in like fashion at certain other specified places. Certain amendments were made to this agreement in 1907, the chief one being the prohibition of trawling in the Sound. *Fiskeri-Beretning for Finansaaret*, 1906-1907, p. 45. *Svensk Författningssamling*, No. 79, År., 1907.

shows how complicated the three-mile limit is among the islands.

The views of Russia with respect to the limits of territorial waters, as expressed during the negotiations with Great Britain in the earlier part of last century, have been referred to (p. 581), and it appears from the Russian Code of Prize Law, 1869 (Art. 21), that the jurisdictional waters, the extent of which

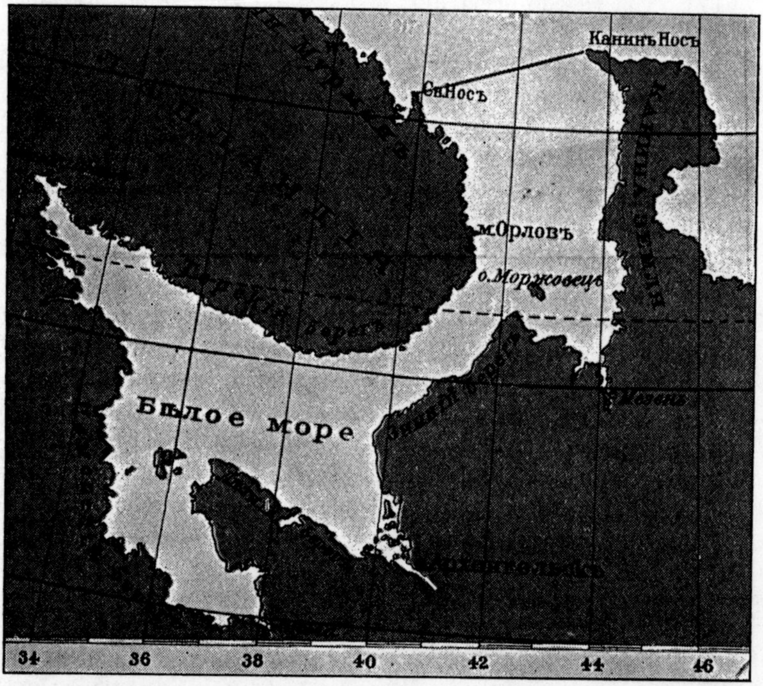

Fig. 22.—*The White Sea, showing the line between Cape Kanin and Cape Sviatoi.*

had been fixed in her treaties at the end of the eighteenth century at the range of guns, are limited to three miles (about 5647 metres) from the shore. The same distance was assigned for customs purposes; and as no general boundary has been prescribed for the exclusive right of fishing, it may be presumed that that right is restricted to the same space.[1] It

[1] *Sixth Supplement to Section* 44 *of Customs Orders*, vol. vi., 1886; *Ordinance of Home Department for the Regulation of the Fishery Supervision on the Murman Coast*, 4th May 1887. See footnote, p. 657.

appears that Russia also claims the White Sea as a *mare clausum*, or *mer fermée*, within a line between Cape Kanin (Kanin Nos) and Cape Sviatoi (Sviatoi Nos), where it is about eighty geographical miles in width.[1] If this claim is now made by Russia, it would probably be difficult for her to make it good before an international tribunal, did such exist. For not only is the mouth of the width stated, but the area included is nearly 30,000 square geographical miles, only about twenty per cent of which is within the ordinary three-mile limit. Until lately the only foreigners who fished in the neighbourhood of the White Sea were Norwegians, but in each summer since 1905 both English and German steam-trawlers have carried on an important fishery in the vicinity of Cape Kanin, but not within the White Sea itself, where the rocky nature of the bottom is said to prevent this method of fishing.[2]

In France, fishing in the sea beyond three miles from low-water mark was declared by a decree of 10th May 1862 to be free all the year round, except for oysters; but certain fisheries were allowed to be temporarily suspended beyond the three-mile limit, if it was found necessary for the preservation of the bed of the sea, or of a fishery composed of migratory fishes.[3] The first Article of the law of 1st March 1888, which originated in the North Sea Convention, states that "fishing by foreign vessels is prohibited in the territorial waters of France and Algeria within a limit which is fixed at three marine miles

[1] *Norsk Fiskeritidende*, 466, 1893; *Revue Général de Droit International Public*, 1894, p. 440.

[2] In July 1910, a British trawler, *Onward Ho*, while engaged in fishing off the Kanin Peninsula, at a distance, according to the skipper, of 40 miles from Russian Lapland, and admittedly much beyond the three-mile limit, was arrested by a Russian cruiser and taken to Archangel, on the charge of illegal fishing. The vessel was released after representations had been made by the British Government, the Russian authorities finding that it had been arrested outside the boundary under the protection of the cruiser. The action was doubtless taken in connection with a new law of 10th December 1909, establishing a limit of 12 miles from the coast for customs purposes,—all vessels, Russian or foreign, being held to be subject to the control of the Russian authorities when within that distance. *Handelsberichten*, 12th May 1910, p. 135.

[3] "Art. 2. Sur la demande des prud'hommes des pêcheurs, de leurs délégués et, à défaut, des syndics des gens de mer, certaines pêches peuvent être temporairement interdités sur une étendue de mer au delà de 3 milles du littoral, si cette mesure est commandée par l'intérêt de la conservation des fonds ou de la pêche de poissons de passage. L'arrêté d'interdiction est pris par le Préfet Maritime."

seawards from low-water mark," with the same arrangement for bays as in the North Sea Convention. The distance stated does not, however, necessarily represent the bounds of the territorial sea, properly so called, the extent of which has never been precisely defined by France.[1] No doubt France, like other countries, reserves her right to a wider limit should occasion arise to make that necessary.

It appears that as early as 1832 the three-mile limit was declared by Belgium to be the boundary of her territorial waters,[2] and by a law promulgated in 1891, and based upon the North Sea Convention, "all foreign boats" were prohibited from fishing within three miles of the Belgian coast.[3]

In the Netherlands also, in connection with the North Sea Convention, the boundary of exclusive fishing has been declared to be at the distance of three miles from low-water mark, and this applies to all foreign fishermen. No distinction has been formally made between the fishery limit and the limit of the territorial sea for political purposes.[4]

In Austria-Hungary, whose coast is confined to the eastern shore of the Adriatic, the three-mile limit has been adopted, subject to certain qualifications respecting the right of fishery under treaties with Italy. The regulations concerning foreign vessels of war authorise a shot to be fired from the nearest battery at any such vessel which does not show its flag on coming within range of the guns, and within the same distance

[1] M. de Chasseloup Lubat, in *Ann. di Agricoltura*, 50. 1891.

[2] Law of 7th June 1832. Heffter, *Le Droit International de l'Europe*, c. ii. s. 75.

[3] "Loi relative à la pêche maritime dans les eaux territoriales," 19th August 1891. A decree of 5th September 1892 regulated foreign fishing-boats when within territorial waters.

[4] Wet van 15 Juni 1883, *Staatsblad*, No. 73; Koninklijk Besluit van 20 March 1884, *Staatsblad*, No. 40, putting in force the North Sea Convention: "Art. 1. De bepalingen dezer overeenkomst, welke ten doel heeft de politie der visscherij in de Noordzee buiten de territoriale wateren te regelen, zijn toepasselijk op allen, die tot de nationaliteit der Hooge contracteerende Partijen behooren. 2. De visschers van elken Staat zullen het uitsluitend recht van visscherij genieten binnen een kring van drie mijlen, gerekend van de laagwaterlijn, langs de geheele uitgestrektheid der kusten van elken Staat en evenzeer langs de eilanden en banken, die daarmede zijn verbonden," &c. Wet van 7th December 1883, *Staatsblad*, No. 202; Wet van 26th October 1889, *Staatsblad*, No. 135, "Tot vaststelling van bepalingen tegen het visschen door opvarenden van vreemde vaartuigen in de territoriale wateren van het Rijk"; the limits, as laid down in the convention of 1882, are applied to all foreign fishing vessels. There are special agreements with Belgium as to the fishings in the Schelde. H. van der Hoeven, *Wetgeving betreffende de Zee- en de Zalmvisscherijen*. Leiden, 1897.

of a fortified port they are prohibited from taking soundings, practising with firearms, &c.; other regulations forbid vessels laden with goods which form the object of a monopoly of the state from approaching within gunshot. By a decree of 23rd August 1846, and a circular of 28th April 1849, it was declared that the expression "range of guns" in these ordinances was equivalent to three marine miles of sixty to a degree. The customs regulations operate within the same limit, but the manifest can be demanded within a farther distance of four marine miles.[1] With respect to the right of fishing, the regulations are somewhat complex. The boundary of exclusive fishing is fixed at three miles,[2] but inasmuch as the fisheries in the Adriatic are carried on almost only by Austrian and Italian subjects, it was found convenient to arrange by treaty for the fishermen of either country to fish within the territorial waters of the other, except within a distance of one marine mile from the shore, and subject to certain restrictions regarding the fisheries for corals and sponges, and the observance of the local regulations.[3] This mutual arrangement with regard to the right of fishery was renewed and continued in a later treaty of 11th February 1906.

The fishings within one marine mile of the shore are reserved to the inhabitants of the commune to which the coast appertains; but in certain specified circumstances fishermen from other places may be allowed to fish within this communal zone. The use of drag-nets and trawl-nets is prohibited in all places where the depth is under eight metres; within the first maritime or communal zone at certain seasons, irrespective of depth, and altogether within five miles of the coast when employed from steamers. Owing to the absence of tides, the shoreward limit is not measured from a low-water mark, but from a line, fixed by local authorities, where the water ceases to be constantly brackish.[4]

[1] Strisower, *Annuaire de l'Institut de Droit International.* 1894.

[2] Verordnung der Ministerien des Handels und des Ackerbaues, im Einvernehmen mit dem Ministerium des Innern, vom 5 December 1884, betreffend die Seefischerei, s. 3.

[3] Handels- und Schiffahrtsvertrag vom 27 Dec. 1878, zwischen Oesterreich-Ungarn und Italien. Schlussprotokoll ad Art. xvii., xviii.; Marchesetti, *La pesca lungo le coste orientali dell' Adria.* Trieste, 1882.

[4] Vorschriften über die See-Fischerei giltig in Oesterreich-Ungarn seit 12 December 1884.

It is doubtful how far the three-mile limit has been adopted in Italy. In a Bill of 1872 a distinction was proposed between the territorial waters and the exclusive fishing waters, but this distinction was not made in the law of 1877.[1] The question was taken up later by the Commission for Fisheries, and the opinions elicited from the local authorities at various parts of the coast, who were consulted, varied, the recommendations for the boundary of the territorial waters (*mare territoriale*) ranging from one and a half miles to ten kilometres, and very commonly the limit suggested was four geographical miles. The boundary recommended for the exclusive fishing waters (*mare pescatorio*) also varied, but in this case the depth of the water rather than the distance from shore was held to be the more important factor in deciding on a limit, an opinion with which the Commission agreed so far as concerned steam trawling. In view of the fishery conventions of the western Powers, the Commission recommended a limit of three miles and ten miles for bays, as in those conventions,[2] but the proposal was not accepted by the Italian Government. The subject was again considered by the Commission in 1904 and 1906, with particular reference to steam trawling and dredging, but no proposition to determine the boundary of the territorial waters for fishing purposes was adopted. A decree of 4th September 1908, however, introduced a limit of three miles,, but only with reference to the use of dredges in some districts of the Tyrrhenian Sea.

With respect to the extent of the territorial sea for political purposes, no definition has been given in Italian laws; it depends therefore upon the general principles of international jurisprudence. It is interesting to note that in some comparatively recent decrees the boundary is stated to depend on the range of guns. Thus, instructions issued by the Minister of Marine in June 1866 commanded the officers of the navy to refrain from all hostile acts in the ports and territorial waters of neutral Powers, and reminded them that the limit of the territorial waters was the range of cannon from the shore; and in a circular from the same Ministry in March 1862 it was stated that the extent of the territorial sea varied

[1] Legge sulla pesca del 4 marzo 1877, No. 3706 (Serie 2a).

[2] *Annali di Agricoltura*, 1891. Atti della commissione consultiva per la pesca, pp. 32, 86.

in different countries and in the opinion of different publicists, but that the general opinion was that the range of guns was the sole rule on the matter.[1] It may be added that by the customs law of 1896, the manifest of vessels may be demanded within ten kilometres of the coast.[2]

In Greece, another of the Mediterranean states, the three-mile limit was adopted in 1869, when a circular of the Minister of Marine prohibited foreigners from fishing within that distance of the shore. Previously, in virtue of a royal decree issued in 1834, foreign boats were allowed to fish for sardines in the Gulf of Corinth, but this concession was withdrawn.[3]

As already mentioned, the three-mile limit is the one in force in all the British colonies, in Japan,[4] in the United States of America, and in some at least of the South American states. The Chilian Government, for example, has defined the extent of the territorial sea belonging to it as one marine league from low-water mark, within which distance the right of fishing is reserved to Chilian citizens or domiciled foreigners. At the same time it is stated that "police administration for the purposes of the security of the State or the carrying out of fiscal regulations extends to a distance of four marine leagues, measured in the same manner."[5]

Quite lately, however, one of the chief states of South America has advanced a claim to a very wide extent of sea along its coasts—so far, at least, as the right of fishery is concerned. In September 1907 the Minister of Agriculture for the Argentine Republic issued a series of ordinances for the regulation of the fisheries,[6] in which it is declared that, with respect to the fisheries, a zone of water up to a distance of ten miles (18,520 metres, or about 10¼ nautical miles) from high-water mark on the land is under the control of the state. The great gulfs and bays are, moreover, included, such as the Gulf of San Matias, the Gulf of St George, and the Gulf of Nuevo,

[1] Definizione del mare territoriale e ordine di vigilare sugli armamenti alla pesca. *Ann. del Ministero di Agricoltura, Industria e Commercio*, i. parte i. 96. Genoa, 1871.

[2] Corsi, in *Fifteenth Ann. Rep. Assoc. for the Reform and Codification of the Law of Nations*, 83.

[3] No. 7, 409, 2nd Dec. 1869. Apostolidès, *La Pêche en Grèce*, 86. Athens, 1888.

[4] Dr Kishinouye, *in litt.*

[5] Civil Code, Articles 593, 611.

[6] Reglamentendo la pesca y caza, *Boletin official*, 20th September 1907.

the closing line in some cases considerably exceeding one hundred nautical miles from point to point, and extending for more than seventy miles beyond a three-mile limit. All living animals in the sea are considered as objects of sea-fishing, with the exception of those which reproduce on the land, as birds, seals (*lobos*), and fish-otters. Within the declared limits the exercise of sea-fishing is free, provided that the regulations are adhered to. The one referring to trawling prohibits that method of fishing by sailing-boats within three miles of the shore, but allows such boats to trawl outside that distance if the meshes of the nets have an aperture not less than 16 centimetres (6¼ inches); steam trawling, on the other hand, is prohibited within five miles of the shore. Commercial fishing is forbidden within the great extent of water referred to unless by vessels entered on the official list (*matricula nacional*), and foreigners are thus excluded. A novel feature, but one in complete harmony with the results of modern fishery investigations, is the reservation of the right to close any area within the limit claimed, so that such area or areas may act as reserves to replenish neighbouring grounds and increase the multiplication of the fish. The right to establish close-times is also reserved, and the sale of undersized fish is prohibited unless for certain specified purposes.

Special regulations are made for sealing. Concessions for this purpose will be granted for a term of five years on various parts of the coast under certain conditions, and it is enacted that for a distance of twenty miles from the coast in such places the right of taking seals is confined to those who have obtained the concession. Penalties for the infraction of the laws are provided, fines varying from five to five hundred pesetas, and offenders may be imprisoned for a period of from one to sixty days.

Later regulations issued by the Minister of Agriculture, applying to that part of the coast between the Rio de la Plata and the Rio Negro, provide that all those engaged or who desire to engage in sea fishing there, must first receive official permission to do so. Within a zone of twelve miles from low-water mark, trawling by steamers is prohibited, but trawling by sailing-boats, and fishing with various kinds of lines and with drift-nets, are allowed; and all vessels employed must fly the national flag, and have their crews partly national, in accordance with the laws.[1] It may be noted that these regulations are declared to be for the purpose of preventing the extermination of certain species of fish, and that the grantees must, when requested, allow officials to be on board for scientific study.

The adjoining state of Uruguay also lays claim to jurisdiction, with regard to fisheries at least, beyond the ordinary three-mile limit in the extensive inlet of the Rio de la Plata, which lies between Uruguay and Argentina, and is nearly sixty miles wide at its mouth, with an estimated area of about 5000 square miles. In 1905 a Canadian sealer, the *Agnes G. Donohoe*, was arrested for the contravention of a presidential decree which prohibits sealing within these Uruguayan waters, but it was subsequently released. The British Government formally protested against this claim to jurisdiction outside the three-mile boundary, which, however, is strongly supported by the Argentine Government, which is equally concerned in its maintenance.[2]

It is evident from the foregoing that most maritime states, and all the great ones, either by treaty or in their municipal laws and decrees, have adopted the three-mile limit, at least for fishery purposes. It is quite appropriate, therefore, to refer to it as the "ordinary" limit, as was done by the Tribunal of

1 Reglamento para las concesiones de pesca en el litoral oceánico de la Provincia de Buenos Aires, 4th June 1909. "Art. 3°. Los concesionarios solo podrán emplear redes arrastradas por vapores en una zona distante no menos de doce (12) millas, contadas desde las líneas de las más bajas mareas. Art. 4°. Dentro de la zona de doce millas hasta la línea de las más bajas mareas, podrán usarse redes arrastradas por veleros. Se declara libre el uso de las líneas, palangres ó espineles, nasas y redes verticales de deriva. Art. 6°. Las personas ó empresas que quisieran usar artes especiales de pesca distintos de los indicados, deberán solicitar permiso especial de la División de Ganadería y obtener la autorización correspondiente. Art. 7°. Las embarcaciones llevarán bandera nacional y sus tripulaciones se compondrán de una parte de individuos de nacionalidad argentina, de acuerdo con las leyes y reglamentos de cabotaje nacional." I am indebted to the courtesy of Mr R. M. Bartleman, the American Consul-General at Buenos Aires, for a copy of these regulations.

2 Reuter's telegrams from Buenos Aires, 21st March, 30th June 1908. *Scotsman*, 23rd March, 2nd July 1908. *La Prensa*, one of the leading journals of Buenos Aires, is quoted as declaring it hard to believe that the British Government has decided to raise a question of such exceptional gravity, seeing the first effect of such action would be to bring about a conflict to which there could be no conciliatory or friendly solution, since the immediate reply, which would be final, would be absolute rejection of the claim put forward—that is, that the waters of the estuary outside the limits of three miles from the coasts are non-territorial.

Arbitration on the rights of seal-fishing in the Behring Sea, though the tribunal did not affirm, and could not affirm, that it found the three-mile limit to be, as a matter of fact, universally accepted.[1] But though it is the ordinary limit, it is not the only one enforced, and it is erroneous to declare, as some of the less instructed writers on international law have stated, that territorial jurisdiction cannot be carried further.[2]

In point of fact, no fewer than four of the maritime states of Europe reject the three-mile limit, while a fifth has in part deviated from it. Norway, Sweden, Spain, and Portugal, all claim to enforce a wider boundary, and Denmark has adopted the old Scandinavian limit in her recent treaty with Sweden (see p. 655). Thus, along nearly 4000 miles of the coasts of Europe, or for about one-third of their whole extent, the three-mile limit is not accepted by the bordering state. The right claimed by these countries to a wider extent of territorial sea has been embodied in treaties between some of them, and has been successfully maintained in specific instances against the opposition of other Powers. It is to be noted, moreover, as is shown later, that their claims to the wider space have been quite lately fully justified and homologated by the most authoritative exponents of international law, the French Institute and the British Association on the Law of Nations, as well as by various international congresses of fishery experts dealing with the subject from a fishery point of view.

We have already stated that Spain in the eighteenth century declared that her territorial sea extended to a distance of six miles from the coast (see p. 569). At that time such a limit must have been regarded as moderate, but during last century, after the principle of cannon range had been commonly translated into one marine league, the right to a zone of double that extent was called in question both by the United States and Great Britain. During the civil war in America the question

[1] Award of the Tribunal of Arbitration, p. 23, "outside the ordinary three-mile limit." The President, Baron de Courcel, has since explained that the tribunal "s'est borné à constater que les parties étaient d'accord pour admettre que l'étendue de trois milles à partir de la côte comme formant dans l'espèce qui lui était soumise, la limite ordinaire des eaux territoriales." M. de Courcel to M. Auber, *App. Ann. de l'Institut de Droit Internat.* for 1894, p. 282. *Vide* Hall, *A Treatise on International Law*, 4th ed., p. 161.

[2] For example, Leoni Levi, "No territorial sovereignty exists or can be claimed beyond the three miles zone." *Internat. Law*, 112.

came to the front, more particularly with reference to the waters around Cuba. In 1862 the American Government intimated that they were not prepared to admit that Spain, without a formal concurrence of other nations, could exercise exclusive sovereignty upon the open sea beyond a line of three miles from the coast; while Spain, relying on the legal principle governing the extent of the territorial sea, argued that the improvement of modern artillery made the three-mile limit ineffective. Two years later a discussion on the subject took place between the British and American Governments, the former desiring that during the existence of hostilities the limit of neutral waters should be greatly extended, so that shots from belligerents might be prevented from falling, not only on land, but within the neutral waters, and limits of ten, eight, and five miles were mentioned.[1] In 1874 the British Government had itself occasion to object to the claim of Spain; and on communication with the Government of the United States, they were informed that that Government had always protested against it, and on the same grounds, that by the law of nations jurisdiction could only extend to one marine league from the coast.[2] Notwithstanding the opposition of the two chief maritime Powers, Spain did not abandon its claim, for by a royal order of 16th May 1881, passed with special reference to the jurisdiction over American vessels in Cuban waters, it was declared that full jurisdiction extended to a distance of six miles from the coast. This limit was also fixed for customs purposes in Spanish waters by royal decrees in 1830 and 1852, and in the general ordinances of the customs in 1884, the six miles being stated to be equivalent to eleven kilometres.[3]

With regard to fisheries, Spain has entered into various treaties with Portugal as to the right of fishing along their

[1] Mr Seward, Secretary of State, to Mr Tassara, 6th December 1862. The same to Mr Burnley, 16th September 1864. Wharton, *A Digest of the International Law of the United States*, i. 105. American ships were charged with pursuing Confederate vessels into British waters, and the balls from the guns they fired had struck objects on shore. The facts were used to show that the hostile acts had occurred within our territorial jurisdiction. Hansard, vol. 173, p. 509; February 1864.

[2] Secretary Fish to Sir E. Thornton, 22nd January 1875. "We have understood and asserted that, pursuant to public law, no nation can rightfully claim jurisdiction at sea beyond a marine league from the coast." *Loc. cit.*

[3] Torres-Campos, in *Fifteenth Ann. Rep. Assoc. for Reform and Codification of the Law of Nations*, 93. Negrin, *Tratado de Derecho internacional maritimo*, 1883.

respective coasts. By a convention in 1878, reciprocity was established in the territorial waters of the two countries, subject to the observance of local regulations and certain specified conditions, as the prohibition of the use of drag or trawl nets ("*artes de Bou* ou *parelhas, chalut, muletas*") within twelve miles from the coast.[1] In another treaty concluded between these Powers on 2nd October 1885, and slightly amended in 1888, two fishery zones were established, the first extending to three miles from the coast, which was exclusively reserved for nationals, and the second, from three to six miles, in which the fishermen of both countries were at liberty to fish. In a later treaty of commerce and navigation, which came into force in October 1893, the zone of exclusive fishing was extended to six geographical miles from the coast of either country—that is, to the extreme boundary of the jurisdictional waters, measured from low-water mark of spring tides ("de la línea de bajamar de las mayores mareas"), and a ten-mile base-line for bays was adopted. Within this space the fishery and its regulation were reserved by each state; but in the frontier rivers, the Miño and Guadiana, the fishery was specially dealt with, as in previous treaties. Each Government also agreed to prohibit certain injurious modes of fishing (*parejas, muletas,* &c.) within twelve miles of their coasts, and a series of regulations, like those of the North Sea Convention of 1882, were included with respect to the entry of the fishing-boats of one of the countries within the territorial waters of the other, and the police supervision of the fishing-boats of either country beyond the six-mile limit.[2] In Spain the reservation of six miles

[1] *Negocios Externos. Documentos apresentados ás Cortes na Sessão legislativa de* 1879 *pelo Ministro e Secretario d'Estado dos Negocios Estrangeiros. Questão das Pescarias,* p. 258. Lisboa, 1879. The volume contains a full discussion of the questions between the two Governments.

[2] Tratado de navegación y comercio entre España y Portugal, firmado en Madrid el día 27 de Marzo de 1893. Apéndice Sexto. Reglamento de policía costera y de pesca. Sec. 1. Disposiciones aplicables á las aguas de cada país. "Art. 1°. La policía costera y de pesca en las aguas jurisdiccionales de España y de Portugal, quedará sujeta á las disposiciones siguientes. Art. 2°. Los límites dentro de los cuales el derecho general de pesca, queda reservado exclusivamente á los pescadores sujetos á las jurisdicciones respectivas de las dos naciones, se fijan en seis millas, contadas por fuera de la línea de bajamar de las mayores mareas. Para las bahías cuya abertura no exceda de diez millas, las seis millas se contarán á partir de una línea recta tirada de una punta á la otra. Las millas mencionadas

was regarded as unjust, since the water off the coast of Portugal was much deeper than off the Spanish coast, and in the following year the Portuguese Government allowed Spanish fishermen to fish, under certain conditions, to within three miles of the coast of Algarbe.[1]

While it is evident that Spain and Portugal claim jurisdiction to the extent of six miles from the coast, it appears that an exclusive fishery to that distance is not enforced against all other nations. It seems that on the Mediterranean coast, the three-mile, and not the six-mile, limit is applied against French fishermen,[2] and the British Government, in the interests of British trawlers, recently intimated that they did not recognise any claims of the Spanish or Portuguese Governments to exercise jurisdiction over British vessels beyond the three-mile limit; and, in point of fact, British and German trawlers now fish off the Portuguese and Spanish coasts up to three miles from the shore.[3] They have developed an important and extensive trawl-fishery there during the last few years; and although the local fishermen strongly object to their presence within waters where they are themselves prohibited to trawl, and it is stated that negotiations on the matter have taken place between the

son millas geográficas de 60 al grado de latitud. Art. 3°. Cada una de los Estados tendrá el derecho de reglamentar el ejercicio de la pesca en sus respectivas costas marítimas hasta una distancia de seis millas de las mismas, límite dentro del cual solamente será permitido á los pescadores nacionales ejercer esta industria." F. López y Medina, *Colección de Tratados Internacionales, Ordenanzas y Reglamentos de Pesca*, pp. 44, 49 (Madrid, 1906). I am indebted to Sir Reginald MacLeod, K.C.B., late Under-Secretary for Scotland, for this volume.

1 *Revista de Pesca Marítima*, ix. 97 (1893); x. 209 (1894). Various regulations have been lately made with respect to trawling beyond the six-mile limit at certain parts of the Spanish coast (*vide* López y Medina, *Primer Apéndice á la Colección de Tratados, &c.*, pp. 34-45. Madrid, 1907), and also on the coast of Portugal (*vide Collecção de Leis e Disposições diversas com relação á Pesca e Serviço maritimo dos Portos*, pp. 28, 54, 276, 535. Lisboa, 1907). In no other countries, it may be added, have more regulations been made restricting all kinds of trawling than in Spain and Portugal.

2 Prof. A. F. Marion, *in litt.*

3 The National Sea Fisheries Protection Association: *Twenty-fourth Ann. Rep. of the Committee of Management*, 1905, p. 7. "Spanish and Portuguese Territorial Limits. Communications were made to the Foreign Office on the subject of Spanish and Portuguese Territorial Limits, and, in reply, the Association was informed that His Majesty's Government did not recognise any claims of the Spanish or Portuguese Governments to exercise jurisdiction over British vessels beyond the three-mile limit."

London and Lisbon Governments, they have not been ordered out of them, and still continue their trawling. Both in Spain and Portugal meetings have been held with reference to the territorial waters, at which resolutions were passed calling for an international arrangement for the extension of the limits to ten or twelve miles; and some unpleasant encounters have occurred between the local and foreign fishermen. On these coasts, however, a limit so extensive would largely prevent foreigners from fishing, owing to the great depth of the water at such distances from the shore. On the other hand, it is argued that as the available fishing-ground is so narrow and small, there is all the more reason why it should be protected from the destructive methods of fishing pursued by the foreign vessels, and preserved as far as possible for the inhabitants of the coast.[1] Quite recently, it appears, the Portuguese Government have regularised their position with regard to foreign trawlers and foreign fishermen generally, by passing a law forbidding them to fish, under severe penalties, within a zone of three sea miles from the shore. They have thus accepted the inevitable, in view of the pressure applied by at least one of the great maritime Powers. With regard to bays, however, the limit specified in the fishery conventions is not adopted. The zone of three miles in respect to bays has to be reckoned according to the principles of international law.[2]

Spain, it may be added, after the victorious campaign of 1859-60, concluded a treaty with Morocco, by which Spanish subjects are allowed to fish on the coast of that country up to

[1] *Fish Trades Gazette*, 10th Dec. 1904, p. 23. London. *Boletin Oficial de la Liga Marítima Española; Vida Marítima, Revista de Navegación y Comercio, Pesquerias, &c.* Madrid. In 1905 no less than forty-five English trawlers, as well as four German trawlers and one Spanish, landed fish at Lisbon and Oporto, which had been caught in neighbouring waters and as far as Morocco, the value being 332,220 milreis, or about £74,750. *Estatistica das Pescas Maritimas, Anno de* 1905. Lisboa, 1907.

[2] A summary of this new law, which received the sanction of the King of Portugal on 26th October 1909, is given in *Mitteilungen des Deutschen Seefischerei-Vereins* for February 1910 (Bd. xxvi. No. 2), from *Diario do Governo*, No. 247, viz.: Portugiesisches Gesetz betreffend das Verbot für fremde Fahrzeuge zum Fischen in den territorialen Gewässern. "Art. 1. In den portugiesischen Territorialgewässern innerhalb einer Zone von 3 Seemeilen, von der Linie des Niedrigstwasserstandes an gerechnet, ist fremden Fahrzeugen das Fischen verboten. In den Buchten ist die Zone von 3 Seemeilen gemäss den Grundsätsen des internationalen Rechts zu berechnen."

the shores, for corals, sponges, and other marine products, as well as for fish.[1]

The extent of the territorial waters claimed by Norway and Sweden is even greater than that claimed by Spain and Portugal, owing to the method of measurement, the distance of four geographical miles being measured either from the coast or from the outermost part of the outermost isle or rock which is not submerged by the sea at high tide. Such isles and rocks are numerous on the Scandinavian coasts, so that the fishermen distinguish the waters "within the rocks" (*inom skärs*) from those "without the rocks" (*utom skärs*) or at sea, and in many places the extent of water reserved by the rule is very considerable. There appears, however, to be a difference in Sweden and Norway as to the precise method of measurement. In Norway such isles and rocks are appropriate for the base-line, if they are not farther from the mainland than eight geographical miles of sixty to a degree; and it seems to follow from the rule that the measurement from the coast or shore must be made at high-water, but this is not expressly said.[2] In Sweden the isle or rock is spoken of as within one geographical league of the coast, and it may be such as is not *continuously* submerged, but is periodically uncovered, which implies a base of low-water.[3] On some parts of the Norwegian coast

[1] Tratado de comercio con el emperador de Marruecos, 20th November 1861. *Revista de Pesca Marítima*, xiv. 149, 1898. López y Medina, *op cit.*, 72.

[2] This is also the interpretation made by Mr Arctander (*Norsk Fiskeritidende*, Tolvte Aargang, 1893, p. 464) of the wording of the ordinances, that the line must be drawn through points that lie above the water at high tide (*flod*), the rule thus differing from the usual one. On the other hand, the Norwegian Department of the Interior, in replying to certain queries from the International Law Association, stated, with reference to the royal ordinance of 1812 (see p. 653), that "it is not expressly said whether the distance is to be reckoned at half-tide, high-water, or low-water"; and they did not suggest which ought to be adopted. *Rep.*, *Seventeenth Conference*, 1895, p. 301. The Danish terms agree with the Swedish. See p. 655.

[3] Professor Auber thus states the practice in Norway: "Nous avons regardé comme tout naturel que, l'île n'étant pas située plus qu'à deux anciens milles marins (deux quinzièmes de degré) de la terre ferme, l'étendue de la mer territoriale doive être compter jusqu'à un mille au delà de l'île, et ainsi de suite d'île en île" (*Annuaire de l'Institut de Droit International* for 1889, p. 139). M. Kleen, on the other hand, speaks of the outermost isle being included "sous la condition que cette île ou ce brisant ne soit pas situé plus loin de la côte qu'une lieu géographique" (*Fifteenth Ann. Rep.*, *Internat. Law Association*, p. 20). The Norwegian law refers to "the island or islet farthest from the mainland, and not covered by the

the territorial sea may thus extend to twelve miles from the mainland. Bays and fjords are, moreover, included in the territorial waters irrespective of whether their width at the mouth is or is not greater than ten miles; and in including these, as much importance is attached to the islands which may lie at their entrance as to the distance between headlands.

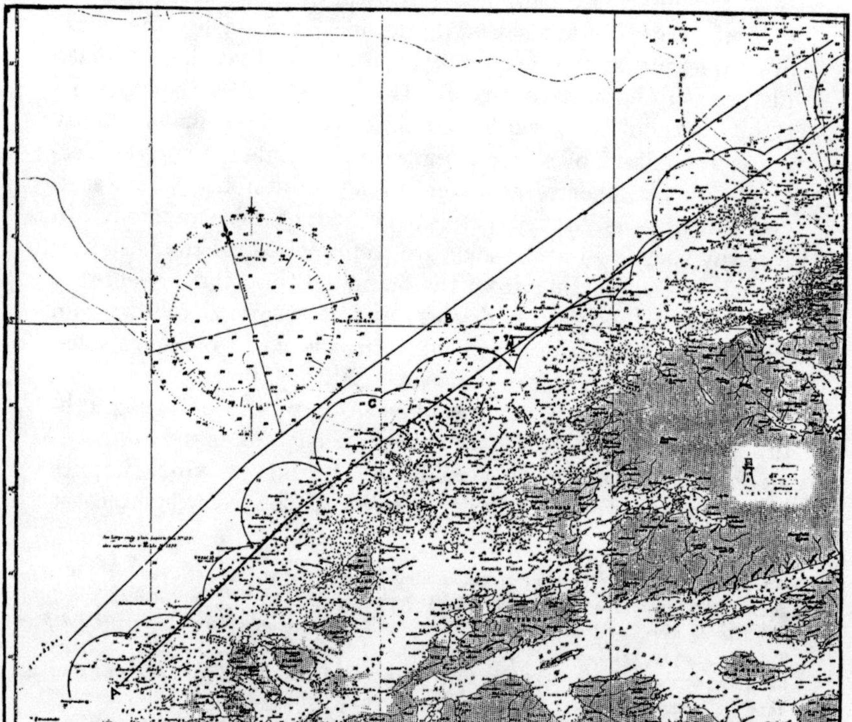

Fig. 23.—*Showing the Limit at Romsdal Amt, Norway.*

A, The base-line; B, the line of closure; C, the three-mile limit.

With regard to large open ways or stretches of sea partly enclosed, no fixed rule has been laid down, but Norway reserves the right in certain cases to exceed the limit derived

sea," while M. Kleen says: "Comme brisant à compter sera alors considéré chacun qui n'est pas *continuellement* submergé par la mer . . . pourvu qu'il soit à découvert périodiquement et que la mer ne le couvre pas *toujours.*"

from the general principle as above explained. On some parts of the coast special laws regulate the extent of the sea in which the exclusive right of fishing is reserved to subjects. The rich cod-banks on the coast of Söndmöre, Romsdal, and Nordmöre are thus included within the territorial waters, the base-line being drawn between various islands, in the manner described above. The first of these was a royal decree of 16th October 1869, which prescribed that a straight line drawn at a distance of one geographical mile (of fifteen to a degree) from and parallel to a straight line drawn between Storholmen and Svinö, shall be taken as the boundary of the waters off the coast of the Söndmöre district, in which the fishing is entirely reserved for the inhabitants of the country. Another royal decree of 9th September 1889 continued this boundary farther to the north-east. It ordained that a line drawn at a distance of one geographical mile from and parallel to a line from Storholmen through Skraapen (outside of Harö), Gravskjær (outside of Ona), and Kalven (the last of the Orskjærens), to the last of the Jevleholme, outside of Grip, was the boundary of the waters off the coast of the Romsdal district, in which fishing is entirely reserved for the inhabitants of the country.[1]

This special line from Svinö (which lies about eight miles north of Stadtland, or Van Staten) to Jevleholm stretches for about eighty-five geographical miles along the coast,[2] the distance between the islets through which the base-line passes being respectively 28, 14½, 7, 23½, and 12 geographical miles, and some of them are over seven miles distant from the mainland or the nearest large island. The extent of water reserved is thus large, the area between the base-line and the boundary-

[1] *Kongelig Resolution* af 16 Oktober 1869: "At en ret linie, trukket i en geografisk mils afstand fra og parallelt med en ret linie mellem Storholmen og Svinö, bliver at betragte som grændsen for den havstrækning udenfor den tilsvarende kyst af Söndmöres fogderi, paa hvilken fiskeriet er landets egen befolkning udelukkende forbeholdt." *Kongelig Resolution* af 9 September 1889: "En linie, trukket i en geografisk mils afstand fra og parallelt med en linie fra Storholmen over Skraapen (udenfor Harö), Gravskjær (udenfor Ona) og Kalven (det yderste af Orskjærene) til yderste Jevleholme udenfor Grip, bliver at betragte som grændsen for den havstrækning udenfor den tilsvarende kyst af Romsdal amt, paa hvilken fiskeriet er landets egen befolkning udelukkende forbeholdt."

[2] From about 62° 20′ N. lat. and 5° 13′ E. long. to about 63° 13′ N. lat. and 7° 35′ E. long.

line being alone about 340 square miles; but the extent of sea included which would be outside the ordinary three-mile limit is much less than might be expected, owing to the great number of isles and islets along the coast. In the accompanying figure (fig. 23), the part of the coast embraced by the law of 1889 is represented, the base-line, the boundary of the reserved waters, and the ordinary three-mile limit being shown. The area of water between the latter and the Norwegian limit amounts, approximately, to 140 square miles. The figure also shows how complicated a three-mile boundary based on the provisions of the North Sea Convention would be on such a coast. It is to be noted further, that within the limits prescribed by the royal decrees a series of stringent regulations have been made for the orderly prosecution of the fishery.[1]

Of much greater international importance is the claim made by the Norwegians to the exclusive right of fishing in the Vestfjord, an arm of the sea which extends between the coast of Nordland and the Lofoten Islands, where from time immemorial the greatest cod-fishing in Europe has been carried on.[2] It is, strictly speaking, a strait, as indicated in the accompanying figure (fig. 24), bounded on one side by a chain of islands and on the other by the mainland, opening to the northwards by several narrow channels, and to the south by a wide mouth about forty-five geographical miles in breadth. The waters of the Vestfjord have for centuries been considered as territorial, and the fisheries within them as reserved for the Norwegian people; but no decree or law has as yet been promulgated respecting the boundary between the reserved waters and the open sea.[3] Locally, however, as at Bodö, it is supposed that

[1] Provisorisk Anordnung angaaende vaartorskefiskeriet ved Söndmöres kyster, 3 Jan. 1870; Lov angaaende vaartorskefiskeriet ved Söndmöres kyster, 6 June 1878; Lov om vaartorskefiskeriet ved Romsdals amts kyst og fjorde, 1 July 1907.

[2] It is referred to in A.D. 888. The fishery is prosecuted from about the middle of January to the end of April; in 1908 over 20,000 fishermen, drawn from all the neighbouring parts of the coast, took part in it. *Aarsberetning vedkommende Norges Fiskerier for* 1908: 4de Hefte, *Lofotfiskeriet*, 1908.

[3] "Le droit exclusif de la pêche dans le golfe du Vestfjord, consacré par un usage plusieurs fois seculaire, n'a jusqu'ici été l'objet d'aucune disposition legislative." Letter of the Minister for Foreign Affairs, 6th August 1908. "The Vestfjord through centuries has been considered as Norwegian territorial waters, but no decree or decision as to the special frontier or limit between this fjord and the open sea has been issued up to the present." Letter from his Excellency M. J.

the line of closure runs from Moskenæs on the west to Stot on the east, which are about forty-five miles apart, and the length of the fjord from this line is about sixty-five miles. As stated below, however, it appears from a letter of the Minister of Foreign Affairs, in 1868, that the line may be drawn from the

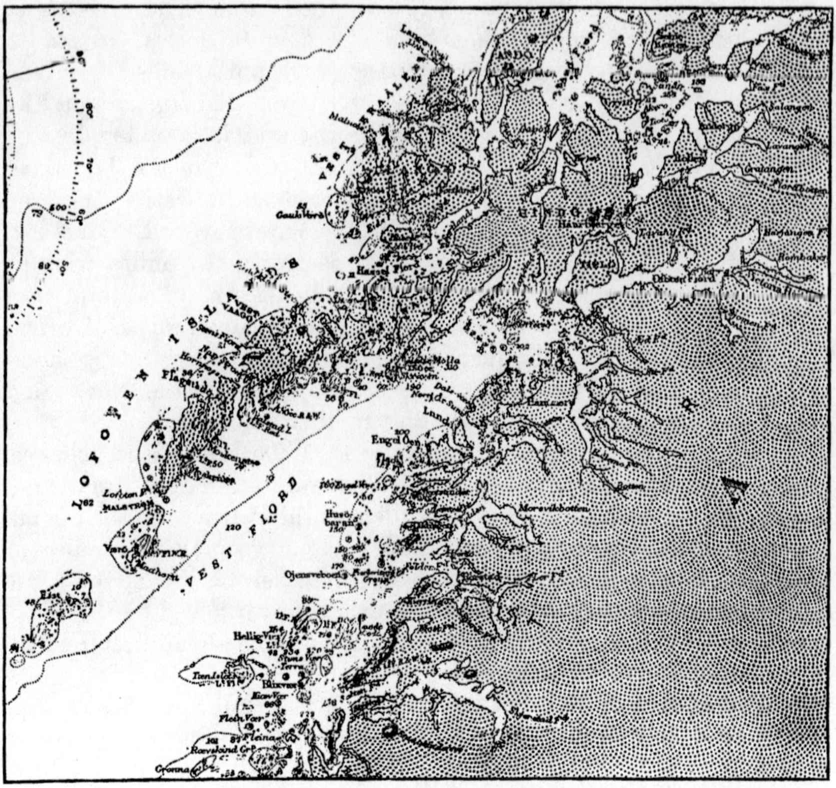

Fig. 24.—*The Vestfjord, Lofoten Islands.*

southern part of Röst, a group of isles situated nearly fifty miles from the mainland and about 110 miles from the

Irgens, the Norwegian Minister, 13th June 1908. Having some difficulty in getting authentic copies of the various Norwegian decrees, I applied to Dr Fridtjof Nansen, then Norwegian Minister in London, and later received full information from three sources—from Mons. J. Irgens, Dr Nansen's successor, and now the Foreign Minister of Norway; by the courtesy of Sir Reginald MacLeod; and through Dr Baty, the Secretary to the International Law Association.

extreme head of the fjord. The total area within a line drawn from the south end of Moskenæsö (Lofoten Point) to Möst Fjord is over 2000 square (geographical) miles, about 900 square miles of this lying outside the ordinary three-mile limit. Within a line from Röst to Kunna the total area is nearly 3900 miles, about half being beyond the ordinary limit.

Another large expanse of sea, the Varangerfjord, in East Finmarken (fig. 25), has been closed, with special regard to whaling, for a distance up to one geographical mile (of fifteen to a degree) outside a line drawn from Kibergsnæs on the north to Jacobs River on the south; and it is stated by the Norwegian Minister for Foreign Affairs that the boundary mentioned has always been considered as indicating the true limit of the territorial waters in the Varangerfjord. This arm of the sea, claimed as territorial, is thirty-two miles wide at the entrance and about fifty miles in length. The total area of the fjord is about 630 square (geographical) miles, of which approximately 225 square miles are beyond the ordinary three-mile limit. Various laws have been made by the Norwegian Government affecting whaling in this quarter.[1]

A Swedish decree of 5th May 1871 concerning the fisheries, defined the extent of the territorial waters from the Norwegian frontier along the coast to Kullen, at the entrance to the Sound, as one Swedish league (equal to four geographical miles of 60 to a degree), reckoned from the coast, or the farthest out island or rock which is not constantly overflowed by the sea;[2] and by the treaty with Denmark in 1899, already referred to,

[1] 5th January 1881; 19th June 1880; 14th June 1890; 17th December 1896; 7th January 1904. In the law of 17th December 1896 the limits are mentioned as follows: "Paa Havstrækningen ved Tromsø Amts og Finmarkens Amts Kyst i en Afstand af indtil én geografisk Mil fra Kysten, regnet fra den yderste Ø eller Holme, som ikke overskylles af Havet, skal det indtil videre være forbudt at jage, anskyde eller dræbe Hval i Tidsrummet fra 1ste Januar til Udgangen af Mai. For Varangerfjordens Vedkommende i Finmarkens Amt bliver Grændsen for den fredede Strækning udad mod Havet en ret Linie trukket fra Kibergnæs til Grændse, Jakobselv, dog saaledes, at det ogsaa udenfor denne Linie skal være forbudt i den ovenanførte Tid at jage, anskyde eller dræbe Hval i kortere Afstand fra Kysten ved Kibergnæs end én geografisk Mil." See also Auber, *Annuaire*, xi. 136, 1892; Kleen, *Fifteenth Ann. Rep. Internat. Law Assoc.*, 17; Aschehoug, *Norges nuvarende Retsforfatning*, 90; Kleen, *Neutralitetens Lagar*, 1889; *Norsk Fiskeritidende*, 1893, 461.

[2] Räknadt från kusten eller längst ut från denna liggande ö eller skär, som ej ständigt af hafvet öfversköljes." *Svensk Fiskeri Tidskrift*, 9e Årg., p. 78.

the same limit is carried on from Kullen to Falsterbo and up to Simrishamn in Christianstad. There does not appear to be any corresponding decree for the eastern coast of Sweden.

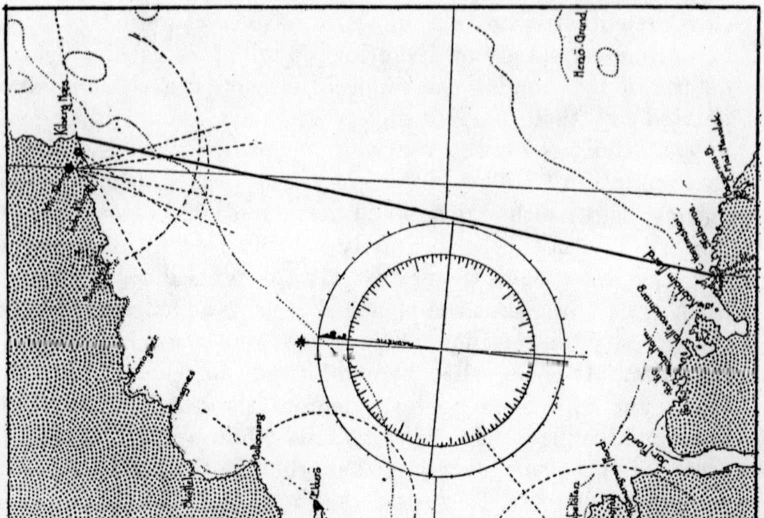

Fig. 25.—*The Varanger fjord.*

Within the territorial waters as described above, Norway claims the exclusive right to the fisheries and all the sovereign rights that are usually exercised in territorial seas, as well as one that is not as a rule included—namely, the right to control all navigation. All vessels within the territorial waters are likewise subject to the control of the customs authorities, while in Sweden the Customs Law of 1877 extends jurisdiction to a distance of one Swedish league from the base-line. The Government does not rest its claim to so large an extent of the bordering sea merely on the principle which is usually held to determine its bounds—the range of cannon fire,—though it is pointed out that the Norwegian boundary is in reality more in conformity with the range of modern artillery than is the three-mile limit. They argue, very truly, that the zone of one marine league, although adopted in conventions between several Powers, has not been definitely established in international law, and they have themselves always refused to agree to a limit so narrow. But the principal reasons advanced are those of necessity and utility. The Norwegian coast is peculiarly irregular. It is engirdled by a multitude of islands, reefs, and rocks, and is broken up by numerous fjords which penetrate deeply into the land. A three-mile limit applied to such a coast on the principle adopted in the North Sea Convention would be intricate, confusing, and impracticable. The boundary would be exceedingly irregular, and patches and strips of extra-territorial water of the most diverse size and form would be intermingled with the territorial water; and in practice it would be extremely difficult or impossible for foreign fishermen to observe the complicated boundary, or for the authorities to enforce it. Constant disputes would result.

Another reason put forward is a moral one. The country is comparatively sterile; the climate is rigorous; the people are poor, and the fisheries are of the utmost importance for their maintenance. A large proportion of the population derive, and have always derived, their livelihood from the sea, "with which they wage a desperate war in the darkness and tempests of winter and spring to gain their daily bread."[1] It is therefore only just that this natural source of food along their coasts should be conserved as much as possible, so long as the manifest rights of other nations are not violated, and that the poor native fishermen, pursuing a hard and laborious calling, which necessity has imposed on them, should be pro-

[1] Auber, *loc. cit.*

tected from the intrusion of foreign vessels, better equipped and with more capital at their disposal. It is further urged that the Norwegian fishermen have enjoyed the wider area for many centuries. From immemorial times the right of fishing has been regarded as pertaining to the land. This principle was enunciated in the old provincial laws (*landskapslagar*) of Sweden in the middle ages, and was continued in the laws of the kingdom since the fourteenth and fifteenth centuries.[1] It is also declared that a smaller extent of territorial sea would interfere with the efficacy of the regulations enforced for the preservation of the fisheries. A lesser boundary would intersect the more important fishing-banks, "making it impossible," to quote the words of the Minister of the Interior, "for the state to regulate the fisheries on the whole bank, and it would be fatal to those fisheries which are necessary for the subsistence of the coast population." This consideration, it is pointed out, is likely to have still more weight in future, owing to the increase of the population and the impoverishment of the fishing-grounds along the coast.

The claim of Norway to the wider extent of territorial sea has been as a rule respected by foreigners, probably owing in the main to the fact that its coasts are but little visited by foreign fishermen, but it has not remained without challenge. The French Government on one occasion complained that a French vessel had been prevented from fishing in the Vestfjord; but the prohibition was justified by Norway on the grounds that by the law of nations the Lofoten fisheries, and especially those in the Vestfjord, which was "part of the territorial sea," belonged exclusively to the inhabitants, and that for centuries no foreign vessels had attempted to take part in them.[2] In communicating the decision to the French Government, the Minister for Foreign Affairs declared that the prohibition

[1] Kleen, *op. cit.;* Egerström, *Sveriges Landtbruksförvaltning*, 1896, p. 37. It is the same in Finland,—J. A. Sandman, *Uebersicht ueber die Seefischerei Finnlands*, p. 145, 1906.

[2] Minister of the Interior to Minister of Foreign Affairs, 28th October 1868 . . . "Cela s'explique : ces pêches, ayant lieu dans un golfe considéré comme faisant partie de la mer territoriale de la Norvège, ont été regardées comme la propriété exclusive du pays. Cela ne peut certainement pas cadrer avec les principes du droit international, qu'on puisse tout à coup amener des changements dans une situation légale qui repose sur une reconnaissance tacite de plusieurs siècles."

applied equally to the adjacent sea and to the entrance to the fjord up to the distance of a marine league (of four miles), measured from the most southerly point of the isles called "Röst"—a group which lies about twenty-six geographical miles west and south of Moskenæs, and about sixty geographical miles from the mainland.[1] In 1870 another foreign Government raised objection to the limits defined off Romsdal by the royal decree of 16th October 1869, on the ground that the base-line drawn between the islands Svinö and Storholmen exceeded eight ordinary marine miles in length, which was the maximum distance according to the Norwegian principle, already referred to, for the inclusion of the "outermost" island. The Norwegian Government, however, declared that by the law of nations it was competent to include a bay or a gulf of "not too large an extent" by drawing the line from one advanced point to another, and that it was necessary to consider local circumstances and what was natural, convenient, and just. The line that had been drawn, they said, coincided with a natural depression in the bottom of the sea which separated the inshore from the offshore fishing-banks, and it formed a natural boundary which could be readily ascertained by the use of a sounding-lead. To adhere strictly to the four-mile line in this case would make the limit intricate and impossible to be observed, and it would pass across the inshore banks. It was also argued that till lately foreign fishermen had never attempted to fish in the neighbourhood, even within a space far more extensive than that comprised in the decree.[2]

Since the period referred to, the limit claimed by Norway is said to have been respected by foreign states and by foreign fishermen; and the Scandinavian Government has officially declared on several occasions, and notably in December 1874 to the British Government, that it would never adhere to any international convention which established a maritime zone of less than four marine miles. It declined to become a party to the North Sea Convention of 1882 for this reason,

[1] Letter of the Minister for Foreign Affairs, 7th November 1868. "Aussi il est défendu aux sujets étrangers de faire la pêche dans ce golfe, et cette défense s'applique également à la mer voisine et à l'embouchure jusqu'à une distance d'une lieue marine à partir du point le plus méridional du group d'îlots dit 'Röst.'"

[2] Minister of the Interior to Minister for Foreign Affairs, 28th January 1870.

and because the line for the closure of bays was in its opinion much too small. The only treaties with foreign countries in which a limit has been fixed are the one between Sweden and Denmark, previously mentioned, in which the Scandinavian boundary is maintained, and one with Mexico, in 1886, for customs purposes, which stipulates for three marine leagues from low-water mark.[1]

It is evident that Sweden and Norway, besides claiming a greater extent of territorial water than other countries, also claim in particular cases to depart from the principles which in general govern their own system of delimitation, in order to include other waters lying off their coasts, when they deem it necessary to reserve the fisheries there for their own subjects. In such cases it is said to be impossible to be guided by geographical rules of an absolute kind, and it is urged that any general international rules on the question should be sufficiently elastic to allow of similar exceptions elsewhere.[2] There is little doubt that the wider area claimed by the Scandinavian states is, from the point of view of sea fisheries, preferable to the narrower zone adopted in the North Sea Convention. It will appear later, that both the authorities on sea fisheries in various countries and the authorities on international law agree as to the inadequacy of the three-mile limit for fishery purposes; and it is hardly probable that the Government of any other country

[1] 20th August 1886. "Art. 7 . . . Les deux parties contractantes conviennent de considérer comme limites des mers territoriales de leur côtes respectives pour tout ce qui se rapporte à l'application des règlements de douane et aux mesures prises pour empêcher la contrebande, une distance de trois lieues marines comptées depuis de la ligne de marée basse." A similar customs treaty, it may be mentioned, was concluded between Mexico and Great Britain on 27th November 1888, in which three marine leagues was stipulated by each country "as a limit of their territorial waters on their respective coasts," strictly for customs purposes. "The two Contracting Parties agree to consider, as a limit of their territorial waters on their respective coasts, the distance of three marine leagues reckoned from the line of low-water mark. Nevertheless, this stipulation shall have no effect, excepting in what may relate to the observance and application of the Custom-house Regulations and the measures for preventing smuggling, and cannot be extended to other questions of civil and criminal jurisdiction or of international maritime law" (Hertslett, *Treaties*). It is of interest to note, however, that the ordinary limit adhered to by the British Government so rigorously in connection with fishery rights, may be legitimately extended by treaty in order to protect the revenue.

[2] Auber, *op. cit.*, 141.

will now seriously contest the right of Sweden and Norway to the larger area they claim, unless under exceptional circumstances. Norway has been fortunate in this respect, that her coasts are rarely visited by foreign fishing vessels; but this immunity is not likely to continue. During the last few years the great feature of the sea fisheries both in Great Britain and also on the Continent has been the enormous development of steam-fishing, particularly trawling (see p. 698). Confined for a time to the North Sea and the neighbourhood of their own coasts, steam fishing-vessels now regularly visit distant quarters in large numbers, and trawlers from England and Germany make the long voyage to the grounds off the White Sea, traversing the whole coast of Norway, in quest of fish. The absence of foreign competition in the fisheries of the Norwegian coast is due largely to the generally rough and rocky nature of the bottom and the great depth of the water, which make trawling difficult or impossible; but there are, no doubt, within the territorial limits, more or less restricted areas where trawling could be carried on with success, and if these be discovered by foreign vessels, and they are outside the ordinary three-mile boundary to which they are accustomed, there is little doubt the question of the Norwegian claim will be raised again. Line-fishing by steamers is now, moreover, greatly developed, and this method of fishing can be pursued, and is now pursued by the Norwegians, in deeper water and on rocky bottom, as in the Vestfjord and off Romsdal. In the summer of 1907, indeed, one or two British trawlers were seized by the Norwegian authorities for fishing within their territorial waters at Finmarken, but were released later.[1]

From the account which has been given above of the recent practice of civilised states it is apparent that the majority of them have adopted the three-mile limit, with a ten-mile base-line for bays, for fishery purposes. There is a tendency,

[1] Foreigners are forbidden to carry on fishing within the territorial waters, the most recent law relative to this subject being that of 2nd June 1906. Instructions to the commanders of the Norwegian cruisers, dated 22nd December 1906, with reference thereto, describe the limit as an "ordinary sea mile" (measured as described), the equivalent distance being stated at 7529 metres, which is equal to 4·065 mean nautical miles, or 4·68 English statute miles. A law of 1908 prohibits trawl-fishing within the territorial waters.

moreover, for this process to be continued and extended, as is shown by the recent treaty between Great Britain and Denmark concerning the ocean around Iceland and the Faröes, and the action of the British Government respecting the six-mile limit on the coasts of Spain and Portugal. It is possible, and indeed likely, that the Spanish and Portuguese Governments have protested against the infringement of what they regard as their just rights; but if they are unable or unwilling to maintain them, and the three-mile limit comes to be the only one observed on their coasts, the usage will settle the matter in the course of time. Up to the present, however, Norway and Sweden have very justly resisted all attempts to impose on them the ordinary limit and bring them into line with other Powers, and they have successfully caused their wider bounds to be respected. The diversity in practice between the Iberian and Scandinavian states and the other states of Europe may be traced to the modes by which the limits were evolved. In the former case, the boundaries were fixed in the middle of the eighteenth century, without special reference to the range of the guns of the time. The three-mile zone, on the other hand, was developed early in last century from the doctrine of Bynkershoek, three miles being then looked upon as approximately the range of cannon.

The general adoption of this limit, as previously said, was due in great measure to the preponderating influence of Great Britain and America in maritime affairs, the lesser states following their example, willingly or with reluctance. It is not too much to say, indeed, that the three-mile boundary in its origin and development is an Anglo-American doctrine, its authors being Washington and Lord Stowell. It is thus of interest to consider the opinions of modern writers on international law on the question, and to see how far they agree with or differ from their predecessors, whose opinions have been previously passed under review. It will be found that, considering the extent to which the three-mile limit has been actually applied in practice, the writers who accept it as the established rule in international law are singularly few, and are for the most part English or American. It will be also noticed how extremely loose some writers, even of high authority, are in their use of the terms "three miles *or* the range of guns," as if they were now synonymous, which they are not. Such looseness of phrase is not absent from some judicial decisions on the question, as in that of Lord Cockburn in the case of Regina *v.* Keyn, previously referred to (p. 591).

Another statement that one not uncommonly finds in the text-books, and to which currency was given by Lord Stowell, is that *since* the invention of firearms the distance at which the power of the state, and therefore the territorial waters, terminated, has usually been recognised as about three miles from the shore. Calvo, a writer of much authority, also makes this statement, affirming at the same time the doctrine of Bynkershoek as the principle of delimitation.[1] In view of the range of modern artillery, he, however, considers this space too small, and is of opinion that it ought justly, on grounds of logic and reason, to be extended; but until this extension has been sanctioned by a majority of states he looks upon the three-mile limit as the established rule of international law. Much the same view is expressed by Bluntschli.[2] He defines the territorial sea according to the range of guns, and says that international treaties or the laws of states may fix more precise limits, such as one marine league from the coast at low-water; but, considering the increased range of artillery, he is disposed to think the three-mile limit insufficient. Phillimore, one of the greatest English authorities, agrees with Calvo.[3] He states that the rule of law may now be considered as fairly established that absolute property and jurisdiction in the adjacent open sea "does not extend, unless by the specific provisions of a treaty, or an unquestioned usage, beyond a marine league (being three miles) or the distance of a cannon-shot from the shore at low tide." The limit, he says, was fixed at a marine league because that was supposed to be the utmost distance to which a cannon-shot from the shore could reach;

[1] *Le Droit International*, i. 349; *Dict. de Droit International*, 501. Bluntschli endeavours to place the doctrine on a philosophical but absurd basis, by stating that the sovereignty over the sea extended originally only to a stone's-throw from the coast, later to an arrow-shot, and then according to the range of firearms.

[2] *Das Moderne Völkerrecht*, s. 307-9.

[3] *Commentaries upon International Law*, I. viii. cxcviii.

and he adds that the great improvements recently effected in artillery seem to make it desirable that this distance should be increased, but he holds that this can be done only by the general consent of nations, or by specific treaty with particular states. Phillimore, like most of the other writers, was apparently ignorant of the fact that the Scandinavian and the Iberian Powers claimed a limit much farther than three miles.

Halleck follows Wheaton in saying that the general usage of nations superadds to bays, &c., an exclusive territorial jurisdiction over the sea for the distance of one marine league, or the range of a cannon-shot, along all the shores or coasts of the state, and that the maxim of law on the subject is *terræ dominium finitur ubi finitur armorum vis,* "which is generally recognised to be about three miles from the shore."[1] On the other hand, Lawrence, in his edition of Wheaton (p. 321), says very definitely that all the space through which projectiles thrown from the shore pass, being protected and defended by these warlike instruments, is territorial and subject to the dominion of the Power that controls the shore: "The greatest reach of a ball fired from a cannon on the land is, then, really the limit of the territorial sea." Bishop, also accepting Bynkershoek's principle, says that a cannon-shot is estimated for the purpose of delimiting the territorial seas at a marine league, but, like so many others, he argues from the improvement of artillery that, "in reason, the distance would now seem to require extension."[2] Woolsey, likewise adopting the three-mile limit "or" cannon range, is of opinion that, "as the range of cannon is increasing, and their aim becoming more perfect, it might be thought that the sea-line of territory ought to be wider," though this author does not think the point likely to become of great importance.[3] Dana expresses the usual vague opinion of the English and American writers in regarding it as "settled that the limit of the territorial waters is, in the absence of treaty, the marine league, *or* the cannon-shot."[4] Sir Travers Twiss also speaks of the range of guns, which, he says, with the common lack of information respecting

[1] *International Law,* 135.
[2] *Commentaries on Criminal Law,* iv. c. 5, s. 74.
[3] *Introduction to the Study of International Law,* s. 56.
[4] Wheaton's *International Law,* 8th ed., p. 359.

some other countries, "by consent is now taken to be a maritime league seawards along the coasts of a nation."[1]

Rather different opinions are expressed by Fiore, an Italian writer of eminence. While pointing out that publicists are not agreed as to the extent of the territorial sea, he thinks it should be determined by the necessity of the case and the nature of the particular rights claimed, as fishing, dues connected with navigation, and defence: for the latter purpose he is of opinion that the zone should increase with the improvement of artillery. With regard to the rights to certain fisheries, he says that the fishing for coral,—an important industry in Italy,—for example, belongs to the people of the neighbouring coast where it is found.[2] Pradier-Fodéré holds strongly to the doctrine of cannon range. The extent of the territorial sea, he says, depends upon the power of artillery from shore; the farthest distance a shot can be thrown, according to the progress of military art, is the limit of the territorial sea, and he adds that this is the principle almost universally adopted, although, "since the invention of firearms," this distance has usually been considered as three miles.[3] Perels, a German writer of eminence, accepts the doctrine of Bynkershoek that the sovereign jurisdiction of a state extends in the sea to the distance of a cannon-shot from the coast, and he says the extension of the boundary-line depends upon the range of cannon-shot at the particular period, but is the same at any period for all coasts. British and American publicists, he adds, have generally adopted three miles as an equivalent, but this has not usually been done by Continental authorities.[4] Another writer, Ferguson, gives a novel explanation of the reason why three miles is generally adopted in practice. He says the distance referred to is presumed to be the range of the coast defences, but on the maxim that *terræ dominium finitur ubi finitur armorum vis*, it should be stated to extend to any point on the sea to which the cannon of actual coast defences on shore can carry a projectile. Since, however, the carrying power of

[1] *The Law of Nations in Time of Peace*, s. 172.

[2] *Trattato di Diritto Internazionale Pubblico*, ii. c. 3, pp. 65-67.

[3] In Fiore, *Nouveau Droit International Public*, note, p. 372.

[4] *Das Internationale Öffentliche Seerecht der Gegenwart*, p. 21 *et seq.*

any given cannon is such a vague measure, the three-mile radius is generally adopted.[1]

In the opinion of Desjardins, the expression territorial sea must be taken in the precise sense given to it by international law. Maritime territory, he says, is only made effectively inviolable at the real range of cannon from the coast, and the laws of police or customs usually applied in time of peace cannot prevail against a principle founded on the nature of things. In his opinion a prize taken beyond three miles from the coast, but within the range of guns, would be illegitimate, while it would be legitimate within the particular limits fixed by a neutral state if beyond the range of guns.[2] Latour, another recent French writer, also argues that the three-mile limit is not necessarily the true one, but that it depends on the actual range of guns from the shore.[3] On the other hand, Professor Kleen, in his work on the laws of neutrality, considers the Scandinavian method of delimiting the territorial sea the proper one, since the extent depends not only on the mainland but on the "adjacent isles." Admitting that the distance from the coast at which the external limit is fixed is, according to the positive international law of to-day, determined by the range of cannon, he thinks this measure is so susceptible of change and controversy that it is desirable to replace it by a fixed one, which ought not to be less than four marine miles. The range of guns is much greater than four miles; and there are some coasts where the geographical configuration requires that a larger area should be subject to the territorial state, in order to avoid collision with foreigners as well as encroachments on the natural rights of the inhabitants. He is of opinion that Bynkershoek's doctrine was wrong in certain respects: it reposed on a basis of brute force; the range of guns differs in different countries and at different times; and the range of the most powerful modern gun is too much to allow a state the exclusive possession of the sea up to that distance from the shore. The range of guns, he says, is admissible in respect of war and neutrality, but in all other respects the distance ought to be fixed and mathematically

[1] *International Law*, 399. [2] *Droit Commercial Maritime*, 10.
[3] *La Mer Territoriale*, 36.

determined independent of military force, and should be the same everywhere.[1]

Another Scandinavian publicist, Professor Aschehoug, also argues for a wide extent of territorial sea under international law, according to the principles previously described. He thinks that it is impossible to exclude from the territorial sea of a people that space which is commanded by their guns on shore; and *vice versa*, this space is necessary to preserve the shores from the projectiles of belligerents. The state has all the rights of sovereignty in this area, as those connected with neutrality, police, inspection, jurisdiction, and the exclusive right of fishery and other usufructs, except the right of forbidding navigation.[2]

The eminent Russian authority, Professor de Martens, expresses a strong opinion that the three-mile limit is now quite inadequate, and that a state has the power to extend it. The only true boundary of the territorial sea is, he says, the range of guns from the coast, Bynkershoek's aphorism—*terræ dominium finitur ubi finitur armorum vis*—forming the only legal and rational foundation for the delimitation. Within the zone so determined the bordering state has exclusive sovereignty and dominion, and the exclusive right of fishing. The limit of the territorial waters ought therefore to change with the modifications in the range of cannon. If at one time the reach of guns was three miles, then the extent of the territorial sea at that time was only three miles. If at the present day, he says, cannon carry to twelve, or even fifteen, miles, the territorial waters extend to the same distance. De Martens, however, thinks that an international agreement with regard to such limits is necessary to ensure the success of the measures of protection established in the open sea for the preservation of the legitimate interests of each nation, especially with regard to fisheries. But he holds that until such an international arrangement has been accomplished, each state has the incontestable right to declare as its territorial sea the waters which are dominated by batteries on its coasts. In view of the necessity of precisely defining

[1] *Neutralitetens Lagar*, i. s. 160; *Annuaire de l'Institut de Droit International*, xii. 140.

[2] *Norges Offentlige Ret*, 79-81; *Annuaire*, xi. 141.

the range of cannon, and the exigencies of international commerce, the bordering state, he says, may limit this distance to a number of miles fixed by law; and he himself advocates a limit of ten miles, instead of three miles, as being more in conformity with the actual range of guns, and better fitted to protect the interests of the coast population who subsist by sea fisheries.[1]

The latest English writer of authority on international law, Mr W. E. Hall, who has given a lucid and philosophical account of the territorial sea, is also of opinion that the three-mile limit is inadequate. The boundary, he says, is generally fixed at three miles, but this distance was defined by the supposed range of guns of position, and the effect of the recent increase in the power of artillery has not yet been taken into consideration, either as supplying a new measure of the space over which control may be efficiently exercised, or as enlarging that within which acts of violence may be dangerous to persons and property on shore. "It may be doubted," he continues, "in view of the very diverse opinions which have been held until lately as to the extent to which marginal seas may be appropriated, of the lateness of the time at which much more extensive claims have been fully abandoned, and of the absence of cases in which the breadth of the territorial waters has come into international questions, whether the three-mile limit has ever been unequivocally settled; but in any case, as it has been determined, if determined at all, upon an assumption which has ceased to hold good, it would be pedantry to adhere to the rule in its present form; and perhaps it may be said without impropriety that a state has the right to extend its territorial waters from time to time at its will with the increased range of guns; though it would undoubtedly be more satisfactory that an arrangement upon the subject should be come to by common agreement." In a later edition of his work, which appeared after the results of the international conferences of publicists, to be presently referred to, were known, he says that it is felt and growingly felt, not only that the width of three miles is insufficient for the safety of the territory, but that it is desirable for a state to

[1] *Revue générale de Droit International Public*, No. 1.

have control over a larger space of water for the purpose of regulating and preserving the fishery in it, the productiveness of sea fisheries being seriously threatened by the destructive methods of fishing which are commonly employed, and in many places by the greatly increased number of fishing vessels frequenting the grounds.[1] A still later writer, Oppenheim, has apparently much the same opinion, for he says that although many states in municipal laws and international treaties still adhere to a breadth of one marine league, the time will come when by common agreement of the states concerned such breadth will be very much extended.[2]

While there is thus some diversity of opinion among modern writers on the law of nations, both as to the actual extent of territorial sea belonging to a state and in respect to the principles which should govern its delimitation in certain cases, there is all but universal acceptance of the rule that in general the limit is determined by the range of guns. Practically all authorities are agreed that this is the historical basis of the demarcation, and the majority of publicists, as Schmalz, Klüber, Reddie, Ortolan, Hautefeuille, Pistoye and Duverdy, Massé, Bluntschli, Pradier-Fodéré, Lawrence, Perels, Desjardins, De Martens, and Aschehoug, adhere to it as the only true principle. This adherence to Bynkershoek's doctrine logically implies that the range of artillery at any particular period governs the extent of the territorial sea at that period, and several authorities, as Ortolan, Lawrence, Perels, Desjardins, and De Martens, accept this view in its bare and absolute form, while others, though willing to agree to it as proper and reasonable, think that a mutual arrangement on the subject is first of all desirable or necessary, or that it applies specially to questions of neutrality. There are very few writers, on the other hand, who are of opinion that the three-mile limit has become established in international jurisprudence as the legal limit, notwithstanding that it is the limit commonly adopted. Calvo and Phillimore are the most important authorities who take this view, but both think the extent is too small and ought logically to be increased owing to the greater range of artillery,—an

[1] *A Treatise on International Law*, 4th edition, 1895, p. 160.

[2] *International Law*, i. 242 (1905).

opinion which is shared by Bishop, Woolsey, Fiore, and Hall. Nearly all those who mention three miles as the boundary of the territorial seas—and they are almost wholly English or American—couple with it the alternative, "*or* the range of cannon," as Wheaton, Manning, Halleck, Phillimore, Bishop, Dana, Twiss, Ferguson, and Woolsey. In this they merely adopt the language used by Lord Stowell at the beginning of last century, and which was quite appropriate at the time. But for more than half a century the range of guns has exceeded three miles, and to use the terms now as if they were synonymous tends only to confusion. Some modern publicists, it may be added, as Kent, Heffter, and Fiore, follow Wolff and Vattel in the opinion that the limit of territorial waters may be extended in certain cases beyond the range of guns.

Moreover, quite lately the subject of the territorial sea has been jointly and exhaustively inquired into by the leading publicists of Europe, and with important results. In 1887 the International Law Association appointed a committee to consider the definition and *régime* of the territorial waters, and two years afterwards the Institut de Droit International followed the same course.[1] A long series of questions was circulated among the members to elicit their opinions on the various points connected with the subject; the whole matter was discussed and considered at various subsequent annual meetings; and the rules as finally adopted and approved by the Institute and the Association may therefore be

[1] The Committee of the Association was composed of ten members—viz., Sir Travers Twiss, President; Sir George Baden-Powell; Hon. D. Dudley Field, New York; Dr F. Sieveking, President of the Hanseatic High Court of Appeal, Hamburg; Mr E. H. Schweigaard, Christiania; Rear-Admiral P. H. Colomb; E. Edouard Clunet, Paris; Dr E. N. Rahusen, Amsterdam; Mr T. H. Haynes; and Mr (now Sir) Thomas Barclay, Paris, who was Secretary. The Committee of the Institut comprised twenty-four members, including Sir Travers Twiss; Professor Westlake; Professor Lorimer; M. Desjardins, Advocate-General of the Court of Cassation; Feraud-Giraud, Judge of the French Court of Cassation; Harburger, Judge of the Court of First Instance at Munich; Hartmann, Privy Councillor, Hanover; Perels, Director of the German Admiralty; Marquis d'Olivart, Ex-Professor of International Law, Madrid; Edouard Rolin, Editor of the *Revue de Droit International;* &c. M. Renault, the Paris Professor of International Law, was appointed "reporter" to the Committee, but this position was soon occupied by Sir Thomas Barclay.

fairly taken as representing the latest views of European publicists.

With regard to the question of the limits of the territorial sea, it was very generally held that a distinction should be drawn between various sovereign rights, as the right of fishery and the rights of neutrals during war. The two limits commonly recognised—namely, cannon range and three miles from low-water mark—were no longer identical. Three miles was now too small a distance for safeguarding the coasts of a neutral from the projectiles of belligerents, and the range of modern artillery fluctuated, and was besides considered to be too great a distance for the exercise of exclusive rights of sovereignty. Sir Thomas Barclay's proposal was therefore to reaffirm the limit of cannon range as the public law of Europe, but to confine its application to the right of the neutral as founded in reason, and to establish another and a lesser boundary for the exercise of the exclusive sovereign rights of the neighbouring state. The former limit was a "zone of respect"; the latter bounded the true territorial sea. There was general agreement that the neutral line or zone of respect should coincide with the actual range of guns; but some were of opinion that the range should be considered not from the coast, on the principle of Bynkershoek, but from the sea, and others that the neutral zone should be measured from the boundary of the true territorial sea, in order to prevent violation of the latter by the bullets of belligerents. Since the range of guns, however, is uncertain and variable, and the line of respect must necessarily vary with it, it was decided finally not to adopt a fixed distance, but to recommend that in case of war the neutral state, taking the range of guns as the basis, should itself fix and declare the extent of its neutral waters beyond the limit of the territorial sea.

There was not the same agreement as to the limit which should be recommended as the boundary of the territorial sea, within which the rights of the state are much more complex, and of which the extent should be precisely fixed. The historical principle of demarcation—the range of cannon—having been transferred to the line of respect, the only other limit in common use was the three-mile limit, and this was the distance at first proposed by Sir Thomas Barclay in the draft rules, mainly because it was the one which was usually recognised by international usage. But the preponderating opinion of Continental publicists favoured a more extended boundary, in view more particularly of the right of fishery, the distances proposed varying from five to ten miles from low-water mark;[1] and Professor Auber, of Christiania, advocated the extension of jurisdiction with respect to fisheries beyond the limit fixed for the territorial sea, to apply equally to subjects and foreigners, each state assigning boundaries for such jurisdiction, either itself or by convention between the Powers interested, and a similar proposal was made by the Canadian representative, who suggested that the jurisdictional zone should extend to nine miles. Owing to these opinions, and also to the report of the Sea Fisheries Committee of the House of Commons in 1893, presided over by Mr Marjoribanks (the late Lord Tweedmouth), which proposed an extension of the territorial waters in the interests of the fisheries,[2] the three-mile limit was abandoned, and one of six miles from low-water mark recommended instead. This particular distance was selected in order to secure a limit which would correspond to that of Spain and the Scandinavian Powers, and thus make the practice in all European countries more uniform.

With regard to bays, the draft proposal was at first to adopt a base-line of six miles from headland to headland, and afterwards one of ten miles, as in the fishery conventions, was proposed. The Institut finally adopted a base-line of twelve miles—*i.e.*, double the width of the territorial zone,—but the International Law Association preferred the old limit of ten miles. The Scandinavian publicists were of opinion that these limits were too small, and that instead of having a fixed and rigid rule for the delimitation of bays, each state should be permitted to fix the boundaries according to the local configuration of the coast and the local requirements. While this suggestion was not accepted, it was admitted that certain

[1] Most of the English members who expressed their opinion, as Sir Travers Twiss, Professor Holland, and Mr Moore, preferred to retain the limit at three miles; Professor Westlake favoured five miles.

[2] *Report from the Select Committee on Sea Fisheries*, 1893; *Seventeenth Rep., International Law Assoc.*, p. 103, 1896; *Annuaire de l'Institut de Droit International*, xiii.

bays whose width exceeded ten miles were necessarily, by their situation, placed under the sovereignty of the neighbouring state, as the Bay of Cancale, the Bay of Chaleur, and the Scottish Firths.[1]

The various rules concerning sovereignty and jurisdiction were applied to straits whose width does not exceed twelve miles, with the following modifications: (1) straits of which the coasts belong to different states form part of the territorial sea of the bordering states, which exercise their sovereignty there up to the middle line; (2) straits whose coasts belong to the same state, and which are indispensable for maritime communication between two or several states other than the bordering state, always form part of the territorial sea of the bordering state, and they cannot be closed; (3) in straits whose coasts belong to the same state, the sea is territorial even though the distance between the coasts is greater than twelve miles, if at each entrance of the strait this distance is not exceeded; (4) straits which serve as a passage from one free sea to another free sea can never be closed. The rules were adopted by the Institut in 1894, and by the International Law Association, with slight amendments, in the following year, when Sir Richard Webster (now Lord Alverstone, the Lord Chief Justice of England) was in the chair.[2] The rules as finally adopted in London are given in Appendix O.

[1] "Il en est ainsi pour les *firths* écossais. . . . Toutes ces baies sont considérées comme étant sous la domination exclusive de l'État riverain." *Annuaire*, 23.

[2] *Annuaire de l'Institut de Droit International*, x., xi., xii., xiii. *Reports, International Law Association*, xv., xvi., xvii.

CHAPTER V.

THE INADEQUACY OF THE THREE-MILE LIMIT FOR FISHERY REGULATIONS.

THE recommendation of the International Law Association and of the French Institute that the territorial waters should be extended to six miles from the shore, or double the width usually enforced, was avowedly made, as we have seen, chiefly in the interests of the sea fisheries; and it may be presumed from the opinions of the majority of accredited writers on the law of nations, as reviewed in these pages, that it is open to any Power so to extend its territorial sea, except in so far as such extension may be opposed to the provisions of treaties with any other Power or Powers. It is undoubtedly the case that in by far the greater number of instances in which the limits of territorial waters, or the rights of the bordering state in the adjacent sea, have been disputed, or have come under discussion, between one nation and another, it was the right of fishery that was at issue. From the reign of James I. this has been the case, and it has been exhibited on all coasts, and in almost all countries. How replete our history is with such disputes may be gathered from foregoing chapters, while nearly all recent international treaties in which limits in the neighbouring sea are dealt with have been concerned with fishery questions. The numerous treaties and agreements with the United States and France respecting the vexed rights of fishing on the coasts of British North America, the North Sea conventions in Europe, and the various other agreements between European Powers, as between Spain and Portugal, Austria and Italy, Denmark and Sweden, Denmark and Germany, Great Britain and France, Belgium and Germany, and with Denmark concerning Iceland, are instances in point. The fishery interest is thus the determining interest, and the one which has made these various conventions desirable.

There appears to be little doubt that, in many cases at least, the three-mile boundary which has been commonly fixed in the fishery conventions is inadequate from the point of view of the fisheries, and this is the opinion of most of the experts and authorities, as is explained below. It must not be forgotten that the three-mile limit was selected, not on any grounds special to fisheries, but because it had been already recognised and put into force in connection with the rights of neutrals and belligerents in time of war, as representing the approximate range of guns at the time. It is in reality a product of the maritime wars in the latter part of the eighteenth and the beginning of the nineteenth century, and its application to the right of fishing is accidental and arbitrary. The boundaries which were formerly proposed as limiting the right to exclusive fishery, independently of any question of the rights of neutrals or the range of cannon, were invariably greater than three miles. The range of vision was employed in Scotland and on the English coast later; its equivalent of fourteen miles was embodied in the Draft Treaty of Union between England and Scotland in 1604, and was proposed again in 1618; and Sir Philip Meadows, the most able opponent of extravagant claims to maritime sovereignty, favoured a similar distance in 1689. Limits of eight miles and ten miles to be enforced against foreigners were fixed in the Fishery Bill passed by the House of Commons in 1660, while as late as 1824 and 1827 the Dutch Government decreed a limit of six miles for their fishermen on the British coasts. We have seen, too, that the wider extent of sea in which rights of exclusive fishery are claimed by the Scandinavian and Iberian states exists in great measure because those Powers established their limit without reference to Bynkershoek's doctrine, and before indeed it became prevalent.

The same need of a wider limit is shown in the municipal legislation of many countries, which was specially designed with the object of preserving sea fisheries, as well as in certain international agreements. There are two classes of sea fisheries which have received special treatment beyond the ordinary limits of territorial waters, and both on the same principle—

viz., that the action of man, if unrestrained, would lead to their destruction and economic extinction. They are those for marine mammals, as seals and cetaceans, and for certain shell-fishes and coral. A considerable number of countries have legislated for the preservation of seals, and some of the enactments at least apply beyond the ordinary limits. Examples may be found in the Canadian statute of 1886,[1] which refers also to whales and porpoises; the Russian law dealing with the sealing industry in the White Sea; the Norwegian law fixing a close-time for whales in the Varangerfjord; and the concurrent international legislation of Great Britain, Sweden, Norway, Russia, Germany, and Holland concerning the Jan Mayen seal fishery in the Atlantic east of Greenland.[2] A recent instance is afforded by the regulations which were prescribed for British and American citizens and subjects by the Tribunal of Arbitration for the purpose of protecting and preserving the fur-seal in Behring Sea. By these regulations the killing, capture, or pursuit of this animal was forbidden within a zone of sixty geographical miles around the Pribilov Islands, comprising about 15,000 square miles of sea; a close-time was fixed between 1st May and 31st July on the high sea within an immense area—viz., north of 35 degrees North latitude and eastwards of 180 degrees West longitude; only specially licensed sailing vessels, with canoes or undecked boats propelled by paddles, oars, or sails, were at liberty to carry on fur-sealing operations where and when the fishing was allowed; the use of nets, firearms, and explosives was forbidden, except shot-guns outside of Behring Sea, and some minor conditions were laid down.[3]

Another instance is the agreements entered into between Russia on the one hand and Great Britain and the United States

[1] 49 Vict., c. 95.

[2] 38 Vict., c. 18; Order in Council, 28th November 1876.

[3] *Award of the Tribunal of Arbitration*, p. 23. Declarations made by the Tribunal of Arbitration, 1893. As the Behring Sea case has been often referred to in recent controversies about the right of fishing, as having affirmed the three-mile limit as the true international boundary of the territorial sea, the facts may be briefly recalled. In 1867 the United States purchased from Russia the territory of Alaska with its dependent islands, &c., and an American company, very powerful financially and politically, was formed in 1870, which obtained a lease of the Pribilov Islands in order to engage in the fur-seal industry. Under the Act of Congress of 1870 which enabled this to be done, it was made unlawful to kill any seals upon the islands, "or in the waters adjacent thereto," except during certain specified

on the other, by which a zone of ten marine miles on all the Russian coasts of Behring Sea and the North Pacific Ocean, and a zone of thirty marine miles round the Commander Islands and Robben Island, were closed to sealing for the fur-seal.[1]

The other class of fisheries referred to, for sedentary animals

months. Sealing vessels, both from the United States and from British Columbia, began to frequent Behring Sea and the waters adjacent to the islands; their competition impaired the practical monopoly of the Company in the markets for sealskins; and in 1886 three British vessels were seized by American revenue cruisers at distances of 70, 75, and 115 miles from the land, and the masters and mates were fined and imprisoned for illegal sealing. Up to 1890 other eleven British sealers were similarly seized and dealt with for fishing at distances between 15 and 96 miles from land, and five others were ordered out of Behring Sea. In the negotiations which followed, the American Government first pled a virtual *mare clausum* for the whole of Behring Sea; then that they had jurisdiction up to 100 miles from land; and lastly, that they had special property in and right of protection over the fur-seals in Behring Sea and frequenting the islands for breeding purposes. The Tribunal of Arbitration decided that they had not this right of protection or property "when such seals are found outside the ordinary three-mile limit." Then the Tribunal, in terms of the treaty appointing them, prescribed the regulations above referred to, leaving to Great Britain the honours of the contest, and to the United States the advantage. The true lesson to be derived from this chapter of international diplomacy, is not that the high tribunal reaffirmed the three-mile limit as the legal boundary of the territorial sea, which they did not do (see letter from Baron de Courcel, the President, p. 664), but that that limit may be set aside and a much wider boundary fixed (in this instance 60 miles) if the protection and preservation of a marine fishery require it. It may be added that of late years pelagic sealing by Japanese has greatly increased in Behring Sea, and since the regulations apply only to British and American subjects, the Japanese carry on their operations up to the ordinary three-mile limit around the Pribilov Islands, and sometimes within it, there having been several encounters with the American patrol-boats involving loss of life, and heavy fines have been inflicted on offenders. In the summer of 1908 a fleet of thirty Japanese schooners, some with sixteen boats, were thus engaged, and according to the Government agent, they effectually blocked the escape of the seals from the islands. The agent says that in the last ten years the seal herds have diminished almost three-fourths, and if the slaughter by the Japanese is not put a stop to, complete destruction of the industry will follow. Thus, while the British are compelled to keep sixty miles off the islands, and can only kill the seals with spears, the Japanese operate up to three miles from shore, and can use firearms or any other method. It is stated that some of the British Columbia sealers are endeavouring to nationalise their vessels in Japan, so that they may be able to fish under the Japanese flag. In April 1910, when the lease of the Company expired, the United States Government did not renew it, but took the seals under their own protection, and an Act was passed prohibiting the killing of the fur-seal unless authorised by the Secretary of Commerce and Labour.

[1] *Parl. Papers, Russia*, No. 1 (1895). Correspondence respecting the Agreement with Russia relative to the Seal Fishery in the North Pacific. Seal Fishery (North Pacific) Act, 1893, 56 Vict., c. 23; Order in Council, 4th July 1893.

connected with the bottom, such as oysters, pearl-oysters, and coral, which are found in shallow water, as a rule, and usually near the coast, have always been considered as on a different footing from fisheries for floating fish. They may be very valuable, are generally restricted in extent, and are admittedly capable of being exhausted or destroyed; and they are looked upon rather as belonging to the soil or bed of the sea than to the sea itself. This is recognised in municipal law, and international law also recognises in certain cases a claim to such fisheries when they extend along the soil under the sea beyond the ordinary territorial limit. Cases in point are the pearl-fisheries on the banks in the Gulf of Manar, Ceylon, which extend from six to twenty-one miles from the coast, and are subject to a colonial Act of 1811, which authorises the seizure and condemnation of any boat found within the limits of the pearl-banks, or hovering near them: boats or vessels navigating the inner passage are prohibited from hovering or anchoring in water deeper than four fathoms, and those navigating the outer passage from hovering or anchoring within twelve fathoms. These pearl-fisheries are very valuable, and have been treated from time immemorial by the successive rulers of the island as subjects of property and jurisdiction; and the laws referred to apply also to foreigners. Another case is the pearl-fisheries in Australia. In Western Australia certain Acts are applied far beyond the three-mile limit, though apparently only against British subjects,[1] and a similar Act, of 1888, applied in Queensland to extra-territorial waters west of Torres Strait. The pearl-fisheries of Mexico and Columbia are also subject to regulation beyond the ordinary three-mile limit. Examples of extra-territorial jurisdiction over beds of the common edible oyster are to be found in the British conventions with France in 1839 and 1867, by which the Bay of Granville was reserved to France (see p. 612), and in the last of these conventions (Article ix.) a close-time was provided in the English Channel; and likewise in the proceedings concerning the Arklow and Wexford banks, off the Irish coast (see p. 621). Coral-beds in the Mediterranean, off the coasts of Algeria, Sardinia, and Sicily, are in a similar way regulated

[1] The Western Australian Pearl and Bêche-de-mer Fishery (Extra-Territorial) Act, 1889.

by Italian and French laws beyond the ordinary three-mile limit.

Even in regard to the class of fisheries for what is termed "floating" fish—that is to say, the ordinary fisheries for sea fishes, carried on usually by nets and lines—there are a number of enactments conferring jurisdiction, or which have conferred jurisdiction, beyond the distance of three miles from shore. Old English and British Acts, previously referred to (p. 608), fixed limits of four-and-a-half and five miles from the coast, within which distance the use of certain apparatus, as drag-nets and trawls, was prohibited. In the Herring Fishery Act of 1808, which provided for the appointment of commissioners for the herring fishery, and for the regulation of the fishery and the curing of herrings, jurisdiction was extended over "all persons" engaged in catching, curing, and dealing in fish in all the lochs, bays, and arms of the sea, and also within ten miles of the coasts.[1] At the Isle of Man an Act of Tynwald prohibited herring-fishing at a certain season within nine miles cf the shore,[2] and other instances might be given where municipal Acts extended jurisdiction beyond the ordinary three-mile limit for similar purposes.

It is, however, in connection with the great development of trawl-fishing from steamers in recent years, that the question of the inadequacy of the ordinary three-mile limit for the preservation and regulation of fisheries has been brought to the front, and it is around this method of fishing that most of the

[1] An Act for the further Encouragement and better Regulation of the British White Herring Fishery, 48 Geo. III., c. 110, s. 60, 46. Section 60: "And whereas it may be useful to provide a jurisdiction for preserving order and settling disputes among persons carrying on the fishery for herrings on the coast and in the lakes of Scotland; be it therefore enacted, That the jurisdiction of the sheriffs and stewarts depute of Scotland, and their substitutes, shall be extended over all persons engaged in catching, curing, and dealing in fish in all the lochs, bays, and arms of the sea within their respective counties and stewartries, and also within ten miles of the coasts of their said counties and stewartries, and that in as full and ample a manner as the same is exercised over the inhabitants of these counties and stewartries; and if any loch, bay, or arm of the sea shall adjoin to two or more counties or stewartries, or any part of the sea shall be within ten miles of the coasts of two or more counties or stewartries, the sheriffs and stewarts of the said counties shall have and exercise a concurrent jurisdiction over such persons as aforesaid, in any such loch, bay, or arm of the sea which shall be in or opposite to their respective counties and stewartries, or any part of the sea within the aforesaid distance of the coast thereof."

[2] *Report of Commission on Sea Fisheries*, 1863, p. lxvi.

controversies affecting the territorial waters, at least in Europe, have gathered.[1] It is therefore necessary to understand something about it, and how it is that it has given rise to demands for the extension of the ordinary limits and for the closure of large areas beyond these limits. It is the most effective and at the same time the most destructive method of fishing ever made use of. It differs from hook-and-line fishing, in which only a few kinds of fish are taken at the same time, according to the size of the hook and the kind of bait, and from gill-net or drift-net fishing, which is adapted, according to the dimensions of the mesh, to capture a particular fish, as herring or mackerel. Trawling consists essentially in dragging along the bottom of the sea a great bag of netting, which captures a large variety of fishes, big and little; and it may involve, at certain places and in certain seasons, the destruction of immense quantities of edible fishes too small to be marketable, and which are thrown back, dead, into the sea.[2] It is a very old method, but until about a century ago it was confined on the British coast to the mouth of the Thames and neighbourhood and to certain localities in the Channel, its headquarters being Barking and Brixham. Trawling was then restricted to shallow water; the boats were small and the trawls were such as a man could carry on his shoulders. At the close of the French war, Brixham trawlers began to migrate eastwards, prospecting for new grounds, fixing their temporary headquarters first at Dover, then at Ramsgate in 1818, and at Harwich in 1828. Continuing their explorations, the Dutch coast was visited about 1830 and the southern part of the Dogger Bank a few years later, and in 1837 a great impetus was given to trawling by the discovery of enormous quantities of soles in the Great Silver Pit, south of the Dogger. Trawlers flocked thither from all quarters; the Brixham men fixed upon Hull, first as their temporary, and then as their permanent home, and from this time North Sea trawling was firmly established. It was not until 1858, little more than half a century ago, that trawlers began to be employed from Grimsby, which is now by far the greatest fishing-port in the world. Gradually the

[1] Trawling, and, in particular, steam-trawling, is practically unknown in America; but in recent years French steam-trawlers have begun to frequent the Newfoundland banks.

[2] *Annual Reports*, Fishery Board for Scotland; *Journal of the Marine Biological Association, &c.*

enlarging fleets of trawlers pushed northwards and eastwards as new grounds were discovered. By 1860 the whole of the Dutch coast and the coast of Schleswig was frequented; ten years later the Danish coast was included, and, for the first time, the whole of the Dogger Bank, as well as large areas north and west of it, off the coast of England and Scotland. About 1875 the Great Fisher Bank, which lies about 200 miles east of the Scottish coast, began to be visited, and in 1891 the English trawlers boldly pushed on to Iceland, where enormous catches of fish were obtained.

During this period, while the fishing-grounds were being vastly extended, great improvements were made in the means of catching the fish and bringing them to market. The trawling vessels gradually increased in numbers, size, speed, and storage capacity; the trawl-net grew larger and more efficient; the use of ice for the preservation of the fish enabled distant grounds to be visited, and the deeper waters of the north necessitated the substitution of steam-power for hand-labour in hauling the nets on board; the "fleeting" system, by which steam-carriers collected the fish each morning and brought them rapidly to market, allowed the fleets of sailing smacks to remain on the grounds constantly fishing for many weeks at a time. Then the industry was revolutionised by the substitution of steam vessels for the sailing smacks, a change which began about 1878; and trawling, which was at first a summer occupation owing to the frailty of the boats, and then a winter pursuit, as plenty of wind was required to drag the heavier nets, became independent of the season, and almost of the weather. A further improvement was the introduction in 1895 of the otter-trawl instead of the unwieldy beam-trawl, the mouth of the net being kept open by the divergence of two boards, one at each side, on the principle of the kite. This allowed the net to be made very much larger, and also to be used in much deeper water, and commercial trawling is now carried on in depths down to about 200 fathoms.

There has thus occurred during the last generation or so an enormous development in the extent and efficiency of trawl-fishing. The British fleet since about 1835 has grown from some 200 small vessels, of twenty to twenty-four tons, and using trawls of from twenty to thirty feet beam, to an aggregate of 3170 vessels in 1907, of which 1609 were steamers and 918 deep-sea sailing smacks.[1] These figures, however, convey but little impression of the real increase in the catching power. It has been computed, both by practical men and by scientific experts, that the modern steam otter-trawler is approximately eight times more effective in catching fish than was one of the large sailing smacks of a generation ago,[2] and thus the British deep-sea trawling fleet in 1907 was equal to about 13,790 of the older sailing smacks. But in addition to these there are the foreign steam-trawlers which fish on the same grounds, for many other countries have followed the English example in developing deep-sea trawling. The aggregate number of such vessels at the end of 1907 was about 634, of which 224 were French, 239 German, and 81 Dutch;[3] and they would represent 5072 sailing smacks, so that the total trawling fleet of Western Europe was then equal to about 18,862 of the sailing trawlers of twenty or thirty years ago, the sailing trawlers in use on the Continent being left out of account. It has been calculated that the area of the sea-bottom which is swept each day by the nets of this great fleet is equal to about 2000 square miles.

Now, this extraordinary extension of trawl-fishing in recent times bears upon the question of territorial waters in two ways. One relates to the impoverishment of the older fishing-grounds near the coast and in the North Sea. The other relates to the incursion of steam-trawlers on foreign coasts as affecting the fishing of the inhabitants of such coasts.

With regard to the first, there have been many inquiries made by Royal Commissions and Parliamentary Committees, as well as by fishery departments and experts, which show that the excessive fishing has depleted the older banks. In the first of these inquiries, which began in 1863, when there were only from 650 to 700 smacks trawling in the North Sea (and then only in a part of it), the reporters expressed their belief

[1] For the earlier periods the statistics are incomplete. In 1863 the number of sailing trawlers was 955, of which 650 to 700 fished in the North Sea, 530 belonging to Ramsgate, Yarmouth, Grimsby, and Hull; in 1883 the aggregate was estimated at 3000, some being large vessels of ninety tons; in 1889 there were 230 steamers and 2323 smacks; in 1899 the steamers numbered 1186 and the smacks 1637.

[2] Garstang, The Impoverishment of the Sea, *Journal Marine Biol. Assoc.*, vol. vii. p. 47, 1900.

[3] Return of the Number of Steam Trawlers registered at Ports in the States of Western Europe in the Year 1907, *Parl. Papers*, Cd. 4236, 1908.

that this method of fishing "in the open sea" was not wastefully destructive, and required no legislative interference, for if any ground were over-fished, the fishing there would become unprofitable, and the trawlers would go elsewhere.[1] The next Commission, in 1878, by which time trawling had greatly developed, came to much the same general conclusions; but they found that a decrease of soles had occurred, and also a decrease of plaice and flounders in some localities, and they recommended that power should be given to the Secretary of State to forbid trawling "in any of the territorial seas," which power was conferred in 1881.[2] This inquiry was noteworthy as first revealing complaints by the trawlers themselves of the diminution of certain fish and the impoverishment of inshore grounds, and for the advocacy by Grimsby smack-owners of the prohibition of trawling at localities where small fish abound, as the inlets on the Dutch and German coast, the Wash, and off Yarmouth, and even within a nine-mile limit all round the shores of the North Sea. At the next Commission of inquiry, in 1883, the complaints of the trawlers were stronger, and the remedies they proposed more drastic. Those of Hull and Grimsby stated that the numbers of flat fishes, particularly soles, had much diminished; that the nearer grounds were impoverished, and that they had to go much greater distances for their supplies of fish. They expressed the belief that most damage was being done by trawling along the coasts, especially on the Continental side of the North Sea, and that the most effectual remedy would be to prohibit trawling within a ten-mile limit around the whole of the North Sea coasts. The conclusions reached by the Commission were that soles had decreased, and also flat fishes and haddocks in many parts of the territorial waters between Grimsby and the Moray Firth, and they recommended that the Scottish Fishery Board should receive powers to regulate or suspend trawling within territorial waters.[3]

[1] *Report of the Commissioners appointed to inquire into the Sea Fisheries of the United Kingdom*, vol. i., 1866. The late Professor Huxley and Mr Shaw Lefevre (now Lord Eversley) were two of the commissioners.

[2] *Report on the Sea Fisheries of England and Wales*, 1879 (C.—2449). The commissioners were Mr Frank Buckland and Mr (afterwards Sir) Spencer Walpole.

[3] *Report of the Commissioners on Trawl-Net and Beam-Trawl Fishing*, 1885 (C.—4328).

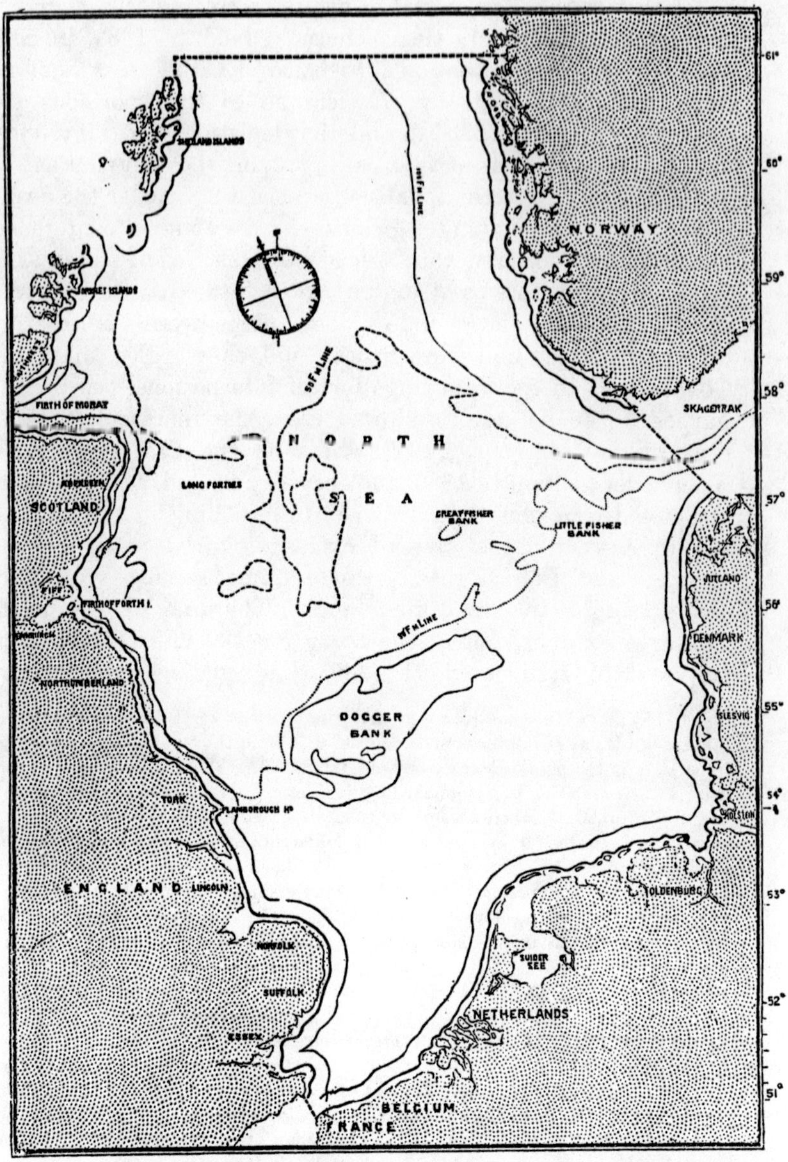

Fig. 26.—*Showing the three-mile limit and a thirteen-mile limit in the North Sea.*

From this time onwards the demand of the trawlers for some legislative restrictions on trawl-fishing increased to a clamour. At a conference of practical fishermen held in 1883, in connection with the International Fisheries Exhibition at London, statements were made by trawlers as to the enormous destruction of under-sized fish and the depletion of the grounds, and a resolution was passed calling upon the Government to bring about an international conference to consider the desirability of recommending legislation.[1] At another conference, in 1888, they declared that a large and distressing diminution of flat-fishes had occurred in the North Sea; that they viewed the future with alarm unless some steps were immediately taken to protect immature fishes; and they called upon the Government to try to arrange for an international law for the purpose.[2] As no result followed from the representations to the Government, the trawl-owners on the East Coast took independent action in 1890, and formally agreed, as a preliminary step, to prevent their trawlers from fishing in the summer within a very large area of extra-territorial water off the German and Danish coasts, where immature fish were generally caught in great abundance. The line of closure of this area extended along the coast for 130 miles, passing, to the west of Heligoland, at a distance varying from twenty

[1] "That taking into consideration that the question of the destruction of immature fish is one of international importance, it is, in the opinion of this meeting, imperative in the public interest that an International Conference be held to consider the desirability of recommending legislation upon the subject; and this meeting of practical fishermen further requests of Her Majesty's Government to take immediate steps to bring about such Conference at the earliest possible date." *Fisheries Exhibition Literature*, vol. iv. pp. 346, 355.

[2] Conference of Representatives of the Trawl-Fishing Industry, held at the Inns of Court Hotel, London, 13th November, 1888. "1. That we find a large and distressing diminution in the North Sea of soles, turbot, plaice, and all flat fish, and view with alarm the future, unless some steps are immediately taken to prohibit the catching of immature fish." 2. "That the Conference petition Her Majesty's Government, urging them to enter into negotiations with all Continental Governments to establish an international law to prohibit the wilful catching of immature fish, and to make it unlawful to offer such immature fish for sale." 3. "That copies of the resolutions be forwarded to the President of the Board of Trade asking for immediate action, and to the President of the National Sea Fisheries Protection Association, asking that Association to undertake the responsibility of a measure for legislation, and to do all they can for the protection of immature fish in and around the coasts of the North Sea and other coasts of the United Kingdom upon which breeding-grounds exist."

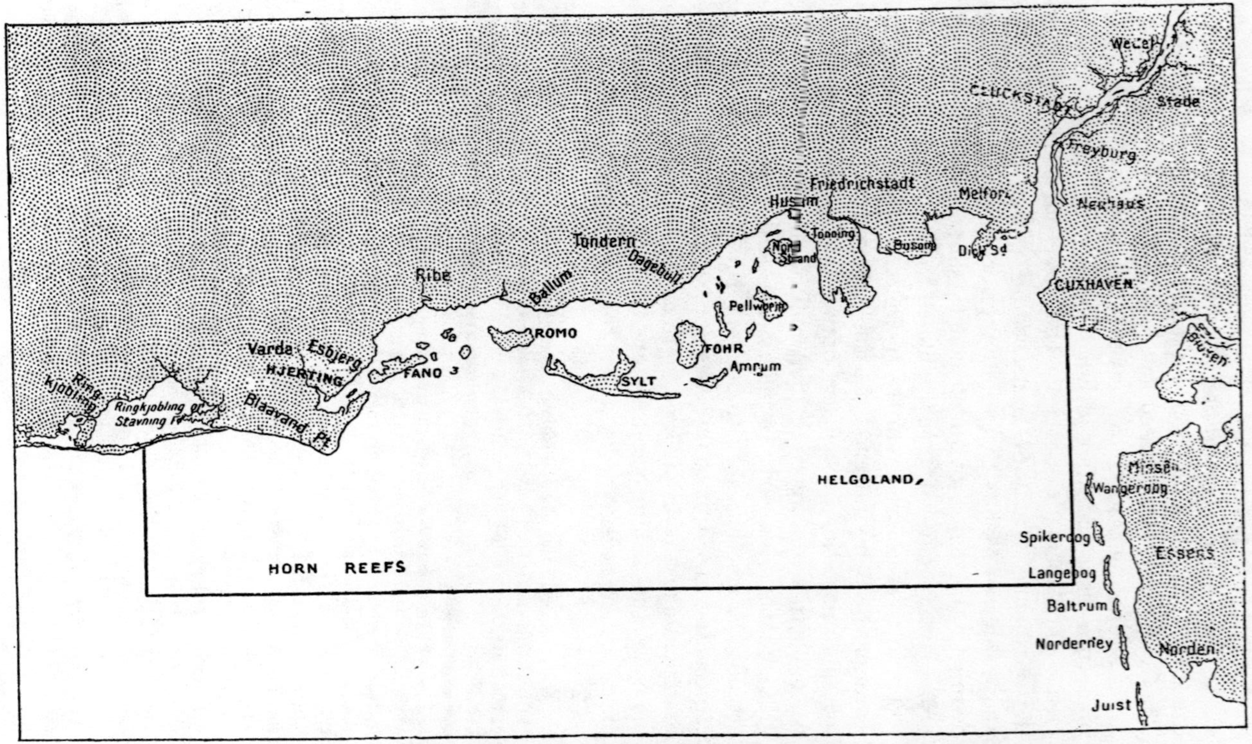

Fig. 27.—*Showing the area of the Small-fish Grounds, which the English trawlers desired to have closed for the preservation of immature fish.*

to over fifty miles from the shore, and embracing no less than about 3600 square (geographical) miles of water lying outside the three-mile limit as defined by the North Sea Convention. The Conference also pressed for legislation of a national and international character to prevent the sale and purchase of immature fish, and they defined what they meant by that term.[1] For some time at least the vessels of the great trawling companies abstained from fishing within the large area above referred to, but the voluntary arrangement fell through owing to the action of independent "single-boaters," and the grounds were never effectually closed. The Government went so far to meet the wishes of the trawlers as to issue, through the Foreign Office, invitations from the National Sea Fisheries Protection Association to various Continental Governments to send delegates to a conference in 1890, and representatives from Belgium, France, Denmark, Germany, the Netherlands, and Spain attended a meeting at Fishmongers' Hall in that year, but no representative of this country was present in an official capacity. Statements of the usual kind were made as to the impoverishment of the fishing-grounds and the necessity of remedial measures in order to keep up the fish supply, and it was

[1] Conference of the Trawl-Fishing Industry of the East Coast Ports, held at Hull, 30th April 1890. 1. "That this Conference of the Trawl-Fishing Industry of the East Coast, consisting of delegates from Hull, Grimsby, Yarmouth, Lowestoft, Scarboro', and Boston, having realised the enormous loss which the trade has sustained year by year through the wholesale capture and destruction of immature and inedible fish, hereby resolves that the time has come when a strong and united effort should be made to put a stop to this growing evil; and as a preliminary step in this direction, it is agreed by the whole of the delegates here assembled, for themselves individually and the Companies, Corporations, Fleets, and Associations they represent, to abstain during the coming summer from fishing on the grounds where immature fish are generally caught in great abundance, such grounds being specified in the next Resolution." 2. "That the Fishing Grounds or Nurseries where experience has found immature fish to be most prolific, and which are referred to in the foregoing Resolution, shall be defined as follows: That part of the North Sea the Eastern Boundary of which is the German and Danish Coasts; the Western Boundary, Longitude 7 deg. 30 min.; the Northern Boundary, Latitude 56 deg.; the Southern Boundary, 53 deg. 50 min." The third resolution defined immature lemon soles, soles, turbot, brill, and plaice; and the fourth expressed the opinion that it was "highly necessary for the future wellbeing of the trade, and for the preservation of an important food-supply, that Parliament should be asked to impose restrictions upon the sale and purchase of immature fish"; and the delegates were instructed to press for legislative interference, national and international.

resolved, in view of an official international conference being called, to circulate a set of questions regarding the scientific and statistical aspect of the subject.[1]

The complaints continuing as to the deterioration of the fisheries, the Government in 1893 appointed a Select Committee of the House of Commons to inquire into their condition and to report as to what remedies might be required. The trawlers again gave strong evidence as to the impoverishment of the grounds in the North Sea from over-fishing, the banks having been "fished out" in succession as they were discovered, so that they were compelled to go to distant regions, as Iceland and the Bay of Biscay, to keep up the supplies. Some of them still pressed for an extension beyond the three-mile limit and the prohibition of trawling within ten miles from the shore, especially on the foreign coasts on the eastern side of the North Sea, and in particular that large areas in the extra-territorial waters should be closed by international agreement. The prohibition of the sale of immature flat fishes was also strongly advocated as an indirect means of closing these grounds. The Committee reported that the evidence of all classes of witnesses, "whether trawlers or linesmen, smack-

[1] International Conference of Representatives of Maritime Powers convened under the auspices of the National Sea Fisheries Protection Association, to discuss the Question of Remedial Measures necessary to be taken for the Preservation and Development of the Fisheries in the Extra-territorial Waters of Europe, 1890. *Minutes of Proceedings.* The Conference passed a resolution that an official international conference of European maritime powers should be held with the view of concluding a convention for the preservation of undersized fish; and another, proposed by Dr P. P. C. Hoek, the delegate for the Netherlands, that before such a conference met, "the different nations interested in the sea fisheries of European waters should collect, with as little delay as possible, sufficient information, scientific as well as statistical, with regard to the damage done by the capture of undersized fish by their fishermen." The author, who was present, conscious of the advantages of international co-operation, if the programme and conditions were appropriate, proposed that Dr Hoek's resolution "should be modified in the way of recommending that a joint scheme of investigation might be drawn up by the countries concerned"; and on the motion of Captain C. F. Drechsel, the delegate for Denmark, who approved of it, the delegates adjourned to consider this proposal. The result, however, was merely the tabling of a resolution, which was adopted, "That the National Sea Fisheries Protection Association be requested to formulate a set of questions with a view to obtaining scientific and statistical information in relation to undersized fish, and forward it to each delegate, in order that he may submit it to his Government for adoption" —with what result does not appear. *Ibid.*, pp. 21, 34, 36, 37.

owners or fishermen, scientific experts or statisticians," showed that a considerable diminution had occurred among the more valuable classes of flat-fishes in the North Sea, which was to be attributed to over-fishing by trawlers in certain localities; and they recommended that the sale of undersized flat-fishes should be forbidden, and that the three-mile limit should be extended for fishery purposes alone, provided it could be effected on an international basis.[1]

It does not appear that any action was taken by the British Government in consequence of this report; and as the trawlers had failed to get the large area off the German and Danish coasts closed to them directly, they got a Bill introduced into Parliament to prohibit the sale of undersized flat-fishes, in the belief that an enactment of that kind would result in closing the grounds indirectly. The reasoning on which they proceeded was this. Trawling, to be remunerative, depends upon the capture of a variety of fishes, and it is not possible by an enlargement of the mesh of the net to allow of undersized flat-fishes escaping, without also and at the same time permitting the escape of numerous large marketable round-fishes, as haddocks, as well as of many marketable soles, and fishing under such conditions would be unprofitable. It was also known that it would be futile to return to the sea the undersized fishes after they had been brought on board, because in commercial trawling they are dead or moribund, and might as well be taken ashore as thrown back into the water. It was admitted that the only effective way to protect the immature

[1] "Your Committee are sensible of the difficulties of making international regulations, but are nevertheless of opinion that the best method for effectively governing the operations of the various classes of fishermen, and, at the same time, for securing, so far as it may be found possible, the proper protection of spawning and immature fish, would be to throw the responsibility of these duties, so far as the waters immediately adjacent to the various countries are concerned, on those various countries; that, for the effective realisation of this object, the present territorial limit of three miles is insufficient, and that, for fishery purposes alone, this limit should be extended, provided such extension can be effected upon an international basis, and with due regard to the rights and interests of all nations. Your Committee would earnestly recommend that a proposition on these lines should be submitted to an international conference of the Powers who border on the North Sea." *Report from the Select Committee on Sea Fisheries*, 377, 1893. The Chairman of the Committee, which consisted of fourteen members, was Mr Marjoribanks (the late Lord Tweedmouth); among the others were Sir Albert Rollit, Mr Buchanan, and Mr (now Lord) Heneage. The report was presented to the House of Commons and ordered to be printed on 17th August 1893.

fish was to prevent the trawl from being used on the grounds; and if this could not be done by direct closure of the area, it might be accomplished by prohibiting the sale of undersized flat-fishes generally; for on these particular "small fish" grounds, or "nurseries," large fishes are so scarce that trawling is remunerative only by reason of the great quantity of small fishes taken. If the sale of these were forbidden, then trawling in such localities would cease. For an enactment of this kind to succeed, it was obviously necessary that it should apply to the whole kingdom, and it was opposed by fishermen on other parts of the coast; and as it was felt to be extremely problematical whether it would secure the cessation of trawling on the small-fish grounds without at the same time injuriously affecting the fisheries on our own coast and raising the price of fish, the Bill was abandoned. Several subsequent Bills of the same kind shared the same fate, usually after a more or less exhaustive inquiry by a Parliamentary Committee. One of those Committees, consisting of thirteen members of the House of Commons, took evidence in 1900 from the representatives of the trawlers and others, of the character previously described, advocates of the Bill admitting that in their view it was a tentative measure, and that the direct closure of the grounds would be preferable. The Committee thought that it was proved beyond all doubt that there was a serious diminution of flat-fishes, particularly in the North Sea; that the ancient fishing-grounds were much depleted; that the evil was a growing one, and that in default of a remedy the consequences would be disastrous to the industry.[1] One of the causes of the diminution was found to be the vast destruction of immature

[1] *Special Report and Report from the Select Committee on the Sea Fisheries Bill*, 1900 (287): "Your Committee think that it is proved beyond doubt that there is a very serious diminution of the supply of certain kinds of flat-fish, particularly in the North Sea. Of late years the total quantity of such fish caught has remained nearly stationary. This fact, when taken along with the enormously increased catching power and the vastly larger area of sea subjected to fishing operations, seems to show that the ancient fishing-grounds are much depleted. The whole of the local evidence, differing in many other respects, is practically unanimous as to this point. It seems clear that the evil is a growing one, and that in default of a remedy the consequences to the fishing industry in the diminished supply of flat-fish will at no very distant future be disastrous." The late Mr (afterwards Lord) Ritchie, President of the Board of Trade, Mr Graham Murray (now Lord Dunedin), and Captain Sinclair, now Lord Pentland, Secretary for Scotland, were members of the Committee.

fish, the direct remedy for which, the Committee said, was either the prohibition of the taking and killing of such fish, or the prohibition of fishing within areas where small fish abound. They were of opinion that the former was practically impossible without prohibiting trawling altogether, while the areas where the small fish congregate could only be closed by a joint international arrangement. The indirect remedy was that proposed by the Bill, and, for reasons such as are stated above, they felt it would not be expedient to pass the Bill into law without further inquiry and investigation. The Committee were of opinion that the subject of the diminution of the fish supply was a very pressing one, and that the situation was going from bad to worse, and they recommended that no effort should be spared, first, to arrange for international treatment of the subject generally, and especially for regulation of the North Sea area; and second, to provide for the adequate equipment of the Government Departments in charge of the subject.[1]

The trawlers still pressed for legislation to deal with the wasteful destruction of undersized fish, and continued to pass resolutions on the subject;[2] and another and somewhat modified Bill was introduced into the House of Lords in 1904 by the Department of Agriculture and Fisheries, and remitted to a Select Committee of that House. The Committee, after taking much evidence of the usual kind, stated their opinion that the ideal manner of protecting the fishing-grounds in the North Sea where young fish abound would be by an international agreement between all the Powers concerned, and they expressed the hope that the Government would not relax its efforts to secure

[1] "Your Committee feel that the subject of the diminution of the fish supply is a very pressing one, and that the situation is going from bad to worse. In their view, no effort ought to be spared (1st) to arrange for international treatment of the subject generally, and especially for regulation of the North Sea area; and (2nd) to provide for the adequate equipment of the Government Departments in charge of the subject, so that they may effectively pursue scientific investigation and ascertain with sufficiency and precision what has been done, either in the way of scientific research or in the matter of practical legislation, by other inquirers and by other countries, with the view of determining whether any, and if so what, legislation may be desirable to effect the objects of the Bill." *Ibid.*, iv.

[2] *E.g.*, "That this conference regards as conclusive the evidence of a widespread diminution of the supply of food fishes in the North Sea and adjacent grounds, and is of opinion that the only practicable remedy is the prevention of landing and sale of immature and undersized fish." Nat. Sea Fisheries Protection Ass., 1902.

such a convention. It was thought that, as the first step towards attaining this result, the Bill ought to be passed into law; but the opposition to it was too strong, and it shared the fate of its numerous predecessors.[1]

The statements of the trawlers that the older fishing-grounds are impoverished, particularly those in the North Sea, are borne out by the results of statistical and scientific inquiries. It was calculated by Professor W. Garstang that the average catch of bottom fishes, per fishing unit, decreased in the North Sea in the ten years 1889 to 1898 from 60·6 to 32·3; or, in other words, that while the average take of each trawling smack in 1889 was sixty tons, it was only about thirty-two tons in 1898.[2] The official statistics published annually by the Board of Agriculture and Fisheries show that the quantity of bottom fishes taken from the North Sea is declining, while on the other hand the quantity landed in this country from distant waters is greatly increasing.[3]

This brings us to the second point, in which the immense development of trawling touches upon the question of territorial waters—namely, the flocking of the trawlers to new grounds on foreign coasts. As the North Sea became, com-

1 *Report from the Select Committee of the House of Lords on the Sea Fisheries Bill* (*H.L.*), 1904 (36). The Earl of Onslow, Lord Tweedmouth, and Lord Heneage were members of this Committee.

2 *Op. cit.*

3 Thus from the year 1903 (when these statistics begin) to 1906 the number of tons of bottom fishes landed on the East Coast of England by first-, second-, and third-class fishing vessels, from the North Sea and from beyond the North Sea, was as follows:—

	1903.	1904.	1905.	1906.
From North Sea . .	260,313	230,975	207,440	217,567
From beyond the North Sea	67,625	78,216	93,395	129,697

The particulars for all coasts are only given for 1906, and they show that almost half of the total supply of bottom fishes in England and Wales come from grounds outwith the North Sea. The figures are: from North Sea, 217,571 tons; from beyond the North Sea, 203,863 tons. Captain Walter S. Masterman, of the Board of Agriculture and Fisheries, in a valuable report on his research work in the North Sea, states that while the total quantity of bottom fishes taken within the North Sea by steam-trawlers and landed on the East Coast of England has decreased in the four years, 1903-1906, by 39,650 tons, or nearly 17 per cent, the decrease in flat fish has amounted to 23,590 tons, or nearly 42 per cent; and that "the decrease has been continuous from year to year, especially in the case of plaice." *Report on the Research Work of the Board of Agriculture and Fisheries in relation to the Plaice Fisheries of the North Sea*, 1908 (Cd. 4227).

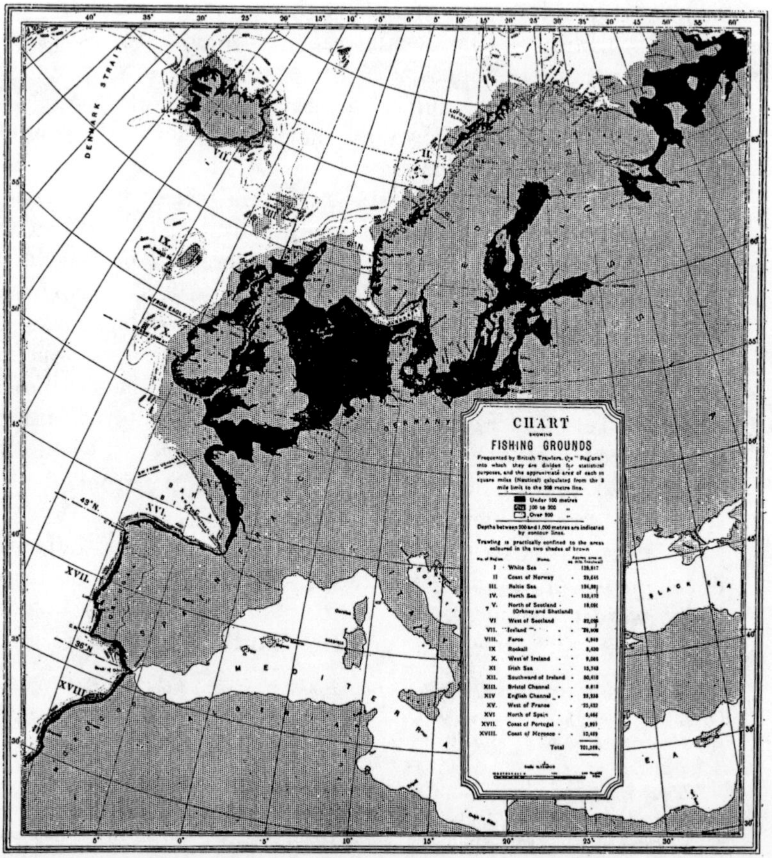

Fig. 28.—*Chart showing the Fishing-grounds frequented by British trawlers. Depths under* 100 *metres represented in black; those from* 100 *to* 200 *metres in shading.* From Report of the Board of Agriculture and Fisheries for 1906.

paratively speaking, more and more exhausted, the vessels were compelled to go farther and farther away in order to maintain the supply.[1] The grounds at Iceland, now so impor-

[1] A leading representative of the trawling industry, Mr G. L. Alward, thus described the process to the Committee of the Lords in 1904. The diminution, he said, was from over-fishing, "first of all in our original old fishing-grounds. We denuded those, and found less year by year as time went on. We then discovered new grounds, with, in process of time, the same result. In going back originally, say to about 1830 to about 1890, we found, at ground after ground, after being fished for a few years, the same results; the fish became scarcer and scarcer." *Report*, p. 78.

tant not only to the British trawlers but to the Germans and the French, were first visited in 1891, and those in the neighbourhood of the Faröe Islands a little later. The operations of the trawlers were at first limited to the south-east coast, but the catches were so enormous, and the enterprise so profitable, that large and seaworthy vessels were specially built for this fishing, which became one of the most important for the English markets.[1] Then the grounds in the Bay of Biscay and those on the coasts of Spain and Portugal began to be frequented, mostly from about the year 1902; and in the next year the operations of the trawlers were extended farther south to the coast of Morocco, as far at least as Agadir (20 deg. N. latitude), and even in some cases to the coast of Mauritania in French West Africa. The vessels fishing in these southern regions, many of them being fitted with refrigerating rooms, land a considerable proportion of their fish in Portugal and elsewhere. A year or two later, in 1905, the enterprising English trawlers opened up new grounds far away to the north-east in Barents Sea, at the very borders of the perpetual ice of the Arctic regions, and increasing numbers make the long double voyage of some 3500 miles thither every summer, and bring back from the neighbourhood of Cape Kanin great quantities of plaice for the English markets.

Thus the great enterprise and energy of British trawlers, supported by large capital, have enabled them to exploit the available grounds from far beyond the Arctic circle almost to the tropics, and it is from those distant regions that an increasing proportion of the fish supply is being drawn.[2] The influx of alien vessels, the most powerful and efficient fishing machines in existence, along these foreign coasts is not, as was naturally to be expected, viewed with satisfaction by the native fishermen. They see the fishing-grounds which they had so long

[1] The quantity brought to England from Iceland and Faröe in 1907 was nearly 117,000 tons, or nearly 26 per cent of the total quantity of bottom fishes landed. *Board of Agriculture and Fisheries Annual Report on Sea Fisheries for* 1907. Schmidt, *Fiskeriundersøgelser ved Island og Færøerne i Sommeren*, 1903, p. 132.

[2] A sidelight is thrown upon the risks as well as the enterprise of their labours by the fact that in 1908 a trawler's crew, on the one hand, fishing on the coast of Africa, fell into the hands of the Moors; while another, whose vessel was wrecked near the White Sea, were saved from starvation by the kindness of Russian Laplanders, who killed reindeer for their sustenance.

been accustomed to consider as their own—in many cases lying within the territorial waters preserved to them by the laws of their own country, though possibly outside "the ordinary three-mile limit"—invaded and exploited by foreigners, and their own livelihood threatened. They fear that what has occurred in the North Sea will happen along their own coasts; that the fishing-grounds, often of limited extent, will be impoverished and exhausted for the sole benefit of the foreigners, and their efforts to maintain themselves and their families rendered difficult or impossible. They observe from their boats the immense hauls of fish made by the huge trawl-nets, and the great waste that is often involved.[1] One cannot be surprised that the fishermen, and those who sympathise with them, feel indignation at the invasion of their waters by foreign trawlers, and that great meetings have been held, as in Spain and Portugal, to demand redress, and that at least the same limit as applies to natives pursuing similar methods should be enforced on the foreigners, or an international conference called to arrange for an equitable limit, or equitable treatment, which would have regard for the rights of all concerned.[2]

From the foregoing description of the problems associated

[1] Trawlers, on discovering new and productive grounds, invariably select out the fish that are most remunerative and throw the rest back into the sea. "Hundreds of thousands of tons" of immature fish are said to have been destroyed in this way in the North Sea, and what has happened at Iceland with regard to mature fish is thus described in a letter from one trawler to another, which was read by the recipient to the Parliamentary Committee in 1893: "Dear Manton, . . . At present the trawlers who are running Iceland are throwing thousands of tons of good mature fish away, which, if some scheme of storage were got up, the fish sorted, and bought for food, would supply thousands in the year. I have been to Iceland, and we have to throw away hundreds of tons of good mature fish, such as haddock, supposed to be too large, and great quantities of cod, ling, and other fish. The fact is, the ground, which is valuable for fishing, is completely rotten with the refuse from the trawlers. We have to haul every two hours, and we have to carry extra hands to get rid of the fish and get the bit below we choose to save. The ground is fairly poisoned, and the plaice-fishing not so brisk, only in odd places; whereas before it was more general where there is any trawling ground" (*Report cit.*, p. 248). The grounds had only been recently opened up when this was written. It is different to-day, when 85 per cent of the fish brought back from Iceland are round fish, chiefly haddocks and cod (*Ann. Rep. Sea Fisheries for* 1906, App., p. 15). It used to be the same in the North Sea, only prime fish being taken, and haddocks, &c., thrown away.

[2] *Vida Marítima, Órgano de la Liga Marítima Española*, 1904, 1905; *Boletin oficial.*

with the modern development of trawling, it will not be difficult to understand the scope and nature of the legislation which has been devised in various countries to preserve the native fisheries for the inhabitants of the coast. It may be said that in practically all of them, trawl-fishing is either entirely prohibited within territorial waters or is subjected to various regulations, for the most part with the view of allowing minor forms of trawling, as that for shrimps, to be carried on. In those countries which have a zone of territorial water extending beyond the ordinary three-mile limit, it is prohibited within that zone, as in Norway, Spain, and Portugal, and even up to twelve miles from the shore; while in some others in which three miles is in use as the ordinary limit for exclusive fishing, trawling is forbidden at distances beyond that limit. In Italy and Austria steam-trawling is not allowed within five miles of the coast. In Scotland and Ireland it is prohibited in certain specified waters, which extend much beyond a three-mile boundary. As recent legislation, or byelaws made with the authority of Parliament, bearing upon these prohibitions have given rise to much controversy, it is desirable to consider them with a little care.

In England, where the administration of the local fisheries around the coast is in the hands of various Sea Fisheries District Committees, numerous byelaws have been made and are in force, with the sanction of the Board of Agriculture and Fisheries, prohibiting or regulating trawling of one kind or another in the waters under the control of the Committees. None of the byelaws appear to apply to parts of the sea beyond the ordinary three-mile zone, though it is open to question whether the wording of the Act, by which the Committees were created, does not give power in that direction.[1]

[1] Sea Fisheries Regulation Act, 1888, 51 & 52 Vict., cap. 54. Section 1 is as follows: "1.—(1) The Board of Trade may from time to time on the application of a county council or borough council, by order, (*a*) create a sea fisheries district comprising *any part of the sea within which Her Majesty's subjects have by international law the exclusive right of fishing*, either with or without any part of the adjoining coast of England and Wales; and (*b*) define the limits of the district," &c. *Sea Fisheries (England and Wales), Annual Reports of the Inspectors; Board of Agriculture and Fisheries, Annual Reports of Proceedings under Acts relating to Sea Fisheries.* An excellent chart, showing the regulations with respect to trawling around the English coast, is published in the *Report from the Select Committee of the House of Lords on the Sea Fisheries Bill*, 1904.

The Irish Fishery Department have made a very large number of byelaws, at various times and under various Acts, for the regulation or prohibition of trawling. Of these some forty-four are at present in force, twenty-two applying to all trawling and twenty-two to steam trawling alone, and one or two of them date from the years 1842 and 1851.[1] Under these byelaws trawling in one form or another is prohibited entirely or under certain conditions at most parts of the coast of Ireland; and on certain parts of the coast not inconsiderable stretches of the sea, beyond the three-mile limit and the limit for bays as defined in the fishery conventions, are closed against this method of fishing. The lines around the coast within which trawling is prohibited, in many instances pass between headlands which may be as much as twenty-six, and even forty-three, miles apart; not infrequently they are drawn, not between headlands, but from one light-ship to another, and these light-ships may be four or five miles from land and twenty miles apart. Sometimes the closing line is placed three miles to the seawards of such base-lines; and they may pass from about two to seven or eight miles outside the limit as defined in the conventions, and in some instances up to ten or eleven miles from low-water mark on the shore.

It is obvious that the principle upon which these lines have been drawn has been one of convenience. They differ entirely from the lines of closure in the two Scottish Firths referred to below, which are *inter fauces terræ* with the lines passing from headland to headland. But all the lines on the Irish coast are well within the range of guns from the shore, and are thus, according to the Law of Nations, within the territorial sea. The aggregate area beyond the ordinary limits of the conventions amounts to a little over 400 square (geographical) miles.

It does not appear that foreign trawlers have been found contravening the Irish byelaws to any great extent. Between June 1904 and September 1905 seven steam-trawlers and one sailing-trawler were captured fishing within the limits, one of the former being registered in a foreign country, and, with regard to it, the official report says "it was found impossible

[1] *Department of Agriculture and Technical Instruction for Ireland: Report on the Sea and Inland Fisheries for* 1907. Part I., General Report, pp. 56-62.

to enforce the order made by the magistrates against the owner and skipper." It is added that "it is thought, however, that means have been found within the existing law of compelling foreign trawlers to observe the byelaws affecting Irish territorial waters."[1]

It is, however, with reference to the legislation for Scotland, under which certain areas are closed against trawling, that the main controversies have been raised. Several statutes gave power to the Fishery Board for Scotland to regulate trawling. The first was an Act of 1881,[2] which empowered the Board of Trade to restrict or prohibit this method of fishing "in any area being part of the sea adjoining the United Kingdom, and within the territorial waters of Her Majesty's dominions, within the meaning of the Territorial Waters Jurisdiction Act, 1878" (see p. 591); which power was transferred to the Scottish Board by subsequent Acts.[3] Then the Sea Fisheries (Scotland) Amendment Act, of 1885,[4] empowered the Board to make byelaws for restricting or prohibiting, either entirely or subject to such regulations as might be provided, any method of fishing "in any part of the sea adjoining Scotland, and within the exclusive fishery limits of the British Islands," when they were

[1] *Report on the Sea and Inland Fisheries of Ireland for* 1904, p. xxv. *Manual of Fisheries (Ireland) Acts.* Section 3 (subsection 1) of the *Steam Trawling (Ireland) Act*, 1889 (52 & 53 Vict., c. 74), gave powers to the Inspectors of Irish Fisheries to make, alter, and revoke byelaws for prohibiting steam-trawling "within three miles of low-water mark of any part of the coast of Ireland, *or within the waters of any other defined areas specified in any such byelaw*, and subject to any conditions or regulations contained in such byelaw." Subsection 2 enacted that "each and every person who uses any trawl-net, or any method of fishing in contravention of any byelaw of the Inspectors of Irish Fisheries made in pursuance of this section," shall be subject to a fine not exceeding five pounds for a first offence, or twenty pounds for a second or subsequent offence, with forfeiture of the gear employed. Section 4 made it unlawful for "any person" to land or sell in Ireland any fish caught in contravention of any such byelaw. Section 1 (subsection 1) of the *Fisheries (Ireland) Act*, 1901 (1 Ed. VII., c. 38), makes "every person who uses any trawl-net or any method of fishing in contravention of any byelaw" of the department made in pursuance of the third section of the Act of 1889, liable on conviction under the Summary Jurisdiction Acts to a fine not exceeding one hundred pounds, with forfeiture of the gear, for the seizure of which any duly authorised officer is empowered to "go on board any vessel propelled by steam employed in fishing." The Irish byelaws must be approved by the Lord-Lieutenant and Privy Council of Ireland.

[2] *Sea Fisheries (Clam and Bait Beds) Act*, 44 & 45 Vict., c. 11.

[3] 48 & 49 Vict., c. 70; 50 & 51 Vict., c. 52.

[4] 48 & 49 Vict., c. 70.

satisfied that such mode of fishing was injurious to any kind of sea fishing within that part, or in order to make experiments and observations to ascertain this, or for fish-culture; and such byelaw was not to be valid until it had been confirmed by the Secretary for Scotland. Several byelaws under this Act were made, prohibiting trawling within certain areas on the coast of Scotland within the ordinary limits.[1] It may well be questioned, in view of the definition of the "territorial waters of Her Majesty's dominions" in the Territorial Waters Jurisdiction Act, and of the "exclusive fishery limits of the British Islands" in the Sea Fisheries Act, 1883,[2] whether these powers were restricted to the three-mile limit and to bays whose width was not greater than ten miles; but it is noteworthy that a byelaw with reference to the Firth of Clyde was not confirmed by the Secretary for Scotland, presumably because it was considered at the time to be *ultra vires*.[3]

In 1889, however, an Act was passed which directly prohibited trawling "within three miles of low-water mark of any part of the coast of Scotland" (except the Solway and Pentland Firths), and within the waters specified in a schedule annexed, except in such parts as might from time to time be permitted by byelaws of the Fishery Board; and the Board was further empowered to forbid trawling within any area or areas in the Moray Firth between Duncansby Head and Rattray Point, which may be regarded as its headlands.[4] The waters specified in the schedule included the areas closed under the then existing byelaws, as well as a number of bays, lochs, and areas, the most important of which was "the waters inside a line drawn from Corsewall Point, in the County of Wigton, to the Mull of

[1] 1st Feb. 1886, 18th April 1887, 25th April 1887, &c. *Manual of Sea Fisheries (Scotland) Acts and Statutory Bye-laws*, pp. 253-257.

[2] See pp. 592, 643.

[3] *Ibid.*, p. 255.

[4] *The Herring Fishery (Scotland) Act*, 1889, 52 & 53 Vict., c. 23. Section 7.—(1) "The Fishery Board may, by byelaw or byelaws, direct that the methods of fishing known as beam trawling and otter trawling shall not be used within a line drawn from Duncansby Head, in Caithness, to Rattray Point, in Aberdeenshire, in any area or areas to be defined in such byelaw, and may from time to time make, alter, and revoke byelaws for the purposes of this section, but no such byelaw shall be of any validity until it has been confirmed by the Secretary for Scotland." The next section prohibits the landing or sale in Scotland of any fish caught in contravention of the Act or byelaws.

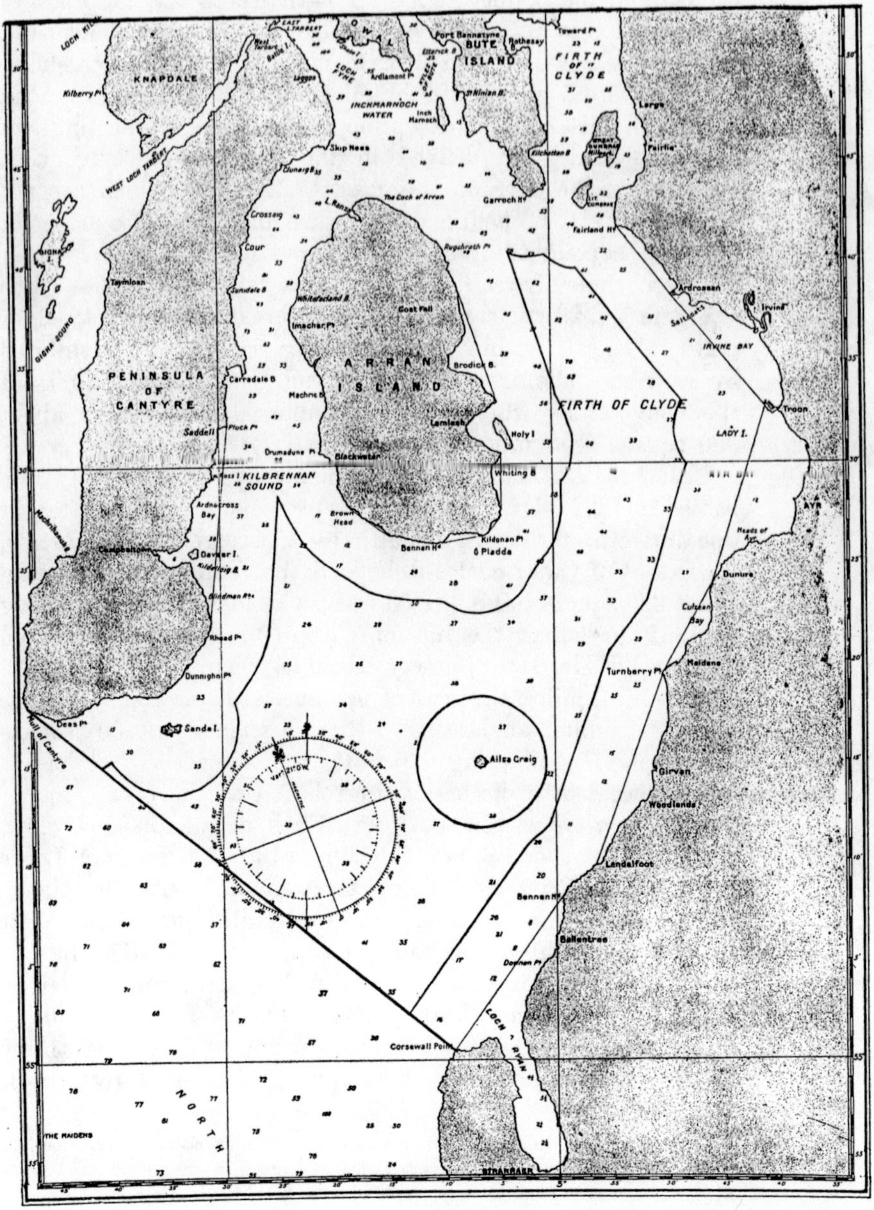

Fig. 29.—*The Firth of Clyde, showing the line of closure and the ordinary three-mile limit.*

Cantyre, in the County of Argyll"—that is to say, the Firth of Clyde. In this Act, it will be noted, nothing is said about bays, save in this schedule, and an examination of the charts shows that the waters specified in the schedule, twenty-five in number, would all, with a single exception, be included in the limits of exclusive fishing as defined in the North Sea Convention. Presumably the bays on the coast of Scotland which are not mentioned in the schedule do not come under the provisions of this Act beyond the distance of three miles from low-water mark on their shores. The exception referred to is the Firth of Clyde (fig. 29), where the line of closure is about twenty-eight miles in length, within which trawling was directly prohibited by the Act. The area of water outside the ordinary limits of the conventions which is thus embraced amounts to about 380 square (geographical) miles.

Under the section referring to the Moray Firth, a byelaw was passed in 1890 giving effect to its provisions within a straight line drawn from the Ord of Caithness to Craighead near Buckie, the extent of water enclosed, beyond the ordinary limits, being about 310 square miles. This was replaced by another byelaw in 1892, in which the line of closure to trawling was from Duncansby Head to Rattray Head, a distance of about 73 geographical miles, the area of sea enclosed between it and the ordinary limits amounting to approximately 1480 square (geographical) miles (fig. 30). It is this byelaw that has of late given rise to discussion in relation to the operations of foreign trawlers within the Moray Firth, as is explained below.

In 1895 another Bill was introduced into the House of Lords by the Lord Privy Seal (Lord Tweedmouth), with the object, among other things, of extending a similar jurisdiction over the waters washing the east coast of Scotland. The line at first chosen in this case was a very long one, running along the open coast from Rattray Head to the Farne Islands, a distance of about 120 miles, and passing a little over thirty miles east of Fife Ness.[1] It was proposed later to give power

[1] "11.—(1) The Fishery Board may, by byelaw or byelaws, direct that the methods of fishing known as beam trawling and otter trawling shall not be used within a line drawn from Rattray Point, in Aberdeenshire, to the Farne Islands, in Northumberland, in any area or areas to be defined in such byelaw, and may from time to time make, alter, and revoke byelaws for the purposes of this section."

to prohibit trawling in any area or areas within eighteen miles of the coast.[1] In the Act as passed the distance was reduced to thirteen miles from the coast in areas under the jurisdiction of the Crown, and no area was to be so regarded unless the powers conferred had been accepted as binding upon their own subjects with respect to such area by all the states who were parties to the North Sea Convention.[2] This section of the Act has remained inoperative, and no byelaws have been made under it; and there appears to be no evidence as to whether the views of other Powers have been obtained.

In the Moray Firth, closed to trawling by the byelaw above referred to, foreign trawlers began to make their appearance first of all in 1895, when a Danish vessel came. Two years later it returned, and a German trawler also, which was prevented from landing its fish at Aberdeen,—an act of the Crown, which was tested by a case in the Court of Session and upheld by it. In 1898 foreign trawlers appeared in the Firth in considerable numbers, and, it was reported, carried on their operations in such a reckless manner as to involve a great deal of damage to the gear of the net and line fishermen.[3] These vessels appear to have been mainly Danish, but there were a few Belgian, Dutch, and German, and they came for the most part intermittently and for brief periods, some of them appear-

[1] *A Bill [as amended in Committee] intituled An Act for the better Regulation of Scottish Sea Fisheries* (52), s. 10, February 1895.

[2] *Sea Fisheries Regulation (Scotland) Act*, 1895, 58 & 59 Vict., c. 42. Section 10.—(1) "The Fishery Board may, by byelaw or byelaws, direct that the methods of fishing known as beam trawling and otter trawling shall not be used in any area or areas under the jurisdiction of Her Majesty, within thirteen miles of the Scottish coast, to be defined in such byelaw, and may from time to time make, alter, and revoke byelaws for the purposes of this section. Provided that the powers conferred in this section shall not be exercised in respect to any areas under Her Majesty's jurisdiction lying opposite to any part of the coasts of England, Ireland, or the Isle of Man, within thirteen miles thereof." (2) provided for a local inquiry to be held. (3) "Provided that no area of sea within the said limit of thirteen miles shall be deemed to be under the jurisdiction of Her Majesty for the purposes of this section unless the powers conferred thereby shall have been accepted as binding upon their own subjects with respect to such area by all the States signatories of the North Sea Convention, 1882."

[3] *Eighteenth Ann. Rep. Fishery Board for Scotland*, Part I., p. xxxii. The information relating to this part of the subject is taken mostly either from the *Annual Reports* of the Scottish Fishery Board or from Hansard's *Parliamentary Debates*.

ing only once or twice in a year. Soon, however, the Firth was invaded by a fleet of trawlers flying the Norwegian flag, although it was known that Norway possessed no steam trawlers,[1] and these vessels fished regularly in the Moray Firth, carrying their fish to Grimsby, where they were landed and sold. It was soon discovered, and admitted, that these trawlers were in reality English, so far as capital, management, and crew were concerned, but they were registered in Norway in order to evade the British statute, and they soon obtained a practical monopoly of trawling in the Moray Firth. In 1901 there were fourteen or fifteen of them, but by 1905 they had increased to twenty-nine or thirty; while the visits of trawlers of other nationalities had diminished to nine in 1903, to six in 1904, and to two in each of the three following years. In 1903 and 1904 thirteen convictions were recorded against foreign trawlers, eight in connection with the Moray Firth and five in connection with the Clyde; in 1905 the number rose to fifteen for the Moray Firth and six for the Clyde. In all these cases the charge was for trawling within the ordinary three-mile limit. In 1905 a case was brought against Martin Olsen, the Norwegian "flag-master" of one of the trawlers registered in Norway, the *Catalonia*, for trawling within the Dornoch Firth in contravention of the Act of 1889, and byelaw No. 2, made under the Act of 1885. The place where the offence was committed was beyond the distance of three miles from the shore, but it was within three miles of the ten-mile base-line across the Dornoch Firth, and therefore within the exclusive fishery limit as defined in the conventions, and within one of the areas scheduled in the Act of 1889. The Sheriff-Substitute at Dornoch sustained Olsen's plea of no jurisdiction, on the ground that the *Catalonia* was registered in Norway, and Norway was not one of the Powers signatory to the North Sea Convention. On appeal to the High Court of Justiciary the decision was reversed, the judges holding that the prohibition in the Act of 1889, being quite general in terms, was applicable to foreigners as well as to

[1] See *Norges Officielle Statistik; Norges Fiskerier*, 1906, pp. 17, 18. Sixteen steam trawlers were on the list as registered in Norway in that year, but "they did not carry on fishing from Norwegian ports," and were not included in the list of *bona fide* Norwegian fishing-vessels.

British subjects, and that it was not for them to draw a distinction which had not been made by Parliament.[1]

This decision was the means of raising the question whether the byelaw did not apply to foreigners equally with British subjects in the whole extent of the Firth, and a series of cases were brought before the Sheriff to test the point. Three prosecutions were instituted, one against Emmanuel Mortensen, a Dane, master of the *Niobe*, of Sandefjord, Norway, for trawling at a point about five miles off Lossiemouth; another

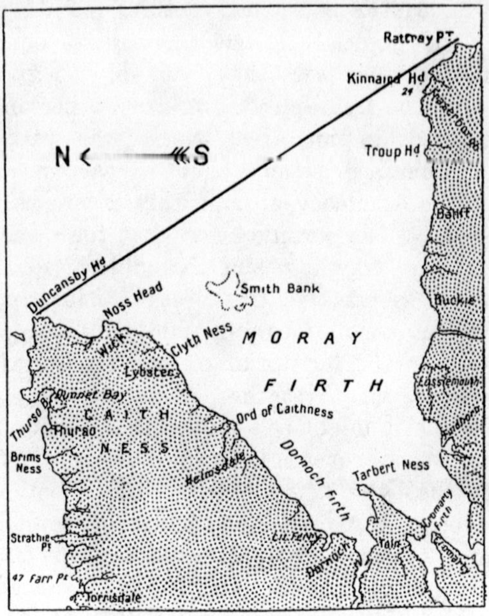

Fig. 30.—*The Moray Firth, showing the line of closure.*

against Thomas Robinson, a British subject, master of the *Verbena* of Stavanger, Norway, for trawling at a point five miles S.S.E. of Garty Point, Sutherlandshire; and the third against Arthur Lambert, a British subject, fishing-master of the *Pinewold,* registered at Sandefjord, Norway, for trawling at a distance of seven miles from Tarbetness. Convictions were obtained in all cases in the Sheriff Court of Dornoch,

[1] *Peters* v. *Olsen*, 7, *Court of Session Reports*, 5th Series (*Justiciary Cases*); 42 *Scottish Law Reporter*, p. 735.

mainly on the same ground as in the above case, that the statute was general and applied to all persons, but Sheriff (now Lord) Guthrie also held that the Moray Firth was within the territorial waters of Scotland.[1]

The case in regard to Mortensen was appealed and was heard by the full bench of twelve judges of the High Court of Justiciary, who unanimously upheld the conviction and dismissed the appeal. The leading opinion was delivered by the Lord Justice-General (Lord Dunedin), who treated the question as one of construction, and of construction only, since the court had nothing to do with whether an Act of the Legislature was *ultra vires* or in contravention of international law; they had only to give effect to it. The terms of the Act, applying to "every person" committing the offence within an area which was precisely defined, made the inference strong that it was meant to apply to all persons whatsoever; and this inference was further strengthened by the consideration that the clear object of the Act was to stop trawling, and that object would be defeated or rendered less effective if the prohibition applied only to British subjects, while leaving those of other nations free. With regard to the territorial or non-territorial character of the place where the *Niobe* had been trawling, Lord Dunedin said that while it might be assumed that within the three-mile limit the territorial sovereignty would be sufficient to cover such legislation, that was not a proof of the counter proposition, that outside the three miles no such result could be looked for. There were at least three points which went far to show that the *locus* was *intra fauces terræ:* (1) the dicta of the Scottish Institutional Writers, as Stair and Bell;[2] (2) the fact that the same statute puts forward claims to analogous places, as, *e.g.*, the Firth of Clyde; (3) there were many instances in decided

[1] "In fact, the Moray Firth, within the line from Duncansby Head to Rattray Point, is not the high seas, but is a bay or area between these headlands *intra fauces terræ*,—between the jaws of the land,—which has been called in England one of the King's Chambers. In law, such an area must be dealt with by the Courts of this country as part of the territorial limits of Scotland, unless the Legislature chooses to enact, in fairness to other countries or for any other reason, that the extent of the space involved is too great to come within the reasonable definition of a bay."

[2] See p. 545.

cases where the right of a nation to legislate for waters more or less landlocked, though beyond the three-mile limit, had been admitted. "It seems to me, therefore," continued Lord Dunedin, "without laying down the proposition that the Moray Firth is for every purpose within the territorial sovereignty, it can at least be clearly said that the appellant cannot make out his proposition that it is inconceivable that the British Legislature should attempt for fishery regulation to legislate against all and sundry in such a place. And if that is so, then I revert to the considerations already stated, which, as a matter of construction, make me think that it did so legislate." He did not think any argument could be drawn from the definition of "exclusive fishery limit" in the North Sea Convention, inasmuch as the Convention, as a whole, did not deal with what was here in question—viz., mode of fishing; and the Act treated subjects and foreigners alike in the matter.

Lord Kyllachy also held that, on the point of construction, the intention of the Act was that in no part of the area should trawling be practised by anybody; the terms were definite and applied to a quite definite area; it would be easier to suppose that the Legislature had reached even an erroneous conclusion as to the extent of its jurisdiction, than that it had resolved deliberately to impose a futile restriction upon its own countrymen and at the same time to create a hurtful monopoly in favour of foreigners. With regard to the territorial or non-territorial character of the Moray Firth, it seemed vain to suggest that according to international law there was any part of it which was simply an area of the open sea, and thus in the same position as if it were situated, say, in the middle of the German Ocean. The whole Firth was *prima facie* a "bay," with two well-marked headlands, and stretching inwards for many miles into the heart of the country. All that could be said against this was that at its outer end the Firth was very wide, and of a size, if not also of a configuration, somewhat beyond what is usually characteristic of bays and estuaries; but that might or might not be so, and the cases of the Bristol Channel, the Firth of Clyde, and the Firth of Forth would have to be considered before the proposition could be affirmed. There was no established rule on the subject in international law, and in particular no rule "so arbitrary and artificial as that of the ten-mile limit measure," for which the appellant contended. Perhaps the most interesting part of Lord Kyllachy's opinion concerned the bearing of the North Sea Convention on the case. If the question had been one of *exclusive fishing privileges*, the bearing of the Convention might have been important. "But exclusive fishing privileges—or, at all events, exclusive fishing privileges as defined by convention—are one thing; territorial jurisdiction, proprietary or protective, is a different thing. . . . There is certainly nothing in the Convention, at least nothing was brought under our notice, which in the least conflicts with the right of the several contracting nations to impose each of them within its territorial limits (whatever these are) restrictions universally applicable against injurious practices or modes of fishing such as are by this statute and byelaw imposed here. In other words, there is nothing in the statute and byelaw in question which at all interferes with the exclusive fishing privileges of the several nations." He could not consent to the argument that the Convention had introduced a new chapter into international law establishing, with respect to the definition of bays and estuaries, new and artificial rules. The other judges who gave their reasoned opinions expressed similar views, both as to the construction of the Act, the possibility or probability that the Moray Firth was a territorial bay by the law of nations, and as to the distinction between the limits of exclusive fishing as defined in the Convention and the right of the bordering state to regulate the fishery beyond that limit and within its territorial waters, provided the regulations applied equally to all.[1]

It is to be noted that although the question was strictly one of the construction of the Act, the judges had necessarily, in reaching its true meaning, to consider certain aspects of international law in relation to the territorial sea. From the above summary of their opinions, it is evident that the most eminent Scottish lawyers are in agreement with the modern publicists whose views have been referred to in a previous chapter, both in rejecting the three-mile limit as the farthest boundary of territorial sovereignty and as to the ten-mile rule (to say nothing of the six-mile theory) for bays. It may, however, be questioned as to how far the doctrine of independent territorial

[1] *Court of Session Reports*, 8 Fraser, p. 93.

regulation of fisheries beyond the limit of exclusive fishing, as defined in the Conventions, will be accepted as applied to the signatories of the Conventions. It is not expressly stated in the Conventions that the waters outside the exclusive fishery limits shall be free and common to all; but that is implied even in the title of the last of them,[1] and the Convention, in point of fact, lays down such regulations for the conduct of the fishery, outside the exclusive fishery limits, as appeared to the signatories at the time sufficient for the equitable enjoyment of the common right. It would be easy to conceive of general regulations being applied independently at particular places by one state, which would have the effect of abridging the common right of the other states, without affecting the interests of its own subjects—on the principle of the invitations which the fox and the stork issued to one another in the fable. That the intention was to leave the fisheries outside the limits mentioned free, except in so far as the regulations agreed upon affected them, is clear from the proceedings at the conference at The Hague. As regards other states, however, such as Norway, which were not signatories of the Conventions, it is equally clear that, up to the utmost bounds of the territorial waters, regulations may not only be imposed on their subjects, but they may be excluded from the fisheries altogether.

The effect of the decision of the High Court of Justiciary was apparently to keep the foreign trawlers out of the Moray Firth for a short time. But very soon a number of them came back again from Grimsby, with express instructions from the owners to fish in the Moray Firth. On 31st January 1907 six masters, all foreigners, of trawlers registered in Norway, were charged at Elgin Sheriff Court with thirteen separate contraventions of the byelaw, committed between 23rd November and 22nd December 1906, at various distances from about five to twelve miles from the coast; on conviction, penalties of £100 or sixty days' imprisonment were imposed, and five of the men went to prison. On 4th February other two masters of foreign trawlers were convicted of a corresponding offence at Wick Sheriff Court. At the trial at Elgin, the Norwegian Vice-Consul

[1] "For the purpose of regulating the police of the fisheries in the North Sea outside territorial waters." The use of the words "territorial waters" and "exclusive fishery limits" indifferently for the same thing is common, but improper.

at Aberdeen read a protest, at the instance of the Foreign Minister of Norway, against the conviction of the masters of three of the Norwegian vessels which he named, provided the trawling with which they were charged had taken place "outside the territorial limits."[1]

Representations were also made to the British Foreign Secretary by the Norwegian Minister in London (Dr F. Nansen), and the men were released on 9th February,[2] the decision of the Scottish High Court being thus in effect set aside. It was subsequently explained that in taking this action Norway was merely making a formal stand for the rights of her flag, since the trawlers had been registered in Norway in a legal way, Norwegian subjects were concerned, and no claim had been put forward on behalf of the British Government to the Moray Firth as being territorial in character. In point of fact, the Norwegian Government was in full sympathy with the policy of keeping the pseudo-Norwegian vessels out of the Moray Firth,[3] and they immediately, after the formal protest referred to, issued orders warning all owners of Norwegian trawlers fishing in the Moray Firth to cease from doing so, and not to expect the support of their Government in case of proceedings being taken against them in Scotland.[4] It does not appear that any advantage was taken of this proceeding for further prosecutions of Norwegians contravening the law; but

[1] "I, George Milne Cook, Vice-Consul for Norway for Aberdeenshire and the adjacent districts, by instructions of Herr Laveland, Minister for Foreign Affairs of Norway, hereby protest, on behalf of the Government of Norway, against any conviction of the masters of the Norwegian trawling vessels *Stroma*, *Sando*, and *Catalonia*, provided the trawling with which they were charged has taken place outside the territorial limits, and I further protest against any punishment or fines being inflicted in the Sheriff Court at Elgin on the said masters."

(Sd.) GEORGE M. COOK.

ELGIN, 31*st January* 1908.

[2] Hansard, vol. 169, pp. 557, 558, 988; vol. 170, pp. 1202, 1206.

[3] A letter appeared in the *Fish Trades Gazette*, on 14th October 1905, from Mr Hans Johnsen, the Fisheries Agent for Norway in Great Britain, stating that he had resigned his membership of the National Sea Fisheries Protection Association owing to the President (Lord Heneage) having prevented him from reading at the annual conference of the Association at Aberdeen, with reference to a resolution regarding the Moray Firth, a letter from the Norwegian fishery authorities. His object in endeavouring to speak on the resolution, he said, "was to clear the Norwegian flag from having anything to do with the piracy practised by Grimsby steam trawl-owners in the Moray Firth, and which the Government of Norway and the Norwegian Fishery Board is highly indignant at."

[4] Hansard, vol. 170, pp. 472, 1206, 1246, 1383.

it was decided to proceed against British subjects who might be found on the foreign vessels which were violating it, and who were undoubtedly under the jurisdiction of British courts. On March 20th twelve cases were brought before the Elgin Sheriff Court, the men charged being the "fishing-masters" of the foreign trawlers,[1] and the only one who appeared was fined fifty pounds for each of three offences, or fifteen days' imprisonment. A little later, on 17th April, fifteen fishing-masters of foreign trawlers, one of which was Swedish, all British subjects belonging to Grimsby, were charged in the same court for trawling within the Moray Firth outside the ordinary limits, and on conviction small fines were imposed. Similar cases were brought against eleven men in July, who were charged with twenty-eight offences committed between 2nd March and 24th June, and still smaller penalties were imposed.[2]

Considerable discussion was evoked by the various occurrences above referred to. Resolutions were passed at various meetings of fishermen in Scotland in favour of the byelaw being strictly enforced, and asking that an international arrangement should be come to if necessary to enable that to be done. At meetings of trawl-owners, on the other hand, held at Grimsby and elsewhere, resolutions to the opposite effect were agreed to, and the Government were requested to maintain the "three-mile international territorial limits as now defined." In the Houses of Parliament also numerous questions were put to Ministers on the subject, and there were several debates of a more or less formal kind. It appears that the Foreign Office had come to the conclusion that the Act of Parliament as interpreted by the High Court of Justiciary was in conflict with international law;[3] and that view having been taken, it was obvious that it would be necessary, if the statute was to have

[1] In these Norwegian vessels there were a "flag-master" and a "fishing-master," the former, nominally in charge of the vessel, being a Norwegian in order to comply with the registration laws, but often, or usually, occupying a humble position, such as cook. The "fishing-master" had the real control and occupied the master's rooms on board. He, like all or most of the crew, was English, resident at Grimsby.

[2] In April the penalties ranged from £10 to £2, 10s., or two to ten days' imprisonment; in July they ranged from £1 or one day to £45 or fourteen days; three cases were dismissed, one was found not proven, and in five the verdict was not guilty; four cases were appealed to the High Court by the Procurator-Fiscal and the appeal sustained. *Twenty-Sixth Ann. Rep. Fishery Board for Scot.*, Part I., App. L., II.

[3] Hansard, vol. 170, p. 472.

equal effect on foreigners, that some international arrangement, such as had been previously recommended by the Select Committees of the House of Commons and the House of Lords,[1] should be reached. It appears that there would have been no difficulty in arranging such an agreement with Norway, which was desirous of entering into negotiations for the purpose; but it was felt by the Foreign Office that, while an arrangement of the kind would not bind other Powers, questions of reciprocity might be raised, and British trawlers might be excluded from similar areas on foreign coasts. They therefore declined to enter upon negotiations with foreign Powers until the whole policy had been carefully considered.[2] One point of view which was taken was indicated in a speech of the Under-Secretary for Foreign Affairs (Lord Fitzmaurice) in the course of a debate in February 1907, which had been initiated by Lord Balfour of Burleigh. He stated that according to the views hitherto accepted by the chief departments of the Government—the Foreign Office, the Admiralty, the Colonial Office, the Board of Trade, and the Board of Agriculture and Fisheries—and apart from the provisions of special treaties, territorial waters were: "First, the waters which extend from the coast-line of any part of the territory of a State to three miles from the low-water mark of such coast-line; secondly, the waters of bays the entrance to which is not more than six miles in width, and of which the entire land boundary forms part of the territory of a State. By custom, however, and by treaty and in special convention, the six-mile limit has frequently been extended to more than six miles."[3] The Lord Chancellor, it may be said, was absent through illness; and the declaration quoted, though it represents what has been the general, but by no means the invariable, attitude of the British Foreign Office in dealing with territorial waters, is not in accordance with the law of nations, as is shown in the foregoing chapters. Nor does it agree with the opinions expressed in a former debate by the late Lord Salisbury, so long the distinguished Foreign Minister of this country, by

[1] See p. 707 *et seq.*

[2] Hansard, vol. 169, pp. 832, 991, 1037; vol. 170, pp. 786, 1246, 1247; vol. 192, p. 832, &c.

[3] *Ibid.*

Lord Halsbury, the former Lord Chancellor, and by Lord Herschell, the then Lord Chancellor (see p. 592), in which Lord Salisbury said "great care had been taken not to name three miles as the territorial limit." Nor is it in agreement with the carefully considered and most explicit reservations made in the Territorial Waters Jurisdiction Act, both in regard to the extent of the territorial waters and the rightful jurisdiction of the Crown beyond three miles from the shore under the law of nations, conferred by Act of Parliament, or by law existing, and the similar reservations in certain other Acts previously referred to. Even more singular is the novel statement as to what constitutes a territorial bay. A six-mile limit of the kind will obviously confer in the great majority of cases no greater extent of sea than the three-mile limit on an open coast, and it is thus opposed to one of the best-recognised principles of international law relating to the subject. The only part of the world where it appears to be in force is in British North America, with reference to subjects of the United States. The history of how it came to be applied at all is told in a previous chapter, in which it is also shown that the British Government as late as 1887 rejected even the ten-mile limit for bays, as involving a surrender of fishing rights, and as being contrary to the law of nations (p. 629), and they have made declarations equally emphatic on other occasions.[1]

But in a subsequent debate Lord Fitzmaurice appears to have qualified his statement, and quoted the observation of Lord Salisbury that where the coast was "folded and doubled," as

[1] Thus, in the "Reply on behalf of Her Britannic Majesty's Government to the Answer of the United States of America," submitted to the International Fisheries Commission at Halifax in 1877, it was said: "It is not understood that the Answer either raises or invites the discussion of any rules or doctrines of international law, save such as bear upon the question of what are to be considered the territorial waters of a maritime State for the purposes of exclusive fishing. The contention of the Answer in relation to these doctrines which requires special attention, is that which asserts that Great Britain and other Powers have traditionally recognised a rule, by which foreigners were excluded from fishing in those bays only which are six miles, or less, in width at their mouths. It is distinctly asserted on the part of Her Majesty's Government *that this alleged rule is entirely unknown to, and unrecognised by, Her Majesty's Government*, and it is submitted that no instance of such recognition is to be found in the Answer or the Brief accompanying the same, and that none can be produced." This was approved of by the Earl of Derby, Foreign Secretary (the Earl of Derby to Mr Ford, August 31, 1877; the same to the same, Oct. 6, 1877).

where bays exist, it was an unsettled question in international law how far territorial waters extend in such cases.[1]

Rather a different view was taken by the Lord Chancellor, a few weeks later, in the course of another debate about the Moray Firth. Lord Loreburn confined himself to saying that the obvious contention of other nations, and one very difficult to encounter, if we tried to make byelaws under our own law in regard to waters within a line from headland to headland eighty-five miles apart, would be that we might be trying to legislate for the high seas.[2] And in a debate in July 1908, the Secretary for Foreign Affairs (Sir Edward Grey) put the matter in an exceedingly lucid manner. Parliament had recognised the contention, he said, that there ought to be special regulations, especially in regard to the Moray Firth, going far beyond the three-mile limit; and, like other members of the Government, he condemned the action of British subjects who, knowing perfectly well the law, made use of a foreign flag to evade the regulations of the Moray Firth, which it was obviously the desire of Parliament should be enforced. But when they came to the question of enforcing the law on foreign subjects, they were placed in a very difficult position. The national policy of this country hitherto "had been to uphold the three-mile limit, but to protest against and to resist by every means in our power the pretension of any foreign country to enforce its own jurisdiction on the sea beyond the three-mile limit." We had contended before international tribunals, as in the Behring Sea Arbitration, that the three-mile limit is the only one we can recognise as the limit of foreign jurisdiction over British vessels; and suppose we attempted to enforce a doctrine going far beyond the three-mile limit on foreign ships, how could we

[1] 11th Nov. 1908. Hansard, vol. 196, p. 236. Very important declarations as to the territorial character of bays will be found in the decision of the Permanent Court of Arbitration at The Hague, on the North Atlantic Fisheries (7th September 1910, Award No. V.), received as these sheets are passing through the press. The application of the three-mile limit to bays was rejected, the following rule being formulated: "In case of bays the three marine miles are to be measured from a straight line drawn across the body of water *at the place where it ceases to have the configuration and characteristics of a bay*. At all other places the three marine miles are to be measured following the sinuosities of the coast." In its practical application to British North America, the Tribunal recommended a ten-mile limit generally, except for certain specified bays (including Chaleurs, Miramichi, Egmont) where special lines, enclosing much larger areas, are proposed.

[2] Hansard, vol. 170, p. 1383. The miles referred to are English statute miles.

contend before an international tribunal for a doctrine precisely the reverse of that which we have always upheld on previous occasions? It followed from this that "if there was to be a modification of the rules relating to trawling in the North Sea, it must be by agreement with foreign Powers"—that was really the practical point upon which the matter turned. But in an important question affecting the interests of the country at large, it was impossible for the Foreign Office to approach other Powers with the view of reaching an agreement until it was quite clear that it was in the interest of a policy which had been adopted, affirmed, and declared by the Government to be a policy which was in the general national interest of the United Kingdom. Judging from the very great force with which the case in such regions as the Moray Firth had been presented, and the strong feeling that existed and which was not confined to the Moray Firth, it had always seemed to him that there was a case for grave consideration as to whether any new regulations were required for the preservation of the fishing industry in the North Sea at large. Trawling was a perfectly legitimate industry in which large capital was invested, and if further restrictions were to be imposed on it, it must be because a really important national interest required it; it would not be right to adopt in the interests of particular localities any special restrictions which might result in diminishing the supply and raising the price of fish. But, having laid down these two principles, Sir Edward Grey thought it was equally true that if the supply of fish from the North Sea is being affected by want of further regulations, then the interests of any particular industry must be subordinated to the general interest, which in the long-run was also the interest of the industry itself. "If it be the case," he proceeded, "that in areas like the Moray Firth, which are important breeding-grounds, the supply of fish is being seriously interfered with by the prosecution of trawling in narrow waters, then it becomes a matter of national interest that we should, as soon as possible, come to some agreement with foreign Powers under which we should be able to make the arrangements which prove to be necessary in the national interest at large." The subject was one requiring the deliberate investigation of the Government, and the investigation was proceeding; and they should know in the course of a reasonable time whether or not the Government thought they had a case for approaching other Powers, and if so what were the grounds and propositions they should ask those Powers to agree to. With regard to bays, the Foreign Secretary said it had generally been understood that the qualification of the three-mile limit applied to bays ten miles wide, and they must be very careful as to how far they pressed the doctrine as to the width of a bay, or laid down an international doctrine on any particular bay. They must think of what the application of it might be in other parts of the world.[1]

In this statesmanlike speech the case was put temperately and fairly. Whether the Moray Firth is or is not a territorial bay, it has been the general practice of the British Government to contend for the ordinary three-mile limit, at least on open coasts, in relation to fishery questions. If there are clear reasons for the extension of this limit at any part of the coast, or in the North Sea generally, in the common interests of the fisheries, as recommended by the Select Committee of the House of Commons in 1893; or for the prohibition of trawling within a great area on the Continental coast, as urged by the English trawlers, and recommended by the Parliamentary Committees of 1900 and 1904; or if it is believed to be necessary to regulate the fisheries in any way beyond the ordinary limit, then obviously the best method is to endeavour to come to an arrangement with the other Powers concerned. There are precedents for this course in British policy. By treaties with France, the British Government agreed to bind British subjects not to fish for oysters or any kind of fish within Granville Bay in waters beyond the ordinary limit. In the interests of the preservation of the fur-seal, in which the United States was mainly concerned, they agreed to prohibit British subjects from taking them within a limit of sixty miles around the Pribilov Islands, and to compel them to observe a close-time on the high seas, and to use only the primitive spear. They have also by treaty agreed to respect various other limits beyond the ordinary three miles in the interest of the preservation of other kinds of seals. The case of the North Sea, or of that inlet of it known as the Moray Firth, is on the same footing as these. The question is not one of the extension of territorial sea *qua*

[1] Hansard, vol. 191, p. 1769.

territorial sea, but of special regulations independent of it, and exclusively relating to the fisheries.

From what has been said in foregoing pages as to the impoverishment of the fishing-grounds in the North Sea, and the various remedies that have been at one time or another proposed by the English trawlers and by Parliamentary Committees with the view of maintaining the fish supply, it might appear that a very good case already existed for approaching foreign Powers with the object of arranging for general regulations beyond the ordinary limit, and one far weightier than that which brought about the conference at The Hague and the North Sea Convention in 1882 (see p. 631).

Two probable reasons may be advanced for the delay in giving effect to the recommendations of the various Committees of Parliament. The first is that a very important international investigation of the North Sea and adjacent waters has been in progress for a number of years and is still going on. On the invitation of the Swedish Government, representatives of Great Britain, Germany, Russia, the Netherlands, Denmark, Sweden, and Norway met at Stockholm in June 1899, and again at Christiania in May 1901, to discuss and arrange an organisation and a programme for an international scientific investigation of the North Sea, the Norwegian Sea, and the Baltic, in the interests of the fisheries; and in July 1902, the first meeting of the body so constituted, the International Council for the Exploration of the Sea, was held at Copenhagen. Since then all the maritime countries of Western Europe, with the exception of France, have engaged in these researches.[1] This country entered into the arrangement with special reference to the fisheries in the North Sea, and with a very practical end in view—namely, to secure a careful inquiry into the effect of the methods of fishing in the North Sea, and to promote a scheme for determining whether

[1] Reports of the British Delegates attending the International Conferences held at Stockholm, Christiania, and Copenhagen, with respect to Fishery and Hydrographical Investigations in the North Sea. *Parl. Papers*, Cd. 1313, 1903. Corresponding "Reports" to 1906 (*Parl. Papers*, Cd. 2966/06, 3033/06, 3165/06). Conseil Permanent International pour l'Exploration de la Mer, *Rapports et Procès-Verbaux des Réunions*, Copenhague. A summary on the subject, by Dr A. T. Masterman, will be found in the Minutes of Evidence, Committee on Fishery Investigations (*Parl. Papers*, Cd. 4304, p. 479, 1908).

protection against overfishing was required; and, if so, where, when, and how such protection should be given.[1] Much strong criticism has been passed as to the origin, the methods, and the programme of these investigations,[2] and while they have naturally resulted in large additions to our knowledge of the physical

[1] "2. The delegates should propose that the scientific investigations shall be accompanied by a practical *exposé* of the steps to be taken in order to bring the exercise of sea-fishing more in accord with the natural conditions regulating the growth and increase of fish in our seas, and thus permanently increase the supply of fish in the markets of the countries adjoining the North Sea. 3. In making this proposal, which they should do at the outset, the delegates should make it clear that the principal object the British Government have in directing them to take part in the Conference, is to secure a careful inquiry into the effect of present methods of fishing in the North Sea; and the delegates should give every assistance in promoting a scheme for determining whether protection against overfishing is needed, and, if so, where, when, and how such protection should be given. 4. The delegates should propose that a thorough scheme for obtaining statistical information with regard to the quantity and quality of fish caught by the different methods of fishing shall be organised, with a view of determining whether protection against overfishing is needed, either by the prohibition of trawling in certain selected areas or the limitation of fishing during certain selected seasons."—Instructions to the British Delegates for the Meeting at Stockholm, 15th June 1899; Reports of the British Delegates, &c., p. 13. *Parl. Papers*, Cd. 1313, 1903; Committee on Fishery Investigations, Minutes of Evidence, &c., p. 278, *Parl. Papers*, Cd. 4304, 1908. The instructions of the British Government to the Delegates for the Meeting in 1901, at Christiania, were of similar tenour:—"His Majesty's Government fully share in the interest shown in the cause of scientific research, but having regard to the importance of the evidence which was laid before the Select Committee of the House of Commons [see p. 709], and which was adopted by them as showing that the supply of fish in the North Sea is decreasing, they are of opinion that the consideration of this subject will admit of no delay, and you should press on your foreign colleagues the importance of entering at once upon the pursuit of investigations calculated to lead to an international agreement. You should in no way discourage or check any desire which you may find to exist for scientific research into problems not so immediately pressing, but his Majesty's Government place in the forefront of their reasons for taking part in the forthcoming Committee the desire that no delay should be incurred in the adoption, by international agreement, of measures for arresting the diminution of the supply of fish in the North Sea, and for restoring, as far as possible, that source of supply to its former abundance." *Ibid.*, p. 278.

[2] *Memorandum drawn up by the Expert Members of the Ichthyological Research Committee*, Report of the Committee appointed to Inquire and Report as to the Best Means by which the State or Local Authorities can Assist Scientific Research as applied to Problems affecting the Fisheries of Great Britain and Ireland (*Parl. Papers*, Cd. 1312, p. xxii, x, 1902). *Evidence of Mr Walter E. Archer, Assistant-Secretary, Board of Agriculture and Fisheries*, Minutes of Evidence given before the Committee appointed to inquire into the Scientific and Statistical Investigations now being carried on in relation to the Fishing Industry of the United Kingdom, pp. 277, 288, 346, 359 (*Parl. Papers*, Cd. 4304, 1908).

and biological conditions of the sea, of the life-history of fishes, and of certain fishery questions, no report has yet appeared dealing with the fundamental problem as to overfishing and any remedies which may be required to safeguard the fish-supply; and it is doubtless such information that is referred to by the Foreign Secretary as essential before Foreign Powers can be approached. An opinion was, however, early expressed as to the particular question of the Moray Firth. The Conference held at Christiania in 1901, at which all the Powers signatory to the North Sea Convention (with the exception of France) were represented, passed a resolution to the effect that "in distinct areas of the sea, as for example the Moray Firth, in which any Government has undertaken scientific experiments in the interest of the fisheries, and in which the success of the experiments is being hindered by the operations of trawlers, it is to be desired that measures be adopted for the removal of such hindrances."[1]

The second probable reason that nothing has yet been done to arrive at an international understanding appears to be that the representatives of the great trawling industry have changed their minds within the last few years. Since foreign coasts have been exploited with immediate financial success to the trawling companies, their interest in the North Sea has diminished. They fear that if the question of fishery regulations beyond the ordinary three-mile limit is opened up with foreign Powers in the interest of the North Sea fisheries, proposals may be made, as a *quid pro quo*, by some of the other Powers for similar regulations on their coasts; and it is evident from the statements made in Parliament that this view has hitherto prevailed.[2] One would have thought that a *quid pro quo* which closed to trawling the great area off the Continental coast, which English trawlers for more than fifteen years have been vainly asking to be closed by international arrangement, would be satisfactory to them. Or that a fishery limit of nine or ten miles on the other side of the North Sea, or all around it, which they thought some years ago to be the best remedy for the

[1] Reports of the British Delegates, &c., *Parl. Papers*, Cd. 1313, p. 72, 1903. The countries represented were Great Britain, Germany, Denmark, Belgium, the Netherlands, Norway, Sweden, and Russia.

[2] Hansard, vol. 169, pp. 992, 996; vol. 170, p. 786; and 11th Nov. 1908.

depletion of the fishing-banks, would meet with their approval. These areas, compared with the whole of the North Sea, are comparatively of small extent (see fig. 26). The area of the North Sea between the three-mile line and a nine-mile limit amounts to about 12,000 square miles, or 7·4 per cent of the whole area beyond three miles from the shore; and the area between the three-mile line and a thirteen-mile limit amounts to about 20,000 square miles, or 12·3 per cent.

Meanwhile, the condition of the fishing-grounds in the North Sea is described as serious by those who ought to know most about it—the trawlers who are daily working there; and if no remedy is timeously applied, the measures which will eventually be necessary will transcend those which are now proposed.[1]

But if it be imprudent to postpone indefinitely the seeking of an international remedy for the depleted fisheries of the North Sea, because the trawling industry fears that retaliatory measures may be proposed against British trawlers on some foreign coasts, it may be questioned, on the other hand, whether the action taken to obviate such measures has always been well-judged or in accordance with the true comity of nations. On strictly selfish grounds, and for immediate profit, it is doubtless justifiable to make every fishing-bank, wherever it is situated, available for the enterprise of British capital, irrespective of the interests of the inhabitants of the adjoining coast, if that can be managed. If, indeed, the resources of the sea were inexhaustible,—if it was impossible for the operations of man to diminish the abundance of fish,—then no limit of exclusive fishing would be necessary: only such regulations would be required as would enable fishing operations to be conducted in an orderly manner. But the condition of the North Sea alone proves the opposite. It shows also, what is well enough understood, that unrestrained trawling on any

[1] Mr Frank Barrett, of Grimsby, thus referred to the condition of the North Sea at the conference of the National Sea Fisheries Protection Association in 1905: "Unless they did something as a counterpoise to the continual trawling which was going on, they would find themselves powerless as regarded that splendid fishing-ground, the North Sea. He did not believe the North Sea, if left to itself, could last for ever. He was one of those who thought it could not last very long; and he thought they should apply the lessons of science in order to rehabilitate the North Sea." *Fish Trades Gazette*, Oct. 14, 1905.

banks will, in course of time, materially reduce their productiveness; and the rapidity of the impoverishment will very largely depend upon the intensity of the fishing and the extent of the grounds. That being so, it may well be said that a measure of protection on the banks which are still productive along foreign coasts would be in the permanent interest of the English trawling industry itself, as well as in the interest of the coast population.[1]

On some of those coasts the local population are dependent on the fish they catch on the neighbouring grounds, which are often of limited extent, and it is reasonable and just that they should endeavour to preserve this supply for their own use and advantage. At Iceland, for example, the area of the possible fishing-grounds between the ordinary three-mile limit and a depth of 200 metres (or 109 fathoms), including places where trawling is not practicable, amounts to about 36,600 square miles, compared with nearly 312,000 square miles between the same limits off the British Isles.[2] It was recently stated in the House of Lords, by Lord Heneage, that the Icelanders, with the view of preserving their fishing-grounds, a few years ago brought forward a law in the *Althing*, or local Parliament, to extend the limit of exclusive fishing to seven miles around their coast. It was also said that in 1901 they passed laws for enclosing extra-territorial waters.

[1] Mr G. L. Alward, one of the leading and most experienced trawl-owners of Grimsby, who was invited to take part in a discussion on sea fisheries in the Zoological Section of the British Association in 1906, thus referred to the subjcet. He said: "There was no doubt that the North Sea was deteriorated as a fishing-ground, and in order to maintain an adequate supply they had had to explore fresh fields. They had shifted the trawling-grounds to the coasts of Faröe, Iceland, and Norway, while others had had to go out into the Atlantic, to the Bay of Biscay, and to the coast of Morocco. But if they had exhausted the 147,000 square miles of the North Sea,—every mile of which had been fished,—and they fished out the area between Norway and Faröe and Iceland, not more than forty or fifty thousand square miles, with the same rapidity, they had to look forward to nothing short of a dearth of fish and a rise in value to famine prices." *Aberdeen Free Press*, 9th August 1906.

[2] According to an interesting table on a chart appended to the *Annual Report of the Board of Agriculture and Fisheries* for 1906 (see fig. 28), the areas, in square miles, between the three-mile limit and the 200-metre line, are as follows: North Sea, 152,473; North of Scotland (Orkney and Shetland), 18,096; West of Scotland, 32,099; West of Ireland, 9066; Irish Sea, 15,743; Southwards of Ireland, 50,416; Bristol Channel, 8613; English Channel, 25,238. The area at Iceland is 36,608, and at the Faröes, 4949 square miles.

As soon as these proceedings came to the knowledge of the English trawl-owners, the National Sea Fisheries Protection Association made a representation on the subject to the Foreign Office, and in consequence of this the Danish Government took action, and the law was prevented from coming into operation.[1] And any such action in the future was effectually prevented by the immediate negotiation of an international convention in which a three-mile limit was fixed for Iceland and Faröe (see p. 647) so far as concerned British fishermen. Then with respect to the coasts of Spain and Portugal, where the available grounds are narrow, amounting altogether between the three-mile limit and the 200-metre line to 15,460 square miles (see fig. 28), intimation has been made by the British Foreign Office, at the instance of the National Sea Fisheries Protection Association, that jurisdiction will not be recognised over British vessels beyond three miles from the shore, and the national regulations in regard to trawling are thus rendered comparatively ineffective. With regard to Norway, moreover, where the area between the three-mile limit and the 200-metre line exceeds 30,000 square miles, it appears that soon after her separation from Sweden, in 1905, the British Foreign Office made the proposal that she should join in the North Sea Convention (which, along with Sweden, she refused to do in 1882), so that the ordinary three-mile limit might be imposed along the Norwegian coast; but the proposal was rejected.[2]

In view of the evidence that has been adduced, the recommendations of the various Committees of Parliament that have inquired into the subject, and the statements made in the House of Commons, it may be assumed that an international conference of the Powers bordering the North Sea will be convened, to consider how fishery regulations may be made more effective, whether by extension of the limits of exclusive fishery or otherwise, as soon as the results of the international fishery investigations justify that course.

[1] Hansard, vol. 169, p. 996; vol. 196, p. 217. I have been courteously informed by Mr Bjarni Sæmundsson, of Reykjavik, a well-known authority on the fisheries of Iceland, that no laws proposing to extend the territorial waters were passed, or proposed, by the *Althing*.

[2] Hansard, vol. 170, p. 786.

APPENDIX A.

(P. 45.)

THE LIBEL REGARDING REYNER GRIMBALD.

De Superioritate Maris Angliæ et Jure officii Admirallatus in eodem.

(Chancery Rolls, Miscellaneous. Treaties and Diplomatic. Bundle 14, No. 15, Mem. 12.)

A vous Seignurs Auditours Deputez par les Roys Dengleterre et de Fraunce a redresser les damages faitz as gentz de lour Roialmes et des autres terres subgiz a lour seignuries par meer et par terre en temps de pees et de Trewes monstrent les Procureurs [1] des Prelatz et Nobles et del Admiral de la meer Dengleterre et des Comunaltes des Citees et des Villes et des Marchanz Mariners Messagers et Pillerins et de tous autres [2] du dit Roialme Dengleterre et des autres terres subgies a la seignurie du dit Roy Dengleterre et daillours sicome de la Marine de Genne Cateloigne Espaigne Alemaigne Selaunde Heylande Frese Denemarch et Norweye et de pluseurs autres leux del empyre qe come les Roys Dengleterre par raisoun du dit Roialme du temps dount il na [3] memoyre du contraire eussent este [4] en paisible possession de la souereigne seignurie de la meer Dengleterre et des Isles esteans en ycele [5] par ordinance et establicement des lois estatuz et deffenses darmes et des vesseaux autrement garniz qe vesseaux de Marchandise et de seurte prendre et sauuegarde doner en tous cas qe mestier serra et par ordinance de tous autres faitz necessaires a la garde des pees droiture et equite entre toute [6] manere des genz taunt dautri seignurie come leur propre [7] par illeqes passanz et [8] par souereigne garde et [9] tote manere de conisance et Justice haute et basse sur les dites loys

[1] On Mem. 1 the words "le dit Roi Dengleterre et" follow "Procurors."
[2] Mem. 1 and 8, "de touz autres de son Roialme."
[3] Mems. 1, 14, and 15, "il ny ad." Mem. 8, "du temps qil ny ad."
[4] Mem. 8, "aueroient este."
[5] Mem. 1, "oue touz les Isles et les apportenaunces."
[6] Mem. 1, the words are "estatuitz et defenses comunes et priuees" and the rest is omitted to "sur toute manere des gentz taunt," &c. Mem. 8, "communes et priuees a garder pays et droiture entre tote manere des gentz tant," &c. Mem. 15, "estatuitz et defences pur gouerner en toute manere," &c.
[7] Mems. 1, 8, 14, 15, "come de lour propre."
[8] Mem. 1, "oue."
[9] Mems. 1, 8, and 15, "oue."

estatuz ordinances et deffenses et par tous autres faitz queux a le gouernement [1] de souereigne seignurie appartenir purront es leux auantdiz. Et A. de B. Admiral de la dite meer deputez par le Roy [2] Dengleterre et tous les autres Admirals par meisme celui Roy Dengleterre [3] et ses Ancestres iadiz Roys Dengleterre eussent este [4] en paisible possession de la dite souereigne garde [5] oue la conisance et Justice et tous les autres appurtenances auantdites horspris [6] en cas dappel et de querele faite de eux a lour souereignes Roys Dengleterre de deffalte de droit ou de mauueis iuggement et especialment par empeschement mettre et Justice faire [7] seurte prendre de la pees de tote manere des genz vsanz armes en la dite meer ou menanz Nefs autrement apparaillees ou garnies qe nappartenoit au [8] Neef Marchande et en tous autres pointz en queux homme poet auoir resonable cause de suspecion vers eux de roberie ou des autres mesfaitz.[9] Et come les Meistres des Neefs du dit Roialme Dengleterre en absence des diz Admirals eussent este en paisible possession de conustre et juggier de tous faitz en la dite meer entre tote manere des gentz solonc les loys estatus et les deffenses franchises et Coustumes.[10] Et come en le primer article de lalliaunce nadguers faite entre les diz Roys en les traitiz sur la darraine pees de Paris soient comprises les paroles qe sensuient en vne cedule anexe ayceste.[11] Primerement il est traite et acorde entre nous et les messages et les procureurs desurdiz en nonn des diz Roys qe yceux Roys serrount lun a lautre desores en auant bons verays et loiaux amys et eydanz countre tout homme sauue lesglise de Rome en tiele manere que si ascun ou pluseurs quicunques ils fuissent voloient deponticer [*sic*] empescher ou troubler les diz Roys es franchises es libertez priuileges es droiz es droitures ou es custumes de eux et de lour Roialmes qils serront bons et loiaux amys et aydanz countre tout homme qi puisse viure et morir a defendre gardir et mainterer [12] les franchises les libertez les priuileges les droiz les droitures et les coustumes desusdites Excepte [13] le dit Roy Dengleterre Monsieur Johan Duc de Braban en Brabant et ses heirs dessenduz de lui et de la fille le Roy [14] Dengleterre et excepte pur le dit nostre seigneur le Roy de Fraunce excellent Prince Monsieur Aubert Roy Dalemaigne [et] ses heirs Roys Dalemaigne et Monsieur

[1] Mem. 1, instead of gouernement, "a la generalte"; Mem. 8, "a la garde."
[2] Mems. 1, 8, and 15, "le dit Roi."
[3] Mem. 1 omits "Dengleterre."
[4] Mems. 1 and 8, "Rois Dengleterre deputez eient este."
[5] Mem. 8, "de la dite seignurie et garde."
[6] Mems. 1, 8, 14, and 15, "forspris."
[7] Mems. 1, 8, and 15 insert "et."
[8] Mem. 15, "a."
[9] Mem. 1, "ou mesfaitz"; Mem 8, "ou de mesfaitz."
[10] The sentence from "Et come" to "Coustumes" is omitted on Mems. 1, 8, and 15.
[11] Mems. 1 and 8 omit "en vne cedule anexe ayceste," and Mems. 1, 14, and 15 omit the whole of the next paragraph, recommencing "Monsieur Reymer Grimbaus." Mem. 8*d*, paragraph commencing "Primerement."
[12] Mem. 8, "et a maintener."
[13] Mem 8, "excepte pur le dit Roy."
[14] Mem. 8, "le dit Roy."

Johan Counte de Henau en Henau. Et que lun ne serra en consail ne en ayde ou lautre perde vie membre estat ne honur temporel [Mem. 12*d*] Monsieur Reymer Grymbaltz Meistre de la Nauie du dit Roy de Fraunce qi se dit estre Admiral de la dite Meer deputez per soun seignur auantdit pur sa guerre countre les Flamaings apres la dite alliaunce faite et affirmee et[1] contre la fourme et la fource de meisme lalliance et lentencion de ceux qi la firent loffice deladmiralte en la dite Meer Dengleterre[2] par commission du Roy[3] de France torsenousement enprist et usa un an et plus en parnant les gentz et[4] marchantz du Roialme Dengleterre et daillours par la dite meer passanz euesque leur biens[5] et les gentz ansi prises liuera a la prison de soun dit Seignur le Roy de Fraunce et lour biens et[6] Marchandises a les Receiuours par meisme celui Roy de Fraunce[7] a ce[8] deputez en les Portz de soun dit Roialme come a lui forfaites et acquises fist amener par soun iuggement et agard[9] et la prise et detenue des dites gentz oue[10] lour diz biens et marchandises et soun dit iuggement et agard sur la forfaiture de eaux et acqueste[11] ait Justice deuant vous Seignurs Auditours en escript par my lautorite de la[12] dite commission sur ladmiralte auantdite par lui ansi vsurpee et par my vne deffense communement faite par le Roy[13] Dengleterre par my soun poer solonc la forme du[14] tiers article de lalliaunce auant dite qi contient les paroles desouzescriptes en requerant que de ce il en fuisse quitz et assouz en grant damage et preiudice du dit Roy Dengleterre et des Prelatz et Nobles et autres desusnomez par quoy les diz procureurs en les nouns de lour diz Seignurs[15] Auditours auantdiz prient que deliuerance dewe et hastiue des dites gentz ouesqe leur biens et marchandises ansi prises et detenues facez estre faite al Admiral du dit Roy Dengleterre a qi la conisance de ce appartient de droit sicome desus est dit ansi qe[16] sans destorbance de vous et dautri[17] puisse de ce conustre et faire ce qe appartient a soun office auant dit et qe le dit Monsieur Reyner soit condampne et destreint affaire dewe satisfaction a tous les diz damagez si auant come etc.[18] Item vous requirent les diz procureurs que come solone

1 Mem. 14 omits "et."
2 Mems. 1 and 8 omit "Dengleterre."
3 Mems. 1, 14, and 15, "du dit Roi."
4 Mems. 8 and 15 insert "les."
5 Mems. 1, 8, and 15 insert "et marchandises."
6 Mem. 1 omits "et."
7 Mem. 1 omits "de Fraunce."
8 Mems. 1, 14, and 15 read (here and elsewhere) "ceo."
9 Mem. 8 omits "et la prise," &c., recommencing, "sur la forfaiture," &c.
10 Mem. 14, "ou."
11 Mem. 8 inserts "et."
12 Mems. 1, 14, and 15, "sa."
13 Mems. 1 and 8, "de par le dit Roi."
14 Mem. 1, "de la"; Mems. 8, 14, and 15, "de le."
15 Mems. 1, 8, 14, and 15 insert "a vous Seigneurs."
16 Mems. 8 and 14, "qil."
17 Mem. 8 inserts "il."
18 Mems. 1, 14*d*, and 15 complete the passage as follows: "Come il purra suffire et en sa deffaute son dit seignur le Roi de Fraunce par qi il estoit deputeez al dit office et qe apres dewe satisfactioun faite as ditz damagez le dit Monsieur Reiner soit si duement punitz pur le blemissement de la dite alliance qe la punicioun de lui soit as autres example [Mem. 8, 'ensample'] pur temps auenir." Mem. 15 ends here. Mem. 8 transposes the next paragraph and the last.

les anxnienes[1] loys franchises et coustumes du Roialme Dengleterre a la garde des queles vostre dit seignur le Roy et ses auncestres Roys Dengleterre soloient estre liez par lour sermentz Lour Admirals de la Meer Dengleterre oue[2] les Maistres et Mariners nefs[3] des Portz de la Marine Dengleterre esteans en les[4] armees des diz Admirals ne deuoient[5] respondre deuant nuls Justices des Roys auantdiz[6] sur fais en la Meer susdite durans lours[7] guerres countre lour enemis et le dit Admiral vostre dit seignur le Roy et plusours des Maistres et Mariners des Portz auantdiz ore esteans en sa Armee countre les[8] enemis Descoce et lour aydans et alliez par expres mandement de vostre dit seignur le Roy soiient accusez deuant vous par gentz de Normandie et de Bretaigne et daillours sur ascuns faitz en la dite Meer en temps de trewes et puis la pees afferme entre les diz Roys Dengleterre et de Fraunce et auant la guerre comencee entre eaux a ce qest dit. Vous plaise surseer es proces countre eux ia comencee et deporter de comencer nouel durant la guerre susdite ansi qils naient mestier de se[9] complaindre a vostre dit seignur et as Prelatz et Nobles de soun dit Roialme par leur serment liez a les dites loys franchises et coustumes garder et maintenir.

APPENDIX B.

(P. 49.)

PROCEEDINGS BEFORE THE AUDITORS DEPUTED BY THE KINGS OF ENGLAND AND FRANCE FOR THE REDRESS OF THE GRIEVANCES BETWEEN THE SUBJECTS OF THE TWO COUNTRIES. 27-33, Edw. I.

(Abstract of Chancery Miscellaneous Roll. Bdle. 5, No. 6.)

RICHARD BUSH *against* REYNER GRŸMAUS.

LIBEL (*Libellus*).

Richard Bush of London complains that a ship called "la Blacoḡ" of London, going from Winchelsea to Dieppe in August 1301, containing goods to the value of £157, was attacked by Michel de Navere

[1] Mem. 1, "auncіens"; Mem. 14, "auncienes."
[2] Mems. 1, 8, and 14, "ne."
[3] Mems. 1, 8, and 14 omit "nefs."
[4] Mem. 8, "leurs."
[5] Mem. 8, "doiuent."
[6] Mem. 8, "deuantdiz."
[7] Mems. 1 and 8, "les."
[8] Mems. 1 and 8, "ses."
[9] Mem. 8, "soy."

and others of Calais, and his said goods taken thither and there disposed of by said Michel and Henry de Ganewe. Said Richard demands restoration of goods and £20 damages.

DENIAL (*Contestatio negativa*).

The said "Cheual̃" asserts that he was not in that country at the time specified, nor for nearly a year afterwards.

REJOINDER (*Repplicatio*).

To the answer of the "chevalier" that he was not admiral till some time after the events specified, the attorneys of said Richard reply that they will advise with their master as to the truth.

William Bush of London loaded a ship called "la Mariote de Seland" at Antwerp for London with goods to the value of £175, 17s. 8d. Michel de Nauere and others of Calais came with three galleys to the foreland of Thanet at the mouth of the Thames in May 1298; took said ship to Calais and there disposed of the goods by the aid of Henri de Ganewe. Said William demands restoration and £20 damages.

To the demand of William Bush the said John[1] replies "en la maniere q̃ il fait a la demande Cecile,"[2] that it does not concern him, but "mos̃ Henri et Michel de Nauare."

Said William further complains that he loaded a ship called "la Blithe" of London in Brabant for London with goods, value £40. John Pederogh seized them at the mouth of the Thames in July 1303, took them to Calais, and there disposed of them by the aid of Edward de Mabusshon. William demands restoration and £8 damages.[3]

Said John replies that at the time specified he was not on the sea at all but in Paris or on the road to Calais.

THOMAS CROS *against* JOHN PAYDRO.

LIBEL.

Thomas Cros of London, executor of the will of Thos. Cros his father, who was executor of Henry Box of London, complains that said Henry loaded the ships William le fiz Henri, Godefroi de Duffle, Michel de Middelborgh, Johan Athelard, Johan le Chaundeler in London, to go to Brabant (which ships were of Brabant) with goods value £672; Michel de Nauuere and others of Calais with three

1 [*Sic*]: not previously mentioned; probably Johan Paderogh. 2 *See* below.
3 Side-note says: "The said goods have been delivered to Will. Bush."

galleys seized said ships off the foreland of Thanet in May 1298, took the goods aforesaid from said ships and in their galleys to Calais, and there disposed of them by the aid of Henry de Genewe. Said Thomas Cros demands restoration and £100 damages.

EXCEPTION REQUIRING DELAY (*Excepčo dilatoria*).

The said John says it is not for him to reply, as the complaint concerns not him but mos̃ Henri de Genes and Michel de Nauare, who are abroad where they cannot be had.

"Watier le Hert de Mallins" and Rose de Salisbery of London loaded at London a ship called the Johan Azelard de Mallins with goods value £28, 19s. 2d. Michel de Nauare and others of Calais with three galleys seized said goods out of said ship, then anchored off the foreland of Thanet (May 1298), took them in their galleys to Calais, and disposed of them by the aid of mons̃. Henri de Genewe. Said Watier and Rose demand restoration and £6 damages.

Cecile atte More of London loaded at London for Brabant the ships William Petersone of Seland, William Henriessone of Seland, Johan le Chandeler, with goods value £158, 19s. Michel de Nauere and others of Calais in May 1298 seized said goods out of said ships (then anchored off Thanet) and disposed of them at Calais by the aid of Henri de Genewe. Cecile claims restoration and £20 damages.

Cecile atte More complains that in July 1303 Johan Pederogh and others seized goods of the said Cecile at the mouth of the Thames out of a ship called "la Blithe de Londres" coming from Brabant, and disposed of them at Calais by the aid of mos̃ Edward de Mabusshon: value £10. Cecile prays restoration and 40s. damages.

Said John replies that at the date specified he was at Paris or on the road to Calais, and not on the sea at all.

Thomas atte Hurst of London loaded at Berwick the "Distaf de Haneford" for London, with goods to the value of £11, 18s. 8d. They were seized by men from Calais off Blakeney on the Tuesday after Saint Bartholomew 1303,[1] and disposed of at Calais. Thomas prays restoration and damages.

The said John [*sic*] says that the above demand concerns "mi sire Reniers de Grimaus" only, for he was then admiral, and said John was on shore at the date specified. Said John was only in the company of said Reniers "en Sellande et en Horlande."

[1] *24th Aug.* 1303, *Saturday.*

To the demand of Thos. atte Hurst touching goods seized from the "Distaf de Haneforde" by Johan Peidroge, Clay Clinkhamer, Piers Hues, and others in 1302 [*sic*], the said "Oudart" [*sic*] replies as he did to the claim of Alayn de Thorndon. [*See below.*]

Aleyn de Thornden, burgess of "Lenn," loaded a ship in Scotland belonging to Nichol de Caith̄ with goods value £133 for Brabant, —mons̄ Odard de Maubusshon, Johan Peidrgroge, Johan de la B . . ge . lour, "soen frere Lani yacop" Gusse Odin, Johan le parker, vaaseur le Mariner, Hirnolet le Man and Petre le Puttere, in August 1304 seized the ship off Kirkele, killed the crew, and disposed of ship and goods at Calais. Aleyn demands restoration and damages, value in all £143.

The said John replies that he and others named in above plaint at the date specified were in Holland and Zeeland. "Car le iour de la Seint Laurence [1] il se combatieront en Selande as Flamens as Baioñois et as Engleis qi estoient en lour aide."

William Quineberge, burgess of Lynn, loaded his own ship, the "Nicholas," at Lynn for Scotland with goods, value £35, 15s. 8d.—Odard de Maubusshon, Johan Perdroge, Johan Huard, Gusse Odin, Simond Danyn, Johan Allestein, Clay Clinchamer, Vaaseur le Mariner, Johan Paye, and Petre le Pottere in August 1303 plundered the ship off Scarborough, killed a mariner, and disposed of the goods at Calais. William demands restoration and £10 damages.

Adam Honson of Gloucester loaded the ship of "Williame de Douere" at Antwerp for England with goods, value £220. Odard de Maubusshon and Johan Peidroge of Calais, in September 1303, plundered said ship in sight of Dover, "et illoeques la Nief deliuereront al auant dit William de Douere" [*sic*]. Adam demands restoration and £60 damages.

Johan de Hetheye, William le Scherman, Rich. le Goldsmith, Johan le Blunt, Will. de Nesse, Johan Gode, and Wauter Top loaded the ship of William Gare called "Michele de Arwe" in London with goods, value £556, 3s. 8d., for Brabant.

Sire Reyner Grimbaud, admiral, on the high seas, the Sunday after Michaelmas 1303,[2] seized said ship and goods and took them "a Roem en Normandie"; sent the crew to Calais, where some were put in prison, and one still remains. Plaintiffs demand restoration and £100 damages.

To the complaint touching "la Michele de Arwe," seized on the

[1] *St Lawrence, Aug.* 10.

[2] *29th Sept.* 1303, *Sunday.*

Sunday after Michaelmas 1304 [*sic*], the "chiualer" confesses he took such a ship in that year but not of the value named: "ains fu prise la dite Nief a la Suyne a la pointe du Jour oue poer des enemys as Ancres." He seized it rightfully, the said ship consorting with the enemies of France. The crew were taken, without force, and letters were found in the ship to those of Bruges concerning money to be received in that town; those put in prison all escaped except Johan de Masworth, who is still there. The "chiualer" deems both persons and goods forfeit to the King of France.

To the demand of John de Masworth for restoration of goods and liberty, the "chiualer" says he is in prison as a malefactor against the King of France, and that the commission of the deputies does not extend to such cases.

ADAM DE FULHAM *against* JOHN PAYDROGE.

LIBEL.

Adam de Fulham of London complains that in the year 1302 men of Calais attacked the "Margarete de Jernemuth" off Orfordenessh going to London, killed the crew, and took the ship and goods to the value of £20 to Calais and there disposed of them. Demands restoration and damages.

DENIAL.

To the demand made by Adam de Fulham against said John and others touching violence done to him between "le Seint Martin et le Chaundeler" in 1302, said John replies as he did to Johan de Chelchethe.

EXCEPTION REQUIRING DELAY.

To another demand of said Adam, said John replies as he did to William Seruat.

JOHN DE CHELCHETHE *against* REYNER DE GRYMAUS.

LIBEL.

John de Chelchethe of London complains that in 1302 John Padrogh and others of Calais attacked the "Margarete de Jernemuth" off Orfordenessh, killed the crew, and took ship and goods to Calais. Demands restoration and damages, value in all £39, 5s. 8d.

EXCEPTION REQUIRING DELAY.

Said John Padrogh replies as he did to William Seruat.

EDMUND LAMBY . . . *against* JOHN PAYDROGE.

LIBEL.

Said Edmund complains as others have done concerning the "Margaret of Yarmouth." His goods therein were of the value of £12.

GILBERT DE ASSHENDON *against* JOHN PAYDROGE.

LIBEL.

Said Gilbert de Asshendon of London complains that the "Distaf de Haneford" loaded at Berwick for London was taken off Blakeney in 1303 (Tuesday after St Bartholomew). Demands restoration and damages, value in all £8, 10s. 4d.

DENIAL.

Said John replies that at the date specified he was on dry land at Calais.

To this demand against Johan Peidroge, Clay Clinkhanner, Piers Hues, Stace Swares, and Johan Huares, Oudart replies as he did to Alein de Thornden.

APPENDIX C.

(P. 65.)

LICENSE FOR FISHING AT THE "ZOWE" BANK IN THE CHANNEL.

(State Papers, Domestic. James I., Vol. 81, No. 3. 1615.)

ROBERT, Baron of Brancepeth, Viscount Rochester, Earle of Somersett, Lord Chamberlaine of his Ma^te^ householde, knyght of the most noble order of the Garter, and one of his Ma^te^ most honorable privie Counsell, provisionally deputed for the government of the Cinque Portes. To all to whom theis presentes shall come, Greeting, Knowe ye that I, according to the auntient ordinances and rules hertofore established and lately revived for the preservacon of the fishing betwixt the subiectes of the Easterne coast of the kingdome of great Britayne and the frenche Fishermen accoastinge those partes, Haue by theis presentes licensed and authorised Reynold Howgatt of the Towne of Treporte, Fisherman, M^r^ of one Fisherboate called the Don de Dieu of about fourteen tonnes, with all her Company and servants of the same Boate, To Fishe at the place called the Sowe upon the English coast and elsewhere upon that coast, in the same sorte as any one of those five boates heertofore tollerated and privileged out of respect for the service of the Frenche king his excellent Matie, for all sortes of Fishe without restrainte of season, soe the same be done and performed with nettes and engines lawfull and accustomed by the English subiectes of that coast. Requiring you and every of you whom it shall concerne not onely to permit and suffer him and his sayd servantes soe to doe without any your unnecessary lett or impeachement. But alsoe to yeilde him and his company all lawfull favor and assistance therein as they shall have occasion, bearinge themselves orderly and peaceably and observing the rules and ordinances sett downe and established for that coast fishing as aforesaid under the penalties therein expressed and conteyned. This license is to endure but untill the first daie of August wch shalbe in the yeare of our Lord God 1616.

Geven under the Seale of Office at Douer Castle the sixt daie of July in the thirteenth yeare of the reigne of our Souereigne Lord, James, by the grace of God of Great Britaine, Frannce, and Ireland, king, Defender of the fayth, &c. (Sd.) R. Somerset.

A la nominacon du Mouns^r^ Villares Houden gouern^r^ du Chatiau et ville de Diep et suit du Roy de Fraunce.

APPENDIX D.

(P. 119.)

PROCLAMATION FOR REUOCATION OF MARINERS FROM FORREINE SERUICES.

(A Booke of Proclamations, published since the beginning of his Majesties most happy Reigne ouer England, &c., Vntill this present Moneth of Febr. 3, Anno Dom. 1609 [1602-1612].)

Whereas within this short time since the Peace concluded betweene vs and the King of Spaine and the Archdukes our good brothers, it hath appeared unto vs that many Mariners and Seafearing men of this Realme hauing gotten a custome and habite in the time of the Warre to make profite by Spoile, doe leaue their ordinary and honest vocation and Trading in Merchantly Voyages, whereby they might both reape conuenient maintenance, and be seruice-able to their Countrey, And doe betake themselues to the seruice of diuers forreine States, vnder the title of men of Warre, to haue thereby occasion to continue their vnlawful and vngodly course of liuing by spoile vsing the seruice of those Princes but for colour and pretext, but in effect making themselues commonly no better then Pirats to robbe both our owne Subiects their Countreymen, and the subiects of other Princes our neighbours, going in their honest Trade of Merchandize: By which courses they doe impeach the quiet traffique of Nations one with other, leaue our Realme vnfurnished of men of their sort, if we should haue cause to vse them, and inure themselues to an impious disposition of liuing by rapine and euill meanes, although by reason of the Uniuersall peace wherein wee are at this present with all Christian Princes and States, they may haue a more plentifull employment in an orderly and lawfull Nauigation, then at any time of late yeeres they conld haue had: We haue thought it necessary in time to preuent the spreading of such a corruption amongst our Subiects of that sort and calling, whereby our Nation will be so much slandered, and our Realme so greatly disaduantaged. Wherefore we doe will and command all Masters of ships, Pilots, Mariners, and all other sort of Seafearing men, who now are in the Martiall seruice of any forreine States, that they doe presently returne home into their owne Countrey, and leaue all such forreine Seruices, and betake themselues to their vocation in the lawfull course of Merchandize, and other orderly Nauigation, upon such paines and punishments as by the Lawes of our Realme may be inflicted upon them, if after this declaration of our pleasure, they shall not obey. And we doe also vpon the same paines straitly charge and command al our Subiects of that profession, that none of them shall from hencefoorth take Letters of Marke or Reprisall, nor serue vnder any that hath such Letters of Marke or Reprisall from any forreine Prince or State whatsoeuer, Nor otherwise employ themselues in any warlike Seruices of any forraine State vpon the Sea, without speciall License obtained from our selfe, or from our high Admirall, as they will answer the contrary at their perils.

And forasmuch as although we are in Peace with all Christian Princes and States, yet during the continuance of the Warre betweene the King of Spain and the Archdukes on the one side, and the vnited Prouinces of the Low-Countreys on the other side, many chances may happen, as some already haue happened, of difficult interpretation to our Officers and Subiects how to behaue themselues in such cases, vnlesse they be explained vnto them: We haue thought it conuenient to make an open declaration how our said Officers and Subiects shall demeane themselues towards the Subiects aswell of the King of Spaine and Archdukes, as also of the States vnited in the cases following.

First our pleasure is, That within our Portes, Hauens, Rodes,

Creekes, or other places of our Dominion, or so neere to any of our sayd Ports or Hauens, as may be reasonably construed to bee within that Title, Limit, or Precinct, there shall be no force, violence, surprise, or offence suffered to be done either from Man of warre to Man of warre, or Man of warre to Merchant, or Merchant to Merchant of either party, but that all of what Nation soeuer, so long as they shall bee within those our Ports and places of our Jurisdiction, or where our Officers may prohibite violence, shall bee vnderstood to be under our protection to bee ordered by course of Justice, and be at peace each with other.

And whereas some of the Men of warre of ech side haue vsed of late, and it is like will vse in time to come, though not to come within our Ports, because there they know wee can restraine violence, yet to houer and hang about the skirts of our Ports, somewhat to Seaboard, but yet so neere our coastes and the entrie of our Harbours, as in reason is to be construed to be within the extent of the same, and there to await the Merchant of the aduerse part, and doe seaze and take them at their going out of our Ports, which is all one in a manner, as if they tooke them within our Port, and will bee no lesse hinderance to the trade of Merchants: Our pleasure therefore and commaundement is to all our Officers and Subiects by Sea and Land, That they shall prohibite, as much as in them lyeth, all such houering of Men of warre of either side, so neere the entrie of any of our Hauens or our Coastes, And that they shall rescue and succour all Merchants, and others that shall fall within the danger of any such as shall await our Coastes in so neere places to the hinderance of Trade and Traffique outward and homeward from and to our Kingdomes. And for the better instructions of our Officers in the execution of these two Articles, Wee haue caused to be sent to them plats of those Limits, within which we are resolued that these Orders shalbe obserued.

And where it hath happened, and is like to doe often, that a Ship of warre of the one side may come into some of our Ports, where there shall bee a Merchant of the other side: In such case, for the benefit and preseruation of the lawfull Trade of Merchants, Our pleasure is, That all Merchants Ships, if they will require it, shall bee suffered to depart out of the sayd Port, two or three tydes before the Man of warre, to the intent that the Merchant may bee free from the pursuite of his aduersary. And if it so happen, that any Ship or Ships of warre of the one side, doe finde any Ship or Ships of warre of the other side in any our Ports or Roades aforesayd; Like as our pleasure is that during their abode there, all violence be forborne: So doe wee likewise commaunde our sayd Officers and Subiects both on Sea and Land, That the Ship of warre which came in first, bee suffered to depart a Tyde or two before the other which came in last, And that for so long time they shall stay and detaine any Ship of warre, that would offer to pursue another out of any our Ports immediately.

And where [*sic*] wee are infourmed, that notwithstanding the seueritie of our Lawes against receiuers of Pirats goods, many of our Officers of our Ports and other inhabitants within and neere vnto them, doe receiue dayly Goods brought in from Sea by such as are indeed Pirats, if they, and the getting of their Goods were well examined: We doe hereby admonish them all, to auoyd the receiuing or buying of any Goods from Sea, coming not into the Realme by lawfull course of Merchandise, for that they shall finde, wee are resolued so to preuent all occasion and encouragement of Pirats to bee vsed by any our Subiects as wee will cause our Lawes to bee fully executed according to their true meaning, both against the Pirats, and all Receuiers and Abetters of them, and their Goods.

Giuen at Thetford the first day of March, in the second yeere of our Reigne of Great Britaine, France and Ireland.

Anno Dom. 1604.

APPENDIX E.

(P. 120.)

DECLARATION OF JURY OF THE TRINITY HOUSE AS TO THE LIMITS OF THE KING'S CHAMBERS.

(State Papers, Domestic. James I., Vol. 13, No. 11. 1605.)

A note of y[e] Headlandes of England as they beare one from another agreeing with the plott of y[e] Description of y[e] Countrye as followeth.

From Holy Iland to the Sowter is South South east. From the Sowter to Whitby is Southeast. From Whitby to Flamborough head is Southeast, and half a point Southerly. From Flamborough head to the Sporne is Southeast easterlie. From the Sporne to Cromar is Southeast, and by East. From Cromar to Wynterton nes is Southeast and by South. From Wynterton nes to Caster nes is South South east. From Casternes to Layestof is South. From Layestof to East nes is South, and half a point to the Westward. From Eastness to Orforthnes is South and by West. From

Orforth nes to the North foreland is South, and one third of a point to the Westward. From the Northforland to the Southforeland is South. From the Southforeland to Dungnes is Southwest and one fourth part of a point to ye Southwards. From Dungnes to Beache is West Southwest, and one fourth part of a poynt to the Southwards. From Beache to Dune noze is West Southwest, and three quarters of a point to the Westwards. From Dune noze to Portland is West and by South Southerly. From Portland to the Start is West Southwest and one fifth part of a point to the Westwards. From the Start to the Ramme is West, and one fourth part of a point to the Northwards. From the Ramme to the Dudman is West Southwest, and one sixt part of a point to the Westwards. From the Dudman to the Lizard is West Southwest, and one third part of a point to the Southwards. From the Lizard to Lands end is West Northwest Northerly. From Lands end to Milford is North and two third parts of a point to the Eastwards. From Milford to S. Dauids head is North and half a point to the Westwards. From S. Dauids head to Beardsie, is North and by East, and one eight part of a point to the Eastwards. From Beardsie to Holly head is North, and one sixt part of a poynt to the Westwards. From Holly head to the Ile of Man is North and by East, and one fifth part of a point to the Northwards.

Wee whose names are heerevnder written being called before the right worshipfull Sir Julius Cesar, Knight, Judge of the Kings Majesties Highe Court of Admiraltie, and there impanelled, and sworne vpon a Jurie to sett downe the bounds, and lymits, howfarre the Kings Chambers, Hauens, or Ports on the Sea coasts doe extend; Do heereby certifie, and sett downe (according to our best knowledge, and vnderstanding) that his Highnes said chambers, Hauens, or Ports are all the Seacoasts within a straight lyne drawne from one head land to the next head land throughout this realme of England. And for the better vnderstanding thereof haue made a plott of the same, and haue therevnto prefixed this our Schedule, shewing how euerie head-land doth beare vpon a right lyne the one from the other according to the said Plott. Dated the 4. of March A°. D^{i}. 1604 [160$\frac{4}{5}$] And in the second yeare of the reigne of our Souueraigne Lord King James, &c.

(Signed) Thomas Milton. William Bygate. John Burrell. William Jones. Peter Hilles. Michael Edmondes. James Woodcolt. Thomas Beast. William Juye. John Skynner. John Wyldes. Henry Hauken. William Cace.

APPENDIX F.

(P. 148.)

PROCLAMATION OF JAMES I. FOR THE RESTRAINT OF FOREIGNERS FISHING ON THE BRITISH COASTS.

(A Booke of Proclamations, &c. 1609 [1602-1612].)

JAMES by the Grace of God King of Great Britaine, France and Ireland, Defender of the Faith, &c. To all and singular persons to whom it may appertaine, Greeting. Although we doe sufficiently know by our experience in the Office of Regall dignitie (in which by the fauour of Almighty God, we haue bene placed and exercised these many yeres) as also by the obseruation which wee haue made of other Christian Princes exemplary Actions, how farre the absolutenesse of Soueraigne power extendeth it selfe, And that in regard thereof we need not yeeld accompt to any person under God, for any action of ours, which is lawfully grounded upon that iust prerogatiue: Yet such hath euer bene, and shalbe our care and desire to give satisfaction to our neighbour Princes, and friends, in any Action which may haue the least relation to their Subiects and Estates, as we haue thought good (by way of friendly premonition) to declare unto them all, and to whom soeuer it may appertaine, as followeth.

Whereas wee haue bene contented since our comming to the Crowne, to tolerate an indifferent and promiscuous kinde of libertie to all our friends whatsoeuer, to fish within our streames, and vpon any of our coasts of Great Britaine, Ireland, and other adiacent Islands, so farre foorth as the permission or vse thereof might not redound to the empeachment of our Prerogatiue Royall, nor to the hurt and damage of our louing Subiects, whose preseruation and flourishing estate we hold our selfe principally bound to aduance before all worldly respects: So finding that our conniuence therein, hath not onely giuen occasion of ouer great encrochments vpon our Regalities, or rather questioning for our Right, but hath bene a meanes of much dayly wrongs to our owne people that exercise the trade of Fishing as (either by the multitude of Strangers, which doe preoccupy those places, or by the iniuries which they receiue most cõmonly at their hands) our Subiects are constrained to abandon their Fishing, or at the least are become so discouraged in the same, as they hold it better for them, to betake themselues to some other course of liuing, whereby not onely diuers of our Coast-townes are much decayed, but the number of Mariners dayly diminished, which is a matter of great consequence to our Estate, considering how much the strength thereof consisteth in the power of Shipping, and vse of Nauigation: We haue thought it now both iust and necessary (in respect that wee are now by Gods fauour lineally and lawfully possessed, aswell of the Island of Great Britaine, as of Ireland, and the rest of the Isles adiacent) to bethinke our selues of good lawfull meanes to preuent those inconueniences, and many others depending vpon the same. In the consideration whereof, as we are desirous that the world may take notice, that we haue no intention to deny our neighbors and Allies, those fruits and benefits of Peace and friendship, which may be iustly expected at our hands in honour and reason, or are affoorded by other Princes mutually in the point of Commerce, and exchange of those things which may not prooue preiudiciall to them: So because some such conuenient order may be taken in this matter, as may sufficiently prouide for all these important considerations which doe depend thereupon; Wee haue resolued first to give notice to all the world, That our expresse pleasure is, that from the beginning of the Moneth of August next comming, no person of what Nation or qualitie soeuer, being not our naturall borne Subiect, be permitted to fish vpon any of our Coasts and Seas of Great Britaine, Ireland, and the rest of the Isles adiacent, where most usually heretofore any fishing hath bene, untill they haue orderly demanded and obtained licenses from vs, or such our Commissioners, as we haue authorised in that behalfe, viz. at London for our Realmes of England and Ireland, and at Edenborough for our Realme of Scotland: Which Licenses, our intention is, shall be yeerely demanded, for so many Vessels and ships, and the Tonnage thereof, as shall intend to fish for that whole yeere, or any part thereof, vpon any of our Coastes and Seas as aforesaid, vpon paine of such chastisement, as shalbe fit to bee inflicted vpon such wilfull offendors.

Giuen at our Palace of Westminster, the 6. day of May, in the 7. Yeere of our Reigne of Great Britaine, &c.

Anno Dom. 1609.

APPENDIX G.

(Pp. 169, 196.)

INSTRUCTIONS BY THE PRIVY COUNCIL OF SCOTLAND FOR THE LEVYING OF THE "ASSIZE-HERRINGS" FROM FOREIGN FISHERMEN.

(Register of the Privy Council of Scotland, vol. xi. p. 592.)

INSTRUCTIONIS givin be the Lordis of Secreit Counsall to Mr Johnne Fentoun, his Majesteis commissionar, who is directit to demand his Majesteis rent of assyse and teynd frome these of Holland, Zeland, Hambruch, Ambden, Rustock, and all utheris strangeris haunting the trade of fisching in his Majesteis seas during this present yeir.

In the first, yow sall prepair your selff and mak you reddie in goode and comelie ordour and equippage and with all possibill haist to go in his Majesteis schip callit *The Charles*, quhairof David Murray is capitane and commander, towardis the North Seas of this Kingdome, quhair the Hollanderis and utheris strangeris hes thair fisching: And at your arryveall thair yow salbe cairfull to inquyre and informe yourselff of the names of the admirallis and vice-admirallis attending the flott, and of the names of thair schippis, of quhat townes and provinceis they ar, and quhat nomber of wauchteris and buscheis is sent oute be every towne, province and estate to attend thair fischeing.

Yow sall be vertew of your commissioun, and attending to the tennour thairof, demand frome the saidis admirallis, and, incaice of thair absence, frome the vice-admirallis, and frome tua or thrie of the waughteris and busches of every estate, his Majesteis rent of assyse and teynd specifeit and contenit in your commissioun for the haill fischeis tane and slayne be thame in his Majesteis watteris and seas this yeir. And yow sall use this requisitoun and demand in fair and gentill termes and with modestie and discretioun.

Yf thay contravert with yow anent the quantitie of this dewytie, yow sall not dispute that poynt with thame, bot, if they mak offer of ane smaller dewytie, althoght it wer bot ane angell for every busche overhead, yow sall accept of thair offer.

Yf thay sall mak offer of the fische outher for the teynd or assyse, yow sall accept of thame, and, gif yow find ony countrey vessellis or boittis thair, yow sall send for thame and putt the fische in thame.

Yf they gif unto yow a delaying answer and crave tyme and

laiser to send to thair superiouris to be advyseit with thame, yow sall accompt of thair delay as ane refuisall, and accordinglie accept sua of it.

Yf it be objectit unto yow that all the busches ar not of a lyke burdeyne, and that consequentlie they aucht not to pay a lyke dewytie for assise and teynd, yow sall in this caise gif defalcatioun to the smaller busches according to your discretioun and be the aduyse of the admirallis, gif thay will concur with yow in that erand; provydeing alwayes that the smallest dewytie to be taine be yow for every busche be not within ane angell.

Yf the admirallis or vice-admirallis for every toun, estate, or province will aggrie with yow for the haill busches under thair charge, yow sall aggrie with thame and gif unto them acquittanceis in name of the haill that thay tak burdeyne for; bot, yf thay remitt yow to deale with every busche apairt, yow sall do the same and gif acquettanceis accordinglie.

Yf refuisall salbe maid unto yow of his Majesties rent and dewytie, yow sall tak instrumentis upoun the said refuisall without forder contestatioun; and, gif obedience be givin and payment accordinglie maid, yow sall lykwayse take instrumentis thairupoun.

Yow sall informe the saidis admirallis, and, incaice of thair absence, the saidis vice-admirallis, of the complaint maid to his Majesteis Counsall be his Majesteis subjectis of Zetland anent the greit oppressioun committit upoun thame be divers personis of the floitt who comes aschoir upoun thair illis of Halff Grunay, Wedderholme, South Grunay, and Lungya, and upoun divers utheris pairtis of the countrey, quhair thay not only enter in kirkis, dimolischeis and brekis doun the daskis and seattis within the same and schamefullie abuses the same, to the offence and dishonour of God, bot with that thay spoyle the countrey people of thair scheip, geis, hennis, eggs, and suche uther commoditeyis as they find upoun the ground, and sumtymes invaidis and persewis thame of thair lyveis; and thairfoir yow sall crave redres and reparatioun to be made for thir wrangis and that the lyke be forborne in all tyme coming.

APPENDIX H.

(P. 251.)

REGLEMENT FOR PREVENTING ABUSES IN AND ABOUT THE NARROW SEAS AND PORTS.

(State Papers, Domestic. "James I., Vol. 11, No. 40. 1604." Charles I., Vol. 279, No. 18. 1634.)

His most Excellent Ma^ty taking into his Royall Consideration, upon the frequent Complaints, as well of his own Subjects, as the Subjects of other Princes and States in Peace and Amitie with his Ma^ty. That his Seas (commonly called the four English Seas) are more infested now a days then heretofore, by men of Warre and such others, who living by spoile haunt those Seas, with ships and vessels of strength warlikely appointed to gett prey and booties, whereby not only his Ma^tye's own Subjects and the Subjects of his friends suffer manifold losses, violences and Injuryes in their persons, ships and goods, but also divers strange Insolencyes indignityes and contempts are committed, tending indirectly and by consequence to the denyall and impeachment of that Soveraignety and especiall and peculiar Interest and property, wch his Ma^ty and his Predecessors time out of mind have had and enjoyed in the said Seas, and soe approved not only by the fundamentall Lawes of this his Kingdome, but by the acknowledgement and assent of the bordering Princes and Nations, as appeareth by undoubted Records. His Ma^ty out of his Princely wisedome and providence (with the Advice of his Privy Councell) hath thought it most necessary, as well for vindicating his own honour and right in the said Seas, as in point of Justice for securing the passage of his Subjects and friends to and frõ his harbours and Ports, and all other Ports [? parts] of his Dominions, to make this open declaration ensuing.

1. That notwithstanding the continuance of ye war between the K. of Spaine on the one side, and the United Provinces of the Low Countryes on the other side, his Ma^ty doth streightly prohibite any force, violence, surprize, or offense to be done or attempted either frõ Man of Warre to man of Warre, or man of Warre to Merchant, or Merchant to Merchant of either Party within the limits wch his Ma^ty will cause to be described in a Plott for that purpose, but that all of what Nation soever soe long as they shall be upon those places or Seas aforesaid, especially within such limits, shall be understood to be under his Ma^tyes Protection, and obliged to be at Peace each with other.

2. Because it appeareth that an especiall occasion of the mutuall spoiles and acts of hostility executed by the said men of Warre each upon other and sometimes upon his Ma^{tyes} own Subjects, or the Subjects of other Nations wch are in Amity with the Soveraignes of the Spoilers, ariseth from the opportunity wch the said Men of Warre have by continuing and abiding in havens, Sea-shoares or Sea-Roades and other harbours of his Ma^{tyes} Kingdomes, whence they gett intelligence of ships and vessels outward and hitherward bound, and accordingly assayle them, where it is most for their advantage, to the great hindrance and interruption of free Commerce and Entercourse, His Ma^{tyes} Will and Pleasure is, That, for the reasons aforesaid, noe shipps of Warre, belonging either to the K. of Spaine, or any his Subjects, or to the said United Provinces, or any of their Subjects shall be permitted or allowed to come, enter, repaire, or arrive in or to any of his Ma^{tyes} Towns, Citties, Sea-Shores, Havens, Harbours, or Sea roades, whatsoever, or there to abide and continue, except they happen to be constrained either by force of Tempest, or buying of Victualls, or other things, or for repairing of shipping, so that they doe no hostile act in the said Places, but demeane themselves honestly and quietly as it becometh Confederates and friends, and so as they stay and remaine not in and about the said Ports any longer then shall be needfull for reparation, and Provision of necessaryes.

3. Albeit his Ma^{ty} doth justly challenge Soveraignety and property in all those his Seas farre beyond the limits hereafter to be described and might with like Justice require from all persons using those his seas a forbearance frõ Injuryes and all hostile actions, yet (in and through all the same) sodenly to tye the hands of his friends and Allyes in open hostility each with other is not for some reasons held convenient at this time. And therefore to avoyde all difficultyes and Colour of Controversies that may be stirred concerning the bounds and extent wherein his Ma^{ty} now professeth to yeild Peace and Security to his friends and neighbours, desiring the same, his Ma^{ty} purposeth to send Plotts of those limits to be affixed in the most publique places of his chiefest Sea-Towns and harbours.

4. Because it is very like, that during the continuance of the Warre betweene the K. of Spaine, and the United Provinces as is aforesaid, each Party may gaine and acquire frõ other in places out of the aforesaid Limitts, ships, and goods, His Ma^{ty} doth declare, That as he will afford to the conquering Partyes, free passage through his Seas for themselves, their ships and prizes, and like free accesse and repaire to all his Ports and harbours, and safe aboad and continuance in the same during their occasions, so his Ma^{ty} shall not understand it to be any breach of his Peace, or violation of that Security wch he intendeth to mainteine, if the enemyes of the

conquering Party shall reconquer or regaine the said Prizes, before the conquering Party shall have brought his said Prizes within any of his Ma^{tyes} harbours, or when after they shall have departed with the said Prizes homewards, or elsewhere from the said harbours, the right of Warre and Law of Nations giving like allowance to either of the said hostile actions, Provided always, that his Ma^{ty} doth not mean hereby to derogate from the Jurisdiction of his Court of Admiralty, but if any action (in forme of Law) shall be lawfully instituted and duly presented in the Admirall Court ag^{t} the said Prizes and the Takers thereof, his Ma^{ty} will cause Justice to be administred in that behalfe with all possible expedition.

5. Whereas mention is often made in the premisses of his Ma^{tyes} Protection within the aforesaid bounds and limits, his Ma^{ty} is now pleased further to expresse his Intention and meaning to that effect, viz. That he shall readyly give his Letters of Safe Conduct under the Great Seale of his Admiralty to any the Subjects of the Princes or States in league and Amity with his Ma^{ty} desiring the same from the Lords Commiss^{rs} of the Admiralty, to whom his Ma^{ty} will referre the Consideration and allowance of such Petitions, the said Letters of Safe Conduct to be conceived in the best forme. And if any man of Warre or other Person whatsoever shall assault or use any violence to any ship or vessell, or the persons therein, within the limits aforesaid his Ma^{ty} will hold such offender being lawfully convicted thereof for a Pirate, and will cause his Officers to inflict such punishment thereupon, as in Cases of Piracy is usuall, if the said offenders can be apprehended within any his Ma^{tyes} Countrey or Dominions, or any other, or any other ships or goods belonging to them, To wch purpose his Ma^{ty} will cause notice to be given from the Court of his Admiralty to all his Officers in Ports and Vice-Admiralls and Captaines of his Forts and ships, But if all this notwithstanding, the said offenders cannot be attached or apprehended, then the Party wronged, upon sufficient testimonyes to be recorded in the Court of Admiralty may take out of the said Court Processe, conteining a Monition for the said pretended offenders, to appeare in the Court of Admiralty within 4 moneths next after the date of the said Processe, there to answer for the pretended wrong or violence, the said Processes to be affixed openly in some eminent place of the Royall Exchange, London. And if the said offenders shall not render their bodyes to Justice, then upon faith made, that the said Processe was duly taken out, and the next day after the date thereof was publiquely affixed as is aforesaid, his Ma^{ty} will by his Letters of Request under his Privy Seale to the Soveraignes of the said offenders, or otherwise, pursue such further proceedings ag^{t} the said offenders, as is agreeable to the Custome amongst Sovereigne States and Princes and the Law of Nations in like Cases.

APPENDIX I.

(P. 289.)

REPORT OF THE ADMIRALTY TO CHARLES I. AS TO THE EMPLOYMENT OF THE SHIP-MONEY FLEET IN WAFTING AND SECURING FOREIGN MERCHANTS PASSING THROUGH HIS MAJESTY'S SEAS, AND IN PROTECTING FOREIGN FISHERMEN WHO ACCEPT THE KING'S LICENSE.

(State Papers, Domestic. Charles I., Vol. 313, No. 24.)

IT may Please your Ma^ty^,

According to your Majesty's commandment, wee, your Commissioners for ye Admiralty have mett and consulted on those two pointes which you were pleased to recommend to our consideration, touching the imploying of your fleete for yor Honor and Proffit. The one for the wafting and securing of Merchants that pass through yor Majesty's seas. The other for protecting all such fishermen in generall as shall exercise that trade by your Majesty's license upon yor seas and coastes.

The first of these that fell into debate was that concerning the fishing, and by Sr Henry Martin it was made evident vnto vs that y^r^ Ma^ts^ father of blessed memory in yeere of his Raigne, was, vpon long and mature deliberacion, satisfied and resolved, that the fishing in his Seas, and upon the coasts of his Dominions, did justly appertain unto him as a right incident to his Crownes, and that in pursuance thereof, he did then sett out his Royall Proclamation, thereby declaring his title, as allso his pleasure, that no stranger of what quality soever should presume to fish there without his expresse license, and so was graciously pleased in the said Proclamation to appoint, that for the Coastes of England and Ireland licenses should be given in London, and for those of Scotland in Edenborough.

And howsoever Sr Henry Martin did allso make it appear unto us that the States of the Vnited Provinces did at that time sende Commissioners into England who presented to his Majesty a paper contayning allegations by wch they did entend to prove continued custom and a present possession of that fishing, mentioning w^t^all som treaties that had bene heretofore betwene the Kinges of Englande and the Dukes of Burgundy in fauor of that their fishing, yet upon the whole matter, and after due deliberation, wee were all of opinion and are so still, that the Right and Royallty of that fishing upon yor Ma^ts^ Coastes doth undoubtedly belong unto yor Majesty by inheritance, so you may iustly prohibit or license all strangers at yor Royall will and pleasure.

This being laid for the ground, wee proceeded (according to your Majesty's directions) to the consideration of what was now fitting to be advised unto yor Majesty vpon this present occasion of yor strength at sea, and are all of opinion, that this season is most propper again not only to set on foote, but to putt in execucion that yor Majesty's so iust clayme, so as then there only remayned our consultation *de modo.*

In this wee are now much guided by that which yor Majesty yor selfe was pleased to declare unto us concerning the protecting of all such fishers as shall take yor license. For it is most certain that the Hollanders will by no meanes be so much induced (be the right what it will) as by consideracions of their owne proffitt and safety. Wee therefore thought itt (and do most humbly offer it to y^r^ Majesty as our opinion) that vnto the Minister or Ministers of the States residing here, it may be intimated and declared, that yor Majesty doth no way relinquish that iust right and clayme of inheritance to the Royall fishings, so divolved unto you from yor Royall Predecessors, but are resolved to defende it as the hereditary right and possession of any other yor Dominions. Yet least they should think you do now challenge it in a tyme that they have most neede of yor favor and grace, it may be tolde them, that it is farr otherwise, for whereas yor Majesty's father did barely offer them licenses, you do now offer them safety and protection w^t^all, and that wch further moved you to do it, in this season, is, that by a third Prince, they are of late interrupted and beaten from that fishing even in sight of yor Majesty's harbours; wherein yor Majesty is prejudiced in honor and Interest, and they in Proffit.

That it is not vnknown to the States how much their enemies are resolved to interrupt that their fishing, as holding it a most certain way and meanes both to weaken and impoverish them.

That by taking licenses from yor Majesty you may justify the drawing yor sword in their defence, and likewise for the maintenance of the said licenses against any notwithstanding any league or treaty whatsoever, wch without that obligation might seeme a breach of that neutrality wch hitherto yor Ma^ty^ hath preserved in yor selfe.

And lastly wee tooke into consideration that in case the Hollanders shall willfully refuse to take those licenses upon so gracious and fauorable conditions from yor Majesty then we were all cleere of opinion, that yor M. should renew and publish the like proclamation to that of the King yor father, and prosecute the settling of that yor right as a thing so highly concerning you in honor, dominion and profit. And so we do humbly conclude this point, with advice, that all such licenses as shalbe granted, be rated according to the tonne or burden of the vessells, so to be licensed.

Touching that of the Wafting of Merchants strangers shippes that shall passe through yor Majesty's seas, we are cleere of opinion that yor M. ought to have a profit by it, seeing that they are thereby preserved from oppression and ruine. But we are not of opinion that this profit should arise by way of a generall Imposition vpon all that passe: for that wold, doubtlesse, draw a iust complaint and clamor from yor neighbour Princes and their subiects. But that it should be taken of such as shall desire waftage, wch yor M. may direct not to be denyed to any of what Christian nacion soever that shall demande it, not being men-of-warre.

And because it wilbe a difficult matter to expresse in any Commission or Instructions a certain somme or duety to be taken of every ship so wafted, for that som shippes are rich, others of lesse value; som will require a short waftage, others a longer. Therefore we are of opinion, that for the value, much is to be left to the discretion of yor Majesty's Generall and commanders, and that som honest hable men may be employed to keepe bookes, and to receave the moneyes of all those waftings wch shall occurr, and be accomptable and answerable for the same. [5 Feb. $\frac{1635}{1636}$. Copy by Windebank.]

APPENDIX K.

(P. 389.)

ABSTRACT OF THE THIRTY-SIX ARTICLES PROPOSED BY THE DUTCH TO ST JOHN AT THE HAGUE, 1651.

State Papers. Foreign. Treaty Papers (Holland), No. 46. 1651.

A BRIEFE Narrative of the Treatie at the Hague betweene the hono^{ble} Oliver St John, Lord Chiefe Justice of the Court of Com̃on Pleas, and Walter Strickland Esq. Embassado^{rs} extraordinary of the Parliament of the Com̃onwealth of England, to the great Assembly of the States Generall of the United Provinces begun upon the 20th of March 1650 [1651] and continued vntill the 20th of June 1651 and then broke of re infecta.

A Drafte of the Treatie which is to be made and entred into with the extraordinary Ambassado^{rs} of the Republique of England.

. . . .

2.

Confederated ffrds for defence &c. & against Dystourbrs &c.

That they shalbe, and remayne confederated friends, vnited, and allyed for the defence, and preservation of the Libertye and freedomes of each others people, and mutuall Comerce Navigacon, and Comon Interests against all those that shall endeavour to disturbe either of the States in the same by water or land in manner as is herevnder declared and expressed.

. . . .

17.

Libertie to dwell in each othrs lands & to enjoy equall privilges wth the Natiues &c.

The subiects, and Inhabitants on both sydes may come, and dwell in each others lands reciprocallye, and take their setled residence there, have their owne houses there to dwell in, and their Warehouses for to bring their goods, wares, and Merchandizes thither, and also vse their trade, and comerce there in all securitye, and without hinderance of any one as well at sea, other waters, as at land, enioyeing there, and every where else, the same, privilidges, Libertie, and freedome, as the Inhabitants, and each others subiects doe respectively enioy there in their own Country, and in case any hinderances happen they shall really, and speedilye be removed.

18.

Free libertie of Fishing &c.

The subiects, and Inhabitants of either, of what qualitie, or condition soever they be, may sayle, and fish every where at sea freely, without any disturbance Licence, Patent, or Passe port, as well herring, as all other sorte of fish, great and small, and the sayd Fishermen being driven out of the sea by storme, Rovers, Enemyes, or any other accident, and coming in, or to any of the other Havens, or Jurisdictions shalbe well, and freindly receaved, and entreated, and may depart thence againe with their ships, fish, furniture for fishing, and other laedings, (in such case, and not haveing broak bulke there,) freely without payeing custome, or any the least duty.

19.

No harboring of Pyrates &c.

Rouers & Cocealrs to be punishd & ye ships & goods restored &c.

For to make the free Navigation, and comerce, on the seas, Rivers, and every where more certeyne, the said Republicke, and Vnited Provinces, shall not receave, nor suffer, or pmitt that any Pyrats, or Searovers, be receaved, kept, or harboured by their subiects, in their respective Havens, Lands, Cittyes, or Townes but shall cause as well the said cencealors, as Rovers, to be psequuted, apprehended, and punished, for terrour to others as is fitt, and the roved ships, goods, Merchandises yet in Esse, and in being, yea though they were there sould, shalbe restored, or made good to the right owners, or to such as have their Assignm[ts], or Lett[rs] of Attorney, who doe sue for, and reclayme the said roved ships, and goods, vpon a iuratory affirmation of the reclaymer till better proofe.

20.

Sufficient securitie by those who goe out vpon pticul[r] comissions.

All pticuler psons on either syde, that goe out upon perticular Comissions, shalbe bound before they may goe to sea, to put in sufficient securitie before the Judge of the place from whence he setts saile.

21.

Both to set out Fleets for scouring the Seas &c.

And to cleare the seas from all Pyrats, and Rovers, of what nation soever they bee, and to defend, and free the Libertie, and freedome of both the Nations Comerce, Navigation, and Freefishing as well in the North sea, Ocean, as Mediterranean sea, and all channells, and Streights runing betweene 'em; the sayd Republicke of England and the Vnited Netherlands shall provide and anually set out to sea a strong fleete at least of . . . [*sic*] Vessells, and the like proportion of men, munition of warr, Victualls, and all necessary furniture, wherewith each vnder his owne Admirall, and flagg, shall crosse, and scoure the said seas, to witt those of England from . . . vntill . . . and those of the Lowe countryes from . . . till . . . beginning the first of . . . and stayeing till the last of . . . and shalbe bound to seaze on, and master all Pyrats that they shall meete with, the ships of either of the nations by them taken to restore to the true owners, and if it be needfull, and requisite to helpe, and seacond each other, each to keepe his taken bootye, or prises for himselfe, and so to cleare, and free the said seas, and channell, or straights from all Pyrats and searovers.

22.

Each pties Fleetes to force to Reparacon hinderers of y[e] Comerce navigacon Fishg &c.

And for the further defence and advancem[t] of the freedome, and Libertie of both the said Nations Comerce, Navigation, and freefishinge in the sayd seas, the sayd fleets and alsoe other men of warr, and comission bearers on either syde, shall not only doe against Pyrats in manner aforesayd, but alsoe against all, and singuler psons, whatsoever they be that shall chance to trouble, molest, hinder, exacte, or against the Lawe of all nations burthen, or charge them, or either of them in the sayd freedome, Comerce, Navigation, and fishing. It is intended neverthelesse that the dampnifyed partie shall first, and aforehand complayne of the same to the undampnifyed partie, and endeavor together by all freindly waies, and intercession, that they who molested them doe make repation to content, But if it be not so done, that then they shall seaze, take, and surprize in the said seas, not onlie with the said Fleete, but alsoe with all the strength of shipping which they can bring to sea the ships, and goods of the Cittie, and of her inhabitants, who have done the said trouble and so continewe vntill that the dampnifyed partye shall have gott full satisfaction, and every thing be putt agayne in full Freedome, that all damage may be recovered, in case they chance to goe beyond or exceed their comission, and charge.

23.

Men of warr to ptect ye Mchts ships of each pty or of ye Allies &c.

The men of warr of either partye meeting or overtakeing any Marchant shipp, or ships at sea, of the other partie, or of the others subiects, or of the Allyes (alsoe comprehended in this Treatye) and haveing both one course, or goeing both one way shalbe bound so longe as they keepe one course togeather to take them vnder their protection, and to defend them against all, and everyone.

24.

Retaking of ships taken in one anothrs Havens.

In case any shipp, or ships of eithers subiects, or of a Newter chance to be taken in the Havens, or Libertyes of the one or the other by a third partie, being no subiects of either partie, they in or out of whose Havens, or Libertyes the said ship, or ships shall be taken, shalbe bound to help with the other party, to endeavor that the sayd taken ship, or ships may be followed, brought back, and restored to the Owners, but all at the charges of the said Owners, or interessed.

25.

Ships forced into Haven through any Misfortune may depart againe freely wthout paying any Dutie &c.

In case any Marchants ships of the subiects of either partye chance to come to harbour in the Land of one or the other by tempest, or by pursuite of Searovers, or through any other necessitye, force, or misfortune, they may sayle out agayne from thence freely at their pleasure, without that they shall therefore be bound to goe on shoare, vnlade, or sell their Merchandizes there, nor to paye for the same any duties, or customes, it shall in such cases be enough if they shew their Maritine lettrs and Passe ports without being subiect to any other search.

26.

None to come into each othrs Havens wth men of warr to a Number wch might cause suspition &c. wthout Leaue &c.

They may not come to, or in, nor stay in the Havens of each others Country with men of warr, and souldiers, to a number which might cause apparent suspition, or ill thoughts, without consent, or leave of those vnder whome the said Havens are, vnlesse they be driven by tempest, or forced to doe soe through necessitye, and to avoyd any dangers of the sea.

27.

Othr men of warre to come & goe freely &c.

For the men of warr of either syde, not being in soe great a number to cause any suspition, the Havens, rivers, and roades of either party, shall be alwayes open and free for to come in, there lye at Ancher, and sayle out agayne without any hinderance, or trouble; the sayd men of warr regulating themselves neverthelesse according to the lawes, and customes of the respective places.

28.

Men of warre not to be searcht onely coming into Hauens to shew their Comissns.

Provided neverthelesse that none of the men of Warr, or such as have Comission on either syde, shalbe subiect to any search, or visitation there, or on the respective coasts, or alsoe in the full sea, further then only to shew each others Comissions, comeing into their respective Havens, and not otherwise.

29.

Like libertie touchg Prizes &c.

All perticular Comission bearers on either side, shall likewise enioy the same freedome, in respect of their owne ships, as alsoe of the prises which they shall have taken from their particular on the comon Enemy, for to bring the said prises to the place where they are bound according to their Comission, which they shalbe bound to informe, or make knowne to the Officers of the place, or to paie any dutye vnto them, or any else there, they shalbe neverthelesse bound to shew their respective Comissions to the sayd Officers.

30.

Goods of eithr pty found in Enemies ships to be prize as well as ye ships.

The goods, wares, and merchandizes of the subiects, and inhabitants of either partie, laeden, and found in Enemyes ships shalbe vnfree, and prise as well as ye ships.

31.

No Assistance to Enems or Rebels by Cōtrabda wares &c.

What serues for victuall or maintenance of Life to be free &c.

It is alsoe expressly agreed, that the parties Contractors shall not give, nor suffer that out of their respective Countries, by their subiects, or other Newters any assistance be done to their respective enemies, or rebells, of any Contrabanda wares, or Marchandises, as are all manner of fyreworks, and what else belongs therevnto, as Cannon, Musketts, Morterpieces Petards, Guns, Granadoes, Sawsiges, . . . , Rests, Bandeliers, Powder Match, Saltpeter, Bullets; all sortes of armes, as Pykes, swordes, Headpieces, Cuirasses, Holberds, and such lyke; as also souldiers Horses, horse furniture, Pistoll cases, Rapiers, Belts, and all furniture, fashioned, and made for vse of warr, with expresse meaning that vnder the name of Contraband, or forbidden goods, there shall not be comprehended wheat, Corne, and other grayne, Pease, Beanes, Wheat [*sic:* Meat?], Salt, Wyne, Oyle, nor generally all that serves for food, and maintenance of lyfe, but shalbe free, as other goods above mentioned, And any of the said Contraband goods, being found in each others ships, they may be confiscated after knowledge of the case before a competent Judge, without troubling any other Wares, or goods.

32.

No carying of anie Portugll goods &c. vpon Penaltie of Losse of ye ships &c.

It is further bespoake, that the subiects, and inhabitants of either side, may not transporte, or carry any Portingall goods, wares, or Merchandises out of America, Asia, or Affrica, or into, or out of Europe, or one parte thereof to another, nor vice versâ from Europe to America, Asia, or Affrick, nor from one part of them to another, upon penaltye of losse of the same ships.

33.

Ships cast away If claymd wthin a yeare & a Day to be wth ye goods restored to the Owners wthout suite.

If any ships either for warr, or marchandise, or other of either partye by storme, or any other misfortune, chance to be stranded, or cast away on the coast of either country, the said ships with their Apparell, and all therein may be reclaymed, and brought back againe within the space of a yeare, and a day, by the right owners or there Assignes, or deputies, and shalbe restored againe to them without any forme of suite onlye payeing for the charges done about 'em, and a reasonable gratuitye or salvage money, and in case upon such, and the like accidents, subiects of either side chance to fall to question, the officers of the respective places shall be bound to doe good, and right Justice betweene the partyes, without deteyning them by any formalitye of processe.

. . . .

APPENDIX L.

(P. 398.)

TROMP'S MEMORANDUM TO THE STATES OF HOLLAND AS TO THE CUSTOM OF STRIKING THE FLAG TO THE ENGLISH. $\frac{\text{27TH FEBRUARY}}{\text{9TH MARCH}}$ 1651.

(Aitzema, *Saken van Staet en Oorlogh, in, ende omtrent de Vereenigde Nederlanden*, Vol. iii. p. 731.)

Wanneer deses Staets Schepen van Oorloge in Zee quamen te ontmoeten een Engelsch Koninghs Schip, op-hebbende de Vlagge als Admirael, Vice-Admirael ofte Schout bij nacht; dat deses Staets-Schepen hare Admiraels Vlagge ende Mars-zeylen streecken en schoten negen, seven of vijf Eer-schoten (daer op de Engelsche antwoordede met gelijcke Eer-schoten) en lieten de Vlagge gestreken hangen tot sij van malkanderen scheyden, met het schieten van drie of een Adieu-schoot; en weynigh van den anderen zijnde, setten de Staetsche de Vlagge wederom op. Doch voor particuliere Konings Schepen streken geen Vlagge, alleen salueerden malkanderen met eenige Eer-schooten. Maer is verscheyden-malen geschiet, dat particuliere Schepen van weynigh geweldt zijnde, oock naer de Vlagge van Staetsche hebben geschoten, uyt hooghmoet, willende hebben dat men soude strijcken: daer meesten tijdt op is gevolgt, dat de Staetsche wederom na haer hebben geschoten en haer tanden laten sien, en geen macht hebbende de Staetsche daer toe te dwingen, moesten met uytlacchen haer Kours gaen; doch is bij haer en die van desen Staet veel tijdts gesien op de meeste macht, en dan discretie gebruyckt. Binnen haer Havenen ende Casteelen komende, salueerden de Casteelen met Eer-schoten (die oock wederom antwoorden) en namen de Vlagge in, en lieten in plaets een Wimpel waijen, soo lange die van desen Staet binnen haer Havenen lagen, in sonderheydt wanneer eenige Konings Schepen daer waren die de Konings Vlagge lieten waeijen. Doch geen Konings Schepen zijnde, is 't verscheyde-malen gebeurt, dat de Gouverneurs van de Casteelen een Expressen aen boort stuyrden uyt courtosie, en gaven consent, dat de Staetsche haer Admiraels Vlagge souden opsetten en laten waijen: mits wederom uyt-zeylende ende de Casteelen passerende, de Vlagge streecken en lieten hanghen, totdat men met Eer-schooten haer hadde gesalueert, en sij gheantwoordt; dan wierde wederom de Staetsche Vlagge op geset.

APPENDIX M.

(P. 404.)

CORRESPONDENCE BETWEEN TROMP AND BLAKE.

(De Zee Betwist. Geschiedenis der Onderhandelingen over de Zeeheerschappij tusschen de Engelsche Republiek en de Vereenigde Provinciën vóór den eersten Zee-Oorlog. Dr M. C. Tideman.)

MONS[R],

Le 19/29 du Mois passé nous entrerencontrans en mer mon invention [*sic*: intention ?] estoit de vous saluer, mais me voyant attacquée de la sorte, et n'ayant peu scavoir la vostre puisque devant ny apres ladite rencontre je n'ay parlé a personne des vostres ne doubtant toutesfois nullemant (selon que m'a tesmoigné Monsr. le Commandeur Born, par les responses qu'il a faictes et données a celuy que je luy envoyois pour luy communiquer mon ordre et sincere Intention) que ne soions amis et bons alliez, fus contraint, comme un homme d'honneur, tant seulement de me defendere, mais d'autant que aujourdhuy, estant a lancre devant Calais on ma rapporté, qu'un de nos Navires le Capiteyne Tuynemans de Middelbourg auroit este emmené a vostre Rade aux d'unes, lequel je croiois estre coulé en fond, comme celuy seul qu'il nous defailloit. C'est pourquoi je vous supplie en toute amitie que ce soit votre plasir, que ledit navire nous soit rendu et mis en main du porteur de ceste, en forme qu'il a este prins, et me promets, que la bonne alliance et union entre Messeigneurs les Estats de Vostre et de nostre Republycque, nostre Religion et mutuelle amitié fera, que ne voudres le refuser, Sur quoy me tiendray obligé de demeurer, comme veritablement je suis,

Monsieur,

Vostre Tres humble Serviteur,
(Signé) M. HARP[TS]. TROMP.

En notre navire *Le Brederode* le 2e Junij 1652 a la Rade de Calais.

The superscription was:—

A Monsieur,

Monsieur N. N. Blake, Collonel et Admirael au Service de Messeigneurs les Estats de la Republicque d'Angleterre, ou en son absence au Commandant a present aux d'unes.

Gardiner (Letters and Papers, 257) gives Blake's reply "retranslated from the Dutch translation." The original, which was appended to

Tromp's letter to the States-General, is given by Tideman, as follows, from *Lias Admiraliteit:* Bijvoegsel bij Tromps brief aan H. Ho. Mo. uit Ostende d. d. 10 Juni 1652.

S^r^,

Y^r^ Letter of the second of June 1652 stilo novo, brought by yor Messenger, was read by mee not without much wonder that you stiling yor selfe a person off honor should insert therin toe great mistakes after yor seeking out the ffleet of the Parliament of the Comonwealth of England instead of performing those usuall respects which off right belong unto them and which yor selve have often done, you were pleased to beginn acts off hostility which you call yor owne defence against the commonwealth, without the least provocation on the part of their servants thus assaulted by you, and at a time when yor Superiours, and their Ambassadors with the Parlyament were in a Treaty and desire of friendshipp with the Comonwealth of England, but that God in whome wee trust, having defeated your purposes of our destruction and some off yor ships taken, you thincke fitt to demaund the same off us as if yor former accord had been as you call it but a salutation and when that fayled, you would second yor high affronts by yor paper to which I doe not thincke fitt to returne any other Answere, But that I presume you will find the Parlyament sensible of these greate Iniuries and of the Losse off the innocent bloud of their Countrymen, And you will find likewise ready to obey their comandts,

Yo^r^ humble Servant,
ROB: BLAKE.

DOWNES, 29*th May* 1652.

APPENDIX N.

(P. 461.)

CONCESSION TO BRUGES TO FISH IN THE BRITISH SEAS.[1]

(State Papers—King's Letter Book, 1664-1670. Foreign Entry Book. Vol. 174, p. 119.)

CAROLVS &c. Omnibus ad quos præsentes literæ pervenerint vel ullo modo spectaverint salutem. Cum in virtutum albo longè Princeps audiat liberalitas, quippe quæ non tantùm beneficia sed ipsam etiam

[1] Differences found in copy, *State Papers, Dom.*, Chas. II., Vol. 339, p. 589, are shown in brackets.

benevolentiam et humanitatem secum comites trahat, Hinc est, quod Nobilissimæ et antiquissimæ civitatis Brugensis summis erga Nos meritis coacti quodammodo, animique Nostri ductum secuti [sicuti], tum maximè accepti hospitij memores, in hoc unum ferimur [feremur] ut priorum prementes Vestigia grati in eam animi non leve argumentum posteris quoquo modo traderemus; Et sanè affectu tam [tum] singulari non tantùm Sacerdotum, Consulum, Senatorum, et summus ille Nobilium ordo, sed universa passim Urbs et Nos et fratres Nostros iniquitate rerum hospites olim factos fovit semper et propensior indies accepit, ut animo Nostro altius infixa recens adhuc amoris tantó hæreat memoria, eaque jure quodam hæreditario ad Successores Nostros deferenda, ne posteris Nostris tantæ benignitatis ingrata tandem obrepat oblivio, Regnis utique [utque] Nostris ejecti benigniori hospitio in tantum recreari cœpimus, ut iniquam [inquam] fortunæ invidiam æquiori animo tulisse videremur, eo saltem nomine non passuri [possum] unquam ut ad priorem statum reduces ingratorum notâ laboremus. Vellemus quidem eâdem alacritate quâ prædicta Civitas Brugensis (Celeberrimum quondam Emporium tum magnificentiâ, amplitudine et fulgore præ cæteris clarum) benevolentiæ et benignitatis fidem coluit, gratum animum testari, & Civitati de Nobis tam bene meritæ pristinam gloriam et splendorem illæsum prorsus, et [est] integrum præstare. Quâ de causâ à Viro Nobis præcipuè dilecto Marco Alberto Dognati Equite [d'Ognati Equiti] Aurato, Regisque Catholici ad renovandam Belgij Dignitatem Commissario, rebusque Nostris singulari curâ intento à charissimo consanguineo Nostro (et) Illustrissimo Marchione [Marchioni] de Castel-Rodrigo Belgij et Burgundiæ Gubernatore de Commercij libertate hoc tempore faciendâ misso [misse] tum literas, tum Monochroma Novi Opificij, Portus, usque ad Oceanum Ductus [ductos] nuper elaborati et in capacem Navigationis formam redacti, grato animo accepimus; Lætique benignitate pristinâ, Regiam aliquam prærogativam quæ non [non non] ingrate spondeat, in predictam civitatem Brugensem conferre meditamur, plenâ potestate & authoritate Nostrâ Regiâ plenè, liberè sponte, ac motu proprio dantes & concedentes sicuti [sicut] per præsentes pro Nobis, Hæredibus et Successoribus Nostris damus et concedimus, ut prædicta civitas Brugensis quocunque demum impedimento obstante Quinquaginta Naves piscatorias in Mare Nostrum in futurum possit deducere, nec non juxta Regnorum Nostrorum Oras et Littora liberè ac secure piscaturam exercere, tum etiam Haleces [Halices] piscesque alios quoscunque captare. Licebit porrò prædictæ Urbis Civibus ad Portus Nostros Littora et flumina cum prædictis Navibus appellere, retia siccanda [seccanda] et resarcienda in terram exponere, periculis hostium tempestatumque sese subducere, necessaria tum ad victum tum ad alia quæcunque in oppidis alijsque locis Regnorum Nostrorum justo pretio coemere, nullâque aliâ ad hoc speciali facultate aut salvi [salvus] conductûs literis habitis aut petitis inde redire liberèque [libere] recedere ita tamen ut dictæ Civitatis Brugensis

Magistratûs literis, præsentium vigore sub sigillo ejus exhibendis, instructi veniant; caveant interim prædictarum Navium piscatoriarum proprietarij, fide prius datâ apud dictum Magistratum per sponsores idoneos, ne per ipsos piscatores, Nautas, aliosvè ad pisces derehendos substitutos, ad loca Nobis et Regnis Nostris inimica hujusmodi onus subrehi sinant [hujusmodi oras sinant et] aut permittant. Volumus igitur et per præsentes decernimus, ut prædicta piscandi libertas juxta numerum Navium supramemoratarum præfatis Urbis Brugensis Civibus solva [sola] semper et integra maneat, et in perpetuum per Nos ac Hæredes et Successores Nostros stabilita continuetur. Nèque quisquam subditorum Nostrorum, cujuscunque statûs, authoritatis, gradûs seu conditionis, huic [hujus] Nostræ liberæ et spontaneæ concessioni [concessionis] gratiæ, favori et privilegio, quoquo modo contravenito. Mandamus igitur et injungimus Fratri Nostro Charissimo Ducé Eboracensi Magno Nostro Angliæ Admiralio [Admirallo] Nec non omnibus et singulis Regnorum Nostrorum Thalassiarchis, Navium Bellicarum capitaneis et Ductoribus Provinciarum, Urbium, Arciumque maritimarum Præfectis et eorum Vicem gerentibus, Judicibus, Officialibus, et alijs quibuscunque Ministris Nostris et juris Administratoribus, &c., ut prædictis piscatoribus in quācunque maris parte vel juxta littora, flumina, Portusve Nostros obviam facti, non modo illis injuriam non inferant, sed eós etiam amicè et benevolè excipiant, ac ubi opus fuerit, ijs opem ferant ijsdemque liberum accessum et recessum reditumque in patriam unà cum Navibus, piscibus, cæterisque bonis suis, nullo facto impedimento seu contradictione quâcunque præstent et permittant. In quorùm omnium majorem fidem [fidem majorem] præsentibus hisce manu Nostrâ Regiâ signatis [signatas] Magnum Nostrum Angliæ Sigillum appendi fecimus. Dabantur, &c., Julij 1666 [*sic*].

APPENDIX O.

(P. 692.)

TERRITORIAL WATERS.

The articles adopted by the Institut de Droit International at Paris in 1894, and accepted with slight modifications by the International Law Association at London in 1895. [*Note.* — The additions to and alterations of the Rules adopted at Paris, which were made at London, are indicated by italic type.]

L'Institut,

Considérant qu'il n'y a pas de raison pour confondre en une seule zône la distance nécessaire pour l'exercice de la souveraineté et pour la protection de la pêche littorale et celle qui l'est pour garantir la neutralité des non-belligérants en temps de guerre;

Que la distance la plus ordinairement adoptée de trois milles de la laisse de basse marée a été reconnue insuffisante pour la protection de la pêche littorale;

Que cette distance ne correspond pas non plus à la portée réelle des canons placés sur la côte;

a adopté les dispositions suivantes:

Article Premier.—L'État a un droit de souveraineté sur une zône de la mer qui baigne la côte, sauf le droit de passage inoffensif réservé à l'article 5.

Cette zône porte le nom de mer territoriale.

Art. 2.—La mer territoriale s'étend à six milles marins (60 au degré de latitude) de la laisse de basse marée *ou de la ligne de laquelle il est parlé dans l'article* 3, sur toute l'étendue des côtes.

Art. 3.—Pour les baies, la mer territoriale suit les sinuosités de la côte, sauf qu'elle est mesurée à partir d'une ligne droite tirée en travers de la baie dans la partie la plus rapprochée de l'ouverture vers la mer, où l'écart entre les deux côtes de la baie est de *dix* milles marins de largeur, à moins qu'un usage continu et séculaire n'ait consacré une largeur plus grande.

Art. 4.—En cas de guerre, l'État riverain neutre a le droit de fixer, par la déclaration de neutralité ou par notification spéciale, sa zône neutre au delà de six milles, jusqu'à portée du canon des côtes.

Art. 5.—Tous les navires sans distinction ont le droit de passage inoffensif par la mer territoriale, sauf le droit des belligérants de réglementer et, dans un but de défense, de barrer le passage dans ladite mer pour tout navire, et sauf le droit des neutres de réglementer le passage dans ladite mer pour les navires de guerre de toutes nationalités. *Il n'est pas dérogé par cet article aux dispositions de l'article* 10.

Art. 6.—Les crimes et délits commis à bord de navires étrangers de passage dans la mer territoriale par des personnes qui se trouvent à bord de ces navires, sur des personnes ou des choses à bord de ces mêmes navires, sont, comme tels, en dehors de la juridiction de l'État riverain, à moins qu'ils n'impliquent une violation des droits ou des intérêts de l'État riverain, ou de ses ressortissants ne faisant partie ni de l'équipage ni des passagers.

Art. 7.—Les navires qui traversent les eaux territoriales se conformeront aux règlements spéciaux édictés par l'État riverain dans l'intérêt et pour la sécurité de la navigation et pour la police maritime.

Art. 8.—Les navires de toutes nationalités, par le fait seul qu'ils se trouvent dans les eaux territoriales, à moins qu'ils n'y soient seulement de passage, sont soumis à la juridiction de l'État riverain.

L'État riverain a le droit de continuer sur la haute mer la poursuite commencée dans la mer territoriale, d'arrêter et de juger le navire qui aurait commis une infraction *pénale* dans les limites de ses eaux. En cas de capture sur la haute mer, le fait sera, toutefois, notifié sans délai à l'État dont le navire porte le pavillon. La poursuite est interrompue dès que le navire entre dans la mer territoriale de son pays ou d'une tierce puissance. Le droit de poursuite cesse dès que le navire sera entré dans un port de son pays ou d'une tierce puissance.

ART. 9.—Est réservée la situation particulière des navires de guerre et de ceux qui leur sont assimilés.

ART. 10.—Les dispositions des articles précédents s'appliquent aux détroits dont l'écart n'excède pas douze milles, sauf les modifications et distinctions suivantes:—

1° Les détroits dont les côtes appartiennent à des États différents font partie de la mer territoriale des États riverains, qui y exerceront leur souveraineté jusqu'à la ligne médiane.

2° Les détroits dont les côtes appartiennent au même État et qui sont indispensables aux communications maritimes entre deux ou plusieurs États autres que l'État riverain font toujours partie de la mer territoriale du riverain, quel que soit le rapprochement des côtes. *Ils ne peuvent jamais être barrés.*

3° *Dans les détroits dont les côtes appartiennent au même État, la mer est territoriale bien que l'écartement des côtes dépasse douze milles, si à chaque entrée du détroit cette distance n'est pas dépassé.*

4° Les détroits qui servent de passage d'une mer libre à une autre mer libre ne peuvent jamais être *barrés.*

ART. 11.—Le régime des détroits actuellement soumis à des conventions ou usages spéciaux demeure réservé.

INDEX.

THE END.

PRINTED BY WILLIAM BLACKWOOD AND SONS.

LaVergne, TN USA
17 November 2010
205168LV00004B/1/P

9 781584 772323